THE ROUTLEDGE HANDBOOK OF ENDANGERED AND MINORITY LANGUAGES

The Routledge Handbook of Endangered and Minority Languages addresses the urgent need for comprehensive language documentation and a deeper understanding of language identity, emphasizing the preservation of endangered languages.

This book argues that safeguarding linguistic diversity enriches global cultural heritage and knowledge. By meticulously documenting minority languages, we not only preserve words and grammar but also the unique cultural narratives they carry. The book also introduces new language learning paradigms that recognize the complexities of multilingual societies, advocating for educational systems that embrace the diverse linguistic backgrounds of students. These approaches aim to create more inclusive and effective learning environments by valuing multilingualism. Exploring the fluid nature of language identity, the book examines how sociopolitical contexts and technology influence it, calling for policies that respect linguistic rights and promote social cohesion. It presents case studies from diverse regions, including the Pacific, Nordic countries, Cornwall, Pakistan, the UAE, and more, offering practical strategies for language preservation and revitalization.

Groundbreaking insights into the use of digital tools, social media, and AI in language preservation, along with the challenges and successes of various revitalization efforts, make this book a valuable resource for researchers, educators, and policymakers committed to fostering linguistic diversity and equity worldwide.

Weixiao Wei is the author of three monographs: *An Overview of Chinese Translation Studies at the Beginning of the 21st Century* (2019), *The History of Chinese Rhetoric* (2022), and *A Notional Analysis of Chinese Academic Discourse on China* (2023). She has also served as editor or co-editor for three Routledge volumes: *The Routledge Handbook of Chinese Studies* (2021), *China's Contemporary Image and Rhetoric Practice* (2022), and *The Routledge Handbook of Descriptive Rhetorical Studies and World Languages* (2023). Her recent projects include two forthcoming handbooks, set for publication in 2025: *The Routledge Handbook of Endangered and Minority Languages* and *The Routledge Handbook of the Sociopolitical Context of Language Learning*. Weixiao's research and teaching focus is on English rhetoric and composition, and she is currently pursuing a PhD at the University of Houston.

James Schnell, PhD (Ohio University, 1982), presently works in administration at Ohio State University after spending three years as a cultural advisor in the Defense Critical Languages & Culture Program at the University of Montana, USA. He retired from the U.S. Air Force at the rank of colonel, with his final 14 years serving as an assistant Air Force attaché at the U.S. Embassy in Beijing, China. Schnell is a three time Fulbright Scholar to Cambodia, Myanmar, and Kosovo; has completed three visiting fellowships at the East West Center (Honolulu); and has taught at universities in the United States and throughout Southeast Asia.

ROUTLEDGE HANDBOOKS OF LANGUAGE LEARNING IN THE GLOBAL CONTEXT

Series Editors

Chris Shei

Swansea University and

Weixiao Wei

University of Houston

ABOUT THE SERIES

Routledge Handbooks of Language Learning in the Global Context is a series of edited handbooks providing cutting-edge research on how current affairs and environmental changes influence language learning and teaching practices. Communicative Language Teaching (CLT), the mainstream language teaching method nowadays, emphasises meaningful interaction and use of language in context. This means that language teachers and learners should be keenly aware of the influence exerted by global context on language, thereby making language learning a dynamic experience which both reflects the change in global contexts and initiates a response at the linguistic, cognitive and sociocultural levels. Language learning, among other things, should contribute to world peace and common prosperity by helping to resolve conflicts and misunderstanding and achieve peace and harmony. Please get in touch with Dr Chris Shei at c-c.shei@swansea.ac.uk to discuss any ideas you might have, either for editing a new handbook in the series, or contributing a chapter that may inform a new handbook.

THE ROUTLEDGE HANDBOOK OF THE SOCIOPOLITICAL CONTEXT OF LANGUAGE LEARNING
Edited by Weixiao Wei and Der-lin Chao

THE ROUTLEDGE HANDBOOK OF ENDANGERED AND MINORITY LANGUAGES
Edited by Weixiao Wei and James Schnell

Find out more about this series at www.routledge.com/Routledge-Handbooks-of-Language-Learning-in-the-Global-Context/book-series/RHLLGC

THE ROUTLEDGE HANDBOOK OF ENDANGERED AND MINORITY LANGUAGES

Edited by Weixiao Wei and James Schnell

LONDON AND NEW YORK

Designed cover image: Cover photo by YQW

First published 2025
by Routledge
4 Park Square, Milton Park, Abingdon, Oxon OX14 4RN

and by Routledge
605 Third Avenue, New York, NY 10158

Routledge is an imprint of the Taylor & Francis Group, an informa business

© 2025 selection and editorial matter, Weixiao Wei and James Schnell;
individual chapters, the contributors

The right of Weixiao Wei and James Schnell to be identified as the authors of
the editorial material, and of the authors for their individual chapters, has been
asserted in accordance with sections 77 and 78 of the Copyright, Designs and
Patents Act 1988.

All rights reserved. No part of this book may be reprinted or reproduced or
utilised in any form or by any electronic, mechanical, or other means, now
known or hereafter invented, including photocopying and recording, or in any
information storage or retrieval system, without permission in writing from the
publishers.

Trademark notice: Product or corporate names may be trademarks or registered
trademarks, and are used only for identification and explanation without intent
to infringe.

British Library Cataloguing-in-Publication Data
A catalogue record for this book is available from the British Library

ISBN: 978-1-032-57428-8 (hbk)
ISBN: 978-1-032-57463-9 (pbk)
ISBN: 978-1-003-43949-3 (ebk)

DOI: 10.4324/9781003439493

Typeset in Times New Roman
by Apex CoVantage, LLC

CONTENTS

Editorial board	*ix*
List of figures	*xi*
List of tables	*xii*
List of contributors	*xiv*

Introduction *Weixiao Wei*	1

SECTION I
Endangered and minority languages in the new global context 7

1 Preserving Indigenous languages in the Pacific region: the role
  of key stakeholders 9
  Govinda Ishwar Lingam

2 Language revitalization case studies from the Nordic countries 31
  Riitta-Liisa Valijärvi

3 Celtic lessons: revitalizing Cornish through the education system 48
  George Wilson

4 Basque and Occitan in the new global context: some reflections
  on language coexistence in multilingual education 62
  Elizabeth Pérez-Izaguirre, Karin van der Worp, and Marie-Anne
  Châteaureynaud

Contents

5 Redrawing language boundaries: nurturing Arabic in the
United Arab Emirates 78
Briji Jose and Bettina Biju Jacob

6 How is Alsatian written?: a case study of the linguistic landscape
in Strasbourg 93
Rei Sugiura

7 The global language – Latin 108
Milena Minkova and Terence Tunberg

SECTION II
Technology, media, and revitalization **121**

8 The role of language attitudes and ideologies in minority language
learning and language revitalisation: perspectives of Polish migrants
learning Welsh 123
Karolina Rosiak

9 Learning from language revitalization movements to promote Uyghur
language resilience in diaspora 140
Rebecca Clothey and Brian McCommons

10 The role of new media in maintaining endangered languages: insights
from Igbo 155
Sopuruchi Christian Aboh

11 Challenges of language survival in digital perspectives: case
and context of India 171
Arimardan Kumar Tripathi

12 Indigenous artificial intelligence: virtual and augmented reality
as tools in the cultural preservation and education of endangered
and extinct languages 188
Cringuta Irina Pelea

SECTION III
Language policy, ideology, and multilingual education **211**

13 "Speak standard Mandarin, write standard characters": mandarin
language promotion and its effect on minority languages in China 213
Britta Ingebretson

Contents

14 Ideological monolingualism and the languages classroom in England   228
    Abigail Parrish

15 Multilingualism in minority schools: new realities   243
    Sabina Zorčič and Lara Sorgo

16 Learning the neighbor's language: regional and minoritized languages as
    a resource in the European educational context   259
    Marija Mandić

17 Challenging standard language ideology in L2 learning contexts for
    endangered and minority languages   274
    Katharine E. Burns

18 Turning toward plurilingualism through a focus on place   288
    Kellie Rolstad

19 Border culture identity   303
    Iván A. Sanchís

20 Textual phenomena addressing youth: orthographic, typographic, and
    ideological aspects of the Cypriot-Greek dialect   317
    Aspasia Papadima

21 "I already know where that place is . . .": the educational linguistic
    landscape of a language at risk   334
    Kayhan İnan and Gülin Dağdeviren-Kırmızı

SECTION IV
Learning endangered and minority languages   **353**

22 Artificial intelligence–assisted language learning for *all* in the new
    global context: threats and opportunities   355
    Cristina A. Huertas-Abril and Francisco Javier Palacios-Hidalgo

23 Raising intercultural awareness in European University Alliances:
    opportunities, challenges and limitations   377
    Cédric Brudermann

24 Rhizomatic approaches: a response to hierarchies, linearity, and isolation
    in language learning   392
    Beatriz Carbajal-Carrera and Rita Prestigiacomo

vii

Contents

25 The non-fiction picturebook as a tool for (re)constructing children's and teachers' representations of endangered languages: design and results of a multimodal educational project for the Aragonese language   407
Iris-Orosia Campos-Bandrés and Rosa Tabernero-Sala

26 Modularity as a practical approach to teaching and learning about the LGBTQIA+ community in Japan and beyond   425
Nobuko Koyama

Index   *440*

EDITORIAL BOARD

Ellen A. Ahlness Researcher with Veterans Health Administration, USA. Research interests: Arctic studies, qualitative methodology, Indigenous environmental and language policy, Inuktitut, reflexivity, and decolonial methodologies.

Pompi Basumatary Assistant Professor of English and Cultural Studies at Christ (Deemed to be University), Delhi, NCR. Research interests: translation studies, colonial studies, knowledge production, folk literature, Bodo community, and creative writing.

Khedidja Chergui Associate Professor of World and Postcolonial Literature, Department of English, L'Ecole Normale Supérieure de Bouzaréah, Algiers. Research interests: literary theory, language and identity, postcolonial literature, and decolonial methodologies.

Lynda Chouiten Full Professor of Literature at the University of Boumerdes (Algeria). Research interests: Francophone literature, Anglophone literature, (post)colonial studies, travel writing, creative writing, women's literature, discourse, power, and translation.

Liubov Darzhinova RGC Postdoctoral Fellow at the Department of English Language Education, the Education University of Hong Kong, Hong Kong SAR. Research interests: language processing, reading, technology-enhanced assessment, and teacher education.

Samuel Despars University of Ottawa, Canada. Research interests: philosophy of law, artificial intelligence, and language rights.

Gabriel D Djomeni Senior Lecturer of Linguistics and African Languages, University of Dschang, Cameroon, Research interests: language description and analysis, language documentation and revitalization, language policy and planning, mother tongue education, sociolinguistics, didactics of languages, and digital humanities.

Editorial board

Sarali Gintsburg Researcher, Institute for Culture and Society, University of Navarra (Spain). Research interests: Arabic language, sociolinguistics, linguistic identities, multimodal analysis, immigrant identities, and minoritized languages in MENA.

Francesca La Morgia Adjunct Professor and Research Fellow, Department of Education Studies "Giovanni Maria Bertin", University of Bologna, Italy.

Amy Leshinsky Assistant Professor of Education at Curry College, Milton, Massachusetts, USA. Research interests: book censorship, literacy education, artificial intelligence, American literature, and social justice.

Ana Sofia Louro School of Arts and Humanities of the University of Lisbon, Portugal; Researcher at Centre of English and American Studies of the University of Lisbon, Portugal.

Craig A. Meyer Associate Professor of English and Director of the Writing Program, Jackson State University, Mississippi, USA. Research interests: rhetoric and composition, popular culture, AI integration, Star Trek, disability studies, and social justice.

Tihomir Rangelov Postdoctoral Researcher at the Max Planck Institute for Evolutionary Anthropology. Research interests: Vanuatu, Melanesian languages, phonetics, phonology, typology, language documentation, description, revitalization, language contact, sociolinguistics, language ecology, Slavic and North Germanic languages.

Violeta Stojičić Full Professor of Linguistics, Department of English, University of Niš, Serbia, and Visiting Professor, University of Applied Sciences, Ventspils, Latvia. Research interests: discourse, systemic-functional linguistics, appraisal theory, and ecolinguistics.

Tanupriya Assistant Professor of English and Cultural Studies at Christ (Deemed to be University), Delhi, NCR. Research interests: cultural studies, gender and language, queer and trans studies, body studies, and life writing.

Sutanovac Vladan Cognitive Science Researcher, Cross-Cultural Pragmatician, Conceptual Semanticist, and Philosopher of Language and Mind at University of Vienna's Faculty of Philological and Cultural Studies and Vienna Cognitive Science Hub.

FIGURES

1.1	Map showing SIDS in the Pacific region	10
6.1	Bilingual top-down street name sign	100
6.2	Monolingual top-down signs	101
6.3	Bottom-up signs in Strasbourg	101
10.1	Map of Igbo land (Oyali 2018: 12)	156
10.2	A sample of an Igbo phrase for the week	167
12.1	Photo: Thomas Moore, as he appeared when admitted to the Regina Indian Industrial School, and Thomas Moore, after tuition at the Regina Indian Industrial School	193
12.2	"Homes are sought for these children"	193
14.1	GCSE entries in modern foreign languages, 2000–2023	229
14.2	Percentage of students entered for the full EBacc, 2009–2022	235
14.3	Number of entries for GCSE Chinese, 1995–2023	237
22.1	Data query in Scopus database	357
22.2	PRISMA flow chart of article identification and screening (adapted from Page et al. 2021)	358
22.3	Network of most recurrent topics using VOSViewer	360
22.4	Distribution of the papers per year	360
23.1	Delineating the contours of a transductive relationship related to GCE within EUAs	384
25.1	Evolution of the introduction of Aragonese in schools, superimposed on the language's vitality map as described by Postlep (2012) in the province of Huesca (Aragon)	409
25.2	Example of the contents of the book	413

TABLES

1.1	Materials in Fijian language available to the public in Fiji	18
2.1	Minority languages of Denmark, including the status of Faroese and Greenlandic	34
2.2	Minority languages of Finland and Aland	34
2.3	Minority languages of Norway	35
2.4	Minority languages of Sweden	35
4.1	Comparison of languages in education in NA and the BAC	70
5.1	Questionnaire responses related to students' Arabic language acquisition in UAE ($n = 114$)	84
6.1	Chronology of the history of Alsace	94
6.2	Survey on language spoken in Alsace, 1926–1962	95
6.3	Basic information of the interviewees	99
6.4	Overall results for language distribution	100
6.5	Language on top-down and bottom-up signs	100
10.1	Fishman's GIDS	158
11.1	Internet companies – selected mergers and acquisitions	176
11.2	Hierarchy of languages in digital space	178
12.1	Overview of findings	195
14.1	The structure of the EBacc	233
14.2	Progress 8 'buckets'	233
15.1	The number and share of students with permanent residence in Slovenia enrolled at Slovene minority schools at the upper secondary level in the last five school years	246
15.2	Self-assessment of language proficiency in students from Slovenia in minority schools in Austria	248
15.3	Self-assessment of Italian language skills	252
15.4	Students' mother tongues	254
20.1	Textism findings from the 'CUTchat' Discord channel	325
20.2	Textism findings from the 'Cyprus University of Technology Secrets' Facebook page	326

Tables

20.3	Written conventions found in CG Textese of the 'and' conjunction	327
21.1	Photographs used as prompts	339
21.2	Participants (students)	340
21.3	Participants (academic/administrative staff)	340
22.1	Inclusion and exclusion criteria	358
22.2	Summary of papers analysed and coded	361
22.3	SWOT matrix	369
24.1	The myth of the average learner	396
25.1	Synthesis of emergent categories arising from the data analysis	416

CONTRIBUTORS

Sopuruchi Christian Aboh is a recipient of the prestigious Hong Kong PhD Fellowship and a PhD candidate in the Department of English and Communication at the Hong Kong Polytechnic University. He is a member of the Research Centre for Professional Communication in English and also affiliated to the Department of Linguistics, Igbo and other Nigerian Languages, University of Nigeria, Nsukka. He is interested in (political) discourse analysis, heritage language learning, multilingualism, language attitudes and stereotypes, and Igbo studies. His research has been published in *Discourse & Society, the Journal of Multilingual and Multicultural Development*, and *Lingua.*

Cédric Brudermann is Professor of English and Applied Linguistics at *Le Conservatoire National des Arts et Métiers* (Cnam), Paris, France. He is a member of the FoAP (Formation et Apprentissages Professionnels, EA 7529) research unit. His research interests include computer-assisted language learning, second language acquisition, curriculum design, instructional technology, and language policy.

Katharine E. Burns is Assistant Professor of Applied Linguistics, Second Language Acquisition, and Hispanic Studies at Carnegie Mellon University, where she is a faculty member in the doctoral program in Applied Linguistics and Second Language Acquisition. Her current research interests include sociolinguistic variation in L2 contexts, bi/multilingual identities, language ideologies, language policy, and heritage and minority language education. She holds an MA and PhD from the Second Language Acquisition and Teaching (SLAT) Program at the University of Arizona, as well as an MA in Spanish language and literature from Marquette University in Milwaukee, Wisconsin. Her teaching experience includes courses on various applied linguistics topics at the graduate and undergraduate levels, as well as Spanish and English language courses in a variety of contexts (domestic, international, heritage, non-heritage).

Iris-Orosia Campos-Bandrés holds a PhD in education and is an associate professor in the area of language and literature didactics at the University of Zaragoza. She is a member of the Reference Research Group ECOLIJ (Communicative and Literary Education in the Information Society. Children's and Youth Literature in the Construction of Identities). She directs the Specialisation

Contributors

Diploma in Aragonese philology, a postgraduate qualification at the University of Zaragoza. Her research interests include aspects related to linguistic and literary education, educational sociolinguistics, and language sociodidactics. She is currently a member of the research group of the state R+D+i project "Non-fictional readings for the integration of citizens in the new cultural ecosystem" (PID2021–126392OB-I00).

Beatriz Carbajal-Carrera is a lecturer in Spanish and Latin American studies at the University of Sydney. She received her PhD in linguistics from the University of Salamanca and Flinders University and holds a bachelor's in Spanish studies as well as a bachelor's in English studies from the University of Salamanca, where she also completed her master's in Spanish as a foreign language. Her research examines the sociocultural, linguistic, and cognitive dimensions of language learning, humor, and emotions in discourse through sociolinguistic and pragmatic approaches. Dr Carbajal-Carrera has participated in international research projects, including a project on language diversity with the *Real Academia Española de la Lengua Española* and a Spanish government–funded project on the phono-pragmatics of emotions. Her work has been published in *System, Spanish Journal of Applied Linguistics, The European Journal of Cultural Studies, Critical Discourse Studies, The European Journal of Humour Research*, and other international peer-reviewed journals.

Marie-Anne Châteaureynaud is Full Professor of Applied Linguistics at the College of Education (INSPE) at the University of Bordeaux. Her research focuses on Occitan, minority languages, sociolinguistics, language learning, language sociodidactics, and plurilingualism.

Rebecca Clothey is Professor and Head of the Department of Global Studies and Modern Languages at Drexel University. Her current research on maintenance and transmission of Uyghur culture spans several countries, including China, the United States, and Türkiye. She was a visiting scholar at Boğaziçi University in Istanbul in 2018–2019 and at Xinjiang Normal University in 2014. Dr. Clothey's research has been funded by Fulbright Fellowships, the Spencer Foundation, and NEH-ARIT, among others.

Gülin Dağdeviren-Kırmızı is Associate Professor of Linguistics at Başkent University, Türkiye. Her work focuses specifically on language endangerment, heritage speakers, family language policy, and second language acquisition.

Cristina A. Huertas-Abril (she/her), associate professor, belongs to the Department of English and German Philologies of the University of Córdoba (Spain), where she teaches at the Faculty of Education Sciences and Psychology. Her research mainly focuses on computer-assisted language learning (CALL), teaching English as a foreign language, bilingual education, and teacher training.

Kayhan İnan is Associate Professor of Turkish Language Teaching at Amasya University, Türkiye. He studied teaching Turkish as a foreign language at Gazi University in Ankara. Since 2021, he has been a visiting scholar at Moldova State University under the abroad program of the Turkish Ministry of Education. His research focuses on Turkish language maintenance, bilingualism, and teaching Turkish as a foreign language.

Britta Ingebretson completed a joint PhD in anthropology and linguistics at the University of Chicago. She is currently Assistant Professor of Chinese and Linguistics in the Department of

Languages and Cultures at Fordham University. Her research focuses on the politics of language use and linguistic difference in China and among Chinese diaspora populations in New York City. She is the director of the Sociolinguistics Lab and a co-director of the Demystifying Language Project and the Bronx Asian American Oral History Project at Fordham. Her work has been published in *Signs & Society* and the *Journal of Linguistic Anthropology*.

Bettina Biju Jacob is a researcher who is a keen observer of Middle Eastern affairs. Her research focuses on the works of American Palestinian author Naomi Shihab Nye, studying how intersectionality works in second-generation migrants living outside of their homelands. Born into an immigrant family in the UAE, her search for identity and roots became a quest she would forever embark on. Currently, she works with an organization that provides language training for AI models.

Briji Jose is an assistant professor at Kristu Jayanti College, India. Her research interests lie in the fields of migration studies, energy, and environmental humanities. She is a second-generation migrant who was raised in the UAE, and her PhD research delves into the Gulf migrations from India, examining how they reshape power dynamics and identities within local cultures. She has presented and published papers in her field and has also held an honorary research position at the Chinese University of Hong Kong.

Nobuko Koyama is Associate Professor of Japanese Language and Linguistics and Coordinator of the Japanese Language Program in the Department of East Asian Languages and Cultures at the University of California at Davis (UCD). She is a faculty advisor for the Japan Children's Home Internship Program (JCHIP), which fosters linguistic, social, and cultural exchanges between UCD students and underprivileged children in Japan. She has much experience in teaching JSL and JFL in Japan, Taiwan, and the United States. As an advocate for diversity, equity, and inclusion (DEI), she is interested in creating, experimenting with, and researching inclusive curricula for Japanese language and culture in the United States. Her research interests also include the benefits and effects of overseas experience (study abroad and overseas internships) by learners of Japanese, Academic Japanese (AJ), and Open Educational Resources (OER). Her OER project *Getting to Know Japanese Language and Culture* (www.youtube.com/@gettingtoknowjapaneselangu265) (with Yuko Kato and Junko Hatanaka) has been widely viewed and used by both teachers and learners of Japanese worldwide.

Govinda Ishwar Lingam holds a PhD in education from Griffith University, Australia. He is Professor of Teacher Education and Associate Dean for Learning and Teaching at the Fiji National University (FNU) in Suva, Fiji. His previous work experience includes teaching at the University of the South Pacific (USP) where he received successive promotions. He served as Professor of Education and Head of the School of Education, President of the Association of the USP Staff (AUSPS), and a member of the USP council and senate. He has published journal articles, book chapters, and books. Recently, he co-authored a book on educational leadership, *Developing School Leaders in the Pacific: Building Capacity to Enhance Student Learning* (Springer Nature, 2023). His research interests include teacher education, professional development, educational leadership, policy, and planning.

Marija Mandić is a researcher at the Institute for Philosophy and Social Theory of the University of Belgrade. She received a PhD from the University of Belgrade (2010) and the Humboldt

Contributors

Fellowship for Postdoctoral Researchers (2016–2018) when she was a visiting scholar at the Humboldt University in Berlin. Her research interests include minority languages and ethnic minorities, multilingualism, language education, ethnic identity, gender, and political discourse, with a special focus on Central and Southeastern Europe. To the study of these, she is applying critical ethnographic, sociolinguistic, and discourse analytical methods. She published the monographs *Discourse and Ethnic Identity: The Case of the Serbs from Hungary* (Peter Lang, 2014), *Minority Languages in Vojvodina: Language Educational Policy, Ideology and Practice* (Ed.) (in Serbian; Akademska knjiga, 2024), and many scientific papers.

Brian McCommons is currently working as a program development and accreditation specialist at the University of Doha for Science and Technology in Doha, Qatar. Brian has over 10 years of experience working in global higher education in the United States, Bolivia, and now the Middle East. His past research focus has been primarily in minority language communities. Currently, his research is focused on first-year student social and academic integration to university from a wellness perspective.

Milena Minkova is Professor of Classics at the University of Kentucky, the home of the Institute for Latin Studies, where the entire Latin patrimony from antiquity until modern times is studied, and this happens in the target language. Minkova has worked on the whole continuity of the Latin tradition. In recent years, she has published on the 12th-century renaissance, Neo-Latin, Latin composition, and Latin pedagogy. Minkova has co-authored (with T. Tunberg) the widely used introductory Latin textbook *Latin for the New Millennium*, as well as a manual in Latin composition, *Readings and Exercises in Latin Prose Composition*, and other books. Minkova's most recent volume is a critical anthology of Neo-Latin *Florilegium recentioris Latinitatis* (Leuven University Press, 2018). Minkova is about to publish (with T. Tunberg) a book pertaining to Neo-Latin prose style entitled *Recentiores non deteriores* (in the series *Supplementa Humanistica Lovaniensia* for Peeters Publishers). Minkova is a regular fellow (since 1998) of *Academia Latinitati Fovendae*, the primary learned society for the promotion of Latin with a seat in Rome.

Francisco Javier Palacios-Hidalgo (he/him), associate professor, belongs to the Department of English and German Philologies of the University of Córdoba (Spain), where he teaches at the Faculty of Education Sciences and Psychology. His research focuses on the teaching of English as a foreign language, language and bilingual education teacher training, educational technologies, teacher digital literacy, and queer pedagogy.

Aspasia Papadima is an associate professor in the Department of Multimedia and Graphic Arts at Cyprus University of Technology. She is the founder and coordinator of the Language and Graphic Communication Research Lab, www.lgcrl.com. Formerly, she worked as a graphic designer in creative and advertising agencies in Greece and as an art director in the field of advertising in Cyprus. She works as both a graphic design consultant and a graphic artist. Her design work has been awarded in global competitions and exhibited locally and abroad. Her research interests include typographic rendering of the Cypriot-Greek, typographic and linguistic landscapes, semiotics, gender, and advertising. She is the author of the book (transl. from Greek) (2020) *Coffee and the Coffeeshop: Coffee Culture and the Semiotics of the Traditional Coffee Shop in Cyprus*, Athens: Kardamitsa Publications. She is a member of the International Association for Semiotic Studies (IASS-AIS), a member of the Hellenic Semiotic Society, and a member of the Cyprus Association of Graphic Designers and Illustrators (CAGDI).

Contributors

Abigail Parrish is Lecturer in Languages Education at the University of Sheffield. Her work draws on her previous career as a school languages teacher and uses self-determination theory to explore student motivation against a background of non-compulsory language learning. She is the Language Learning Editor of the Center for Self-Determination Theory. Her other main research interest is in language policy.

Cringuta Irina Pelea is Lecturer in Communication Studies at Titu Maiorescu University, Romania. Her primary research interests are cultural studies, social justice, and communication sciences. She is the editor of the volume *Culture-Bound Syndromes in Popular Culture* (Routledge, 2023) and, among other publications, has recently contributed to the *Routledge Companion to Literature and Social Justice* (2023) with a chapter on Romania's social movements for civil rights and democracy. Her current research project examines genocide narratives and testimonies of war survivors through AI, holographic, and immersive technologies and has been presented at Tampere University, Finland (DIGIKÄKI, Digital History and Handwritten Sources, May 2024). Her future work is expected in *Fashioning the Asian Century: Aesthetics, Sustainability and Popular Culture* (Bloomsbury, 2025) and *Future of Media in Asia* (Springer, 2025).

Elizabeth Pérez-Izaguirre holds a diploma in social education (University of the Basque Country, UPV/EHU), a BA in social anthropology (UPV/EHU), an MA in international relations (University of Kent), and a PhD in education (UPV/EHU). She is currently an associate professor at the Faculty of Education, Philosophy, and Anthropology at the University of the Basque Country (UPV/EHU). She is a member of the Department of Didactics and School Organization. Her research interests are focused on education in general, including multilingualism and the teaching of minority languages, from a qualitative and ethnographic perspective. Some of her other areas of interest include ethnographic research in art and art learning. She is a member of the AKTIBA research group and has been a visiting scholar at the University of Bordeaux; Case Western Reserve University; University of California, Berkeley; and University of Nevada, Reno.

Rita Prestigiacomo is a lecturer at the Graduate School of Biomedical Engineering at the University of New South Wales, Sydney, Australia. Rita received her PhD in education from the University of Sydney and holds an honors degree in foreign languages and literature from the Catholic University of the Sacred Heart in Milan, Italy. She has extensive teaching experience in languages other than English. Her current research focuses on co-design, curriculum development, and pedagogy in higher education. Currently, she is working on several educational research projects on students' identity and sense of belonging within the field of engineering.

Kellie Rolstad is Associate Professor of Applied Linguistics and Language Education at the University of Maryland. She previously worked as a bilingual teacher in the Los Angeles Unified School District. Her research concerns language variation, plurilingualism, and democratic education and has appeared in the *Bilingual Research Journal, Bilingual Review, Teachers College Record, Hispanic Journal of Behavioral Sciences, Educational Policy*, and in major edited collections. Professor Rolstad earned her PhD in education at UCLA, where she also earned degrees in linguistics (BA) and applied linguistics (MA). She currently serves as an associate editor for the *International Multilingual Research Journal.*

Karolina Rosiak is an assistant professor at the Celtic Studies Research Unit, Faculty of English, at Adam Mickiewicz University in Poznań, Poland. Her research examines the sociolinguistics of

xviii

Contributors

the Welsh language and linguistic aspects of Polish migration to Wales, with particular focus on language attitudes and ideologies and motivation to learn minority languages. She is also interested in cultural ties between Wales and Poland.

Iván A. Sanchís holds a BA in English philology (Univ. of Seville), an MA in second language teaching and European literature (Univ. of Huelva, Spain) and a PhD in Hispanic studies in the United States (Univ. of Seville). He has worked at Florida International University, University of Huelva, and Univ Pablo de Olavide (Seville) in the field of language and literature. He combined his research with the teaching of Spanish and English languages and the design of language courses in these two languages for specific purposes and linguistic and cultural immersion. Since 2020 has been working as a full-time professor at Facultad de idiomas, Univ. Autónoma de Baja California, in Ensenada, Mexico. Along with his teaching and research activity, he is coordinating a course diploma (160h) for teachers of Spanish as L2 and the center of official examinations of Instituto Cervantes Diploma de español como lengua extranjera (DELE). He is a member of different research groups in his area and was granted the National Researchers System scholarship.

Lara Sorgo holds a PhD in language and interculturality from the University of Primorska (Slovenia). Since 2020 she has been working as a researcher at the Institute for Ethnic Studies in Ljubljana. Her research focuses on minority protection, ethnic studies, and language policy. In particular, she explores the Italian national community and inter-ethnic relations, the situation and use of the Italian language, and the model of education in the ethnically mixed area of Slovene Istria. As part of her work, she attends international conferences and actively collaborates with other research institutions in Europe.

Rei Sugiura is a PhD student in applied linguistics at the Faculty of Language and Information Sciences of the University of Tokyo. She received a research grant from the Japan Society for the Promotion of Science (JSPS) Research Fellowship for Young Scientists (2023–2026). Her interest is in language in border regions, especially the France and Germany border, Alsace. She has submitted her master's dissertation on linguistic landscape in Strasbourg. She also has experience studying the ongoing phonetic variation of Japanese in urban areas. She is currently working on language variation and change in the Alsace region. Her thesis focuses on the phonetic variation of French spoken in Alsace.

Rosa Tabernero-Sala is Associate Professor of Language and Literature Didactics at the University of Zaragoza. She is the head researcher of the reference research group ECOLIJ (Communicative and literary education in the information society. Children's and Young Adult Literature and construction of identities). She is the director of the master's degree in reading, books, and readers for children and young adults at the University of Zaragoza (www.literaturainfantil.es/). She also directs the collection of Prensas Universitarias de Zaragoza [Re]pensar la educación. Her research interests include mainly aspects related to linguistic and literary education. She is currently the principal researcher of the project "Non-fictional readings for the integration of citizens in the new cultural ecosystem" (PID2021–126392OB-I00).

Arimardan Kumar Tripathi started higher education with a Master of Arts in language technology in 2005 and was later awarded his MPhil degree with "Semantic Net-Based Hindi Information Retrieval System" and PhD with "Anaphora Related Discourse Analysis and Natural Language Processing." He has published several books and papers in Hindi and English as sole and co-author/

editor. He has been the editor of a web magazine, *HindiTech* since 2010. Simultaneously, he has presented papers and delivered lectures all over India, focusing on Indian languages and language technology. As a professional researcher, he has worked on corpus management, machine translation, knowledge-based language processing, and digital documentation of Indian languages for institutions such as the Central Institute of Indian Languages, Microsoft India, North Eastern Hill University, and Shillong, along with his current affiliation with the Centre for Endangered Languages, Visva-Bharati, Santiniketan, West Bengal, India.

Terence Tunberg completed his doctoral studies in the Department of Classics and the Pontifical Institute for Mediaeval Studies at the University of Toronto in 1986. He began to devote himself to spoken Latin as a graduate student and has since then regularly taken part in seminars for spoken Latin in Europe and North America. In 1998 he was elected fellow of the *Academia Latinitati Fovendae*, the Rome-based international organization for maintaining the use of Latin. He has moderated the Conventiculum Latinum Lexintoniense, an annual immersion seminar in spoken Latin, for more than two decades. Together with Milena Minkova, he teaches in the *Institutum Studiis Latinis Provehendis* at the University of Kentucky, a two-year post graduate curriculum in which Latin literature and Latin composition are taught entirely in Latin. He has published extensively on prose style in classical and Neo-Latin, as well as the history of Ciceronianism. Together with Milena Minkova, he has written a manual of Latin prose composition, entitled *Readings and Exercises in Latin Prose Composition*. Tunberg is about to publish, in co-authorship with Milena Minkova, a book pertaining to Neo-Latin prose style entitled *Recentiores non deteriores* (in the series *Supplementa Humanistica Lovaniensia*).

Riitta-Liisa Valijärvi is Associate Professor of Finnish and Minority Languages at University College London and Associate Professor of Finnish and Finno-Ugric Languages at Uppsala University, Sweden. Her research areas are socio-cultural linguistics, language revitalization and reclamation, minoritized languages (including Meänkieli, West Greenlandic, and North Sámi), music, and language documentation and description, as well as nonbinary and gender-inclusive language.

Karin van der Worp holds a doctoral degree in education (UPV/EHU, Basque Country), a master's degree in teaching Spanish language and culture (RuG, The Netherlands), a master's degree in applied linguistics (RuG), a bachelor's degree in Romance languages and cultures (RuG), and a bachelor's degree in pedagogy (UPV/EHU). She is a professor at the UPV/EHU University of the Basque Country at the Faculty of Education, Philosophy and Anthropology in the Department of Research Methods in Education. She is a member of the research group DREAM (Donostia Research on Education and Multilingualism). Her research interests include multilingualism in the workplace and in education and minority languages. She has presented her work at national and international conferences and has published several articles in international academic journals.

George Wilson holds an MA in comparative education from the UCL Institute of Education and works as Head of English Programmes for the British Council in France. He has over 20 years of teaching and teacher training experience in French and Australian universities and is the author of a report into regional language policy in France and the UK published in the academic journal *Current Issues in Language Planning*. His work focuses on multilingual education, inclusive education practices, and regional language revitalization.

Contributors

Sabina Zorčič holds a PhD in applied linguistics from the University of Ljubljana (Slovenia). As the researcher at the Institute of Ethnic Studies in Ljubljana, she has published scientific research articles dealing with language choice, language competence, linguistic and national identities, native speakers, and minority and trans-border schooling (especially regarding Austrian Carinthia). She is involved in the national and international projects at the institute and at the same time is the editor-in-chief of the scientific journal *Treatises and Documents, Journal of Ethnic Studies*.

INTRODUCTION

Weixiao Wei

In an era marked by rapid globalization and technological advancement, the intricate interplay between language, identity, and education has never been more pivotal. This book is born out of a profound recognition of these dynamics and seeks to address the critical need for comprehensive language documentation, innovative language learning methodologies, and an enhanced understanding of language identity.

The preservation of linguistic diversity stands at the forefront of this book's mission. With thousands of languages at risk of extinction, language documentation efforts are essential not only for safeguarding cultural heritage but also for enriching the global tapestry of human knowledge. The chapters within this volume underscore the significance of meticulously documenting endangered and minority languages. By doing so, we preserve not only words and grammar but also the unique worldviews and cultural narratives embedded within these languages.

Equally important is the evolution of language learning paradigms. Traditional methods often fail to capture the complexities of multilingual and multicultural societies. This book introduces forward-thinking approaches that embrace the linguistic richness of learners, advocating for educational systems that recognize and leverage the diverse linguistic repertoires of students. By fostering an environment that values multilingualism, we can create more inclusive and effective language learning experiences.

Language identity, another central theme of this book, is explored through various lenses, revealing its fluid and dynamic nature. The chapters delve into how sociopolitical contexts, community perspectives, and technological influences shape language identity. They call for policies and practices that honor the linguistic rights and identities of all individuals, promoting social cohesion and respect for diversity.

By addressing these interconnected themes, this book hopes to make contributions to the fields of sociolinguistics, language education, and cultural studies by providing valuable insights and practical strategies for researchers, educators, and policymakers dedicated to fostering linguistic diversity and equity in an increasingly globalized world.

The preservation and revitalization of languages, especially those facing endangerment, is a pressing concern in today's globalized world. As linguistic diversity dwindles under the pressures of dominant languages and cultural assimilation, efforts to maintain and rejuvenate endangered and minority languages become increasingly critical. The following chapters of this book delve

DOI: 10.4324/9781003439493-1

into various case studies and theoretical analyses that address these challenges across different regions and contexts.

Chapter 1, by Govinda Ishwar Lingam, opens the discussion with a focus on the Pacific region, highlighting the crucial role of key stakeholders – governments, speech communities, higher education institutions, and international organizations – in preserving indigenous languages. Through a detailed examination of the impact of colonization and the contemporary efforts in countries like Fiji, the chapter underscores the importance of collective action to safeguard linguistic heritage against the encroachment of dominant languages such as English.

In Chapter 2, Riitta-Liisa Valijärvi shifts the lens to the Nordic countries, exploring language revitalization efforts in Finland, Sweden, Norway, Denmark, and the associated territories. This chapter frames language reclamation as a decolonial process intertwined with cultural and environmental contexts. By reviewing various revitalization strategies, including education programs and social media initiatives, Valijärvi provides a comprehensive overview of the successes and ongoing challenges in these efforts.

George Wilson's Chapter 3 narrows the focus to Cornwall, examining the revitalization of the Cornish language through educational systems. By tracing the historical decline and revival efforts, Wilson draws valuable lessons from other Celtic regions to propose strategies for enhancing Cornish-language education. This chapter emphasizes the integration of educational initiatives within broader language planning frameworks to support the language's long-term sustainability.

Chapter 4, authored by Elizabeth Pérez-Izaguirre, Karin van der Worp, and Marie-Anne Châteaureynaud, explores the interplay between print media and language ideologies in Pakistan. The chapter investigates how English dominance and the marginalization of local languages, such as Punjabi and Sindhi, are reflected in official policies and newspaper discourse. The analysis reveals a gap between policy and public sentiment, advocating for more inclusive language policies to strengthen local language education.

Briji Jose and Bettina Biju Jacob's Chapter 5 delves into the language dynamics in the United Arab Emirates, where the dominance of English poses a threat to Arabic. The chapter discusses how migrant populations influence Arabic language usage and explores strategies to enhance Arabic proficiency among second-generation migrants. Through a mixed-method approach, the chapter suggests policy adjustments to better integrate Arabic in the UAE's multilingual landscape.

Rei Sugiura's Chapter 6 examines the linguistic landscape of Strasbourg, focusing on Alsatian, a Germanic language with a contested status. The study highlights the visibility and perception of Alsatian in public signage and street names, revealing both the language's resilience and the challenges it faces in maintaining its presence and identity in contemporary Alsace.

Chapter 7, by Milena Minkova and Terence Tunberg, shifts to a broader perspective with a discussion on Latin. The chapter explores Latin's historical significance and its enduring role in global communication. By examining Latin's stability and its revival as a "living language," the authors argue for its continued relevance in facilitating dialogue across time and space, contributing to both historical understanding and contemporary engagement.

In Chapter 8, Karolina Rosiak investigates the role of language attitudes and ideologies in the learning of minority languages, specifically Welsh, by Polish migrants in Wales. The chapter explores how different attitudes and beliefs about language affect learning motivation and revitalization efforts. Rosiak's findings highlight the importance of considering sociolinguistic factors when developing language policies aimed at adult learners.

Rebecca Clothey and Brian McCommons's Chapter 9 focuses on the Uyghur language, examining the impact of repressive policies in China and the efforts of Uyghur communities in the diaspora to maintain their language. By comparing these efforts with successful revitalization

Introduction

movements, such as those for the Aymara language, the chapter offers insights and recommendations for bolstering Uyghur language resilience outside of China.

Chapter 10, authored by Sopuruchi Christian Aboh, explores the role of new media in sustaining endangered languages, with a focus on Igbo. The chapter highlights how platforms like Facebook and Instagram are used to promote and maintain Igbo while also discussing the impact of digital tools like podcasts in language teaching. The chapter advocates for increased support for technology-based language pedagogy and community engagement to ensure the continued vitality of the Igbo language.

As we delve deeper into the complexities of language preservation and policy, Chapter 11 explores the challenges that minor languages face within the digital landscape, focusing on India. Arimardan Kumar Tripathi presents an insightful examination of how digital advancements and cloud computing predominantly benefit major languages, thereby marginalizing less widely spoken ones. This disparity becomes evident as minor language speakers, such as the Birhor community, must often adapt to dominant languages like Bangla, Hindi, or English to fully engage with digital technologies. The chapter highlights how this trend threatens the survival of minor languages by reducing their visibility and functionality in the digital realm, where English and other major languages continue to dominate.

Moving from the digital to the technological, Chapter 12, by Cringuta Irina Pelea, investigates the role of Indigenous artificial intelligence in the preservation and revitalization of endangered and extinct languages. This chapter provides a groundbreaking analysis of how virtual reality (VR) and augmented reality (AR) can be leveraged to maintain cultural heritage and language vitality. Pelea explores whether these technologies can bridge the gap between Indigenous and non-Indigenous cultures, offering a global overview of pioneering projects that utilize VR and AR for language preservation. The discussion includes both the potential benefits and the challenges of integrating such advanced tools into Indigenous language revitalization efforts.

Shifting focus to East Asia, Chapter 13, authored by Britta Ingebretson, examines the impact of China's language policies on minority languages. Despite constitutional provisions for linguistic diversity, the promotion of Standard Mandarin (Putonghua) has led to the marginalization of regional languages through various policies in education, media, and urban development. Ingebretson's chapter explores the effects of these policies on language ideologies and speaker attitudes, revealing how economic incentives and prestige associated with Mandarin influence the valuation of minority languages and their preservation efforts.

In England, Abigail Parrish addresses the consequences of ideological monolingualism on language education in Chapter 14. The prevalent belief that English should be universally spoken or learned undermines the perceived value of other languages. Parrish's chapter critically examines how this monolingual ideology affects language learning uptake and achievement, arguing that overcoming such beliefs is crucial for recognizing the broader benefits of language education and addressing the current language learning crisis in schools.

Chapter 15, by Sabina Zorčič and Lara Sorgo, explores the new realities of multilingualism in minority schools within the context of Europe's inclusive educational policies. Their research highlights how minority education programs, originally designed for minority groups, are now attracting speakers of majority languages. The chapter examines the implications of this trend on linguistic competence and multicultural awareness, using case studies from Slovene secondary schools in Austria and Italian primary schools in Slovene Istria to illustrate the impact of increased participation by speakers of majority languages.

In Chapter 16, Marija Mandić investigates how regional and minoritized languages are positioned as resources within the European educational context. Her analysis provides a historical

3

and contemporary overview of European language policies, noting how regional languages are often relegated to cultural roles rather than being recognized for their instrumental value. The chapter critiques the educational models that incorporate these languages, arguing that while they contribute to social cohesion and cultural balance, they remain constrained by prevailing monoglot ideologies and face challenges from the dominance of English.

Katharine E. Burns, in Chapter 17, addresses the role of standard language ideology (SLI) in language learning contexts for endangered and minority languages. Her chapter examines how SLI perpetuates the belief in a single, standardized form of language as superior, impacting language teaching and learning practices. Burns highlights the need for a shift towards recognizing learners as emergent bilinguals with diverse linguistic repertoires, advocating for approaches that counteract SLI and incorporate sociolinguistic insights into language education.

Turning to educational innovations, Chapter 18 by Kellie Rolstad proposes a linguistically informed approach to education that integrates plurilingualism with place-based learning. Rolstad's chapter critiques traditional curricula for their lack of critical language awareness and suggests replacing "translanguaging" with "plurilanguaging" to better align with current research and policy. By combining place-based frameworks with plurilingualism, the chapter advocates for a model that bridges classroom instruction with authentic linguistic and cultural contexts, aiming to enhance educational practices and support diverse linguistic identities.

In Chapter 19, Iván A. Sanchís explores the concept of border culture identity through the lens of individuals living between Mexico and California. This chapter examines the linguistic and cultural dynamics of this border region, focusing on the interplay between English, Spanish, and indigenous languages. Sanchís highlights the marginalization of indigenous languages and the challenges faced by these communities, arguing for a broader interpretation of heritage language and greater institutional support for border communities.

In Chapter 20, Aspasia Papadima investigates the textual phenomena associated with the Cypriot-Greek dialect among youth. Her study of "Textese" – a hybrid linguistic code used in digital communication – examines orthographic, typographic, and ideological aspects of this informal language variant. Papadima's ethnographic research sheds light on how contemporary digital practices shape language use and cultural identity among Greek-Cypriot youth, offering insights into the evolving nature of Cypriot-Greek in a globalized context.

As we approach the final chapters of this volume, the examination of innovative and pressing issues in language education and preservation continues to unfold. Chapter 21, authored by Kayhan İnan and Gülin Dağdeviren-Kırmızı, investigates the educational linguistic landscape of the Autonomous Territorial Unit (ATU) of Gagauzia, where Gagauz, Russian, and Romanian function as official languages. Their study reveals a significant misalignment between the language policies set forth and the actual linguistic practices observed within educational settings. Through an in-depth analysis, the chapter highlights how Russian has emerged as the functionally dominant language, revealing a discrepancy between policy intentions and on-the-ground realities in language representation and pedagogy.

In Chapter 22, Cristina A. Huertas-Abril and Francisco Javier Palacios-Hidalgo delve into the realm of artificial intelligence–assisted language learning (AIALL) and its implications for democratizing language education in the contemporary global landscape. Their comprehensive review of 60 articles published from 2013 to 2023 evaluates the strengths, weaknesses, opportunities, and threats associated with AIALL tools. The chapter argues that while AIALL has the potential to enhance personalized learning and promote social equality, it also faces challenges such as unequal accessibility and high financial costs. The authors advocate for leveraging AIALL to support a more inclusive and critical approach to language education.

Introduction

Chapter 23, by Cédric Brudermann, addresses the role of European University Alliances (EUAs) in fostering intercultural awareness among students. As EUAs integrate diverse languages and cultures into their educational models, Brudermann explores the pedagogical strategies necessary to address cross-cultural communication challenges. By proposing the incorporation of global citizenship education (GCE) initiatives, the chapter outlines potential benefits and limitations in enhancing students' intercultural competencies through language and culture-based learning.

In Chapter 24, Beatriz Carbajal-Carrera and Rita Prestigiacomo challenge traditional hierarchies and linearity in language learning through the lens of rhizomatic approaches. Drawing from the botanical metaphor of rhizomes, the authors advocate for a non-hierarchical, interconnected model of knowledge that empowers learner agency and fosters critical literacy. The chapter provides an integrative review of how rhizomatic principles can address the limitations of conventional language learning frameworks, offering insights into their past contributions and future potential.

Chapter 25, by Iris-Orosia Campos-Bandrés and Rosa Tabernero-Sala, examines the use of non-fiction picturebooks in the educational context of the Aragonese language, a minority language facing challenges of intergenerational transmission and institutional support. Their multimodal project, "O nuestro charrar," seeks to reconstruct both teachers' and students' representations of Aragonese through innovative educational resources. The chapter evaluates the design and outcomes of this project, highlighting how non-fiction picturebooks can influence perceptions and support the language's educational efforts.

Finally, in Chapter 26, Nobuko Koyama addresses the integration of LGBTQIA+ issues into Japanese language education. The chapter critiques the traditional, prescriptive nature of foreign language textbooks and advocates for modular, critical approaches that reflect the evolving realities of gender and sexuality. By proposing practical, ready-made modules for educators, Koyama aims to promote inclusivity and diversity within language classrooms, challenging outdated norms and encouraging meaningful dialogue about LGBTQIA+ identities.

In conclusion, this volume traverses a wide array of contemporary issues in language education, from the challenges of preserving endangered languages in digital and educational contexts to the innovative integration of technology and critical perspectives. The chapters collectively highlight the need for a nuanced and inclusive approach to language policy, pedagogy, and practice, highlighting the importance of aligning educational strategies with the diverse needs and realities of learners and communities. Through these explorations, we hope to contribute valuable insights and practical solutions to advance language education and preservation in an increasingly interconnected and dynamic world.

SECTION I

Endangered and minority languages in the new global context

1
PRESERVING INDIGENOUS LANGUAGES IN THE PACIFIC REGION
The role of key stakeholders

Govinda Ishwar Lingam

Introduction

Language is a vital cultural indicator of the identity of people all over the world, including those living in the Pacific region. However, the use of many Indigenous languages is shrinking. The United Nations record on languages demonstrates that many languages may disappear by the end of the century (United Nations 2023). This is alarming, as the Pacific region is the home of many Indigenous languages. Without concrete protection by stakeholders, most of these languages are likely to dwindle in use to the point where they could become extinct. Their status contrasts markedly with those languages that are flourishing and spoken by many people throughout the world, such as the English language, because they have gained significance.

This chapter attempts to specifically discuss the role of the key agencies, namely governments, communities, higher education institutions, professional societies, speech communities, and significant others (hereafter 'stakeholders') to actively engage in preserving Indigenous languages from extinction. The geographical scope of the discussion focuses on six of the Pacific small island developing states (PSIDS). The linguistic situation of each country in the PSIDS and the wider Pacific region is beyond the scope of the present chapter. The chapter begins with brief background information about the PSIDS to help readers better understand the context, followed by a discussion on their cultural and linguistic colonisation. Next, the chapter provides brief case studies of the linguistic situation in a few selected countries, Vanuatu, Solomon Islands, Kiribati, Nauru, and Niue, before turning to a more detailed analysis of the linguistic situation in Fiji. The chapter also highlights the significance of Indigenous languages and the role of international agencies, such as UNESCO, as development partners together with other relevant stakeholders to promote, preserve, and reinvigorate the Indigenous languages. This is followed by some discussions on possible initiatives by stakeholders to sustain Indigenous languages. Finally, the chapter concludes by emphasising the need for appropriate support from the key stakeholders to safeguard the Indigenous languages in the PSIDS for a sustainable future.

DOI: 10.4324/9781003439493-3

Background

A necessary first step in discussing the language issue is a brief background of the region, namely the PSIDS. The classification criteria used by the United Nations (Hein 2010) for small island developing states is applied to include only those countries which fall under this category in the Pacific region (Figure 1.1).

These SIDS fall under three major regions: Melanesia, Micronesia, and Polynesia. For the purpose of this chapter, the discussion focuses on the three Melanesian island groups of Vanuatu, Solomon Islands, and Fiji; two Micronesian island groups of Kiribati and Nauru; and a single Polynesian island, Niue. In total, the region comprises small island nations and territories, as shown in Figure 1.1. Some of these nation states are made up of one main island, whereas others are archipelagos. According to Webb (2020), these nations are categorised by various indexes such as 'developing' or 'least developed'. As mentioned earlier, a relatively recent term to describe these islands is small island developing states (Hein 2010). The PSIDS face various development challenges and constraints, including language documentation, education, and financial management due to their economic vulnerability and ecological fragility (Hein 2010).

Apart from their small size, these islands are notable for their isolation from the other major regions of the world. One striking feature of the PSIDS is the 'immensity of the ocean over which they are scattered, about one-third of the earth's surface' (Lingam et al. 2015: 338). Furthermore, Jenkins (1993: 19) describes the Pacific region as 'Vast tracks of ocean divided up into jigsaw-like geometric shapes and appearing to cover a sizeable proportion of the surface of the planet earth. The many islands appear almost a scattering dot'. He goes on to note that it is 'a region so diverse

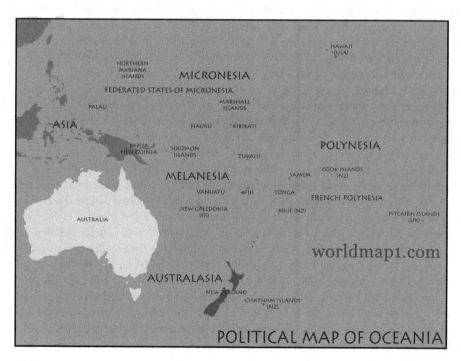

Figure 1.1 Map showing SIDS in the Pacific region

Preserving Indigenous languages in the Pacific region

and disparate in its communities and cultures' that the provision of any services in such a scattered geographical context is a mammoth challenge.

Because of smallness and remoteness, these countries experience situations and challenges that are very different from those of a developed country. These same characteristics mean the economies of these island nations are very limited. For this reason, from the time they were colonised, PSIDS have depended on external aid from countries and agencies outside the region, as well as on Western ideas in a wide range of areas. Without aid packages, developments in all sectors of the economy, including education, would be difficult. The region is also characterised by wide-ranging diversity in terms of not only geography and social, economic, historical, political, and educational development but also more obviously culture, ethnicity, and language. The last mentioned is the focus of the discussion in this chapter.

As Marti (2006: ix) succinctly states:

Each language is an epistemological and axiological universe. Each language offers original metaphors, ideas, and symbols for understanding and expressing the world, society, and human experience. Each language is a vehicle for values, ethics, and aesthetics expressing desires and utopias.

From this point of view, language is a treasure for the whole of humanity. It therefore is important to encourage all stakeholders to work collaboratively to ensure all Indigenous languages are safeguarded.

In terms of language, the region is probably the most linguistically diverse and complex of any region in the world. Lynch (1998: 25) states succinctly:

There are, or were, almost fourteen hundred distinct languages spoken in the Pacific or about one quarter of the world's languages spoken in the Pacific. And these fourteen hundred languages are spoken by not much more than 0.1 percent of the world's population! Further, so far we can tell, these languages do not all belong to a single language family.

There may be more Indigenous languages in the PSIDS than Lynch's estimation. Certain aspects of the language may not have been fully captured in depth and richness when recording in the past, as most documentation was achieved using a traditional pencil-and-pen style of recording (Seifat et al. 2018). This is a challenge for researchers, policy makers, and others who have a vested interest in undertaking research in the field of language in the region. It is noteworthy that the documentation of languages has increased over the past decades via surveys conducted by missionaries, linguists, local activists, and other stakeholders, and we now have a more accurate estimate of Indigenous languages in the PSIDS and beyond (Francois 2018).

The growth of digital technology has greatly enhanced the work, specifically in terms of recording, storing, and accessing multimedia records pertaining to different languages (Seifat, et al. 2018; Francois 2018). Databases such as Glottolog and Ethnologue help summarise these findings, and PSIDS languages are well represented in a number of online archives, such as the PARADISEC (Francois 2018; Hammarström et al. 2017). Online archives are useful, but they need to be periodically maintained. The cost of maintaining digital archives is a big challenge due to ongoing changes in the technology (Seifat et al. 2018). Thus, archives themselves are potentially endangered in keeping up with technology. For the PSIDS, this is a grave issue due to their limited financial resources to support costly initiatives. One of the advantages of having language documented and archived is that the language archive materials could be used later to assist the revitalisation of moribund or extinct languages (Sammons and Leonard 2015).

In future, more technological developments are likely to happen, and with high-quality tools, a lot more will be possible in terms of documentation, analysis, and flourishing of endangered and minority languages (Hieber 2015; Jones 2019). Development of endangered language technology in the age of cloud-based application and the use of online tools such as TypeCraft, ELAN, and FLEX are other alternatives to demonstrate how technologies can be applied to revitalise endangered language (Jones 2019). As reported by Tanzer and his colleagues (2024), the use of translation machines such as machine translation from one book (MTOB) has greatly enhanced language translation work. Such a method could be usefully utilised to leverage qualitative data pertaining to small speech communities. At the moment, there are no Indigenous language computational tools available in the PSIDS, and having them would surely boost the maintenance of Indigenous languages. The combined use of the old technologies and new ones by various stakeholders in the PSIDS would be a milestone achievement for safeguarding loss of their Indigenous languages.

Even though language documentation by linguists continues, for example, through collaborative workshops and web-based projects, there is still a lot more work required in the PSIDS to document their endangered and rapidly dwindling linguistic diversity (Francois 2018). In addition to language diversity between nations, many nations have considerable language diversity within their borders. Indeed, most PSIDS have more than one Indigenous language due to the linguistic differences among their population.

Globally it is estimated that between 35% and 42% of languages are still substantially undocumented, including PSIDS Indigenous languages (Francois 2018, Seifat et al. 2018). Language documentation efforts need to speed up due to pressure of colonial languages, such as the use of English leading to accelerating loss of Indigenous languages (Francois 2018). A combined effort of all stakeholders such as governments; higher education institutions (HEIs), especially language scholars for their dissertations; and professional societies and foundations can help increase the state of documentation of Indigenous languages of the PSIDS. As mentioned earlier, due to financial constraints, the PSIDS need to source funds from elsewhere to document their Indigenous languages, although the lack of local expertise may hinder work in this invaluable area (Tamata 2022). However, the existence of powerful organisations in developed countries such as the Volkswagen Foundation, the Arcadia Foundation, and the Max Plank Society through its various institutes could help in the research and documentation of languages. Such renowned organisations that could undertake big initiatives such as research and documentation of languages do not exist in the PSIDS. Even high-quality language journals are not easily accessible and affordable in the PSIDS to anyone with a vested interest in knowing more about research in languages. Subscription costs are too high for most local academics and graduate students.

The next section focuses on cultural and linguistic colonisation with reference to a few selected countries of the PSIDS.

Cultural and linguistic colonisation

Most of the countries in the Pacific region, including the PSIDS, were colonised by countries such as the United Kingdom, USA, Germany, and France. This section briefly summarises the cultural and linguistic history of a selection of PSIDS, with a focus on the impact of colonisation on their Indigenous languages.

Vanuatu, a small island developing state, is unique in having a history as a colony of both France and the United Kingdom. As a result, people there use both English and French as the official languages today. Together the population of less than a million people speak an estimated 138 Indigenous languages (Francois et al. 2015). Vanuatu is regarded as one of the world's most linguistically diverse nations. This diversity is well captured even in the constitution of Vanuatu, which reads: 'We the people of Vanuatu, proud of our struggle for freedom, determined to safeguard the achievement of this struggle, cherishing our ethnic, linguistic, and cultural diversity, hereby proclaim the establishment of the united and free Republic of Vanuatu' (Constitution of the Republic of Vanuatu 2006: 5).

Bislama is the only national language of Vanuatu and widely used as the lingua franca. It is closely related to both Tok Pisin in Papua New Guinea and Solomon Islands Pijin and is classified as Melanesian Creole (Crowley 1980, 2004; Terril 2002). Along with the languages of the colonisers, Britain and France, the Bislama language unites all people in Vanuatu. This is because not all ni-Vanuatu speak both French and English: some are Francophone and others Anglophone. Instruction in Bislama and other Indigenous languages takes place especially at the pre-school and primary school levels (Vanuatu Ministry of Education 2012). Despite Bislama being designated as the only national language, privilege is still accorded to both English and French as the media of instruction in education. Moreover, some Indigenous languages in Vanuatu are moribund – that is, spoken by a few elders who remain alive – and as such, these languages are almost extinct (Francois 2012). According to statistics, only 81 known languages are still active, 17 are considered moribund, and 8 are already extinct (Charpentier 2006; Lynch and Crowley 2001; Vari-Bogiri 2008). Towards the end of the 19th century and during the 20th century, the spread of diseases killed many people, which resulted in loss of many languages and dialects (Codrington 1885; Francois 2012). The situation in Vanuatu clearly reflects the heterogeneity of its languages, especially in the use of both English and French in addition to many other local Indigenous languages. Charpentier (2006) notes that various factors such as mobility of the people and political policies have favoured European languages over the Indigenous languages.

Solomon Islands became a British colony in 1893 and gained independence in 1978. Together with Vanuatu, Fiji, and other parts of the wider Pacific region, it belongs to the geocultural region known as Melanesia. Solomon Islands has 71 recognised Indigenous languages, 16 of which are classified as significantly endangered (Simons and Fennig 2018). It is reported that the average size of each language is around 9,000 speakers (Early 2007). Solomon Islands is also home to Solomon Islands Pijin. As mentioned earlier, this language is similar to Tok Pisin in Papua New Guinea and Bislama in Vanuatu, which are varieties of Melanesian Creole. Solomon Pijin is English-based creolising and is now the major lingua franca throughout the country (Early 2020).

Initially, because British colonial rule was de facto, involving minimum intervention, use of the vernacular languages was common in all parts of the country (Burt 1998). After World War Two, however, the British government took control of education, and the English language became the sole medium of instruction in schools and for all official purposes and key functions. In terms of education, Early (2020: 87) highlighted that 'English competency and literacy is regarded as the key learning outcome for all schools and all supporting mechanisms (curricula, classroom resources, assessment, teacher education, and development) are operated in English only'. As far back as the 1980s, Solomon Islanders saw the English language as a language of power and advancement, and, as a result, the role of vernacular languages diminished (Tryon and Hackman 1983). It is reported that there are a number of endangered languages in Solomon Islands, and Lavukalevu is one of them because it has a very small language community (Terril 2002).

In Micronesia, the small island developing state of Kiribati was colonised by three imperial powers: the British in 1788 and later the Japanese, followed by the Americans. It gained independence in 1979. Kiribati comprises 33 islands, most of which are uninhabited, and has a population of about 100,000 (Ohi and Ingram 2022). It is one of the most remote and geographically dispersed countries in the Pacific region. Economically, Kiribati is one of the least developed countries in the world, ranking 40th among 43 nations in the Asia-Pacific region (Webb 2020). The nation relies heavily on the sale of fishing licences to companies based in other countries such as Japan, Korea, Taiwan, and China (Webb 2020). Another source of income that Kiribati relies on heavily is aid from foreign development partners.

Kiribati has two main dialects, Northern and Southern, spoken across the nation, but Te-Kiribati (known as Gilbertese while Kiribati was a colony) is the standard national language that unites Kiribati people (Ohi and Ingram 2022). For Kiribati, the linguistic story following colonisation is somewhat different from that of other island nations. Initially, the British colonial government stipulated that the language of instruction should be Te-Kiribati by withholding the offering of the English language (Ohi and Ingram 2022). As a result, in the colonial era, the vernacular language remained prevalent in the country. Later, English became the language of instruction in schools throughout Kiribati and gained recognition over the Te-Kiribati language. All official events and ceremonies held in the country use the English language for communication purposes (Ohi and Ingram 2022). In recent years, the Kiribati government through the education ministry is encouraging citizens through government agendas, policies, and classroom teaching practices to attain better English language proficiency. This would provide them a more promising future due to the high possibility of an impending diaspora because of rising sea level (Ohi and Ingram 2022).

Another nation in Micronesia, Nauru, is a tiny island of only 21 square kilometres, located in the Western Pacific. It was colonised by Germany in 1878, when German became the language of instruction in schools. Later, Australia, New Zealand, and the United Kingdom carried out a joint administration of Nauru, and English became the language of instruction in schools. The Nauruan language, like other local Indigenous languages, has not had the chance to be used in various modern contexts, and as such, following independence, the English language continues to encroach on the domain of the Nauruan language. For example, television programmes such as news, musical shows, and documentaries are predominantly presented in English (Baker 2012). Over the years, the status of the English language has continued to grow, and it is envisaged that the Nauruan language is endangered. One of the notable reasons for this is that the speech community is small, numbering only a few thousand (Baker 2012).

Niue is part of the Polynesian group of islands. It is a small island nation with fewer than 2000 residents. Contact with the Europeans began around the late 17th century. As a former New Zealand colony, it enjoys a unique constitutional arrangement with New Zealand and shares common citizenship and a single currency (Lingam and Lingam 2015). Because the country lacks critical resources, there has been a huge exodus of Niueans to New Zealand. New Zealand Niueans far outnumber Niue-resident Niueans, yet all of them identify as Niueans. The official languages in Niue are Niuean and English.

Niueans are now experiencing a dilemma when attempting language maintenance initiatives in an English-dominant context, namely New Zealand. As a result, the Niuean language, which is already endangered, could become extinct in future (Starks 2008). Some web-based forums are dedicated to Niueans, allowing them to share everything related to their culture, including language (Sperlich 2005). However, as the forums attract users of English, too, this initiative appears to be harming the Niuean language rather than saving it (Sperlich 2005). The New Zealand government offers a wide range of support to Niue. Like other countries in the Pacific, Niue depends heavily on development partners for most development work, including education, due to its limited economic resources.

Fiji is part of Melanesia. It became a British colony in 1874 and was a colony for almost 104 years before it achieved independence in 1970. Initially the colonial rule in Fiji was guided by policies to preserve the Indigenous way of life, including language – 'paramountcy of Indigenous interests becoming the guideline and mantra of colonial policy in Fiji' (Lal 2006: 4). Over time, the colonial government established schools and trained teachers. It mandated the medium of instruction in schools was to be English. After achieving independence, Fiji continued with the education system the colonial government had set in place. Although the independent government gradually phased in reforms to modernise the education system, the education system remains very much a manifestation of the system that existed in the colonial era, including with English as the medium of instruction in education (see the case study that follows for further discussion). It also dominates media and government.

Generally, the situation described for the previous countries resonates with the experience of the other countries in the PSIDS. For the colonial administration across the countries in the region, English in particular and French, especially in French colonies, were used to enhance social cohesion and political stability. As a result, English in all PSIDS has become an invaluable language in education because it promises a better future, especially in terms of employment (Ohi and Ingram 2022). The English language has also gained popularity in almost all other spheres of life.

The spread of the English language has had a detrimental effect on local cultures and languages (Phillipson 1992). Colonisation negatively impacted not only Indigenous people's languages but also their histories, lands, and other aspects connected to their daily living. They are still struggling to maintain and restore their traditions and local cultures, including languages, due to the huge devastation experienced over the many years of imperialism and colonialism. As a result, Indigenous languages and cultures, including knowledge, have been suppressed, subjugated, or silenced, while the discourses and power of the West have gained recognition (Nabobo-Baba 2012; Phillipson 1992).

Looking back at these transformations brought about by European imperialism stirs a wide range of feelings and attitudes – both positive and negative – throughout the Pacific region. Due to the growing concern about Western influence, Pacific scholars formed an initiative known as the Rethinking Pasifika Education Initiative for and by Pacific People (RPEIPP) in the last decade (Nabobo-Baba 2012). The main purpose was to indigenise education on the basis of Pacific peoples' Indigenous cultures such as, language, values, and leadership (Nabobo-Baba 2012; Sanga 2006, 2011). Unfortunately, since then, not much has been achieved to give greater recognition to Pacific knowledge systems and cultures, including languages in the education systems.

One constructive way forward for governments and other stakeholders of the PSIDS is to use the UNESCO's (2011) methodological guideline known as the Language Vitality and Endangerment (LVE) tool to gather relevant information about a particular Indigenous language. The tool consists of nine factors that determine the extent of vitality/endangerment of a language. Based on the analysis of the data, informed decisions could be made on measures to be taken for language maintenance or revitalisation. The tool has been applied in several contexts, and researchers have found it to be useful. Some researchers have added additional factors to cater to their unique context. Through this approach governments, language communities, linguists, educators, and other stakeholders could better prioritise and strategise the safeguarding measures of any Indigenous language. The next section offers a detailed analysis of the language situation in Fiji.

Language: A case study of Fiji

The 2017 Population and Housing Census showed that Fiji had a total population of 884,887, of which 1.2% are Rotumans, 57% Indigenous Fijians, and 38% Indo-Fijians, the remainder being minority groups (Fiji Bureau of Statistics 2018). The main languages are English, Fijian, and Hindi, while other languages are spoken by the minority groups living in Fiji, such as Rotumans, who live in the northernmost island of Fiji. Also, there are other minority languages of people who have migrated to live in Fiji. For example, the people of Kioa Island and Rabi Island are originally from Tuvalu and Kiribati, respectively, and they speak their own languages as well as Fijian.

Even though Rotuma is within the Fiji group, it is linguistically and ethnically distinct. The Rotuman language is one of the endangered languages reported by UNESCO. The teaching and learning of Rotuman language is carried out only in schools located in Rotuma. Children whose parents migrate elsewhere in Fiji do not have access to Rotuman language learning. With a population of less than 2000 still living on the Island, the Rotuman language needs to be strongly reinforced and taught to all school-aged Rotuman children at whatever cost. Based on the small number of people speaking the language, other appropriate measures need to be put in place by the stakeholders to sustain the language. Otherwise, the language will further diminish in status and possibly become extinct.

As stated earlier, in Fiji, the combined population of all ethnic groups is still not even 1 million. The total population of Indigenous Fijians (known as iTaukei), including both those living in Fiji and those abroad, is likely to be less than half a million (Fiji Government 2019). This indicates that the number of Indigenous people speaking the Fijian language is relatively small. The Standard Fijian (SF) language is referred to as *Vosavakaviti or Vosavakaviti Raraba*, and the Fiji government (2010) changed the official name of SF from Fijian to iTaukei to clearly reflect that it is the language of the Indigenous people of Fiji. Furthermore, the SF language is a mixture of different communalects rather than one related to a particular geographical area, and there are approximately 300 Fijian dialects (Tamata 2022). With respect to the Fijian language, several studies, including documentation of the language, have been carried out during colonial and post-colonial times. Some linguists have produced documentation of different communalects, such as Nadrau (Kikusawa 2001), Wayan (Pawley and Sayaba 1990), and the whole area of Fiji (Geraghty 1983). This demonstrates the positive contribution linguist stakeholders can make to safeguarding language loss. More linguists who speak the Indigenous language are needed to enhance documentation and translation work.

Fiji also has a substantial population of speakers of Hindi and other Hindustani languages; however, they have their roots in India, so, fortunately, their languages are spoken by millions of people and as such are sustainable. Fiji Hindi is not the standard Hindi, and there have been many debates around this issue. However, local academics and linguists perceive that Fiji Hindi is a legitimate language for the people of Fiji (Delaibatiki 2021; Pillai 1990; Shameem et al. 2022). This language is well maintained by the Girmitya descendants, but there was fallout by the public when one of the radio stations switched from standard Hindi to Fiji Hindi, and its CEO had to provide justification on the change through debates and interviews (Shameem et al. 2022). Shameem and her colleagues (2022) report that the popularity of standard Hindi is slowly shrinking because it uses Devnagari script, which people are not good at unless they have studied Hindi at school. The Universal Roman Code with some adaptations could be effectively used towards orthography of Fiji Hindi to help the language continue to survive, and some work towards this initiative has already begun (Shameem et al. 2022). A workshop on this initiative was held in New Zealand which was funded by UNESCO New Zealand (Shameem et al. 2022). Such initiatives require funding, and unfortunately this is a challenge in Fiji and other PSIDS.

Even though Hindi and Fijian languages are part of the national curriculum and recognised along with English in the 2013 constitution of Fiji, they are not taught in all primary and secondary schools throughout the country. This is because the education ministry has not made it compulsory.

Another challenge is the unavailability of qualified vernacular language teachers. Each school has the discretion to choose which vernacular language to teach (Fiji Islands Education Commission 2000). For example, a school that is managed and owned by the Sangam denomination encourages the teaching of the Tamil language. Similarly, a school owned and managed by the Methodist Church teaches the Fijian language. A positive development at the primary school level is the introduction of Conversational Fijian and Conversational Hindi to those students who do not speak Hindi or Fijian at home (Tamata 2022). However, only a few sessions are allocated for this per week. At the primary school level, the language policy from the education ministry states that teachers are to teach lower primary children in the vernacular languages, but this is rarely followed in practice, reflecting a large dissonance between policy and practice. A lack of adherence to the language policy in the curriculum could eventually reduce children's interest in their own language, with the result that local people in the not-too-distant future could be incapable of speaking their Indigenous language fluently.

On a positive note, in 2017, the Fiji government launched a mobile app called iVolavosa to enable other communities to learn the language and for fostering healthy relationships among all communities (Fiji Government 2019). In addition, the national media capabilities, especially television and radio broadcasts, play an important role in promoting and protecting Indigenous languages. There are two television service providers and a total of 11 radio stations in Fiji. Of these radio stations, three specifically air programmes in the Fijian language. Of the remaining radio stations, equal numbers air Hindustani and English language programmes. The television services have a number of channels which provide entertainment, cultural, and news programmes in Fijian, Hindustani, and English languages. In 2022, Fiji TV One launched the first-ever iTaukei language channel, known as the *Na Lololo* TV channel (Fijian Holdings Limited 2022). This channel airs programmes associated with Fijian language, culture, traditions, and challenges of everyday life. It is interesting to note that one of the Fijian programmes specifically focuses on the Fijian language and is known as *Vueta Na Vosa*, meaning raising the language (Tamata 2022). An academic from the University of the South Pacific, Dr Paul Geraghty, normally participates in the programme and discusses pertinent issues relating to the Fijian language. He has depth and breadth of knowledge about the iTaukei language and is a fluent speaker. Such initiatives by the TV service provider are good in terms of safeguarding the language from becoming endangered. With respect to Hindustani, a lot of entertainment, religious, and cultural programmes from India and locally produced programmes are aired at different times of the day.

Another interesting development in 2024 is the launching of the Rotuman News program by one of the stakeholders, Fiji TV (Low 2024). The news program is titled *Filo Ne Rogrogo* and is aired on the *Na Lololo* TV channel. As mentioned earlier, the Rotuman language, which is largely spoken by the Rotuman people, has been recognised as an endangered language by UNESCO and linguistic experts. Presenting the news in the Rotuman language gives a clear indication of the importance of promoting and protecting the unique Rotuman linguistic heritage. Such initiatives by stakeholders can make a huge difference as part of the efforts to preserve the Rotuman language. In future, television companies could include a program on the Rotuman language like that on the Fijian language, that is, *Vueta Na Vosa*. This will be a positive step towards motivating the Rotuman people to think about the consequences of their language loss, and as speakers of the language, they would realise the need to maintain their own language as a mark of their identity in the world.

Besides television and radio, newspapers also play a significant role in keeping a language alive. In the case of Fiji, *Nai Lalakai* and *Shanti Dut* are the two vernacular newspapers, which are published weekly. The *Fiji Times* and *Fiji Sun* are both in English and are published daily. The

Table 1.1 Materials in Fijian language available to the public in Fiji

Media	Title	Producer
Radio	*Bogi ni Tusitib ena walu* 'Tuesday nights T 8'	Radio Fiji
TV	*Vueta na vosa* 'Raising the language'	Fiji TV
DVD (play)	*Lakovi* 'Marriage proposal'	iTaukei Trust Fund
DVD (play)	*Keteketeqele* 'The basket of soil'	iTaukei Trust Fund
DVD (play)	*Na iLululu* 'Handshake'	iTaukei Trust Fund

Source: Tamata 2022: 151

production of two vernacular newspapers is commendable, as the public gets an opportunity to read and also contribute articles in their respective languages for publication. Such publications can be digitally archived for future use. Even more online language materials and cultural programs could be made available for the local public and Fijians in diaspora communities. There are now some materials in the Fijian language available to the public.

It is pleasing to note that some materials in the Fijian language are stored and available to the public. With the advancement of technology, especially the use of digital technology, more materials in the Fijian language could be documented and stored safely, which hitherto was not possible. As mentioned earlier, the iTaukei Trust Fund Board members could commit more funds to ensure more materials are available in the Fijian language in future.

The government of Fiji commended the United Nations for launching the International Year of Indigenous Languages and stated that it is committed to protecting the Indigenous languages in Fiji. Keeping the Indigenous languages alive leads to other benefits, especially when applying traditional knowledge in areas such as environment, climate change, and biodiversity, given that so much knowledge is contained in the vernacular.

The period following the COVID-19 pandemic saw an increasing rate of migration of people from the Pacific region, especially from Fiji to Australia and New Zealand. An exodus of skilled and experienced workers such as nurses, teachers, and tradespeople could increase the number of people using the English language in their everyday conversation and neglecting their own vernaculars. The younger generation of the Fiji Indian diaspora, such as those living in New Zealand, shows patterns of shifting to adopt the English language (Shameem et al. 2022). On the other hand, Tamata (2022) reports that Fijians abroad celebrate Fijian language week and other cultural events, even though they may be speaking the language of that particular context. Because of the use of the English language in the workplace, those Fijians living abroad may further adopt the use of the English language in their homes to help their children better adjust to school when they begin their studies. The largest concentration of Pacific communities lives in New Zealand and Australia. The high rate of migration of the speech communities could have a detrimental effect on the usage of some Indigenous languages in the future.

Both Fijian and Rotuman languages are part of the school curriculum, and this platform at least ensures some protection for these Indigenous languages. The Fiji government is proud that broadcasts in the Fijian language via TV and radio enabled communities to better prepare themselves during natural disasters, especially climate-induced disasters. At the international level, the Fiji government, as part of the COP23 Presidency, introduced the use of the Indigenous word 'talanoa' (Fiji Government 2019). The term 'conveys a core Fijian cultural principle; that issues, no matter how great or small, can be resolved and consensus can be reached through discussion and listening to one another' (Fiji Government 2019: 3). Likewise, the Indigenous word 'Bula', which means hello/welcome, is used by the national carrier, Fiji Airways, and resorts to greet tourists. Even though some of these initiatives are small, they make a positive contribution towards longevity of the language.

In contrast to the Indigenous languages, the English language is prominent throughout the curricula in Fiji because it is the compulsory language in all schools. It is an examinable subject in all internal and external examinations. Moreover, it is the language of instruction in higher education institutions (HEIs). For example, English is the official language of the University of the South Pacific (USP), which is owned by 12 member countries in the Pacific region. At HEI in Fiji, English language proficiency is a requirement for completing any program of study unless specified otherwise. Overall, the English-language programs dominate not only in the television services but also in the radio stations. Anecdotal evidence shows that most families tune into English radio stations and watch English television programs. To date, English continues to dominate in all spheres of life, following on from the prominence given to the language during the colonial era in Fiji.

Significance of Indigenous languages

Apart from confirmation of people's identity the world over, language also plays an integral part in learning at all levels of education. When children are immersed in their first language in their early years, they are likely to do well academically. Conversely, immersing children in another language can adversely affect their cognitive, linguistic, and educational development. Research findings on language learning and teaching have shown that education in the medium of the student's mother tongue has a significant role in predicting their success in learning. If teaching is delivered in a learner's mother tongue, then the learners are unlikely to face any difficulties in understanding the concept taught, as the delivery is done in a language which they understand better. On the other hand, if teaching is delivered in a foreign language, then the learners will face challenges, as they may not properly comprehend what is being delivered.

Yet although learning concepts in foreign language may demotivate a learner, it is also important to remember that knowledge of a foreign language allows speakers to communicate with the outside world, which opens a window of opportunities. According to Mustapha and Argungu (2019), effective communication is possible when speakers speak the same language. This is very true in Fiji's context. As a multi-racial country, Fiji has classrooms full of students from diverse linguistic backgrounds. Hence, if teachers and students speak the same language, then effective communication will take place. However, if either of them is not proficient in the target language, then communication breakdown and misunderstanding between the two groups will occur (Mustapha and Argungu 2019). The use of the English language could be a factor contributing to the low levels of students' learning outcomes.

In a study on the effect of first language maintenance on successful English and academic achievement among students in Fiji, Fujioka-Kern (1994) found a significant correlation between literacy in the first language and overall academic achievement in all the groups she tested. As far back as the 1970s, similar studies in other settings affirm that children learn better when using their mother tongue rather than a foreign language, specifically English (Bamgbose 1976; Mugler and Lynch 1996; Siegel 1996; Tabouret-Keller 1997). Colonisation and more recently globalisation have affected the learning experiences of higher education students in the South Pacific, and some of the problematic areas identified relate to the use of the English language and the Western teaching and learning pedagogies adopted by the local education systems (Clarence 2003). Several other writers have reported that the differences between two cultural forces – mainly Western education and students' home cultures – contribute to the learning gap for students in the Pacific region (Clarence 2003; Taufeʻulungaki 2004; Thaman 2009).

Based on feedback from the teachers in Fijian primary schools, the Fiji Islands Education Commission (2000) recommended mandating Fijian language as a medium of instruction in schools. The basis for this recommendation was that teachers indicated students found it difficult to understand what they teach in English, so they frequently have to use the Fijian language instead. Now that English has been emphasised as the medium of instruction in schools for many decades, parents, students, and other stakeholders are strongly invested in its use in education and pay scant attention to the vernacular languages for academic purposes. In Fiji, parents tend to encourage their children to learn and speak the English language from a very early age. Children are exposed to online games and other English programs available on online platforms. Some parents even go to the extent of talking to the children in English at home. They buy books written in English to help their children excel in the language and perform well academically. Such an emphasis both at home and at school reinforces the attitude that the English language is more important than Indigenous languages.

Having English as the language of instruction used in schools is culturally undemocratic because it ignores the learners' culture, especially their language, in the teaching and learning process, and this is deemed unethical (Korman 1974). As mentioned earlier, language plays a vital role in learning but in most countries in the Pacific region, English is mainly used in the teaching and learning process. The experience of Kiribati illustrates the negative impact of this practice on learning. Its official policy is that only 20% of education is to take place in the Kiribati language, with the remaining 80% in English (Ohi and Ingram 2022). Despite this policy, students and teachers are encouraged to always speak in English. The education ministry in Kiribati encourages the culturally undemocratic use of a language that is foreign to the learners as well as teachers. According to Thaman (2009: 2),

> learning in a foreign language such as in English or French has become the rule rather than the exception, as the structure as well as the processes of schooling continue to neglect the languages of the communities that send students to school.

The effect of this practice is illustrated through anecdotal evidence from Kiribati teachers on in-service training at USP: from their experience in teaching at senior secondary school, the students faced difficulties with the use of English language and were struggling with their studies. This illustrates that the foreign language contributes to students failing their examinations or scoring low marks.

From the author's work experience in the Pacific region, students are not confident or fluent in English and have little knowledge of how to speak and write in it. Using it contributes to the culturally undemocratic nature of schools in Kiribati and other parts of the PSIDS. A flow-on effect is that the use of English language is a factor in dissipating I-Kiribati and other Pacific Island peoples' values such as customary practices, mutual respect, and spiritual faith.

The same effect is evident in other countries in the Pacific region (Puamau 2004; Sanga 2000; Thaman 2009). Local Tongan academic Taufe'ulungaki (2004) strongly argues for the importance of having local languages as part of the school curriculum. She states that using vernacular language has the effect of 'revitalizing and maintaining both the language and culture of its speakers, improv[ing] classroom interactions and consequently the quality of learning' (2004: 30). Because teachers are the key transmitters of knowledge to students, Sanga (2000: 6) argues that teachers need to 'establish a basis for communication, they must deal with differences between cultures of home and school, and they must value their students' cultural values, speech rules and learning systems'.

More than this, it can contribute to social marginalisation of the communities involved. Yet, despite the compelling evidence that using children's home language at school improves their performance, most governments in the PSIDS continue to emphasise the use of English language as the medium of instruction in schools.

Thus, safeguarding and protecting all languages is a necessity across the entire PSIDS. The issue is particularly acute where a language is spoken by a minority group: the continued growth in the use of English could gradually lead to the extinction of such languages, and as a result these groups could lose their traditional values, identity, and cultural roots. A clear example comes from the small island of Rotuma, which has been politically affiliated with Fiji since 1881 and has Rotuman as its distinctive Indigenous language. This language is ranked by UNESCO as one of the world's endangered languages.

Like Rotuman, several other Indigenous languages spoken in other countries in the PSIDS are in danger of extinction because not many people speak these languages, and at the same time more people are using the English language as a lingua franca to communicate with others who have a different mother tongue. The English language has grown in popularity for this purpose because of globalisation, which sees many people travelling, as well as living and working with people from diverse linguistic backgrounds.

Another broader influence comes from the use of English as the medium of instruction in primary and secondary schools and from there into the HEIs of all countries of the PSIDS. The required use of English in education institutions is a clear testimony to its significance in all facets of life. It is on this basis that English has become a language of communication in the PSIDS that is more widely used than the local Indigenous languages.

International and regional support for Indigenous languages

Based on the premise that many Indigenous languages throughout the world, including those in the Pacific region, are endangered, the United Nations General Assembly has declared the decade from 2022 to 2032 the International Decade of Indigenous Languages. The intent of this declaration is specifically to promote, revitalise, preserve, and reinvigorate Indigenous languages throughout world. As succinctly stated by the United Nations (2023: 3–4), the purpose is:

> to draw attention to the critical loss of indigenous languages. . . . The Decade is an opportunity to expose and address the severe loss of indigenous people's languages locally, regionally, and globally. It is a chance for the entire world community to come together and commit to bringing indigenous languages back from the brink of dormancy or extinction.

It is necessary, therefore, to take some urgent steps at local, regional, and global levels to keep all Indigenous languages alive.

Recently, at the Conference of Pacific Education Ministers (CPEM), held in Auckland, New Zealand, from 20 to 22 March 2023, ministers discussed two key issues relating to language learning and teaching. First was the question of how language policies could improve the literacy of our students; the second question was how we can help students to learn languages such as English and French without marginalising Pacific languages. The French language is taught only in French-dominated areas such as Vanuatu. Even though the ministers want vernacular languages to be taught in schools, the emphasis is still on foreign languages and English in particular. Some of the constraints they highlighted in teaching vernacular languages include the lack of trained teachers and resource materials.

A more general problem is that Indigenous issues are given little attention in contemporary times due to the dominance of Western knowledge in all parts of the globe. For instance, at the 1990 World Conference on Education for All, in Jomtien, Indigenous people were seen as clients who needed to become literate by using the English language to improve their educational achievement and enable them to contribute to the gross national product (Thaman 2009). Similarly, at the World Commission on Indigenous Education held in Sydney, Australia, the need to hear the voices of Indigenous peoples in all spheres of intellectual life was emphasised, but little action was taken to leverage this to an appropriate level (Thaman 2009). Prior to this, a UNESCO-sponsored conference in Rarotonga, Cook Islands, which was attended by educators from the Pacific region including Māori and Australian Aboriginal educators, reaffirmed the role of Pacific cultures in educational development (Thaman 2009), but again, not much was achieved.

At the 2016 Indigenous Language Conference organised at USP, the participants recognised the importance of safeguarding Pacific languages (Willams 2016). But guaranteeing a sustainable linguistic future for the Pacific region requires every echelon of society and government to commit substantially to this goal. Every new generation needs to understand the value of their language, to be able to stand up for their linguistic rights in their schools, in organisations, and in international negotiations (Willams 2016).

In view of the current status of languages in the Pacific region, appropriate initiatives need to be formulated and enforced to promote Indigenous languages. This has significant implications for stakeholders such as internation organisations, HEIs, communities, and governments in that they all have a role to play in providing additional support to boost the use of Indigenous languages in educational systems and beyond to sustain them.

Initiatives sustaining Indigenous linguistic futures

As noted in previous sections, Indigenous languages of the Pacific region are at risk of becoming endangered and possibly extinct in future. To address this issue, all key stakeholders – such as governments, HEIs, and other international organisations and development partners – need to play an active role in saving local languages from extinction, considering that many are already endangered.

Higher education institutions

HEIs and schools are potential settings for language revival and for promoting Indigenous languages that are less commonly spoken or are not currently taught. HEIs – specifically those responsible for teacher education and training – can offer studies in Indigenous languages. Governments and even other agencies within the region and beyond could support such institutions in a variety of ways. They could incentivise students to take up these language studies as electives or majors through offering scholarships and some promise of secured jobs, for example, as interpreters, after completing their studies.

In the last decade, USP has taken some constructive steps in introducing Indigenous language courses, reducing the focus on English. For example, it offers a diploma in vernacular language in one of the following languages: Fijian, Hindi, Cook Islands Māori, Tongan and Niuafo'ou, and Vagahau Niue (USP 2024). It is also possible to complete degrees in either of the two major languages spoken in Fiji, Fijian and Hindi. The development of both iTaukei and Hindi language programs was funded by the iTaukei Trust Fund Board and Indian High Commission, respectively (Tamata 2022). In the Bachelor of Arts and Graduate Certificate in Education program, students can take English plus a vernacular language as their majors. In this program, student teachers are professionally prepared on the didactics related to vernacular language education. At the moment, the vernacular language programs are available for students in Cook Islands, Fiji, Niue, and Tonga to complete a diploma in vernacular language. Fijian speakers can take their studies further to the level of a postgraduate diploma in Fijian language. There are plans to introduce a masters and doctor of philosophy in vernacular languages (Tamata 2022). It is notable that, even though USP offers studies in Fijian and Hindi languages, the enrolments in these two programs are very low because students and even parents feel that mastering these languages would not really help them to secure a lucrative job within or outside Fiji. Conversely, they see knowing English as helpful in securing seasonal work overseas, such as in Australia and New Zealand.

The steps that USP has taken so far to include some Pacific vernacular languages in study programs are generally positive. However, one disadvantage is that these programs are only offered as in-country projects rather than being available as or part of the mainstream programs. When a sufficient number of students is available, then the courses are conducted based on the university's business model. With this model, which rests on making profit, it is unlikely that a sufficient number of students will be available at any point in time to run the in-country projects. In addition, while the programs help to sustain some of the languages spoken by the locals, many other Indigenous languages of local minority groups are not included in USP's programs of study. What efforts can be made to support the sustainability of those languages?

The number of HEIs in the Pacific region is slowly growing. At one time, USP was the only HEI available for 12 island nations in the Pacific – Fiji, Cook Islands, Tokelau, Nauru, Kiribati, Solomon Islands, Samoa, Vanuatu, Tuvalu, Niue, Marshall Islands, and Tonga. In the last two decades, a few more countries, including Fiji, Tonga, Samoa, Solomon Islands, and Vanuatu, have established their own HEIs. In addition to their normal offerings, these institutions could play a crucial role in advocating for the teaching and learning of local languages. Their support would enable some of these local languages to receive the attention they deserve and at the same time help sustain them. USP, as the premier regional institution, has modelled a way that other HEIs in the region can include Indigenous language studies in their programs.

Non-governmental organisations

It is interesting to note that a Centre for Pacific Languages, based in Auckland, New Zealand, has been established. This non-government organisation offers online, 10-week courses in Samoan, Cook Islands Māori, Vagahau Niue, Tongan, Fijian, and Rotuman. The Centre is also responsible for providing translation services in Samoan, Tongan, Vagahau Niue, Cook Islands Māori, Fijian, Rotuman, Tuvaluan, Te Kiribati, and some dialects of Indigenous languages in Papua New Guinea. The Centre is a lead organisation in promoting activities associated with Pacific languages and culture in New Zealand.

In the same vein, each country in the region could set up a similar institution to be responsible for promoting all Indigenous languages spoken in that country, especially those in danger of extinction. For example, such an institution could liaise and provide educational justification to the media companies such as TV to run programs in Indigenous languages such as musical shows, news, and documentaries. Otherwise, they will run programs which will enable them to make maximum profit. Such an organisation could be a means of providing all languages with resources for language learning, along with additional language support to minority groups with their smaller language communities. Further, such institutions could assist governments in formulating suitable policies to promote Indigenous languages. All of these types of activities would help safeguard and protect the Indigenous languages across the Pacific region.

Policies for language learning and teaching

Over recent decades, governments in the Pacific region have been struggling to introduce policies that address the linguistic challenges of sustaining local languages. For instance, in 2012 the Council of Ministers endorsed the Vanuatu National Language Policy 2012 (Vanuatu Ministry of Education 2012), and the education ministry has since worked towards implementing the policy. In addition to utilising English and French, the policy focuses on using island vernacular and/or Bislama as the instructional language for grades K–3. With a similar intent, the language policy in Fiji encourages mother-tongue literacy, but this is not really enforced in practice at the lower primary level in Fiji schools. Generally, experience shows that instruction in schools can be carried out effectively in more than one language in any educational setting (Baldauf and Kaplan 2006; Taylor-Leech 2013).

In Tonga, the current language policy was developed in 2004 with a top-down approach with little community participation and consultation. The policy states that Tongan is to be the only language used in Classes 1 to 3 of primary school. In Class 3, English should be informally introduced through songs and poems, taking about 60 minutes of class time per week. English is to be formally introduced in Class 4 and limited to only 20% use, compared with 80% use of Tongan. In the last two years of primary school, use of English should then increase to 30% in Class 5 and 40% in Class 6. For all levels of high school (Forms 1 to 7), English and Tongan are to be equally used, at 50% each (Tonga Ministry of Education 2004).

Despite this policy, past research findings identified that the top schools – especially the government-run schools – continue to teach in English only (Otsuka 2007). Anecdotal evidence indicates support for this practice in the wider community. As far back as the 1990s, Taufe'ulungaki (1999) reported that parents of students at Tonga High School once petitioned to remove Tongan as a subject from the school, as they believed it was a waste of time. Even today, the current prime minister has proposed a language policy of bringing the use of English back to Class 1. In response, Tongan academic Dr Taufe'ulungaki told Radio New Zealand:

> The Tongan language is one of the strong indicators of our identity as Tongans. Tonga is the home of the Tongan language and if Tonga does not privilege its own language in its home country, who else would privilege the language?
>
> (Hopgood 2021)

In most countries in the Pacific region, what the processes of developing and implementing language policies seem to have in common is that they have followed a typical top-down model. In Vanuatu, the language policy overlooks the community's opposition to schooling in the vernacular and its even stronger feelings against Bislama. There appears to be an ongoing debate on the issue. To effectively promote the implementation of such a policy, genuine consultation at the grassroots level is vital. This approach would be consistent with the increasing preference for policy-making at all levels of the organisation and systems and for close consultation at the grassroots level. Such an approach to language policy development would surely promote an understanding of the relevance of teaching students' mother tongue in schools and a wider acceptance of the practice.

A proper language policy that takes account of these issues needs to be formulated and enforced. To this end, it is worth considering these suggestions from Subramani (2000: 290):

> Language policy and planning should be viewed as a deliberate effort to influence the attitudes of citizens with respect to language instruction. Because decisions about teaching languages affect language status, language boundaries, and language communities, all stakeholders, together with Ministry of Education and teacher training institutions, should be involved in the initial planning. Unplanned language policies usually have a detrimental effect on the mother tongue, the vernaculars and the learning of a second language.

With the enforcement of a well-planned language policy, schools could offer teaching in an Indigenous language as part of the school curriculum. Schools could also organise and run other activities to promote the Indigenous languages in the communities they serve. For their part, governments could support educational institutions and communities in such initiatives in various practical ways such as through funding and sponsorship.

As the English language continues to expand its role as the global lingua franca, it is imperative that Indigenous languages be given due attention by policy-makers. Without such initiatives, the linguistic and cultural colonisation of Indigenous and local communities will continue throughout the Pacific region. Furthermore, ongoing scholarly dialogue about this agenda – the politics and practice of language learning and teaching – warrants specific attention from everyone with a vested interest in promoting Indigenous languages in schools and teacher education programs (Biesta et al. 2020).

Resources and qualified teachers

If teachers are to effectively teach in any Indigenous language, both they and their students need an abundance of suitable resource materials. Based on the author's work experience in the Pacific region, the shortage of such resource materials is an endemic problem in most schools. A clear illustration of this point comes from the tiny atoll of Nauru, where the official language is Nauruan, while English is the language of instruction. Teaching in the Nauruan language is severely hampered by the lack of suitable resource materials and even of qualified teachers to teach in what could be another fast-dying language (Baker 2012).

As Nauru's experience indicates, another major obstacle to promoting and protecting Indigenous languages is the unavailability of teachers qualified to teach these languages. The current generation of teachers were themselves students at either English or French schools and then received their teacher training in either English or French. As a consequence, their entire educational knowledge and experience are grounded in either English or French, and they lack the level of proficiency and didactics required to educate children in their vernacular language. This lack of proficiency, combined with the lack of resources for them in those languages, such as no standardised orthographies, dictionaries, and other materials, clearly places heavy constraints on teachers' ability to implement a policy that promotes Indigenous languages.

To address these obstacles, governments in the PSIDS together with development partners could give priority to funding initiatives that promote Indigenous languages, especially those on the verge of becoming extinct, by developing and providing language textbooks and other learning resources. Education ministries could come up with short- and long-term solutions with respect to the training of language teachers and producing suitable resource materials. For example, they could take a somewhat flexible approach to the teacher shortage by appointing local people to teach until a qualified teacher is available. Such support from principal stakeholders is necessary to revitalise the endangered Indigenous languages.

Funding

Because the Pacific region is not economically rich, it relies heavily on financial support from development partners, overseas governments, and other agencies to bring about improvements in education and other sectors. The so-called characteristics of 'small island developing states', such as those in the Pacific region, are recognised as bringing particular challenges to 'education for development' related to scale, geography, and institutionalism (Crossley 2010). In particular, the issues associated with the remote and small nature of countries in this region mean governments have to confront the challenges of limited resources – whether they be fiscal, human, infrastructure-related, or curricular – in their respective school contexts. In addition, leaders of schools in the least developed, remote islands face an added burden of meeting the same accountability requirements as their urban counterparts, while they have limited financial resources along with a lower tax base and per capita grant.

Because our peoples in the Pacific deserve much better, international agencies and industrialised nations might consider contributing to shifts in policy and understanding in ways that promote Indigenous language learning and teaching in schools and communities in the Pacific region. As they have done for funds for climate change activities in the region, international agencies such as UNESCO and developed nations could set aside more funds for these PSIDS to use in initiating activities for promoting and sustaining Indigenous languages. All countries in the Pacific region have commercial banks, which could allocate grants for those intending to advance their studies in vernacular languages. Already Westpac Bank in Fiji provides an education grant to students who present the best posters and essays on the theme of 'Women's and Girls' Education'. This could be a model for commercial banks and other corporations to set up a similar initiative related to revitalising endangered languages, given this is imperative in terms of maintaining people's identity.

Yet in providing assistance, some donor agencies diplomatically request certain concessions in return. Vanuatu, for example, gained substantial financial support from the Chinese government in recent times, while it also signed a memorandum of understanding to help include the learning and teaching of Chinese Mandarin as a foreign language in Vanuatu's primary and secondary schools (Lingam 2022). The Chinese government has also promised that it will prepare a pool of Chinese-language teachers and develop Chinese-language textbooks and learning materials. This case clearly demonstrates how politics influences language policies and how the Chinese government can afford to train teachers and provide relevant resources for teaching a Chinese language.

Another significant development is the establishment of the Chinese Institute at USP, which offers the study of Chinese language (Lingam 2022). In addition to being available at the main Laucala campus in Fiji, the programme is offered in the campuses of Tonga, Kiribati, Vanuatu, and Solomon Islands. The Chinese government promotes the inclusion of Chinese language in the education systems of as many countries as possible for their long-term benefit. French is becoming another popular language in the region. In light of these trends, governments of the countries in the PSIDS need to promote Indigenous languages in their respective countries with greater conviction.

Language exhibitions

Language exhibitions could be another means to uplift the level of appreciation and interest and at the same time better understanding of any language. In Fiji's case, there are very few linguists, and this adversely impacts language-related research and other activities such as language exhibitions.

Preserving Indigenous languages in the Pacific region

Language exhibitions are not an innovation. One has been held, for example, in Minpaku, Japan, at the National Museum of Ethnology (Kikusawa 2019). Since 2019, the iTaukei Trust Fund Board in Fiji has been planning to set up a cultural centre, but this has not happened so far. As mentioned earlier, there are different communalects of Fijian spoken throughout the country. Each communalect has unique characteristics, and this could form part of the content of the exhibition. As suggested by Tamata (2022: 156) 'Interactive and digital exhibitions would attract young people, in particular, sound and video materials must be included'. Inspiring young people with insightful exhibitions using advanced technology would be a pragmatic way to influence them to take responsibility to safeguard and sustain their language. Other vital information about the culture and language could be available in the exhibition not only for the speakers of the language but also for others, including tourists. Such exhibitions would help speakers of the language to gain more insights and knowledge about their language. In addition, there are 'sources of unity and pride in a language exhibition' (Tamata 2022: 153). This can help with language maintenance. The iTaukei Trust Fund Board, traditional leaders, and chiefs are other key stakeholders who could play an active role in preserving their Indigenous language and culture in Fiji. Similar exhibitions could be planned and conducted in other PSIDS.

Conclusion

Language is an important *eyedentity* (emphasis using the optical principle) for all people, including those living in the PSIDS. As this chapter has shown, the PSIDS are linguistically and culturally very diverse and share similar colonial histories and the consequences of colonialism on their culture and language. In addition, the number of Indigenous languages spoken varies widely from country to country, and overall, the speech communities are small. This chapter has also highlighted the linguistic situation in a few selected countries in the PSIDS to illustrate the dwindling situation of the Indigenous languages. A more in-depth analysis with particular attention to the linguistic situation in Fiji demonstrates some positive developments in the Indigenous iTaukei language, especially with an increase in the content of this language in media such as television. However, the Rotuman language needs a lot more attention from stakeholders. In the context of PSIDS, it is readily apparent that the growth of dominant languages such as the English language places at risk the future of the many diverse Indigenous languages, with their relatively small number of speakers.

Additionally, the chapter has shown how the use of new and old technologies by the stakeholders can greatly enhance their efforts to intensify language preservation and documentation. The use of the UNESCO (2011) tool LVE could greatly assist stakeholders in deciding on the interventions needed to revitalise endangered Indigenous languages. In this regard, a combined effort of the stakeholders can help towards preserving the Indigenous languages, and the chapter has especially highlighted some constructive interventions to sustain the Indigenous languages. Different communities are likely to respond to such initiatives in different ways, and flexibility may be needed in terms of their implementation in the PSIDS.

It should not be forgotten, however, that the speakers and communities speaking the language have a key role to play in maintaining and passing on the language to the next generation. Where the tradition of the locals is strong, the vernacular languages will continue to be spoken and remain alive. Without the concerted efforts of all stakeholders, more Indigenous languages of the PSIDS could become endangered and possibly extinct in future. As theorist Stuart Hall (2005) points out, globalisation is increasing the flow of ideas, leading to changes around the world in a compressed time. This means everyone throughout the world is experiencing changes in all areas – including culture and language – much faster now than ever before. This fast pace of change is one of the characteristics of 'New Times' that Hall describes, and this could adversely impact Indigenous languages in the PSIDS.

References

Baker, X. (2012). 'English Language as Bully in the Republic of Nauru'. In V. Rapatahana and P. Bunce (Eds.), *English Language as Hydra: Its Impacts on Non-English Language Cultures* (pp. 18–36). Short Run Press.

Baldauf, R. B. and Kaplan, R. B. (Eds.). (2006). *Language Policy and Planning in Fiji, The Philippines and Vanuatu*. Great Britain: MPC Books Ltd.

Bamgbose, A. (1976). *Mother Tongue Education: The West Africa Experience*. London: Hodder and Stoughton.

Biesta, G., Takayama, K., Kettle, M. and Heimans, S. (2020). 'Teacher Education between Principle, Politics, and Practice: A Statement from the New Editors of the Asia-Pacific Journal of Teacher Education'. *Asia Pacific Journal of Teacher Education*. 48(5): 455–459.

Burt, B. (1998). 'Tradition and Christianity: The Colonial Transformation of a Solomon Islands Society'. *The Journal of the Royal Anthropological Institute*. 4(4): 820–821.

Charpentier, J. M. (2006). 'The Future of the Languages of Vanuatu and New Caledonia'. In D. Cunningham, D. E. Ingram and K. Sumbuk (Eds.), *Language Diversity in the Pacific: Endangerment and Survival* (pp. 131–136). MPG Books Ltd.

Clarence, A. (2003). 'Of Gaps and Bridges: Educational Challenges for the Pacific'. *Directions: Journal of Educational Studies*. 25(1 and 2): 17–27.

Codrington, R. H. (1885). *The Melanesian Languages*. Oxford: Oxford University Press.

Constitution of the Republic of Vanuatu (2006). *Laws of the Republic of Vanuatu: A Consolidated*, 6th ed. Vanuatu: Government of Vanuatu.

Crossley, M. (2010). 'Context Matters in Educational Research and International Development: Learning from the Small States Experience'. *Prospects*. 40: 421–429.

Crowley, T. (1980). *Beach-la-Mar to Bislama: The Emergence of a National Language in Vanuatu*. Oxford: Oxford University Press.

Crowley, T. (2004). 'Bislama Reference Grammar'. *Oceanic Linguistics*. 44(1): 301–305.

Delaibatiki, N. (2021). 'Fiji Hindi: It's a Legitimate Language for People of Fiji'. *Sun Fiji*. May 29: 9.

Early, R. (2007). 'Language Sizes in Melanesia'. In J. Siegel, J. Lynch and D. Eades (Eds.), *Language Description, History, and Development* (pp. 439–456). John Benjamins Publishing Co.

Early, R. (2020). 'Adjusting Language-an-Education Practices in a Multilingual Society: A Solomon Islands Case Study'. In S. Johansson-Fua, R. Jesson, R. Spratt and E. Coxon (Eds.), *Relationality and Learning in Oceania: Contextualising Education for Development* (pp. 87–101). Brill Sense.

Fiji Bureau of Statistics (2018). *2017 Population and Housing Census*. Suva: Fiji Government Printer.

Fiji Government (2010). *Republic of Fiji Islands Government Gazette, Volume II*. Suva: Fiji Government Printer.

Fiji Government (2019). 'International Year of Indigenous Languages High-level Event of the General Assembly: Fiji Statement'. *fiji.pdf* (unmeetings.org)

Fiji Islands Education Commission (2000). *Learning Together: Directions for Education in the Fiji Islands*. Suva: Fiji Government Printer.

Fijian Holdings Limited (2022). *Fiji TV Launched First Ever iTaukei Language Channel-Na Lololo TV*.021728554.PDF (spx.com.fj).

Francois, A. (2012). 'The Dynamics of Linguistic Diversity: Egalitarian Multilingualism and Power Imbalance among Northern Vanuatu Languages'. *International Journal of the Sociology of Languages*. 214: 85–110.

Francois, A. (2018). 'In Search of Island Treasures: Language Documentation in the Pacific'. In B. McDonell, L. Andrea, Berez-Kroeker and G. Holton (Eds.), *Reflections on Language Documentation 20 Years after Himmelmann 1998* (pp. 276–294). France: HAL-Open Science.

Francois, A., Lacrampe, S., Franjieh, M. and Schnell, S. (Eds.). (2015). *The Language of Vanuatu: Unity and Diversity*. Australian National University: Asia-Pacific Linguistic College of Asis and the Pacific.

Fujioka-Kern, Y. (1994). *The Effect of First Language Maintenance on Successful English and Academic Achievement among Students in Fiji*. Unpublished MA thesis. Suva: The University of the South Pacific.

Geraghty, P. (1983). *The History of the Fijian Language*. Honolulu: University of Hawaii Press.

Hall, S. (2005). 'The Meaning of New Times'. In D. Morley and K. H. Chen (Eds.), *Stuart Hall: Critical Dialogues in Cultural Studies*. USA: Routledge.

Hammarström, H., Sebastian, B., Robert, F. and Martin, H. (Eds.). (2017). *Glottolog 3.1*. Jena: Max Planck Institute for the Science of Human History. http://glottology.org/.

Hein, P. (2010). *Views and Perspectives of the Committee for Development Policy on United Nations Support for Small Island Developing States*. United Nations: Department of Economic and Social Affairs.

Hieber, D. W. (2015). 'Review of Endangered Languages and New Technologies'. *Language Documentation and Conservation*. 9: 344–350.

Hopgood, S. J. (2021). 'Tongan Academic Concerned about Proposed Language Policy'. *Radio New Zealand*. www.rnz.co.nz/international/pacific-news/438409/tongan-academic-concerned-about-proposed-language-policy

Jenkins, D. (1993). 'Regional Collaboration in Teacher Education'. *Pacific Curriculum Network*. 2(1): 19–20.

Jones, M. C. (Ed.). ((2019). *Endangered Languages and New Technologies*. Cambridge: Cambridge University Press.

Kikusawa, R. (2001). 'A Sketch of the Syntactic Structures of Nadrau Fijian'. *Journal of Asian and African Studies*. 62: 35–90.

Kikusawa, R. (2019). 'Utilising Visual Materials for Introducing the Languages of the World and the World of Language'. In N. Sonoda (Ed.), *Conservation of Cultural Heritage in a Changing World* (pp. 195–204). Osaka: National Museum of Ethnology.

Korman, M. (1974). 'National Conference on Levels and Patterns of Professional Training in Psychology: Major Themes'. *American Psychologist*. 29: 301–313.

Lal, B. (2006). *Islands of Turmoil: Elections and Politics in Fiji*. Canberra: Asia Pacific Press.

Lingam, G. I. (2022). 'Teaching and Learning of Indigenous Languages in the Pacific: Are We Doing Enough in Teacher Education?'. *Asia-Pacific Journal of Teacher Education*. 50(5): 447–452.

Lingam, G. I. and Lingam, N. (2015). 'Are They Fit for Leading? Teachers' Perceptions of Leadership Practices of Niuean School Principals'. *International Studies in Educational Administration*. 43(1): 3–15.

Lingam, G. I., Raturi, S., and Finau, K. (2015). 'Pacific Island Countries: Improving Educational Reach with Information and Communications Technology'. In M. Crossley, G. Hancook and T. Sprague (Eds.), *Education in Australia, New Zealand and the Pacific* (pp. 335–360). England: Bloomsbury Academic.

Low, E. (2024). 'Fiji TV Officially Launches Rotuman News Programme'. *Fiji One News*.

Lynch, J. (1998). *Pacific Languages: An Introduction*. Honolulu: University of Hawaii Press.

Lynch, J. and Crowley, T. (2001). *Languages of Vanuatu: A New Survey and Bibliography*. Australian National University: Pacific Linguistics.

Marti, F. (2006). 'Foreword'. In D. Cunningham, D. E. Ingram and K. Sumbuk (Eds.), *Language Diversity in the Pacific: Endangerment and Survival* (pp. ix–xi). MPG Books Ltd.

Mugler, F. and Lynch, J. (Eds.). (1996). *Pacific Languages in Education*. Suva: Institute of Pacific Studies.

Mustapha, G. H. and Argungu, I. A. (2019). 'Importance of Language Teaching and Communication'. *International Journal of Research and Innovation in Social Sciences*. 3(8): 513–515.

Nabobo-Baba, U. (2012). 'Transformations from Within. Rethinking Pacific Education Initiative. The Development of a Movement for Social Justice and Equity'. *The International Education Journal: Comparative Perspectives*. 11(2): 82–97.

Ohi, S. and Ingram, P. (2022). 'Preparing I-Kiribati for the Future: Probing the English Language Research-policy Nexus in Kiribati'. *Asia Pacific Journal of Education*. 42(3): 478–496.

Otsuka, Y. (2007). 'Making a Case for Tongan as an Endangered Language'. *The Contemporary Pacific*. 19(2): 446–473.

Pawley, A. and Sayaba, T. (1990). 'Possessive Making in Wayan, a Western Fijian Language: Noun Class or Relational System?'. In J. Davidson (Ed.), *Pacific Island Languages: Essays in Honour of G. B. Milner* (pp. 147–171). School of Oriental and African Studies.

Phillipson, R. H. L. (1992). *Linguistic Imperialism*. Oxford: Oxford University Press.

Pillai, R. (1990). 'Adhura Sapana'. In I. Gaskell (Ed.), *Beyond Ceremony: An Anthology of Drama from Fiji* (pp. 195–256). Suva: University of the South Pacific.

Puamau, P. (2004). 'Re-thinking Educational Reform in the Pacific'. *Directions: Journal of Educational Studies*. 26(1): 21–41.

Sammons, O. and Leonard, W. (2015). 'Breathing New Life into Algonquian Languages: Lessons from the Breath of Life Archival Institute for Indigenous Languages'. In *Papers of the Forty-Third Algonquian Conference: Actes du Congres des Algonquinistes, 207–204*. Albany: SUNY Press.

Sanga, K. (2000). *Learning from Indigenous Leadership*. USP: Institute of Education.

Sanga, K. (2006). *Brief Summary of the Rethinking Pacific Education Initiative for & by Pacific Peoples* (RPEIPP): *Report to NZAID*. NZ: Wellington.

Sanga, K. (2011). 'Indigenous Pacific Emerging Educational Metaphors'. *Paper Presented at the 12th International Conference on Diversity*. University of British Columbia, Vancouver.

Seifat, F., Evans, N., Hammarstrom, H. and Levinson, S. C. (2018). 'Discussion: Language Documentation Twenty-five Years on'. *Language*. 94(4): 324–345.

Shameem, N., Goundar, F. and Khan-Janif, J. (2022). 'Orthography Development of Girmit Hindustani, a Case Study of Fiji Hindi'. *Directions: Journal of Education Studies*. 36(1): 99–115.

Siegel, J. (1996). *Vernacular Education in the South Pacific*. Canberra: AUSAID.

Simons, G. F. and Fennig, C. D. (Eds.). (2018). *Ethnologue: Languages of the Americas and the Pacific*, 21st ed. Dallas, TX: SIL International.

Sperlich, W. (2005). 'Will Cyber Forums Save Endangered Language? A Niuean Case Study'. *International Journal of the Sociology of Language*. 172: 51–77.

Starks, D. (2008). 'The Changing Roles of Language and Identity in the New Zealand Niuean Community: Findings from the Pasifika Languages of Manukau Project'. *International Journal of Bilingual Education and Bilingualism*. 9(6): 374–391.

Subramani (2000). 'Learning Languages Together'. In *Fiji Islands Education Commission* (pp. 290–300). Suva: Fiji Government Printer.

Tabouret-Keller, A. (1997). *Vernacular Literacy: A Re-evaluation*. Oxford: Clarendon Press.

Tamata, A. (2022). 'Potentials of a Fijian Language Exhibition Based on Fijian GIS Data'. In K. Ritsuko and S. Fumiya (Eds.), *Fijian Languages: Cultures and Their Representation* (pp. 149–158). Osaka: National Museum of Ethnology.

Tanzer, G., Suzgum, M., Visser, E., Jurafsky, D. and Melas-Kyriazi, L. (2024). 'A Benchmark for Learning to Translate a New Language from One Grammar Book'. https://lukemelas.github.io/mtob?fbclid=IwAR0H ncezCiZ-z07TPF8PcTO-IJvO_0eVZSaiUJRziJKE1TPtckV9cTlXTLk

Taufe'ulungaki, A. M. (1999). 'The Teaching of Vernacular Languages in the Pacific with Special References to Tonga'. *Pacific Curriculum Network*. 8(2): 2–4.

Taufe'ulungaki, A. M. (2004). 'Language and Culture in the Pacific Region: Issues, Practices and Alternatives'. *Journal of Educational Studies*. 27(1): 12–42.

Taylor-Leech, K. (2013). 'Timor-Leste: Sustaining and Maintaining the National Languages in Education'. In R. B. Baldauf, R. B. Kaplan, N. M. Kamwangamalu and P. Bryant (Eds.). *Language Planning in Primary Schools in Asia* (pp. 185–204). London: Routledge.

Terril, A. (2002). 'Why Make Books for People Who Don't Read? A Perspective on Documentation of an Endangered Language from Solomon Islands'. *International Journal of the Sociology of Language*. 155/156: 205–219.

Thaman, K. H. (2009). 'Towards Cultural Democracy in Teaching and Learning with Specific References to Pacific Island Nations (PINs)'. *International Journal for the Scholarship of Teaching and Learning*. 3(2): 1–9.

Tonga Ministry of Education (2004). *Tonga Educational Policy Framework 2004–2009*. Tonga: Ministry of Education.

Tryon, D. T. and Hackman, B. D. (1983). *Solomon Islands Languages: An Internal Classification*. Canberra: ANU Printing Press.

UNESCO (2011). *UNESCO's Language Vitality and Endangerment Methodological Guideline: Review of Application and Feedback since 2003*. UNESCO's Culture Sector.

United Nations (2023). *Why Indigenous Languages Matter: The International Decade on Indigenous Languages 2022–2032*. United Nations, Department of Economic and Social Affairs.

University of the South Pacific (USP) (2024). *USP Handbook*. Suva: University of the South Pacific.

Vanuatu Ministry of Education. (2012). *Vanuatu National Language Policy 2012*. Vanuatu: Vanuatu Ministry of Education.

Vari-Bogiri, H. (2008). 'Safeguarding Endangered Languages in Vanuatu: A Case Study'. *Paper Presented at the UNESCO/UNU Conference on Globalisation and Languages: Building on over Rich Heritage*. Tokyo, Japan, 27–28 August 2008.

Webb, J. (2020). 'Kiribati Economic Survey: Oceans of Opportunity'. *Asia & the Pacific Policy Studies*. 7(1): 5–26.

Willams, F. (2016). 'Carving Out Institutional Space for Multilingualism in the World's Most Multilingual Region: The Role of Linguistics at the University of the South Pacific'. *Current Issues in Language Planning*. 17(3): 351–368.

2

LANGUAGE REVITALIZATION CASE STUDIES FROM THE NORDIC COUNTRIES

Riitta-Liisa Valijärvi

Introduction

The purpose of this chapter is to explore language reclamation and revitalization from a Nordic perspective. The Nordic countries – Finland (including Aland), Sweden, Norway, Denmark (including Greenland and Faroe Islands), and Iceland – are often seen in the international press as a utopia in terms of democracy, freedom of speech, human rights, work–life balance, standard of living, and gender equality. They have excellent education systems (cf. Finland's success rate in the Pisa studies) and near 100% literacy. The Nordic countries share a religion, Lutheranism, although they are becoming increasingly secular. One could describe it as being culturally Christian without necessarily believing in God. Furthermore, the Nordic countries all have advanced welfare state systems with bursaries, benefits, and free or affordable healthcare. Values in the Nordic region have been liberal (e.g. LGBTQAI+ rights), and climate change is a key concern for policy makers. Except for Finnish, the national majority languages of the region are Scandinavian. There are many domestic, regional, and international forums through which cooperation at the formal governmental and sub-governmental level take place (e.g. the Nordic Council).

When focusing on Nordic exceptionalism, the international audience often forget about their colonial histories and discriminatory policies, such as the colonization of Greenland by Danes–Norwegians from the 1700s onwards and Greenlanders' conversion to Christianity; Sámi residential schools where children were punished for speaking their language and expressing their culture; the loss of Sámi lands; government-funded eugenics and its dark and painful legacy (e.g. Persson 2018); national state- and church-backed assimilatory policies in the 1800 and 1900s; and the marginalization of Jews, Roma, and Tatars. Furthermore, national romanticism and nationalism from the 1800s in, for example, Finland and Norway, paved the way for independence but also focused on creating a unified and homogenous nation where minorities were less visible.[1] More recently, the rise of right-wing populism and anti-migration is a concern in the region, while climate change threatens the Indigenous cultures of the region in Greenland and Sápmi (the traditional Sámi-speaking area).

The colonial and assimilatory practices have led to the current situation where certain languages spoken in the region are threatened or require additional support. A positive development has been the ratification of the European Charter for Regional and Minority Languages (ECRML).[2] It was

DOI: 10.4324/9781003439493-4

signed by Denmark (2000), Finland (1994), Norway (1993), and Sweden (2000). Unfortunately, the charter does not specify which languages require protection, which has been a point of contention alongside the voluntary nature of the charter. The EU does, however, monitor the extent to which the charter has been implemented. For example, Sweden has received repeated criticism in the Council of Europe's evaluation reports concerning its failure to protect national minorities' languages and cultures (Council of Europe 2020). Minority language policies are now coded in law (e.g. Swedish law on national minorities and minority languages),[3] thanks to speakers and activists who have been working tirelessly for recognition and support. However, this does not mean that the situation has been solved or a Nordic utopia: there is still a considerable need to improve linguistic and cultural policies and practices in the Nordics and an urgency to address the policy–practice mismatch.

Because of the shared commonalities and shared history, it is worthwhile to discuss the Nordic region as a whole when examining language reclamation and revitalization. More specifically, this chapter addresses the following questions:

1. Which languages are endangered or minoritized in the Nordic countries?
2. What are some of the revitalization measures that have been implemented in the region?
3. What are some of the ways in which speaker communities reclaimed and revitalized their languages in the region?
4. What are some of the challenges that remain in the revitalization of endangered and minoritized languages in the Nordic region?

This introductory section is followed by a theoretical section. In the third section, I discuss the complexities of the linguistic situation in the Nordic countries by attempting to list the numbers of speakers for the various minoritized languages and describing their history and status. I will touch upon some of the general challenges in improving the linguistic vitality of these languages. The fourth section contains a selection of language revitalization, reclamation, and maintenance case studies from the region. This chapter concludes with a section where I summarize the case studies in this chapter and discuss potential future endeavors in the region in the field of language reclamation and revitalization.

Note that the goal of the chapter is to give an overview of research on the types of reclamation and revitalization activities that have taken place, not to provide exhaustive information about each activity or organization. I will illustrate the developments and challenges through well-studied instances of language reclamation and revitalization.

Theory

The overall approach in this chapter adopts a decolonial lens to socio-cultural linguistic practices (cf. Bhambra 2014) and challenges the prevailing perception of the Nordic countries as homogenous and utopian (cf. Lóftsdottir and Jensen 2016; Keskinen et al. 2019; Stoltz et al. 2021). The goal is to draw attention to the ongoing effects of linguistic imperialism, that is, the effect of majority cultures' expansion at the expense of linguistic and cultural minorities (Philipson 1992, 2009), which in the Nordic context has led to a linguistic and cultural erasure. The majority cultures and languages in question are the national state languages Danish, Norwegian, Swedish, and Finnish. In other words, it is important to focus on language revitalization to right historical wrongs (see Skutnabb-Kangas and Phillipson 2022). Furthermore, being able to use one's language and culture are closely linked to mental and physical wellbeing both in terms of physical indicators (e.g. lower rates of heart disease, high blood pressure, and diabetes) as well as mental and behavioral indicators (e.g. lower rates of drug and alcohol abuse, and suicide) (e.g. Winsa 2005; Schweitzer et al. 2010; Walsh 2018; Huss 2023). Additionally, this chapter ties in with the work of truth and reconciliation commissions in the region, such as the ongoing Truth and Reconciliation Commission Concerning the Sámi People in Finland and the recently concluded Truth and Reconciliation Commission for Tornedalians, Kvens and Lantalainens (SOU 2023).[4] These state-sanctioned commissions aim to give voice to the speakers and highlight, for example, the processes of language endangerment through interviews with community members.

Language reclamation refers here to "larger effort by a community to claim its right to speak a language and to set associated goals in response to community needs and perspectives" (Leonard 2012: 359), which is by its very nature decolonial (Leonard 2017). Language reclamation can happen on an individual level as a type of emancipation and desire to explore one's linguistic heritage. Revitalization, on the other hand, can have the goal of creating new speakers or reversing language shift (Hinton 2001: 5; Hinton et al. 2018). Revitalization measures can vary from the more formal (e.g. North Sámi as a school subject) to informal (e.g. singing or listening to songs in Meänkieli) and can take place online or offline. Language revitalization can happen as a bottom-up process (initiated by community members themselves) or as a top-down process (led by the government or some other official body). Moreover, there are numerous factors that affect the need for, and success of, revitalization measures, such as and whether it targets children or adults, whether the focus is on spoken or written language, or whether it takes place in an urban setting or in the traditional area surrounded by traditional culture. There can be tension between older and younger generations or new[5] and traditional speakers. Older speakers may want to use more conservative language, while younger generations may include loan words from the majority language in their speech or use innovative grammar.

In language revitalization it is important that there are realistic goals: it may not always be possible to achieve full fluency, and in some cases it may consist of symbolic linguistic measures, such as signage, name changes, or use of greetings (e.g. Grenoble and Whaley 2006). Here the term *ethnolinguistic identity gratification* is useful (Vincze and Moring 2018). It refers to the speakers being able to express and assert their linguistic identity or background in various contexts and can be as powerful as becoming fluent in the language of one's ancestors. The role of language planning and maintenance is also important in the revitalization process, as various language boards, corpus planning initiatives, and standardization measures, including the creation of an orthography, in the Nordic region show. Both language planning and inter-generational differences relate to the issue of purism (Sallabank 2018); that is, what is regarded as an acceptable or desired way of speaking or which variety should form the basis of the standard or receive the most resources.

Aikio-Puoskari (2018) highlights the need for community agency and a holistic socially sensitive and culture-based approach to revitalization of Sámi languages, which is also the perspective in this chapter. More specifically, the communities decide what benefits them, and language, culture, and the environment are intertwined and cannot be separated from each other. Moreover, this chapter echoes Grenoble and Whaley's (2021) framing of language as a nexus of social activities (that language is always used in specific social contexts), and language revitalization as an endeavour that promotes community members' wellbeing is based on sustainability and takes into consideration the multilingual realities of the speakers (cf. Pietikäinen et al. 2010; Laakso et al. 2016).

The focus in this chapter is on minoritized Indigenous, transnational, and regional languages in Nordic countries, more specifically what are sometimes referred to as historical minorities, rather than the languages of more recent migrant communities. A minoritized language may be spoken in only one country (e.g. Inari Sámi in Finland), be regional and be spoken in two or more countries (e.g. North Sámi in Finland, Norway, and Sweden), be spoken in two countries but be a minority in one and the majority language in the other (e.g. Swedish in Finland, Finnish in Sweden), or be transnational and spoken in several countries without being associated with one specific region (e.g. Yiddish, Romani).[6]

Languages, stakeholders, and challenges

The information in Tables 2.1–2.4 is taken primarily from Ethnologue, and the speaker numbers are based on estimates (Eberhard et al. 2023). I have included the languages from the ECRML as well as the historical minoritized languages that are striving for recognition (e.g. Elfdalian). An additional complication in the enumeration or classification of endangered languages are the different varieties of Sámi and Romani that are not always specified in official documents, as well as the status of Faroese and Greenlandic as minoritized languages vs national languages. Meänkieli and Kven are still sometimes classified as dialects of Finnish and listed as moribund. Furthermore, Ethnologue's first language (L1) concept is problematic in relation to bilingualism and new speakers. Finally, census data does not include exact figures on the number of speakers, and the speaker numbers in Tables 2.1–2.4 are thereby simply estimates. Stakeholders include not only community members and activists but also broadcasting companies, publishers, universities, researchers, activists, and funding bodies.

Table 2.1 Minority languages of Denmark, including the status of Faroese and Greenlandic

Language	Estimated and approximate number of L1 users	Status (Eberhard et al. 2023)
German (in Northern Schleswig)	37,800	dispersed
Danish Sign Language	5,000	developing
Faroese	21,000 in Denmark, 50,000 in Faroe Islands	unestablished in Denmark, institutional in Faroe Islands
Greenlandic (kalallisuut)	7,000 in Denmark, 50,000 in Greenland	dispersed in Denmark, national/institutional in Greenland

Table 2.2 Minority languages of Finland and Aland

Language	Estimated and approximate number of L1 users	Status (Eberhard et al. 2023)
Swedish (Finland Swedish)	288,000	institutional
Inari Sami	400	threatened
North Sami	1,700	threatened
Skolt Sami	300	shifting
Karelian (different varieties)	5,000 (estimates vary)	moribund
Finnish Romani	10,000	developing
Finland–Swedish Sign Language	300	moribund
Finnish Sign Language	5,000	developing
Mishar Tatar	700?	–

Language revitalization case studies from Nordic countries

Table 2.3 Minority languages of Norway

Language	Estimated and approximate number of L1 users	Status
Kven	1,500	moribund
Lule Sami	500	threatened
North Sami	20,000	provincial
Romani Vlax	500	dispersed
Romanes (Scandoromani)	100	moribund
South Sámi	300	threatened

Table 2.4 Minority languages of Sweden

Language	Estimated and approximate number of L1 users	Status
Elfdalian	2,400	shifting
Finnish	46,000	dispersed
Gutnish	2,000–5,000	–
Jämtska/Jämtmål	30,000	–
Yiddish, Eastern	3,000	shifting
Meänkieli	30,000	moribund
Romani, Kalo	1,650	developing
Romani, Tavringer/Scandoromani	100	nearly extinct
Romani, Vlax	12,500	threatened
Sámi, Lule	4,000	threatened
Sámi, North	2,000	threatened
Sámi, Pite	20–40	nearly extinct
Sámi, South	300	threatened

Denmark, Faroe Islands, and Greenland

The total population of Denmark is 5,530,000, and the official language of the country is Danish. Table 2.1 includes the figures for Faroese and Greenlandic, as they are protected by the ECRML. The exact number of potential Romani speakers in Denmark is not known. There are no Yiddish speakers left in Denmark.

West Greenlandic (Kalaallisut) is the official language in Greenland, although in practice Danish is used in various contexts (e.g. by tradesmen) and at the sixth-form (high-school) level. Greenlandic has two regional minority variants, East Greenlandic (Tunumiisut) and Polar Eskimo (Inuktun), but these two lack a written standard (Fortescue 2022). Oqaasileriffik – the Language Secretariat of Greenland – is responsible for language maintenance, digital tools, and dictionaries. It is possible to study translation and interpreting and teacher education, among other things, at the University of Greenland. The broadcasting company Kalaallit Nunaata Radioa has Greenlandic content, as does the bilingual newspaper *Sermitsiaq*. The range of popular culture products is limited in Greenlandic, but the language is used actively online.

Yet Greenlandic verbal and cultural practices are threatened (Johannsen 2021), and the education system does not fully support the maintenance of Greenlandic (Wyatt 2009). UNESCO's World

Atlas of Languages classifies Greenlandic as 'endangered/unsafe'[7] due to the overall small size of the speaker population. This is a general issue in the Arctic, where speaker populations are small and live far apart, and the speakers are multilingual and their proficiency in the different languages varies depending on topic and context (Grenoble 2018: 351). This is a challenge not only for Greenlandic but also for Sámi languages, Kven, and Meänkieli in the Nordic Arctic. Additionally, many speakers have left their traditional areas and moved to cities or from Greenland to Denmark.

Faroese is classified as 'endangered/unsafe' by the UNESCO Atlas of World Languages. It is characterized by dialectal variation and bilingualism and is not fully standardized. Málráðið – the Faroese Language Board – is responsible for the development and maintenance of the language.

The German minority in Denmark is bilingual; the majority speaks the South Jutish dialect of Danish at home, with family, and with neighbors, and many do not feel fluent in German; dialects and standard versions of Danish and German are all used, and codeswitching is common (Tarvet 2022: 181–184), which shows that purist and national language policies have not worked for the hybrid boarder region (Tarvet 2022: 178). The rights of the minority are included in the Copenhagen-Bonn Declarations of 1955.

Finland and Aland

The overall population of Finland is 5,530,000, and the two official languages are Finnish (spoken by most of the population) and Swedish (5.2% of the population). All the minoritized languages of Finland can be found in Table 2.2.

Swedish enjoys official status, which means all Finnish speakers learn Swedish in school, there is Swedish-medium education to from primary school to university, all government services are available in the language, and there are established Finland–Swedish cultural institutions. It is the main language of Aland. Despite Finland–Swedish often being seen as a successful case of minority-language policy and practice, there has been debate about the status of Swedish in Finnish schools and society (e.g. Hult and Pietikäinen 2014).

The main body responsible for language planning and maintenance in Finland is the Institute for the Languages of Finland (Kotus). However, the Sámi Language Council of the Sámi Parliament is responsible for developing Sámi languages, offering terminology advice, and taking part in pan-Nordic collaboration. YLE, the Finnish Broadcasting Company, publishes news in all three Sámi languages, Karelian, and Romani.

Karelian varieties spoken in Finland are somewhat invisible in society and not well known (Sarhimaa 2017). The Karelian community hopes to be included in the constitution to legitimatize revitalization measures (Rytkönen 2022). The University of Eastern Finland is responsible for the language and provides tuition and produces materials. As a result of the war in Ukraine, it has been difficult to maintain contact with the Karelian speakers in Russia, and previous active collaboration with Petrozavodsk State University has ended (Kämppi 2022).

There are three different Sámi languages in Finland. Skolt Sámi was spoken in four villages, and when the Petsamo area was ceded to the Soviet Union after WWII, the Skolt Sámi were evacuated to other villages in Finnish Lapland. The Skolt Sámi Cultural Foundation works actively to revitalize the language and runs Tä´lvvsijdd, the Skolt Sámi Cultural Centre. The Inari Sámi live around lake Inari, while North Sámi are a transnational community. Some of the revitalization measures implemented for Sámi feature and include language nests and music, media, and education. The Giellagas Institute at the University of Oulu is responsible for researching and teaching Sámi languages.

There are two sign languages in Finland: Finnish Sign Language and Finland–Swedish Sign Language. The latter is endangered, and so a state-funded a project, Lev i vårt språk (Live in

Language revitalization case studies from Nordic countries

our language) 2015–2017, 2018–2020, and 2022 was set up to revitalize the language. The project included university courses, interpreter training, language documentation, and measures to strengthen identity.[8] For information about transmission of sign languages in the Nordic countries, see Bergman and Engberg-Pedersen (2010).

The Roma started arriving in Finland during the 1500s and were marginalized for many years. Finnish Romani is spoken by about a third of the Roma population in Finland, but many of the speakers are elderly; the language is characterized by variation (Granqvist 2012; Hedman 2017). The Finnish government has set up a revitalization program for Romani (Opetushallitus 2022). The lack of qualified teachers and teaching materials suitable for different ages has previously been an issue (Soininen 2014).

Tatar speakers in Finland were merchants who arrived in the 1800s when Finland was part of Russia (Bedretdin 2017; Wassholm 2020). The Tatar-speaking community is small, but they have been able to maintain their language and culture. The success has been attributed to highly organized activities and funding. Yiddish, on the other hand, speakers also arrived in Finland during the 1800s (Muir 2000, 2004). The Yiddish-speaking community are, however, undergoing language shift from Yiddish via Swedish to Finnish.

Norway

The population of Norway is 5,420,000, and the official languages are Norwegian (with two written standards, Bokmål and Nynorsk) and Sámi (North, Lule, and South Sámi).

Most of the speakers of North Sámi live in Norway. It is an official language in Troms og Finnmark and eight additional municipalities. North, Lule, and South Sámi are taught in school as a first language, second language, and foreign/new language; for Lule and South Sámi there are no medium of instruction programs (see e.g. Albury 2016; Vangsnes 2022). The Sámi Parliament of Norway is responsible for revitalization of the language and culture and the development of Sámi teaching and learning materials. The case studies include a discussion about Sámi languages in the Norwegian education system. The broadcasting company NRK has programs and news in Sámi languages and Kven.

The Kven language is closely related to northern Finnish dialects, and, in Norway, the language is sometimes considered the same as Finnish. The Kainun Institutti – Kvensk Institutt – is responsible for the revitalization of Kven. The case studies include corpus development and immersion methods for Kven.

Scandoromani mixes Norwegian/Swedish/Danish and Romani in various ways (Carling et al. 2014). There is interest in revitalization of the variety in Norway. Romani Vlax is the transnational variety spoken elsewhere in Europe.

Sweden

Sweden has a total population of 10,219,000, and the official language of the state is Swedish. Its national minority languages – Finnish, Meänkieli, Sámi (all varieties), Romani (all varieties), and Yiddish – are protected by legislation, while Elfdalian, Gutnish, and Jämtska are regarded as dialects and do not have the same status (cf. Parkvall 2015). The Swedish Institute for Language and Folklore is responsible for the maintenance and revitalization of national minority languages, except for Sámi languages that fall under the Sámi Parliament. There are newly established language centers for Meänkieli (two offices in Kiruna and Övertorneå), Finnish (Uppsala), Yiddish (Stockholm), and Romani (Stockholm). These centers organize activities, produce materials and promote the languages. The Swedish broadcasting company SVT broadcasts programs in Sámi languages, Finnish, and Meänkieli.

Large numbers of Finns migrated to Sweden in the late 60s and 70s for work. Their descendants are keen to revitalize their languages and pass them on, but there are a range of challenges, including the lack of qualified teachers (e.g. Lainio 2017; Vuorsola 2022). The Meänkieli dialect of Finnish is spoken in Finland, while Meänkieli in Sweden has started to develop into its own distinct variety and is recognized as a language in the country; people with Meänkieli heritage feel unseen and forgotten in Swedish society (Lipott 2015; see Valijärvi et al. 2022 for a full bibliography).

Yiddish in Sweden has diverse origins, and the role of Hebrew in the Sweden Jewish community is growing, while the speaker numbers for Yiddish are declining (Lebenswerd 2016). Yiddish is learnt through strong grassroots initiatives and Jewish organizations, and it has managed to stay alive despite all odds (Schulman and Milani 2023). Several varieties of Romani are spoken in Sweden, which further complicates revitalization (for the history of Roma and Romani in Nordic countries, see Selling 2022).

Elfdalian is an example of a variety that is regarded as a dialect by some and a language by others. It has been included here to respect the perspective of activists and to highlight the way in which the language situation in the Nordics is dynamic (cf. Valijärvi et al. 2022 for a discussion about the past status of Meänkieli). Ulum Dalska – Organization for the Preservation of Elfdalian – was established in 1984 and is working to secure recognition for the variety by the Swedish state. They organize regular intensive language courses, and the Elfdalian Language Committee, Råðdjärum, has developed an orthography for the language (see Sapir 2017; Karlander 2020; Lundell 2023). There have been financial incentives for young speakers to learn Elfdalian, and the language has been used in preschools.

Iceland

Iceland does not have a historical minority language, and Icelandic is spoken by most Icelandic people. Some of the regent migrant groups include speakers of Polish and Lithuanian.

Case studies

The following case studies have been chosen to achieve maximum variety in the type of activity, type of language (Indigenous, regional, transnational), and country. The purpose is not to provide one case study from each country but to highlight the methods. The choice has also been made based on the availability of recent salient and relevant research on various methods. It is not possible to include every case study in this overview.

Formal education and teaching materials

Formal education in schools and at universities is not without its challenges even in the Nordic countries. Most of the minoritized languages are taught in schools with varying success. The main issues are the lack of teachers and teaching materials or the lack of opportunities for studying the language outside a certain area or school (see e.g. Hermansen and Olsen 2020).

Vangsnes (2022) offers an interesting projection on the future number of speakers based on the number of pupils currently studying Sámi languages in schools. The total numbers of pupils in the school system for Sámi languages in the year 2020/2021 were: first language 1,011, second language 834, and third/foreign language 677: a total of 2,522. The mathematical model by Vangsnes

(2022) predicts an increase in speaker numbers for Lule and South Sámi in Norway, while the future of North Sámi is uncertain.

The Sámi Education Institute (SAKK) – Sámi oahpahusguovddáš (SOG) – is a vocational college in Finnish Sápmi that offers multidisciplinary classes, workshops, and degree programs for adults. Their curriculum, based on Sámi languages and culture, promotes nature-based occupations and employment. Sámi University of Applied Sciences – Sámi allaskuvla – operates under a similar premise and has been hailed as model for Indigenous language and culture education (Porsanger 2017). It is this type of holistic Sámi education that may work best in practice (see also Tanabe 2018).

Instead of offering language tuition in traditional classrooms, some have recommended that schools should focus on ensuring that their curriculum is in line with the culture of the region or the target-language culture (Keskitalo et al. 2013; Sarivaara et al. 2019). This creates a sustainable, interconnected, culturally informed learning environment that supports linguistic reclamation and revitalization in a formal setting. For an additional critical discussion, see Nutti (2013) on Sámi maths teaching, Axell (2020) on technology education, or Ekeland (2017) on Sámi history in textbooks.

Poromaa Isling (2020a, 2020b) has studied the challenges of the invisible Tornedalian minority who speak or whose heritage language is Meänkieli in the Swedish school system. He uses the term *decolonial pockets* (Poromaa Isling 2020a) to describe the resistance from within. The curriculum does not take into consideration the existence of the Meänkieli language or the associated Tornedalian culture. It is up to the students to use the language on their own as an act of resistance outside formal classes.

The colonial legacy is often discernible in school teaching materials, where minority cultures and languages are not represented (e.g. Spjut 2020; Raattamaa Visén and Hallesson 2023). This type of marginalization or misrepresentation continues to restrict cultural and linguistic expression, which in turn has an impact on inclusive teaching practices.

Language nests and master–apprentice programs

Language nests are early childhood language immersion programs (e.g. Grenoble and Whaley 2006: 52–55) During language nest activities, children and members of older generations meet and do activities in the target language to solve interrupted intergenerational transmission. The idea is to focus on local practices and cultural activities, such as making crafts or cooking together. There have been language nests for Inari Sámi, Skolt Sámi, and Karelian in Finland and language-nest style activities for many of the other languages of the region.

Pasanen (2015, 2018) studied the effectiveness of the two Inari Sámi language nests that were opened in 1997. Using 100% immersion, children started to understand key input after a few months and were able to speak at their own pace (see Pasanen 2015: 228–250). She writes: "It is impossible to imagine a more powerful sign of reversing language shift or a more healing phenomenon for the community of an endangered language than when small children start to speak the language" (Pasanen 2018: 366).

In Norway a language nest method has been applied to the revitalization of Kven in two nurseries (kindergartens) in northern Norway. Niiranen (2014) interviewed parents, staff, and municipal decision makers about the Kven language nest activities during the period 2009–2011. She notes that one of the challenges is the language skills of the staff members, while a positive factor is the interest of the staff in initiating and maintaining these activities. A Finnish staff member could lead some of the activities, as the languages are closely related, and some parents felt that it was enough to include culture and phrases. The role of parents was highlighted in Niiranen's (2014) study: to achieve fluency, the language would need to be used in the home. For the role of nurseries in Sámi revitalization, see Aikio-Puoskari (2018) and Rasmussen (2022).

For adults, the immersive master–apprentice method has been used to revitalize Inari and Skolt Sámi in Finland and Lule and South Sámi in Sweden, among others. The goal of the intensive master–apprentice courses is to train adults to become high-level bilinguals and thus active users of Sámi who transmit the language to the next generation. The model developed during the CASLE project involves both formal study and practical immersive doing (Olthuis et al. 2013; Aikio-Puoskari 2018: 358, see also Pasanen 2019, Rasmus and Lane 2021; also Niiranen 2021 for Kven master–apprentice activities). These immersive approaches are perhaps the most effective methods of creating new speakers.

Social media

Social media is a powerful bottom-up way to reclaim and revitalize a language. In the informal forum, questions of language rights and identity can be discussed whilst also experimenting with the language on a small scale and multilingually. Social media also enables the use of the language with people outside one's geographical area, such as in urban centers (cf. Dankertsen 2022). While this section focuses on social media, more traditional media (such as newspapers, radio, and TV) continue to be essential for revitalization, decolonization, network building, information spreading, and agency (e.g. Viinikka-Kallinen 2010; Cocq and DuBois 2019) and are indicators of ethnolinguistic vitality.

Cocq (2015) studied the use of North and South Sámi hashtags and status updates on social media (see also Barrett and Cocq 2019). She describes the role of social media: "More than a tool for communication, an indigenous language functions as a symbol of identity, and its visibility in a majority society is part of revitalization efforts and a way of questioning minority/majority relations" (Cocq 2015: 274). Practically it can be used to ask about linguistic items and support others who are reclaiming their language. In other words, the choice to use Sámi-language hashtags and to post associated content partially in Sámi enables ethnolinguistic identification (cf. Vincze and Moring 2018), even in the absence of fluency or confident skills during one's language reclamation journey.

Ackermann-Boström's (2021) analysis of social media posts shows that young Meänkieli users are generally positive towards Meänkieli and language maintenance while experiencing exclusion by not only the majority society but by other, more competent Meänkieli speakers. Furthermore, in a survey conducted by Moshnikov (2022) about the use of Karelian online, 40% of the respondents were found to use the Karelian language online daily, especially on Facebook and Instagram. More content would be welcome to increase visibility and support the revitalization of the Karelian language. The Finnish-speaking minority in Sweden also actively uses social media for linguistic activism (Liimatainen and Carlsson 2023).

Language planning: corpora, terminology, orthography, and standardization

This section contains case studies of various language planning initiatives that have been used to support the revitalization of minoritized and endangered languages in the Nordic region. The role of documentation and corpora is essential in language revitalization. For a language to be revived, we need data about its use, including variation. Useful instruments in this process are various language technology tools and applications, such as machine translation, speech recognition, spellcheckers, corpus tools, and paradigm generators, developed in the region, especially by Giellatekno in Norway (Trosterud 2013; see also Domeij et al. 2019).

New terminology needs to be developed for a minoritized language to be used in all spheres of life; while an orthography makes it possible to write a language, it also carries symbolic significance. For example, Kuusi et al. (2022) studied a series of courses that were delivered to Karelian translators of Finnish. The translators drew upon all their linguistic resources to create neologisms when translating Wikipedia pages and fiction. The significance of an orthography was obvious to the marginalized and small Pite Sámi community in Sweden when it was finally launched in 2019 (Sunna et al. 2019; see also Valijärvi and Wilbur 2011). An orthography was developed for Elfdalian to unify the script and aid in revitalization but also to improve its status; the process of creating the orthography was not straightforward and involved disagreement about conventions (Sapir 2017).

Standardization may indeed be challenging due to different varieties, interest groups, or even intralinguistic variation, as is the case for Meänkieli (see Lainio and Wande 2015; Valijärvi et al. 2022). For Kven, a corpus was created that fed into a grammatical description; in this grammatical description, a decision was made to allow parallel and dialectal forms (Keränen 2018; Lane et al. 2022). As part of this Ausbau process, Kven was distinguished from Finnish through the use of loanwords from Norwegian (Niiranen 2022). Similar documentation and standardization efforts are underway for Meänkieli in Sweden.

Music

Music has played an important role in the emancipation and resistance of Sámi, as well as a linguistic and cultural revival (e.g. Ridanpää and Pasanen 2009; Hilder 2017; Ramnarine 2017). Music functions as a locus for acquiring the language and makes the language and culture appeal to a younger audience through a modern genre, for example, through Sámi rap (Pietikäinen and Dufva 2014). Two prominent examples of this are the two Sámi language rappers, Ailu Valle and Amoc. Ailu Valle raps in North Sámi, Finnish, and English about destructive nature of Western influence and highlights the importance of Indigenous ways of thinking. He has received an award for his work for children and young people, more specifically for the support of their minority identity, in Finland. Amoc, on the other hand, raps in Inari Sámi about monsters and other horror themes and combines his musical output with activism and language teaching.

Pop music covers in Sámi can be used in teaching; they are easily sharable and have an interactive element if uploaded on YouTube (Dlaske 2017). Literature can also serve a similar empowering purpose (e.g. Prokkola and Ridanpää 2011; Heith 2012 on the significance and production of Bengt Pohjanen for Meänkieli and Molnár Bodrogi 2019 for Kven and Meänkieli literatures).

Yiddish is often revived through music (Margolis 2022). For instance, Kahn (2020) classifies the use of Yiddish in heavy metal music (the Swedish band Dibbukim) as an instance of post-vernacularity: the language is not a vernacular, a spoken language, anymore, but it bears symbolic value and is used as part of performances that celebrate Ashkenazi Jewish heritage and facilitate the learning of words and phrases.

Semiotic reclamation or symbolic revitalization

The minoritized language communities in the Nordics have not only developed orthographies, applied for ISO language codes, or set up versions of Wikipedia in the language but have also adopted flags and anthems and redrawn maps to distinguish themselves from others. This symbolic recognition and identification are sometimes the first steps in one's language reclamation journey.

One instance of reclamation is the changing one's name from a majority-language name to a minority-language name and thus asserting ethnolinguistic belonging despite the absence of fluency (e.g. Ekholm and Muir 2017; also Valijärvi et al. 2022). Another way is ensuring visibility in the linguistic landscape. For example, in Greenland, signage includes colors, symbols, and images from the local culture and environment (Valijärvi and Kahn 2020), while the placement and role of Greenlandic in the written part of the signage raises its status. For German signage in Denmark, see Tarvet (2022); for Sámi, see Salo (2012) and Pietikäinen and Moriarty (2014).

An interesting project in this respect is the Swedish-medium podcast *Proud to be Ummikko*, created by Daniel Fjellborg. *Ummikko* means "monolingual" or "non-speaker" in Meänkieli. The podcast focuses on what it is like to have lost one's own language, Meänkieli, and whether language skills are essential to one's identity.

Concluding remarks

The challenges in Nordic language revitalization are language variation and multilingualism, ensuring holistic approaches and setting realistic expectations, and availability of qualified teachers or language masters, as well as access to a range of popular culture products in the language. Reclamation may be hindered by marginalization and invisibility in society. More research is needed on the effectiveness of the existing methods, activities, and resources, such as various immersive summer programs, cultural activities (e.g. the role of dance and handicrafts), teaching materials, and the role of variation in learning. While Sámi languages, especially North Sámi, have been studied extensively, the revitalization of Sign Languages, Meänkieli, Yiddish, Romani, and Tatar in the Nordic countries has received less attention. A future research agenda should include cocreation of materials and research studies where speakers, activists, educators, parents, and scholars work together.

Notes

1 Decolonial processes led to Iceland becoming independent from Denmark in 1944, while the Faroe Islands have had home rule since 1948, and Greenland received home rule in 1979 and self-governance in 2008. Faroe Islands, Greenland, and Iceland are not members of the European Union. Åland has been an autonomous and demilitarized part of Finland since 1920.
2 www.coe.int/en/web/european-charter-regional-or-minority-languages/about-the-charter
3 Lag (2009: 724) om nationella minoriteter och minoritetsspråk. www.riksdagen.se/sv/dokument-och-lagar/dokument/svensk-forfattningssamling/lag-2009724-om-nationella-minoriteter-och_sfs-2009-724/
4 I acknowledge my own position as a Finnish-speaking Finn here. I lived in Sweden for a long time and regard myself as a member of the Finnish minority there. I have worked with speakers of Pite Sámi, North Sámi, Meänkieli, West Greenlandic, and Yiddish. I am a member of a panel that assess language revitalization project funding applications for the Swedish Institute for Language and Folklore.
5 New speaker refers here to "individuals with little or no home or community exposure to a minority language but who instead acquire it through immersion or bilingual educational programs, revitalization projects or as adult language learners" (O'Rourke et al. 2015: 2).
6 Romani speakers arrived in the Nordic region first in the 1500s and in several groups from the early 1900s. Several varieties of Romani are spoken in the region. Yiddish speakers arrived in the Nordic region in the 1600–1700s, although their free movement was banned until the mid-1800s.
7 https://en.wal.unesco.org/
8 https://livs.humak.fi/

References

Ackermann-Boström, C. (2021). '"Språket fick jag inte med mig som liten" Unga meänkielibrukares samtal om språkbevarande på sociala medier'. *Tidskrift för genusvetenskap* 42(4): 32–50.

Aikio-Puoskari, U. (2018). 'Revitalization of Sámi languages in three Nordic countries: Finland, Norway, and Sweden'. In L. Hinton, L. Huss, and G. Roche (Eds.), *The Routledge Handbook of Language Revitalization* (pp. 355–363). New York: Routledge.

Albury, N. J. (2016). 'Holding them at arm's length: A critical review of Norway's policy on Sámi language maintenance'. *Journal of Home Language Research* 1: 1–16.

Axell, C. (2020). 'Broadening the horizons of technology education: Using traditional cultural artefacts as learning tools in a Swedish Sámi school'. *Design and Technology Education* 25(2): 192–216.

Barrett, J. and Cocq, C. (2019). 'Indigenous storytelling and language learning: Digital media as a vehicle for cultural transmission and language acquisition'. In C. Cocq and K. Sullivan (Eds.), *Perspectives on Indigenous Writing and Literacies* (pp. 89–112). Boston: Brill.

Bedretdin, K. (2017). 'Preserving of mother tongue, religious and cultural identity of Tatar migrants (the case of the Tatar community in Finland)'. *Istoricheskaia ètnologiia = Historical Ethnology* 2(2): 233–242.

Bergman, B. and Engberg-Pedersen, E. (2010). 'Transmission of sign languages in the Nordic countries'. In D. Brentari (Ed.), *Sign Languages* (pp. 74–94). Cambridge: Cambridge University Press.

Bhambra, G. (2014). 'Postcolonial and decolonial dialogues'. *Postcolonial Studies* 17(2): 115–121.

Carling, G., Lindell, L. and Ambrazaitis, G. (2014). *Scandoromani: Remnants of a Mixed Language*. Leiden: Brill.

Cocq, C. (2015). 'Indigenous voices on the web: Folksonomies and endangered languages'. *The Journal of American Folklore* 128(509): 273–285.

Cocq, C. and DuBois, T. A. (2019). *Sámi Media and Indigenous Agency in the Arctic North*. University of Washington Press.

Council of Europe (2020). 'Seventh evaluation report on Sweden. Committee of Experts of the European Charter for Minority and Regional Languages'. https://rm.coe.int/swedenecrml7-en3c-pdf/16809fbaab (Accessed 20 June 2024).

Dankertsen, A. (2022). 'Young city Sámi in Norway and Sweden: Making space for urban Indigenous identities'. In M. Berg-Nordlie, A. Dankertsen, and M. Winsvold (Eds.), *An Urban Future for Sápmi? Indigenous Urbanization in the Nordic States and Russia* (pp. 107–146). Berghahn Books.

Dlaske, K. (2017). 'Music video covers, minoritised languages, and affective investments in the space of YouTube'. *Language in Society* 46(4): 451–475.

Domeij, R., Karlsson, O., Trosterud, T. and Moshagen, S. (2019). 'Enhancing information accessibility and digital literacy for minorities using language technology: The example of Sami and other national minority languages in Sweden'. In C. Cocq and K. Sullivan (Eds.), *Perspectives on Indigenous Writing and Literacies* (pp. 113–137). Boston: Brill.

Eberhard, D. M., Simons, G. F. and Fennig, C. D (Eds.). (2023). *Ethnologue: Languages of the World. Twenty-sixth Edition*. Dallas, TX: SIL International. Online version: www.ethnologue.com (Accessed 15 February 2024).

Ekeland, T. G. (2017). 'Enactment of Sámi past in school textbooks: Towards multiple pasts for future making'. *Scandinavian Journal of Educational Research* 61(3): 319–332.

Ekholm, L. K. and Muir, S. (2017). 'Name changes and visions of "a new Jew" in the Helsinki Jewish community'. *Scripta Instituti Donneriani Aboensis* 27: 173–188.

Fortescue, M. (2022). 'Greenlandic dialect classification'. *Dialectología* 2022: 155–168.

Granqvist, K. (2012). 'Romanikielen historiaa Suomessa'. In P. Pulma (Ed.), *Suomen romanien historia* (pp. 272–287). Helsinki: Suomalaisen Kirjallisuuden Seura.

Grenoble, L. A. (2018). 'Arctic Indigenous languages: Vitality and revitalization'. In L. Hinton, L. Huss, and G. Roche (Eds.), *The Routledge Handbook of Language Revitalization* (pp. 345–354). New York: Routledge.

Grenoble, L. A. and Whaley, L. J. (2006). *Saving Languages: An Introduction to Language Revitalization*. Cambridge: Cambridge University Press.

Grenoble, L. A. and Whaley, L. J. (2021). 'Toward a new conceptualisation of language revitalisation'. *Journal of Multilingual and Multicultural Development* 42(10): 911–926.

Hedman, H. (2017). *Suomen romanikieli: kenttäselvitys romanikielen asemasta, kielitaidosta ja kieliasenteista Suomessa*. Helsinki: University of Helsinki.

Heith, A. (2012). 'Platsens sanning. Performativitet och gränsdragningar i tornedalsk litteraturhistoria och grammatik'. *Nordlit* 30: 71–85.

Hermansen, N. and Olsen, K. (2020). 'Learning the Sámi language outside of the Sámi core area in Norway'. *Acta borealia* 37(1–2): 63–77.

Hilder, T. R. (2017). 'Sámi festivals and Indigenous sovereignty'. In F. Holt and A.-V. Kärjä (Eds.), *The Oxford Handbook of Popular Music in the Nordic Countries* (pp. 363–378). New York: Oxford University Press.

Hinton, L. (2001). 'Language revitalization: An overview'. In L. Hinton and K. Hale (Eds.), *The Green Book of Language Revitalization in Practice* (pp. 3–8). Leiden: Brill.

Hinton, L., Huss, L. and Roche, G. (Eds.). (2018). *The Routledge Handbook of Language Revitalization.* New York: Routledge.

Hult, F. M. and Pietikäinen, S. (2014). 'Shaping discourses of multilingualism through a language ideological debate: The case of Swedish in Finland'. *Journal of Language and Politics* 13(1): 1–20.

Huss, L. 2023. 'Språkförlustens konsekvenser. Om språk, kultur och välbefinnande'. In SOU 2023:68 (Ed.), *Som om vi aldrig funnits. Tolv tematiska forskarrapporter. Aivan ko meitä ei olis ollukhaan. Kakstoista temattista tutkintoraporttia* (pp. 153–202). Stockholm: SOU. www.regeringen.se/rattsliga-dokument/statens-offentliga-utredningar/2023/11/sou-202368/ (Accessed 20 June 2024).

Johannsen, S. B. (2021). 'Revitalisering af inuitisk tradition i Grønland: Etnopartikulær nichereligion eller New Age-tendens med globalt udsyn'. *Religionsvidenskabeligt tidsskrift* 71: 1–17.

Kahn, L. (2020). 'Yiddish metal as a manifestation of postvernacularity'. In R.-L. Valijärvi, C. Doesburg, and A. Digioia (Eds.), *Multilingual Metal Music: Sociocultural, Linguistic and Literary Perspectives on Heavy Metal Lyrics* (pp. 9–26). Bingley, UK: Emerald.

Kämppi, M.-L. (2022). 'Karjalan kielen elvytys on vaikeutunut Itä-Suomen yliopistossa, kun yhteydet Venäjän Karjalaan on katkaistu'. https://yle.fi/a/3-12376503 (Accessed 20 June 2024)

Karlander, D. (2020). 'When political institutions use sociolinguistic concepts'. *International Journal of the Sociology of Language* 263: 13–18.

Keränen, M. (2018). 'Language maintenance through corpus planning – the case of Kven'. *Acta borealia* 35(2): 176–191.

Keskinen, S., Skaptadóttir, U. D. and Toivanen, M. (2019). 'Narrations of homogeneity, waning welfare states, and the politics of solidarity'. In S. Keskinen, U. D. Skaptadóttir, and M. Toivanen (Eds.), *Undoing Homogeneity in the Nordic Region: Migration, Difference, and the Politics of Solidarity* (pp. 1–18). London: Routledge.

Keskitalo, P., Määttä, K. and Uusiautti, S. (2013). *Sami Education.* Frankfurt am Main: Peter Lang GmbH, Internationaler Verlag der Wissenschaften.

Kuusi, P., Riionheimo, H. and Kolehmainen, L. (2022). 'Translating into an endangered language: Filling in lexical gaps as Language Making'. *International Journal of the Sociology of Language* 274: 133–160.

Laakso, J., Sarhimaa, A. Åkermark, S. S. and Toivanen, R. (2016). *Towards Openly Multilingual Policies and Practices: Assessing Minority Language Maintenance Across Europe.* Multilingual Matters.

Lainio, J. (2017). 'Situationen för Sveriges östersjöfinska nationella minoritetsspråk finska och meänkieli 2016'. *Multiethnica* 36–37: 13–27.

Lainio, J. and Wande, E. (2015). 'Meänkieli today: To be or not to be standardised'. *Sociolinguistica* 29: 121–140.

Lane, P., Hagen, K. Anders Nøklestad, A. and Priestley, J. (2022). 'Creating a corpus for Kven, a minority language in Norway'. *Nordlyd* 46(1): 159–170.

Lebenswerd, P. J. K. (2016). 'Jewish Swedish'. In L. Kahn and A. Rubin (Eds.), *Handbook of Jewish Languages* (pp. 618–629). Leiden: Brill.

Leonard, W. Y. (2012). 'Framing language reclamation programmes for everybody's empowerment'. *Gender and Language* 6(2): 339–367.

Leonard, W. Y. (2017). 'Producing language reclamation by decolonizing "Language"'. *Language Documentation and Description* 14: 15–36.

Liimatainen, T. and Carlsson, N. (2023). 'Våga finska! Sverigefinsk språkaktivism på sociala medier, Sveriges nationella minoritetsspråk – nya språkpolitiska perspektiv'. In T. M. Milani and L. Salö (Eds.), *Sveriges nationella minoritetsspråk: Nya språkpolitiska perspektiv* (pp. 67–96). Lund: Studentlitteratur.

Lipott, S. (2015). 'The Tornedalian minority in Sweden: From assimilation to recognition: A 'forgotten' ethnic and linguistic minority 1870–2000'. *Immigrants & Minorities* 33(1): 1–22.

Lóftsdottir, K. and Jensen, L. (2016). 'Nordic exceptionalism and the Nordic "Others"'. In K. Loftsdóttir and L. Jensen (Eds.), *Whiteness and Postcolonialism in the Nordic Region* (pp. 1–11). London: Routledge.

Lundell, J. (2023). *Between the Private and a Public Place: Lived Experiences in Contemporary Elfdalian Revitalisation.* MA dissertation. Uppsala University.

Margolis, R. (2022). *Yiddish Lives on: Strategies of Language Transmission.* Montreal: McGill-Queen's University Press.

Molnár Bodrogi, E. (2019). 'Dissenting narratives of identity in Saami, Meänkieli and Kven literatures'. *The Romanian Journal for Baltic and Nordic Studies* 11(1): 19–55.

Moshnikov, I. (2022). 'The use of Karelian language online: Current trends and challenges'. *Eesti ja soome-ugri keeleteaduse ajakiri* 13(2): 275–305.

Muir, S. (2000). 'Yiddish in Helsinki and its Swedish component'. *Nordisk judaistik* 21(1–2): 139–148.

Muir, S. (2004). *Yiddish in Helsinki: Study of a Colonial Yiddish Dialect and Culture.* Helsinki: Finnish Oriental Society.

Niiranen, L. (2014). 'Kveenin kieli ja kulttuuri kahdessa päiväkodissa Pohjois-Norjassa – kielen elvyttämistä ja vähemmistökulttuurin välitystä'. *Lähivertailuja* 24: 151–182.

Niiranen, L. (2021). 'Minority language learning in Kven through conversation'. *Acta borealia* 38(1): 5–22.

Niiranen, L. (2022). 'Making a difference – Ausbau processes in Modern Written Finnish and Kven: How a group of loanwords marks a divergence between the Kven language and Modern Written Finnish'. *Nordic Journal of Linguistics* 2022: 1–33.

Nutti, Y. J. (2013). 'Indigenous teachers' experiences of the implementation of culture-based mathematics activities in Sámi school'. *Mathematics Education Research Journal* 25(1): 57–72.

Olthuis, M.-L., Kivelä, S. and Skutnabb-Kangas, T. (2013). *Revitalising Indigenous Languages: How to Recreate a Lost Generation.* Bristol: Multilingual Matters.

Opetushallitus. (2022). *Suomen romanikielen elvytysohjelma toimenpide-esityksineen: Mo džiivel romani tšimb! = Eläköön romanikieli!* Helsinki: Opetushallitus.

O'Rourke, B., Pujolar, J. and Ramallo, F. (2015). 'New speakers of minority languages: The challenging opportunity – foreword'. *International Journal of the Sociology of Language* 231: 1–20.

Parkvall, M. (2015). *Sveriges språk i siffror: vilka språk talas och av hur många?* Stockholm: Språkrådet, Morfem.

Pasanen, A. (2015). *Kuávsui já peeivičuová. 'Sarastus ja päivänvalo': Inarinsaamen kielen revitalisaatio.* Helsinki: Suomalais-ugrilainen Seura ja Helsingin yliopisto.

Pasanen, A. (2018). '"This work is not for pessimists" – Revitalization of inari Sámi language'. In L. Hinton, L. Huss, and G. Roche (Eds.), *The Routledge Handbook of Language Revitalization* (pp. 364–372). London: Routledge.

Pasanen, A. (2019). 'Becoming a new speaker of a Saami language Through intensive adult education'. In A. Sherris and S. D. Penfield (Eds.), *Rejecting the Marginalized Status of Minority Languages* (pp. 49–69). Bristol: Multilingual Matters.

Persson, C. (2018). *'Då var jag som en fånge': statens övergrepp på tornedalingar och meänkielitalande under 1800-och 1900-talet.* Övertorneå: Svenska tornedalingars riksförbund – Tornionlaaksolaiset: Met Nuoret.

Philipson, R. (1992). *Linguistic Imperialism.* Oxford: Oxford University Press.

Philipson, R. (2009). *Linguistic Imperialism Continued.* London: Routledge.

Pietikäinen, S. and Dufva, H. (2014). 'Heteroglossia in action: Sámi children, textbooks and rap'. In A. Blackledge and A. Creese (Eds.), *Heteroglossia as Practice and Pedagogy* (pp. 59–74). New York: Springer.

Pietikäinen, S., Huss, L., Laihiala-Kankainen, S., Aikio-Puoskari, U. and Lane, P. (2010). 'Regulating multilingualism in the North Calotte: The case of Kven, Meänkieli and Sámi languages'. *Acta borealia* 27(1): 1–23.

Pietikäinen, S. and Moriarty, M. (2014). 'Spatial interaction in Sámiland: Regulative and transitory chronotopes in the dynamic multilingual landscape of an indigenous Sámi village'. *The International Journal of Bilingualism* 18(5): 478–490.

Poromaa Isling, P. (2020a). 'Tornedalian teachers' and principals' in the Swedish education system: Exploring decolonial pockets in the aftermaths of Swedification'. *Nordic Journal of Comparative and International Education* 4(1): 84–101.

Poromaa Isling, P. (2020b). 'Young Tornedalians in education: The challenges of being national minority pupils in the Swedish school system'. *Education in the North* 27(1): 92–109.

The Routledge Handbook of Endangered and Minority Languages

Porsanger, J. (2017). 'Building Sámi language higher education: The case of Sámi University of applied sciences'. In E. A. McKinley and L. T. Smith (Eds.), *Handbook of Indigenous Education* (pp. 969–995). Singapore: Springer Singapore.

Prokkola, E.-K. and Ridanpää, J. (2011). 'Following the plot of Bengt Pohjanen's Meänmaa: Narrativization as a process of creating regional identity'. *Social & Cultural Geography* 12(7): 775–791.

Raattamaa Visén, P. and Hallesson, Y. (2023). 'De nationella minoritetsspråken i läromedel'. In T. M. Milani and L. Salö (Eds.), *Sveriges nationella minoritetsspråk: Nya språkpolitiska perspektiv* (pp. 245–278). Lund: Studentlitteratur.

Ramnarine, T. K. (2017). 'Aspirations, global futures, and lessons from Sámi popular music for the twenty-first century'. In F. Holt and A.-V. Kärjä (Eds.), *The Oxford Handbook of Popular Music in the Nordic Countries* (pp. 277–292). New York: Oxford University Press.

Rasmus, S. and Lane, P. (2021). 'New speakers of Sámi: From insecurity to pride'. In L. Grenoble, P. Lane, and U. Røyneland (Eds.), *Linguistic Minorities in Europe Online*. Berlin: De Gruyter Mouton.

Rasmussen, T. (2022). 'Samiske barnehagers rolle i språkrevitaliseringa'. *Nordlyd* 46(1): 205–217.

Ridanpää, J. and Pasanen, A. (2009). 'From the Bronx to the wilderness: Inari-Sami rap, language revitalisation and contested ethnic stereotypes'. *Studies in Ethnicity and Nationalism* 9(2): 213–230.

Rytkönen, A.-P. (2022). 'Karjalan kielen asema on Suomessa heikko – professori: "Perustuslaki antaisi kielelle olemassaolon oikeutuksen"'. https://yle.fi/a/3-12501465 (Accessed 20 June 2024).

Sallabank, J. (2018). 'Purism, variation, change and 'authenticity': Ideological challenges to language revitalisation'. *European Review* 26(1): 164–178.

Salo, H. (2012). 'Using Linguistic landscape to examine the visibility of Sámi languages in the North Calotte'. In D. Gorter, H. F. Marten, and L. Van Mensel (Eds.), *Minority Languages in the Linguistic Landscape* (pp. 243–259). London: Palgrave Macmillan UK.

Sapir, Y. (2017). 'The revitalization of Elfdalian'. In N. Ostler, V. Ferreira, and C. Moseley (Eds.), *Proceedings of the 21st FEL Conference: Communities in Control: Learning Tools and Strategies for Multilingual Endangered Language Communities* (pp. 50–57). Foundation for Endangered Languages.

Sarhimaa, A. (2017). *Vaietut ja vaiennetut – Karjalankieliset karjalaiset Suomessa*. Helsinki: Suomalaisen Kirjallisuuden Seura.

Sarivaara, E. K., Määttä, K., and Uusiautti, S. (2019). *Indigenous Adult Language Revitalization and Education*. Cambridge Scholars Publishing.

Schulman, S. and Milani, T. M. (2023). 'Slaget om jiddisch – språkligt medborgande mot alla odds. In T. M. Milani and L. Salö (Eds.), *Sveriges nationella minoritetsspråk: Nya språkpolitiska perspektiv* (pp. 97–124). Lund: Studentlitteratur.

Schweitzer, P., Fox, S. I., Csonka, Y. and Kaplan, L. (2010). 'Cultural wellbeing and cultural vitality'. In J. N. Larsen, P. Schweitzer, and G. Fondahl (Eds.), *Arctic Social Indicators: A Follow-up to the Arctic Human Development Report* (pp. 91–108). Copenhagen: Nordic Council of Ministers.

Selling, J. (2022). *Romani Liberation: A Northern Perspective on Emancipatory Struggles and Progress*. Central European University Press.

Skutnabb-Kangas, T. and Phillipson, R. (Eds.). (2022). *Handbook of Linguistic Human Rights*. Oxford: Wiley-Blackwell.

Soininen, M. (2014). 'Romanien perustuslaissa turvattujen kielellisten oikeuksien toteutuminen'. *Oikeusministeriö*. https://julkaisut.valtioneuvosto.fi/handle/10024/76520 (Accessed 20 June 2024).

SOU. (2023). *Som om vi aldrig funnits – exkludering och assimilering av tornedalingar, kväner och lantalaiset. Slutbetänkande av sannings- och försoningskommissionen för tornedlingar, kväner och lantalaiset*. Statens offentliga utredningar 2023:68. 15 November 2023. Stockholm. https://www.regeringen. se/rattsliga-dokument/statens-offentliga-utredningar/2023/11/sou-202368/ (Accessed 10 October 2024).

Spjut, L. (2020). 'Nationella minoriteter i grundskolans läromedel 2011–2019'. *Nordidactica* 2020(4): 60–87.

Stoltz, P., Mulinari, D. and Keskinen, S. (2021). 'Contextualising feminisms in the Nordic region: Neoliberalism, nationalism, and decolonial critique'. In S. Keskinen, P. Stoltz, and D. Mulinari (Eds.), *Feminisms in the Nordic Region: Neoliberalism, Nationalism and Decolonial Critique* (pp. 1–21). Cham, Switzerland: Palgrave Macmillan.

Sunna, A., Päiviö, A. M. and Niia, A.-K. (2019). 'Nu har pitesamiskan eget skriftspråk'. https://sverigesradio. se/artikel/7283047 (Accessed 20 June 2024).

Tanabe, Y. (2018). 'Sámi language revitalisation and higher education: The case of Sámi University College, Norway'. *Japanese Journal of Northern European Studies* 14: 27–36.

Tarvet, R. (2022). 'Between openness and authenticity: The current state of linguistic identity in the German minority of North Schleswig'. In P. Thaler (Ed.), *Like Snow in the Sun? The German Minority in Denmark in Historical Perspective* (pp. 175–193). Germany: De Gruyter.

Trosterud, T. (2013). 'A restricted freedom of choice: Linguistic diversity in the digital landscape'. *Nordlyd* 39(2): 89–104.

Valijärvi, R.-L., Blokland, R., Kangas, E., Ackermann-Boström, C. and Kuoppa, H. (2022). 'Meänkieli'. In L. Grenoble, P. Lane, and U. Røyneland (Eds.), *Linguistic Minorities in Europe Online*. Berlin: De Gruyter Mouton.

Valijärvi, R.-L. and Kahn, L. (2020). 'The linguistic landscape of Nuuk, Greenland'. *Linguistic Landscape* 6(3): 265–296.

Valijärvi, R.-L. and Wilbur, J. (2011). 'The past, present and future of Pite Saami: Sociological factors and revitalization efforts'. *Nordic Journal of Linguistics* 34(3): 295–329.

Vangsnes, Ø. A. (2022). 'Projections for Sámi in Norway'. *Nordlyd* 46(1): 259–272.

Viinikka-Kallinen, A. (2010). 'Substance through your own language: The minority media connect, strengthen and inform'. In H. Sulkala and H. Mantila (Eds.), *Planning a New Standard Language: Finnic Minority Languages Meet the New Millennium* (pp. 178–202). Helsinki: Finnish Literature Society.

Vincze, L. and Moring, T. (2018). 'Towards ethnolinguistic identity gratifications'. In E. H. Gruffydd Jones and E. Uribe-Jongbloed (Eds.), *Social Media and Minority Languages: Convergence and the Creative Industries* (pp. 47–57). Bristol: Multilingual Matters.

Vuorsola, L. (2022). *Speak Your Own Language – On Tensions Regarding Finnish in Sweden*. PhD thesis. University of Stockholm. https://su.diva-portal.org/smash/get/diva2:1702263/FULLTEXT01.pdf (Accessed 20 June 2024).

Walsh, M. (2018). 'Language is like food – links between language revitalization and health and well-being'. In L. Hinton, L. Huss, and G. Roche (Eds.), *The Routledge Handbook of Language Revitalization* (pp. 5–12). New York: Routledge.

Wassholm, J. (2020). 'Tatar pedlars in the Grand Duchy of Finland in the late nineteenth century'. *Studia Orientalia* 8(2): 8–24.

Winsa, B. (2005). 'Language policies: Instruments in cultural development and well-being'. *International Journal of Circumpolar Health* 64(2): 170–183.

Wyatt, T. (2009). 'The role of culture in culturally compatible education'. *Journal of American Indian Education* 48(3): 47–63.

3
CELTIC LESSONS
Revitalizing Cornish through the education system

George Wilson

Introduction

According to UNESCO (Moseley 2010), there are 129 vulnerable or endangered regional languages on the continent of Europe and this number is growing. In an effort to combat this international issue, the Council of Europe formulated the European Charter for Regional or Minority Languages (1992) setting out the steps European states should take to support language revitalization. The measures focus on regional and national education systems, since these become increasingly important as intergenerational transmission diminishes (Baker 2003). Indeed, as Hodges notes, 'minority language transmission through education is undoubtedly at the very epicenter of contemporary language-planning infrastructures throughout Europe' (2012: 355).

Nonetheless, using national education systems to promote regional-language learning is challenging, and this chapter contends that it is vital for European regions to learn lessons from one another in order to succeed in regional-language revitalization through education. To illustrate this thesis, the chapter will study the example of Cornish, one of Europe's most endangered languages. It will consider what lessons Cornwall Council can learn from other Celtic regions to help it successfully embed the language within the region's education system and thus facilitate its revival. Indeed, Wales, Scotland, Brittany, Northern Ireland, Eire and the Isle of Man all have valuable experience in supporting their respective languages in this way.

First, the chapter will provide a brief introduction to the Cornish language before moving on to examine Cornwall Council's education strategy for language revitalization. It will then study some of the lessons to be learnt, focusing on the importance of stakeholder support and on how to negotiate the complex ideological web underpinning European education systems. Ultimately, it will question the extent to which language revitalization can realistically be achieved through education systems and consider the implications this may have for the Cornish context and beyond.

The Cornish language

Decline

Cornish is a part of the family of Celtic languages, which includes Scottish Gaelic, Irish Gaelic, Manx, Welsh and Breton. The language developed out of the Common Brittonic language

DOI: 10.4324/9781003439493-5

during the early Medieval period, going on to prosper in the geographical region of Cornwall and reaching its apogee in the 14th century with an estimated 38,000 speakers (Judge 2007). However, it experienced a steady decline after this period due, in large part, to the erosion of Cornwall's traditional semi-independence from the English. Two bloody episodes inflicted demographic shocks on the language community: the slaughter of 2,000 Cornish people in 1497 after tax protests and the execution of 10% of the duchy's male population after resistance to the introduction of the English Prayer Book in 1549 (Judge 2007). The political turmoil around the Reformation impacted the language's status as a medium of trade by cutting the region's traditional ties with Brittany, while the growth of the tin-mining industry saw an influx of non-Cornish speakers into the region, which further diluted the language community (Judge 2007). By the late 18th or early 19th century, the language had 'faded altogether from everyday vernacular usage' and was, to all intents and purposes, extinct (Sayers, Davies-Deacon and Croome 2019).

Rebirth

However, such was not to be the fate of the Cornish language, and it was successfully revived over the course of the 20th century. This volte-face was thanks to the determined efforts of various academics working at the end of the 19th and the beginning of the 20th centuries who took a keen interest in collecting and restoring what remained of their ancestral tongue (Judge 2007). Chief among these was Henry Jenner who, in 1904, published *A Handbook of the Cornish Language*. This publication allowed people to learn the language, with Cornish first becoming a mode of written communication in specialist journals such as *Old Cornwall* before gradually becoming a spoken tongue once again. By the 1930s, a small number of people were able to converse in Cornish, and one particularly important revivalist, Robert Morton Nance, was even raising his daughter through the language, thus creating the first native speaker of Cornish in well over a century (Judge 2007). The number of Cornish speakers continued to grow during the decades that followed, and the language became progressively more vital until, in 2010, UNESCO finally upgraded Cornish's status from 'extinct' to 'critically endangered' (Moseley 2010).

Cornish today

Today, Cornish is a living language once again. It is difficult to estimate the exact number of Cornish speakers, but Mackinnon's 2001 study found that the language 'is being used across a range of everyday purposes' (p. 37) and identified ten families using it to raise their children, thus creating a new generation of native speakers. A 2008 survey suggested there were approximately 627 people with varying degrees of fluency, of which around 80 spoke it as their main language (Burley 2008). The 2021 census shows that 464 people claimed Cornish as their first language, a figure which has remained relatively constant since 2011 (Cornwall Council 2022). These figures are encouraging, considering the fact that the language was all but dead only a few short decades ago. Nonetheless, such limited intergenerational transmission means that future growth inevitably depends on the education system. Cornwall Council recognizes this fact, and its Language Strategy pledges accordingly to create 'An accessible education programme from pre-school to higher and adult education' (Cornwall Council 2004: 10) in order to support the revitalization of the language.

The Cornish education strategy

Pre-school provision

This education strategy theoretically involves offering Cornish language learning at the pre-school level before gradually developing such provision at primary and secondary levels (Cornwall Council 2017). Regional language education can take on many forms, from second language teaching through to bilingual and immersion education. As Grenoble and Whaley explain, however, 'Most linguists and educators would agree that total-immersion programs are the best option for revitalizing a language' (2005: 51), and this is the stated goal for pre-school education in Cornwall (Cornwall Council 2017). In reality, however, providing any form of pre-school education involving Cornish has so far proved problematic. The Tregenna Nursery Group does offer an initiation to the language through second-language project work to a handful of pupils (Broadhurst 2023), and the two Cornish Magi Ann apps, designed by Golden Tree Productions and launched in 2017, have allowed around 2,000 nursery children to hear stories told through Cornish (Rogerson 2023). However, there is only one bilingual pre-school in Cornwall. Emilie Champliaud founded *Skol Veythrin Kerenza* in 2009, running it originally as a parent group every Saturday, then as the childcare provider for Cornwall College and, more recently, as a child-minding company. As of September 2023, she has set up *Skol Veythrin Sen Jowan* in its place to offer four days of bilingual pre-school education per week, working on a basis of 50% English and 50% Cornish (Champliaud 2023). While such initiatives show a commitment to bilingual education, the numbers of children in pre-school education who are learning through Cornish is negligible: there is currently only one child enrolled in the nursery. The work of Grenoble and Whaley (2005) suggests that this is to be expected, as the success of such programs depends on significant financial resources, community good-will and a critical mass of speakers demanding such pre-school provision for their children. These prerequisites have not yet been met in Cornwall, and the goal of immersion education seems a long way off. Settling for an initiation program like the one offered in primary education may yet prove a more achievable short-term goal.

Primary and secondary school provision

Cornwall Council aims 'to establish and develop extended opportunities for children and young people to learn Cornish within Cornwall's primary and secondary schools' as a foreign language, and 'to develop opportunities for children to gain primary education through the medium of Cornish – in terms of immersion education' (Cornwall Council 2017). As central government funding has fluctuated over the last 15 years, so too has the scope of the projects undertaken (Sayers, Davies-Deacon and Croome 2019). There are currently no plans to introduce immersion primary education. The strategy prior to the COVID-19 pandemic was for the social enterprise Golden Tree Productions to support the roll-out of one term of Cornish teaching in clusters of primary schools. Cornwall Council's 2019–20 Mid-Year Update (2020a) shows that Cornish was being taught as a second language for one term per year in 16 primary schools in two clusters around Penzance and Liskeard and that a new cluster was about to be launched around Camborne. This model was, however, very dependent on direct interventions in the schools by Golden Tree Productions, and, when COVID-19 forced schools to close in 2020, the organization decided to shift their approach to an accreditation model under the banner of 'Go Cornish' (Cornwall Council 2020b). The hope was that this new approach would allow for a more scalable and sustainable model that would be less reliant on the organization's direct interventions (Broadhurst 2023). The Go Cornish program is designed to give teachers who do not necessarily speak Cornish the tools to introduce the language through school routines, such as taking the register, and through simple teaching activities (Golden Tree Productions 2023). There are three levels to the program, with schools applying for bronze, silver and gold certifications, and six schools have already obtained the bronze standard (Rogerson 2023). This approach is certainly extending reach, with 43 primary schools currently enrolled and a potential audience of 8,266 primary pupils receiving an introduction to the language (Rogerson 2023). Maintaining the interest of teachers and school leaders in the long term, however, remains challenging (Cornwall Council 2023b).

At secondary level, meanwhile, there is no formal provision in place for the teaching of Cornish but the language is sometimes taught as an extracurricular activity or 'as part of wider language awareness or diversity classes and activities' (Council of Europe 2018). Cornwall Council's 2020–21 mid-year review shows that there was a plan to 'Deliver Cornish in at least one secondary school' (Cornwall Council 2020b), but this objective has since been abandoned because of the resources required to produce teaching resources (Rogerson 2023). There is no legal reason why Cornish could not be taught as a second language (Sayers, Davies-Deacon and Croome 2019), and the challenge at secondary level is therefore to gain a place for it on the curriculum. While the best solution would be to make the regional language compulsory, like in Wales or Ireland, Cornwall Council lacks the power to do so because it is merely a local council and not a devolved or sovereign government. It therefore has no legislative control over the education system and can do little more than lobby the national and local education authorities. Nonetheless, the fact that there is now a nationally accredited qualification in spoken Cornish administered by the Welsh Joint Education Committee (WJEC) could facilitate its introduction, since McArdle and Teare (2016) found that a lack of accreditation was a deterrent for schools considering teaching Manx on the Isle of Man. Furthermore, it may be hoped that the establishment of Cornish immersion pre-schools in the future might one day create cohorts of bilingual students whose parents will exert pressure on the education authorities to provide bilingual programs in primary and secondary education. Robertson (2018) and Clague (2009) have shown that parental demand did indeed have such an effect in Scotland and the Isle of Man respectively.

Adult learning provision

Alongside the school system, Cornwall Council also aims to 'maintain and increase the numbers of adults who speak Cornish' by developing 'a comprehensive system of community-based adult learning classes . . . both directly and in partnership with third-party providers' (Cornwall Council 2017: 16). To achieve this objective, it pledges to undertake quality assurance and teacher training and has created an online database of available classes. Cornwall Council estimates that there are now 254 adults learning Cornish through evening classes and 1,820 active users on the Memrise app for learning Cornish (Rogerson 2023). In 2022, 90 students took Cornish Language Board exams, and, in 2021, 12 passed the WJEC qualifications, although none did in 2022 or 2023 due to staff shortages (Rogerson 2023). Although Clague (2009) argues that resources are better focused on children because adults are poor language learners and are reluctant to use their skills, the Council's dual approach mirrors those of the other Celtic regions. Moreover, it is supported by Struble's and Fishman's theoretical frameworks, which highlight the importance of building a mass of adult speakers to allow for teaching, community-use and intergenerational transmission (Grenoble and Whaley 2005). The Learn Welsh program, which currently provides classes for 15,260 adults (Learn Welsh 2023), appears to be a good model for the coordination of adult programs, and its focus on Welsh for employment may provide a useful example for Cornwall to follow in helping to create professional domains of use in the future.

This is therefore an exciting period for Cornish, where future education provision is being actively shaped. Factors that have arisen in other Celtic regions will now be examined and their implications for Cornwall considered, with particular focus on the role of different stakeholders in shaping provision.

Celtic lessons

The importance of state support

First, the successful introduction of Cornish into the education system is inevitably highly dependent on UK government support. Cornwall, unlike Wales, Scotland or Northern Ireland, does not have devolved control over its education system, which means that curriculum decisions are made in London by the national government and not in Truro by a regional body. While Cornish could legally be taught as a second language at all levels of the system, any widespread introduction would require government funding on a scale not previously forthcoming (ELEN 2019). This reticence is perplexing, since the government officially recognizes the importance of revitalizing the language and has granted it level-two status in the Council of Europe's European Charter for Regional or Minority Languages. This means it has a responsibility to create a favorable environment for the learning of Cornish (Tresidder 2015) and to provide 'primary education at the absolute minimum as an integral part of the curriculum' (Croome 2015: 115). While such recognition is undoubtedly valuable, not least in validating the community's efforts at revitalization (Grenoble 2015), the government is not currently meeting these commitments – the existing primary provision is certainly not integral to the curriculum. Furthermore, true guarantees for educational provision are reserved for languages with level-three protection under the European Charter for Regional or Minority Languages, such as Welsh, Scottish Gaelic or Irish in Northern Ireland. It is therefore essential that Cornwall Council continue to lobby for level-three recognition to ensure both funding and a meaningful place for Cornish in the curriculum. Indeed, compiling a case for level-three protection has been identified by Cornwall Council as one of its key strategic priorities in 2023 and 2024 (Cornwall Council 2023a).

Neoliberalism: an ideological hurdle

One explanation for the UK government's reticence to support the provision of Cornish-language education is the neoliberal ideology that has dominated education planning since the 1980s. This ideology, with its associated new public management approach, emphasizes the need for 'quantifiable outcomes' (Sayers 2012) and argues that curriculum planning ought to be based on economic productivity and educational utility. As a result, 'educational policies have sought to prioritize the need for children to learn functional skills' (Tresidder 2015: 216) and for schools to perform well in league tables. McManus (2016) suggests that this pressure has led Northern Irish schools to shift efforts away from the teaching of Irish Gaelic towards 'easier' subjects that secure better grades in the all-important national GCSE exams that mark the end of compulsory education. McEwan-Fujita (2003), meanwhile, traces how a neoliberal campaign depicting Gaelic education as pointless and wasteful was waged in the Scottish media to undermine revitalization efforts. Languages whose economic rationales are not immediately obvious have therefore had difficulty maintaining their places in increasingly packed curricula, particularly at the secondary level. Indeed, in 1984, Cornish was being taught as a subject in two secondary schools, but, by the year 2000, it was only taught as an extracurricular activity (Mackinnon 2001). Croome (2015) pinpoints neoliberalism as a causal factor, showing that teachers perceived Cornish as a 'risky' subject because of the pressure to demonstrate good exam results in core subjects. It is therefore important that the Cornish revitalization movement make a successful case for the language's social and economic utility.

Playing the neoliberal game

Indeed, other Celtic regions have succeeded in embedding their languages in the curriculum by making clear economic arguments for teaching them and thus tackling neoliberalism on its own terms. For instance, McEwan-Fujita highlights how Scottish education authorities rebranded Gaelic as 'useful and valuable in business and national education' (2003: 232) to reflect Margaret Thatcher's efforts to commodify Scotland's regional particularity and thus cash in on the development of mass tourism in the 1980s. Similarly, Wilson argues that 'the Isle of Man Government views Manx as one of a number of ways of distinguishing the island from its global competitors, especially in the banking and financial services sector' (2009: 21) and highlights its use in national branding campaigns. Cornwall Council clearly understands the importance of framing an economic rationale for teaching Cornish, declaring that the region's prosperity can be enhanced 'through sustaining and enhancing Cornwall's distinct natural environment, heritage, culture and image' (Cornwall Council 2004: 20) and recognizing 'the importance of the Cornish language as a unique asset which has been central to the defining of Cornwall's distinct heritage and culture' (Cornwall Council 2019: 3). Such arguments should carry weight in Cornwall, where tourism is estimated to be worth £2.4 billion a year (Cornwall DMC 2023). Furthermore, the teaching of a language ultimately creates a marketplace for that language 'in the form of jobs for teachers, teacher-aides, teacher-trainers, curriculum and materials developers, and so forth' (Cooper 2010: 162). This, in turn, spurs student and parental interest in the language: Hodges' 2012 study of the Rhymni Valley revealed that 25% of parents with children in Welsh-medium education perceived Welsh as an economic advantage for their children. Enhancing Cornish education would therefore, in turn, reinforce the economic arguments for teaching it and ultimately fuel parental demand.

Leveraging parental demand

Education as a marketplace

While neoliberalism presents challenges for the teaching of Celtic languages, it has also paradoxically made the introduction of such provision possible by placing parental choice at the heart of the education system. For instance, the 1986 Education Act allowed Welsh parents to choose their children's school, which led to an increase in the number of Welsh immersion schools (Jones and Martin-Jones 2003). Similarly, the Education (Scotland) Act 2016 obliges Scottish local authorities to provide Gaelic-medium primary education if parents of at least five children request it (Robertson 2018). This is driving growth in Gaelic provision across the whole of Scotland and not just in the Gaelic heartlands. The Breton example, meanwhile, shows that parents can pressure education authorities into providing immersion and bilingual education even where no such legislative mechanisms exist (Hifearnáin 2011). Oakes (2011) found that, despite administrative barriers set up by the French state to deter the establishment of new Breton immersion schools, parental demand has led to a growth in semi-official ones called *Diwans*. The subsequent competition between *Diwans* and state providers is, in turn, leading to an increase in the number of state immersion schools (Oakes 2011). These examples suggest that, if sufficient numbers of Cornish parents were to demand Cornish immersion education, the very market forces that have previously undermined provision could lead to its growth. Indeed, in 2019, Cornwall had more academy schools than the national average (Sayers, Davies-Deacon and Croome 2019). These private education operators are designed to promote parental choice, and their prevalence in Cornwall shows that a liberal education market is already thriving in the region. However, evidence currently suggests that such parental demand for Cornish education is lacking. Sayers argues that 'a wide public mandate had never underpinned the revival' (2012: 115), citing a 2007 survey showing that 8% of respondents were unaware of the Cornish language and a further 50% were indifferent to creating opportunities for greater use. It is therefore vital that Cornwall Council succeed in sparking parental demand for Cornish education in order to fuel future growth.

Casting Cornish as a marker of identity

One way of triggering parental demand would be to emphasize the symbolic value of the language as a marker of Cornish identity. For instance, when Eire became independent in 1922, Irish was portrayed as a touchstone for national identity. The new constitution gave it the status of first official language and it became a 'symbolic representation in the company of emblems such as the shamrock and the harp for many Irish citizens' (Ceallaigh and Dhonnabháin 2015: 180). Irish education continues to enjoy widespread support, and Watson argues that 'people learn Irish and support its promotion because of this sense of identity' (in *idem*, p. 180). Dunmore (2018) found that 59% of respondents already considered Cornish an important symbol of regional identity, and further lionization of the language seems possible today, with studies suggesting that large-scale in-migration is fueling a revival in Cornish identity. Carkeek (in Deacon 2013) found that a total of 52% of respondents identified as either equally Cornish and British (18%), more Cornish than British (17%) or only Cornish (17%). Similarly, a 2011 school survey found that 41% of 15- to 18-year-olds in six Cornish schools defined themselves as Cornish (Deacon 2013). Aldous and Williams conclude that 'identification with Cornish ethnicity may be increasing over time' (in Dunmore 2018: 22), although whether this identity is based on ethnicity or civic identification remains an open question (Sayers 2012). Cornwall Council has already begun to tap into this renascent regional identity to win parental support for Cornish education. Indeed, the Council's language learning program is called 'Go Cornish', and its website clearly states that 'By having an appreciation of the Cornish language, we can all gain a greater sense of place and cultural awareness' (Golden Tree 2023) before going on to emphasize the language's place in the landscape, history and culture of the region. Moreover, Wilson shows that, on the Isle of Man, such messaging has been particularly effective in winning over parents who have recently migrated from 'larger, more heterogeneous (and anonymous) places' (2009: 18). Many of them 'felt that a Manx language education would give their children a better sense of place or belonging' (p. 22), and Grenoble and Whaley explain this trend by arguing that 'globalizing forces have triggered reacting forces as some people seek to assert, or better to reassert, their unique cultural identity' (2005: 3). The Council's efforts to assimilate the Cornish language with Cornish identity are therefore a promising tactic for garnering parental support amongst old and new residents alike.

Emphasizing the benefits of bilingualism

Another technique for generating parental demand for Cornish education would be to publicize the cognitive benefits of bilingualism more widely and thus emphasize its importance as a form of cultural capital. Goalabré shows that many Scottish and Breton parents with children in immersion education saw the 'additional skill of bilingualism as desirable because of its perceived benefits for their children's intellectual development' (2011: 134). This sentiment was echoed on the Isle of Man, with some parents in Wilson's 2009 sample even stating that the Manx language itself was incidental and that they would have opted for French or Spanish immersion programs if these had been available. Furthermore, his respondents' belief in such cognitive benefits echoed the information literature distributed by the Manx language officer. This observation has interesting implications for Cornwall, since it suggests that campaigns by authorities can help raise awareness of the advantages of bilingualism and thus generate parental interest in immersion schemes. These findings support Goalabré's assertion that 'The educational field is one area where strategic and socially orientated choices can be found, with many parents calculating and evaluating the best options for their children' (2015: 53). She cautions, however, that such instrumental motivation is not likely to have long-lasting benefits for the language itself as, without a parental commitment to use the language as a home language, the bilingualism acquired will be very limited and will fail to contribute to community use.

Associating Cornish teaching with academic quality

The introduction of Cornish education may also stimulate further parental demand if it becomes associated with academic excellence, as has been the case in other Celtic contexts. For instance, 28% of parents in Hodges' (2012) sample cited high educational standards as their main reasons for choosing Welsh-medium schools. Their logic was captured in one parent's observation that 'it's almost like having a [private]-school education in the national system', citing 'the discipline of the children and the pride and expectations of the teachers' (p. 366). In Brittany, meanwhile, Timm (2009) found that parents believe Breton-immersion schools offer a higher standard of education because they are less closely linked with the centralized national education system. New Cornish-language sections and immersion schools would inevitably begin with smaller classes and close authority supervision, and such selling-points could therefore be touted to attract parents in the UK's liberal education marketplace. However, Goalabré (2015) cites a plethora of research studies showing that immersion schools are most likely to attract middle-class parents, arguing that these parents traditionally place higher value on academic quality and the benefits of childhood bilingualism. This phenomenon could be particularly problematic in Cornwall because the revitalization movement has historically been heavily middle-class (Hirner in Sayers 2012), and yet Cornwall is one of the poorest areas of the UK. It is therefore important that Cornwall Council consciously raise awareness of the benefits of Cornish-immersion programs among all socio-economic groups to ensure that the teaching of Cornish garners widespread parental support and can serve as a positive vector of social inclusion and mobility.

Language community engagement

While both the state and parents have important roles to play in introducing Cornish into the education system, another key stakeholder is the language community itself. For all Celtic languages, an important contribution made by these speakers has been linguistic standardization (Mackinnon 2001), which has allowed for the sharing of teaching materials, the employment of peripatetic teachers and the movement of staff and students from one school to another. Such standardization has, however, often proved controversial. In Brittany, it created a form of 'neo-Breton' so distinct from the multiple regional dialects that it is 'frequently unintelligible to many of the native

Breton speakers' (Jones in Nolan and Hornsby 2010: 316). While standardization allowed the language to be taught in schools, it divided the language community between the younger, urban speakers who had learnt the language in the classroom and the older, rural, native speakers, with the two versions coming to 'represent different ways of life, outlooks and mentalities' (Jones in Timm 2009: 727). Furthermore, standardization has negatively impacted the self-perception of traditional speakers who, 'Intimidated by the intellectualization of their language . . . , are quick to denigrate their own variety of Breton with the words "we don't speak properly here"' (Hornsby 2007: 195). In Cornwall, there is also scope for standardization to divide the language community. The acrimony between the speakers of the six different varieties of the revived language long deterred funding bodies and prevented the introduction of the language into formal education until a compromise was reached in 2008 and a new Standard Written Form (SWF) was created for use in education (Tresidder 2015). Unfortunately, the expansion of education provision seems to be contributing to a drift in the Standard Written Form towards the Kemmyn version, and Sayers and Renkó-Michelsén (2015) warn that this risks reviving old hostilities. It is therefore important that Cornwall Council implement its education strategy with tactful respect for and recognition of the different forms of Cornish so as not to alienate the tiny number of speakers whose unity of purpose is so important to the teaching and wider use of the language. If the introduction of immersion education can be successfully negotiated in the future, it may be hoped that a new generation of 'neo-native' Cornish speakers will ultimately make the language their own and move it beyond such academic arguments about form, unconsciously breaking the hard-won rules with the immunity from reproach which comes from native-speaker status.

Teacher engagement

The final group whose support is fundamental to the establishment of Cornish-language education is the teaching community. The lack of any legal obligation to teach Cornish means that headteachers can decide whether or not to do so. Furthermore, studies show that teachers' attitudes towards their subjects have a significant effect on students' attitudes (Croome 2015 cites research by Flores 2001 and Nespor 1987). The success of Cornish education may therefore hinge on the enthusiasm of teachers. At first glance, the situation seems encouraging: Croome found that 72% of Cornish headteachers surveyed in 2015 said that they would like to introduce Cornish into their schools, and there is a high uptake of the Go Cornish program. Good will is not, however, enough to ensure effective language teaching, and Stephen, McPake and McLeod (2012) argue that a lack of training in Scotland and a failure to share best practices resulted in questionable teaching strategies that negatively impacted Gaelic language learning. Other regions have, however, taken successful steps to overcome such issues. For instance, Wales has a scheme allowing teachers preparing to teach Welsh to take a sabbatical to study the language and its pedagogy (Prys Jones and Jones 2014). On the Isle of Man, a materials writer has been employed, procedures for the sharing of best practice have been established and online solutions for the pooling of resources have been found (McArdle and Teare 2016). Cornwall Council still has much work to do in equipping teachers with the skills and materials to teach Cornish effectively, but the Go Cornish program provides introductory training sessions and materials for primary teachers (Sayers, Davies-Deacon and Croome 2019). As the Council argues, such efforts always need to be underpinned by significant involvement from the higher-education sector (Cornwall Council 2004). A Cornish Language Practice Project was set up at Plymouth University in 2014 to train early-years teachers, but this EU-funded scheme came to an end after only one year (Champliaud 2023). It is therefore vital that Cornwall Council be given the means to extend opportunities for comprehensive training in the effective delivery of Cornish education and that the higher education sector be encouraged to take an active role in this process.

This chapter has so far demonstrated that Cornwall can learn much from other Celtic regions to optimize the introduction of Cornish into the education system. It has considered the importance of garnering the support of stakeholders such as the national government, parents, the language community and teachers and has looked at how this can be achieved. Nonetheless, the most important question remains the extent to which the revitalization of these languages through education has been successful in other regions and whether it could ultimately be successful in Cornwall.

Can education really revitalize Cornish?

Overall, the widespread teaching of Celtic languages has certainly increased the numbers of young people able to communicate in them. In Ireland and Wales, for instance, the vast majority of students study the local language to the end of secondary education (Prys Jones and Jones 2014; Ó Murchú 2016). This is a significant achievement which will help safeguard the existence of the languages for future generations. Nonetheless, the fact that they are being learnt widely as second languages or used in immersion education does not necessarily mean that they are consolidating their positions as community languages or that the intergenerational transmission so vital to language revitalization is taking place. As Hifearnáin underlines, 'There is a difference between children acquiring competence in the language and those same children necessarily becoming active speakers outside the classroom as a result of that linguistic competence' (2013: 123). This is illustrated in Wales, where a 2011 study found that, 'while 98% of informants have contact with Welsh within school, only 24% of these speakers use Welsh outside of school' (in Price and Tamburelli 2016: 190). Similarly, Baker (in *idem*) reported that Welsh-medium pupils make little use of Welsh in informal communication outside of school. Similar results were reported in Goalabré's 2015 study of Scottish Gaelic and Breton. These findings therefore suggest that, while Cornish-education provision, both as a second language and as a medium of instruction, is a positive step in spreading knowledge of the language, it will not automatically lead to wider revitalization.

The limits of education

There are several reasons why the use of a language in the education domain does not necessarily lead to family or community use. First, the language acquired through education is limited in terms of level and range. Ceallaigh and Dhonnabháin show that 'Even though [Irish] immersion students display fluency and confidence in their L2 use, the level of L2 accuracy and the range of L2 competencies achieved are less than native-like' (2015: 188), and Ní Mhaoláin concludes that 'one of the recognized weaknesses of the Irish immersion system is that a full language context cannot be created within the classroom because the natural context is not there' (in Ceallaigh and Dhonnabháin 2015: 25). Mac Aogain argues, however, that 'the reason that school Irish doesn't survive very well in everyday life is not because it is school Irish but because there is nothing to do with it' (in Benjamins, Company and Central 2020: 30). He thus emphasizes the importance of creating a range of societal domains in which the language can be used. Another issue is that the education domain is an official one, and so, as Price and Tamburelli suggest, 'the formal register learned by informants is wholly inappropriate for casual application' (2016: 201). Their study concludes that, 'The informants' lack of informal Welsh holds implications for their ability to use Welsh in every-day environments' (p. 201). Moreover, they argue that use in education can also result in a form of 'inverted diglossia' wherein the language becomes negatively associated with this formal domain and English gains status 'as the language of rebellion against the established rules of the adult world' (p. 192). In their view, this explains why teenage boys are less likely to use the language outside of the classroom than their female classmates. Finally, Maguire (in Clague 2009) suggests that children in Northern Ireland are reluctant to use Irish in the home after a certain age because they become aware of their parents' linguistic limitations. This finding is echoed in Clague's study of the use of Manx within the home by immersion students (2009). It is therefore clear that education cannot bear the full burden of language revitalization, and this has significant implications for Cornish which, as a revived language, is disproportionately reliant on the education system to embed it in society.

The importance of wider language planning

The best solution to these problems would be to actively encourage the use of Cornish in a range of societal domains to prevent it becoming too closely associated with formal education alone. Such efforts are being made in each of the Celtic regions for their respective languages. One solution has been the creation of what Abbi (1995) describes as 'new linguistic markets' where education leads to employment opportunities in teaching, journalism or the civil service. This is a positive development and should be encouraged through extensive vocational education in the Celtic languages. However, employment remains a formal domain and will not necessarily ensure that Cornish becomes a community language. More promising initiatives are the extracurricular programs established by Welsh education authorities which offer opportunities for pupils to socialize in Welsh (Prys Jones and Jones 2014). Judge (2007), meanwhile, emphasizes the need for language speakers to be able to identify one another and build networks within the wider community. The harnessing of social media could potentially help in this aim. Cornwall Council therefore needs to support community-based social activities running parallel to formal education and allow for visibility within the community to allow children to develop a more natural, informal register and make active use of the language in their everyday lives. This is, however, challenging given the limited pool of volunteers available within the community (Cornwall Council 2023b). Such initiatives will be particularly important in Cornwall given that the language was reconstructed as an academic exercise. It is now in desperate need of a living population to break its rules and rebuild them in its image.

Conclusion

This chapter has used the example of Cornwall to illustrate how important the sharing of experience between different European regions can be to the effective use of education systems to revitalize regional languages. It has drawn on examples from different Celtic contexts to highlight factors that Cornwall Council should consider in order to ensure that its Cornish-language education provision is effective.

First, it needs to continue lobbying the UK government, whose control over the education system makes it central to the success of the revitalization program. In particular, the obtention of level-three protection under the Charter for Regional or Minority Languages would guarantee its place as a formal part of the education system. To acquire this, the Council needs to continue playing the neoliberal game, emphasizing the economic utility of the language as an essential part of the Cornish brand and capitalizing on parents' power to choose the type of education their children receive. Parental demand can be fostered by linking the language to Cornish identity in the public consciousness, by selling the benefits of bilingualism and by ensuring that Cornish education becomes synonymous with enhanced academic quality. The Council will need to be careful, however, to guarantee that Cornish education does not become a reserve of the middle classes but promotes social inclusion and mobility.

The Council will also need to work tactfully with the language community, notably encouraging them to nurture the Standard Written Form which, after so many years of acrimony, has made the entry of Cornish into the formal education system a viable possibility. Finally, it must foster the support of the teaching profession, providing high-quality training and facilitating the sharing of materials and best practice.

It is clear from other Celtic contexts, however, that the education system alone cannot bear the full responsibility for revitalizing a language – this will result in a stilted version whose usage is not that of a fully-fledged community language. It is therefore essential that education planning go together with wider acquisition planning, emphasizing the importance of use in numerous domains, including the family.

The Cornish language is at a crucial point in its long history, and the decisions that stakeholders make in the near future will determine whether it flourishes or dies. If Cornish is successfully introduced into the education system and takes root in the community, its example will hopefully provide its own Celtic lessons to other European nations struggling to revive their regional languages through education and may ultimately help stem the tide of language extinction that threatens to engulf Europe in the coming years.

Bibliography

Abbi, A. (1995) 'Small languages and small language communities', *International Journal of the Sociology of Language*, 116(1): 175–186.

Baker, C. (2003) 'Language planning: A grounded approach', in J. Dewaele, A. Housen and L. Wie (eds) *Bilingualism: Beyond Basic Principles*, Clevedon: Multilingual Matters, pp. 88–111.

Benjamins, J., Company, P. and Central, P. E. (2020) 'Irish', in J. Edwards (ed) *Minority Languages and Group Identity: Cases and Categories*, Philadelphia: John Benjamins Publishing Company, pp. 105–1227.

Broadhurst, K. (2023) 'Cornish: Can an Indigenous language become a fixture in the local primary curriculum?', in C. Blyth (ed) *'Other' Voices in Education – (Re)Stor(y)ing Stories*, Singapore: Springer.

Burley, S. (2008) *A Report on the Cornish Language Survey Conducted by the Cornish Language Partnership* [online]. Available at: https://docplayer.net/219074273-A-report-on-the-cornish-language-survey-conducted-by-the-cornish-language-partnership-july-2008.html [Accessed April 2020].

Ceallaigh, T. J. Ó. and Dhonnabháin, Á. N. (2015) 'Reawakening the Irish language through the Irish education system: Challenges and priorities', *International Electronic Journal of Elementary Education*, 8(2): 179–198.

Champliaud, E. (2023) *Discussion on pre-school education* [phone call] (Personal communication, 20 December 2023).

Clague, M. (2009) 'Manx language revitalization and immersion education', *Cultural Survival*, 2: 165–198.

Cooper, R. L. (2010) 'Acquisition planning', *Language Planning and Social Change*, 157–163.

Cornwall Council (2004) *Strategy for the Cornish Language*, Truro: Cornwall County Council.

Cornwall Council (2017) *Strateji an Yeth Kernewek 2015–25/Cornish Language Strategy 2015–25* [online]. Available at: www.cornwall.gov.uk/media/25229704/cornish-language-strategy-2015-2025.pdf [Accessed March 2020].

Cornwall Council (2019) *Cornish Language Policy* [online]. Available at: www.cornwall.gov.uk/media/40801945/cc-cornishlanguagepolicy-20191017.pdf [Accessed April 2020].

Cornwall Council (2020a) *Cornish Language Strategy Operational Plan 2019/20 – Mid-Year Update* [online]. Available at: www.cornwall.gov.uk/media/40759106/forum-reports-20181110.pdf [Accessed March 2020].

Cornwall Council (2020b) *Cornish Language Strategy Operational Plan 2020/21* [online]. Available at: https://kalenderkernewek.weebly.com/uploads/2/5/6/6/25661447/cornish_language_operational_plan_2020-21_-_mid_year_update_nov_20.pdf [Accessed December 2023].

Cornwall Council (2022) *Identity, Ethnicity, Language and Religion: 2021 Census Topic Summary* [online]. Available at: www.cornwall.gov.uk/media/t4nh3d3x/2021-census-identity-ethnicity-language-and-religion-topic-summary.pdf [Accessed December 2023].

Cornwall Council (2023a) *Cornish Language Strategy Operational Plan 2023/24* [online]. Available at: www.cornwall.gov.uk/media/nifjvj3b/cornish-language-operational-plan-2023-24.pdf [Accessed December 2023].

Cornwall Council (2023b) *Written Evidence Submitted by Cornwall Council* [online]. Available at: https://committees.parliament.uk/writtenevidence/119170/pdf/ [Accessed December 2023]

Cornwall DMC (2023) *What Is the Value of Tourism to Cornwall?* [online]. Available at: https://cornwall-dmc.co.uk/news/what-is-the-value-of-tourism-to-cornwall/ [Accessed December 2023].

Council of Europe (1992) *European Charter for Regional or Minority Languages*, Strasbourg: Council of Europe.

Council of Europe (2018) *European Charter for Regional or Minority Languages: Fifth Periodical Report Presented to the Secretary General of the Council of Europe in Accordance with Article 15 of the Charter* [online]. Available at: https://rm.coe.int/ukpr5-en-revised/168077fb40 [Accessed April 2020].

Croome, S. (2015) 'Accommodation and resistance in the implementation of a minority language: A survey of headteacher attitudes across primary schools in Cornwall', *SOAS Working Papers in Linguistics*, 17: 113–145.

Deacon, B. (2013) 'Are Cornish politics celtic?', in *'The Politics of the Celtic Fringe' Symposium, 21st June 2013 Penryn*.

Dunmore, S. (2018) 'A Cornish revival? The nascent iconization of a post-obsolescent language', *Journal of Historical Sociolinguistic*, 1–34.

ELEN (2019) [press release] June 2019. Available at: https://elen.ngo/2019/07/09/uk-government-announce-funding-for-cornish-language-elen-support-must-be-long-term-and-substantial/ [Accessed April 2020].

Goalabré, F. (2011) 'The choice of Bilingual schools in language shift situation in Brittany and in the Western Isles of Scotland', *Proceedings of the Harvard Celtic Colloquium*, 31: 118–136.

Goalabré, F. (2015) 'Immersion education and the revitalisation of Breton and Gaelic as community languages', *Policy and Planning for Endangered Languages*, 1: 48–66.

Golden Tree Productions (2023) *Go Cornish* [online]. Available at: https://gocornish.org/ [Accessed December 2023].

Grenoble, L. A. (2015) 'Leveraging language policy to effect change in the Arctic', in M. C. Jones (ed) *Policy and Planning for Endangered Languages*, Cambridge University Press, pp. 1–17.

Grenoble, L. A. and Whaley, L. J. (2005) *Saving Languages: An Introduction to Language Revitalization*, Cambridge: Cambridge University Press.

Hifearnáin, T. H. (2011) 'Breton language maintenance and regeneration in regional education policy', in C. Norrby and J. Hajek (eds) *Uniformity and Diversity in Language Policy: Global Perspectives*, Multilingual Matters, pp. 93–108.

Hifearnáin, T. Ó. (2013) 'Institutional Breton language policy after language shift', *International Journal of the Sociology of Language*, (223): 117–135.

Hodges, R. S. (2012) 'Welsh-medium education and parental incentives – the case of the Rhymni Valley, Caerffili', *International Journal of Bilingual Education and Bilingualism*, 15(3): 355–373.

Hornsby, M. (2007) 'Néo-breton and questions of authenticity', *Sociolinguistic Studies*, 6(2): 191–218.

Jones, D. V. and Martin-Jones, M. (2003) 'Bilingual education and language revitalization in Wales: Past achievements and current issues', in J. W. Tollefson and A. B. M. Tsui (eds) *Medium of Instruction Policies: Which Agenda? Whose Agenda?*, Routledge, pp. 43–69.

Judge, A. (2007) *Linguistic Policies and the Survival of Regional Languages in France and Britain*, Basingstoke: Palgrave Macmillan.

Learn Welsh (2023) *2021–2022 Statistics Learn Welsh Data* [online]. Available at: https://learnwelsh.cymru/about-us/statistics/2021-2022-statistics/ [Accessed December 2023].

Mackinnon (2001) *Cornish Language Study* [online]. Available at: www.cornwall.gov.uk/media/21486827/independent-study.pdf [Accessed April 2020].

McArdle, F. and Teare, R. (2016) *The Manx Gaelic Language in Education in the Isle of Man*, Mercator European Research Centre on Multilingualism and Language Learning.

McEwan-Fujita (2003) *Gaelic in Scotland, Scotland in Europe: Minority Language Revitalization in the Age of Neoliberalism*. PhD thesis. University of Chicago.

McManus, C. (2016) 'Irish language education and the national ideal: The dynamics of nationalism in Northern Ireland', *Nations and Nationalism*, 22(1): 42–62.

Moseley, C. (ed) (2010) *Atlas of the World's Languages in Danger*, Paris: UNESCO.

Nolan, S. and Hornsby, M. (2010) 'The regional languages of Brittany', in J. Fishman (ed) *Handbook of Language and Ethnic Identity*. 2nd ed., New York: Oxford University Press, pp. 310–322.

Oakes, L. (2011) 'Promoting language rights as fundamental individual rights: France as a model', *French Politics*, 9(1): 50–68.

Ó Murchú, H. (2016) *The Irish Language in Education in the Republic of Ireland*, Mercator European Research Centre on Multilingualism and Language Learning.

Price, A. R. and Tamburelli, M. (2016) 'Minority language abandonment in Welsh-medium educated L2 male adolescents: Classroom, not chatroom', *Language, Culture and Curriculum*, 29(2): 189–206.

Prys Jones, M. and Jones, C. (2014) *The Welsh Language in Education in the UK*, Mercator European Research Centre on Multilingualism and Language Learning.

Robertson, B. (2018) *The Gaelic Language in Education in Scotland*, Mercator European Research Centre on Multilingualism and Language Learning.

Rogerson, S. (2023) *Discussion on primary, secondary and adult education with Language Officer of Cornwall Council* [email exchange] (Personal communication, 21 December 2023).

Sayers, D. (2012) 'Standardising Cornish: The politics of a new minority language', *Language Problems and Language Planning*, 36(2): 99–119.

Sayers, D., Davies-Deacon, M. and Croome, S. (2019) *The Cornish Language in Education in the UK*, Mercator European Research Centre on Multilingualism and Language Learning.

Sayers, D. and Renkó-Michelsén, Z. (2015) 'Phoenix from the Ashes – Reconstructed Cornish in relation to Einar Haugen's four-step model of language standardisation', *Sociolinguistica*, 29(1).

Stephen, C., McPake, J. and McLeod, W. (2012) 'Playing and learning in another language: Ensuring good quality early years education in a language revitalisation programme', *European Early Childhood Education Research Journal*, 20(1): 21–33.

Timm, L. (2009) 'Language, culture and identity in Brittany: The sociolinguistics of Breton', in M. J. Ball and N. Müller (eds) *The Celtic Languages*, London: Routledge, pp. 712–752.

Tresidder, M. (2015) 'Rediscovering history and the cornish revival: Changing attitudes to obtain language policies', in M. C. Jones (ed) *Policy and Planning for Endangered Languages*, Cambridge University Press, pp. 205–221.

Wilson, G. N. (2009) '"But the language has got children now": Language revitalisation and education planning in the Isle of Man', *Shima: The International Journal of Research into Island Cultures*, 3(2): 15–31.

4

BASQUE AND OCCITAN IN THE NEW GLOBAL CONTEXT

Some reflections on language coexistence in multilingual education

Elizabeth Pérez-Izaguirre, Karin van der Worp, and Marie-Anne Châteaureynaud

Introduction

Nowadays educational systems in Europe are recommended by the European Union to teach at least one foreign language – and preferably two – next to the local languages of the country. These educational recommendations follow up on the modern advances in technology and the increasing demand for international communication and mobility. Multilingual education in global contexts confronts education with the need to manage and organize relationships between different languages at school. Not only is it important to manage the local and foreign languages of the curriculum, but also the differing first languages of the students should be taken into account in order to guarantee a correct development – or at least maintenance – of the competences in those languages in the case of, for instance, migrant students (Siguán 2002).

This challenge is even greater when minority and majority languages and the lingua franca, usually English, need to coexist, as language policies and schools must design and implement a curriculum including the teaching of each language, converting the educational system in at least a trilingual one. Not only do schools have to respond to the international needs of communication in foreign languages; the minority languages should also be supported. The growing recognition of minority languages has actually encouraged multilingualism (Gorter 2013).

On primary and secondary school levels, this multilingualism is most of all present in terms of languages of the curriculum, struggling to provide enough hours to dedicate to all of the languages, and the presence of students with first languages other than the ones of the curriculum. At higher educational levels, universities usually have to navigate between two forces, global competitiveness and innovation, on the one hand, and local attractiveness and diversity, on the other hand (Yanaprasart 2020), creating a conflict between internationalization and contextualization (Gajo and Berthoud 2020). Their ranking depends in part on successful internationalization, which in terms of language use often requires the use of English (e.g. for applying to international research funds, publishing in academic high-impact journals, etc.). On the other hand, universities are often funded by the local taxpayers, which makes the promotion of local languages a priority.

Following the idea of Cenoz (2009), in this chapter, we understand multilingual education as the teaching of more than two languages with the aim of developing communicative competence in

DOI: 10.4324/9781003439493-6

several languages. The mere presence of linguistically diverse students is not sufficient to consider education multilingual; an effort has to be made to develop the linguistic competences in order to consider education truly multilingual. The criteria to consider an educational system multilingual are not that straightforward; to what percentage should the system be multilingual in order to be considered such? Moreover, should this percentage be measured in terms of numbers of languages taught or numbers of hours spent on each language?

Different educational variables can have an influence on the degree of multilingualism in education, varying on a "continua of multilingual education" from less to more multilingual (Cenoz 2009: 31). The term "continua" indicates that it considers all those variables on a scale with different positions. The continua allows us to realize comparisons of the relative degree of multilingualism, in relation to linguistic, sociolinguistic and school specific dimensions.

As a first variable, we find the school context itself. Within this context, it has to be taken into account that the teachers might have different levels of multilingualism, with varying proficiency in different languages, and different levels of training in multilingual education. Moreover, the linguistic planning of schools might differ in terms of the presence of more than one language as school subjects, the integration of the different languages in syllabus design and lesson planning, the intensity of instruction and the age of introduction. Furthermore, several languages might be used as language of instruction throughout the several subjects of the curriculum.

A second variable refers to the linguistic distance between the languages used. The languages can have more or less relation because of their origin and have similarities or differences at a typological level. This linguistic distance influences multilingual education in terms of program design and the need to dedicate more or fewer hours to a language. In general terms, the more distant the languages, the more difficult it might be for schools to establish multilingual programs.

A third variable to take into account is the sociolinguistic context of the school on a macro and micro level. The difference in status of languages at an institutional level, the use of the different languages in the media and the distribution of speakers of the different languages, as well as the general linguistic landscape, indicate the level of social multilingualism on a macro level. On the micro level, we find the interpersonal relationships an individual establishes with others in time, such as parents, siblings, peers and neighbors, and the languages in which they shape these relationships.

Actually, for any educational institution – whatever the degree of multilingualism is – an effort should be made to provide teaching to pupils in a linguistically inclusive way, as "language is vital to content access and academic achievement for all students, enabling them to engage in higher-order thinking to help them reach their academic potential and foster their linguistic and cognitive abilities" (Bergroth et al. 2022a: 9). This is not only a concern to be taken into account by language teachers but in fact by all teachers, who all should aim at providing linguistically sensitive teaching (LST) at schools (Bergroth et al. 2022a).

LST refers to the linguistic dimension in education in the broadest sense of the word, focusing on inclusive education, considering the coexistence of multiple languages at school an opportunity rather than a problem. It seeks to move away from monolingual classrooms towards plurilingual pedagogies as an intrinsic part of educational institutions. LST acknowledges the role of languages in learning, identity and well-being of the students. LST includes not only the languages taught at school but also the languages that students, teachers and the society bring to school, since they all can serve as a vehicle and a tool for developing knowledge. LST does not consider these languages in isolation, to be taught separately from other subjects and other languages (Bergroth et al. 2022[a]). LST concerns all teachers, not only language teachers, as all teachers need to be aware of the crucial role that languages play in their teaching practice, regardless of the subject they teach.

Moreover, not only teachers as individuals but also the entire educational community should be involved in LST. Even students can become principal actors by actively bringing their languages into the classroom and respecting the languages of their peers. LST should take place throughout the whole school, within the classroom, in whole school activities, at the organizational level and in contact with the wider society but should also be supported at the educational policy level. LST would be an asset for education and the personal and academic development of the pupils (Bergroth et al. 2022a).

LST is in line with other multilingual ideas such as the focus on multilingualism (Cenoz and Gorter 2011), where students are considered multilingual speakers with their own particular fluid linguistic competence, using their linguistic repertoire in a complex and dynamic way while engaging in a specific social context. It also encompasses the idea of pedagogical translanguaging (García 2009), where the competence of multilingual speakers to navigate between several languages in an integrated system is built on as a pedagogical strategy to serve as a mean for scaffolding for language learning.

Changing monolingual frameworks into more multilingual-sensitive ones remains a challenge. Taking into account this complex reality of multilingual education, this chapter will focus on a comparison of the multilingual education systems of two nearby contexts: New Aquitaine (France) and the Basque Autonomous Community (Spain).

Both contexts deal with the challenge of the inclusion of majority languages, minority languages and English. In schools in New Aquitaine, the minority languages Occitan and Basque coexist with French as the majority language and English, while in the BAC, Basque as a minority language coexists with Spanish as the majority language and English. Both cases differ in the education and language policy support that minority languages receive: while in New Aquitaine, the teaching of Basque and Occitan is optional, French is compulsory, and English is not compulsory but in practice taught at most schools, in the BAC, the teaching of Basque is compulsory and reinforced by the educational system, and it coexists with Spanish and English as compulsory languages. Moreover, due to immigration, some students have mother tongues other than the ones of the curriculum, and these should also be given a place among the other present languages.

This work is part of a cross-border cooperation supported by the Euskampus structure of excellence, which enables the involved universities (University of Bordeaux and University of the Basque Country) to carry out research into the languages of these territories. For several years the cross-border team has been carrying out qualitative research into the teaching of Basque and Occitan languages in a multilingual context. They have interviewed Basque and Occitan teachers and pupils as part of a study of the sociolinguistic context in schools.

The aim of this chapter is to compare both cases from a global and multilingual perspective. The context of New Aquitaine will be described in the second section, the context of the BAC will be covered in the third section, and a comparison will be made in the fourth section. This chapter will conclude with a final section providing conclusions and reflecting on the possibilities of the language curriculum to improve the coexistence of minority languages, majority languages and the lingua franca.

Sociolinguistic and educational context of New Aquitaine

The New Aquitaine region is located in the southwest of France in the Cantabric sea border and is home to several minority languages, including Basque in the south and Occitan and Poitevin Saintongeais in the north. We are interested here in the case of Basque and Occitan, as the presence of those languages is the strongest one in education.

Basque, or Euskara, is a pre-Indo-European language of unknown origin present in both the Spanish and the French area. The Spanish area is called Hegoalde in Basque (southern Basque Country), comprising the Basque Autonomous Community and Navarre. In the BAC, Basque has been a co-official language since 1979 and since 1982 in some areas of Navarre. In the French Basque Country, called Iparralde (northern Basque Country), Basque is present in more or less half the area of the Pyrénées Atlantiques. However, the only official language is French. According to the VII Sociolinguistic Survey of the Basque language in 2023 (Basque Government 2023), only 20.1% of the northern Basque Country is Basque-speaking, while 9.4% are Basque receptives (they understand but do not speak Basque) and 70.5% non-Basque speakers.

The Occitan language is a Romance language, and it occupies a third part of the southern French territory (32 departments), 12 Italian valleys and the Val d'Aran in Spain. Occitan comprises several dialects, three of which are spoken in Aquitaine: Limousin in the northeast, Languedoc in the east and Gascon in the majority of the territories. Throughout the Occitan area, Occitan has been a written language since the Middle Ages and was also the language of the court and literature from the 11th century with the texts of the troubadours and a legal language.

A survey carried out in New Aquitaine and Occitania, territories where Occitan is spoken (OPLO 2020), shows that the number of Occitan speakers is estimated to be around 7% of the population. The other regions where Occitan is spoken have similar numbers of speakers as New Aquitaine and Occitania, except Val d'Aran, where Occitan is an official language and taught extensively. In contrast with the rest of the regions, in Val d'Aran, about 60% of the global population is Occitan speakers.

The minority languages are taught in both public and private education, but the French context is specific and strongly influenced by monolingualism, and only French is compulsory. In France, French is the language of the republic, and the majority of schooling is in French (apart from bilingual or immersive schools). It is important to note that since the Deixonne law in 1951 authorized the teaching of so-called regional languages in France (Palacín Mariscal 2017), Basque and Occitan have been taught. It should be pointed out that in the same highly monolingual French context, the sociolinguistic and educational situations of Basque and Occitan are different.

The situation for teaching Basque is different overall, as it benefits from clearer recognition of its identity (a single name for the language, whereas in Occitan there are several designations: Gascon, Limousin, Languedoc, etc.), a more circumscribed territory and a more proactive local policy. In the case of Occitan, the geographical extent of the language and the diversity of variants and situations in the different departments make the transmission of the language in schools more fragile.

The education stages and existing linguistic models are as follows. In nursery schools (aged 3 to 6), pupils have access to bilingual teaching (50/50) in state schools, while immersive teaching is provided in private schools. Bilingual education in Nouvelle Aquitaine often refers to French and Occitan or French and Basque teaching. In the case of Occitan, some nursery schools offer an awareness program. In nursery schools, language awareness is recommended to develop pupils' phonological skills and open them up to otherness with an intercultural education. Although this teaching is highly valued in research, it is not yet practiced in all schools and is often absent from primary education (ages 6–10).

In primary education, in the same way, bilingual teaching exists in state schools and immersive teaching in private schools. It should be noted, however, that there are more bilingual and immersive schools in Iparralde (half a department) than in the Occitan area, which is much larger (four and a half departments). The main linguistic model proposes teaching a foreign language (usually English) from the start of primary school at the age of 6 and provides for 54 hours per year up to the start of college (ages 11–15). In some schools, two foreign languages can be taught (mainly Spanish but also in some cases German).

At secondary level (11–18), there are more Basque than Occitan schools offering bilingual courses in the public sector and immersive courses in the private sector. However, Occitan is mainly taught as an optional subject (2 hours a week). In general, at secondary level (from 11 to 18), English will be taught systematically as LV1 (First Living Language) for 3 to 4 hours a week and LV2 (Second Living Language) for 2 hours a week; at lycée (ages 15–18), LV1 and LV2 are taught for 5.5 hours a week, and other language options may be added (another foreign language, an ancient language or a regional language).

Last, although researchers have shown the value of taking pupils' languages into account (Châteaureynaud 2022), there is little multilingual practice in the classroom, and so-called allophone pupils (migrants who do not speak French) benefit from a special scheme: the UPE2A, which takes them out of the ordinary classroom for a few hours a week for a year to have hours of French as a language of instruction to promote their inclusion.

These pupils can benefit from this scheme during a year before joining the mainstream class. On arrival, their level is assessed by a specialized teacher to determine their level of schooling and prior learning, and they are then sent to a mainstream school where they will be placed in a UPE2A. However, in a mainstream class, little account is taken of their language of origin and prior learning. Teaching conditions and monolingualism ideology do not really allow teachers to build on the skills already in place in the mother tongue to help pupils progress in learning the language of schooling. Compared with their European counterparts, the majority of French teachers have large class sizes and a high number of teaching hours per week, and teaching conditions do not allow sufficient time for joint work. For the pupils, it can lead to learning difficulties, even failure at school, and a feeling of insecurity and rejection. The monolingual ideology that is still highly present in French schools does not encourage making references to other languages. In 2018, the Evascol report stated that the results of a survey on the schooling conditions of allophone pupils confirm that the pace at which French is learnt does not match the institutional provision, which is limited to 1 year in a traditional UPE2A (despite the 2012 circular recommending long-term learning), or the pace of teaching, which is often dense and fast paced.

However, research into plurilingualism has gradually led to the emergence of teaching practices such as linguistically sensitive teaching (language awareness, comparison of languages, intercomprehension, etc.) that enable the languages of origin of newly arrived pupils to be better included. In-service and initial teacher training is needed to take better account of the languages and cultures of origin and to ensure the genuine inclusion of these newly arrived pupils, who should be able to appropriate French as the language of schooling without losing their language and culture of origin. These inclusive practices with allophone pupils are also used in bilingual classes in Occitan and Basque.

At university, all students must study English. However, the three universities – the University of Bordeaux Montaigne (UBM), the University of Pau and Pays de l'Adour (UPPA) and the University of Bordeaux (UB) – offer courses in Occitan and Basque but in very different ways. UBM and UPPA offer optional courses in Occitan, and UB offers training for future bilingual primary school teachers. For Basque, there is a complete course at UBM, in addition to optional courses, and training for bilingual primary school teachers at UB.

In general, it could be said that the fact that Occitan is not compulsory weakens the whole program because the Occitan competes with other options. Before the latest reform, the lycée (15–18) was able to offer more teaching options, which could subsequently encourage students to continue learning Occitan in higher education.

At university, the opportunities are limited, and so are the candidates. Few students enroll in Occitan courses or teacher training courses (Pérez-Izaguirre, Châteaureynaud, and Amiama 2021: 164)

Teaching conditions, pedagogical continuity and the resources allocated to the teaching of these languages are still a cause for concern. The Union of Occitan teachers (Fédération des Enseignants de Langue et Culture d'Oc) (Verny 2009) highlights that (1) there is a growing decline in the attractiveness of regional language teaching, due to the interplay of coefficients and competition with other options, and (2) timetables are unattractive for students.

Sociolinguistic and educational context of the Basque Autonomous Community

It is important to situate the linguistic situation of the BAC in a specific historical and political context. The BAC is administratively dependent on Spain; it is located in the north, bordering the south of France. It is part of a larger, cross-border territory called Euskal Herria, Basque Country, which includes the aforementioned south of New Aquitaine, called Iparralde, and the north of Spain, called Hegoalde. These are the northern and southern parts of the Basque Country, which share the Basque culture and language.

In the BAC, since Franco's dictatorship (1939–1975), Basque was forbidden in the public sphere and, therefore, also in the educational system. The transmission of the language, which had never had an official status, was lost during that period, although some clandestine schools did transmit the language during that time (Biota Piñeiro and Zabaleta Imaz 2018).

From the transition to democracy, the Autonomous Communities were established in Spain and the BAC was one of those that achieved the co-official status of Basque and Spanish in the linguistic field, as well as the transfer of important competences in the field of education from the central state to the Basque government. Thus, in 1982, the Law for the Normalization of Basque was approved, and since then, every student in the BAC has the right to receive his or her education in Basque or Spanish. In 1983, three linguistic models were proposed, which at that time responded to certain needs of the population (Maia 2012). The linguistic models are as follows:

- Model A: Instruction is in Spanish and Basque is taught as a subject.
- Model B: Instruction is in Spanish and Basque, moderately flexible depending on the center.
- Model D: Instruction is in Basque, and Spanish is taught as a subject.

Model D was intended for people who already knew Basque to be taught in their language. However, over the years, a very marked social trend has been promoted in which model A has almost disappeared, model B is becoming less and less popular and model D prevails in most schools. In the 2017/2018 academic year, 80% choose model D (ISEI-IVEI 2021). There are several reasons to explain this movement or general trend towards model D, and although it is not the purpose of this chapter to delve into these reasons, it is important to highlight two elements: (1) that Basque is increasingly demanded by public institutions, as well as in some private ones, as an indispensable requirement to access a public position and (2) that Basque has established itself as the vehicular language of schools in general. In general, it can be said that the schools have achieved the effect of normalizing the language, since two out of every three of the new 300,000 speakers of Basque are so thanks to the school (ISEI-IVEI 2021). In fact, the number of Bascophones has increased in the last 40 the years in almost all regions.

This movement of Basque language learning within the educational system contrasts with the sociolinguistic reality. According to the VII Sociolinguistic Survey (Basque Government,

Government of Navarre, OPLB 2023), although knowledge of Basque in general has increased, mainly thanks to the school, the use remains low. In fact, only 22% of the population aged 16 and over in the BAC uses Basque as much or more than Spanish. Some of the reasons that have to do with this phenomenon are the languages used in the relationship networks, as well as the ease of speaking the language. Interest and motivation are also important, but the networks become central to increasing the use of the language.

It is also important to understand the BAC context within a global migratory perspective. Following ISEI-IVEI (2021), 11.7% of the total students enrolled in compulsory education are of migrant background and constitute 12.5% of the total number of students enrolled in the public school system. Until recently, this also concentrated 73% of the migrant students in the only existing Spanish track, and student background in this track was characterized by lower socio-economic indicators and greater failure rates than their native classmates (Basque Government 2018). However, in 2022 the Basque government approved a New Decree for Admission and Scolarisation of Students for all schools receiving public funds (Basque Government 2022a). This decree has been applied starting with the 2023/24 academic year and applies the Index for Vulnerability, which enables identification of vulnerable students and to define the percentage that each school should have. The decree is designed to equally distribute diversity and vulnerability in education centers and avoid socioeconomic or other kinds of segregation. The Index for Vulnerability includes criteria such as developmental delay, language and communication development disorders, attention or learning disorders, severe lack of knowledge of the learning language, being in a situation of socio-educational vulnerability, high intellectual abilities and having joined the education system late or personal conditions or school history (Basque Government 2022b).

With respect to immigrant languages, as a general rule, it is important to say that, apart from Spanish or English, these are not taught at school, although they can be considered through different plans of the center. In general, when a student arrives and does not know Basque and/or Spanish, they have certain hours per week dedicated to a Program for Linguistic Reinforcement to the learning of one or both languages so that they can acquire these and be able to receive the education that corresponds to them by age (Basque Government 2023).

As mentioned, in the BAC, Basque as a minority language coexists with Spanish as the majority language and English. The teaching of Basque is compulsory and reinforced by the educational system and coexists with Spanish and English as compulsory languages. Compulsory education in the BAC ranges through ages 6–16, although most children attend early education starting at 3 years old. Primary education (6–12) and secondary education (12–16) are the subsequent compulsory education stages. The following two years are baccalaureate (16–18), which are considered secondary education but are not compulsory. These are specialization years for artistic, humanities, social science, natural science or technical streams, which become important if students opt for higher education (Basque Government 2020).

From kindergarten onwards, students and their families choose the language of schooling, with certain restrictions. As already mentioned, schools using public funds tend to offer an education mainly in Basque, including Spanish and English as subjects or even gradually including English as a vehicular language in other subjects. Some schools opt for an integrated treatment of languages, and others apply the CLIL method, although this is not yet generalizable.

One of the instruments used by schools to define their linguistic identity is the School Linguistic Project. This project, which is developed by the school, allows for a program per year for each of the languages in which the subjects are taught, and must be prepared by the school itself. This project considers the language planning and organization of teacher training, in coherence with the sociolinguistic reality and linguistic competence of the teachers, taking a multilingual approach (Basque Government 2016).

As for higher education, the three universities present in the BAC, University of the Basque Country (UPV/EHU), University of Deusto and Mondragon University (MU), offer courses in Basque, Spanish and English. Most of the offer of the public university, the UPV/EHU, is bilingual and can be accessed both in Spanish and Basque, while taking courses in English is also a possibility, with similar situations in the other two private universities.

Methodology

The approach of this chapter is qualitative (Nieto and Recamán 2009) because it gathers data in a natural context, based on observation and interviews with the public concerned. The work is based on several years of surveys in the areas concerned. We have used data collection methods from the human sciences – questionnaires and semi-structured interviews – to gain a better understanding of the situation of language teaching in the school context. This is a non-experimental exploratory study designed to identify and describe the characteristics and relevant phenomena of a specific population in an objective and comparable way (Nieto and Recamán 2009).

The aim of the field study is to gain a better understanding of the contexts in which Occitan and Basque are taught on either side of the Pyrenees, to show the specific features linked to the history and language policies of each country and their practical impact on the conditions in which these languages are taught and passed on to pupils.

Since 2018, with several projects such as *Euskocc* and *Pyrenlang*, data has been collected: Interviews, observations and shared social diagnostic sessions were carried out with Occitan and Basque teachers and pupils. The conclusions of these data collections over the years, together with an extensive literature review on the topic, have formed the basis for the comparison between the contexts as presented in the chapter.

Comparison between New Aquitaine and the Basque Autonomous Community language education

In Table 4.1, a comparison of the treatment of different languages in NA and the BAC is provided for the different educational stages.

Before comparing both cases, just a few notions regarding the legal educational context are necessary for a correct interpretation. In NA, the only official language is French, while in the BAC, both Spanish and Basque are official. This monolingual versus bilingual framework should be taken into account as an important difference on the basis of the educational system. In NA, the French national program CECRL defines the legal educational framework, while in the BAC, each school can set up their own linguistic project within the framework of the Autonomous Community.

First of all, from the table it is clear, and of course logical, that at all compulsory educational stages in both contexts the local majority language is obligatory. The main difference is that in the BAC, Spanish – although compulsory as a subject – is not always the language of instruction, since many schools offer education through the medium of Basque. In NA, the compulsory language French is both a subject as well as the official language of instruction. This fact is in line with the monolingual language policy in NA versus the bilingual language policy of the BAC. In tertiary education, in the case of the BAC, Spanish is no longer compulsory, and although studies through the medium of Spanish are offered, studies could also be entirely carried out in the minority language Basque without using any Spanish.

Table 4.1 Comparison of languages in education in NA and the BAC

Educational stage	NA/ BAC	Local majority language	Local minority language(s)	Foreign language(s)	Students with other L1
Pre-school	NA	French compulsory	In some schools Occitan and Basque optional	Language awareness	Migrant students in ordinary schools
	BAC	Spanish offered	Basque offered	English offered	Migrant students in ordinary schools
Primary	NA	French compulsory	In some schools Occitan and Basque optional	Majority English, some Spanish	Special groups UPE2A
	BAC	Spanish compulsory at all schools as a subject; some schools offer Spanish as medium of instruction	Basque compulsory at all schools as a subject; most schools offer Basque as medium of instruction	English compulsory; used in some schools as medium of instruction	Program for linguistic reinforcement for Basque and/or Spanish. Migrant students mainly in Spanish model until 2022; new decree on Index of Vulnerability
Secondary	NA	French compulsory	In some schools Occitan and Basque optional	Majority English LV1 and Spanish LV2, some German LV2 Few other foreign languages: Portuguese, Italian, Russian, Chinese, etc.	Special groups UPE2A
	BAC	Spanish compulsory at all schools as a subject; some schools offer Spanish as medium of instruction	Basque compulsory at all schools as a subject; most schools offer Basque as medium of instruction	English compulsory; used in some schools used as medium of instruction Other optional foreign languages, mainly French	Program for linguistic reinforcement for Basque and/or Spanish Migrant students mainly in Spanish model until 2022; new decree on Index of Vulnerability
Tertiary	NA	French compulsory	Occitan and Basque optional	English, some Spanish	Migrant students in ordinary schools
	BAC	Studies through the medium of Spanish offered	Studies through the medium of Basque offered	Studies through the medium of English offered	Migrant students mainly in Spanish model

Note: This table was elaborated by the authors based on the information presented in the previous sections.

Regarding the minority languages, the main difference between NA and the BAC lays in the fact that in the BAC, the minority language is obligatory in compulsory education and thus offered by all schools, whereas in NA, it is a mere option, and only some schools offer this option. In fact, in the BAC, the minority language is used as language of instruction in one of the most popular models of compulsory education, the D model. Again, a clear link can be seen with the monolingual language policy of the NA, not providing other languages than French as compulsory, and the bilingual language policy of the BAC providing the same right and presence for both the minority and the majority language. In fact, in the BAC, the D model, in which the minority language is used as language of instruction, has become the most popular model of compulsory education over the last decades. Afterwards, in tertiary education, in the BAC, students can opt for doing many studies through the medium of Basque, while in NA, studying in these languages is merely optional.

When it comes to foreign languages, although in NA, officially the only compulsory language is French, in practice all schools teach English as a subject. Some schools also offer Spanish as a foreign language, or even German. Other foreign languages are less often offered. In tertiary education, studies can be done in English, or also some in Spanish. In the BAC, English is compulsory as a subject, and often schools use it as a medium of instruction for specific subjects. Other foreign languages are offered only optionally in some schools, with the prevalent foreign language French. In tertiary education, some studies are offered through the medium of English.

It should thus be noted that despite the monolingual French context, two foreign languages (including English) – although formally not compulsory – are taught in practice from middle school (age 11) in France, whereas in the BAC, in a multilingual context, only English is compulsory, and learning another foreign language remains optional.

When it comes to (migrant) students with L1s other than the languages of the curriculum, in compulsory education, attention is paid to their linguistic reinforcement from primary education onwards. In line with the corresponding language policies, in NA, this reinforcement is focused on the majority language, French, while in the BAC, this reinforcement is directed towards both Spanish and Basque. In practice, in the BAC, until recently, migrant pupils usually attended Spanish models, but with the recent new decree on the Index of Vulnerability, migrant students are supposed to be equally distributed among the different schools and models, probably bringing up new changes in the very near future.

Discussion and conclusion

This chapter aimed to make a comparison between the multilingual education systems of two nearby contexts: New Aquitaine (France) and the Basque Autonomous Community (Spain). Both contexts deal with the challenge of the inclusion of majority languages, minority languages and foreign languages at school, as well as the presence of migrant languages. In schools in New Aquitaine, the minority languages Occitan and Basque coexist with French as the majority language and English as the main foreign language, while in the BAC, Basque as a minority language coexists with Spanish as the majority language and English as the main foreign language. Both cases differ in the education and language policy support that minority languages receive: while in New Aquitaine, the teaching of Basque and Occitan is optional, French is compulsory, and English is not compulsory but in practice taught at most schools, in the BAC, the teaching of Basque is compulsory and reinforced by the educational system and coexists with Spanish and English as compulsory languages.

The results of the comparison between the two different contexts carried out in the previous section underlines the need to reflect on the differing situations of multilingual education and the possibilities of the language curriculum to improve the coexistence of minority languages, majority languages and foreign languages.

First of all, it is necessary to understand how the context in which languages are taught varies from one country to another. The status and recognition of a language has an important impact on the way it is taught. In France, where there is no language status other than for French, the other languages of France have a fragile and partial recognition, and their teaching remains difficult. In Spain, the status of Basque as a co-official language alongside Spanish, the national language, offers many more prospects, and the teaching of the language of the territory is widespread, as in the autonomous communities of the Basque Country (BAC and Navarre) and similarly for Catalan in Catalonia. It also seems that the recognition of the languages of the region leads to a de facto multilingualism in the classroom, which also encourages the study of foreign languages.

In fact, multilingualism in Spain is a daily reality for many pupils, with teaching hour rates that enable language acquisition. In France, bilingual Basque and Occitan schools are still in the minority, and the status of foreign languages other than English is less than ideal. A monolingual ideology is often blamed for the difficulties French pupils have with foreign languages and the cuts in language options. This raises questions about the different situations on either side of the Pyrenees, where several languages are concerned: Basque, Occitan and Catalan.

Their respective locations to the north and south of this natural border lead us to wonder about the origin of this difference in linguistic vitality and teaching conditions. One possible explanation could be found in both the historical and legal layers. In France, the revolutionary period developed the concept of the universality of the French language, and French is the only language of the republic. "*Liberté, Egalité Fraternité*" [Liberty, Equality, and Fraternity] were the values promoted during this period and associated solely with French. In order to disseminate this new ideal, the other languages of France were openly refuted: Breton, Basque, Occitan and others, as shown in the report by Abbé Grégoire who, in 1794, wrote a "*Rapport sur la nécessité et les moyens d'anéantir les patois et d'universaliser l'usage de la langue française.*" Republican values spread by associating the use of other French languages with counter-revolution and an outdated, archaic world. These notions, which were very much present in the public education system designed and implemented by the Ferry laws, prohibited the use of these languages, which were then the languages of a large proportion of pupils entering school, despite the movements of the Occitan cultural renaissance. With the passage of time and societal changes such as industrialization, the rural exodus and the wars, the other languages of France were confined to the private sphere and only French was taught and valued. In 1951, when the teaching of Corsican, Occitan, Basque and others was authorized, regional languages were already much less widely transmitted in families than they had been in the previous century. Foreign languages were not taught in primary education until the late 90s, and the languages of migrant pupils are now beginning to be given a little more consideration. It could be argued that the French language has benefited from a form of sacralization, a process that has undermined all others, both those of France and those of other countries, particularly those of immigrants.

In Spain, the situation seems to be different: languages and cultures have been able to be passed on despite societal changes. The Spanish language was not as early associated with the values disseminated in education, and there was probably not as much centralization as in France, so the other languages were passed on. At the turn of the 19th and 20th centuries, for example, in Basque Country (particularly in Hegoalde), there was a strong emergence of a collective awareness of the importance of the language and a structuring of its support. Later on, at the time of Franco's dictatorship, open repression of the Basque language led speakers to lay even greater claim to their languages because, as Santiago de Pablo (2009: 53) points out, "la represión franquista no fue sólo política sino también lingüística y cultural. [The repression of Franco was not only political but also linguistic and cultural]". Then the transition to democracy and the birth of the Autonomous Communities led to co-officiality and the implementation of a language policy, particularly in education, to make it more widespread, thus creating generations of multilingual pupils who study Spanish, Basque, English and sometimes other languages. As Zabaleta summarized (2019: 7):

> Toutefois, ces caractéristiques communes font également apparaître des dynamiques contraires. Si, suite à une première phase d'unification linguistique de la France et de l'Espagne, voire de répression linguistique à l'égard de la langue basque dans les sphères publiques de ces deux États, une phase différente est apparue à partir de la deuxième moitié du XXème siècle. En Espagne, la transition démocratique initiée à la fin de la dictature franquiste a permis une nouvelle division du pouvoir qui s'est traduite par la création de Communautés autonomes nouvelles dont l'autonomie politique a été reconnue et qui ont reçu d'importants transferts de compétences. Si l'Espagne post-franquiste s'est caractérisée par une plus grande autonomie et par la mise en place par les Communautés autonomes de politiques linguistiques en faveur de la langue basque, le cas de la France a été plus mitigé. La décentralisation administrative initiée en 1982 ne s'est pas traduite par l'instauration d'un bilinguisme institutionnel et la révision de la Constitution française du 25 juin 1992 a réaffirmé la primauté du français en disposant que la langue de la République est le français.
>
> [However, these common characteristics also reveal opposing dynamics. Following an initial phase of linguistic unification in France and Spain, and even linguistic repression of the Basque language in the public spheres of these two States, a different phase emerged from the second half of the 20th century onwards. In Spain, the democratic transition initiated at the end of the Franco dictatorship led to a new division of power, resulting in the creation of new Autonomous Communities whose political autonomy was recognised and which received significant transfers of powers. . . . While post-Franco Spain was characterised by greater autonomy and by the implementation by the autonomous communities of linguistic policies in favour of the Basque language, the case of France was more mixed. The administrative decentralisation initiated in 1982 did not result in the introduction of institutional bilingualism, and the revision of the French Constitution on 25 June 1992 reaffirmed the primacy of French by stating that "the language of the Republic is French."]
>
> (27)

He underlines how, despite the initial similar patterns of repression of the minority languages in both states, the flourishing of bilingualism afterwards has not been equal.

The example of Occitan in Val d'Aran is quite typical in this sense, since all pupils are taught Occitan, Catalan, Castilian, English and others in different ways, according to the specific region they find themselves in.

From a legal background, the status provided to languages has an impact on the way they are transmitted and, in particular, on the way they are taught. With the example of Basque and Occitan, which are co-official in Spain but not official in France, for various historical reasons, it is clear that the teaching of minority languages is an indication and possibly a guarantee of plurilingual practices. It has to be remarked, though, that in the NA, despite the monolingual framework and the absence of the obligation of teaching other languages than French, English teaching is a common practice for almost all schools in this context, while this is not the case for the teaching of the minority languages. It thus seems that foreign languages reclaim their space relatively easily in the educational system compared to the local minority languages. Perhaps because of globalization and the added value of knowing English on the international market, such a lingua franca needs less support from language policies than do minority languages, whose value is more often narrowed down to a local use.

In the European Commission's report on language teaching in Europe, it states that "in most European countries, legislation officially recognizes at least one regional or minority language" (2023: 23), but some countries, such as France, do not recognize regional and minority languages as official languages, which changes the situation for the teaching of these languages on the ground. This chapter compared the situation of border minority languages, Occitan and Basque, and the resulting situations of plurilingualism in schools. From the comparison it is clear that the fact that a regional language has been given its own status truly changes the conditions in which it is taught and therewith the plurilingualism of pupils, which is not limited to a foreign language. The teaching of minority languages thus seems to encourage the emergence of efficient plurilingualism. In accordance with Cenoz (2009), the sociolinguistic context of the school in terms of the difference in status of languages at an institutional level indicates the level of social multilingualism on a macro level and influences the multilingual level of education.

According to the same report of the European Commission (2023), the amount of instruction time devoted to foreign languages in the contexts under study is small as compared to the total instruction time in most other countries, especially in the NA, where English is not officially recognized as a language of education, although in practice it is taught.

We could think that providing solid spaces to languages in the educational system, starting with the local minority and majority languages, could also better develop into a truly multilingual system including foreign languages and even providing breathing spaces for other L1s of the pupils, following up on ideas such as linguistically sensitive teaching. It is clear that due to migration, more and more language diversity is present among the pupils, and there is a clear need to take into account their mother tongues in order to obtain the best academic results but also general well-being of the students and their families.

Moreover, studies on translanguaging have shown how scaffolding between the different languages of the students' repertoire could improve the language competence in various languages of the students (Cenoz and Gorter 2021). The plurilingual reality of both contexts could serve as an enriching input for translanguaging practices. However, especially in monolingually framed educational systems, but even in multilingual framed ones, teachers still can appear reluctant towards letting other languages than the language of the subject into the classroom. They fear that, especially in the case of the minority languages, those could be endangered by admitting the use of other languages in the classroom.

Cenoz (2009) argues that pedagogical translanguaging could help schools to get to the more multilingual end of the continua of multilingual education. As is clear from the comparison carried out, on this continua, the linguistic planning of schools plays a crucial role, by including more than one language as school subjects, the intensity of instruction and the age of introduction and the use of the languages as language of instruction throughout the several subjects of the curriculum. Moreover, the fact that the BAC manages to include the minority language at the same level as the majority language, despite the linguistic distance between the languages – a factor that usually complicates multilingual education – can serve as a good example of how multilingual education can take place.

All this requires not only changes in the educational legal framework but also in the preparation of teachers, who will need training to teach in multilingual classes (Bergroth et al. 2022b), something that is not yet common among teachers in Europe (European Commission 2023). Also, teachers should be trained in their awareness of the importance of the linguistic element involved in all teaching (Bergroth et al. 2022a). The early introduction of several languages should be advocated for, since now "learning a foreign language as a compulsory subject starts relatively late in primary education. . . . This explains why the proportion, which concerns students in the whole of primary education, is relatively low" (European Commission 2023: 107).

All in all, multilingual education faces challenges to include additional foreign languages to the – sometimes not even equally balanced – local linguistic repertoire and to be sensitive towards all other languages that pupils might bring to the class from their home environments, a challenge that needs to be reflected upon, in today's glocal society, where the local and the global are closer related than ever. A first starting point for such a reflection could be the implementation of reflection tools in teacher education, such as the ones provided in the guide provided by Bergroth et al. (2022a) *Linguistically Sensitive Teacher Education: Toolkit for Reflection Tasks and Action Research.* Specific tools should be implemented to create awareness among future teachers, in-service teachers and, finally, also policy makers in order to overcome challenges in multilingual education.

The findings of the present chapter argue in favor of developing pupils' plurilingual skills. On the one hand, there are many educational opportunities to help pupils become aware of the richness of linguistic diversity and of their own ability to participate in this linguistic richness and to appreciate its benefits by opening up to other languages and cultures. Often referred to as plural approaches, or multilingual pedagogies, these classroom activities help to develop sensitivity to languages, openness to other cultures and a sense of otherness. Their aim is to promote social justice and inclusion. These cross-curricular activities, which can be used in a wide range of disciplines, have already been identified within the approach to the teaching and learning of languages of the Council of the European Union. Research (Escudé 2014) has shown the benefits of intercomprehension and the need to train teachers in this. Catalano and Hamann (2016: 275) adds that:

> Multilingual pedagogies such as language study and reflection, multilingual microteachings, translanguaging, service-learning, digital storytelling, multimodal multilingual inquiry projects, and many more illustrate ways in which teacher education programs can prepare future teachers to realize the possibilities and improvements that could be made for their increasingly diverse student bodies.

Developing training for teachers, greater mobility for teachers and pupil and international gatherings of pupils around linguistic and cultural themes could help to develop linguistic biodiversity and multilingualism. Focusing on teacher training and projects on multilingualism without excluding minority languages in the territories concerned could offer a real added value to education systems and could be a guarantee of future cooperation.

References

Basque Government. (2016). *VI Mapa Sociolingüístico [VIth Sociolinguistic Map].* www.eustat.eus/elementos/ele0018800/vi-mapa-sociolinguistico/inf0018828_c.pdf

Basque Government. (2018). *La escolarización del alumnado de origen extranjero en el sistema escolar de la CAPV [The Schooling of Students of Foreign Origin in the School System of the Basque Autonomous Community (BAC)].* https://www.euskadi.eus/contenidos/documentacion/inn_doc_esc_inclusiva/es_def/adjuntos/diversidad/La_escolarizacion_alumnado_origen_extranjero.pdf

Basque Government. (2020). *Guía para las Familias [Guide for Families].* www.euskadi.eus/contenidos/informacion/sistema_educativo_vasco/es_def/adjuntos/Guia_para_las_familias_c.pdf

Basque Government. (2022a). *DECRETO 132/2022, de 2 de noviembre, de modificación del Decreto 1/2018, de 9 de enero, sobre la Admisión y la Escolarización del Alumnado tanto en Centros Públicos Dependientes del Departamento Competente en Materia de Educación como en Centros Privados Concertados, en Educación*

Infantil, Educación Primaria, Educación Secundaria Obligatoria, Bachillerato y Formación Profesional Básica, de Grado Medio y de Grado Superior de la Comunidad Autónoma del País Vasco, así como en los Centros Públicos de Titularidad Municipal que Impartan Formación Profesional Básica [DECREE 132/2022, of 2 November, Amending Decree 1/2018, of 9 January, on the Admission and Schooling of Students Both in Public Centres Dependent on the Department Responsible for Education and in Subsidised Private Centres, in Early Education, Primary Education, Compulsory Secondary Education, Baccalaureate and Basic, Intermediate and Higher Vocational Training in The Autonomous Community of the Basque Country, as Well as in Public Centres under Municipal Ownership That Provide Basic Vocational Training]. www.legegunea.euskadi.eus/eli/es-pv/d/2022/11/02/132/dof/spa/html/webleg00-contfich/es/

Basque Government. (2022b). *Nuevo Decreto de Admisión y Escolarización del alumnado [New Decree on Admission and Schooling of Pupils].* www.euskadi.eus/noticia/2022/nuevo-decreto-admision-y-escolarizacion-del-alumnado/web01-ejeduki/es/

Basque Government. (2023). *Marco Conceptual del Programa EUSLE [Conceptual Map of EUSLE Programme].* www.euskadi.eus/contenidos/informacion/inn_edu_inc_pd_prom_intercult/es_def/adjuntos/EUSLE_2023_urria_c.pdf

Basque Government, Government of Navarre, and OPLB. (2023). *VII Encuesta Sociolingüística 2021. Comunidad Autónoma de Euskadi. Informe Resumen [VIIth Sociolinguistic Survey. 2021. Basque Autonomous Community. Summary Report].* www.euskadi.eus/contenidos/informacion/eas_ikerketak/es_def/adjuntos/VII-ENCUESTA-SOCIOLINGUISTICA_resumen-.pdf

Bergroth, M., Dražnik, T., Llompart Esbert, J., Pepiot, N., van Der Worp, K. and Sierens, S. (2022a). *Linguistically Sensitive Teacher Education: Toolkit for Reflection Tasks and Action Research.* www.doria.fi/bitstream/handle/10024/183724/Linguistically%20Sensitive%20Teacher%20Education_%20Toolkit%20for%20Reflection%20Task%20and%20Action%20Research%202022.pdf?sequence=1&isAllowed=y

Bergroth, M., Llompart, J., Pepiot, N., van Der Worp, K., Dražnik, T. and Sierens, S. (2022b). Identifying space for mainstreaming multilingual pedagogies in European initial teacher education policies. *European Educational Research Journal*, 21(5), 801–821.

Biota Piñeiro, I. and Zabaleta Imaz, I. (2018). La Renovación Pedagógica al Servicio de la Escuela Pública Vasca: el Colectivo Adarra [Pedagogical Renovation at the Service of the Basque Public School: The Adarra Collective]. In P. Dávila (Ed.), *El Profesorado y la Renovación Pedagógica en el País Vasco [Teachers and Pedagogical Renovation in the Basque Country]* (pp. 85–129). Delta Publicaciones. https://addi.ehu.es/bitstream/handle/10810/27173/La%20renovaci%C3%B3n%20pedag%C3%B3gica%20en%20PV_interior%20%20-%20Adarra.pdf

Catalano, T. and Hamann, E. T. (2016). Multilingual pedagogies and pre-service teachers: Implementing "language as a resource" orientations in teacher education programs. *Bilingual Research Journal*, 39(3–4), 263–278. https://doi.org/10.1080/15235882.2016.1229701

Cenoz, J. (2009). *Towards Multilingual Education. Basque Educational Research from an International Perspective.* Multilingual Matters.

Cenoz, J. and Gorter, D. (2011). A holistic approach in multilingual education: Introduction. *The Modern Language Journal*, 95(3), 339–343. https://doi.org/10.1111/j.1540-4781.2011.01204.x

Cenoz, J. and Gorter, D. (2021). *Pedagogical Translanguaging.* Cambridge University Press.

Châteaureynaud, M. A. (2022). *Sociodidactique du Plurilinguisme et de l'Altérité Inclusive.* Peter Lang.

Council of the European Union. (2019). Council recommendation of 22 May 2019 on a comprehensive approach to the teaching and learning of languages (2019/C 189/03). *Official Journal of the European Union.* https://eur-lex.europa.eu/legal-content/EN/TXT/PDF/?uri=CELEX:32019H0605(02)

de Pablo, Santiago (2009). Lengua e Identidad Nacional en el País Vasco: Del Franquismo a la Democracia [Language and National Identity in the Basque Country: From Franquism to Democracy]. In Lagarde (Ed.), *Le discours sur les "langues d'Espagne" [Discourse on Languages in Spain].* Perpignan University Press. https://doi.org/10.4000/books.pupvd.303.

Escudé, P. (2014). De l'intercompréhension comme moteur d'activités en classe [From intercomprehension as an engnie for classroom activities]. *Tréma*, 42. https://doi.org/10.4000/trema.3187

European Commission, European Education and Culture Executive Agency (2023). *Key Data on Teaching Languages at School in Europe.* Publications Office of the European Union. https://data.europa.eu/doi/10.2797/529032

Gajo, L. and Berthoud, A. C. (2020). Issues of multilingualism for scientific knowledge: Practices for assessing research projects in terms of linguistic diversity. *European Journal of Higher Education*, 10(3), 294–307. https://doi.org/10.1080/21568235.2020.1777451

García, O. (2009). *Bilingual Education 21st Century. A Global Perspective*. Wiley-Blackwell.

Gorter, D. (2013). Multilingual interactions and minority languages: Proficiency and language practices in education and society. *Language Teaching*, 46(4), 1–17. https://doi.org/10.1017/S0261444812000481.

ISEI-IVEI. (2021). *Panorámica del Sistema Educativo Vasco [Overview of the Basque Education System]*. https://isei-ivei.hezkuntza.net/documents/635622/0/Diagn%C3%B3stico+del+sistema+educativo_25_de_junio.pdf/10d8346f-bc09-487c-abf9-997682509687

Maia, J. (2012). Linguistic school models in the Basque country. In P. Salaburu and X. Alberdi (Eds.), *The Challenge of a Bilingual Society in the Basque Country* (pp. 137–155). Jon Benjamins Publishing.

Nieto, S. and Recamán, A. (2009). Investigación y conocimiento científico en educación [Research and scientific knowledge in education]. In S. Nieto and M. J. Rodriguez (Eds.), *Investigación y evaluación educativa en la sociedad del conocimiento [Research and Educational Evaluation in the Knowledge Society]* (pp. 81–159). University of Salamanca.

OPLO (Office Publique de la Langue Occitaine – Public Office of Occitan Language). (2020). *Résultats de l'enquête sociolinguistique relative à la pratique et aux représentations de la langue occitane en Nouvelle-Aquitaine, en Occitanie et au Val d'Aran [Results of the sociolinguistic survey on the practice and representations of the Occitan language in Nouvelle-Aquitaine, Occitanie and Val d'Aran]*. OPLO. https://www.ofici-occitan.eu/wp-content/uploads/2020/09/OPLO_Enquete-sociolingusitique-occitan-2020_Resultats.pdf

Palacín Mariscal, I. (2017). Ikastolen Elkartea, example of effective transfrontier cooperation under the European language charter. *Oñati Socio-Legal Series*, 7(6), 1343–1370. https://ssrn.com/abstract=3074342

Pérez-Izaguirre, E., Châteaureynaud, M. A. and Amiama, J. F. (2021). Teachers' view on the elements that enhance and hamper Basque and Occitan teaching in southern France: An exploratory approach. *Diaspora, Indigenous, and Minority Education*, 15(3), 151–165. https://doi.org/10.1080/15595692.2021.1929154

Siguán, M. (2002). Las Razones de la Educación Monolingüe [Reasons for monolingual education. In F. Etxeberria Balerdi and U. Ruiz Bikandi (Eds.), *¿Trilingües a los 4 años? [Trilingual at 4?]*. IBAETA Pedagogía.

Verny, M. (2009). Enseigner l'occitan au XXIe siècle. Défis et enjeux. *Tréma*, 31, 69–83. https://doi.org/10.4000/trema.962

Yanaprasart, P. (2020). Language of knowledge and knowledge of language. Towards plurilingual sciences? *European Journal of Higher Education*, 10(3), 257–275. https://doi.org/10.1080/21568235.2020.1777450.

Zabaleta, E. (2019). *Le Droit de la Langue Basque – Étude Comparée France, Espagne -[Basque Language Law: Spain – France Comparative Study]*. Université de Pau et des Pays de l'Adour.

5

REDRAWING LANGUAGE BOUNDARIES

Nurturing Arabic in the United Arab Emirates

Briji Jose and Bettina Biju Jacob

Introduction

The contemporary globalized milieu is characterized by extensive cross-border migrations, particularly in relation to labor mobility and economic opportunities. Following the discovery of oil, the Middle Eastern nations have emerged as pivotal regions, attracting migrants from diverse global locations. The United Arab Emirates (UAE) is a Gulf region with a consistent migration inflow for over five decades. The expat population makes up 88.52% of the entire population, outnumbering the native population of the country (GMI 2024). The UAE has commonly been perceived as a multilingual and multicultural cosmopolitan urban space characterized by interaction among diverse ethnic groups who are nevertheless demarcated by racial distinctions. Researchers in the field discuss this phenomenon as a small group of highly internally stratified locals sitting on top of a large group of migrants in an organizational structure described as ethnocratic (Longva 2006). Labor migrants in the UAE have been recognized as temporary citizens as they cannot legally attain formal citizenship and exist on a contractual basis. This status is intricately connected to both official and popular perceptions of Emirati national identity, which often depict the native population as homogeneous, particularly from an external perspective (Akinci 2020b). Arabic is central to the Emirati identity as it becomes a symbol of power and a tool for unification in the post-oil formation of the Gulf Cooperation Council (GCC).[1] Arabic is 'the lifeblood that circulates in the hearts and minds of the peoples of twenty-five nations and carries with it the blueprint of a whole civilization' (Sayed et al. 2017). During the formative stages of these modern nations, Arabization emerged as a phenomenon aimed at promoting the extensive use of Arabic in oral and written communication. This encompassed policies such as establishing Arabic as the official language of the country, the medium of official instruction, and the standardization of terminology in language textbooks across various Arabic-speaking nations. Article 7 of the UAE's constitution stipulates Arabic as its official language, primarily spoken by the minority native population.

In recent years, the tension between Arabic and English, the latter being used as a lingua franca in cosmopolitan UAE, has been a well-noted phenomenon. English, a double-edged sword, becomes essential for communication in a region populated by multi-ethnic migrants. However, English's pervasive use also poses a risk, threatening the loss of Arabic, which is inherently linked to the Emirati culture and identity. The chapter builds on the existing literature by examining the

DOI: 10.4324/9781003439493-7

various factors contributing to the decreased usage of Arabic in modern UAE. It focuses explicitly on the majoritarian migrant community and explores the intertwining realities of Arabic language loss and concerns about migrant domination. The chapter offers a diverse perspective by reframing migrants not as obstacles but as potential advocates for preserving the nation's native language. It particularly emphasizes the role of second-generation migrants (SGM) in promoting Arabic by assessing their comprehension of Arabic and the complex social dynamics in which they are situated. SGM refers to individuals born and raised in the migrant land, with their parents having migrated there initially for job opportunities. The chapter seeks to investigate the gaps in the existing migrant language policies, pedagogy, and migrant-native language politics that have led to SGM's inability to speak Arabic, thereby furthering its declining usage in the nation. The findings point to the challenges and obstacles that cosmopolitan UAE faces in nurturing Arabic and forefronts the role of migrants in promoting the language.

An integral feature of the Arabic language is that it exhibits diglossia with its multiple spoken dialects. Charles Ferguson's seminal publication *Diglossia* (1959) identified Arabic as a prime example of what he defined as diglossia in languages. Within the dialects of the language, Ferguson highlights the presence of a 'high'-status language (H) used in formal contexts and a 'low'-status language (L) or a vernacular variety. In Arabic, these variations are complex as 'classical Arabic, the language of the Qur'an, Hadith, and Classical poetry set at one end, the uneducated dialects and vernaculars on the other end, with Modern Standard Arabic (MSA), educated dialects, and enlightened dialects all spread in-between' (Altoma 1974: 280). Other Arabic speakers perceived Emirati colloquial Arabic (CA) or Khaleeji Arabic as a form of 'corrupted' language compared to long-standing sophisticated forms of Egyptian and Levant Arabic (Piller 2017). The standardization of Arabic in the form of MSA used in popular media platforms, taught in schools, and used in formal communication was a strategic move by its speakers to propagate the notion of a unified imagined community. This complex feature of the Arabic language has received scholarly attention, looking into aspects of language propagation and teaching methodology, primarily focusing on the national population (Gallagher 2022). With the UAE's rapid modernization and consistent inflow of migrants, the language dynamics have significantly shifted with time. Various other languages like Farsi, Hindi, Malayalam, Sinhalese, Tagalog, and Urdu are also widely spoken in the multilingual nation. As previously mentioned, English emerged as a resolution by assuming the role of a lingua franca within a predominantly multinational expatriate community.

Migrants and language usage in the UAE

A review addressing language-related issues in the UAE reveals a concern over specific themes. Studies on the Arabic language examine the socio-economic shifts brought in by globalization that rapidly led to the emergence of dual-language politics in Arab nations. Within the nation, Arabic came to be viewed as a language of cultural authenticity, tradition, and religion, while English represents modernity, internationalism, and material status, promoting two distinct worldviews. Findlow (2006) argues that this linguistic-cultural dualism is intrinsic to the contemporary UAE's collective identity and establishment of a nation-state. Language education has always been invoked as an essential instrument of nation-building, and the UAE has invested immense resources into its education system. Scholars highlight a notable transition from conventional Arabic-medium instruction to a bilingual curriculum, where Arabic and English literacy is highly regarded (Al-Bataineh 2021). An interconnection between educational reforms and promoting bilingual education in the UAE is intrinsically tied to the community's loss of the Arabic language

(Al-Issa and Dahan 2020; Findlow 2006). Al-Bataineh (2021) further adds that as public and private higher education is exclusively maintained in English, 'the status of Arabic is lowered and relegates its domains to local uses, while elevating the status of English and extending its domains to what is perceived to be quality education' (216). The strong connection between the job market, technology and foreign languages is, among other reasons, contributing to the decline of Arabic (Al-Shamsi et al. 2009). The wide use of English as the lingua franca in the region looms as a threat to the linguistic, religious, cultural, and social identities of the native population.

The perception of language threat is further revealed as Emirati students continue to receive poor results in their Arabic examinations, and studies reveal anecdotal narratives from the native population that observe the increasing use of English among themselves (Malek 2015). Myhill (2014) argues that Arabic literacy in the UAE and other Gulf countries is extremely low when adjusted for per capita income. The slow degradation of a language is of grave concern as not only words are lost, but ideas, ways of knowing, and cultural diversity also vanish with it. Language is an expression of a community's identity and contains the collective wisdom, traditions, and cultural heritage of a community. Its loss is intricately connected to the disappearance of valuable ways of knowing and the nuanced understandings of the world encoded within these languages. Al-Issa and Dahan (2020) argue that 'linguistic genocide' is occurring in the UAE on an immense scale where media and formal education have been identified as the primary culprits (Skutnabb-Kangas 2001). The authorities have actively attempted to implement language policies and projects to sustain and grow Arabic in the UAE. The Dubai Prime Minister and Ruler, Sheikh Mohammed bin Rashid Al Maktoum, approved the establishment of the Consultative Council for Arabic Language in 2012. He has also launched the Mohammed bin Rashid Arabic Language Award to encourage exceptional contributions in serving the Arabic language and outstanding experiences in disseminating and educating the Arabic language (Razem 2020). Despite these attempts, Arabic faces challenges in asserting its prominence and flourishing within the multilingual context of the nation.

Recent research has focused on identifying gaps in the Arabic language education system and reforming language policies for language propagation. It surrounds the native Emirati population and the current evolving language politics, often overlooking the perspectives and experiences of the larger migrant population. Expatriate language experiences in this context are a severe gap that needs to be addressed and offer a broad scope for exploration. This research focuses on exploring the language usage among the non-Arab migrant community and their interaction with the Arabic language. Arabic's role as the national and cultural language of their host land is significant in understanding the language politics that these migrants are embedded in. The reviewed literature indicates that the restructured educational policies designed to align with the socio-economic landscape and the growing multi-ethnic expatriate workforce represent the foremost articulated concerns posing a threat to the Arabic language (Al-Issa and Dahan 2020; Tibi and McLeod 2014). An integral feature of UAE's migrant population is that they are viewed as 'guest workers' or 'temporary citizens' as they cannot attain formal citizenship and exist on a contractual basis. Even though Gulf migrants do not integrate with the native population, it does not impede them from staying in the country for long periods. The aftermath is a growing population of second-generation migrants born in the country and spend most of their lives there. The immigration and integration policies in most GCC nations do not entitle citizenship to foreigners born in the country. The immigration policy in the UAE states that expatriate residents must sponsor SGM children with a minimum income criterion that needs to be renewed yearly. Parents can only sponsor visas for their sons until they are 18 years of age and as long as their daughters are not married. New revisions in these policies, such as removing profession-based restrictions for expatriate workers to sponsor family visas

Redrawing language boundaries

and introducing Golden Visas, demonstrate flexibility in the previously rigid immigration systems (UAE Government Portal 2023).

'Migrants are incorporated into the economic structure but are excluded from the social structure: separation, not integration or assimilation, is the goal' (Weiner 1982: 16). Researchers have extensively explored the migrant exclusion in the Gulf with the region's prevailing citizenship laws and tight regulations around naturalization (Vora 2013). The natives enjoy different rights and responsibilities that come with legal citizenship, such as free education, free healthcare, employment priority, access to property loans, and a host of other welfare benefits, accompanied by performances of national identity that further the segregation. The migrant-native divide is inherent within the legal frameworks of 'guest workers,' socio-political understandings and language differences that have delineated boundaries over time. This chapter focuses on the language politics of the SGM population who grew up in the host land, navigating and finding meaning and belongingness despite the constant state of temporariness. Unlike first-generation migrants with nostalgic notions of returning home, SGM return migration is meaningless, as they never migrated. Studies conducted on SGM in countries like the USA, Canada, and Sweden indicate a direct correlation between prolonged residence duration and increased levels of assimilation and acculturation within the host country (Portes and Rivas 2011). Literature on multi-ethnic migrants in the Arab World shows higher levels of transnational behavior where many migrants leave, return, and leave again, viewing the host country as an economic pitstop (Ali 2011). Syed Ali's research on SGM concludes that all migrants, irrespective of nationality, experience exclusion and structured impermanence as they are legally and socially treated as foreigners despite growing up there. He argues that, in return, migrants receive a tax-free income while living in a nearly crime-free, consumer-oriented society.

The linguistic interactions of multi-ethnic migrants are embedded within a web of power politics of ethnicity and social class, a factor that warrants recognition. Expatriates from Western nations like the USA, UK, and Australia tend to possess higher levels of income and mobility than other migrant groups, which impacts their interactions with the host land. Assigning Western expats under the defined label of a Gulf 'migrant' is complicated, as their motives for migration, duration of stay, and socio-cultural expectations differ significantly. It influences their language preferences, usage, and interaction, which differ from those of the other migrant population. A recent report states that from 2000 to 2020, the migration corridor between South Asia, Southeast Asia, and the Gulf has grown more than any other global migration corridor (UNDESA 2021). The SGM population in UAE primarily comprises of individuals from South-Asian and Arab backgrounds. For non-Emirati Arab migrants hailing from countries such as Syria, Lebanon, Palestine, and Egypt, Arabic functions as a familiar and native language despite variations in dialects. Syed Ali's (2011) research explores the language politics and migrant identity of the Arab SGM population, which is also further discussed in the paper. Vora's (2013) study on the South Asian SGM population from India, Bangladesh, Pakistan, and Sri Lanka focuses on the dissonances and challenges of cultural duality that migrants experience. Both their research stress that all migrants, regardless of nationality, face the same forces of exclusion as their identities are limited to the domain of the economic, which, unlike culture and nation, is not considered central to belonging. With the exception of Arab SGM, nearly all other SGM populations are exposed to English and their native language as their first and second languages. Arabic then becomes a third language formally taught in the school setting.

For analytical clarity, the chapter focuses on the predominant South Asian SGM population, characterized by shared socio-economic backgrounds and schooling environments. In the UAE, labor migrants from India constitute 27.49% of the total migrant force, forming the primary labor force in the country (GMI 2024). For practical purposes and to limit over-generalizations, the study specifically focuses on the Indian SGM population which forms a diverse data set in itself. Vora's (2013) study suggests that Indian SGM in the UAE retain their native cultural identity by knowing their native language and practices as they do not merge with the locals. For many of these children, transnationalism becomes a coping strategy to fit into a host society that does not incorporate them beyond economic matters. This is precisely because, in migrant-dominated nations like the UAE, there is a prevalent concern regarding demographic shifts, linguistic homogenization, and the potential erosion of the host language with extensive migrant interaction. The chapter discusses how this fear has further led to the erosion of Arabic with the complex interplay between the minority Arabic native speakers, multilingual socio-cultural settings and exclusion of migrants. This study points to how a renewed outlook can change what is perceived as obstacles to language propagation into opportunities for the revitalization of Arabic.

Methods

The study employs a mixed-method approach using online questionnaires and semi-structured interviews to explore the usage of the Arabic language among the SGM population. The eligibility of the respondents for the questionnaire and the interviews were limited to second-generation Indian migrants who were born and raised in the UAE. The study targeted young adults aged between 18–30 years who had completed their schooling in the country under similar national language policy regulations and social environments. The online questionnaire used a *Likert scale* to measure the respondent's level of agreement or disagreement with the questions asked. The Likert scale is a measuring scale typically containing 5 to 7 values and can usually be of two types: ordinal or interval. This questionnaire uses the ordinal scale, where each consecutive value is greater or better than the previous one; the values range from 1 to 5, where 1 represents the lowest and 5 represents the highest value. The mean, median, and mode are calculated to analyze the results and give a comprehensive value. The questions were formulated to measure the migrant's understanding and relationship with their host language, Arabic. For example, the survey included statements like, 'I can speak and understand Arabic fluently' and 'I found the need to use Arabic in the social environment I grew up in.' The respondents attached a value according to their response to the question. A snowball sampling technique was used, and the questionnaire was distributed across groups eligible to take the survey through the digital medium of a Google Form.

A total of 114 responses were collected and used for analysis. A total of ten semi-structured interviews were also conducted, enabling respondents to describe their relationship with Arabic and their migrant land in detail. The interviews began by understanding the family background of the individuals and their motives to stay in the country as 'non-nationals.' Questions that probe into their childhood and school experience in the country gave insights into their relationship with the natives and host culture. The researchers specifically explored their opinions on Arabic as a language and its influence on their lives as migrants. The data underwent coding and categorization, revealing patterns and dissimilarities as the analysis progressed. All the respondents attended private schools in the UAE, and none had studied with the native Emirati population. All the respondents were fluent in English and their mother tongue, though some said they could not read and write in their native language. The participants agreed that they were taught Arabic in school for 10–12 years but could not converse in the language, which will be extensively discussed in the findings. An extensive review of the migrant literature and migrant language policies in the UAE adds to the research findings. The 12-item online survey in English allowed access to a large number of Indian SGM in the UAE. It elicited data on language knowledge and attitudes towards

Arabic while the interviews ensured an in-depth understanding of the issue. As researchers of the study and being SGM ourselves, our residency in the UAE facilitated our access to participants. Our collective experiential knowledge and empirical observations acquired during our residency are crucial in informing this research.

Results

The following table presents the significant results from the online questionnaire, which is further analyzed by combining data from the interviews in the discussion section.

Discussion

In the UAE, where diverse, multilingual migrants interact, language choices in social settings have implications for its culture and speakers. As mentioned earlier, English has been adopted as the primary medium of communication at all levels of the Emirati society. To further understand the complexity of migrant interaction and loss of Arabic, this chapter begins by investigating the competency of Arabic among Indian SGM in the UAE. per the language policies set by the UAE's Ministry of Education, Arabic was mandated as a compulsory subject for non-native speakers across all private schools (Randall and Samimi 2010). Razem (2020) argues that the state recommends that non-Arab expatriates study Arabic as an Additional Language (AAL) from Grade 1 to Grade 9, and schools should provide lessons four times a week. The Knowledge and Human Development Authority (KHDA) policy of AAL aims to enhance 'their (expatriates') understanding of the local culture and give them significant opportunities and advantages in later life.' Though AAL is not explicitly mentioned as a policy, schools that do not provide it are fined, as it is a violation under the Executive Council Resolution No. (2) of 2017 (Razem 2020). A migrant host language policy exists and has been implemented; however, its efficacy must be evaluated. Data from the interviews reveal that most Indian SGMs learn English as their first language in school while being exposed to their native tongue (Malayalam, Tamil, Hindi, Telugu) within their home spaces at an early age. All the interviewed respondents were proficient in English, while most were passively fluent in their native tongues. Arabic becomes the third or sometimes even fourth language that SGM children are exposed to in schools. As a language compulsorily taught in schools at an early age, the research raises questions about the level of Arabic competency among the SGM population, which is largely linked to language loss.

Arabic language competency among SGM in UAE

The findings from the online survey indicate that Indian SGM who completed their schooling in the UAE were formally taught the language in school and were exposed to it at an elementary level. As Table 5.1 depicts, the statement 'I speak and understand Arabic fluently' is rated on the 5-point Likert scale, with the mean score being 1.1 with a standard deviation of 0.8. The results indicate their inability to comprehend Arabic, which is also reflected in the interview responses. This phenomenon is intricately linked to Arabic's diglossia, migrant-native language politics, and problematic teaching methodology, which are further elaborated upon. The inability of SGM to converse in the national and cultural language of their migrant land forms the base assumption for this study. The response to the statement, 'I can read and write Arabic,' was comparatively favorable, as the mean value is 3.6, with a standard deviation of 1.1. The interview results also show that most respondents could read and write basic words in the language due to their early exposure to the Arabic alphabet but could not

Table 5.1 Questionnaire responses related to students' Arabic language acquisition in UAE (*n* = 114)

Questions	Mean	Median	Mode	Standard Deviation
I can speak and understand Arabic fluently	1.7	2	1	0.8
I can read and write in Arabic	3.6	4	4	1.1
I think studying Arabic in school is required for non-nationals/migrants in the UAE	3.6	4	3	1.1
I found the need to use Arabic in the social environment I grew up in	2.5	2	2	1.2
I talk and socially interact with the native community in the UAE	2.3	3	2	1.1
I think I would have better employability opportunities if I was fluent in Arabic	4.0	4	4	1.03
I think I would be able to identify with my migrant land if I knew Arabic	3.4	3	3	1.2
I think language is important to relate to culture and to be a citizen of a country	4.2	4	4	0.8

comprehend it. This interesting phenomenon is reiterated by Mariam, a 25-year-old female respondent who studied and continues to live in the UAE with her family:

> So, I can read and write Arabic because I was taught letters in school. But if you tell me to read something and ask me if I understood the meaning? I would have no idea because I cannot understand the meaning of the Arabic text. This was how it was taught to us in our schools.

For most SGMs like Mariam, this is a common, frustrating and striking experience as they cannot comprehend a language they can somehow read. Jose's (2023) analysis of Deepak Unnikrishnan's novel *Temporary People*[2] also highlights this phenomenon as it is portrayed explicitly in the story 'Tongue, Flesh.' The narrative revolves around an SGM boy who demonstrates proficiency in orally reciting Arabic words from his textbook but struggles to grasp their meaning despite repeated inquiries, which is discussed in the paper (Jose 2023). Literature in the field also supports this notion extending beyond Indian SGM to encompass various multi-ethnic migrant parents who have expressed concerns regarding their children's inadequate proficiency in Arabic despite years of schooling in the language (Clarke et al. 2007). To explain this from an applied linguistics perspective, Peter Skehan (1998), in his work, *A Cognitive Approach to Language Learning*, interrelates psycholinguistic and cognitive aspects of language learning. A principal element of Skehan's (1998) discussion on the cognitive bases of language acquisition is the assumption that second language (SL) learners no longer have access to the language acquisition device with which they learned their first language; hence, second language learning is a cognitive learning process. In this case, for most SGMs, Arabic becomes the third or fourth language they are exposed to within their setting, which is attributed to a cognitive learning process.

JB Carroll's (1990) research on foreign language aptitude and his four-factor aptitude model can be applied to understand this phenomenon further. The model includes phonemic coding, grammatical sensitivity, inductive language learning ability and associative memory. The beginning stage of language learning is phonemic coding, which deals with the ability to code an unfamiliar sound so that it can be retained. This is partially what has happened with the case of Indian

SGMs in the UAE, as their exposure to the Arabic alphabet at a very young age enabled them to connect sounds to symbols. They can connect the language phonemes to form morphemes, but learning is restricted to this stage. The next stage of grammatical sensitivity prompts the learner's capacity to identify the functions that words perform in sentences. The inductive language learning ability allows the learner to extract from the given corpus to create new sentences. Finally, the associative memory enables the capacity to form links in the memory. The flawed Arabic teaching methodology for SGM in their classrooms is restricted to only the first primary stage of learning, and it does not move forward, which explains their linguistic predicament. As Wen and Skehan (2011) argue for language acquisition, three competing requirements of accuracy, complexity, and fluency are absent in Arabic language acquisition among SGM learners. The case depicts a form of passive multilingualism where parts of the language are known. However, the speaker is unable to attain agency over it in terms of understanding or speaking it. In the limited research on the cognitive aspects of multilingualism, this case opens up avenues for exploration, especially in applied linguistics. It further points to the need to identify a renewed teaching methodology to address this gap that inhibits Arabic acquisition among SGM. The research acknowledges that migrant learners' proficiency in their first and second languages can influence their acquisition of Arabic, leading to linguistic interference. Pronunciation, grammar, and vocabulary may be significantly affected by the migrant's acquired language patterns. To further elucidate the background of lacking this language competency, Jacob, a 26-year-old male respondent who studied and currently works in the UAE as a mechanical engineer, says,

> I learnt the language for 12 years, but I cannot speak it. In school, most of us studied Arabic just for the sake of passing exams. It was not taken as a serious subject and the need to learn it was not felt by any of us. Even if I knew the language, there was no point because I wasn't going to any Arab's house, and we did not have any Arab friends.

Jacob's response highlights three central aspects regarding the incapacity of SGM to speak Arabic, findings that are echoed in other responses as well. In relation to the native learner's difficulty in acquiring Arabic, the lack of immersion time, teaching expertise, and suitable curricula are all factors that have been discussed (Thomure 2019), which can be extended to SGMs who face similar issues. Respondents, in retrospect, identified a problematic foreign language teaching methodology within their Arabic classrooms that did not fit the learner's needs. Indian SGM join English-medium schools where they primarily engage in English and are exposed to their native language within their home spaces. Despite growing up in the UAE, Arabic remains a foreign language for them, primarily encountered during their AAL classes. The predominant focus of research on language policies in the UAE has centered on improving teaching methodologies for native Arabic speakers. However, a discernible gap persists in addressing the teaching of Arabic to non-Arab SGM that is tied to their incapacity to acquire the language despite it being formally taught.

The diglossic characteristic of Arabic is another significant issue. In SGM private schools, most Arabic teachers are migrants from different Arab nations like Egypt, Lebanon, and Syria and bring their regional dialectical variations of the language with them. These dialects are markedly different from the spoken forms of Emirati Arabic, as well as the MSA prescribed for formal literacy instruction (Tibi and McLeod 2014). While this has been changing with the recent Emiratization of the UAE workforce, non-Emirati teachers still outnumber local Arabic-medium teachers (Weber 2011). This adds a layer of complexity of teaching Arabic to non-Arab SGM, taking in the diglossic nature of the language. Carroll et al. (2017) study on Emirati language use in the UAE reveals that Emiratis primarily use colloquial Arabic (CA) in their home and social spaces, which is considered a low-status variety. They only engage in a few literacy practices using Modern Standard Arabic. Though MSA has been identified as the formal medium of instruction in language classes, the reality is that Emiratis predominantly use CA as the oral means of communication among one another. Language policymakers need to consider the functional aspect of learning Arabic for these migrant children in their immediate surroundings. There is a need to address the complexity of Emirati Arabic literacy, which faces a double danger of the larger loss of the Arabic language and its colloquial variety. Language policies need to prioritize the resolution of this catch-22[3] situation to establish a consensus regarding the usage and formal instruction of the language, particularly tailored for foreign learners. Jacob's response also reveals another significant aspect of the value attached to the Arabic language in these classroom spaces. As he says, Arabic was primarily learnt and ended at the level of examinations, and language use was restricted to AAL classrooms. Nazeem, a 20-year-old male respondent enrolled in university, also adds, 'We would all get good marks for Arabic exams as we memorized all the words and answers. We just didn't know where to apply what we learned.' Cultural attitudes towards language is also a valid factor that can significantly influence SGM language choices and proficiency. If these migrants perceive Arabic as practically applicable or socially advantageous, they may prioritize learning and using it in their everyday setting. As Nazeem reiterates, the lack of immersion in the host language is a primary concern for Arabic incompetency among migrant children. This is intricately embedded within the land's language loss and native-migrant politics, which is explored in the following section.

Native-migrant language politics

Despite Arabic being the national language of the land, as discussed earlier, its position to an SGM is not as a second language but as a foreign language. Responses from the interviews suggest that respondents rarely found any functional or socio-cultural significance of the language in their lives as migrant children. Rahul, a 22-year-old male respondent pursuing his college education in the UAE, opines, 'In today's globalized world, English is sufficient in modern spaces for interaction and acceptance. It would have been good to study Arabic, but just like any other foreign language.' His response demonstrates that Arabic has no personal or utilitarian implications for him in his current socio-cultural setting. As Ferguson (1959) argues, English is likely to enjoy its status due to the social, educational, political and economic forces shaping its use, while Arabic is likely to continue to decline because of the absence of similar powerful forces supporting its use. Acknowledging the cultural norms surrounding the use of the Arabic language is essential for effectively facilitating its acquisition among SGM. Concurrently, the declining state of Arabic can also be intricately linked to the migrant-citizen dichotomy entrenched within the socio-cultural and legal frameworks of the nation, as previously discussed. This divide constrains the immersion of migrants in the host language and impedes language propagation, which is further explored.

It can be deduced from the analysis of the survey statement, 'I think language is important to relate to culture and be a citizen of a place,' where the responses had a high positive mean value of 4.2 with a minimum deviation of 0.8 that asserts that there is a positive relation between the two. These results interestingly stand in contrast to the results of, 'I think I would be able to identify with my migrant land if I knew Arabic,' where the mean value was 3.4 with a standard deviation of 1.2, making it difficult to draw conclusive results. Though most of the respondents agree that the native language of a land is significant for migrants, when it comes to their experiences in the UAE, the responses deviate from their former opinion. This phenomenon is essentially interconnected with the language usage and socio-cultural setting within the nation, where Arabic is restricted to the minority native population or the Arab migrants of the land. The respondents, Jacob and Nazeem, subtly alluded to the underlying socio-political dynamics between migrants and natives; as they say, they do not have anybody to speak to even if they learn the language. The questionnaire's statements, 'I found the need to use Arabic in the environment I grew up in' and 'I talk and interact with the native Arab community in UAE,' received mean values of 2.5 and 2.3, respectively, with a high standard deviation. The differentiated opinion on these statements makes it difficult to draw conclusive results but points to the complexity of language practices in the UAE. On the one hand, the dominant use of English as the lingua franca impedes their need to access the host language for interaction. Furthermore, the lack of Arabic language acquisition among SGM is closely intertwined with the dearth of opportunities for immersion in the host language. The region's socio-cultural settings and citizenship politics support a phenomenon entrenched within the migrant-native divide.

Sociolinguistic theory suggests that within any social setting, tangible elements like culture, religion, or language are essential not only to the extent that they reinforce the nation's identity but also because they differentiate the ingroup from the outgroup (Triandafyllidou 1998). Language acts beyond communication, associating power and identity with the group that exercises it, as Arabic is significant to the national identity. Since the formation of the modern nation, the Arabic language has played a gatekeeper role in differentiating migrants from the natives, which was central to the legal migrant policies of the land. Historically, Arabic has played a significant role in constructing the UAE as a nation and co-creating an Emirati Arab identity. 19th and 20th-century theorists of Arab nationalism highlight this concept as

Individuals who belong to an Arab country and speak Arabic are Arabs. They are, despite the name of the country of which they are officially a citizen, despite the religion they practice or the confession they belong to, they are despite their origin, their ancestry or the roots of the family they belong to. They are Arabs, period.

(al-Husrī 1985, cited in D'Anna and Amoruso 2020: 262)

Arabic was pivotal in delineating the migrant-citizen divide, particularly amidst the continual influx of diverse migrant populations into the nation. It is driven by a concern that prolonged interaction between migrants and natives could lead to the dilution or homogenization of their indigenous cultural identity, which is rooted in Arabic. Society creates an ingroup that is prioritized and defined by its capacity to interact with each other through its cultural language. It also helps members within the group to adopt and maintain social practices that define their community (Meyerhoff 2018). Those who spoke the Emirati Arabic language were seen as the true nationals of the land and formed the ingroup. The temporary migrants retained their native identities as language became a barrier to accessing the ingroup; thus, they formed the Other-non-Arabic speakers. Interviews with the respondents pointed to how language became a significant marker of their identification with the local population. Alan, a 23-year-old male respondent, describes the nationals as, 'Oh, they wear long kanduras,[4] speak mostly only in Arabic and come in expensive cars wearing Rolex watches.' Akinci's (2020a) study reinforces that accent and proficiency in Emirati Arabic are crucial in shaping a cohesive Emirati identity. The Gulf nationals become active agents in the reproduction of boundaries and socio-cultural identity through regular performances that are seen as necessary in a country with a majority migrant population. These constructed boundaries are not concrete, and Akinci's (2020b) findings show how it is possible for Arab migrants who hail from other Arab nations find ways to navigate these complex structures by various means. Their daily linguistic and cultural proximity and interaction with Emiratis aid in acculturation.

For non-Arab SGM, this is a complex affair as they are far removed from the language and the native community. The respondent, Jacob, referred to the native Emirati population as Arabs, with whom he hardly interacted despite living in the same city. Arabic played a historical functional role in differentiating an ingroup (citizen/national) and an outgroup (migrant/non-national). In the UAE, the segregation of social spaces in the city for nationals and migrants is also a standard and well-noted phenomenon in this area of research (Cook 2021; Vora 2013). A combination of varied aspects like urban planning, migration policy, socio-economic and racialized segregation, work-life routines and symbolic experiences of space all come together in the division of spaces within the city (Cook 2021). Jason, a 29-year-old male respondent who works as an accountant, reiterates this point:

> You know, even as children, certain common playing areas were restricted to the Arab-speaking community in which we were not included. Also, there are certain cafes here where only the local community go, and they mostly speak Arabic, which we don't understand.

These socially segregated spaces within the city embed and reiterate the national-migrant divide in which language plays a central role. As Phillipson (1992) argues, the process of inclusion and exclusion reflects the perceived values associated with each language. Education in the country also functions in producing a citizen and non-citizen divide as it creates 'parochial national identities among foreign resident children, who are trained not to hold claims to the UAE but rather to the 'homelands' represented by their passports' (Vora 2013: 157). Entry into public schools is reserved only for citizens of the country, while private schools are where most migrant children study. Indian private schools are niche spaces where SGM children grow up interacting with only their community members. As SGM children, they do not attach a functional value to Arabic due to the lack of interaction with the Arab-speaking community. An apparent lack of immersion in the foreign language also leads to their inability to acquire it.

Over time, as the migrant population expanded and became enmeshed in the power dynamics characterized by limited interaction and immersion in the national language, English emerged as a remedial solution. English gradually replaced Arabic's educational and social functions in modern UAE for practical communication. On the run to preserve the socio-cultural identity of the nation threatened by the growing migrant population, a closed group mentality paved the way for the deterioration of Arabic. Consequently, language use became restricted to a minority population with limited access to the outgroup that formed the majority. As the majority increasingly utilized English for communication, Arabic emerged as an endangered and threatened language in modern UAE with its limited speakers. The chapter's findings underscore a paradoxical phenomenon wherein the effort to protect Arabic has resulted in its restriction and the absence of conducive social environments for its growth. We argue that the revival of Arabic in the contemporary migrant-majority UAE can be facilitated by the very migrants who are perceived as posing a threat to language loss and Emirati identity.

As highlighted in the analysis, the migrant language policy gaps and the evolving linguistic landscape in contemporary UAE are linked to the decline of Arabic. The findings underscore the potential of Indian SGM, which can be further extended to all SGMs who have been raised in the nation and have been adequately immersed in Emirati culture to restore the endangered Arabic language. It also acknowledges that these migrant learners can also encounter a host of other challenges like linguistic interference, cultural differences and socio-economic factors, all of which can impede their language acquisition process. However, research has shown that passive speakers who grow up actively listening or engaging in the language are comparatively the best targets for language revitalization efforts. These SGM who have never really migrated but grew up in the UAE will have the potential to acquire near-native conversational skills compared to those who have no knowledge of the language and culture. It is a promising transactional process as Arabic language acquisition benefits SGM in many aspects. For most SGM, there is no notion of 'going back' to their native lands as they never migrated. 'The benefits of being in Dubai generally outweighed the precariousness of living on three-year visas that conceivably could be cancelled for any reason' (Ali 2011: 561). The study participants also agree that as children, they get accustomed to a specific Gulf culture that becomes difficult for them to obtain in their homelands. Economic opportunities, multiculturalism and consumption patterns are aspects of the UAE culture that this group identifies as home.

Employment in the country becomes a way to extend their temporary stay where the practical value of Arabic is highlighted. Akhila, a 28-year-old female respondent working as a chemical engineer, commented, 'I spent my entire life growing up in the UAE; it was only during my search for jobs that I understood the value of speaking Arabic.' Akinci's (2020b) research also supports this notion as he argues that non-Emirati Arab migrants have an advantage in employability compared to South Asian migrants due to their linguistic and cultural proximity to the national population (Akinci 2020b). The interview results also suggest that most respondents agree that they do not hold any advantage in the job market despite having lived in the country all their lives. Their precarious position is highlighted as they are treated as any outsider or foreigner applying for the job, disregarding their presence and experiences within the community. Respondents also added that language becomes significant in forming better relationships with the nationals and higher authorities within their workspaces. They identify how promotion and even pay scales could affect how they fit into the social ingroup, marked by their ability to communicate in Arabic. In the UAE's current socio-political climate, migrants who could speak Arabic and English were ranked higher and had more access to opportunities in society than migrants who were only fluent in English and their native tongue. Multilingualism also becomes an essential tool for most migrant communities as it is a strategy to negotiate their complex layered identities and form new group relationships. In a society where Arabic is linked to national and cultural identity, the host language significantly influences migrant identities. The acquisition of Arabic by SGM proves advantageous for native and migrant populations.

Language policy and planning (LPP) for migrants in the UAE necessitates an extensive examination of the existing language ideologies and politics, as evidenced in this research. While the formulation of a comprehensive policy is beyond the scope of the paper, the research findings emphasize the necessity of reassessing current migrant host language policies and point out their ineffective implementation. As discussed, it is essential to address and act on the existing linguistic socio-cultural hierarchies at the migrant school level by embracing and advocating for a multilingual pedagogical approach. This entails ensuring that English, Arabic, and the migrant's native language are accorded equal importance, without any language being given precedence over the others. Arabic education has traditionally followed a rigid approach to teaching the language. The contemporary scenario necessitates a shift towards incorporating creative materials that mirror real-world Arabic usage in interactions tailored explicitly for the SGM population. Arabic language teachers can actively organize activities and incorporate flexible and culturally sensitive teaching methodologies to accommodate the needs of multi-ethnic migrant learners. A conscious promotion and identifying clear motives for students to interact in the language will help in its acquisition. Educators who are critically informed about migration and its associated aspects can provide spaces that not only promote literacy development but also empower transnational migrant identities. It is imperative to grant migrants a degree of flexibility in their Arabic usage, which can facilitate the language's growth rather than preserve a 'discrete mono-language fixed in time' (Otsuji and Pennycook 2014: 84). Additionally, there are currently few social incentives for the migrant population to learn Arabic in the UAE, which can be introduced to incentivize the propagation of Arabic within the region. Encouraging the creation of multilingual, inclusive environments for interaction, whether in formal or informal settings, can facilitate the immersion of Arabic for migrants.

Conclusion

One of the main objectives of UAE's Vision 2021 was that Arabic will re-emerge as a dynamic and vibrant language, expressed everywhere in speech and writing as a living symbol of the nation's progressive Arab-Islamic values (Razem 2020). The longevity of the Arabic language is integrally tied to the Emirati identity and the value system the nation has actively strived to preserve. The political and economic power that oil has brought in has enabled the country to progress rapidly, and its socio-cultural impact is just beginning to be addressed. The decline of the Arabic language in modern UAE has been tied to the growing majority of the migrant population, which utilizes English as the dominant tongue, which has marginalized the use and growth of Arabic. This chapter suggests an alternative viewpoint by reframing the migrant population not as a threat but as an opportunity to propagate the degrading national language, Arabic. It acknowledges the existing migrant language policy mandating Arabic instruction for all SGMs during their schooling, presenting a potential solution to this linguistic challenge. Through an evaluation of Arabic proficiency among SGMs, the chapter reveals a discernible deficiency despite formal exposure to the language during early education. It intrinsically explores the inadequacies of migrant teaching methodologies, Arabic's diglossic feature, and the complex linguistic and socio-political landscape shaped by the migrant-native divide, all of which impede the propagation of Arabic. The findings further draw connections to the overall erosion of Arabic stemming from its limited utilitarian value and constrained social interaction to foster its growth. By identifying a gap in the migrant language policy embedded in migrant-native politics, the chapter advocates for the imperative reassessment of existing policies and pedagogical approaches tailored to the needs of the growing SGM population. A policy revisal to enhance host language literacy among the migrant population is a mutually beneficial endeavor as it enhances the vitality of Arabic and opens up opportunities for migrants. 'There is no such thing as a difficult or easy language. Languages need immersion. They need the right techniques and styles to be taught' (Thomure 2019). In a nation where English is the lingua franca, and the migrant-native divide hinders spaces for language propagation, immersion is an essential strategy that must be consciously enabled to revive the language. The findings serve as a starting point for understanding SGM language practices and highlight the need to rethink existing policies specifically targeted to their needs. It opens up avenues to explore linguistic opportunities and challenges that the migrant population encounter in their multilingual settings. The chapter recommends steps to be taken by the LPP to make Arabic instruction more relevant and accessible for SGM. It becomes integral to preserve such heterogeneous languages as entire worldviews of accumulated wisdom, including philosophical beliefs and observations about life, will disappear in its absence.

Acknowledgments

We thank all the participants who generously shared their experiences and partook in our study. We would also like to thank Angela Antony for her assistance with the quantitative analysis of the collected data.

Redrawing language boundaries

Notes

1 The Gulf Cooperation Council, is a regional, intergovernmental, political, and economic union comprising of the Arab states Bahrain, Kuwait, Oman, Qatar, Saudi Arabia, and the United Arab Emirates.
2 Deepak Unnikrishnan's debut novel, *Temporary People* (2017), comprises a series of interconnected stories depicting the lives of Gulf migrants in the UAE. Through this collection, the author delves into themes of migration, identity, struggles, and thess human experience, drawing inspiration from his own upbringing in the UAE.
3 A catch-22 situation is a term used to refer to a dilemma in which one's desired outcome is impossible to achieve due to contradictory constraints or circumstances. The term originates from Joseph Heller's novel, *Catch-22.*
4 A long traditional garment worn by the male nationals of the region.

References

Akinci, I. (2020a). 'Dressing the nation? Symbolizing Emirati national identity and boundaries through national dress'. *Ethnic and Racial Studies.* 43(10): 1776–1794.
Akinci, I. (2020b). 'Culture in the 'politics of identity': Conceptions of national identity and citizenship among second-generation non-Gulf Arab migrants in Dubai'. *Journal of Ethnic and Migration Studies.* 46(11): 2309–2325.
Al-Bataineh, A. (2021). 'Language policy in higher education in the United Arab Emirates: Proficiency, choices and the future of Arabic'. *Language Policy.* 20(2): 215–236.
Al-Issa, A., & Dahan, L. S. (2020). 'Language and identity construction in the United Arab Emirates: Challenges faced in a globalized world'. In *The Routledge Handbook of Arabic and Identity* (pp. 233–244). Routledge.
Al-Shamsi, F. S., Aly, H. Y., & El-Bassiouni, M. Y. (2009). 'Measuring and explaining the efficiencies of the United Arab Emirates banking system'. *Applied Economics.* 41(27): 3505–3519.
Ali, S. (2011). 'Going and coming and going again: Second-generation migrants in Dubai'. *Mobilities.* 6(4): 553–568.
Altoma, S. J. (1974). 'Language education in Arab countries and the role of the academies'. In *Linguistics in South West Asia and North Africa* (pp. 279–313). Mouton.
Carroll, J. B. (1990). 'Cognitive abilities in foreign language aptitude: Then and now'. In *Language Aptitude Reconsidered* (pp. 11–29). Parry and Stansfield.
Carroll, K. S., Al Kahwaji, B., & Litz, D. (2017). 'Triglossia and promoting Arabic literacy in the United Arab Emirates'. *Language, Culture and Curriculum.* 30(3): 317–332.
Clarke, M., Ramanathan, V., & Morgan, B. (2007). 'Language policy and language teacher education in the United Arab Emirates'. *TESOL Quarterly.* 41(3): 583–591.
Cook, W. R. A. (2021). 'A tale of two cafés: Spatial production as de facto language policy'. *Current Issues in Language Planning.* 22(5): 535–552.
D'Anna, L., & Amoruso, C. (2020). 'Complex identities: Arabic in the diaspora'. In *The Routledge Handbook of Arabic and Identity* (pp. 259–272). Routledge.
Ferguson, C. A. (1959). 'Diglossia'. *Word.* 15(2): 325–340.
Findlow, S. (2006). 'Higher education and linguistic dualism in the Arab Gulf'. *British Journal of Sociology of Education.* 27(1): 19–36.
Gallagher, K. (2022). 'Early language education in the United Arab Emirates'. In *Handbook of Early Language Education* (pp. 893–921). Springer International Publishing.
Golden Visa. (2023, October 23). *U.A.E Government Portal.* https://u.ae/information-and-services/visa-and-emirates-id/residence-visas/golden-visa
Jose, B. (2023). 'Language and identity formations of second-generation migrants in Deepak Unnikrishnan's temporary people'. In *Strategies for Cultural Assimilation of Immigrants and Their Children: Social, Economic, and Political Considerations* (pp. 69–85). IGI Global.
Longva, A. N. (2006). 'Nationalism in pre-modern guise: The discourse on Hadhar and Badu in Kuwait'. *International Journal of Middle East Studies.* 38(2): 171–187.
Malek, C. (2015, October 12). 'Arab children snubbing Arabic, Dubai workshop hears'. *The National.* www.thenational.ae/uae/education/arab-children-snubbing-arabic-dubai-workshop-hears.
Meyerhoff, M. (2018). *Introducing Sociolinguistics.* London: Routledge.

Myhill, J. (2014). 'The effect of diglossia on literacy in Arabic and other languages'. In E. Saiegh-Haddad & R. M. Joshi (Eds.), *Handbook of Arabic Literacy* (pp. 197–223). Springer.

Otsuji, E., & Pennycook, A. (2014). 'Unremarkable hybridities and metrolingual practices'. In *The Global-Local Interface and Hybridity: Exploring Language and Identity* (pp. 83–99). Blue Ridge Summit: Multilingual Matters.

Phillipson, R. (1992). *Linguistic Imperialism*. Oxford: Oxford University Press.

Piller, I. (2017). 'Dubai: Language in the ethnocratic, corporate and mobile city'. In *Urban Sociolinguistics* (pp. 77–94). Routledge.

Portes, A., & Rivas, A. (2011). 'The adaptation of migrant children'. *The Future of Children*. 21(1): 219–246.

Randall, M., & Samimi, M. A. (2010). 'The status of English in Dubai'. *English Today*. 26(1): 43–50.

Razem, R. J. (2020). 'Parents' attitudes towards the implementation of Arabic as an additional language in Dubai: An exploratory case study'. *Theory and Practice in Language Studies*. 10(8): 849–862.

Sayed, M., Salem, R., & Khedr, A. E. (2017). 'Accuracy evaluation of Arabic text classification'. *In 2017 12th International Conference on Computer Engineering and Systems (ICCES)*: 365–370.

Skehan, P. (1998). *A Cognitive Approach to Language Learning*. Oxford: Oxford University Press.

Skutnabb-Kangas, T. (2001). 'The globalisation of (educational) language rights'. *International Review of Education*. 47: 201–219.

Thomure, H. (2019). 'Arabic language education in the UAE: Choosing the right drivers'. In K. Gallagher (Ed.), *Education in the United Arab Emirates: Innovation and Transformation* (pp. 75–93). Springer.

Tibi, S., & McLeod, L. (2014). 'The development of young children's Arabic language and literacy in the United Arab Emirates'. In *Handbook of Arabic Literacy: Insights and Perspectives* (pp. 303–321). Springer.

Triandafyllidou, A. (1998). 'National identity and the other'. *Ethnic and Racial Studies*. 21(4): 593–612.

UNDESA. (2021, January 15). 'International Migration 2020 Highlights'. *United Nations Department of Economic and Social Affairs (UNDESA)*. www.un.org/en/desa/international-migration-2020-highlights

United Arab Emirates Population 2024. (2024, January 2). *Global Media Insight*. www.globalmediainsight.com/blog/uae-population-statistics/.

Unnikrishnan, D. (2017). *Temporary People*. India: Penguin Random House.

Vora, N. (2013). *Impossible Citizens: Dubai's Indian Diaspora*. London: Duke University Press.

Weber, A. S. (2011). 'Politics of English in the Arabian Gulf'. *FLTAL 2011 Proceedings*: 60–66.

Weiner, M. (1982). 'International migration and development: Indians in the Persian Gulf'. *Population and Development Review*. 8(1): 1–36.

Wen, Z., & Skehan, P. (2011). 'A new perspective on foreign language aptitude research: Building and supporting a case for working memory as language aptitude'. *Ilha do Desterro: A Journal of English Language, Literatures in English and Cultural Studies*. 60(4): 15–43.

6

HOW IS ALSATIAN WRITTEN?

A case study of the linguistic landscape in Strasbourg

Rei Sugiura

Introduction: Alsace as a border region

Alsace is a border region between France and Germany and a frontier area where French and German languages and cultures meet (Reutner 2017). The regional language of Alsace, Alsatian, is predominantly spoken within Alsace and is a minority language marginalized by French and German, the region's two prominent languages. This chapter addresses how Alsatian, which has been perceived primarily as a spoken language, is written in the streets of Strasbourg. It aims to answer the following two questions: what are the similarities and differences between Alsatian and the way regional languages are written in other regions? What attitudes do people have toward the Alsatian language written in public spaces?

In order to interpret the complex issues of Alsatian, it is essential to follow the context in which Alsace is positioned at the border region and understand how Alsatian has been regarded. European history has a record of "bordering," "de-bordering," and "re-bordering" (Yndigegn 2011). Alsace is a region that has moved between the borders of two states. Depending on the results of the war – the Thirty Years War (1618–1648), the Franco-Prussian War (1870–1871), World War I (WWI; 1914–1918) and WWII (1939–1945) – Alsace has experienced a national border change no less than four times and belonged to two political regimes. Table 6.1 summarizes Alsace's history from the 8th century BCE to the present in terms of political domain and governance structure.

The regional language of Alsace

This chapter will identify how Alsatian is represented in Strasbourg and how it is perceived by the local people. In this section, I discuss three aspects relevant to understanding how Alsatian appears in the public space of Strasbourg: (1) the evolution of the number of Alsatian speakers in the Alsace region, (2) Alsatian in education, and (3) the power relations between French and regional languages in France. But first I present the linguistic aspects of Alsatian.

The term "Alsatian" refers to several Germanic varieties subdivided into Franconian and Alemannic (Philipp & Bothorel-Witz 1990; Gardner-Chloros 1991). Alsatian does not have a standard pronunciation and orthography. Thus, locals often describe Alsatian as a plural form of "*les dialects alsaciens*" (Alsatian dialects). Alsatians state that there are as many dialects in Alsace as there

DOI: 10.4324/9781003439493-8

Table 6.1 Chronology of the history of Alsace (Huck et al. 2007, p. 8)

Period	Year	Political sphere	State/government framework
8th century BC–1st century BC	800 years	Celtic	
1st century BC–5th century AD	550 years	Romaine (Celtic and Germanic)	Roman structures
5th century–10th century	500 years	Germanic	Merovingian dynasty Carolingian Empire
10th century–17th century	700 years	Germanic	Holy Roman Empire
17th century–1870	200 years	French	French (kingdom and republic)
1870–1918	48 years	Germanic	2nd German Empire (Reichsland ElsaßLothringen)
1918–1940	22 years	French	French Republic
1940–1945	4.5 years	Germanic	Germany: Nazi Germany
1945–today	80 years	French	French Republic

are towns and villages (Keck & Daul 2016, p. 7). This remark is not too far from reality. Alsatian is classified into five varieties from north to south, with a more extensive classification scheme (i.e., Rhenish Franconian, South Franconian German, Northern low Alemannic German, Southern low Alemannic German, and High Alemannic German (see Keck & Daul 2016, p. 7 for the details).

The evolution of the number of Alsatian speakers

Alsatian has been a people's every language in Alsace for a long time. L'Institut national de la statistique et des études économiques (INSEE: National Institute of Statistics and Economic Studies) et al. (1999) reported that 500,000 speakers use Alsatian. Compared with other more endangered languages, such as those listed in the Atlas of the World's Languages in Danger (United Nations Educational, Scientific and Cultural Organization [UNESCO] 2010), it may seem that Alsatian will not soon disappear. But after the end of WWII, the Nazis' influence helped to impose a negative public image on Alsatian, so people preferred to speak French to show that they were well integrated into France. Consequently, French became the dominant language in Alsace. As such, the transmission of Alsatian to younger generations was interrupted, and the number of Alsatian speakers continues to decrease.

Table 6.2 shows survey results on language use among the Alsatian population that INSEE conducted from 1926 to 1962 (Huck et al. 2007; Huck 2015, pp. 171, 191, 210, 292). According to the table, in 1926, a large percentage of the respondents (67.91%) stated they "speak only Alsatian," but after 1931, the number of respondents who stated they used Alsatian and French, or German and French, increased. I could assume that Alsatian was spoken among the local population even after WWII when Alsatian speakers became multilingual. The same questionnaire form has not been used since the 1962 survey. Perhaps it was no longer necessary to survey language use in Alsace since French became a dominant language. In 1962, the largest number of respondents reported speaking French and Alsatian, indicating a trend of Alsatians moving toward the use of French.

In the 2000s, three different organizations conducted the following surveys: (1) Office pour la Langue et les Cultures d'Alsace et de Moselle (OLCA: Association for the Language and Culture of Alsace) in 2012, (2) Institut français d'opinion publique (IFOP: French Institute of Public Opinion) in 2020, and (3) Collectivité européenne d'Alsace (CeA: European Collectivity of Alsace) in 2022. OLCA surveyed the language situation in Alsace in 2012 (Office pour la langue et la culture

Table 6.2 Survey on language spoken in Alsace, 1926–1962 (Huck et al. 2007; Huck 2015)

Year	Total respondents	"Which language do you usually use? French, Alsatian, German, or another language, which one?" (%)								
		French only	French + Alsatian	French + German	French + Alsatian + German	Alsatian only	Alsatian + German	German only	another language	n/a
1926	1,153,396	9.86	6.39	0.45	2.93	67.91	2.76	1.11	1.33	7.22
1931	1,199,977	5.60	4.78	2.93	35.16	7.44	32.70	3.79	0.65	6.92
1936	1,206,754	6.23	5.42	3.18	40.79	6.53	29.37	2.72	0.23	5.51
1946	1,122,153	4.91	3.41	2.36	52.02	6.17	24.20	1.26	–	–
1962	1,026,800	13.30	19.10	1.50	46.77	5.60	13.06	0.46	–	–

d'Alsace 2012). It reported that 43% of respondents spoke Alsatian well, 33% spoke or understood Alsatian a little, and 25% did not understand Alsatian. A closer look at the results shows that the percentages of Alsatian speakers vary widely by generation, with a greater prevalence of speakers in the older age groups and fewer speakers in the younger age groups. A more nuanced look at the OLCA report reveals that the percentage of dialect speakers among survey participants by age group is as follows: 12% of respondents aged 18–29, 24% aged 30–44, 54% aged 45–59, and 74% aged 60 or older. Comparing the results of surveys from the 1900s and 2000s, we can conclude that the number of Alsatian speakers is gradually declining and Alsace is facing the problem of a declining Alsatian inheritance.

Alsatian in education

In Alsace, two types of programs are in charge of regional language education: *Association pour le Bilinguisme en Classe dès la Maternelle* (ABCM: Association for Bilingualism in the Kindergarten Classroom) and *Quatre parcours Tomi Ungerer* (Four Tomi Ungerer courses). ABCM is a private kindergarten, whereas Quatre Parcours Tomi Ungerer is public. ABCM was founded in 1991 and was the only bilingual institution in Alsace. ABCM offers bilingual classes in French and German. Alsatian is regarded as oral, whereas German is taught as a written form of Alsatian (Harrison 2016). This conception of regional language education is based on Pierre Deyon's publication in 1982. Deyon published the "circulaire sur la langue et la culture régionales en Alsace (circular on regional language and culture in Alsace)" in 1982. Deyon stated that German as "'expression écrite' de 'l'alsacien que parle la majorité des habitants de cette région'" (the "written expression" of the Alsatian spoken by the majority of the region's inhabitants) (Deyon 1985, p. 10). The new program for learning Alsatian, Quatre Parcours Tomi Ungerer, was founded in 2023. They offer immersion classes in Alsatian, French, and German. We do not yet know the school's detailed curriculum.

ABCM and Quatre Parcours Tomi Ungerer have differing conceptions of regional language education, reflecting a conflicting view on this concept of regional language education in Alsace. Compared with other regions of France, the notion of "bilingual" for regional language education in Alsace is distinctive. Regional language education usually means French and regional languages, such as Basque, Breton, Corsica, and Occitan. However, bilingual education in Alsace means teaching French and German. Préfecture de la région Grand Est & Académie de Strasbourg (2018) officially declared that the regional language of Alsace has two forms, *l'allemand standard*

(Standard German) and *les dialectes pratiqués en Alsace* (the dialects practiced in Alsace). This statement concerning Alsatian as a dialect consequently underestimates Alsatian's linguistic and social status.

The power relations between French and regional languages

To understand the power relation between the national and regional languages in France, it is important to comprehend the historical background of French in the French Republic. France is well known for its monolingual policy, which is based on the slogan "*Une nation, une language*" (One nation, one langue) (Hélot 2003). The French Revolution should always be mentioned when we discuss language standardization in France (Connor 2019). Regional language speakers were discriminated against and treated as ignorant, thoughtless, or even as members of the counter-revolution. As Abbé Grégoire stated in a speech to *Le Comité de salut public* (Committee of Public Safety) in 1794,

> Le fédéralisme et la superstition parlent bas Breton; l'émigration et la haine de la République parlent allemand; la contre-révolution parle l'italien et le fanatisme parle le basque.
>
> (De Certeau, Julia, & Revel 1975, pp. 10–11)

> (Federalism and superstition speak Low Breton; emigration and hatred of the Republic speak German; the counter-revolution speaks Italian and fanaticism speaks Basque.)
>
> (Connor 2019, p. 254)

A plurality of languages has been regarded as a threat to the cohesion of the French Republic. The French government declared the status of the French language in its constitution as the language of the Republic in 1992: Article 2: *La langue de la République est le français* (The language of the Republic shall be French) (France 2008). The French government is unwilling to formulate a language policy to protect regional languages. The first official recognition of regional languages was in 2008 when the government amended the French constitution by adding Article 75–1: *Les langues régionales appartiennent au patrimoine de la France* (Regional languages are part of France's heritage) (France 2008). This clause emphasizes that a regional language is not for its speakers but can serve as a property for all French citizens regardless of the place and their language skills. Another critical background is la *loi Toubon*, the Toubon law, enacted in 1994. This law guarantees the right to use French and that French should be used in all official government publications, advertisements, and workplaces.

This section highlighted the declining numbers of Alsatian speakers and the challenges in regional language education. Investigating how much Alsatian is written in public spaces leads to understanding the current visibility of the language and stimulates further exploration its potential vitality. The following section explains the linguistic landscape (LL) research as a theoretical framework.

Theoretical framework: linguistic landscape studies

Landry and Bourhis (1997), pioneers in the development of the study of language in public spaces, asserted that in a bilingual or multilingual environment, the presence or absence of one's language on public signs influences how connected one feels as a part of a language group (p. 27). The first phase of LL research was based on Landry and Bourhis's (1997) idea to reveal ethnolinguistic vitality by observing the LL. These early studies focused on counting and comparing which languages were written and how many (see Backhaus 2007). They developed analysis concerning dichotomies, such as "governmental versus private signage" and "top-down versus bottom-up signage," and many of these early studies attempted to tackle language policies.

The second wave of LL research started around 2010, the scope of which adopted a semiotic perspective and began to look at the authorship, readership, function, and materiality of signs through qualitative research (Van Mensel, Vandenbroucke, & Blackwood 2016). Though scholars have attempted to employ theoretical perspectives for understanding LL studies (see Ben-Rafael et al. 2010, pp. xvi–xix, for the details), there is no single established and unified theory or methodology for the field. Fundamental to those LL studies is keeping a grounding in fieldwork of empirical observation in public spaces (Kallen 2023, p. 45). This study combines the quantitative research used in the first wave with the qualitative research used in the second wave of LL studies, which I describe in detail in the methodology section.

Cenoz and Gorter (2006) conducted the first study to assess how a solid and active language policy to protect local minority languages could produce trickle-down effects on commercial signage (Van Mensel et al. 2016, p. 436). They compared LL in two multilingual cities in Friesland (Netherlands) and the Basque Country (Spain), where two minority languages, Frisian and Basque, are spoken. They revealed that using Basque in bilingual signs in Donostia had an informative role and an essential symbolic function related to affective elements and the feeling of Basque as an identity symbol (Cenoz & Gorter 2006, p. 79). In the case of a minority language, it may be employed for so-called tokenistic use (Van Mensel et al. 2012, p. 321). A minority language is often used to append an "authentic" impression. The presence of the language in the public space does not reflect actual language vitality in this case.

In an LL study focusing on the use of regional languages in France, Blackwood (2011) conducted a comparative study of LL in Breton, the regional language of Brittany, and Corsican, the language of Corsica. Blackwood (2011) categorized all signs into "top-down" and "bottom-up," which was proposed by Ben-Rafael et al. (2006, p. 14). Blackwood (2011) reveals that Breton is present in the street name, and half of all Breton signs are found at the major underground railway station in Brittany. In Brittany's public spaces, both top-down and bottom-up signs are written in Breton. Monolingual Breton signs tend to be in bottom-up items, whereas multilingual signs in Breton and French are generally top-down items. In Corsica, Blackwood (2011) reported that Corsican has 17 times more monolingual signs than Breton in Brittany. These Corsican signs include many Corsican descriptions of products made in Corsica sold in souvenir shops. Hornsby (2008), who also conducted research in Brittany, asserted that using Breton in public spaces was meant to attract tourists. This interpretation of the use of local and minority languages is reported in many places, for example, Wales (Coupland 2012), Ireland (Kallen 2009; Moriarty 2012), the Northern Calotte (Salo 2012), German-speaking Belgium (Van Mensel & Darquennes 2012), and Italian and French coastal cities (Blackwood & Tufi 2012).

Bogatto and Hélot (2010) conducted the first LL studies in Strasbourg. Their research aimed to explore the notion of multilingualism in urban spaces; thus they focused on the LL around the central station area as the gateway to the city. They recorded shopfront signs and observed multilingual signs in French, the most predominant, and Alsatian, German, English, Arabic, Mandarin, Thai, and Turkish. Alsatian was employed on street names in public signs and for restaurant names on private signs. This research examined LL in other areas in Strasbourg. In the methodology section, I provide a background on the selection of the study site.

Methodology

Linguistic landscape

This study investigates how Alsace's regional language is employed in public spaces using field-work conducted in Strasbourg. The data were recorded in July and August 2019, and a follow-up study was conducted from 2023 to 2024. Quantitative LL data were recorded around squares in the center of Strasbourg: Place Kléber, Place de la Cathédrale, and Place Gutenberg. The Place Kléber is a principal square in the center of the commercial area in Strasbourg. This square has approximately 40 stores, including restaurants, cafes, boutiques, and bookstores, and has been used as a starting point for citizens' protests, marches, or assemblies. The symbol of Strasbourg, the Cathédrale Notre-Dame-de-Strasbourg, stands in the Place de la Cathédrale. Nowadays, the cathedral is a main attraction, with many souvenir shops, Alsatian cuisine restaurants, and cafes in its surroundings. Place Gutenberg has shops, bars, and restaurants. Historical, political, cultural, and religious events are often centered in these squares, and they remain the center for locals and visitors.

This study offers a different Strasbourg study from that of Bogatto and Hélot (2010). This study was conducted in the cathedral and surrounding squares – Strasbourg's cultural, traditional, and religious center. Traditionally, the cultural center of a European city is the cathedral and the surrounding square, and Bogatto and Hélot (2010) studied the LL of the central train station, the gateway for tourists. Strasbourg's railroad station was built in 1883, making it a newly constructed and more multiethnic area in terms of Strasbourg's city history. This study shed light on the LL in the cultural center of Strasbourg, which is why I chose the area around the square as the research site. Following Ben-Rafael et al.'s (2006, p. 14) categorization, all the signs in the city are categorized into "top-down" and "bottom-up." Government offices and municipal administration erect top-down signs, including street name signs, traffic signs, posters, and announcements for events offered by public agencies. Some public posters were identified with a logo *Strasbourg.eu*. All other signs are categorized as bottom-up signs, including various forms of print as well as hand-writing from small handwriting boards to large commercial posters. Names of shops and restaurants are not included in the table, as some are difficult to categorize due to a mixture of languages or coined words. Ultimately, I recorded 68 top-down and 266 bottom-up signs.

In Strasbourg, temporary LL signs dramatically appear at the start of the Christmas season. There are over 300 stalls in each square for Christmas decorations, artworks, crafts, and food. The Christmas market in Alsace attracts tourists from all over the world. Many English and German signs designed for international travelers are present in this area (e.g., Hot mulled wine and *Weißer Glühwein*). Strasbourg is quite touristy during this period. Therefore, these seasonal LL signs are excluded from the LL data in Strasbourg. Instead, they are introduced for qualitative analysis.

Informal interview

The interviews conducted in 2024 are complementary to LL studies, which aim to reveal how Alsatians perceive Alsatian as it is written in the public space. As will be discussed later in the results section, the LL study reveals that Alsatian is prominent in public signs, especially in street names. Therefore, to answer the question of how Alsatian in public signs is received by the population, I will examine how bilingual street names are received by the people living in Alsace. I conducted interviews using snowball sampling, interviewing a total of 18 individuals. I asked, "Que pensez-vous des noms de rue bilingues, alsaciens et français (What do you think of bilingual Alsatian and French street names)?"

Table 6.3 Basic information of the interviewees

	Gender (F = female, M = male)	Age in 2024	Alsatian language proficiency (fluent, passive, little)
Anna	F	77	fluent
Benjamin	M	73	passive
Corentin	M	71	little
Denise	F	69	fluent
Enzo	M	67	fluent
Fanny	F	62	fluent
Gabriel	M	53	fluent
Hugo	M	52	fluent
Ian	M	45	passive
Jérémy	M	44	fluent
Kristeen	F	41	little
Louis	M	33	little
Maxime	M	27	passive
Nicolas	M	21	little
Océane	F	20	little
Pauline	F	20	little
Questa	F	15	little
Romane	F	13	little

It should be noted that this research cannot provide a wide-ranging description of the variety of attitudes that may exist among different ethnic groups, age groups – from schoolchildren to older adults – new immigrants and older immigrants, or attitudes of people with specific political alignments. What my research can do is dive into the linguistics of a multilingual city to revisit the key questions to sample and view the range of opinion about language and identity in Alsace. Table 6.3 provides information on the interviewees' gender, age, and Alsatian language proficiency. All names of interviewees were anonymized to protect their privacy and guarantee anonymity.

Results and discussion

Linguistic landscape in Strasbourg

Table 6.4 shows the overall results for language distribution in LL. French is the most prominent language on both private and public signs. Table 6.5 shows language combinations in public and private signs. Half of public signs are monolingual, while one-third are trilingual. The second and third dominant languages are English and German. There are neither French and German bilingual signs nor German monolingual signs, and Alsatian occupies only a little space. This finding is not surprising. As French is the only official language of the French Republic, the results overlap with those of other cities in France, as Blackwood (2015) observed.

Alsatian is always present as a toponym. In Strasbourg, all street name signs are written in French and Alsatian. French is written in capital letters at the top, and Alsatian in lowercase or italics at the bottom (Figure 6.1). As indicated in the previous section, most Alsatian speakers are either bilingual or multilingual. Given this sociolinguistic context, Alsatian in public spaces is optional for conveying information to inhabitants. For instance, direction signs are written only in French (Figure 6.2).

Table 6.4 Overall results for language distribution

	French	English	German	Alsatian
Top-down	68	25	21	10
Bottom-up	262	74	57	2
Total	330	99	78	12

Table 6.5 Language on top-down and bottom-up signs

Language	Top-down	Bottom-up
French only	33	180
French + English + German	20	47
French + Alsatian	10	2
French + English	4	19
French + German	–	8
French + English + German + Italian + Spain + Chinese + Russian	1	–
English only	–	4
French + Arabic	–	2
French + English + Chinese	–	2
French + English + German + Spanish	–	1
French + English + German + Spanish + Italian + Russian + Japanese	–	1
Total	68	266

Figure 6.1 Bilingual top-down street name sign. Left to right: Quai au Sable in French and Sandplätzel in Alsatian; Rue du Jeu des Enfants in French and Kinderspielgass in Alsatian

Figure 6.2 Monolingual top-down signs. Left to right: the sign indicates directions to the cathedral, visitor center, central station, and tourist area called Petite France; Promenades en bateau indicates the direction of a sightseeing boat's boarding point

Figure 6.3 Bottom-up signs in Strasbourg: Left to right: a large sign with Alsatian *flammekueche* and *tarte flambée* in French, and detailed descriptions of the menu and ingredients in French and German

In bottom-up signs, Alsatian is used only in traditional Alsatian cuisine. A traditional Alsatian cuisine, *tarte flambée*, is expressed in French, *tarte flambée*, and Alsatian, *flammekueche* (Figure 6.3). In the largest letters on signs, Alsatian and French notations are written on the side. Since French is written from left to right, it could be interpreted that *tarte flambée* takes precedence over *flammekueche*. However, letters on a more detailed signboard (right side) are written in French and German, and Alsatian is eliminated. This could suggest that Alsatian *flammekueche* is written as a symbol to provide passers-by with an authentic impression of Alsace. In this sign, Alsatian has an informative role and a symbolic function, which is quite similar to the usage reported in other studies. Regarding the regional language policy, this can be seen as tokenistic use, as Van Mensel et al. (2012) described. From the perspective of a visitor to Alsace unfamiliar with the history of Alsace and the regional language, it may not be easy to immediately distinguish between German and Alsatian, as in the case of the *tarte flambée* stand. The Alsatian language found on private signs, employed symbolically rather than functionally, is rare and is overtaken by predominant languages such as French, German, and English.

Let us compare Blackwood's (2011) study in Brittany and Corsica with this research in Alsace. Brittany has top-down and bottom-up signs written in Breton. Monolingual Breton signs are often bottom-up, while multilingual Breton and French signs are top-down in Brittany. In Corsica, there are many monolingual Corsican signs. Within the Strasbourg research site of this study, there were no monolingual Alsatian signs in either the top-down or bottom-down LL; in street names representing top-down, Alsatian is always written below French. Furthermore, in the bottom-up LL, very few are written in Alsatian, and there were the names of traditional Alsatian cuisine.

I have thus far analyzed the language practices found in Strasbourg's linguistic landscape. One seasonal but influential LL for Alsace is the LL signs during the Christmas market. The Christmas tradition is closely tied with Alsace's tradition. Therefore, some traditional names for cuisine related to Christmas use Alsatian vocabulary which does not have a French translation. Alsatians have a tradition of making biscuits called *Bredele*, which is sold in many stalls at the Christmas market. Moreover, the Place Broglie has a big gate marked *Christkindelsmärik*, which is the Alsatian name for the Christmas market. Christmas markets are traditionally held in various towns and villages in Alsace where local people sell homemade sweets and goods. Today in Alsace, especially in Strasbourg, the market bears more commercial color and is aimed at tourists. There are many signs in English and German during this period. Nonetheless, like in the example of *Bredele* and *Christkindelsmärik*, some signs are written in Alsatian. These examples indicate that using Alsatian is tied with Alsace's tradition.

Interviews

The interview aims to reveal how the local people in Alsace perceive Alsatian as it is written in the public space. As noted in the previous section, Alsatian appears prominently in public signs in the form of street names. Therefore, in my interviews, I asked the question "*Que pensez-vous des noms de rue bilingues, alsaciens et français* (What do you think of bilingual Alsatian and French street names)?" This question attempted to reveal how locals perceive bilingual street names, which cannot be revealed by observation of the LL alone.

When initially looking at the interviews, I found that no individuals demonstrated a negative attitude towards bilingual street names. While the interviews do not cover all demographics, there were no instances of individuals expressing a negative perception towards Alsatian. For example, out of 18 people, 13 began their responses with phrases like "It is a good idea. I like it. I think it is nice. It is important (*C'est une bonne idée. C'est bien. Je trouve que c'est sympa. Oui c'est très important*)," and three ended their responses with only these reactions: "*C'est bien*" (name/gender/generation/Alsatian language proficiency: Corentin/M/70s/fluent), "*Ça c'est très bien*" (Ian/M/40s/passive), and "*Oui ça c'est bien*" (Kristeen/F/little).

Next, I organize the emerging characteristics while quoting people's narratives. Narratives linking the uniqueness of Alsace's region with the presence of Alsatian in street names were observed. Fanny (F/60s/fluent) stated, "*C'est intéressant. C'est une richesse en effet* (It is interesting. It is indeed a richness)." This remark indicates the connection between the region's characteristics and the presence of Alsatian. Similarly, Maxime (M/20s/passive) expressed that the bilingual street names indicate that Alsace is different from other parts of France (*"Ce n'est pas juste un coin comme les autres en France.*/It is not just any corner like any other in France"). Denise (F/60s/fluent) also mentioned that bilingual street names serve as reminders of Alsace's special identity (*"Moi, je trouve que c'est une bonne chose pour effectivement rappeler qu'il y a une identité particulière ici*/For me, I think it is a good thing to indeed remind that there is a particular identity here").

Some individuals mentioned that the bilingual street names are part of Alsace's history and culture, and they serve as a means to trace both. Louis (M/30s/little) remarked that bilingual street names are normal because they are part of Alsatian culture (*"Je pense que c'est normal parce que c'est pour une partie de la culture alsacienne*/I think it is normal because it is for a part of Alsatian culture"). Gabriel (M/50s/fluent) also expressed the idea that Alsatian street names are part of history (*Ça fait partie de notre histoire*/It is part of our history"). Jérémy (M/40s/fluent) similarly mentioned that bilingual street names allow one to discover what streets were called in the past (*"On trouve bien comment à l'époque la rue s'appelait parce que je ne sais pas ça a été changé*/We can easily find what the street was called at the time because I do not know if it has been changed"). Romane (F/10s/little) also suggested that through street names written in Alsatian language, we can learn how places were referred to in the past (*"Je trouve que c'est bien comme ça on sait ça disait à l'époque. Il y a longtemps comme ça se disait en alsacien*/I think it is good like this, we know what it was called at the time. A long time ago, that's how it was said in Alsatian"). From these narratives, we can discern the notion that the history inherent in toponyms is reflected in the names written in Alsatian. Furthermore, while noting Alsace's history of changing hands between two countries, Benjamin (M/70s/passive) and Enzo (M/60s/fluent) pointed out translation errors in translating Alsace's street names into Alsatian, French, or German.

Two university students, Nicolas (M/20s/little) and Pauline (F/20s/little), expressed views that perceive Alsatian as a thing of the past – they think that street names hold little significance. Nicolas remarked that from a utilitarian perspective, nobody reads Alsatian names, suggesting they are solely for decorative purposes. He stated, *"Du point de vue purement utilitaire, personne ne lit le nom alsacien, c'est vraiment pour faire joli* (From a purely utilitarian point of view, nobody reads the Alsatian name; it is really just for decoration)." Meanwhile, Pauline indicated that neither she nor others particularly care about bilingualism. She expressed, *"Je m'en fiche aussi. Je pense que tout le monde s'en fiche* (I don't care either. I think everyone doesn't care)." She acknowledged the presence of Alsatian names as positive but remarked that since hardly anyone speaks Alsatian in present-day Alsace, there are no readers (*"Parce qu'aujourd'hui, comme je dis, presque plus personne ne parle alsacien. Donc si c'est là, pourquoi pas ça rappelle en alsacien c'est bien, mais personne ne va le lire*/Because today, like I said, almost no one speaks Alsatian anymore. So if it's there, why not, it's a reminder in Alsatian, it's good, but nobody will read it"). Nicolas and Pauline currently live in Strasbourg for university, indicating their limited daily interaction with Alsatian speakers. Therefore, it can be inferred that reading or speaking Alsatian is perceived as a thing of the past due to its minimal engagement in present-day daily life.

In contrast, Anna (F/70s/fluent) suggested that Alsatian street names could benefit young people, and preserving some street names is also possible (*"C'est pas mal déjà pour les jeunes quoi, puis se garder un petit peu quand même quelques noms des rues. . . . C'est une idée régionale*/It's not bad already for the younger generation, to keep at least a few street names. . . . It's a regional idea"). This remark implies the idea of creating opportunities for young people to engage with Alsatian, given the decline in Alsatian speakers among the younger generation. Additionally,

Questa (F/10s/little) expressed that Alsatian street names are beneficial for those who speak Alsatian rather than French (*"Franchement, c'est bien parce qu'il y a des personnes qui ne parlent pas forcément le français et qui parlent plus alsacien*/Frankly, it's good because there are people who don't necessarily speak French and who speak more Alsatian"). Despite not speaking Alsatian herself, Questa's opinion likely reflects the influence of her paternal grandparents, who are Alsatian speakers.

Furthermore, I observed two intriguing narratives regarding the relationship between Alsace, Germany, and France. Océane (F/20s/little) prefaced her remarks by stating that while place names may not seem significant, they evoke the history of Alsace. She emphasized the importance of not forgetting history, saying, *"Ce n'est pas une grand-chose, mais ça rappelle l'histoire de l'Alsace. Je trouve que c'est important de ne pas oublier l'histoire justement* (It's not a big deal, but it recalls the history of Alsace. I think it's important not to forget history, precisely)." Reflecting on the history of German and French attempts to "steal" Alsace's identity, she believes that preserving the remnants of Alsatian identity left in Alsace today is crucial (*"Parce que l'Alsace a beaucoup changé de pays et . . . il y a tellement de fois que l'Allemagne et la France ont voulu voler l'identité de l'Alsace que je trouve important maintenant qu'on garde le peu de chose qui reste en Alsace, et qui sont de la culture alsacienne*/Because Alsace has changed countries a lot, and . . . there have been so many times that Germany and France have tried to steal Alsace's identity that I think it's important now to keep the few things that remain in Alsace, which are part of Alsatian culture"). It can be inferred from such statements that she believes Alsace's identity, detached from Germany and France, is preserved in its place names.

On the other hand, Hugo (M/50s/fluent) suggested that when considering Alsace's history, instead of bilingual signage in French and Alsatian, trilingual signage including German should be adopted (*"Pour moi, les panneaux, ils devraient être trilingues*/For me, the signs should be trilingual"). Hugo argued that while French serves as the language of the republic, Alsatian represents the regional and indigenous language of Alsace. Furthermore, he emphasizes the necessity of German due to Alsace's existence within the Germanic environment, similar to Switzerland and Germany (*"ils devraient être français parce que c'est . . . on fait partie de la République française, c'est la langue de la république et devraient être alsacien parce qu'on est en Alsace. C'est notre langue régionale vernaculaire et puis ils devraient aussi être allemand parce qu'on est dans un environnement germanique à la Suisse et à l'Allemagne pour qu'il soit compréhensible aussi dans leur sens l'espace germanique*/They should be in French because . . . we are part of the French Republic, it's the language of the republic. They should be in Alsatian because we are in Alsace. It's our regional vernacular language. They should also be in German because we are in a Germanic environment close to Switzerland and Germany so that it's also understandable in the Germanic space"). Hugo's perspective, articulated through the issue of language representation in street names, highlights Alsace's connection not only to France but also to neighboring countries like Switzerland and Germany, emphasizing its ties to the Germanic linguistic sphere.

This interview aims to observe how people perceive the Alsatian language written in public spaces. I observed various attitudes toward written Alsatian. Some people were observed to perceive Alsatian in public spaces as part of their history and culture. These remarks suggest they view the regional language as part of their Alsatian "heritage." One interviewee described it as the culture of Alsace "left behind" in Alsace. Although street names have a practical purpose and are used to help pedestrians understand directions, two individuals expressed doubts about this practicality. These statements might be influenced by the infrequency of encountering people who use Alsatian, especially in urban areas of Alsace. The facts that French and Alsatian are always written together, with French written above, and that there are no monolingual Alsatian speakers also likely leads to this perception. Regarding the relationship between the ability of Alsatian language proficiency and their perception, it is challenging to draw definite conclusions due to the small number of interviewees. However, it can be said that rather than whether they can use Alsatian, the environment in which they are exposed to Alsatian speakers influences how much value they place on Alsatian in public spaces.

Conclusion

This study investigates how the regional language of Alsace, Alsatian, sometimes considered a spoken language, appears as a written language in public spaces of Strasbourg. It aims to answer two questions: what are the similarities and differences between Alsatian and the way regional languages are written in other regions? What attitudes do people have toward the Alsatian language written in public spaces? In most cases, French is the most prominent language in Strasbourg's public spaces, similar to other cities in France. Alsatian is always visible as a toponym on street name signs in public spaces in Strasbourg. On the other hand, Alsatian is not found on other top-down signs, such as those indicating the direction of tourist areas and instructing caution. In bottom-up signs, Alsatian is rarely seen on other signs; the only exception is the Alsatian names of traditional dishes, such as *Flammekueche*. However, menus are not written in Alsatian. This example of LL can be understood as a tokenistic use of a regional language, as Van Mensel et al. (2012) reported.

The interviews shed light on the perception of bilingual street names in Alsace, offering a multifaced understanding of the significance of language in public space. Some participants expressed sentiments of pride and attachment to their regional identity, viewing bilingual street names as a means of honoring Alsace's unique heritage. While some younger interviewees expressed apathy towards Alsatian, others recognized its value in preserving regional identity and facilitating communication for Alsatian speakers. In addition, one interviewee highlighted the geopolitical background of Alsace and the trilingual road signs to reflect Alsace's historical ties to both France and Germany. This interview provides some insight into the way Alsace locals think about Alsatian as it is written in the public space. Their narratives suggest gradations, depending on the generation and the degree of contact with Alsatian in their daily lives.

Acknowledgements

This work was supported by Grant-in-Aid for Japan Society for the Promotion of Science (JSPS) Fellows (Grant Number JP23KJ0652).

References

English references

Backhaus, P. (2007) *Linguistic Landscapes: A Comparative Study of Urban Multilingualism in Tokyo*. Bristol: Multilingual Matters.
Ben-Rafael, E., Shohamy, E. and Barni, M. (2010) 'Introduction: An Approach to an "Ordered Disorder"'. In E. Shohamy, E. Ben-Rafael and M. Barni (Eds.), *Linguistic Landscape in the City* (pp. xi–xxviii). New York: Multilingual Matters.
Ben-Rafael, E., Shohamy, E., Hasan Amara, M. and Trumper-Hecht, N. (2006) 'Linguistic Landscape as Symbolic Construction of the Public Space: The Case of Israel'. *International Journal of Multilingualism*. 3(1): 7–30.

Blackwood, R. (2015) 'LL Explorations and Methodological Challenges: Analysing France's Regional Languages'. *Linguistic Landscape*. 1(1–2): 38–53.

Blackwood, R. and Tufi, S. (2012) 'Policies vs Non-Policies: Analysing Regional Languages and the National Standard in the Linguistic Landscape of French and Italian Mediterranean Cities'. In D. Gorter, H. F. Marten and L. Van Mensel (Eds.), *Minority Languages in the Linguistic Landscape. Palgrave Studies in Minority Languages and Communities* (pp. 109–126). London: Palgrave Macmillan.

Blackwood, R. J. (2011) 'The Linguistic Landscape of Brittany and Corsica: A Comparative Study of the Presence of France's Regional Languages in the Public Space'. *Journal of French Language Studies*. 21(2): 111–130.

Bogatto, F. and Hélot, C. (2010) 'Linguistic Landscape and Language Diversity in Strasbourg: The Quartier Gare'. In E. Shohamy, E. Ben-Rafael and M. Barni (Eds.), *Linguistic Landscape in the City* (pp. 275–291). Bristol: Multilingual Matters.

Cenoz, J. and Gorter, D. (2006) 'Linguistic Landscape and Minority Languages'. *International Journal of Multilingualism*. 3(1): 67–80.

Connor, J. E. (2019) '"The Langue d'Oc Is Bringing People Together": Debating the Place of Regional Languages in France'. *Journal of Linguistic Anthropology*. 29(2): 249–270.

Coupland, N. (2012) 'Bilingualism on Display: The Framing of Welsh and English in Welsh Public Spaces'. *Language in Society*. 41(1): 1–27.

France (2008) 'Constitution of October 4, 1958 (as Amended Up to the Constitutional Law No. 2008-724 of July 23, 2008, on the Modernization of the Institutions of the Fifth Republic)'. France.

Gardner-Chloros, P. (1991) *Language Selection and Switching*. Oxford: Clarendon Press.

Harrison, M. (2016) 'Alsatian versus Standard German: Regional Language Bilingual Primary Education in Alsace'. *Multilingua*. 35(3): 277–303.

Hélot, C. (2003) 'Language Policy and the Ideology of Bilingual Education in France'. *Language Policy*. 2: 255–277.

Hornsby, M. (2008) 'The Incongruence of the Breton Linguistic Landscape for Young Speakers of Breton'. *Journal of Multilingual and Multicultural Development*. 29(2): 127–138.

Kallen, J. L. (2009) 'Tourism and Representation in the Irish Linguistic Landscape'. In E. Shohamy and D. Gorter (Eds.), *Linguistic Landscape: Expanding the Scenery* (pp. 270–283). London: Routledge.

Kallen, J. L. (2023) *Linguistic Landscapes: A Sociolinguistic Approach*. Cambridge: Cambridge University Press.

Landry, R. and Bourhis, R. Y. (1997) 'Linguistic Landscape and Ethnolinguistic Vitality: An Empirical Study'. *Journal of Language and Social Psychology*. 6: 23–49.

Moriarty, M. (2012) 'Language Ideological Debates in the Linguistic Landscape of an Irish Town'. In D. Gorter, H. F. Marten and L. Van Mensel (Eds.), *Minority Languages in the Linguistic Landscape* (pp. 74–88). Basingstoke: Palgrave Macmillan.

Philipp, M. and Bothorel-Witz, A. (1990) 'Low Alemannic'. In C. V. J. Russ (Ed.), *The Dialects of Modern German: A Linguistic Survey*. London: Routledge.

Salo, H. (2012) 'Using Linguistic Landscape to Examine the Visibility of Sámi Languages in the North Calotte'. In D. Gorter, H. F. Marten and L. Van Mensel (Eds.), *Minority Languages in the Linguistic Landscape* (pp. 243–259). Basingstoke: Palgrave Macmillan.

UNESCO (2010) *UNESCO Project: Atlas of the World's Languages in Danger*. Paris, France: UNESCO Publishing.

Van Mensel, L. and Darquennes, J. (2012) 'All Is Quiet on the Eastern Front? Language Contact along the French-German Language Border in Belgium'. In D. Gorter, H. F. Marten and L. Van Mensel (Eds.), *Minority Languages in the Linguistic Landscape* (pp. 164–180). Basingstoke: Palgrave Macmillan.

Van Mensel, L., Marten, H. F. and Gorter, D. (2012) 'Minority Languages through the Lens of the Linguistic Landscape'. In D. Gorter, H. F. Marten and L. Van Mensel (Eds.), *Minority Languages in the Linguistic Landscape* (pp. 319–323). Basingstoke: Palgrave Macmillan.

Van Mensel, L., Vandenbroucke, M. and Blackwood, R. (2016) 'Linguistic Landscapes'. In O. Garcia, N. Flores and M. Spotti (Eds.), *Oxford Handbook of Language and Society* (pp. 423–449). Oxford: Oxford University Press.

Yndigegn, C. (2011) 'Between Debordering and Rebordering Europe: Cross – Border Cooperation in the Øresund Region or the Danish – Swedish Border Region'. *Eurasia Border Review*. 2(1): 47–59.

How is Alsatian written?

French references

De Certeau, M., Julia, D. and Revel, J. (1975) *Une Politique de La Langue. La Révolution Française et Les Patois* (A Politics of Language. The French Revolution and Patois). Paris: Gallimard.

Deyon, P. (1985) *Juin 1982–juin 1985. Le programme "Langue et culture régionales en Alsace"* (June 1982–June 1985. The "Regional Language and Culture in Alsace" Program). Bilan et perspectives. Strasbourg: Académie de Strasbourg.

Huck, D. (2015) *Une Histoire des Langues de L'Alsace* (A History of the Languages of Alsace). Strasbourg: La Nuée Bleue.

Huck, D., Bothorel-witz, A. and Geiger-Jaillet, A (2007) *L'Alsace et ses Langues. Eléments de description d'une situation sociolinguistique en zone frontalière* (Alsace and Its Languages. Elements of Description of a Sociolinguistic Situation in a Border Area) (pp. 1–73). Strasbourg: Université de Strasbourg.

INSEE, Barre, C. and Vanderschelden, M. (1999) *Insee – Population – L'enquête "Etude de l'histoire familiale" de 1999* (INSEE – Population – The 1999 "Family History Study" Survey). INSEE.

Keck, B. and Daul, L. (2016) *L'alsacien pour les Nuls* (Alsatian for Beginners). France Blue Alsace.

Office pour la langue et la culture d'Alsace (2012) *Étude sur le dialecte alsacien* (Study of the Alsatian Dialect). Office pour la langue et la culture d'Alsace.

Préfecture de la région Grand Est and Académie de Strasbourg (2018) *Convention opérationnelle portant sur la politique régionale plurilingue dans le systemème éducatif en Alsace Période 2018–2022* (Operational Agreement on the Regional Multilingual Policy in the Educational System in Alsace Period 2018–2022). Préfecture de la région Grand Est et Académie de Strasbourg.

Reutner, U. (2017) 'Alsace'. In U. Reutner (Ed.) *Manuel des francophonies* (Francophonies Manual) (pp. 131–148). Berlin and Boston: De Gruyter.

7

THE GLOBAL LANGUAGE – LATIN

Milena Minkova and Terence Tunberg

The chapter proposes to explore several aspects of the globality of Latin and from there its relevance to the modern global world. Latin is marked by time limits that extend far beyond the narrow time span with which it has been traditionally defined by Classics as a discipline. This traditional time span typically has a terminus set at the 2nd century CE, or in any case before the end of antiquity. It is also significant to note that this limited and limiting perception is changing as we are writing these lines. With the acceptance of an open time span comes open spatial understanding: Latin does not only pertain to the Mediterranean region or the territories of the Roman Empire but to our whole planet and in a certain way to real and imagined places beyond it. So the history of expression and communication in the Latin language is indeed a story of time and space mobility. Yet the language structure of Latin itself is remarkable for a kind of stability. Although Latin has always admitted new words (especially nouns) to indicate new concepts, for most of its history it has been based on canonical texts. As a result, the structure, syntax and morphology of Latin have changed relatively little over time compared to national languages. This stability constitutes the basis for intertextual communication without time and space limits. One final consideration is the growing contemporary interest in so-called 'living Latin' (which has its roots in a post–World War II movement aiming at establishing spoken Latin as means of promoting peace and understanding between peoples). Seen from these perspectives, Latin offers not only a common means for dialogue with people around the globe but also for conversing with those who have lived and written centuries ago and in whose writings we may indeed find insights that help us understand our modern problems.

The concept of Latin as a global language – beyond the traditional concept of Classics

We have a very different conception of Latin and the whole discipline named Classics (and rather ineptly so named) than many, or perhaps most Latinists, who see the study of Latin as something more or less limited to the study of the ancient world and its literature. The ancient Roman contribution to Latin is of course fundamental – but it is a mere beginning. Latin literature flourished in the Middle Ages, Renaissance, and early modern eras. The language of Caesar and Cicero performed new functions and came to be used in ways unimagined by the ancient Romans.

DOI: 10.4324/9781003439493-9

Latin in the early modern period became the vehicle for sciences as sophisticated as ballistics and hydrodynamics. Latin exclusively provided the academic and philosophical vocabulary for the expression of Europe's most refined thoughts. The scholarly and scientific works in Latin pertain, among other things, to encyclopedias, typography, philology, law, theology, philosophy, political, economic, and social sciences, arts, medicine, mathematics, engineering, astronomy, astrology, physics, alchemy, chemistry, anthropology, sports, paleontology, geology, language, style, texts, and editions (IJsewijn with Sacré 1998). Latin was the language in which fundamental concepts, such as gravity and the heliocentric solar system, received their first explicit expression. Latin, along with some revived terms from ancient Greek, supplied the language of botany and zoology. Latin was the international language of cartography, geography, history, and ethnography, the sciences through which the discoveries of Renaissance explorers gradually began to erode the entirely Eurocentric mindset which had previously been typical of western intellectuals. Latin, and not any of the nascent national tongues, was the primary linguistic vehicle for all of this before about 1750 CE. But medieval and Renaissance Latin was not merely the language of scholars, scientists, and philosophers; it also produced an astoundingly rich creative literature – including works widely recognized as masterpieces, ranging from the stories of the Venerable Bede and the *Carmina Burana* to Thomas More's *Utopia* and Erasmus' *Praise of Folly*. Just to mention some of the most important genres of the period – we find, among other types of writing, heroic, descriptive, bucolic, lyrical, epigrammatic poetry, satires, hymns, psalms, fables, dramas, declamations, orations, historiography, biography and autobiography, literary letters, dialogues, travel journals, and fictional prose. Even as the language of creative literature, Latin still rivalled the national languages in the Renaissance (Moss 1994).

Latin in the span of temporal perpetuity

One of the important aspects of the globality of the Latin language, therefore, is its uninterrupted existence through millennia (Minkova 2022, 223–225). In our Latin instruction we strive to take account of this. A usual mental exercise for the Classics students at the University of Kentucky is to ask them to visualize, in practical terms, the space needed for fitting paper copies of the works of all ancient authors of Latin – this would be just a wall of library shelves, admittedly fuller if Christian authors of the late antiquity are included. Then the students are invited to conjecture what space would contain everything written in Latin afterwards – during the Middle Ages, Renaissance, early modern, and modern periods. Nobody actually knows the answer, and no catalog has been done or is possible. However, given the tremendous range of Latin writings, especially during the Neo-Latin period (from Petrarch up to our times), it may very well be that several buildings, or more, should be needed. Jürgen Leonhardt asserts that of all writings that have come down to us, those belonging to ancient Rome (inscriptions included) constitute at most 0.01% of all Latin heritage – and about 80% of this minuscule percentage consists of Christian texts (Leonhardt 2013, 2). So it would be absurd to exclude 99% of the Latin patrimony and conceive Latin only as belonging to ancient Rome. It makes sense to embrace Latin in its chronological perpetuity. It is a fact that there has never been any time, from the period of Plautus (3rd–2nd century BCE) to the present day, when there were not at least some people expressing themselves in Latin. So, in a real sense, this mode of expression has continued without interruption to our own time – even if in some periods it has been rather tenuous and limited.

A significant development in this continuum seems to have taken shape from the 6th to the 9th centuries CE: Latin, at least as we know it from written texts, gradually ceased to be the native speech of any people or nation (Wright 1996). Yet the knowledge and use of Latin was retained, partly through the demands of liturgy and religious usage and partly because most of the Germanic peoples, who settled in the regions that once belonged to the western Roman empire, lacked cultures based on writing. So Latin continued to be employed for public documents. Latin maintained its role as the primary language by which the liberal arts and sciences were communicated throughout the Middle Ages and Renaissance. Latin was the language of teaching and disputation in the schools and universities founded during the medieval centuries. Throughout this immensely long period of time, the literate and educated in Europe were, of course, always a small percentage of the total population. But for virtually all of the educated class, Latin was an absolute necessity, and for nearly all of them Latin had to be learned in schools. Their goal was not merely to be able to read the works of Latin authors, the Latin sources of the liberal arts and theology, but also to be able to use Latin themselves as a language of communication in both writing and speaking. But, although people typically learned Latin in the Middle Ages and Renaissance in order to use it, and although new Latin words were coined for new entities, the syntactical and idiomatic norms for expression in Latin were no longer evolving in the same way they were evolving in French, German, and other vernacular tongues. The norms of Latin (not always observed, of course, with perfect consistency) were fixed in texts. For the Middle Ages, the normative texts were the Scriptures and Church Fathers. Since the Renaissance, the standard for prose was found in the works of Caesar, Cicero, Livy, and others of their contemporaries or in works of later Latin writers (including Neo-Latin authors) who followed the usage of these classics.

Wilfried Stroh, a distinguished classical scholar and well-known proponent of communicative Latin, puts the concept of *mors immortalis* ('immortal death') in the center of his history of Latin (Stroh 2007). According to Stroh, in the 1st century CE, Latin was petrified in the form it existed, and in this sense it died. However, since then Latin was reborn several times: in the works of the Christian authors of the late antiquity, in the Carolingian renaissance during the 9th century, and especially during the Renaissance of the 14th–16th centuries. In the early Renaissance, the Italian humanists regarded Cicero, the famous Roman orator and statesman, who had flourished in the last century before the Common Era, not only as a model of language purity but also of civic virtue. The pure modes of expression employed by some of Cicero's contemporaries and immediate successors, such as Caesar and Livy, were also considered essential models for Latin prose. In the widely diffused, often-printed *Elegantiae* ('On the Correct Usage of Latin') by the famous humanist Lorenzo Valla (a work actually written shortly before the invention of printing in the mid-15th century), the exemplary classical Latin prose writers were identified as the Roman authors who had flourished in the 150-year period from Cicero's life to the time of Quintilian (whose authoritative textbook on the art of rhetoric was composed in the latter part of the 1st century CE). The phrases, constructions, and idioms that came from a variety of writers who flourished in this period were considered *probatae Latinitatis* (exemplary Latin). By combining these canonical elements in different ways, each modern writer would stay within the norms of pure Latin while expressing one's own individuality in the actual combination of classical elements. This concept of 'modern' Latin was preferred by the illustrious humanist and philologist Poliziano (1454–1494) over the point of view of the strictly Ciceronian humanists, who wanted to imitate only one classical model – Cicero. Poliziano did not oppose the imitation of Cicero but proposed a more viable (in the eyes of many humanist writers of Latin like Erasmus) eclectic model for the use of a non-vernacular language. Poliziano urged the student of Latin eloquence to study deeply the works of Cicero and other classical Latin authors, and when their words and language structure had been thoroughly assimilated, only then to begin swimming without any aid to flotation, that is – only then to begin composing on one's own (DellaNeva 2007, 4).

The global language – Latin

This puristic attitude toward Latin on the part of the humanists of the Renaissance (whether they were Ciceronian or eclectic) must be appreciated in a cultural context. In the universities of the later Middle Ages, from the 13th century onward, the academic Latin, typically known as 'scholastic Latin', especially in the fields of theology, law, and dialectic and speculative grammar, began to evolve into a highly specialized technical jargon, whose vocabulary and construction diverged sharply even from the usage of Christian and scriptural Latin. The humanists abhorred this Latinity as an aberration (IJsewijn 1990, 22–53). Many agreed with Lorenzo Valla that the scholastic Latin presented the intellectual world with the danger that the international language, whose norms were understandable to all because they were based everywhere on the same canonical texts, would now evolve into specialized 'dialects' of Latin. Classical Latin, pointed out Valla in his *Elegantiae*, had a big advantage over Classical Greek in that it had never been divided into dialects. So, the humanists' response to the Latin of the scholastics, actualized through educational institutions and the publication of new writings, was to propagate a Latin based much more closely on the structural norms of Classical Latin.

Speaking very generally, this Renaissance classicization of Latin was amazingly successful. Of course, we can find exceptions. In the field of canon law, for example, a kind of scholastic Latin descended from medieval usage has persisted right down to the present. A few Latin works published in the early modern period exhibit obvious influence from a vernacular language, such as Peter Martyr's early 16th-century *De orbe novo decades* ('Decades of the New World'). There are some deliberately and humorously macaronic or hybrid texts, such as the *Epistulae obscurorum virorum* ('Letters of Obscure Men'), also published in the early 16th century. And we must always make allowances for new (or medieval) nouns and adjectives to express post-antique entities or instruments (an approach to word-choice sanctioned by most major humanists). Nevertheless, it will be clear to anyone who has read somewhat extensively in the vast ocean of Latin produced after 1500 that most early modern and modern Latin prose written from the 16th century onwards typically follows the classicizing structure, expression, and syntax advocated by the great teachers like Valla, Poliziano, and Erasmus. Even in the philosophical Latin of Spinoza and Descartes, although it retains nouns and adjectives devised by medieval scholastic philosophers to express logical or abstract concepts, the syntax and structure of sentences usually follow the classical norms mentioned previously. So it is hardly surprising that the rules and instructions in most modern textbooks of Latin prose composition reflect the approach and precepts of Valla or the moderate Ciceronians – and never the usage of ecclesiastical or medieval Latin.

Jozef IJsewijn (IJsewijn 1990) rightly asserts that Latin was no more 'living' in the Middle Ages than in the humanist period. In both periods it was a 'dead language' (i.e., no-one's native speech) but used by the groups of society educated in literature and employed in the arts and sciences or the Church. The main difference between the two periods, as far as Latin was concerned, was the approach to the sources upon which usage of the language of the learned should be based. Indeed, IJsewijn and others have suggested with good reason that the classicizing norms introduced originally by the humanists helped to ensure Latin's continuing (and, for some periods, flourishing) use for centuries to come. The norms for literary Latin became much more uniform for authors educated in widely different regions; the influence of local vernaculars became less conspicuous in most literary texts; academic Latin became somewhat more consistent across various disciplines; the teaching of elementary Latin in nearly all parts of Europe was gradually distilled into principles based on the grammatical norms discernable in Cicero and Caesar, which could be learned without extreme difficulty by a motivated student (D'Amico 1984); and from the Renaissance to the present there has been a tendency to simplify and to standardize the norms for pronunciation (Tunberg 2022).

The humanists felt a close contact and an uninterrupted connection with the ancient Latin heritage. Petrarch, the earliest humanist and both Latin and Italian writer, actually wrote letters to Cicero and other ancient authors and felt free to address them. Petrarch conceived a continuity between them and his own times, looking at the time in the middle and defining it as the Middle Ages. Lorenzo Valla, whose contribution (in his *Elegantiae*) to the restoration of the Latin language and its former shape is perhaps the greatest, uses first person plural when he talks about the ancient Romans and his contemporaries – Valla's 'we' seems to include people from both epochs belonging to the same cultural continuum. A few of the so-called Ciceronians went too far by admitting in their expression only words and constructions used by Cicero and shunning any other, albeit classical, authors. This was an extreme position, which faced pushback from scholars like Erasmus of Rotterdam (1466–1536), who wrote a satirical dialogue named *Ciceronianus* ('The Ciceronian') in which he described the pains and ridiculous predicament of a person so truly devoted to Ciceronianism that he could not write a simple note in Latin to his friends or utter a sentence in Latin for fear that he might commit a mistake. Fortunately for the continuation of Latin, this extreme tendency remained extreme and never became a norm.

Actually, Erasmus of Rotterdam, who lived long after the era of the western Roman empire but was a versatile Latin author of no less stature than any of the ancient Romans, is a shining example of this rebirth. Erasmus was Dutch, but we would not be wrong if we say that Erasmus was Latin and a true citizen of the Republic of letters. Erasmus did not live in one place but traveled widely throughout Europe and communicated with different humanists in different countries in no other language than Latin. Perhaps the most famous is the friendship that Erasmus had with Thomas More during Erasmus's sojourn in England – their communication was entirely in Latin. Erasmus did indeed use Latin as his own language. Erasmus' Latin is rich, classical, various, and authentic. It owes much to the writings of Cicero but also to many other classical authors, as well as to the Christian authors of the late antiquity. Erasmus is a giant to be equaled only with Cicero. In fact, Erasmus' corpus of writings is much more extensive than that of Cicero (something that might be said of the Latin literary production of quite a few humanists). Erasmus edited and wrote a commentary on the New Testament, and he published a large range of declamations, among which is the masterpiece entitled *Praise of Folly*; many works on moral philosophy and education; and a number of scholastic dialogues used to familiarize the students with the use of Latin language but which also touch on important issues for humanity and are relevant even today. Erasmus published a huge collection of several thousand proverbs related to the entire Latin and Greek patrimony, a book on synonyms and variety of expression, and a very big collection of letters. Latin in the 15th, 16th, and 17th centuries – and in even later periods – was not at all less real Latin than the Latin of the Romans. Many of these works, especially those produced the 18th century and even later, remain unexplored – in fact, it could be said that the Latin heritage of that period still remains a vast and unknown continent.

Geographical limits/unlimitedness of Latin

If we consider Latin in its temporal continuity from antiquity to modern times, its spatial understanding will also be much wider than in the concept of Latin as a language whose meaningful existence stopped in the 2nd century CE. As we saw in the section about the temporal perpetuity of Latin, the texts written in Latin in the post-antique period significantly surpass the quantity of texts created during ancient times; there is also significant expansion of themes and ideas. Once we accept the chronological universality of Latin, its spatial understanding becomes drastically wider.

The global language – Latin

The experience of Europeans and their horizons widened dramatically after 1500, as they were exposed to new lands and cultures, which had been unheard of before that date. New perspectives arising from contact with the peoples and cultures of Asia, Africa, and the Americas permeate the huge body of Latin produced after 1500. Not only did Europeans write in Latin about these peoples and cultures, but we even find some authors originating from these very peoples and cultures, which had recently been made known to Europeans, employing Latin themselves as the vehicle to express their points of view.

Latin was the language of choice for Juan Latino, the sub-Saharan–born Black poet, son of slaves, and Latin professor at the University of Granada, who composed a short epic poem *Austrias carmen* ('The Song of John') about the victory of the Holy League of Catholic states under the leadership of Don Juan of Austria over the Ottoman army at Lepanto in 1571. In a prefatory elegy to the epic, Juan Latino states that because of the use of Latin language, he is indeed Latin.

The geographical fluidity in the creation of Latin works is visible in the poem of the Guatemalan Jesuit Rafael Landívar *Rusticatio Mexicana* ('Mexican Country Life') that could be defined as a descriptive epic. Landívar, born in Guatemala, had to emigrate to Italy when the Company of Jesus was expelled from the Americas in 1767. Suffering from homesickness, exacerbated by the fact that a strong earthquake shattered Guatemala City in the meantime, Landívar uses the Latin language to return to his native land, as well as to resurrect it from the ruins. With exquisite Latinity, full of love and nostalgia, Landívar describes the floating gardens, a miracle of the region, the volcanos, the animals, the plants, the minerals, the production of indigo and sugar, even the local games. For Landivar, whose linguistic proclivities were undoubtedly influenced by his Jesuit background, Latin was the chosen language to cross imposed boundaries and to allow for travel when physical travel was not possible, as well as to reconstruct his motherland.

Works written in Latin literally circumnavigate the globe through their themes and the fate of their authors. Let us take as an example the Italian Jesuit Giovanni Pietro Maffei (1536–1603). After having spent some time doing research in the Portuguese archives, Maffei wrote a monumental sixteen-book Latin history of the Portuguese exploration and expansion around the world called *Historiae Indicae* ('History of the Indies'). The work, which was composed in Latin not merely because Maffei was a Jesuit but also so that it would reach an international audience and cross linguistic boundaries, engages with South America; touches on Africa; and extensively discusses Asia, especially India, China, and Japan. Although Maffei is European, it is to be noted that he shows true appreciation of the achievements of other populations. For example, when talking about China in Book Six, Maffei repeatedly praises different aspects of the organization of the Chinese society: not only the fertile land but the hard work and industriousness of the Chinese people that allow for excellent agriculture; the incredible beauty of the Chinese cities; and the technical skill with which the Chinese have built roads in most difficult places, a feat to be compared with the engineering mastery of the ancient Romans. It is also curious that Maffeius makes the first mention in the western literature of one of most widespread beverages in the world, known today as tea. Such works are invaluable sources about the contacts between populations and cultures.

In a very different cultural milieu writes the Flemish humanist and an ambassador of the Holy Roman Empire in the Ottoman Empire, Oghier Ghiselin de Busbecq (1522–1592). In four very long *Epistolae Turcicae* ('Turkish Letters') directed to a fellow diplomat and written in a beautiful Latin, he tells about his experiences in Constantinople and beyond. Busbecq, a passionate researcher of the Greco-Roman past, is certainly at odds with the total lack of appreciation of the classical heritage on the part of the Turks. Yet he leads the reader through a completely different, un-European world without using any intemperate language about the Turks and the Ottoman empire threatening the European order but rather expressing his admiration for the efficiency in the organization of the Turkish society.

Latin not only traverses the globe, but it also travels vertically in the universe. The German mathematician, astronomer, and optician Johannes Kepler, in his *Somnium* ('Dream'), published in 1643, which is both a science fiction novel and a scientific treatise on lunar astronomy, in a multi-layered narrative describes a journey from Iceland to the moon. The work was carefully conceived throughout Kepler's life, and its purpose is to provide a glimpse of Earth from the perspective of the lunar surface in support of the heliocentric theory.

Once the travels throughout the world and beyond had started, it was only the next step to set out to imaginary worlds, to seek better places. The most famous of these writings documenting the journey of the mind is *Utopia*, first published by the English statesman Thomas More in 1516. It cannot be stressed too strongly that *Utopia* is a work entirely in Latin, and in manifold and subtle ways it is deeply connected to the whole tradition of writing in Latin and to the Latinate culture of the humanists, who were More's contemporaries. Its allusions and puns cannot be appreciated without recourse to the Latin and ancient Greek languages. Literally a 'No-place' (the very title itself is a Neo-Greek pun), it provides a picture of a communal society without private property that even today evokes consideration without a final determination whether such society is to be sought after or avoided.

An anagram of Utopia is Potu, an imaginary land inhabited by highly intelligent trees described in the 18th-century *Nicolai Klimii iter subterraneum* ('Subterranean Journey of Nicolaus Klimius'). It is a testament to the globality of the Latin literature that the author Ludvig Holberg is considered the father of Danish literature. The novel leads not only to fantastic lands but also to a new form of intelligent life devoid of the limitations of humankind.

Latin as a mechanism for global communication and exchange

Toward the end of the 17th century, Latin began to lose its position as universal language and an undisputed means of communication in the fields of education, scholarship, church and diplomacy (IJsewijn 1990, 41–49; Fransen 2017). A new cultural reality evolved, in which the ability to produce written texts in Latin for an international learned elite became steadily less necessary. With the strengthening of the national identities, the national tongues gained a more prominent position – this was facilitated by the rising bourgeois classes associating themselves with the respective national tongues, the trend toward secularism, especially after the French Revolution, and the challenge the Reformation posed for the leadership of the Catholic Church. Nevertheless, treatises in the fields of mathematics, physics, and in humanistic subjects still continued to be written in Latin. Latin has never ceased to be the official language of the Roman Catholic Church. Latin has continued to supply essential elements in the terminology of botany and zoology. The use of conversational Latin still persisted in the classroom and in some scholarly exchange – there are plenty of sources documenting this (Minkova 2014). This use of Latin as a spoken language continued in many German gymnasia and in some Dutch schools during the 19th century (Van Bommel 2013). Latin was typically the language of teaching in seminaries of the Catholic Church until the time of the second Vatican Council in the 1960s. The survival of Latin is seen by some as the language fully realized and spoken in small scholarly groups (Leonhardt 2013, 289). There have also been periods of great revival and undertaking with regard to the global fate of Latin. Several times, the idea of Latin as an international language has been advanced (Stroh 2007, 293–294). In the beginning of the 19th century, the Spanish priest Miguel Maria Olmo published a booklet *De lingua Latina et de civitate Latina fundanda* ('About the Latin Language and the Establishing of Latin

The global language – Latin

Community of Citizens'), in which he proposed to create an entirely Latin community and laid out plans about the establishment of Latin as an international language (Olmo 1816).

But not until the years following the destruction and the divisions of World War II did a real movement for the promotion of Latin as a global language gain strength. The soul of this movement was Jean Capelle, rector of the University of Nancy in France and professor of electrical and mechanical engineering. A work of his that was published in English in the mid-50s of the last century begins with words that are strikingly valid for the present day. Capelle writes about the need for international peace, the inevitability of economic and social connections on a world scale, and borders being rendered obsolete as a result of technological progress (Capelle 1953, 37). Capelle advocated for the role of Latin as a sole possible international language, as a significant factor of progress, of fraternity, and of peace (Capelle 1953, 40). It is significant that a person outside the discipline of Classics – perhaps with a wider perspective than the classicists – proposed this mission for Latin: Latin as a mechanism to promote peace and understanding. It is also important that Capelle did not limit himself to mentioning the so-called classical authors but also referred to such pillars of human knowledge and progress as Kepler, Descartes, Newton, Leibnitz, Bernoulli, and Euler. Due to the Capelle's efforts, the First International Congress of Living Latin was celebrated in 1956 in Avignon. Delegates from 22 countries attended, including New Zealand, South Africa, Turkey, Romania, Syria, Finland, and Venezuela (Beach 1957, 120). These comprise various geographical areas, socio-economic and political systems, and cultural backgrounds. The congress made a resolution to use restored classical norms in pronunciation of Latin with more uniformity and recommended creating lexica of modern terms. More importantly, though, it ignited the sparks for further initiatives in which Latin, as a living language with a tradition that spans the centuries from antiquity to modern times and extends around the globe, unites people and provides them with opportunities to conduct a dialogue both with this tradition and among themselves.

In 1967, *Academia Latinitati Fovendae*, an international learned society for the promotion of Latin, was founded in Rome. A congress was celebrated in 1970 in Romania behind the Iron Curtain and in 1977 in Senegal in Africa. Latin as an instrument of both written and oral scholarly communication was to be promoted truly globally. The following decades (now more than a half century) saw a wide range of initiatives ranging from the active use of Latin as a didactic tool to its use as a living global language sometimes expected to revive the fundamentals of humanity (Coffee 2012).

After limiting the universal role of Latin in the Catholic Church liturgy and education upon the Second Vatican Council in 1962, the same year Pope John XXIII promulgated the Apostolic Constitution *Veterum Sapientia* (on the promotion of the study of Latin). Two years later Pope Paul VI with Motu Proprio *Studia Latinitatis* founded the *Pontificium Institutum Altioris Latinitatis* within the Pontifical Salesian University in Rome (Motu Proprio *Studia Latinitatis* 1964). The Institute, although largely in the ecclesiastic realm, attracts students from around the world – some of its classes are conducted in Latin, and dissertations can also be written in Latin.

Circuli Latini, informal groups of Latin speakers, were formed in different European locations, and at the same time journals and full-immersion Latin seminars were founded. Caelestis Eichenseer O.S.B. started spoken Latin seminars in Germany in 1973 – he had already inaugurated the publication of the Latin journal *Vox Latina* in 1965. The radiologist and fervent proponent of Latin as an all-European language (again, it seems that non-classicists may have a much wider perspective on the fate of Latin) Guy Licoppe began publishing the Latin periodical *Melissa* in Belgium in 1984 and organizing all-Latin classes. In the north, the Finnish Latinist and Jyväskylä professor Tuomo Pekkanen broadcasted news in Latin on the Finnish radio starting 1989 for thirty years. Reginald Foster O.C.D. conducted in Rome for decades, *sub arboribus* (under the

115

trees), classes both in Latin and in English that were highly formative for the students. The Italian teacher and scholar Luigi Miraglia first near Naples, then in Rome, finally in Frascati, not far from Cicero's villa in Tusculum, scene of the greatest Ciceronian philosophical work, established the full-immersion school *Academia Vivarium novum* with lofty humanistic goals.

One of the authors of this chapter, the University of Kentucky professor Terence Tunberg, after participating European full-immersion Latin seminars, decided to inaugurate a similar venue in North America. Thus, the first all-inclusive and all-Latin seminar in the western hemisphere, *Conventiculum Lexintoniense*, was founded in 1996 in Lexington, Kentucky (Minkova and Tunberg 2012). Five years after that, because of the interest in a similar venture during the academic year, the graduate certificate curriculum in Latin studies was established at the University of Kentucky, and it has been thriving for more than 20 years. This curriculum is devoted to the study of the entire Latin patrimony in its continuity from antiquity until modern times and provides full immersion into the language it studies (Minkova and Tunberg 2006). It has attracted students from six continents and currently is being offered both in person and online in order to accommodate those who want to be part of it but cannot translocate to Kentucky. However, the repercussions of the Lexington seminar went far beyond the University of Kentucky. Many of the numerous participants (some years there were up to 80 participants) went on and founded their own seminars. This led to the thriving of active Latin in North America. If we compare the attitudes toward active Latin in 1996 and in 2024, there appear to be significant differences. In 1996, cultivating Latin as a living language was considered a matter for lunatics, while in 2024 active Latin is everywhere and very much in vogue, especially on the high school level.

'Oral Latin', as it is often called, is a frequent topic on listservs for Latin teachers. It has often been the subject of special sessions and mini workshops at conferences for teachers and professors, including the annual American Classical League Institute and the Annual Meeting of the Society for Classical Studies (previously American Philological Association). The *Standards for Classical Language Learning* developed by a joint committee sponsored by the Society for Classical Studies and the American Classical League and completed in 1997 may perhaps be taken as sort of national statement for the United States classical studies community about the teaching of Latin and Greek. Apparent in this statement of standards is the effect of the interest in active Latin that was already beginning to manifest itself in North America by the end of the 1990s. The document unambiguously recommends that students of the classical languages learn to 'use orally, listen to, and write Latin or Greek as part of the language learning process' (*Standards*, accessed March 8, 2024). There is also a steadily growing interest in the study of Latin as global literature that means including Neo-Latin studies, truly multicultural and interdisciplinary in their essence and thus related meaningfully to our present concerns, in the discipline of Classics.

Dialogicality

Several influential teachers of Latin have emphasized that the primary utility of teaching Latin as a communicative language is a pedagogical one and that this utility is especially focused on the beginning stages of learning Latin, especially with younger learners (Wills 1998; Gruber-Miller 2006). Such educators argue that using Latin communicatively with students from the start allows them to de-emphasize formal descriptive grammar almost entirely, or to a very large degree. Not unreasonably, they insist that Latin can be effectively taught through natural immersion, with very little explanation or description of linguistic features. The process of learning Latin, according to this view, should be much like the way a child learns the native tongue or, failing that, at least like the way one might pick up a lot of conversational usage in another language by simply living in

The global language – Latin

a foreign country for a number of years. They argue further that treating Latin as a conversational medium with students from the start allows Latin teachers to make use of all the newest methods and approaches that are being developed in the field of second language acquisition.

We will be the first to agree that second language acquisition theory might have a lot to offer Latin teachers, especially those who teach younger children, especially in the very beginning stages of learning Latin. But most second language acquisition theory known to us is aimed at languages that are still in a fluid state of syntactical development, whose norms are the standards of current native speakers and change a bit each generation and are not entirely drawn from a series of canonical and perennial texts. They are also aimed at students whose goal (at least in the short term) is not to read, let alone to appreciate in a meaningful way, complicated and sophisticated literature in the language being learned. Latin is indeed a bit different. We as Latinists need to recognize these differences. The norms of 'correct' (i.e. canonical) expression in Latin are not evolving in the same way they do in the vernacular languages but are defined in texts. Latin teachers, moreover, typically focus more exclusively and universally on the reading and understanding of literary texts and do so earlier in the learning process than do their colleagues who teach the national languages. This focus on canonical texts (either pagan or Christian) has, as we have pointed out, been a constant factor in the use of Latin since antiquity. A teacher of French or Spanish, for example, has achieved something if their student can go to a country where the language is used and communicate with the locals – even if no one would mistake the visitor for a native speaker. But this level of proficiency – or its equivalent, if we could find one – is ephemeral for the Latin student. There is no country where the native language is Latin. The primary goal for teachers and students of Latin is the literary language and a better knowledge of our intellectual heritage. Even if one prefers to lead students to reading unadulterated literary texts gradually, we would argue that these texts and the linguistic and cultural knowledge connected with them must remain among the primary reasons for the study of Latin. So, we readily acknowledge the potential utility of second language acquisition theory for beginning learners of Latin, but we must adapt this theory to the special needs of Latin. Certain approaches and techniques, therefore, which are not so prominent any more in national language pedagogy, including a more pronounced focus on grammar and a preoccupation with reading literary texts, have evolved for good reasons in the teaching of Latin (and Greek) and can remain prominent without necessarily conflicting with a communicative approach.

Moreover, if the only utility for communicative Latin (read, write, listen, speak) consisted of a better way to teach the fundamental vocabulary and structures of the language, then someone might argue that after the learners have reached this basic acquisition, the need for communicative Latin diminishes and nothing would really be lost if an instructor simply abandoned the communicative focus once the students begin to study unadapted literature. But, for us, the important progression is nearly the opposite. We agree that a communicative approach (which may or may not involve total immersion) can be valuable from the very beginning of Latin learning, but we insist that the real power of using Latin as the meta-language shows itself at a more advanced stage, when students are confronting continuous unadulterated text, communicating with the author in the author's language and discussing with each other the author's work in the author's language. Our focus on communicative Latin is part of a wider conception of Latin and not merely aimed at beginning language pedagogy. In fact, our interest in communicative Latin is not just a matter of pedagogy in the strict sense: for us it is a way to create a more intimate and instinctive relationship with the language itself and its literature. The conventions providing for a stable and universally understandable use of this language for a virtually unlimited extent of time and space have been established and in place since the Renaissance.

Looking forward

Among students and teachers of Latin, therefore, as we have pointed out at several points in our discussion, interest in using Latin communicatively in speaking and writing as a complement to the study and understanding of Latin literary texts has seen a significant revival in the last two decades. Clearly this interest is in part connected to new understanding of language acquisition and new ideas about the effectiveness of communicative language pedagogy (Avitus 2018; Patrick 2015), but it is also to be linked to a wider appreciation among Latinists for the fact that Latin continued to be an actively used language for a millennium and a half after it ceased to be the native tongue of any particular group of people. But we will almost certainly never return to the situation of the Middle Ages or of the 16th and 17th centuries when Latin was the international language of the scientific and learned world in the west and areas affected by the west. Yet such a goal need not be part of the agenda for Latinists. Latin will not be prevented from becoming an 'endangered' language simply by expanding and widening the community of users of Latin. The secure survival of Latin will depend on maintaining and strengthening its role as an essential discipline in the study of humanities, culture, and literature. And the same is probably true of other 'classical' languages, such as Sanskrit, whose usage continued to flourish, even across cultural/linguistic boundaries, long after the cadre of 'native speakers' faded away.

References

Avitus, A. G. (2018). 'Spoken Latin: Learning, Teaching, Lecturing and Research'. *Journal of Classics Teaching*. 19.37: 46–52.

Beach, G. B. (1957). 'The Congress for Living Latin: Another View'. *The Classical Journal*. 53.3: 119–122.

Capelle, J. (1952). 'Le latin ou Babel'. *L'education nationale*. 23 Oct.: 7–8; and its English translation: Capelle, J., transl. by Th. H. Quigley. (1953). 'Latin or Babel'. *The Classical Journal*. 49.1: 37–40.

Coffee, N. (2012). 'Active Latin: *Quo tendimus*'. *Classical World*. 105.2: 255–269.

D'Amico, J. (1984). 'The Progress of Renaissance Latin Prose'. *Renaissance Quarterly*. 37.3: 1–32.

DellaNeva, J. (Ed.), transl. by B. Duvick. (2007). *Ciceronian Controversies*. The I Tatti Renaissance Library, 26. Cambridge, MA: Harvard Press.

Fransen, S. (2017). 'Latin in a Time of Change: The Choice of Language as Signifier of a New Science?'. *Isis*. 108.3: 629–635.

Gruber-Miller, J. (Ed.). (2006). *When Dead Tongues Speak. Teaching Beginning Greek and Latin*. American Philological Association Classical Resources Series 6. Oxford: Oxford University Press.

IJsewijn, J. (1990). *Companion to Neo-Latin Studies*, Part I. Leuven: Leuven University Press, Peeters Press.

IJsewijn, J. with D. Sacré. (1998). *Companion to Neo-Latin Studies*, Part II. Leuven: Leuven University Press.

Leonhardt, J. (2009). *Latein. Geschichte einer Weltsprache*. München: C.H. Beck; with revised English edition: Leonhardt, J., transl. by K. Kronenberg. (2013). *Latin: Story of a World Language*. Cambridge, MA-London: The Belknap Press of Harvard University Press.

Minkova, M. (2014). 'Conversational Latin: 1650 to Present'. In P. Ford, J. Bloemendal, and C. Fantazzi (Edd.). *Brill's Encyclopaedia of the Neo-Latin World*, Macropaedia (pp. 83–86). Leiden-Boston: Brill.

Minkova, M. (2022). 'Various Dimensions of the Universality of the Latin Language'. In C. Rico and J. Pedicone (Edd.). *Transmitting a Heritage: The Teaching of Ancient Languages from Antiquity to the 21st Century* (pp. 223–232). Jerusalem: Polis Institute Press.

Minkova, M. and T. Tunberg. (2006). 'De Kentukiano instituto studiis Latinis provehendis': Pars I, T. Tunberg, 'De Instituti ortu et ratione', Pars II, M. Minkova 'De methodis didascalicis quae in Kentukiano instituto studiis Latinis provehendis adhibentur'. In A. C. García et M. D. A. Saiz (Edd.). *Acta selecta decimi Conventus Academiae Latinitati Fovendae (Matriti, 2–7 Septembris 2002)* (pp. 283–289). Romae: Academia Latinitati Fovendae – Matriti: Instituto de Estudios Humanísticos de Alcañiz.

Minkova, M. and T. Tunberg. (2012). 'Active Latin: Speaking, Writing, Hearing the Language'. *New England Classical Journal*. 32.2: 113–128.

Moss, A. (1994). 'Being in Two Minds: The Bilingual Factor in Renaissance Writing'. In R. Schnur (Ed.). *Proceedings of the Eighth International Congress of Neo-Latin Studies, Copenhagen, 12 August to 17 August 1991* (pp. 61–74). Binghamton: State University of New York Press.

'Motu Proprio *Studia Latinitatis*'. (1964). *Acta Apostolicae Sedis*. Annus LVI, ser. III, v. VI: 225–231.

Olmo, M. M. (1816). *De lingua Latina colenda et de civitate Latina fundanda liber singularis. Accedit epistola auctoris ad Barberium Vemars, cum responsione Barberii.* Toulouse: Douladoure.

Patrick, R. (2015). 'Making Sense of Comprehensible Input in the Latin Classroom'. *Teaching Classical Languages*. Spring: 108–131.

Standards for Classical Language Learning (North America): http://department.monm.edu/classics/cpl/standards.pdf (accessed March 8, 2024).

Stroh, W. (2007). *Latein ist tot, es lebe Latein! Kleine Geschichte einer grossen Sprache*. Berlin: List.

Tunberg, T. (2022). 'Observations on the Spoken and Extempore Use of Latin in the Late Medieval and Early Modern Period'. In C. Rico and J. Pedicone (Edd.). *Transmitting a Heritage: The Teaching of Ancient Languages from Antiquity to the 21st Century* (pp. 57–72). Jerusalem: Polis Institute Press.

Van Bommel, S. P. (2013). *Classical Humanism and the Challenge of Modernity. Debates on classical education in Germany c. 1770–1860.* Utrecht University: PhD dissertation.

Wills, J. (1998). 'Speaking Latin in Schools and Colleges'. *Classical World*. 92: 27–34.

Wright, R. (Ed.). (1996). *Latin and the Romance Languages in the Early Middle Ages*. University Park, PA: The Pennsylvania State University Press.

SECTION II

Technology, media, and revitalization

8

THE ROLE OF LANGUAGE ATTITUDES AND IDEOLOGIES IN MINORITY LANGUAGE LEARNING AND LANGUAGE REVITALISATION

Perspectives of Polish migrants learning Welsh

Karolina Rosiak

Introduction

The present chapter addresses the importance of considering the role language attitudes and ideologies play in adult migrants learning a minority language of their host communities. Encouraging minority language learning is viewed as an essential component of the broader language revitalisation and maintenance strategies. The mobility within contemporary societies demands proficiency in English, as skills in it are considered essential for international communication and employment opportunities, and also in other major world languages. For years, second language acquisition research has predominantly concentrated on English and other 'big' (state) languages, such as Spanish or Chinese. However, in linguistically diverse regions worldwide, the significance of local indigenous minority languages cannot be overstated. They play a crucial role in fostering social cohesion, enhance one's cultural and social capital, and occasionally have economic value (Olko 2021). In these regions, while contributing to the economic growth of the region, immigration can also potentially undermine the position of the minority and/or endangered languages by introducing more non-speakers into the community. Hence, immigration may pose a threat to minority language revitalisation efforts. It is important, therefore, to encourage migrants to embark on the process of learning the local minority language.

Language revitalisation is a complex, dynamic process that requires taking into consideration a multitude of factors, such as language vitality, types of communities, and motivations behind the revitalisation itself (Grenoble 2021; Flores Farfán and Olko 2021). However, strategies for language revitalisation primarily focus on the methods for passing on the language and creating new speakers (O'Rourke et al 2015). These methods include community-based programmes, master-apprentice programmes, and bilingual or immersion programmes in informal and formal education settings. These include teaching minority languages to children in schools as well as to adults (Grenoble and Whaley 2006; Unterriner et al 2021). The teaching and learning of minority

DOI: 10.4324/9781003439493-11

languages not only encounters practical challenges such as limited learning materials, grammars, and dictionaries but also a scarcity of qualified teachers and opportunities to practice the newly acquired language skills outside the classroom. The decision to learn a minority language in adulthood is influenced by a wide array of sociolinguistic factors, such as the status of minority languages on the linguistic market (Bourdieu 1991) and individuals' language attitudes (i.e., overt explicit statements about selected aspects of a language) and language ideologies (i.e., covert beliefs about a language). As discussed in the following, different language ideologies and attitudes occur at different stages of familiarity with a minority language (O'Rourke and DePalma, 2017; Rosiak 2023). Considering the significant role that the adult learners play in the revitalisation of minority languages, it is vital to consider how ideologies and attitudes impact their motivation to learn a minority language. This is especially the case when formulating language revitalisation policies and strategies, in particular those that are related to lifelong language education. Drawing on the qualitative data from ethnographic studies on post-2004 adult Polish migrants in Wales conducted between 2014 and 2018 (Rosiak 2016, 2022, 2023; Rosiak and Zydorowicz 2023), I intend to offer insights into ways attitudes and ideologies influence the process of learning Welsh.

Minority language learning motivation and international migration

Language acquisition and education and increasing the number of language users are all important aspects of the strategies aimed at revitalisation and maintenance of minority languages. Ample sociolinguistic research implicitly delves into individuals' motivations for learning minority languages and how they acquire language proficiency, such as Smith-Christmas et al. (2018), Nance (2015), Pujolar and Puigdevall (2015), and Dołowy-Rybińska (2020). In general, to date, three main contexts have been explored in sociolinguistic studies on minority language learning motivation (Rosiak 2023). The first context encompasses learning autochthonous minority languages within their native communities. This includes both heritage and the migrant learners (e.g., Dołowy-Rybińska 2020; Perales and Cenoz 2002). The second context involves learning heritage languages outside the indigenous communities (e.g., Walsh and Ní Dhúda 2015). Finally, the third context encompasses learners of minority languages as foreign languages. In addition, there is a growing body of research that integrates sociolinguistics with motivational models specifically employed in applied linguistics (Petit 2016; Nance et al 2016; Flynn and Harris 2016; Flynn 2020).

Research on international migrants learning autochthonous minority languages is still an emerging field, predominantly studied through a sociolinguistic lens employing the new speaker framework. A comparative study of migrants learning Welsh and Galician by Bermingham and Higham (2018) demonstrated that minority language learning is often pursued with the aim of achieving social mobility and improving communication skills. Their motivations may also stem from a sense of pride and a wish to accumulate economic capital. Bermingham and Higham (2018) contend that immigrant new speakers claim the language without necessarily adopting the ethnicity or identity traditionally associated with it. Yet ethnolinguistic categorisations persist, and migrants' assertion of the ownership of the language may be meet with resistance by the members of the host community. As a result, migrant new speakers may not perceive themselves as legitimate or authentic speakers of the language, which impacts their sense of confidence and their relationship with new speaker status. With respect to this, Augustyniak (2021) examined how migrant learners of Basque construct their identities and position themselves in relation to "Basqueness" as a group identity. She demonstrates the correlation between the usage of Basque by migrants and the ideologies of authenticity, legitimacy, and ownership. In her study, migrant learners of Basque perceived learning the language as a means to social integration and, to some extent, as an economic as well as professional advantage. Accordingly, Rosiak's (2016, 2018) study among Polish migrants in Wales yielded similar findings. The participants reported that acquiring even basic skills in Welsh facilitated a greater understanding of the host communities, also increasing their sense of belonging. They also received positive feedback from traditional Welsh speakers, which contributed to their perception of being accepted. Some also reported the perceived economic benefits of learning Welsh.

Within the field of language policy and planning, Higham (2020) investigated the attitudes of civil servants, language tutors, and international immigrants in Wales towards adult migrants learning Welsh. Higham puts forward a model for integration, which aims at providing international migrants with opportunities to learn both English and Welsh as a way to foster their citizenship. Higham's (2025) study of four refugees learning Welsh revealed that the participants viewed learning the minority language primarily as their personal integration projects. However, they have also recognised that learning Welsh can lead to social and economic benefits, such as increased employment opportunities.

Several studies integrated sociolinguistics and language learning motivation research models employed in applied linguistics. Flynn and Harris (2016) examined motivations among adult learners in Dublin, including some who were born and educated outside of Ireland. Based on the findings, they have proposed a provisional classification of learner motivations. O'Rourke and DePalma (2017) have explored the motivation of edutourists (Yarymowich 2005) to learn Galician, noting that their participants were driven by interests in Galician culture and personal connections rather than purely instrumental or economic factors. They emphasise that learners of minority languages are typically less motivated by prospective instrumental and economic benefits of the newly acquired language skills compared to learners of dominant languages. Finally, Rosiak (2023) argues that integrativeness, language ideologies, and language attitudes are crucial factors in understanding the motivation of adult learners to take up minority languages. Hence, due to their relevance, these concepts should be included in the theoretical frameworks for the study of language learning motivations.

Research on adult learning of minority languages further reveals complex motivational dynamics surrounding this process and highlights a tendency toward integrative motives. However, these studies predominantly concentrate on individual motivations and to a lesser extent on the societal factors influencing decisions to take up a minority language. Yet, given that minority and minoritised languages often possess lower status positions on the linguistic market (Bourdieu 1991), the decision to learn or not learn them is closely tied to identity. This decision is, additionally, shaped by the personal and societal language attitudes and ideologies (Woolard 1998; Dołowy-Rybińska and Hornsby 2021). Specifically, dominant language ideologies, the ideology of authenticity, and the ideology of utility, as will be discussed subsequently, play influential roles in the shaping of these motivations. The remainder of this chapter discusses language attitudes and ideologies and presents a case study on the attitudes of adult Polish migrants toward the Welsh language. This also includes the language ideologies that have influenced their language learning motivation.

Language attitudes and language ideologies

Coined by French philosopher Destutt de Tracy (1754–1836) at the end of the 18th century, the term 'ideology' originally referred to a science of idea. Over time, it has undergone significant evolution and accumulated various new meanings and connotations (Woolard 1998: 5–9). Although in the European scholarship, particularly the Marxist school of thought, language ideologies have been studied since the early 20th century, the western English-speaking tradition began exploring the relationship between language and social interaction only a few decades later (Piller 2015: 2–3). In the realm of linguistics, the concept of language ideologies was initially introduced by Michael Silverstein. He defined them as "any sets of beliefs about language articulated by the users as rationalisation or justification of perceived language structure and use" (Silverstein 1979: 193). In other words, they refer to the beliefs about language that have a significant impact on the broader social dynamics. Indeed, Woolard (1994) perceives the study of language ideologies as a "bridge between linguistic and social theory" (p. 72). The rationale behind this is that it establishes a connection between language behaviour and political and economic dimensions of social inequality.

Since Silverstein's seminal publication a substantial body of literature has explored the notion of language ideologies. This applies, in particular, to such fields as linguistic anthropology, language sociology, and the sociolinguistics of minority languages. As the research and understanding of the term have expanded in linguistics, so did its definition (cf. Irvine 1989; Gal and Woolard 1995; Heller 2007). Following Boudreau and Dubois (2007), the term 'language ideology' is used throughout this chapter to refer to:

> a set of beliefs on language or a particular language shared by members of a community. . . . These beliefs come to be so well established that their origin is often forgotten by speakers and are therefore socially reproduced and end up being 'naturalised', or perceived as natural or as common sense, thereby masking the social construction process at work.
>
> (p. 104)

The community that shares specific language ideologies may consist only of speakers of a particular language. However, the same ideologies are frequently shared by neighbouring communities as well. They are enacted and perpetuated in everyday life through opinions, practices, and discourses. Importantly, these ideologies are closely connected to the social, economic, and educational attributes associated with the speakers of a given language, their accents, dialects, or vocabulary in particular (cf. Dołowy-Rybińska and Hornsby 2021: 105). Consequently, they also impact the linguistic choices individuals make. These choices concern not only the language they use in daily interactions but also the actual content of their utterance. Needless to say, language ideologies that exist in a given community may also influence the decision-making of individuals concerning which language to learn.

It is crucial, therefore, to make a clear distinction between language ideologies and language attitudes (King 2000: 168). Admittedly, the two concepts are a community-level phenomenon. However, language attitudes are additionally shaped by a wide array of specific factors pertaining to the individuals themselves. These individual factors include the socio-demographic variables, personality characteristics, social identities, and situational circumstances. At the community level, language attitudes are influenced by language standardisation, (ethnolinguistic) vitality, status, and solidarity (Kircher and Zipp 2022: 6–13). Furthermore, unlike the covert nature of language ideologies, language attitudes are overt and explicit statements expressed as opinions, prejudices even, about the particular languages or the selected aspects of a language (Dołowy-Rybińska and Hornsby 2021: 106; King 2000: 168). However, people's articulated attitudes may not reflect their opinions. Dauenhauer and Dauenhauer (1998) note the frequent gap between verbally expressed attitudes (overt, public attitudes) and "unstated but deeply felt emotions and anxieties" (covert, private attitudes) (p. 62). Thus, overt attitudes may not necessarily predict behaviour and practices (Garrett 2010: 23). Language attitudes are learned through observation and instrumental learning, often at a young age (Garrett 2010: 22). However, they are also dynamic and may change over time.

This occurs in response to changes in the status and prestige of a given language, language variety, or its users, as well as a result of the language planning initiatives (Kircher and Zipp 2022: 6).

The role of language attitudes has gained considerable recognition in second language acquisition research. Attitudes are integrated into theoretical frameworks on language motivation, the most prominent being Gardner and Lambert's (1972) distinction between integrative and instrumental orientations (attitudes). Originally, in the socio-educational model of language learning motivation, attitudes towards the target language were conceptualised as an element of the integrative motivation, which reflected individual interest in the target language community and culture (Gardner and Lambert 1972: 517). Later, however, integrative motivation was redefined as consisting of integrativeness and integrative orientation. Integrativeness has been defined as:

> a genuine interest in learning the second language in order to come closer to the other language community. At one level, this implies an openness to, and respect for other cultural groups and ways of life. In the extreme, this might involve complete identification with the community (and possibly even withdrawal from one's original group), but more commonly it might well involve integration within both communities.
>
> (Gardner 2001: 5)

In contexts where English, a global lingua franca, is learned as a foreign language, integrative orientations were found to play a lesser role. However, they play a significant role in the minority language learning, as learning these languages is rarely done for instrumental purposes, as shown by O'Rourke and DePalma (2017) and Flynn and Harris (2016).

In minority language revitalisation contexts, Sallabank (2013: 62) outlines six key concepts and discourse markers that signal language attitudes: (1) general approval of the language, expressed as 'I like speaking . . .'; (2) commitment to language use ('I want to maintain . . .'); (3) emphasis on ethnic heritage, expressed as 'We owe it to our forefathers to maintain . . .'; (4) considerations of economic and social factors voiced through statements that the language '. . . offers advantages in seeking good job opportunities'; (5) family and local considerations ('. . . is important in family life'); and (6) personal ideological perspectives ('. . . provides a range of aesthetic experiences in literature').

A plethora of research on language ideologies and attitudes exists. In this regard, research on indigenous minority and minoritised languages has largely focused on the examination of standard language ideology, ideology of authenticity, and ideology of legitimacy, as these play a focal role in shaping language revitalisation as well as maintenance policies (e.g., Jaffe 2008; McLeod and O'Rourke 2015; Costa 2015; Dunmore 2019). Understanding the inner workings of these ideologies and navigating them is essential for effectively addressing the challenges of language revitalisation. Literature on language ideologies in the context of migration and multilingual societies tends to frame migrant languages as minority languages in relation to the dominant ones (McCubbin 2010: 458). A number of studies exploring the concept of new speakers focus on minority language acquisition by migrants who settle in indigenous minority language communities (Bermingham and Higham 2018; Augustyniak 2021; Rosiak and Zydorowicz 2023).

While language ideologies and attitudes have a substantial influence on the decision to study languages, to date a limited amount of research into the impact of language ideologies and attitudes on language learning motivation exists. The present chapter, therefore, discusses the ideologies that shape motivations to engage in minority language learning along with those that come into play during the process of gaining skills and proficiency in the language. First, however,

I provide background information and outline the local context for the acquisition of Welsh among adult migrants.

Adult international migrants engaging in Welsh language learning

Wales and the Welsh language

Wales, a devolved country within the United Kingdom, is a bilingual country with Welsh and English as its official languages. The process of devolution led to the establishment of the National Assembly of Wales in 1999, endowed with the authority to decide on internal affairs within the so-called devolved areas. These include, but are not limited to, public administration, economic development, health, social care, and the Welsh language. Hence, for the first time in history, Welsh language policy was included in the broader social policies established and implemented by the Welsh government based in Cardiff. Over the years, the Assembly's powers were expanded, which culminated in its official renaming as Senedd Cymru/Welsh Parliament in 2020.

The legitimation and institutionalisation of the Welsh language was a gradual process, largely spurred by language activism (May 2000: 105–111). The Welsh Language Act of 1993 marked the point at which both Welsh and English were granted equal status in public business and the administration of justice in Wales. A significant milestone occurred, however, in 2011 when the Welsh Language (Wales) Measure, which conferred official status upon the Welsh language in Wales, was passed (Hodges and Prys 2019). As a result, Wales is officially bilingual, recognising Welsh (de jure) and English (de facto) as its official languages. According to the 2021 National Census, 17.8% (i.e., 5,873,000 usual residents) of the population of Wales aged 3 or older can speak Welsh. However, these estimates are contradicted by the Annual Population Survey of 2022, which calculates this number to be 29.5% (i.e., 900,600 usual residents). Such a significant discrepancy may stem from the different methodologies used in the two surveys and the fact that the census data was collected during the COVID-19 pandemic.

Over the decades, Welsh language revitalisation efforts have predominantly centred around its inclusion in formal education. Although the first state-funded designated bilingual schools in Wales opened in the 1950s, Welsh only became a compulsory subject in all schools in Wales as part of the National Curriculum under the Education Reform Act of 1988. Consequently, the following years saw a significant increase in the number of Welsh speakers in the 3–15 years-of-age group (May 2000: 105–106). The mandatory Welsh-language education and language training in the workplace continues to be the cornerstone of Welsh-language policy. This is further evidenced by *Cymraeg 2050: A Million Welsh Speakers* (Welsh Government 2017a), the most recent strategy that very ambitiously aims to double the number of Welsh language speakers. The strategy consists of three interrelated themes. Their aim is to increase the number of speakers and the use of Welsh as well as to create the conditions that would further facilitate the use of the Welsh language.

Within Theme 1 of the strategy, the government underscores not only the importance of transmitting the language within the family but also of the role of statutory and post-statutory education in increasing the number of new speakers of Welsh:

The contribution of speakers who acquire Welsh outside the home is vital to the success of our strategy. Creating the right conditions for new learners of all ages to develop and use their skills is a key objective – from the early years, through every stage of compulsory education and post-16 provision, to opportunities for adults to learn Welsh.

(Welsh Government 2017a: 17)

In addition, Welsh is described as a cultural treasure of Wales, and the government expresses the desire for the language to be relevant and meaningful for all residents of the country, irrespective of their ethnic and linguistic backgrounds (Welsh Government 2017a: 60). Hence, the strategy encompasses both those born in Wales and immigrants from other parts of the UK and abroad. This provision in the document made it necessary to update the English to Speakers of Other Languages (ESOL) policy for Wales (Welsh Government 2019a: 15), which now recognises the importance of Welsh for social integration and acknowledges its potential as a useful skill in the workplace. Lately, however, the Welsh government seems to be moving away from shaping its own migrant integration policy along the lines of Westminster government (Higham 2020). Nevertheless, language provision in Wales still remains separate to a large extent. The ESOL courses offered by numerous educational institutions aim at international migrants, whereas the Learn Welsh courses organised by the National Centre for Learning Welsh (NCLW) are designed for fluent English speakers (implicitly UK-born citizens) who want to learn Welsh (Higham 2025: 117). In 2018, however, representatives of the ESOL provision and the NCLW worked together to design a Welsh for Speakers of Languages Other than English (WSOL) course that would meet the needs of refugees, asylum seekers, and English learners. The result of this cooperation is the *Croeso i Bawb – Cwrs Blasu Cymraeg* (Welcome to All – Welsh Taster Course) coursebook, which has to date been translated into a number of migrant languages. At present, however, it is a 10-hour taster course. Consequently, should they wish to learn Welsh, adult migrants have to enrol in a Welsh for Adults course organised by the National Centre for Learning Welsh.

International migration and the Welsh language provision

Wales is an immigration country. Both internal and international migration has been the primary factor behind the population growth in Wales over the past three decades. Indeed, the population growth recorded in the 2021 National Census is attributed to the positive net migration (Welsh Government 2022a: 5). The 2021 National Census results showed that Polish migrants continue to be the most common non-UK born residents in Wales, with over 25,000 individuals. Other top nationalities include India, Germany, Ireland, Romania, and Pakistan. In a 2017 report, the Welsh government has acknowledged that immigration is the primary solution for addressing the socio-economic problems arising from the demographic decline in the longer run (Welsh Government 2017b: 20). Two years later, in 2019, the Welsh government introduced the Nation of Sanctuary – Refugee and Asylum Seeker Plan (Welsh Government 2019b) with the aim of reducing problems experienced by irregular migrants and aiding their integration with the host communities. As shown by Higham (2020), however, there exists a noticeable gap between the official declarations of the Welsh language's significance to Welsh society and culture and actual language provision for the international migrants. Although small steps have been taken to improve Welsh language provision for migrants (cf. Croeso i Bawb – Cwrs Blasu Cymraeg mentioned earlier), to date, no national government plan or policy regarding Welsh language provision for migrants has been published (Higham 2025). That such a policy is needed is supported by the 2021 National Census. It has provided evidence for an increase in the immigrant population in Wales as well as in the numbers and percentages of the individuals reporting Welsh language skills who also belong to ethnic minorities (Welsh Government 2023).

When devising language plans and strategies, it is crucial to consider the motivations of (potential) learners and the challenges they encounter before embarking on the language learning journey as well as during the language learning process. Adults' choice to pursue minority language learning is influenced by a number of sociolinguistic factors. The most prominent ones include the status of the minority language in the community, its ethnolinguistic vitality, and language ideologies and attitudes. Furthermore, minority language motivation is closely tied to the identity and desire to belong to a cultural community. Building on this, the following section will analyse the particular language ideologies and attitudes that influence motivation as well as the process of learning minority languages.

Ideologies in minority language learning

Based on the studies on new speakers and the motivation to learn Welsh by Polish adult migrants to Wales (Rosiak 2016, 2018, 2023; Rosiak and Zydorowicz 2023), the present section discusses those language ideologies and attitudes that were found to have the strongest influence on the process of learning Welsh. As previously mentioned, Poles have constituted the largest migrant group in Wales over the past two decades. Although a considerable number of Poles reside in the rural areas of Wales, such as Llanybydder in Ceredigion, the largest Polish communities can be found in the urban centres – Cardiff, Wrexham, Llanelli, and Merthyr Tydfil. The data used in the following analysis originates from the ethnolinguistic studies conducted between 2014 and 2018 among 39 Polish participants, who at the time lived in Aberystwyth (Ceredigion) and various locations across the county of Gwynedd in northwest Wales. Both regions are characterised as Welsh language heartlands, surpassing the national average of the percentage of the population claiming proficiency in Welsh (Welsh Government 2022b: 14). Hence, the participants had the opportunity to observe Welsh being naturally used in the community by traditional and language learners alike. None of the participants had family ties to Wales or knowledge of the Welsh language prior to arriving. Their decisions regarding whether to learn Welsh or not were based on their own experiences within host communities and influenced by their existing attitudes and ideologies. Moreover, the motivation of some participants to learn Welsh was strongly associated with identity and desire to integrate into a new cultural community. The factors identified as having the strongest impact on the decision-making and language learning processes included the ideology of utility, the ideology of authenticity, and attitudes towards Welsh language communities and culture.

Ideology of utility

The term 'ideology of utility' is employed here to describe the belief that learning minority languages does not bring any tangible or discernible benefits, as these languages are going to die out sooner or later, and their use is restricted to specific geographical areas, where the local community speaks a majority language alongside the minority language (Rosiak 2023: 43). This belief is often associated with the perception of the minority language as having minimal practical value, or 'utility'. Hence, this ideology may hinder motivation to even begin learning a minority language. However, the ideology of utility was also found to be at work in a study by Pérez-Izaguirre and Cenoz (2021: 155) among immigrant students of Basque during their second year of secondary education. Indeed, this ideology was prevalent among a number of Poles, who frequently did not

Language attitudes in minority language learning

consider acquiring the Welsh language essential for achieving integration. The restricted 'utility' of the language served as a demotivating factor in the decision to learn Welsh. Consider the following extracts from the interviews:

(1) I think that the Welsh language will die its natural death sooner or later, it will be a sort of curiosity, a tourist attraction, there'll be someone still speaking it, there'll be an old man leading the groups of tourists and saying something in Welsh, and they'll be recording him. It's a matter of years. For me this language is completely useless. (GC40M)
(2) I'd rather bet on practical use of what I'm learning, so I cannot see any concrete use for Welsh, because Welsh is used in. . . . Is it used anywhere outside of Wales? (AA203M)

The participant in extract (1) has a firm conviction that Welsh is in significant decline, which demotivates him from learning the language, whereas in (2) we see a transposition of the perception of English as a global language onto Welsh – as a minority language. English is versatile and can be used worldwide. Hence, according to the participant's viewpoint, language learning should prioritise a language that can be used globally. The limited geographical area wherein a language is used daily by a local or national community makes learning that language seem impractical. Moreover, certain potential learners of Welsh may lack motivation, as they already share a common language for communication with the locals, English, as shown in extracts (3), (4), and (5).

(3) ymm If I really needed it, if they only spoke Welsh, I would definitely learn it. But because they also speak English, most people, basically everyone . . . but if I had to learn it, if I needed it to live here, I'd definitely learn it. (AA202M)
(4) When I came here and saw how often the language is used here, and by saying that I mean that the language is used sporadically and in situations when the people really want to communicate in Welsh, they don't have to do it, I decided that perhaps it [learning Welsh] is not my priority. (AA19M)
(5) For a Welsh cultural life it's [speaking Welsh] important but I don't think you need Welsh for everyday life, because everyone here speaks English anyway (AC39M)

However, learning a minority language goes beyond mere communication, defined as the exchange of information. It entails becoming a member of a cultural community and contributes to developing feelings of belonging. The participant in quote (6) highlights that despite the dominance of English, one cannot understand a large part of Welsh history, culture, and national identity without Welsh. Indeed, there is an intricate yet distinct relationship between English and Welsh cultures. Despite the fact that the two cultures interweave, they largely remain separate. Without proficiency in Welsh, one is unable to fully engage in those aspects of Welsh social and cultural life that are available only through the medium of Welsh. As a result, a conscious choice has to be made which spheres of life and culture a newcomer to Wales wants to participate in.

(6) So it's a question of which environment or community you want to be part of, because, you know, there's a huge overlap between the two [language] groups, it's not that you have one group speaking only Welsh and the other speaking only English. People who speak Welsh can speak English and you have a lot of place for manoeuvre here. But true, there are things that belong only to the Welsh speakers. (GA27F)

Considering that the ideology of utility tends to demotivate potential learners from pursuing the language, it should be accounted for in the initiatives focused on attracting new learners of minority languages.

Ideology of authenticity

The concept of "authenticity" originates from the notion of an ideal speaker of a specific language variety or dialect associated with a particular location and can be traced back to the early studies in dialectology and anthropology (Bucholtz 2003: 399). It is also connected to the early studies in language revitalisation, where linguists focused on collecting linguistic data from the remaining native speakers perceived as the authentic and legitimate speakers of the language (O'Rourke and Pujolar 2013: 52). Moreover, the ideology of authenticity, alongside its opposite, anonymity, are central to the research on new speakers of minority languages (O'Rourke and Walsh 2020). This concept is also pivotal in the discussions on native-speakerism in language teaching (Lowe and Pinner 2016; Vogl and De Wilde 2022). According to Woolard (2008), the ideology of authenticity:

> locates the value of a language in its relationship to a particular community. That which is authentic is viewed as a genuine expression of such a community . . . , a speech variety must be perceived as deeply rooted in social and geographic territory in order to have value.
>
> (p. 304)

Hence, for it to be recognised as authentic and have value, a particular language variety must be 'from somewhere' in speakers' consciousness (Woolard 2008: 304).

The ideology of authenticity can affect both language learners or new speakers and traditional or native speakers (O'Rourke et al. 2015; O'Rourke and Pujolar 2013; Woolard 2008). On the one hand, learners may perceive themselves as lacking in naturalness or native-like proficiency, leading to demotivation and constraining their minority language acquisition and use. On the other hand, it might cause traditional speakers to establish a social closure – an identity control mechanism that affirms their status as authentic speakers, which new speakers or learners may perceive as demotivating (O'Rourke et al 2015: 1; McEwan-Fujita 2010). That social closure may be manifested by turning into the dominant language during a conversation when noticing the lack of fluency or linguistic mistake on the part of the new speaker or learner. O'Rourke and Walsh (2020) reported in their study that the ideology of authenticity was frequently demonstrated by the new speakers who avoided code-switching and using English discourse markers, on the one hand, and strived to emulate a traditional Gaeltacht dialect as the authentic variety, on the other hand.

Similar findings were documented in the Welsh context, where learners of Welsh report challenges in practicing their language skills outside the classroom within the community. Pritchard-Newcombe (2007: 39) distinguishes four main reasons for these challenges to arise: (1) traditional speakers' tendency to switch to English, (2) code switching and code mixing, (3) the speed of speech, and (4) dialect differences. The phenomenon of native speakers' reluctance to converse with learners is well described in literature (Trosset 1986; Pritchard-Newcombe 2007). Pritchard-Newcombe (2007: 43–44) attributes this reluctance to the native speakers' insecurity about their own language skills and feelings of inferiority. She argues that since many native Welsh speakers did not receive formal education in Welsh, they may feel hesitant and insecure when speaking with learners, who often possess a command of grammar and vocabulary and use academic language. Consequently, to native speakers, the learners may sound 'too posh', 'too correct', or 'too good'. Trosset (1993: 29–30) suggests that this phenomenon stems from the rules of politeness, which require English to be used when speaking to strangers or when at least one person in the group is not a Welsh speaker. This phenomenon was observed and experienced by one of the participants in my study of Polish migrants in Aberystwyth. Despite initially wanting to learn at least basic Welsh, the use of English by his Welsh-speaking friends discouraged the participant from pursuing Welsh language learning:

(7) Well, and then, as I said, I realized that this is a linguistic practice that is present here and that those people who have decided to learn Welsh try to use this language when they can. Of course, when we talk to bilingual people who speak English and Welsh, they always switch to English. This group of people with whom we have some contact always switches to English, but if there is an opportunity for them to talk in Welsh, they use this language. I think it wouldn't be difficult for me to find someone to talk to, but it would be difficult for me, ymm, maybe, ymmm . . . but to ask for such patience in this language that the person would want to continue with let's say conversations from beginners to more advanced ones, but when I meet people who speak Welsh, they are very willing to talk in Welsh, but not necessarily in the form of learning, but more of a conversation. (AA19M)

The participant notices that in his environment, the issue lies not so much in a scarcity of traditional speakers willing to converse in Welsh but rather in a shortage of people prepared or trained to talk to beginner learners. The same participant noticed that switching to English is also a norm in other social situations, such as ordering food in a restaurant:

(8) And now, working in [fast food chain] I look and talk to people who take orders, and it's quite rare that a person would start the conversation in Welsh, because if they did, we would have to apologize and ask to switch to English. But this happens quite rarely. More often, two or more people talk to each other in Welsh, and when a waiter approaches or they go to the cash register, they automatically have the habit of switching to English and starting communication in this language. (AA19M)

To sum up, the participant's experience with traditional Welsh speakers switching to English in both his personal and professional life prompted the participant to reconsider his decision to learn Welsh.

Pritchard-Newcombe (2007: 39) lists dialect differences as one of the reasons for native speakers' reluctance to converse with learners. However, my data indicates that speaking a dialect different from that of one's interlocutor does not necessarily result in the social closure and decreased motivation for the learner or the new speaker, as shown in extract (9).

(9) Sometimes it happens that they ask me if I had learned Welsh, because they assume that I had learned it in the north, for example, or in some dialect, which they do not entirely understand, so they often assume that, ok, she said it that way, but maybe it's correct where she comes from, but they understand what I mean and they don't think that I have learned the language, and you know, they are extremely happy when they realise that you're learning Welsh. (GA27F)

When it comes to the spoken language, Welsh has not yet developed a national standard. Instead, a broad distinction between north and south Welsh is made, each characterised by distinctive language features and smaller local dialects. The participant in extract (9), who at the time of the interview was a proficient speaker of Welsh, observed that when her interlocutors detect difference between her Welsh and theirs, they often presume she is still an 'authentic' speaker originating from a different region of Wales and thus speaking a different dialect of the language. Such experiences appear to act as motivating factors for the advanced learner to persist in language learning.

Authenticity in speaking minority languages, including Welsh, also entails accepting code-switching and code-mixing as natural phenomena in bi/multilingual communication (Bullock and Toribio 2009: 2). Yet learners tend to perceive such linguistic practices in a negative light and often resort to extreme measures (for example, by using hyper-correct grammar and formal vocabulary) to avoid it (Pritchard-Newcombe 2007: 50–51). This, in turn, has the completely opposite effect to that intended. Due to the fact that their language now differs significantly compared to that of the traditional speakers, it is perceived as inauthentic and triggers the feelings of inferiority discussed previously. Consequently, learners' confidence in their language skills is affected negatively and they are discouraged from using the language in the community. As shown by extract (10), code-switching is also perceived as a sign of an incomplete, impure language or a language in decline.

(10)   Welsh is not a rich language, they don't say. . . . There's a generation of older people, who speak Welsh naturally, they don't use any English words, but ¾ of the population uses English words in Welsh sentences. I was learning Welsh for about six months. In general, Welsh is not difficult to learn because phonetically it's like Polish, so you can learn it, and you can read everything, and I can still read some books with my children. But it was difficult for me to concentrate on it, to think in Polish, because I was learning it through Polish, and say a sentence in Welsh, where suddenly you had to use an English word in a Welsh sentence because there was just no Welsh word for it. (AC34F)

The belief that Welsh is an incomplete language with words missing discouraged this participant from continuing to learn the language. However, another participant noted that although she tried to avoid anglicisms and code-switching at the beginning of her language learning journey, as she became more proficient, she recognised that code-switching is necessary when speaking Welsh casually:

(11)   You can write an MA in Welsh, go to a lecture about Welsh politics, understand every word, but go to a pub 30 miles of where you live and ask something easy and it may happen that you wouldn't understand the answer. It's rather shocking and sometimes depressing, in particular when somebody speaks really fast. So that's one thing. And I had to learn that when you don't know how to say something in Welsh, just say it in English, it's the norm, nobody will mind it, apart from some huge enthusiasts of linguistic purism. But even if you talk like that, it can only add authenticity to your language. (GA27F)

In other words, according to the participant, code-switching is a natural element of speaking Welsh, and to be accepted as an 'authentic' speaker of Welsh, one must learn how to code-switch.

Attitudes towards target language community and culture

Language attitudes play a crucial role in shaping motivations to learn a particular language and, thus, in the efforts to revitalise minority languages. Polish migrants in Wales tended to express their attitudes towards Welsh in terms of economic and social factors, family, and local considerations

Language attitudes in minority language learning

as well as personal ideological perspectives (Sallabank 2013: 62). Various conceptualisations of attitudes were often intertwined within a single excerpt or statement. There was a general consensus among the participants that the knowledge of Welsh is extremely beneficial on the job market, as certain positions are not available to non-Welsh speakers:

(12) It's easier to find a better job [when you speak Welsh] (AA19M)
(13) I started learning mainly to find a better job, because Welsh is often required for office work or . . . or at least they want you to be learning it. Why? Because I decided that since I've been living here for so long I should try and learn it. Before that I studied English in college for a few years, passed my exams. And then I decided it was time for Welsh, so I enrolled on a course with a friend. Three hours, once a week. We passed the exams. (GB26F)

The metaphor of 'opening doors' was frequently employed to illustrate greater opportunities the knowledge of Welsh affords in terms of social interactions, social acceptance, integration, and employment opportunities, as shown in extracts (14) and (15).

(14) It's not a matter of communicating but understanding and rapport. It's a matter of finding a cultural community rather than sheer communicating, exchanging information. I think it opens doors. (AA27F)
(15) It opens doors, it opens a lot of doors, and it helps meeting people who are in a similar situation, and . . . I think it's important to show that I'm interested in your language, your culture. I think it comes from a kind of respect I feel for this place. And I think it's worth it. (GC38F)

Extract (15) illustrates that the participant views learning Welsh not solely as a chance for expanding their social circles but also as a sign of respect for the host community and a display of interest in the local community and culture. Furthermore, quote (16) exemplifies the belief that showing respect by learning the local language fosters reciprocal feelings.

(16) Yes, certainly. 100%. You feel more accepted, they trust you more, they accept you more [when you speak Welsh]. (GC36F)

The presence of a family member, friend, or a colleague who spoke Welsh tended to elicit positive attitudes towards the language and served as a significant influence in the decision to learn it, whether through formal instruction or informal interactions. Individual personal connections to the language foster positive attitudes, both overt and covert ones, thereby play a significant role in promoting the learning and use of Welsh.

(17) First of all, because I live here and I've always liked learning foreign languages. I knew that sooner or later I'd start learning Welsh. Secondly, because part of my husband's family speak Welsh, his sister, his dad, he didn't speak Welsh fluently but he learned it and now he's fluent. I also worked with a person who spoke fluent Welsh and I often heard her speaking Welsh on the phone, which also inspired me. (GC382F)

Finally, positive attitudes were also expressed as personal ideological considerations, such as a kind of self-fulfilment or a better understanding of local culture. See extract (18).

(18) I began learning in January 2011 mainly to just give it a crack, to understand street signs, learn basic phrases, and so on, but once I started learning it was difficult to stop. There's always something. . . . I keep thinking, perhaps I'll be able to chat with someone [in Welsh], perhaps I'll be able to read a book, and so on, so basically I've been studying Welsh for three and a half years now. (GC382F)

Based on participants' experiences, even rudimentary proficiency in Welsh not only facilitates communication and integration but also grants improved access to the local community and its rich cultural heritage. Positive attitudes toward the Welsh language and its speakers facilitated minority language acquisition among Polish migrants. Language learning symbolised a wish to integrate into the Welsh-speaking community, open up to the local culture, and show respect toward the host communities, acknowledging the role of Welsh within the complex cultural and linguistic situation in Wales.

Conclusion

The purpose of this chapter was to show the role language attitudes and ideologies play in the acquisition of languages in general and motivations to learn minority languages, in particular. As demonstrated, language ideologies and attitudes influence minority language learning at various stages. The ideology of utility appears to be the main disincentive for learning a minority language. The belief that investing time and effort into learning a local minority language will not yield immediately recognisable benefits akin to those gained from acquiring 'major' languages such as English and Spanish prevents many people from taking up a minority language. This was certainly the case with Polish migrants in Wales and their perceptions of Welsh. Those who had only mastered a few basic phrases were more inclined to mention the perceived lack of aesthetic appeal in the Welsh language and its perceived limited utility as the reasons hindering them from developing language skills further. Other ideologies come into play once a person commits to learning a minority language and acquires proficiency. The ideology of authenticity is particularly complex, as it may affect both language learners or new speakers and traditional or native speakers. Equally, it may both discourage a person from engaging in language learning and motivate them to work on their proficiency.

Our experience as young language learners undoubtedly shapes our motivations to pursue language learning as adults (Dörnyei 2019). However, the decisions we make as adults concerning languages we decide to learn are heavily influenced by their position on the linguistic market and our own language attitudes and ideologies. Indeed, this was certainly evident among Polish migrants and their motivations to learn Welsh. Therefore, these factors demand thorough research and attention from language educators and planners alike.

References

Augustyniak, A. (2021). 'Migrant learners of Basque as new speakers: Language authenticity and belonging'. *Languages* 6: 2–19. https://doi.org/10.3390/languages6030116

Bermingham, N. and G. Higham. (2018). 'Immigrants as new speakers in Galicia and Wales: Issues of integration, belonging and legitimacy'. *Journal of Multilingual and Multicultural Development* 39(5): 394–406. https://doi.org/10.1080/01434632.2018.1429454

Boudreau, A. and L. Dubois. (2007). 'Français, acadien, acadjonne: Competing discourses on language preservation along the shores of the Baie Sainte-Marie'. In A. Duchêne and M. Heller (Eds.), *Discourses of endangerment: Ideology and interest in the defence of languages* (pp. 98–120). London: Continuum.

Bourdieu, P. (1991). *Language and symbolic power* (G. Raymond & M. Adamson, Trans.). Polity Press.

Bucholtz, M. (2003). 'Sociolinguistic nostalgia and the authentication of identity'. *Journal of Sociolinguistics* 7(3): 398–416.

Bullock, B. E. and A. J. Toribio. (2009). 'Themes in the study of code-switching'. In B. E. Bullock and A. J. Toribio (Eds.), *The Cambridge handbook of linguistic code-switching* (pp. 1–17). Cambridge: Cambridge University Press.

Costa, J. (2015). 'New speakers, new language: On being a legitimate speaker of a minority language in Provence'. *International Journal of the Sociology of Language* 231: 127–145. https://doi.org/10.1515/ijsl-2014-0035

Dauenhauer, N. M. and R. Dauenhauer (1998). 'Technical, emotional, and ideological issues in reversing language shift: Examples from Southeast Alaska'. In L. A. Grenoble and L. J. Whaley (Eds.), *Endangered languages: Current issues and future prospects* (pp. 57–99). Cambridge, UK: Cambridge University Press.

Dołowy-Rybińska, N. (2020). *"No One Will Do This for Us": The Linguistic and cultural practices of young activists representing European Linguistic minorities.* Berlin: Peter Lang D. https://doi.org/10.3726/b17208

Dołowy-Rybińska, N. and M. Hornsby. (2021). 'Attitudes and ideologies in language revitalisation'. In J. Olko and J. Sallabank (Eds.), *Revitalising endangered languages. A practical guide* (pp. 104–126). Cambridge: Cambridge University Press. https://doi.org/10.1017/9781108641142.008

Dörnyei, Z. (2019). '"From integrative motivation to directed motivational currents: The evolution of the understanding of L2 motivation over the decades"'. In M. Lamb, K. Csizér, A. Henry and S. Ryan (Eds.), *The Palgrave handbook of motivation for language learning* (pp. 39–62). Cham: Palgrave Macmillan.

Dunmore, S. (2019). *Language revitalization in Gaelic Scotland. Linguistic practice and ideology.* Edinburgh: Edinburgh University Press.

Flores Farfán, J. A. and J. Olko. (2021). 'Types of communities and speakers in language revitalization'. In J. Olko and J. Sallabank (Eds.), *Revitalizing endangered languages: A practical guide* (pp. 85–103). Cambridge: Cambridge University Press. https://doi.org/10.1017/9781108641142.007

Flynn, C. J. (2020). *Adult minority language learning: Motivation, identity and target variety.* Bristol & Blue Ridge Summit: Multilingual Matters. https://doi.org/10.21832/9781788927048

Flynn, C. J. and J. Harris. (2016). 'Motivational diversity among adult minority language learners: Are current theoretical constructs adequate?'. *Journal of Multilingual and Multicultural Development* 37: 371–384. https://doi.org/10.1080/01434632.2015.1072204

Gal, S. and K. Woolard. (1995). 'Constructing languages and publics. Authority and representation'. *Pragmatics* 5: 129–138. https://doi.org/10.1075/prag.5.2.01gal

Gardner, R. C. (2001). 'Integrative motivation and second language acquisition'. In Z. Dörnyei and R. Schmidt (Eds.), *Motivation and second language acquisition* (pp. 1–20). Honolulu, HI: University of Hawaii Press.

Gardner, R. C. and W. E. Lambert. (1972). *Attitudes and motivation in second-language learning.* Rowley, MA: Newbury House.

Garrett, P. (2010). *Attitudes to language.* Cambridge: Cambridge University Press.

Grenoble, L. A. (2021). 'Why revitalize?'. In J. Olko and J. Sallabank (Eds.), *Revitalizing endangered languages: A practical guide* (pp. 9–32). Cambridge: Cambridge University Press. https://doi.org/10.1017/9781108641142.002

Grenoble, L. A. and L. J. Whaley. (2006). *Saving languages. An introduction to language revitalisation.* Cambridge: Cambridge University Press.

Heller, M. (2007). 'Bilingualism as ideology and practice'. In M. Heller (Ed.), *Bilingualism: A social approach* (pp. 1–24). London: Palgrave Macmillan. https://doi.org/10.1057/9780230596047_1

Higham, G. (2020). *Creu Dinasyddiaeth i Gymru. Mewnfudo Rhyngwladol a'r Gymraeg* [Creating citizenship for Wales. International immigration and the Welsh language]. Cardiff: Gwasg Prifysgol Cymru.

Higham, G. (2025). 'Developing personal integration projects through a Welsh language provision for adult migrants in Wales'. In J. Simpson and S. Pöyhönen (Eds.), *Minority Language Learning for Adult Migrants in Europe.* New York and London: Routledge.

Hodges, R. and C. Prys. (2019). 'The community as a language planning crossroads: Macro and micro language planning in communities in Wales'. *Current Issues in Language Planning* 20(3): 207–225. https://doi.org/10.1080/14664208.2018.1495370

Irvine, J. T. (1989). 'When talk isn't cheap: Language and political economy'. *American Ethnologist* 16: 248–267. https://doi.org/10.1525/ae.1989.16.2.02a00040

Jaffe, A. (2008). 'Language ideologies and the Corsican language'. *Ethnologie française* 38(3): 517–526.

King, K. A. (2000). 'Language ideologies and heritage language education'. *International Journal of Bilingual Education and Bilingualism* 3(3): 167–184. https://doi.org/10.1080/13670050008667705

Kircher, R. and L. Zipp. (2022). 'An introduction to language attitudes research'. In R. Kircher and L. Zipp (Eds.), *Research methods in language attitudes*. Cambridge: Cambridge University Press.

Lowe, R. J. and R. Pinner. (2016). 'Finding the connections between native-speakerism and authenticity'. *Applied Linguistics Review* 7(1): 27–52.

May, S. (2000). 'Accommodating and resisting minority language policy: The case of Wales'. *International Journal of Bilingual Education and Bilingualism* 3(2): 101–128. https://doi.org/10.1080/13670050008667702

McCubbin, J. (2010). 'Irish-language policy in a multiethnic state: Competing discourses on ethnocultural membership and language ownership'. *Journal of Multilingual and Multicultural Development* 31(5): 457–478. https://doi.org/10.1080/01434632.2010.502966

McEwan-Fujita, E. (2010). 'Ideology, affect, and socialisation in language shift and revitalization: The experiences of adults learning Gaelic in the Western Isles of Scotland'. *Language in Society* 39: 27–64.

McLeod, W. and B. O'Rourke. (2015). '"New speakers" of Gaelic: Perceptions of linguistic authenticity and appropriateness'. *Applied Linguistics Review* 6(2): 151–172.

Nance, C. (2015). '"New" Scottish Gaelic Speakers in Glasgow: A phonetic study of language revitalisation'. *Language in Society* 44: 553–579.

Nance, C., W. McLeod, B. O'Rourke and S. Dunmore. (2016). 'Identity, accent aim, and motivation in second language users: New Scottish Gaelic speakers' use of phonetic variation'. *Journal of Sociolinguistics* 20(2): 164–191. https://doi.org/10.1111/josl.12173

Olko, J. (2021). 'Economic benefits: Marketing and commercializing language revitalization'. In J. Olko and J. Sallabank (Eds.), *Revitalizing endangered languages: A practical guide* (pp. 140–155). Cambridge: Cambridge University Press. https://doi.org/10.1017/9781108641142.010

O'Rourke, B. and R. DePalma. (2017). 'Language-learning holidays: What motivates people to learn a minority language?'. *International Journal of Multilingualism* 14: 332–349. https://doi.org/10.1080/14790718.2016.1184667

O'Rourke, B. and J. Pujolar. (2013). 'From native speakers to "new speakers" – problematizing nativeness in language revitalization contexts'. *Histoire Épistémologie Langage* 35(2): 47–67.

O'Rourke, B., J. Pujolar and F. Ramallo. (2015). 'New speakers of minority languages: The challenging opportunity-foreword'. *International Journal of the Sociology of Language* 231: 1–20. https://doi.org/10.1515/ijsl-2014-0029

O'Rourke, B. and J. Walsh. (2020). *New speakers of Irish in the global context. New revival?* New York and London: Routledge.

Perales, J. and J. Cenoz. (2002). 'The effect of individual and contextual factors in adult second-language acquisition in the Basque country'. *Language, Culture and Curriculum* 15: 1–15. https://doi.org/10.1080/07908310208666629

Pérez-Izaguirre, E. and J. Cenoz. (2021). 'Immigrant students' minority language learning: An analysis of language ideologies'. *Ethnography and Education* 16(2): 145–162.

Petit, K. (2016). 'Successful learners of Irish as an L2: Motivation, identity and Linguistic Mudes'. *Studia Celtica Posnaniensia* 1: 39–56. https://doi.org/10.1515/scp-2016-0003

Piller, I. (2015). 'Language ideologies'. In K. Tracy, C. Ilie and T. Sandel (Eds.), *The international encyclopedia of language and social interaction* (pp. 917–927). Chichester: Wiley-Blackwell, Wiley, Vol. 2.

Pritchard-Newcombe, L. (2007). *Social context and fluency in L2 learners. The case of Wales*. Clevedon, UK: Multilingual Matters. https://doi.org/10.21832/9781853599965

Pujolar, J. and M. Puigdevall. (2015). 'Linguistic *Mudes*: How to become a new speaker in Catalonia'. *International Journal of the Sociology of Language* 231: 167–187.

Rosiak, K. (2016). 'The Welsh language and social integration from the point of view of the new Polish emigration to Wales'. *Zeszyty Łużyckie* 50: 315–332.

Rosiak, K. (2018). 'Polish new speakers of Welsh: Motivations and learner trajectories'. *Language, Culture and Curriculum* 31(2): 168–181. https://doi.org/10.1080/07908318.2017.1415925

Rosiak, K. (2022). 'Migration, demography, and minority language learning: A case of Wales'. *Adeptus* 19: 1–23. https://doi.org/10.11649/a.2752

Rosiak, K. (2023). 'The role of language attitudes and ideologies in minority language learning motivation. A case study of Polish migrants' (de)motivation to learn Welsh'. *European Journal of Applied Linguistics* 11(1): 26–52. https://doi.org/10.1515/eujal-2021-0018

Rosiak, K. and P. Zydorowicz. (2023). '"It sounds like elves talking"– Polish migrants in Aberystwyth (Wales) and their impressions of the Welsh language'. *Applied Linguistics Review* 14(4): 823–845. https://doi.org/10.1515/applirev-2020-0027

Sallabank, J. (2013). *Attitudes to endangered languages. Identities and politics*. Cambridge: Cambridge University Press.

Silverstein, M. (1979). 'Language structure and linguistic ideology'. In P. R. Cline, W. Hanks and C. L. Hofbauer (Eds.), *The elements: A parasession on linguistic units and levels* (pp. 193–247). Chicago: Chicago Linguistic Society.

Smith-Christmas, C., N. P. Ó Murchadha, M. Hornsby and M. Moriarty (Eds.). (2018). *New speakers of minority languages. Linguistic ideologies and practices*. London: Palgrave Macmillan.

Trosset, C. (1993). *Welshness performed: Welsh concepts of person and society*. Tucson: University of Arizona Press.

Trosset, C. S. (1986). 'The social identity of Welsh learners'. *Language in Society* 15(2): 165–191.

Unterriner, J., L. Marean, P. Keskitalo, Z. Zahir, P. Bommelyn and R. Tuttle. (2021). 'Teaching strategies for language revitalization and maintenance'. In J. Olko and J. Sallabank (Eds.), *Revitalising endangered languages. A practical guide* (pp. 235–256). Cambridge: Cambridge University Press.

Vogl, U. and T. De Wilde. (2022). 'Teachers as foreign language makers: On standard language ideology, authenticity and language expertise'. *International Journal of the Sociology of Language* 274: 107: 131.

Walsh, J. and L. Ní Dhúda. (2015). '"New speakers" of Irish in the United States: Practices and motivations'. *Applied Linguistics Review* 6(2): 173–193. https://doi.org/10.1515/applirev-2015-0009

Welsh Government. (2017a). *Cymraeg 2050: A million Welsh speakers*. https://gov.wales/sites/default/files/publications/2018-12/cymraeg-2050-welsh-language-strategy.pdf

Welsh Government. (2017b). *Brexit and fair movement of people*. https://gov.wales/sites/default/files/publications/2018-10/brexit-and-fair-movement-of-people.pdf

Welsh Government. (2019a). *ESOL policy for Wales*. https://gov.wales/sites/default/files/publications/2019-11/english-for-speakers-of-other-languages-esol-policy-wales.pdf

Welsh Government. (2019b). *Nation of sanctuary – refugee and asylum seeker plan*. www.gov.wales/sites/default/files/publications/2019-03/nation-of-sanctuary-refugee-and-asylum-seeker-plan_0.pdf

Welsh Government. (2022a). *Demography and migration in Wales (Census 2021)*. www.gov.wales/sites/default/files/pdfversions/2022/11/5/1669371058/demography-and-migration-wales-census-2021.pdf

Welsh Government. (2022b). *Welsh language in Wales (census 2021)*. www.gov.wales/sites/default/files/pdf-versions/2022/12/3/1671609478/welsh-language-wales-census-2021.pdf

Welsh Government. (2023). *Welsh language by population characteristics (census 2021)*. www.gov.wales/sites/default/files/pdf-versions/2023/6/4/1686213046/welsh-language-population-characteristics-census-2021.pdf

Woolard, K. (2008). 'Language and identity choice in Catalonia: The interplay of contrasting ideologies of linguistic authority'. In K. Süselbeck, U. Mühschlegel and P. Masson (Eds.), *Lengua, nación e identidad. La regulación del plurilingüismo en España y América Latina* (pp. 303–323). Frankfurt am Mein/Madrid: Vervuert/Latinoamericana.

Woolard, K. A. (1994). 'Language ideology'. *Annual Review of Anthropology* 23: 55–82.

Woolard, K. A. (1998). 'Introduction: Language ideology as a field of inquiry'. In K. A. Woolard, B. B. Schieffelin and P. V. Kroskrity (Eds.), *Language ideologies. Practice and theory*. Oxford: Oxford University Press.

Yarymowich, M. (2005). '"Language tourism" in Canada. A mixed discourse'. In F. H. Baider, M. Burger and D. Goutsos (Eds.), *La Communication touristique. Approches discursives de l'identité* (pp. 257–273). Paris: L'Harmattan.

9
LEARNING FROM LANGUAGE REVITALIZATION MOVEMENTS TO PROMOTE UYGHUR LANGUAGE RESILIENCE IN DIASPORA

Rebecca Clothey and Brian McCommons

Introduction

UNESCO's World Atlas of Languages lists some 3,000 endangered languages worldwide (UNESCO 2021). With language intrinsically tied to culture, many communities that experience a decline in the use of their native language perceive it as a sign that their culture is dying. Languages represent not just a form of communication but also the cultural knowledge of that language, including ecological, historical, or spiritual knowledge. However, Crystal (2000) estimates that at the current rate of language death, the world is in danger of losing nearly half of all accumulated knowledge. Because of this, community members often look for ways to maintain, transmit, and revitalize their language use through younger generations. Attempts to do so include development of community centers that teach the mother tongue, social activism to create awareness of the native language and culture, and cooperation with the local or national government to support policies that will facilitate language education in the mother tongue.

The first step in saving a language is to identify the specific threats to the language and reverse the shift. Considering there are roughly 7,000 languages in the world (Lewis and Simons 2016), each with different contexts and issues, there is no single method to achieve this goal. It is possible, however, to explore how other language communities were able to overcome such threats and learn from their examples. This chapter demonstrates this process by examining the increasing threats to the Uyghur language in the Uyghur homeland and actions taken in diaspora to prevent the death of the Uyghur language outside of China. These are considered in comparison with successful approaches that were used by the Aymara language communities in undertaking language revitalization efforts.

Brief background of the Uyghurs and Uyghur language policy in China

China is an ethnically diverse nation with 56 officially recognized ethnic groups, including some 113 million ethnic minority people who speak up to 100 different mother tongues. Among these are the Uyghurs. Most Uyghurs are Muslim, Indigenous to China's northwestern Xinjiang Uyghur

DOI: 10.4324/9781003439493-12

Autonomous Region (XUAR). Their mother tongue, Uyghur, is distinct from China's national language, Chinese (i.e., Mandarin or *putonghua*) and uses a different written script. Although Uyghurs constitute a majority within XUAR, they are recognized as an ethno-national minority group within the larger population of China, where Han are the majority.

As a culturally diverse nation, maintaining a balance between minority rights and national identity has been a fraught goal in China, and policies toward that aim have frequently shifted. XUAR's diversity has always presented a challenge to the state-making efforts of the Chinese state (Gupta and Veena 2016). The transmission of cultural traditions between generations frequently occurs through education (May 2011; Mchitarjan and Reisenzein 2014). Yet Uyghur language use has gradually been reduced in the formal curriculum in schools in XUAR in favor of the national language, Chinese.

From the late 1970s until the implementation in XUAR of a 'bilingual education' policy in the early 2000s, there was a parallel education system being followed. Some schools used one of the region's minority languages as a medium of instruction, and Chinese was taught as a second language, while in other schools, Chinese was used as a medium of instruction, and English was taught as a second language (Simayi 2014; Sunuodula and Feng 2011). Where available (generally in urban areas), Uyghur parents could choose what type of school they wanted their children to attend. Chinese curriculum schools were assumed to lead to better economic opportunities later, but Uyghur curriculum schools would ensure the continuity of the Uyghur language across generations (Dwyer 2005; Tsung 2014).

In the early 2000s, the government of XUAR began implementing a 'bilingual education' (双语教育) policy, which they claimed would ensure better Chinese skills among the linguistic minority population than the Uyghur curriculum schools did (Dwyer 2005). In fact, in recent years the bilingual education policy in practice has led to 'monolingual education' in Chinese for increasing numbers of Uyghur students who have begun to study most, and in many cases all, of their classes in Chinese. Uyghur has instead been relegated to the status of a second language in schools that offer it at all (Baranovitch 2020; Klimeš and Smith Finley 2020). According to Baranovitch (2020), some regions in XUAR have completely banned the use of Uyghur even outside the classroom. This trend mirrors a general shift in language policy in China since the 1990s from a pluralistic approach that emphasized linguistic and ethnocultural diversity to an integrationist approach emphasizing assimilation and unity (Baranovitch 2020).

Liu (2012) suggests that bilingual education was recognized by the central government in order to build bridges between minorities and the Han. However, there are no bilingual schools in XUAR specifically to teach one of the regional ethnic minority languages to Chinese-speaking Han students (Sunuodula and Feng 2011; Tsung 2014). Thus, the burden has been on ethnic minority students such as Uyghurs in XUAR to adapt to the majority Han ways and language. This point is also clear in that the government's bilingual teacher education program trains Uyghur teachers or members of another non-Han ethnic group to teach in Chinese (Liang and Zhang 2007) but does not train Han teachers to teach in Uyghur or any other local language (Clothey 2016).

Implementation of the bilingual education policy has also been controversial. When the policy was introduced, even those universities in XUAR that had previously offered a full comprehensive curriculum in both Chinese and Uyghur suddenly abandoned all Uyghur language instruction (Baranovitch 2020; Schluessel 2007). This meant a loss of employment for Uyghur professors who were not able to teach their content in Chinese (Dwyer 2005; Schluessel 2007). Additionally, many K–12 Uyghur schools also suddenly switched the curriculum from Uyghur to Chinese in the middle of the school year when the policy was implemented. A contact of one of the authors was in middle school in XUAR's capital city Ürümchi when his school changed from a Uyghur to a Chinese curriculum in the middle of the school year. He said his school had to cancel final exams in the first year after the language change because the students had not learned enough Chinese at that point to even read the new textbooks. Over time, most Uyghur curriculum schools have merged with bilingual schools, reducing the options for formal Uyghur language instruction even further (Baranovitch 2020).

When languages are not integrated into the formal school curriculum and thus approved institutionally, they become devalued (Hu 2013; Fishman 1991; May 2011). Even in the early years of the bilingual education policy, some Uyghurs expressed concern about the marginalization and potential loss of their language as a result. Research conducted in 2014 reflected that by then Uyghur children were often speaking Chinese rather than Uyghur among themselves, even outside of school (Clothey and Koku 2017).

Increasing restrictions on Uyghur cultural expression

In addition to language, increased restrictions on other expressions of Uyghur culture began to be seen throughout XUAR when, after the 9/11 terrorist attacks in the United States, the Chinese government started overtly associating Islamic knowledge and identity with violent separatism and terrorism ('Learning and Identifying' n.d.; Roberts 2020; Smith Finley 2021). Following violent clashes in July 2009 between Han, Uyghurs, and the People's Armed Police in Ürümchi, China amplified its approach, adopting the Xinjiang Uyghur Autonomous Region Regulation on De-extremification[1] in March 2017.

Although many scholars dispute the characterization of Uyghurs as Islamic terrorists (e.g., Roberts 2018; Rodrıguez-Merino 2019; Smith Finley 2013), state-sanctioned ethnic repression targeting Turkic Muslims in XUAR, including ethnic Uyghurs and others, has resulted in multiple forms of extrajudicial detention, internment, incarceration, and forced labor in recent years (Klimeš and Smith Finley 2020). A Chinese document released in 2017 identified 75 factors that could be deemed indicative of religious extremism by the Xinjiang Uyghur Autonomous Region Committee of the Communist Party of China and could thus lead to incarceration ("Learning" 2017). These include some common Islamic practices such as congregating to pray outside a mosque, "participating in religious activities . . . without justifiable reasons," and women wearing veils. The list also includes some very vague and innocuous ones such as having a "big" beard or suddenly abstaining from drinking and smoking. As a consequence, many aspects of Uyghur cultural identity are now conflated with terrorism in China, and Uyghur cultural expressions (such as participating in traditional Uyghur weddings or funerals, publishing Uyghur books, teaching Uyghur language, etc.) can put Uyghurs at risk of incarceration (Clothey and Mahmut 2024).

At the same time, many aspects of Islam and Uyghur culture have disappeared in the Uyghur homeland. In education, references to Uyghur cultural life have been replaced in textbooks with highlights of Han Chinese culture and social life (Klimeš and Smith Finley 2020; Mahmut and Smith Finley 2022). Uyghur literature and folklore has also largely disappeared from these textbooks (Mahmut and Smith Finley 2022). Many of the Uyghurs who had edited these textbooks have also been incarcerated (Ayup et al. 2023). Yalqun Rozi, who had been head of the committee to compile Uyghur textbooks for the Xinjiang Education Press since 2001, was accused of "incitement to subvert state power" in 2016 after his textbooks fell out of favor for including too much Uyghur content. He was sentenced to 15 years in prison (Mahmut and Smith Finley 2022). Over 435 intellectuals and scholars who were important Uyghur cultural leaders, including professors of Uyghur literature, anthropologists, writers, and musicians, are also among the detained (Harris 2019; UHRP 2019a, 2019b). As the Uyghur intellectual community disappears, the prospects for Uyghur cultural continuity, including in literature and the arts, is diminished, thus marginalizing the language further. Finally, in 2017, Uyghur's status as an official language of XUAR was removed, despite the fact that Uyghurs still make up the majority of the region's population (Ayup et al. 2023).

As this brief discussion on the current situation of Uyghur language in the Uyghur homeland reveals, policy shifts in XUAR due to the broader political environment are impacting many aspects of Uyghur cultural life, and these in turn also relate to the sustenance of the Uyghur language in society. Research by Fishman (1991) shows that a language will no longer be maintained among the third generation of families living in a different linguistic context. As fewer Uyghur children in their homeland are learning their mother tongue formally, the language is becoming less prominent in XUAR society. Uyghurs in diaspora are therefore understandably concerned that formal channels for transmitting aspects of their culture and language to the next generation in their home region are no longer available, with many keen to ensure the language continuity in diaspora. How to do this successfully remains a question, as this chapter will discuss.

Literature review

Language death

Linguists do not agree on exactly how many languages are currently spoken in the world, but general estimates are around 7,500 (Lewis and Simons 2016). The rate at which languages are dying has accelerated over the past 500 years as different language speaking communities interact more frequently through migration, colonization, or globalization (Wiecha 2013). According to Crystal, "a language is only considered alive as long as there is someone to speak it" (2000: 2). Unfortunately, he and others estimate that a language dies every two weeks (Crystal 2000; Wiecha 2013). Languages do not, however, die suddenly. It is more likely that the number of speakers of a language shifts over time and slowly dies.

Language shift

Language shift is a gradual process whereby a community of speakers shifts over time to speaking a different language other than their mother tongue (Baker and Wright 2017). Such a shift can occur due to out-migration of an ethnic group or as the result of a social or political shift favoring a dominant cultural group. For example, often languages that are perceived to be of higher status, due to the possible economic or political benefits gained from speaking them, spread at the expense of other languages that are perceived by their own speakers to be of a lower status (Baker and Wright 2017). Language policy choices in education are also important because they help shape the patterns of language use among children (Kymlicka and Patten 2003).

In the case of Aymara examined here, there have been periods of oppression which directly resulted in the decline of their language. Oppressive forces also pertain to the sociopolitical environment currently faced by the Uyghurs in XUAR, where, as discussed, state-sanctioned policies of cultural infringement have increased in recent years.

Reversing language shift

In creating a model for reversing language shift, Fishman (2001) argues for identifying the general functions of the language as well as the functions that are threatened by the shift. These functions are broken down into power functions (government policies, mass media, higher education, etc.) and non-power functions (family, friends/neighbors, and community education programs). As specific functions of the threatened language are removed, the language becomes more compartmentalized and used less flexibly moving through generations.

Often, and as in the current case of the Uyghurs, resources and the sociopolitical environment do not favor the threatened language. The minority language communities must then either use the limited resources available or seek alternative forms of funding (e.g., NGOs, international organizations, local or foreign governments). Considering the sociopolitical and economic challenges faced by minority language communities, reversing language shift requires (1) prioritizing language functions and (2) creating links between these functions (Fishman 2001). Past successes of language movements show a focus on non-power functions through promotion of the heritage language in the family home and through community-driven education programs.

In addition to Fishman's (2001) theory on reverse language shift, Kondo-Brown (2006) provides the following best practices for promoting minority languages.

1. Using *only* the heritage language (HL) at home while not forcing the language on the child. This includes playing games in the language, interaction with literacy activities, and family activities. Conversely, research shows that children tend to shift towards the non-HL when an authoritarian tone is used to demand HL use.
2. Creation of and exposure to a peer group where the HL is the primary language of communication.
3. Contact with institutions that value the HL. These include weekend language schools and community organizations as well as government agencies (e.g., schools). Research shows that when formal schooling devalues the HL, children tend to shift towards the non-HL both in the school and at home.

In addition to the practices outlined by Kondo-Brown (2006) previously, there is growing research in the role of media in promoting minority languages (Cormack 2005; Clothey 2017; Myers 2008). With the growth of information and communication technology, 'media' now includes the internet and social media in addition to the more traditional forms of media (i.e., television, radio, and newspaper). Minority language communities tend to be located in less developed regions. Investing in media in these communities adds jobs to the region, adds a means of communication between the state and the local community, and can lead to the empowerment of the minority group (Cormack 2005).

The various factors surrounding each community, however, may make implementing the previous practices difficult or, in some cases, impossible. Some communities do not have reliable access to internet or television, which may limit the ability to use media as a tool for promoting language transmission. For example, 63% of Indigenous people in Australia have access to internet in the home compared to 91% of non-Indigenous Australians (Walker et al. 2021). However, in some cases, radio offers a more accessible alternative to the internet and TV (Clothey 2015).

While reversing a language shift may be a goal of the community, the benefits to the individual, particularly those in development stages, should not be overlooked. For example, students who have a positive perception of ethnic identity perform better in school when they recognize value placed on their ethnicity. Gharaei et al.'s (2018) research shows that it is not enough to speak the language – schools and communities should actively show value to the ethnicity. This may be best achieved by targeting non-power functions of the language.

Research methodology

This study uses a comparative case study approach. Comparative case studies emphasize comparison within and across contexts and involve the analysis of "the similarities, differences and patterns" across cases that share a common focus (Goodrick 2014: 1). This approach is particularly well suited to research about practice and policy, because it enables an understanding of how and why particular programs or policies work or fail to work (Bartlett and Vavrus 2017; Goodrick 2014).

One unique challenge facing Uyghurs in supporting cultural continuity in exile is that they are not a typical diaspora community. Most prominent diaspora communities that seek to maintain their culture and language have a territorial homeland from which they have been politically estranged but to which they maintain hopes of return (Roberts and Clothey 2024).

With that in mind, we selected the case of Aymara, an Indigenous language in Andean South America that has survived language shifts towards the colonizing language of Spanish as well as Quechua, another Indigenous language in the region. It was selected as a basis for comparison because Aymara speakers are not confined to one country, nor are they a majority in any country, but rather they are spread throughout South America. This presents a challenge somewhat similar to that of diasporic Uyghurs.

In the cases discussed here, the linguistic community is currently or was facing a threat of language decline and has taken actions to reverse or prevent this. Aymara communities experienced the threat of language extinction and took actions as a community to address the challenges through developing various programs and support networks. These efforts were developed in different communities in different regions throughout South America and took decades to progress to the point of gaining government support. Through a comparative case study approach, the various actions of Aymara communities will provide a lens for analyzing similar actions undertaken by Uyghurs in diaspora, another community whose language and culture is facing a critical situation. The context for the Aymara case is drawn from relevant literature and policy documents. Aymara programs are described and analyzed in order to consider what strategies might work for the Uyghur community.

Data for analyzing the Uyghur case were collected through ethnographic fieldwork conducted in Istanbul by one of the authors between 2016 and 2019 and multiple in-depth interviews with 20 Uyghur thought leaders in the community. Participants were selected based upon their role in language and cultural maintenance within the Uyghur community. These included academics, Uyghur language teachers, principals, and board members of Uyghur-established NGOs. For privacy purposes, data provided in this chapter are reported in aggregate rather than through direct quotes of any individuals.

Comparing the Uyghur and Aymara cases

The Uyghur case: maintaining language resilience in diaspora

Because of the current restrictions on various cultural milieu, many Uyghurs in diaspora are concerned that formal channels for transmitting aspects of their culture and language to the next generation in their home region are no longer available. Oppressive policy measures in the Uyghur region have also led to the out-migration of Uyghur people in recent years. Some Uyghurs who have returned to their homeland from abroad have also become victims of restrictive policy measures, being incarcerated once in China, or prevented from leaving China again. Because of this, Uyghurs in diaspora are reluctant to return to their home region, even to visit family members (Clothey 2022). Therefore, unlike many other ethnic groups who live in diaspora, opportunities to reinforce cultural and linguistic ties among the second generation abroad by returning to the home region to visit family members are either very limited or non-existent.

The Uyghur exile community is spread throughout the world and is estimated to number around 700,000, but it could be larger due to poor documentation in most of the countries where Uyghurs reside (Roberts 2020). The majority of Uyghurs outside of China live in Central Asia and Türkiye. While the largest Uyghur diaspora community is found in Kazakhstan, most Uyghurs there are from earlier migrations in the late 19th and mid-20th centuries. In contrast, Türkiye has the largest population of newly arrived Uyghurs, thus constituting a group of people who bring a living memory of Uyghur cultural traditions from their homeland. Thus, it is an important location for Uyghur cultural continuity outside of China. It is estimated that over the last decade, some 30,000 new Uyghur exiles have settled in Türkiye (Beydulla 2020; Emet 2018).

The Uyghur diaspora in Türkiye faces some issues similar to any diaspora community in maintaining its language outside of their home region, especially one under a centralized education system where localized school policy is not likely to adapt the methods or curriculum to a growing ethnic refugee population (Gharaei et al. 2018). In Türkiye, there are few, if any, opportunities for Uyghur children to study Uyghur language formally. The language of instruction in Turkish government schools is Turkish. Additionally, though Uyghur is taught in Turkic language and literature departments at some universities in Türkiye, Uyghur professors in those departments report that they rarely enroll Uyghur students, who tend to study STEM fields (Clothey 2022).

Furthermore, Uyghur being a Turkic language also causes some unique challenges for Uyghur language survival within the Uyghur diaspora in Türkiye. Although Turkish is relatively easy for Uyghurs to learn due to the linguistic similarities, once learned, the languages are also easy to intermingle. Many Uyghur parents in Istanbul raised this issue about their own children, whom they noted did not speak either language well and often code-switched between Uyghur and Turkish. Some concerned Uyghur parents in Türkiye also speak Turkish, and not Uyghur, to their children at home, because they believe it will ease their children's integration into their new host country. However, this also will lead to a rapid decline in Uyghur language ability among the next generation.

Because of these concerns, an increasing number of independently run Uyghur language classes have been opened in Türkiye since 2017. Most of these are weekend Uyghur language classes that attract Uyghur children in the local community nearest to where the classes are offered (see also Clothey 2022). However, despite the keen desire among many people within the Uyghur diaspora community in Türkiye to prevent the loss of their language, the ability of non-formal Uyghur language education within Istanbul cannot address the problem alone. For starters, the language classes themselves have limitations. Because of the nature of the diaspora community in Türkiye – most people moved there because of necessity, and not always with a plan – there are few Uyghur linguists or education specialists there. Therefore, most of the Uyghur language teachers are passionate, but they do not have professional teaching credentials (Roberts and Clothey 2024). Furthermore, the classes are elective and remain outside of the formal Turkish school system. Parents have to want their children to study Uyghur in order to enroll them. Although many within the Uyghur diaspora community desire their children to study Uyghur, as described previously, some parents also view such efforts as detrimental to integrating into Turkish society.

Also problematic is a lack of textbooks for learning Uyghur within diaspora. New Uyghur texts from XUAR are presently impossible to obtain in Türkiye due to the restrictions in China. At the time of research, Istanbul had three bookstores run by Uyghurs which sold Uyghur books. At one time these bookstores were able to import new titles or restock from XUAR once supplies ran short, but that is no longer true. Therefore, one of the concerns within the diaspora community relevant to their language survival is obtaining Uyghur language texts, especially for children who are learning the language.

To meet demand, some booksellers produce 'reprints' of Uyghur books that are already available within Istanbul; often these can be reprinted 'on demand' and shipped worldwide. In addition, many Uyghur language teachers in Istanbul and elsewhere have written and produced their own curriculum materials, tailored for their own classroom needs and according to their own teaching philosophy. This means that there is now a plethora of independently written and produced books for Uyghur children to learn Uyghur – though most of them are not based on a formal educational pedagogy. Unfortunately, children's literature written in Uyghur is also still limited. This problem had been identified by Uyghurs in Xinjiang even prior to 2016 (see, e.g., Clothey and Koku 2017). Foundational readers for children learning to read Uyghur are available now in Uyghur bookstores in Istanbul, but stories for children and teenagers who are already literate are not easy to find.

Uyghur language teachers within Türkiye and abroad communicate through social media apps to share resources and discuss challenges and solutions for teaching Uyghur to youth in diaspora. Additionally, to further coordinate language maintenance and transmission efforts, several topical conferences and workshops have been held in Türkiye in recent years in which Uyghur language educators based in many countries discussed challenges and methods for addressing Uyghur language preservation among the diaspora. These events represent a genuine effort to pull together the community in support of a common cultural maintenance goal. However, these events will also not reverse the trend of language decline alone.

The Aymara case

Aymara is an Indigenous language spoken in the Andean region of South America. While the majority of the roughly 2 million Aymara speakers live in western Bolivia, there are also large communities in Peru and Chile. Although Uyghur is officially concentrated under one government in XUAR, Aymara spans multiple governments, more like the Uyghurs in diaspora, who are spread throughout Europe, Australia, North America, and Central Asia. Aymara was the most widely spoken language on the South American continent prior to the arrival of the Spanish conquistadors. While the estimate of 2 million Aymara speakers worldwide may not represent a need for urgent action, the portion of speakers on the continent has been steadily declining, as, similarly to many post-colonial regions, the Aymara language faced a slow downturn in speakers over the centuries following the arrival of the conquistadors. As cities became more developed, young Aymara migrated from rural to urban spaces for economic opportunity. Bilingual Aymara parents saw this economic opportunity as well and prioritized Spanish-speaking skills in their children. Not only were the Aymara losing speakers to Spanish, but they were also losing speakers to the other widely spoken Indigenous language, Quechua (Hornberger and Coronel-Molina 2004).

The case of Aymara highlights the intergenerational issues faced by shifting languages. Indigenous people in Bolivia, for example, were not recognized as full citizens until the 1950s. Prior to this (and continuing after), the government did not recognize Indigenous culture or language. As a result, generations from Indigenous backgrounds growing up during this time did not have access to formal education in their first language, as Spanish speakers did. As there was little available formal education, there was less focus on reading and writing in the language (Hornberger and Coronel-Molina 2004). These now elder generations in many cases live in rural communities that have not needed to learn Spanish. As a result, there is a largely non-literate elder population who are only able to *speak* Aymara but are not literate in the language. As the younger generation migrates more towards cities, the intergenerational communication becomes limited. The Aymara community appears to recognize that both these migration patterns present a threat but also that the literacy of the elder population needs to be improved. The benefits of a literate population include the ability to disseminate the language more widely in written form as well as being able to navigate healthcare, education, and social rights, which are becoming more widely available in Aymara as Indigenous rights improve. For example, the Bolivian government implemented a law in 2009 declaring that all public policies and services be available in two languages: Spanish and the Indigenous language most prevalent in the respective region (Georgieva et al. 2009).

In the 1930s, Indigenous communities in the Andean region recognized the importance of speaking Spanish as a means of defending their civil liberties. Despite Peru, Ecuador, and Bolivia promoting Spanish-only education, the 1930s and 1940s saw the informal development of bilingual education practices among the Indigenous communities. This meant that children and adults were learning to read and write in both Spanish and Aymara – Spanish in formal spaces and Aymara in informal spaces led by community members. As bilingual education grew in Indigenous communities, so did the numbers of Aymara who were bilingual in their native language and in Spanish. While these programs were initially not officially supported at the national level, their development and support within the local community demonstrated practices that were targeting non-power functions first.

Throughout the 1960s and 1970s, community activists were unsuccessful in introducing Indigenous languages into formal public education; thus bilingual education remained largely informal. In 1978, however, a major breakthrough occurred with the Proyecto Experimental de Educacion Bilingue de Puno (PEEB-P). This project, begun in Puno, Peru, by Aymara and Quechua communities, was co-financed by a German government organization, GTZ (Association for Technical Cooperation). The GTZ has largely invested in projects in Latin America, specifically in the field of bilingual education, in countries where there is a lack of support from the national government (Lopez 2014). The aim of this specific program was to teach Quechua and Aymara students in their native language for four years before transitioning and assimilating to Spanish. In addition, the program was involved in publishing texts in the Indigenous languages, collecting stories and folklore from the communities, and developing and producing teaching materials. Not only were they successful in these goals, but the program also resulted in great interest from linguists and researchers from around the world. As the long-term goal of the program was assimilation into Spanish-speaking society, it drew controversy in its initial stage. However, the program became a model for bilingual education worldwide (Burman 2018; Lopez 2014).

Eventually, as was the goal when these bilingual programs began, Indigenous communities were armed with the linguistic power of Spanish to push for civil rights in public spaces. With the growth and recognition of community-developed bilingual education and the attention from local and international organizations, Indigenous leaders were able to gain state support for intercultural bilingual education throughout South America. The governments of Peru and Ecuador officially recognized bilingual education and provided funding to support it in 1972 and 1981, respectively (Hornberger 2000, 2006). In 1994, Bolivia implemented bilingual education nationwide (Hornberger and Coronel-Molina 2004), and two years later, bilingual education reached higher education in Bolivia. In 1996, a consortium of six nations developed the Program for Professional Development in Bilingual Intercultural Education for the Andean Region (PROEIB-Andes). The goal of this program was to support and train educators from various Indigenous communities in the Andean region in intercultural bilingual education practices. This includes short-term courses for Indigenous leaders, avenues for publication, and maintaining a library of Indigenous language resources (PROEIB-Andes 2020). The program is held within the University of San Simon in Cochabamba, Bolivia and currently offers a masters' degree in intercultural bilingual education (Hornberger and Swinehart 2012).

Another effort that has been relatively successful specific to the Aymara community is the growth of Radio San Gabriel, an Aymara language radio station in Bolivia. The Aymara were able to utilize mass media [a power function of the language per Fishman (2001)] to implement community-education programming (a non-power function). The radio station was originally started in the 1950s by Christian missionaries aiming to reach rural communities. After the Aymara community largely adapted the radio station as their own, they shifted the mission of the station from one that spread the word of God to one that recognizes, values, and promotes the cultural expression of the Aymara people (Hornberger and Swinehart 2012). The station provided an avenue to disseminate news that affects this population. In 1986, the station added the Sistema de Autoeducación de Adultos a Distancia (SAAD) program, which aimed to provide adult education to the Aymara community through radio, print, and TV ("Radio San Gabriel" n.d.). Educators who received training from the Bolivian government began visiting the rural Aymara communities to facilitate connections between the communities and the radio station and apply the lessons being delivered over the airwaves (Velasquez 1999). This program also provided print material in the Aymara language to supplement the radio programming.

In 2006, policy support for Indigenous rights grew as a result of the election of the first Indigenous president in South America, Evo Morales. This included both increased support for Indigenous language education but also sociopolitical support through laws targeting racism as well as requiring availability of public services in multiple Indigenous languages.

A real threat to the Aymara language still exists, but the Indigenous communities as a whole are actively taking steps to reverse this language shift by targeting both the power and non-power functions of the language. This includes the development of community schooling programs, literacy programs for adults, creating and sustaining Aymara language media, and partnerships with institutions of higher education. Additionally, as momentum for learning the Aymara language grew within the community, they were able to successfully advocate the government for its support. The movement made great strides in Bolivia after the election of Evo Morales in 2006, but continued efforts must be made, as his predecessors may not offer the same support.

Discussion and recommendations

A common thread in the Uyghur and Aymara cases is that they started with community programs. The Aymara communities started by developing and growing their own language schools, which eventually gained state support and funding. These programs began small, included community volunteers, and grew slowly. In the case of the Uyghurs in Türkiye, there does not seem to be a cohesive plan by the various community schools. They do, however, appear to have the support and motivation to develop an effective community to preserve their language and culture.

The recommendations for the Uyghur community based on the successes of Aymara include: (1) prioritize non-power language functions (e.g., through community schools and education through media), (2) develop collaborations with higher education institutes, and (3) coordinate efforts through community activism.

(1) Prioritize non-power language functions

Despite not having the support of the state initially, Aymara leaders taught bilingual education independently, as they recognized the need for Spanish-language abilities to create change in the public sector. These informal bilingual practices were developed through the community with support from an outside organization. The initial bilingual program was a success, and after gaining international recognition, they were able to gain state support. The international recognition, however, was a result of the success of a co-financed project with the German government. Despite not having support from the Bolivian government, alternative funding sources were found. This demonstrates the necessity of financial support for minority language movements, whether through NGOs, international organizations, or governments.

The Aymara community also successfully utilized media. Large portions of Aymara do not have access to internet or television in the rural regions of Bolivia, but the Aymara instead utilized and expanded Radio San Gabriel for education. Cormack (2005) describes the benefit of such media outlets, particularly in rural areas. Furthermore, the Aymara community demonstrates an ability to promote the language through a medium (i.e., radio) that is often seen by others as antiquated, through the combined focus of education programming and educators who facilitate connections from the radio station to reading and writing. This also demonstrates the need to make use of media tools already in use by the community (Clothey 2017).

Not only does an initial approach to community building closely align with Fishman's recommendations on prioritizing non-power functions to reverse language shift, but it is also the most realistic considering Türkiye's context. The highly centralized nature of the Turkish education system leads to curriculum decisions being highly contentious. Türkiye has the largest number of Syrian refugees in the world, and Arabic is now offered as a medium of instruction in some Turkish schools (Nimer and Aparcik 2023). One factor benefiting Arabic-speaking advocates has been the temporary notion of these refugees; the argument is that they will eventually return to their home country (Unutulmaz 2019). The Uyghur refugee community is significantly smaller than the Syrian refugee community, they do not have an independent state to return to, nor are they Indigenous to Türkiye. As such, the Turkish government is likely motivated to assimilate Uyghurs to Türkiye rather than using resources to support their linguistic needs.

However, developing strong community programs can be done without the direct support of the state. Creating family involvement in community education programs creates a bridge for students to foster positive relationships between the school and home. In the Aymara case, members of the small rural communities developed their own bilingual education programs. Most parents or guardians of Uyghur children in Türkiye do speak the language, and their continued involvement in community schools will be beneficial to the promotion of language use in the home.

Furthermore, this does not preclude the potential for independent Uyghur language programming offered through other venues, such as online. As with young people everywhere, most Uyghur youth are active social media users, and Uyghur language media are already available online, for example, through Instagram and YouTube. In fact, social media has exploded in recent years with popular youth-run accounts like Uyghur Collective and Tarim Network, which link diaspora Uyghur youth from across the globe and "provide spaces for expression and connection around what Uyghur identity means and what Uyghur culture can look like" (Anderson 2024: 185). However, one complaint of Uyghur parents is that existing media do not target Uyghur children, the population that most needs to strengthen their Uyghur language skills if the language is to survive into future generations. This could be done, for example, by creating cartoons or publishing new children's books in Uyghur on topics and in formats that are appealing to younger children.

(2) Develop collaborations with higher education institutes

In addition to developing community programs for language development, the Aymara case exemplified university partnerships as a valuable resource for language movements. Through developing programs with local universities, the Aymara language movement was able to establish avenues to preserve and standardize their languages. Not only did the government develop the Indigenous University of Bolivia (UNIBOL), which delivers its curriculum in the Indigenous languages of Bolivia, but the Spanish-speaking University of San Simon, for example, offers language programs that are specifically designed to train individuals in language pedagogy so they may transmit the language from one generation to the next.

One issue expressed by Uyghurs in Türkiye was their lack of language teacher training programs. While most of the teachers at the language schools are Uyghur, most also lack pedagogical knowledge on effective language teaching. A similar situation arose during the development of bilingual education programs in Bolivia. With the support of the University of San Simon, the Indigenous communities were able to develop bilingual teacher training programs. There are already university-level Uyghur language programs in Türkiye; therefore, partnering with local universities to develop pedagogical programs to transmit the language could also be a next step. Utilizing online resources for teacher training would enable scaling even further to a wider number of language teachers across the diaspora.

(3) Coordinate efforts

The case of the Aymara language demonstrates that multiple approaches to language revitalization may occur simultaneously. Aymara speakers in South America span a large geographical area across multiple nations. Efforts that were successful in one region (PEEB-P, for example), may not have been known to Aymara communities in other regions. These non-power community-based approaches can often lead to power functions of the language, and coordination between Aymara-speaking communities may have accelerated the process. As described, Aymara in Peru, Ecuador, and Bolivia all gained recognition from their respective governments, but nearly a decade apart. Had there been more coordination between the Aymara communities, things like PEEB-P or radio programs may have been adapted by more Aymara communities.

The Uyghur community in diaspora already has a very energetic activist community throughout the world (see, e.g., Frangville 2021; Musapir and Steenberg 2024). Individual activists post frequently on social media about widespread actions of the Chinese government against Uyghur cultural survival in XUAR and lobby governments in the West. This activity has garnered the attention and action of many western governments and led to passing legislation condemning China for their treatment of Uyghurs. Focusing some activist attention on the efforts to maintain the survival of the Uyghur culture in diaspora could generate support and funding avenues from governments and non-governmental organizations that will enable the Uyghur community-based efforts to grow not only in Türkiye but beyond.

Conclusion

Language should not be viewed solely as a means of communication. Language represents so much more, from culture to history to knowledge. Language represents knowledge, and when a language dies, the embedded knowledge is also lost. Understanding this function of language is critical in understanding the importance of keeping languages alive.

This comparative case study identifies a language that is in the beginning stages of a shift. While Uyghur speakers in Türkiye are motivated to reverse the shift quickly, they do not appear to have a strategic plan in place to do so, and many of the efforts are ad hoc. Based on successful language revitalization efforts by the Aymara, we offer recommendations to the Uyghur community in Türkiye on how to effectively build on the structures that are already in place. As discussed in this chapter, efforts for language revitalization often begin at the community level and, if successful, may cross into political spaces where power is gained. The case of the Aymara showed how long efforts to make the leap from community activism to government support can take. To accelerate this process, we argue for greater coordination between various communities seeking to revitalize the same language. However, sustainable funding will also be critical for successful implementation. With over 3,000 languages currently categorized as endangered (UNESCO 2021), it is important for communities to start addressing the threats to their language starting with quality programs for the non-power functions of the language and building up from there.

Note

1 For more information, see the webpage of The International Uyghur Human Rights and Democracy Foundation, www.iuhrdf.org/content/xinjiang-uyghur-autonomous-region-regulation-de-extremification (Accessed: 3 August 2021).

References

Anderson, E. (2024). 'Ensuring the Resilience and Vitality of Uyghur Lifeways and Language in Diaspora'. In R. Clothey and D. Mahmut (Eds.), *Uyghur Identity and Culture: A Global Diaspora in a Time of Crisis.* (pp. 181–186). Routledge.

Ayup, A., Tekin, S. and Sidick, E. (2023). 'Linguistic, Cultural, and Ethnic Genocide of the Uyghurs in Xinjiang, China'. In T. Skutnabb-Kangas and R. Phillipson (Eds.), *The Handbook of Linguistic Human Rights, 1st ed.* (pp. 342–355). John Wiley & Sons, Inc.

Baker, C. and Wright, W. (2017). *Foundations of Bilingual Education and Bilingualism, 6th ed.* Bristol, UK: Multilingual Matters.

Baranovitch, N. 2020. 'The "Bilingual Education" Policy in Xinjiang Revisited: New Evidence of Open Resistance and Active Support among the Uyghur Elite'. *Modern China.* 48(1): 1–33. DOI: 10.1177/009770042096913

Bartlett, L. and Vavrus, F. (2017). 'Comparative Case Studies: An Innovative Approach'. *Nordic Journal of Comparative and International Education (NJCIE).* 1(1).

Beydulla, M. (2020). 'Experiences of Uyghur Migration to Turkey and the United States: Issues of Religion, Law, Society, Residence, and Citizenship'. In R. Jureidini and S. F. Hassan (Eds.), *Migration and Islamic Ethics: Issues of Residence, Naturalization and Citizenship.* Boston: Brill.

Burman, A. (2018). *Indigeneity and Decolonization in the Bolivian Andes: Ritual, Practice, and Activism.* Lanham, MD: Lexington Books.

Clothey, R. (2015). 'ICT and Indigenous Education: Emerging Challenges and Potential Solutions'. In J. Jacob, Sheng Yao Cheng, and M. Porter (Eds.), *Indigenous Education: Language, Culture and Identity* (pp. 63–76). Springer.

Clothey, R. (2016). 'Community Cultural Wealth: Uyghurs, Social Networks, and Education'. *Diaspora, Indigenous and Minority Education.* 10(3): 127–140.

Clothey, R. (2017). 'The Internet as a Tool for Informal Education: A Case of Uyghur Language Websites'. *Compare: A Journal of Comparative and International Education.* 47(3): 344–358. DOI: 10.1080/03057925.2017.1281103.

Clothey, R. (2022). 'Education and the Global Politics of Cultural Survival for Uyghur Immigrants in Turkey'. *Journal of Language, Identity, and Education.* DOI: 10.1080/15348458.2022.2045202.

Clothey, R. and Koku, E. (2017). 'Oppositional Culture, Cultural Preservation and Everyday Resistance on the Uyghur Internet'. *Asian Ethnicity.* 18(3): 351–370. DOI: 10.1080/14631369.2016.1158636.

Clothey, R. and Mahmut, D. (2024). 'Introduction: Maintaining Cultural Identity in a Changing Political Landscape'. In R. Clothey and D. Mahmut (Eds.), *Uyghur Identity and Culture: A Global Diaspora in a Time of Crisis* (pp. 1–18). Routledge.

Cormack, M. (2005). 'The Cultural Politics of Minority Language Media'. *International Journal of Media and Cultural Politics.* 1(1): 107–122.

Crystal, D. (2000). *Language Death.* Cambridge University Press.

Dwyer, A. (2005). *The Xinjiang Conflict: Uyghur Identity, Language Policy, and Political Discourse.* Washington, DC: East-West Center.

Emet, E. (2018). *21. Yüzyıl Uygur Dramı: Göç.* Ankara: Akçağ Basım Yayım Pazarlama A.Ş.

Fishman, J. A. (1991). 'Limitations on School Effectiveness in Connection with Mother Tongue Transmission'. In J. A. Fishman (Ed.), *Reversing Language Shift: Theoretical and Empirical Foundations of Assistance to Threatened Languages* (pp. 368–380). Clevedon, PA: Multilingual Matters.

Fishman, J. A. (Ed.). (2001). *Can Threatened Languages Be Saved?* Clevedon: Multilingual Matters.

Frangville, V. (2021). 'Testimonies and the Uyghur Genocide Metanarrative: Some Reflections from the FIELD'. *HAU: Journal of Ethnographic Theory*. 12(12). DOI: 10.1086/720368

Georgieva, S. V., Vasquez, E., Barja, G., Garcia Serrano, F. and Larrea Flores, R. (2009). 'Establishing Social Equity: Bolivia, Ecuador, and Peru'. In E. Gacitúa-Marió, A. Norton, and S. V. Georgieva (Eds.), *Building Equality and Opportunity Through Social Guarantees: New Approaches to Public Policy and the Realization of Rights* (pp. 143–174). World Bank.

Gharaei, T., Thijs, J. and Verkuyten, M. (2018). 'Ethnic Identity in Diverse Schools: Preadolescents' Private Regard and Introjection in Relation to Classroom Norms and Composition'. *Journal of Youth and Adolescence*. 48(1): 132–144.

Goodrick, R. (2014). 'Qualitative Data Analysis'. In K. Newcomer, H. Hatry, and J. Wholey (Eds.), *Handbook of Practical Program Evaluation* (pp. 561–595). John Wiley & Sons, Inc.

Gupta, S. and Veena, R. 2016. 'Bilingual Education in Xinjiang in the Post-2009 Period'. *China Report*. 52(4): 306–323. DOI: 10.1177/0009445516661885.

Harris, R. (2019, January 17). 'Cultural Genocide in Xinjiang: How China Targets Uyghur Artists, Academics, and Writers'. *The Globe Post*. https://theglobepost.com/2019/01/17/cultural-genocide-xinjiang/

Hornberger, N. (2000). 'Bilingual Education Policy and Practice in the Andes: Ideological Paradox and Intercultural Possibility'. *Anthropology & Education Quarterly*. 31(2): 173–201.

Hornberger, N. (2006). 'Voice and Biliteracy in Indigenous Language Revitalization: Contentious Educational Practices in Quechua, Guarani, and Māori Contexts'. *Journal of Language, Identity, and Education*. 5(4): 277–292.

Hornberger, N. and Coronel-Molina, S. (2004). 'Quechua Language Shift, Maintenance, and Revitalization in the Andes: The Case for Language Planning'. *International Journal of The Sociology of Language*. (167): 9–67.

Hornberger, N. and Swinehart, K. (2012). 'Bilingual Intercultural Education and Andean Hip Hop: Transnational Sites for Indigenous Language and Identity'. *Language in Society*. 41(4): 499–525.

Hu, D. (2013). 'Cultural Endangerment and Education: Educational Analysis on the Change of Cultural Transmission of Dongba Dance of Naxi People in Lijiang, Yunnan, China'. *Frontiers of Education in China*. 7(2): 169–194.

Klimeš, O. and Smith Finley, J. (2020). 'China's Neo-totalitarian Turn and Genocide in Xinjiang'. *Society and Space*. www.societyandspace.org/articles/chinas-neo-totalitarian-turn-and-genocide-in-xinjiang?fbclid=IwAR28fYUFeOPffZMwJCMA8pMwHAgyUMxOyjwaYRMBIqfMutI573mGGmUJMmg

Kondo-Brown, K. (Ed.). (2006). *Heritage Language Development: Focus on East Asian Immigrants*. Amsterdam, The Netherlands: J. Benjamin's Publishing.

Kymlicka, W. and Patten, A. (2003). 'Language Rights and Political Theory'. *Annual Review of Applied Linguistics*. 23: 3–21.

'Learning and Identifying 75 Religious Extreme Activities in Parts of Xinjiang'. (n.d.) (trans. by Darren Byler). https://xinjiang.sppga.ubc.ca/chinese-sources/onlinesources/identifying-religious-extremism/

Lewis, M. and Simons, G. (2016). *Sustaining Language Use: Perspectives on Community-Based Language Development*. Dallas, TX: SIL International.

Liang, Y. and Zhang, J. (2007). 'Bilingual Teacher Training among Minority Teachers in Xinjiang' Xinjiang Shaoshu Minzu Shuangyu Jiaoshi Peixun Tanwei'. *Journal of Xinjiang Normal University*. 28(3): 128–131.

Liu, Y. P. (2012). 'Xinjiang Uyghur Autonomous Region Preschool, Elementary and Secondary Bilingual Education Development Plan' Xinjiang Weiwu'er Zizhi Shaoshu Minzu Xueqian he Zhongxiaoxue Shuangyu Jiaoyu Fazhan Guihua'. *Xinjiang Educational Information*. www.xjedu.gov.cn/jgsz/syjxgz/2012/48245.htm

Lopez, L. E. (2014). 'Indigenous Intercultural Bilingual Education in Latin America: Widening Gaps Between Language and Practice'. In R. Cortina (Ed.), *The Education of Indigenous Citizens in Latin America* (pp. 19–49). Abingdon, UK: Multilingual Matters.

Mahmut, D. and Smith Finley, J. (2022). 'Corrective Re-Education as (Cultural) Genocide: A Content Analysis of the Uyghur Primary School Textbook *Til-Adabiyat*'. In M. Clarke (Ed.), *The Xinjiang Emergency: Exploring the Causes and Consequences of China's Mass Detention of Uyghurs* (pp. 155–180). Manchester University Press.

May, S. (2011). *Linguistic and Minority Rights, 2nd ed*. New York, NY: Routledge.

Mchitarjan, I. and Reisenzein, R. (2014). 'Towards a Theory of Cultural Transmission in Minorities'. *Ethnicities*. 14(2): 181–20.

Musapir and Steenberg, R. (2024). 'Family or Freedom? The Changing Landscape of Uyghur Diaspora Activism'. In R. Clothey and D. Mahmut (Eds.), *Uyghur Identity and Culture: A Global Diaspora in a Time of Crisis*. (pp. 142–163). Routledge.

Myers, M. (2008). *Radio and Development in Africa: A Concept Paper*. Ottawa, Canada: IDRC.

Nimer, M. and Aparcik, D. (2023). 'Education and Language Policies toward Syrians in the Turkish State: Incorporation of Former Imperial Subjects into the Neo-Ottomanist Political Regime'. *Comparative Education Review*. 67(3): 630–649.

PROEIB-Andes. (2020). *Centro Interdiscipliario PROEIB-Andes*. www.proeibandes.org/

Radio San Gabriel. (n.d.). *Historia*. www.radiosangabriel.org.bo/rsg/?q=es/node/18

Roberts, S. and Clothey, R. (2024). 'A Transnational Perspective on Uyghur Cultural Maintenance and Preservation'. In R. Clothey and D. Mahmut (Eds.), *Uyghur Identity and Culture: A Global Diaspora in a Time of Crisis* (pp. 59–76). Routledge.

Roberts, S. R. (2018). 'The Biopolitics of China's "War on Terror" and the Exclusion of the Uyghurs'. *Critical Asian Studies*. 50(2): 232–258.

Roberts, S. R. (2020). *The War on the Uyghurs: China's Internal Campaign against a Muslim Minority*. Princeton University Press.

Rodrıguez-Merino, P. A. (2019). 'Old "Counter-revolution," New "Terrorism": Historicizing the Framing of Violence in Xinjiang by the Chinese State'. *Central Asian Survey*. 38(1): 27–45.

Schluessel, E. (2007). '"Bilingual" Education and Discontent in Xinjiang'. *Central Asian Survey*. 26(2): 251–277.

Simayi, Z. (2014). 'The Practice of Ethnic Policy in Education: Xinjiang's Bilingual Education System'. In J. Leibold and Y. B. Chen (Eds.), *Minority Education in China: Balancing Unity and Diversity in an Era of Critical Pluralism* (pp. 131–160). Hong Kong University Press.

Smith Finley, J. (2013). *The Art of Symbolic Resistance: Uyghur Identities and Uyghur-Han Relations in Contemporary Xinjiang*. Leiden, The Netherlands: Brill Publishing.

Smith Finley, J. (2021). 'Why Scholars and Activists Increasingly Fear a Uyghur Genocide in Xinjiang'. *Journal of Genocide Research*. 23(3): 348–370.

Sunuodula, M. and Feng, A. W. (2011). 'Learning a Third Language by Uyghur Students in Xinjiang: A Blessing in Disguise?'. In A. Feng (Ed.), *English Language in Education and Societies Across Greater China* (pp. 260–283). UK: Multilingual Matters Ltd.

Tsung, L. (2014). 'Trilingual Education and School Practice in Xinjiang'. In J. Leibold and Y. B. Chen (Eds.), *Minority Education in China: Balancing Unity and Diversity in an Era of Critical Pluralism* (pp. 161–186). Hong Kong: Hong Kong University Press.

UNESCO. (2021). *The World Atlas of Languages*. https://en.wal.unesco.org/world-atlas-languages

Unutulmaz, K. O. (2019). 'Turkey's Education Policies towards Syrian Refugees: A Macro-level Analysis'. *International Migration*. 57(2): 235–252.

Uyghur Human Rights Project (UHRP). (2019a). *Detained and Disappeared: Intellectuals under Assault in the Uyghur Homeland*. https://docs.uhrp.org/pdf/Detained-and-Disappeared-Intellectuals-Under-Assault-in-the-Uyghur-Homeland.pdf

Uyghur Human Rights Project (UHRP). (2019b, May 21). *Detained and Disappeared: Intellectuals Under Assault in the Uyghur Homeland*. https://uhrp.org/press-release/update-%E2%80%93-detained-and-disappeared-intellectuals-under-assault-uyghur-homeland.html

Velasquez, J. R. (1999). 'Una visión de la radio educativa en Bolivia'. *Revista Ciencia Y Cultura*. 3(5): 22–30.

Walker, R., Usher, K. Jackson, D., Reid, C., Hopkins, K., Shepherd, C., Smallwood, R. and Marriott, R. (2021). 'Addressing Digital Inequities in Supporting the Well-Being of Young Indigenous Australians in the Wake of COVID-19'. *International Journal of Environmental Research and Public Health*. 18(4): 2141. DOI: 10.3390/ijerph18042141

Wiecha, K. (2013). 'New Estimates on the Rate of Global Language Loss'. *The Rosetta Project*. http://rosettaproject.org/blog/02013/mar/28/new-estimates-on-rate-of-language-loss/

10

THE ROLE OF NEW MEDIA IN MAINTAINING ENDANGERED LANGUAGES

Insights from Igbo

Sopuruchi Christian Aboh

Introduction

Out of the 7,168 living languages in the world today, 3,072 are endangered (Eberhard et al. 2023). The number of endangered languages is predicted to increase by the end of the 21st century (Derhemi and Moseley 2023) owing to the low intergenerational transfer of Indigenous languages from the older to the younger generation. Arguably, this lack of intergenerational transfer of languages affects all continents. Earlier studies on the degrees of endangerment by continent indicate that there are approximately 131 endangered languages in North America, 164 in Eurasia, 104 in Australia, and 185 in Africa (Brenzinger 2007; Moseley 2007). Based on Eberhard et al.'s (2023) estimate, we can observe that these numbers have increased in recent years. Endangered languages on these continents indicate that language endangerment is a global phenomenon.

Looking more closely at the situation in Nigeria, out of 520 Indigenous languages, 130 are considered endangered (Eberhard et al. 2023). As is the case in several countries, one striking phenomenon in the Nigerian context is the endangerment of a major Indigenous language. Of the three major Nigerian Indigenous languages, Hausa, Igbo, and Yoruba, only Igbo was considered endangered. It was predicted by the United Nations Educational, Scientific and Cultural Organization (UNESCO) to be extinct by 2050 (Eke 2023). Igbo is a member of the Kwa group, a branch of the Niger-Congo language family. Its speakers are Indigenous to 5 (out of the 36) states in Nigeria: Abia, Anambra, Ebonyi, Enugu, and Imo. They also have several thousand speakers in parts of Delta and River states (see Figure 10.1 for a map of the areas where Igbo is the mother tongue). UNESCO's prediction of Igbo extinction in 1996 served as a wake-up call to Igbo people to explore mechanisms to maintain and revitalize the language. This was evident with the convening of metalanguage meetings; the organization of Igbo conferences; the sensitization of Igbo parents to the need to teach their children how to speak, read, and write in Igbo; and increasing research related to Igbo language and culture.

DOI: 10.4324/9781003439493-13

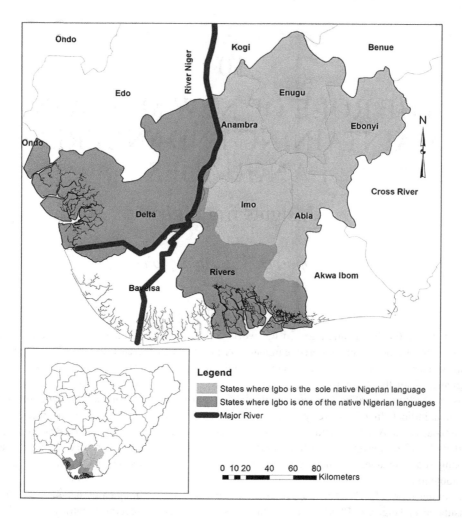

Figure 10.1 Map of Igbo land (Oyali 2018: 12)

Globally, in light of the linguistic and cultural loss resulting from language endangerment, linguists have engaged in various language documentation, maintenance, and revitalization projects. A recent recommendation to reverse language loss and promote the intergenerational transfer of Indigenous languages is to use these languages in new media technologies, such as Facebook, YouTube, Skype, and interactive websites, which can serve as a tool for teaching these languages and increasing their use in day-to-day communication (Cormack and Hourigan 2007). By capitalizing on new media and technology, language revitalization advocates hope to improve the retention and active use of endangered languages among the youth and their communities.

This chapter focuses on how new media technologies such as Facebook, WhatsApp, podcasts, Instagram, Skype, and Zoom have been utilized to maintain the Igbo language. In particular, it draws insights on the efforts of BBC News Igbo and *Ọjị Abịala* (an Igbo podcast) to increase the use of Igbo on the internet and teach Igbo to heritage learners as a way of transmitting Igbo to learners in the diaspora. In what follows, I first provide an overview of Igbo as an endangered language. Then I discuss new media and language maintenance. Before concluding the chapter, I will demonstrate how new media has been used to maintain the Igbo language using BBC News Igbo and *Oji Abịala* as reference points.

Igbo as an endangered language

Definitions of language endangerment abound in literature, and different scholars use varying assessment scales to determine whether a language is endangered. In all these definitions, scholars agree that an endangered language is one that is not being acquired by many children as a first language, indicating minimal intergenerational transmission (Austin and Sallabank 2011). One of the most cited reasons a language may not be transmitted to the younger generation is a shift to a majority language (O'Shannessy 2011), one of the sociolinguistic outcomes of multilingualism and intense language contact. This is also the case in Nigeria where a triglossic hierarchy exists; Standardized English, the country's official language, performs 'high' prestige functions and is seen as the language for upward social mobility, while Nigerian Pidgin (the mid language) is spoken by nonacrolectal Nigerians and serves interpersonal functions. Indigenous languages perform 'low' functions because of their unofficial use. Thus, parents show more positive attitudes toward English than toward Indigenous languages.

Scholars have proposed various scales and frameworks based on the level of intergenerational transmission to assess the degree of endangerment. UNESCO's language vitality and endangerment framework highlights six categories: 1. Safe (language is spoken by individuals of all age groups), 2. Vulnerable (most children speak the language, but it might be limited to specific domains like home), 3. Definitely endangered (children no longer acquire the language as mother tongue in the home), 4. Severely endangered (grandparents and older generations speak the language; while the parent generation may understand it, they do not speak it to their children or among themselves), 5. Critically endangered (the youngest speakers are grandparents and older, who speak the language partially and infrequently), and 6. Extinct (no speakers left) (see Austin and Sallabank 2011 for an overview). Grenoble and Whaley's (2006) six-stage framework: safe, at risk, disappearing, moribund, nearly extinct, and extinct, though it has different nomenclatures, largely covers the same ideas as UNESCO's framework. In his study, Wurm (2003) uses five levels of language situations to assess the degree of language endangerment: 1. potentially endangered (children begin preferring the dominant language), 2. endangered (very few children speakers), 3. seriously endangered (the youngest speakers are [over] middle age), 4. terminally endangered or moribund (few elderly speakers), and 5. dead (no speakers left). These stages of language endangerment indicate that language death is not abrupt (except in rare cases of genocide leading to the death of all speakers of a language) but a gradual process that involves a decline in intergenerational transmission, reduced domains of language use, and decreased linguistic vitality. As Grenoble (2011: 35) argues, 'a key characteristic of language endangerment is that use of the local language is limited, not only regionally but also functionally'.

Anchoring on the domains of use and level of intergenerational transfer, Fishman (1991) proposes an eight-level Graded Intergenerational Disruption Scale (GIDS) for assessing the vitality of a language, as presented in Table 10.1.

Fishman (1991) further categorizes these levels into two broad continua: levels 1–4 represent the 'strong side', while 5–8 are the 'weak side'. The critical stage is 6 because a language moving toward level 5 is developing, while a language tilting toward level 7 is undergoing a severe language shift. Fishman remarks that language revitalization typically starts with stages 7 or 6, while language revival begins with stage 8. Based on these frameworks of assessing language

Table 10.1 Fishman's GIDS

GIDS level	Description
1	The language is used in official domains such as education, mass media, and religion at the national level
2	The language is used for regional mass media and governmental functions
3	The language is used for local and regional work by both ingroup and outgroup
4	Literacy in the language is transmitted via education
5	The language is used orally by all age groups and is effectively used in written form in the whole community
6	The language is used orally by all age groups and is learned by children as their L1
7	The parent generation is competent in the language but not transmitting it to their children
8	The remaining speakers are members of the grandparent generation

endangerment, scholars (e.g., Azuonye 2003; Eke 2023; Igboanusi 2006) who have studied Igbo's level of endangerment agree that Igbo is endangered. For instance, Azuonye (2003: 44) clearly states that Igbo is a 'very seriously endangered language' owing to 12 factors broadly categorized into reduced competence and usage, adverse language policies and standardization, and cultural erosion. Igboanusi (2006: 446) argues that the endangerment of the Igbo language does not stem from an immediate threat to its existence but rather from its diminishing role in education, media, and entertainment due to the pervasive influence of the English language. This position indicates there is an intergenerational transfer of the Igbo language to the younger generation; however, it is facing an increasing decline in its use in official domains. Igboanusi's position may be influenced by the number of Igbo speakers, which is estimated to be 20–25 million. The problem with this number is that he did not clearly specify whether it refers to the total number of people who identify as Igbo or those who speak Igbo, because several people identify as Igbo but cannot speak the language. According to the Central Intelligence Agency (2023), 15.2% of Nigeria's 2023 estimated population of over 230 million is Igbo, indicating that approximately 35 million people are Igbo. When we compare the 2006 census report at the time Igboanusi reported his study, which estimated the population of Nigerians to be over 140 million, we can conclude that as of 2006, 14.2% of Nigerians are Igbo. These figures indicate that the number quoted by Igboanusi represents the number of Igbo people and not necessarily those who speak the language. Such a huge number may 'give the illusion that the language is not seriously threatened' (Quinn 2013: 2). Given that the number Igboanusi stated indicates those who identify as Igbo, we can argue that the number of Igbo speakers is lower because there are many Igbo people who cannot speak their language, especially young ones born outside Igbo-speaking areas and those whose parents did not expose them to Igbo (Aboh 2022).

A common viewpoint in the discourse on the vitality of Igbo is that it is unsafe and experiences a fair degree of endangerment. As with other endangered languages, the factors contributing to the endangerment of the Igbo language are economic, attitudinal, historical, and political. From an economic perspective, migration to non-speaking areas in Nigeria and the diaspora and the ideology that Igbo is less useful in upward social mobility are factors exacerbating the endangerment of Igbo. Many Igbo parents do not speak Igbo to their children because of its perceived low value in the linguistic marketplace (Bourdieu 1977) and lack of pressing communication needs to speak Igbo in a non-Igbo speaking environment. This situation is not only observed among people in non-Igbo-speaking areas; it has also been reported among several parents in Igbo-speaking areas (Nwaozuzu 2015). These children in question become 'terminal speakers' (Dorian 1981), with passive language knowledge and minimal productive skills. Terminal speakers operate virtually all their linguistic activities through the use of English, the dominant language, rather than Igbo. Such speakers, with respect to this, are sometimes referred to by fluent Igbo speakers as *Ndị Igbo khaki* ('inauthentic' Igbos) or 'my mama say I be Igbo' (my mother said I am Igbo), highlighting their limited proficiency in the Igbo language and their disconnection from the cultural and linguistic heritage of their ethnolinguistic group.

Such linguistic-based stereotypes can perform both positive and negative functions. Positively, these can motivate them to learn the language to avoid future negative stereotyping. They can also spur parents to make efforts to expose their children to Igbo later in their lives. This is evident in the practice of parents residing in non-Igbo-speaking states enrolling their children in universities located in Igbo-speaking areas so that they will have the opportunity to learn the Igbo language and culture (Aboh 2022). Negatively, stereotypes weaken the motivation to learn Igbo because of negative feedback. These terminal speakers would prefer not to practice speaking the language to eliminate any situation of embarrassment or destructive criticisms. As Quinn (2013: 1) notes:

> Reduction of the range of domains in which an individual can be exposed to the language commonly results in a feedback effect: otherwise fluent speakers who have knowledge or performance gaps are judged as imperfect speakers by more broadly experienced speakers, leading the former to avoid situations of language use even more, and so intensify the process of contraction.

The reduction in the range of domains in which Igbo is used results from the range and depth of the power of English in Nigeria (Kachru 2017). Given that English is the language used in education and mass media and because of its prestige as a global language (Crystal 2003), it has contributed to the decline in the transfer of Igbo to the younger generation. The negative attitudes of Igbo people toward their language are evident in Ohaneze Ndigbo's (a group that protects Igbo people's interest in Nigeria) meetings, where despite linguistic intelligibility of all the members, English is used as the medium of communication in place of Igbo (Aboh 2022).

Historically, Igbo language endangerment has been attributed to the Nigerian–Biafran War of 1967–1970, which led to the killings of over 3 million Igbos (Madiebo 1980), reducing the number of Igbo speakers. The impact of the civil war did not only restrict the geographical expansion of the Igbo language but also had a noticeable psychological effect on many L1 speakers who, to this day, perceive the language as having lower status when compared to English, Hausa, and Yoruba (Igboanusi 2006). Before the war, the Biafran territory included all five southeastern states and some parts of Akwa Ibom, Delta, and Rivers states, which are Indigenous to the Igbo-speaking people. However, after the war, several parts of Rivers and Delta declared themselves non-Igbo to gain political autonomy and avoid the punishment meted out to Igbo people. Among such punishments was the seizing of the money they had in the banks and giving them only 20 pounds (Eke 2023). The toponyms in these regions were altered to dissociate them from their Igbo origin. For instance, in Port Harcourt, toponyms such as *Umuokoro* (children of Okoro) and *Umuigbo* (Igbo people) were changed by prefixing an 'r-' to them, which resulted in 'Rumuokoro' and 'Rumuigbo', respectively (Ihemere 2007). This shift in identity and the declaration of their dialect as different languages have reduced the Igbo-speaking population and contributed to its status of endangerment. The Igbo orthography controversy, which lasted between 1929 and 1961, also negatively impacted the use of Igbo in education and mass media and further contributed to its endangerment (Akaeze et al. 2021).

Another cause of Igbo language endangerment is political. Although the Nigerian Construction (1999 as amended) and the National Policy of Education (NPE) (1977, revised 1981, 1998, 2004) recognized Igbo as one of the major languages that can be used to conduct the business of the National Assembly and serve as the medium of instruction in the first three years of primary education (Aziza 2016), the implementation of these policies has been lacking, leading to the continued decline of the Igbo language. A language may not progress if it does not have a strong presence in the educational system (Crystal 2000). This non-implementation is due to the government's poor commitment to promoting and preserving Indigenous languages like Igbo, evident by the use of 'escape clauses' (Kamwangamalu 2016) such as 'when adequate arrangements have been made' and 'when government develops instructional materials and qualified teachers available' (cf. Aboh 2022) in the language-in-education policies. In their study on the use of mother tongue education in Nigeria, Igboanusi and Peter (2016) found that Igbo is not the medium of instruction in many schools in Igbo-speaking areas. They reported that Igbo parents deregister their children from schools that they perceive do not emphasize English language teaching and speaking. In many schools with English as the medium of instruction, students are punished for speaking Igbo. This negative attitude toward mother tongue education may have resulted in minimal reactions by Igbo people against the Nigerian Educational Research and Development Council's (NERDC) decision to make Igbo an optional subject for the West African Senior Secondary Certificate Examination (WASSCE). Making Igbo optional in WASSCE has amplified low interest and literacy in the language. These factors, ranging from economic to political, have affected the speaker base of Igbo. Its limited domain of use illustrates the endangered state of Igbo and the need for efforts to maintain and revitalize it. Having discussed Igbo as an endangered language, the next section focuses on new media and language maintenance.

New media and language maintenance

When a language is endangered, there are three possible reactions: 1. do nothing, 2. document it before it becomes extinct, or 3. engage in revitalization and maintenance activities (Romaine 2007). Linguists often aim for the last two options because they believe that the loss of a language is a loss of diversity. In addition to different documentation activities involving working with a few last speakers of an endangered language to describe its linguistic features and create a dictionary, linguists have also made efforts to revitalize and maintain endangered languages by promoting their daily use among speakers and encouraging intergenerational transmission. Language maintenance is defined as the 'efforts to support or strengthen a language which is still vital, i.e., which is still acquiring young speakers, but where incipient decline is starting to be apparent' (Hinton 2011: 291). In other words, young people are the future of endangered languages because their ability to speak these languages improves their vitality. This definition indicates that language maintenance is needed in the early stages of low intergenerational transmission of languages. This suggests that language revitalization is expedient when young people do not speak the language in question. Whether language maintenance or revitalization, it is crucial to note that none of these efforts can be successful without the active participation of the endangered language communities.

Attempts to maintain and revitalize endangered languages have led language revitalizationists to embrace new media technologies. One of the questions asked during the early years of the development of the research area on language endangerment and technology was, 'Can the web save my language?' (Buszard-Welcher 2001: 331). After two decades of research in this area, new media is crucial for reversing language loss and language maintenance (Jany 2018). Browne (1996: 59) identifies seven purposes for Indigenous language media: 1. to save the language; 2.

to increase speakers' self-esteem; 3. to fight negative ideologies; 4. to work for greater coherence, which can result in political influence; 5. to provide an audio-visual symbol of an Indigenous community; 6. to provide a platform for creativity; and 7. to create employment opportunities. These purposes highlight the importance of media in identity enhancement, empowerment, and community cohesion, which are crucial for maintaining endangered languages. However, Browne (1996) notes that these functions can be achieved through committed and concerted efforts to develop electronic media outlets or utilize existing ones to promote the use and maintenance of the languages in question.

Similarly, Moriarty (2011) argues that the media can contribute to elevating the prestige of an endangered language, assisting in developing language resources by spreading new vocabulary, and promoting language learning by enhancing exposure to the language in public and private settings. For instance, Peterson (1997) posits that the prevalence of Setswana as compared to Ikalanga in Botswana can be attributed, in part, to its representation in the media. Similarly, Galla (2009) remarks that new media is the new frontier of language revitalization and maintenance because creating resources for language pedagogy is cost effective, easy and convenient. Wagner (2017) adds that with new media, learners of endangered languages will have access to learning materials and multimodal resources, such as audio, video, and interactive games. These multimodal resources are significant in attracting young learners as they are essential for maintaining or revitalizing languages. Because these resources are available, they increase the frequency with which learners are exposed to the language, which may improve their linguistic and communicative competence. New media also increases the pride of speakers of endangered languages and provides them with the opportunity to lead the fight for the survival of their ethnolinguistic groups as part of social change. In other words, using new media to teach the history and traditional values of Indigenous communities is one of the sovereign features of online language resources, as they allow speakers of Indigenous languages to reject dominant ideologies and reclaim Indigenous identities (Wagner 2017). As a West African proverb puts it, 'until the lions have their own historians, the history of the hunt will always glorify the hunter'. This proverb is a key way of communicating the importance of multiple viewpoints. From a colonial perspective, the proverb resists colonizer's control over the African narrative and encourages Africans to tell their own stories.

Several new media technologies, such as interactive websites and social media platforms, can be used to support endangered languages. Holton (2011: 375) distinguishes between two broad types of these technologies: 1. products, which 'are created by a group of developers or authors for a specific user community or audience' and 2. online technologies, which 'foster communities of language learners and language users'. Product technologies include multimedia, computer-assisted language learning (CALL), electronic dictionaries, web portals, and commercial off-the-shelf tools. Holton (2011) argues that while the developer of CALL products may focus on helping learners become fluent in the endangered language, other products focus mainly on learning about the language. The argument here is not that other products may not be used to learn the language but that the goal for their development is primarily to preserve the language. Examples of online technologies include: email and text messaging, interactive websites, word-of-the-day, podcasts, audio-video conferencing, and web-based language courses. Interactive websites, such as blogs, wikis and social networking services, such as Facebook, X (formerly Twitter), and WhatsApp, foster a virtual language community and allow for the exchange of online multimedia content. Word-of-the-day involves a teacher posting a word or phrase in the endangered language on social media or websites to make learners learn a new word daily. Podcasts often come in the form of audio or video recordings posted on the internet to communicate aspects of the culture or language of endangered languages. The advantage of podcast episodes is that they improve learners' listening skills. Audio-video conferencing technologies such as Skype and Zoom and web-based language courses are crucial because they eliminate the barrier caused by distance and physical borders and allow individuals to learn endangered languages from different locations (see Holton 2011).

Several studies have explored the usefulness of these new media technologies in language maintenance. For instance, de Graaf et al. (2015) examined how new technologies were used to preserve Frisian, a language that was seriously endangered between the 16th and 19th centuries. Frisian is a Germanic language spoken in the Netherlands, northwest Europe. Dutch displaced the language in the official, educational, and religious domains. It ceased to be used in written form until revitalization efforts began at the end of the 19th century. As part of its revitalization, de Graaf et al. (2015) report that the Tomke project, which started in 1996 and was used for pre-school education, involved cartoon characters and films typically made for children to promote multilingualism. In addition, interactive websites (Studio F and Freemwurk) with videos, audio, and interactive games served as teaching and learning resources to improve students' competence in Frisian. Traditional and new media such as the Frisian monthly cultural journal, Facebook, and X were also used by *Algemiene Fryske Ûnderrjocht Kommisje* (General Frisian Education Commission), a cultural institution in Leeuwarden, to promote knowledge of Frisian culture and increase the use of Frisian online. de Graaf et al. (2015) conclude that through new technologies, the number of Frisian speakers and their pride in the language has increased.

Another instance where technologies such as radio, television, and the internet positively influence an endangered language is the case of Kashubian, a language spoken by the Kashubs in Poland. Out of 500,000 people who identify as Kashubian, only 80,000 use it in everyday life. The endangerment of Kashubian was caused by the migration of many speakers to cities where Polish or German are predominantly used, and during the communist era, in Poland (1945–1989), Kashubian was forbidden in public life and schools. However, following the fall of communism in 1989 and the Polish Act on the National and Ethnic Minorities and Regional Language in 2009, which recognized Kashubian as a regional language in Poland and approved it as a school subject, the status of Kashubian has increased and facilitated its use in new media. It is used in radio and TV broadcasting, and its use on the internet has provided the opportunity for its use both orally and in writing. Its use on the internet, especially by young people, has enabled Kashubians to connect with others, learn about their culture, increase their interest in the language, and help with its maintenance (see Dołowy-Rybinska, 2013).

Valijärvi and Kahn (2023) explored the significance of YouTube, Facebook, and X for endangered languages. They showed how hashtags on X were used to raise awareness of Indigenous and endangered-language issues among Sami speakers, where hashtags such as #gollegiela (golden language) and #aarjel ('south' for South Sami) were used as a strategy to make Sami people to be proud of their language. Emphasizing the importance of hashtags in language maintenance, Cassels (2019: 30) notes that they 'empower language users to broadcast their identities and align themselves with cultural and linguistic communities'. Valijärvi and Kahn (2023) remarked that Facebook groups and YouTube are also new media resources used to create awareness about endangered languages, emphasize the need to transmit them to the younger generation, and provide opportunities to speakers of endangered languages to use their language without the constraints of standardization or linguistic purism. They added that podcasts in endangered languages, like Māori podcasts, can improve the listening and knowledge skills of endangered language communities.

These cases highlight how technology and new media can be deployed to maintain and revitalize endangered languages. The use of endangered languages in new media can potentially increase their socioeconomic status. With the monetization features of YouTube, Facebook, and X, individuals would be motivated to use these languages continuously. Constant use increases young people's exposure to the language and may motivate them to acquire it. However, it is worth noting that new media technologies alone cannot successfully maintain or revitalize languages without the concerted efforts of the endangered communities. Fishman (1991) argues that while media can be utilized for language maintenance and revitalization, it is important to note that computer programs, email, search engines, the internet as a whole, chat boxes, or any similar tools cannot replace the value of in-person communication with one's family within an authentic community setting. Since new media cannot automatically create new speakers of endangered languages, revitalizing and maintaining these languages rely on the active engagement and participation of community members, especially parents and educators. This active engagement is needed so that the major languages will not displace endangered languages in the media as well (Cunliffe 2019).

Igbo language and new media

As already stated, doing nothing about endangerment would only result in the extinction of that language. As Riggins (1992: 3) maintains, 'What better strategy could there be for ensuring minority survival than the development by minorities of their own media conveying their own point of view in their own language?' New media has been deployed to increase the use and learning of Igbo as an endangered language. For instance, Igbo Facts and History on X educates Igbo people on Igbo history and culture and uses the hashtag #IgboProverbFriday to invite Igbo people to tweet an Igbo proverb every Friday. Several Facebook pages exist that educate people on how to say specific sentences and words in Igbo. In this section, we will look at how BBC News Igbo and *Ọjị Abịala* (an Igbo podcast) have deployed new media, particularly Facebook, Instagram, Skype/Zoom, podcasts, and WhatsApp, to maintain the Igbo language.

BBC News Igbo

BBC News Igbo is a Facebook- and Instagram-based media platform established by the British Broadcasting Corporation World Service in February 2018 to encourage people to use Igbo more and to increase awareness of Igbo culture. The media platform publishes only in Igbo. Described as the 'twenty-first-century public sphere of the Igbo', its existence has contributed to increasing the pride of its community members in their language and culture and this has managed to attract the young audience, who are crucial for language maintenance (Eke 2023: 97). The thought that BBC, a UK-owned broadcasting service, is investing in Igbo, would encourage its people to value their language and expose their children to it. As of the time of writing this chapter (February 2024), BBC News Igbo has 1.7 million followers on Facebook and 220,000 followers on Instagram. The establishment of BBC News Igbo provided an alternative for young Igbo people to write in their language and be exposed to it despite the decline of Igbo-language newspapers and Igbo-based programs on radio and television stations. As Holton (2011) argues, having a platform where individuals write in an endangered language can promote literacy development.

On its website (www.bbc.com/igbo), the contents are categorized into *Akụkọ* (Stories), *Egwuregwu* (Sports), *Ihe nkiri* (Videos), and *Nke ka ewuewu* (Most viewed/read). The written stories capture events in politics, education, interviews, and foreign affairs and aim to inform readers of the latest socioeconomic issues. They serve to improve the Igbo reading and comprehension skills of the readers. The Stories section also includes general questions addressed to the audience, asking them to provide the completion of a proverb; the name of a plant or animal in their dialect, and their opinions on education-, politics-, and health-related issues. These questions aim to encourage the audience to use Igbo in their responses, which will improve their writing skills and promote the use of the Igbo language. As Crystal (2000: 138) remarks, 'An endangered language will progress if its speakers can write their language down'. The Sports section reports mainly football-related news. Its hilarious football headlines drawn from Igbo idioms and proverbs have endeared BBC News Igbo to many Igbo people. The Videos section includes on-the-spot coverage of events such as elections, community events such as Kingship coronation and New Yam festivals, and interviews with prominent Igbo people. This section helps improve the listening skills of the audience. The most-viewed section includes the four items that have received the highest views since the establishment of the program. Apart from speaking, BBC News Igbo can be argued to improve audience's Igbo reading, writing, and listening skills. Given that Igbo has been made optional in schools, BBC Igbo could serve as a platform for people to informally learn Igbo, especially regarding its lexemes and culture. It also provides Igbo linguists with data for corpus linguistics research that can be used to study the synchronic linguistic features of Igbo. Given that all of its contents are in Igbo, BBC News Igbo has contributed to the neologisms of Igbo words and the popularization of new and existing Igbo expressions. These neologisms contribute to the growth of Igbo, thereby ensuring its survival. Outakoski et al. (2018) argue that instead of restricting the potential for growth and advancement of Indigenous languages, the emergence of new media provides them with new opportunities for dissemination and promotion.

Eke (2023) conducted a comprehensive study of the impact of BBC News Igbo on the revitalization of the Igbo language. Qualitative content analysis was employed to analyze BBC News Igbo stories published on Facebook in August 2020 (totaling 176) and the (meta)comments on these stories. Semi-structured interviews were used to elicit opinions on the potential of BBC News Igbo to revitalize the Igbo language from three BBC News Igbo presenters and three Igbo language enthusiasts. Online survey responses, aimed at ascertaining the extent to which BBC News Igbo has enhanced prestige and acquisition of Igbo language skills among its audience, were also obtained from 125 participants drawn from 1,528 commenters on stories published in August 2020. The study found that 58% of the participants reported that using BBC News Igbo has made them courageous about speaking Igbo. Participants also indicated that they had a sense of belonging and were proud that they could use Igbo on social media, suggesting that there is a move away from the association of Igbo with being old-fashioned and backwards-looking to modernism. For instance, one of the participants remarked: 'My approach to Igbo language now is that of taking pride in communicating with [in] my language' (Eke 2023: 133).

When asked about their views on BBC News Igbo, participants reported that it helped to promote and preserve the Igbo language and culture and served as a platform for learning the same. A participant noted:

> When I have my classes I encourage people to look at BBC News Igbo; I direct them there because all their interviews, everything is in Igbo, even their subtitles are also in Igbo language, that will also help people to know how to spell, how to write Igbo language.
>
> (Eke 2023: 135)

Eke (2023) found that interview responses from BBC News Igbo presenters and Igbo language enthusiasts on the benefits of the program on the Igbo language revealed themes including digitization and promotion of Igbo, revival of interest in the Igbo language and culture, and provision of access and resources for learning the Igbo language. The study concluded that BBC News Igbo has enhanced the prestige of the Igbo language. Nwammuo and Salawu (2019: 91) reached a similar conclusion that BBC News Igbo, through its 'wide range of stories and topics that concern local

I absolutely love *Ọjị Abịala*! I started this program 2 months ago without knowing any Igbo (except for a few words) and now I know enough to carry a daily conversation. The structure of the program is very helpful as I get to listen to the lessons as well as have one-on-one conversations with my conversation tutor. This allows for me to hear and speak Igbo on a consistent basis. It has helped me tremendously.

(Chioma, Uppsala)

These learners emphasized how the program has improved their Igbo listening and speaking skills and increased the frequency of exposure to Igbo. Ngozi remarked that her confidence in speaking Igbo has also increased. These responses indicate how *Ọjị Abịala* has facilitated the learning of Igbo by individuals who are not in Igbo-speaking areas. By helping increase the number of Igbo speakers, *Ọjị Abịala* helps maintain the Igbo language.

In addition to the one-on-one classes, *Ọjị Abịala* also organizes ten-week group Igbo classes twice or thrice a year via Zoom for those who are not directly registered in the program but would like to learn basic Igbo. Holton (2011) found that audio-video conferencing helps in language learning. Each cohort is added to a WhatsApp group where they can practice what they have learned and ask Igbo-related questions. To obtain learners' responses on the impact of the technology-based ten-week Igbo course on their Igbo language skills, I distributed online questionnaires to 67 learners who enrolled in the group classes in 2022. A thematic analysis of their responses resulted in two themes: improved confidence/motivation and enhanced proficiency. These themes indicate that several learners reported that they generally felt more confident using Igbo after completing the course because of improved speaking and comprehension skills, grammar, and vocabulary knowledge.

Apart from one-on-one Igbo language teaching, *Ọjị Abịala* also utilizes its Instagram page (@igbopodcast), which has about 20,000 followers, to post its word/phrase or verb for the week (see Figure 10.2).

For verbs, it provides examples of how the verb is used in present, past, and future tenses; commands; and common idioms or proverbs. In this way, followers learn new verbs and phrases and improve their knowledge of verb conjugation in Igbo. Holton (2011) argues that word/phrase of the day/week is crucial in learning and maintaining an endangered language. The Instagram page also teaches linguistic and cultural issues such as constructing questions, forming negations, Igbo traditional titles, and how to welcome guests in Igbo. Posts asking followers to provide an Igbo translation of a short English expression or what a certain item is called in Igbo are made to promote followers' use of Igbo. In addition to Instagram, *Ọjị Abịala* also uses podcasts (https://obodofullcircle.com/episodes#podcasts), streamed by over 180,000 people, to teach Igbo language and culture. At the time of writing this chapter, the podcasts had 55 episodes, including topics such as the Igbo alphabet, grammatical categories, verbal systems and tones, listening comprehension, and Igbo cultural concepts such as *nwadiala* (denoting affiliation to maternal family) and *dada* (dreads). The podcasts help listeners learn about the Igbo language and culture while performing other duties such as driving to work, doing house chores, or exercising. In the Māori context, Valijärvi and Kahn (2023) argued that podcasts are essential in combating language loss.

Apart from teaching Igbo, *Ọjị Abịala* also promotes the use of Igbo and the emergence of new literary works in Igbo by L1 speakers. In May 2023, it organized an Igbo investigative play competition. The competition, which received about ten entries, gave cash awards to the winner and the first and second runners-up. Such competition may motivate Igbo speakers to be proud of their language, knowing that it can provide economic benefits. Through the affordances of new media, people [which] can be listened to from anywhere in the world', has encouraged Igbo people to speak the language; thus, increasing its vitality. These submissions indicate the positive impact of Indigenous media, such as BBC News Igbo, on maintaining and revitalizing the Igbo language. This program provides a means for the Igbo community to have their language and culture represented and celebrated, thus promoting a sense of pride and self-esteem among its speakers.

Ọjị Abịala (an Igbo podcast)

One of the benefits afforded by teleconferencing technologies, such as Skype and Zoom, and social media platforms, such as Instagram and WhatsApp, is that they bridge the geographical distance between two or more individuals, which has facilitated endangered language pedagogy. *Ọjị Abịala* (with its sister brand known as *Obodo*) deploys the affordances of new media to teach Igbo as a heritage language to Igbo people born in the diaspora from over 20 countries by connecting them to L1 Igbo speakers in Nigeria. Learners' ages ranged from 6 to 60 years. As Moriarty (2011: 454) remarks, through new media, 'diasporic communities can maintain cultural and linguistic links with their place of origin across physical and social spaces, thus aiding the maintenance of linguistic and cultural identities among people who otherwise would have little or no face-to-face contact'. My review of this online teaching platform is based on my experience as a former conversation partner in the program, information obtained from the platform's website (https://obodofullcircle.com/), and the survey responses I obtained from 67 learners in the program. The primary motivation cited by the learners for learning Igbo is to understand and respond when their uncles, aunts, and cousins speak Igbo to them; connect to their heritage; and learn about Igbo culture. Since its inception in 2018, the program has improved the Igbo language skills of more than 700 learners.

Ọjị Abịala can be described as a master–apprentice language learning program where learners (maximum of four) are assigned to an L1 speaker of Igbo, referred to as a 'conversation partner'. Each learner and conversation partner meet one hour per week (any day between Friday and Monday) via Skype. The classes are recorded, which allows learners to revisit them at their convenience. The modules for the classes focus on linguistic and cultural issues aimed at improving learners' language skills and knowledge of Igbo culture. Learners are expected to submit assignments on Tuesdays and Thursdays on WhatsApp, which could be saying something about their day in Igbo or reading a short Igbo text or listening to Igbo music and making sense of what they heard. Emphasizing the importance of music in endangered language pedagogy, Moriarty (2011) notes that it provides teachers with more relevant resources than formal language texts and allows learners to participate and enjoy the medium despite their literacy level. Once their assignments have been submitted, the conversation partner offers feedback. The essence of the weekday assignments is to improve learners' use of Igbo and expand their knowledge beyond the one-hour classes. WhatsApp also allows learners to ask their conversation partners how to construct specific sentences in Igbo, which aids in improving their Igbo vocabulary. Commenting on the program's impact on Igbo language proficiency, two learners remarked:

> I have always been pretty competent in my level of comprehension in listening but struggled with my ability to speak as fluently as I would like. I was tired of whining about this as a life goal and decided to make it a reality. Since joining the program, my speaking proficiency has increased tremendously. I am more confident and much more likely to respond in Igbo when others speak to me instead of my previous inclination to respond in English.
>
> (Ngozi, Texas)

The role of new media in maintaining endangered languages

Figure 10.2 A sample of an Igbo phrase for the week

Ọjị Abịala promotes the use of Igbo and provides opportunities for intergenerational transfer of the language, thereby contributing to maintaining the Igbo language. *Ọjị Abịala* is a great example of how media can be used to teach a less commonly taught language like Igbo. This can provide insights into how new media can be deployed to teach endangered languages in Nigerian schools and beyond.

Conclusion

This chapter has offered a glimpse into the decline in the intergenerational transmission of the Igbo language and how new media such as Facebook, Instagram, Skype, Zoom, and WhatsApp have been deployed to promote the use of Igbo and teach it as a heritage language to the Igbo born in the diaspora. The new media roles discussed in this chapter are in line with the advantages of new media in maintaining and revitalizing endangered languages in the literature (see Browne 1996; Holton 2011; Valijärvi and Kahn 2023). We discussed how new media can contribute to producing Igbo neo-speakers through a master-apprentice language learning system. BBC News Igbo and *Ọjị Abịala* not only enhance the prestige of the Igbo language but also provide a platform for the Igbo community to engage with and celebrate their language and culture. One possible implication of the two cases presented in this chapter for Indigenous language teaching in Nigeria is that they support the benefits of computer- and mobile device–assisted language learning. These cases hope to spur educational officials and policymakers to provide schools with appropriate tools to facilitate a technology-based language pedagogy. For stakeholders such as policymakers, educators, and community leaders who engage in language revitalization efforts, I propose these actionable steps or best practices to support the role of new media in maintaining endangered languages.

First, stakeholders should collaborate with technology experts to develop digital tools for language maintenance, such as mobile applications and leveraging the affordances of artificial intelligence. Second, given that new media helps bridge the distance between teachers and learners, language learning materials must also be digitized to enable learners to assess them despite their location. Libraries, especially in Nigerian language institutes, need to be digitized to improve access and facilitate the learning of Nigerian languages without geographical constraints. These digitized libraries can serve as repositories of learning resources and cultural heritage. Third, to support the role of new media in maintaining endangered languages, there is a need to engage the community through the organization of workshops and seminars where community members will be educated on the need to use their Indigenous languages at home and in the new media. Parents who speak endangered languages need to be encouraged to promote the use of their Indigenous language at home and be proud of it. Last, there is a need for the government and non-governmental organizations to financially support the successful implementation of new media in maintaining languages.

Owing to the fact that a language cannot be successfully maintained or revitalized if there are no new young speakers, new policies need to be introduced to promote additive bilingualism owing to its cognitive advantage (Austin and Sallabank 2011). The government should introduce educational policies that encourage the learning of Indigenous languages in schools. Status planning should be implemented for endangered languages to ensure their use in media, education, and commerce. In line with Aboh (2022), I argue for a bottom-up approach to the revitalization of Nigeria's endangered languages, which involves speakers of these languages playing an active role in preserving and promoting their Indigenous languages. Therefore, it is essential for the Igbo community to actively engage with and support Indigenous media platforms such as *Ọjị Abịala* and BBC News Igbo to ensure the continued growth and development of the Igbo language.

The usefulness of new media in maintaining endangered languages discussed in this chapter does not suggest that there are no potential drawbacks. Cunliffe (2019) argues that the new media can also reinforce the dominance of most languages, such as English. Furthermore, another challenge would be getting people willing to fund schools to utilize new media in teaching Indigenous languages. These potential setbacks notwithstanding, I contend that social media, compared to traditional media, provides more opportunity for speakers of endangered languages to use their languages and may also motivate them to develop technologies that would enable them to use the language online (see also Browne 1996).

English references

Aboh, S. C. (2022). 'On the parameters of the power of English in Nigeria: A bottom-up approach towards revitalizing Nigerian languages'. *Cogent Arts & Humanities*. 9(1): 1–22. https://doi.org/10.1080/233119 83.2022.2118447

Austin, P. K. and Sallabank, J. (Eds.). (2011). *The Cambridge Handbook of Endangered Languages*. Cambridge: Cambridge University Press.

Aziza, R. O. (2016). 'Towards a revitalization of Urhobo: An endangered language of Delta State, Nigeria'. In G. N. Devy, G. V. Davis, and K. K. Chakravarty (Eds.), *The Language Loss of the Indigenous* (pp. 207–220). London: Routledge.

Azuonye, C. (2003). 'Igbo as an endangered language'. *Uwa Ndi Igbo: Journal of Igbo Life and Culture*. 3: 41–68.

Bourdieu, P. (1977). 'The economics of linguistic exchanges'. *Social Science Information*. 16(6): 645–668.

Brenzinger, M. (Ed.). (2007). *Language Diversity Endangered*. Berlin: Mouton de Gruyter.

Browne, D. (1996). *Electronic Media and Indigenous Peoples: A Voice of Our Own?* Ames, IA: Iowa State University Press.

Buszard-Welcher, L. (2001). 'Can the web help save my language?'. In L. Hinton and K. Hale (Eds.), *The Green Book of Language Revitalization in Practice* (pp. 331–345). San Diego, CA: Academic Press.

Cassels, M. (2019). 'Indigenous languages in new media: Opportunities and challenges for language revitalization'. *Working Papers of the Linguistics Circle of the University of Victoria*. 29(1): 25–43.

Central Intelligence Agency. (2023). *The World Factbook: Nigeria*. Retrieved from www.cia.gov/the-world-factbook/countries/nigeria/#people-and-society

Cormack, M. and Hourigan, N. (2007). 'Introduction: Studying minority language media'. In M. Cormack and N. Hourigan (Eds.), *Minority Language Media: Concepts, Critiques and Case Studies* (pp. 1–16). Clevedon: Multilingual Matters.

Crystal, D. (2000). *Language Death*. Cambridge: Cambridge University Press.

Crystal, D. (2003). *English as a Global Language*, 2nd ed. Cambridge: Cambridge University Press.

Cunliffe, D. (2019). 'Minority languages and social media'. In G. Hogan-Brun and B. O'Rourke (Eds.), *The Palgrave Handbook of Minority Languages and Communities* (pp. 451–480). London: Palgrave Macmillan. https://doi.org/10.1057/978-1-137-54066-9_18

de Graaf, T., van der Meer, C. and Jongbloed-Faber, L. (2015). 'The use of new technologies in the preservation of an endangered language: The case of Frisian'. In M. C. Jones (Ed.), *Endangered Languages and New Technologies* (pp. 141–149). Cambridge: Cambridge University Press.

Derhemi, E. and Moseley, C. (Ed.). (2023). *Endangered Languages in the 21st Century*. London: Routledge.

Dołowy-Rybińska, N. (2013). 'Kashubian and modern media: The influence of new technologies on endangered languages'. In E. H. G. Jones and E. Uribe-Jongbloed (Eds.), *Social Media and Minority Languages: Convergence and the Creative Industries* (pp. 119–129). Clevedon: Multilingual Matters.

Dorian, N. C. (1981). *Language Death: The Life Cycle of a Scottish Gaelic Dialect*. Philadelphia: University of Pennsylvania Press.

Eberhard, D. M., Simons, G. F. and Fennig, C. D. (2023). *Ethnologue: Languages of the World*, 26th ed. TX: SIL International.

Eke, I. W. (2023). *Exploring the Impact of BBC News Igbo on Revitalisation of Igbo Language* (PhD Thesis). North-West University (South Africa).

Fishman, J. A. (1991). *Reversing Language Shift: Theoretical and Empirical Foundations of Assistance to Threatened Languages*. Clevedon: Multilingual Matters.

Galla, C. K. (2009). 'Indigenous language revitalization and technology: From tradition to contemporary domains'. In J. Reyhner and L. Lockard (Eds.), *Indigenous Language Revitalization: Encouragement, Guidance and Lessons Learned* (pp. 167–182). Flagstaff: Northern Arizona University Press.

Grenoble, L. A. (2011). 'Language ecology and endangerment'. In P. K. Austin and J. Sallabank (Eds.), *The Cambridge Handbook of Endangered Languages* (pp. 27–44). Cambridge, MA: Cambridge University Press.

Grenoble, L. A. and Whaley, L. J. (2006). *Saving Languages: An Introduction to Language Revitalization*. Cambridge: Cambridge University Press.

Hinton, L. (2011). 'Revitalization of endangered languages'. In P. K. Austin and J. Sallabank (Eds.), *The Cambridge Handbook of Endangered Languages* (pp. 291–311). Cambridge: Cambridge University Press.

Holton, G. (2011). 'The role of information technology in supporting minority and endangered languages'. In P. K. Austin and J. Sallabank (Eds.), *The Cambridge Handbook of Endangered Languages* (pp. 371–399). Cambridge: Cambridge University Press.

Igboanusi, H. (2006). 'Is Igbo an endangered language?'. *Multilingua*. 25: 443–452. https://doi.org/10.1515/MULTI.2006.023

Igboanusi, H. and Peter, L. (2016). The language-in-education politics in Nigeria. *International Journal of Bilingual Education and Bilingualism*. 19(5): 563–578. https://doi.org/10.1080/13670050.2015.1031633

Ihemere, K. U. (2007). *A Tri-generational Study of Language Choice and Shift in Port Harcourt*. Florida: Universal Publishers.

Jany, C. (2018). 'The role of new technology and social media in reversing language loss'. *Speech, Language and Hearing*. 21(2): 73–76. https://doi.org/10.1080/2050571X.2017.1368971

Kachru, B. B. (2017). *World Englishes and Culture Wars*. Cambridge: Cambridge University Press.

Kamwangamalu, N. M. (2016). *Language Policy and Economics: The Language Question in Africa*. London: Palgrave Macmillan.

Madiebo, A. (1980). *The Nigerian Revolution and the Biafran War*. Enugu: Fourth Dimension.

Moriarty, M. (2011). 'New roles for endangered languages'. In P. K. Austin and J. Sallabank (Eds.), *The Cambridge Handbook of Endangered Languages* (pp. 446–458). Cambridge: Cambridge University Press.

Moseley, C. J. (2007). *Encyclopedia of Endangered Languages*. London: Routledge.

Nwammuo, A. and Salawu, A. (2019). 'Are radio programmes via indigenous languages the solution? A study of Igbo scholars' assessment of the effectiveness of the British Broadcasting Corporation (BBC) in promoting African languages'. *African Renaissance*. 16(1): 83–99.

O'Shannessy, C. (2011). 'Language contact and change in endangered languages'. In P. K. Austin and J. Sallabank (Eds.), *The Cambridge Handbook of Endangered Languages* (pp. 78–99). Cambridge: Cambridge University Press.

Outakoski, H., Cocq, C. and Steggo, P. (2018). 'Strengthening Indigenous languages in the digital age: Social media – supported learning in Sápmi'. *Media International Australia*. 169(1): 21–31. https://doi.org/10.1177/1329878X18803700

Oyali, U. (2018). *Bible Translation and Language Elaboration: The Igbo Experience* (PhD Thesis). University of Bayreuth (Germany).

Peterson, L. (1997). 'Tuning in to Navajo: The role of radio in native language maintenance'. In J. Reyhner (Ed.), *Teaching Indigenous Languages* (pp. 214–221). Flagstaff: Northern Arizona University.

Quinn, C. M. (2013). 'Endangered Languages'. In C. A. Chapelle (Ed.), *The Encyclopedia of Applied Linguistics* (pp. 1–5). Oxford: Wiley-Blackwell. https://doi.org/10.1002/9781405198431.wbeal0369

Riggins, S. H. (Ed.). (1992). *Ethnic Minority Media: An International Perspective*. London: Sage.

Romaine, S. (2007). 'Preserving endangered languages'. *Language and Linguistics Compass*. 1(1–2): 115–132. https://doi.org/10.1111/j.1749-818X.2007.00004.x

Valijärvi, R.-L. and Kahn, L. (2023). 'The role of new media in minority- and endangered-language communities'. In E. Derhemi and C. Moseley (Eds.), *Endangered Languages in the 21st Century* (pp. 139–157). London: Routledge.

Wagner, I. (2017). 'New technologies, same ideologies: Learning from language revitalization online'. *Language Documentation and Conservation*. 11: 133–156.

Wurm, S. A. (2003). 'The language situation and language endangerment in the Greater Pacific area'. In M. Janse and S. Tol (Eds.), *Language Death and Language Maintenance: Theoretical, Practical and Descriptive Approaches* (pp. 15–47). Amsterdam/Philadelphia: John Benjamins.

Igbo references

Akaeze, C. M., Aboh, S. C. and Ugwuoke, P. E. (2021). *Fundamentals of Contemporary Igbo Prose Fiction (Ntọala Ọdịnịigha Igbo Ọlọrọohụrụ)*. Obosi: Pacific Publishers Ltd.

Nwaozuzu, G. (2015). *The Efforts of Igbos Toward the Promotion of Their Language and Culture (Agbambọ Ndị Igbo na Nkwalite Asụsụ na Omenala ha)*. A lead paper presented at the 9th Chief Dr. F. C. Ogbalu memorial lecture, Nnamdi Azikiwe University, Awka, Nigeria. Nnamdi Azikiwe University, Awka, Nigeria.

11

CHALLENGES OF LANGUAGE SURVIVAL IN DIGITAL PERSPECTIVES

Case and context of India

Arimardan Kumar Tripathi

Introduction

India is a deep, multilingual country with various shades of its multilingual nature. The democratic setup, complex geography, varying education standards, different religions, races, identities, priorities and policies of governments, globalization, and now the internet have influenced Indian multilingualism intensively. As far as number is concerned, during the data collection process of the 2011 Indian census, the total number of mother tongues recorded was 19,569. After their classification on linguistic grounds, the number was rationalized as 1369. Further, 1474 languages were placed in the category of 'other' languages. Based on the total mother tongue population of 10,000 or more, the number of mother tongues has been recorded as 121. Of these, 22 languages are listed in the Eighth Schedule of the Constitution, and their speaking population is 96.71%, and the remaining 99 mother tongue speakers share only 3.29% of the total population (Census of India, 2011). Apart from the current list of 22 languages, there is a constant demand to add new languages/dialects to the list of the Eighth Schedule. Besides this, there are 87 languages in printing, and radio programs are broadcast in 71 languages. Along with two official languages at the Union level, 32 languages are used as official languages in various states. Forty-seven languages are used as a medium of instruction in schools (Tripathi & Singh, 2021, pp. 19–20). The National Education Policy (NEP)-2020 reiterates the need for elementary education in all mother tongues. Even the country's currency is bilingual, and its value is communicated through 15 languages. The question arises: won't people slip on the flat path after passing through so much roughness? Does the process of Indian digitization achieve its intended objectives only in English? Of course not.

Multilingualism has always been an asset of Indian society, and many categories of language use exist in our language planning system and practices within society, such as Official Languages, Three-Language Formula, Classical Languages, and Eighth-Schedule Languages. In the meantime, a new category, the Endangered Language, appeared for the first time in NEP-2020, which is probably the consequence of UNESCO's list of endangered languages declared in 2009. Further, NEP-2020 has suggested many steps to look into the issues of marginal languages and for their betterment. The policy also talks about protecting and promoting unscripted and endangered

DOI: 10.4324/9781003439493-14

languages in light of the 197 endangered Indian languages list declared by UNESCO in 2009 (Tripathi, 2022, June, p. 97). Contrary to these facts, English has been pivotal in Indian research and development, higher education, administration, and the judiciary. English has persisted in Indian public affairs to varying degrees of use and importance and has been found indispensable for running its political system (Karat, 1972, p. 1). Simultaneously, English is the primary language of cloud computing and machine learning as well. Thus, the dominance of English increased multiply in the process of its interface at the mass level, especially in the case of digitalization. The mother tongue of the information revolution has often been English, and its entire appearance comes against the Indian linguistic ecology. By its very nature, information and communication technology poses the challenge of limiting Indian socio-cultural diversity, narrowing the natural flow of Indian democracy, especially for the regional ethnic societies. The sense of a digital divide is taking place within society intimately and can be observed clearly on a larger scale, as the grass-rooted Indian multilingualism and their expressions, sentiments, and desire to live in digital surroundings are impossible only in English. Since people at a large scale from grassroots society are coming under the ambit of digitalization, the question of the language of communication and its entire growing processes becomes more relevant than ever, as the prevalence of intensive multilingualism on the ground is a primary need, and the Indian constitution well supports these at several levels, especially provisions for the protection of the interests of minorities to ensure the betterment of marginal people. As such, Article 29 (1) states that any section of the citizens residing in the territory of India or any part thereof having a distinct language, script, or culture of its own shall have the right to conserve the same. Article 29 (2) states that no citizen shall be denied admission into any educational institution maintained by the state or receiving aid out of state funds on grounds only of religion, race, caste, language, or any of them, and Article 30 (1) states all minorities, whether based on religion or language, shall have the right to establish and administer educational institutions of their choice. (Government of India, 2022a, p. 15). Therefore, it is the constitutional responsibility of governments to protect and promote the marginal languages in digital space as well.

Dilemma of Indian digitalization

India, as an independent nation, is now 76 years old. Of course, it has a rich linguistic and cultural tradition, and despite many distortions, it is ready again to take care of the legacy where languages and cultures hold a prominent place. Filling the gap of hundreds of years within this limited period is not easy, but also, one cannot absolve oneself of one's responsibilities by holding foreign invaders responsible. The Indian distortion period had long phases, where the British were the last to hand over the legacy to the Indians formally on 15 August 1947. However, British officials started working towards fulfilling Indian aspirations in research and technological innovations on the verge of Indian freedom. During the government of British India, then–Education Adviser Sir John Sargent prepared a comprehensive report, the 'Sargent plan,' on the status and the prospects of education in India. Consequently, the Central Advisory Board of Education (CABE) convened a high-powered committee in 1943, with Sir Sargent as the chairman, to prepare a plan for technical education in the country. One of the committee's recommendations was to create suitable institutions for technical education under the overall guidance of the All India Council of Technical Education (AICTE) (Ghosh, 2022, p. 15). The process started through this, and later, the Sarkar Committee submitted an interim report in 1946 and recommended setting up four higher institutes of technology (HITs) in the four regions of India. Accordingly, Kharagpur was selected to establish the Eastern HIT in West Bengal. J. C. Ghosh, former director of the Indian Institute of Science,

Bengaluru, was appointed the first director of the Institute. The governing body of the eastern HIT Kharagpur, in its meeting on 5 May 1950, decided to change the name Higher Institute of Technology to Indian Institute of Technology (IIT). Consequently, then–Education Secretary Dr. Tara Chand and Education Minister Maulana Abul Kalam Azad decided to name Indian Institute of Technology, Kharagpur, and the Ministry issued a notification in this regard on 11 November 1950 (Ghosh, 2022, pp. 15–16). Thus, the Indian Institute of Technology Kharagpur was the first IIT in India, and accordingly, several IITs were established in phases in the country.

It feels necessary to note here that the current Indian-origin chief executive officer (CEO) of Google (Alphabet Inc.), Sundar Pichai, is an alumnus of this institute. Further, many such research and innovation-based institutions emerged at a broader scale in phases, and currently, 23 Indian Institutes of Technology (IITs), 25 Indian Institutes of Information Technology (IIITs), and 32 National Institute of Technology (NITs) are working under public funding mechanisms (Government of India, 2022b), while many private players are running research institutes and universities in the country, which are conducting research primarily on technology development and cutting-edge innovations. Notably, the paradigm shift for the IT revolution was the period after the liberalization policy adoption in the 1990s, when IT emerged rapidly in the country. An open economy attracted many investors in research and teaching, and consequently, Indian youth became one of the main ingredients of the IT revolution worldwide. The starting years of the 21st century became decisive for IT, and it started occupying a remarkable share of the Indian economy. Three software service companies, Infosys, TCS, and Wipro, had more than USD10 billion in annual revenues; each employed nearly one lakh employees in 2007 (Sadagopan, 2007, p. 17). Per the study, India has a large, educated English-speaking workforce and produces about 350,000 computer professionals annually. Its IT sector has experienced rapid growth. Per a NASSCOM study, software exports recorded USD17.2 billion in 2004–05. Employment in the sector grew by 30% per year between 1999–2000 and 2003–04 (Bist, 2007, p. 706). Several multinational companies were established in India. In 1998, Microsoft established a software development center in Hyderabad and Motorola a design center in Delhi. After the policy change of allowing companies to have 100% ownership without the need for an Indian partner, IBM, which had returned to India in 1992 as an equal partner of the Tata group, bought off Tata group's share and became the sole owner of IBM (India) in 1999. By 2010, the number of IBM employees in India was around 85000, second only to the number of its employees in the USA. By 2010, other large multinational operating development centers in India were Accenture, Cisco, Dell, GE, Oracle, Adobe, SAP, Philips, HP, and Google (Rajaraman, 2012, p. 53).

Meantime, the Centre for Developing Advanced Computing (C-DAC) was established by the government of India in 1988 for research and development-related objectives in IT. Currently, it is working with 12 centers located all over India under the Ministry of Electronics and Information Technology, Government of India (C-DAC, 2022). It is a core research institute for digital innovations, and one of these fields includes language computing as an applied field of computer science and artificial intelligence (AI) research. In the early stage of language computing research, it was necessary to develop fonts for Indian scripts, along with corpora building, dictionaries, and optical character recognisers (OCR) for Indian languages. Most Indian languages use a non-Roman script, which has clearly dominated digital processing. The Graphics and Intelligence-Based Script Technology (GIST) department of C-DAC did major research on font development and enabled Indian languages to be processed through computing. Further, products in speech technology, such as speech-to-text and text-to-speech, were also researched for the major languages of the country. However, the basic focus of language computing remained a priority in developing the machine translation (MT) system in Indian languages or pairing it with English.

However, India's institutional history of MT is 30–35 years old. IIT, Kanpur, and later IIIT, Hyderabad, played a central role in the rule-based model of the MT system. Based on this, dozens of institutions in the country submitted several projects, but C-DAC, Pune, later did important work in the research on MT. Out of these, MANTRA-Rajbhasha worked on translating the proceedings of Parliament per its method, that is, human-aided machine translation, which was developed to translate circulars, orders, office memorandums, and resolutions in administrative, financial, agriculture, small-scale industries, health, security, information technology, banking, and education from English to Hindi (M.H.A., 2022, p. 64). It was financed by the Department of Official Language, Government of India, and developed at C-DAC, Pune. But later, at the evaluation level, it was observed that the level of translation by this package is not up to expectations. One reason for this is the lack of a wide corpus of words and sentences, so Hindi states should use this package and give feedback so that the Mantra software can be improved (M.H.A., 2022, p. 64). While working towards Indic computing, there was an effort to enable the domain names of websites in regional languages, and in its first attempt, nine scripts, Bengali, Devanagari, Gujarati, Gurmukhi, Kannada, Malayalam, Oriya, Tamil, and Telugu, were chosen (PTI, 2017). The role of Roman script cannot be undermined in the venture because once a trend gets established, the alternatives become secondary. Considering the fact there were constant efforts to enhance the list of languages of 8th schedule of Indian Constitution, starting with 5 languages, now a total of 22 languages are available to use in the .bharat domain (Abbas, 2021).

Despite all these attempts, no MT system that is widely accepted at the societal level could be developed in the country. There was even a period when the then government almost stopped funding research in MT because the expected results were not being achieved. Although MT is not a simple task as it has many challenges so far, why only machine, even human, translation has still been questioned at many accuracy parameters. Nevertheless, a big reason for MT not reaching society was that all the research until then was rule based; many rules were made based on the grammar of respective languages. The two languages targeted in translation may have opposite linguistic systems and cultural contexts; hence, the challenges in MT were many times greater than those in human translation. Amidst all this, Google continued to grow in MT research based on its high quality standard and global reach. Notably, the Indian center was the first research and development center of Google outside the USA (Rajaraman, 2012, p. 53). The Indian government silently accepted the role of Google Translate, even for the translation of official documents (M.H.A., 2022, p. 64), and therefore, Google enriches its MT research based on the corpus by extracting linguistic data from the internet, and it has been categorically accepted by the Indian government in words such as – "Google takes the translated sentences in memory so that if similar text comes in future, it gives correct translation (M.H.A., 2022, p. 66)." For a long time, our position as common users of language technological facilities in Indian languages was limited and our prime tendency was to keep English on one side of the scale, compare Indian languages with it, and shed tears only on the backwardness of our languages. Hence, there was no other way except to accept the dominance of Google in language computing, which is a significant challenge and a discouraging phase in emerging minor and multilingual Indian languages in the digital space.

Despite this, Indian youth have been playing a crucial role in shaping the IT industry not only in India but also in other countries. A survey stated that 17% of youth work in the IT industry (Mishra et al., 2018, p. 22). It is important to note that the IT industry considers Indian languages a secondary medium of instructions in the workplace, and English again dominates here, irrespective of the mother tongue of the professional in the IT revolution. Hence, Indian youth have been switching to English for higher education and employment worldwide, which continues so far, as the natural language of teaching and research in IT is English. Hence, marginal languages in particular and most Indian languages in general, which have prominent positions with 96.71% speakers in the total population, are struggling on this front, and English is dominating here, too (Census of India 2011, 2018, p. 12).

Internet and power hierarchy

The power balance between well-equipped technological platforms and their alternative emergence has been uneven in the overall IT market, and the rise of alternative technologies in the digital space has never been easy. After the rise of smart mobile phones, the trend of using the internet shifted to mobile platforms instead of computers. Considering this market orientation, Google acquired a mobile operating system, Android, and by making it user friendly, it is reaching more users and has a market share of more than 95.73% of Indian mobile users (Statcounter, 2024). To compete, the government of India has launched BharOS, an alternative mobile operating system, claiming that poor people of the country will be the primary beneficiaries of a robust, indigenous, dependable, and self-reliant digital infrastructure (PIB, 2023a, p. 2). However, its acceptance so far on the practical ground is still awaited. Before it, advanced efforts in developing search engines and internet browsers were also made in India so that much of what Google does today, such as data exploitation and machine learning, could also be done in India. However, the rise and fall of an Indian search engine, guruji.com, which was emerging as a multilingual interface based on Indian languages, could not compete with Google and finally closed (Firstpost, 2006). The digital world emerged and was shaped as a parallel world that shares its structure with that of humans. Still, despite being a product of human activities, the digital world has created its own rules of existence, and this tendency is overruling the human world. The computing process and ecosystem of digital tools promote monolingualism, as managing more than one language(s) during the development process of any software's interface, user manuals, and installation guidelines increases the efforts of developer and user, hence, more extensively used languages become more resourceful and digitally lesser-used languages become lesser day by day and may become digitally extinct at specific points of time in the future. Due to lack of open linguistic data on marginal languages, there is a minimal possibility that any private player will be involved in digitizing these languages, as they have a limited population and, therefore, a limited market. Major global platforms using public data are becoming more powerful by acquiring free data from the internet, and their machine-learning resources are increasing rapidly. They are finally rising to the highest levels compared to their competitors in the relevant market. Let us consider two US-owned big tech companies, i.e., Google and Facebook which are working in the field of language computing or several digital-human interfaces, with the help of the following table, how they have acquired their competency strength by merging emerging companies of the relevant fields in their business group.

Let us consider the significant popular digital platforms such as Picasa and YouTube and the mobile OS Android, which emerged in the competition as separate startups but were later acquired by Google. Similarly, Instagram and WhatsApp came into the digital market independently but are now under Meta or Facebook's umbrella. The purchase price of merged companies or products is less relevant than the circumstances of the new startups, in which they become ready to be merged with Google or Facebook, which plays a crucial role in becoming more powerful. This is a challenge for any new venture, as they either have to be afraid of developing any new product in competition of these large and resourceful companies or whenever a company like Google or Facebook comes forward with the desire to buy such emerging companies, then new company gets ready for it easily. However, the merger with major internet companies increases

The Routledge Handbook of Endangered and Minority Languages

Table 11.1 Internet companies – selected mergers and acquisitions

Name of group	Year	Companies	Area of operation	Purchase price (USD billions)
Google	2004	Picasa	Photo service	0.01
	2004	Where 2 Technology	Mapping service	N/A
	2005	Android	Mobile software	0.05
	2006	YouTube	Videos, media	1.65
	2008	Doubleclick	Internet advertising	3.10
	2009	Admob	Mobile advertising	0.75
	2011	Motorola Mobility (2014 sale to Lenovo for USD2.9 billion)	Mobile devices	12.50
	2013	Waze	GPS navigation software	0.97
	2013	Boston Dynamics	Military robots	N/A
	2014	Nest Labs	Thermostats; fire alarms	3.20
	2014	Skybox Imaging	Satellite technology	0.50
	2014	Deep Mind Tech.	Artificial intelligence	0.80
	2016	Apigee	Predictive analytics	0.63
Facebook	2009	FriendFeed	Social networking aggregator	0.05
	2010	Hot Potato	Social media platform	0.01
	2011	Beluga	Messaging	0.01
	2011	Gowalla	Social network	N/A
	2011	Snaptu	App developer	0.07
	2012	Instagram	Photo and video portal	1.00
	2013	Parse	App platform	0.09
	2014	WhatsApp	Messaging service	19.00
	2014	Oculus VR (virtual reality)	Virtual reality	2.00
	2015	Surreal Vision	Augmented reality	N/A
	2015	Pebbles	Augmented reality	0.06

Source: Dolata, 2017, p. 12.

their market and consumer orientation competency; consequently, the possibility of aligning new startups with more prominent companies naturally increased. Interestingly, these have been called a gang of FANG (Facebook, Amazon, Netflix, Google) (Bigo et al., 2019, p. 195). As an interface between the digital world and cross-linguistic consumers, they are becoming increasingly powerful, and their ecosystem is one in which major languages gain and minority languages are being discouraged from mainstream digital facilities. Google's market share in the search engine industry declined by approximately 0.6% from 2018 to 2020. Considering the expansion of Bing and Yahoo's market share and the antitrust investigations Google faces, it is predicted that Google's market share will decline at a rate of 0.7% in the future (Si et al., 2022, p. 2171). However, overall, Google's profit has grown as it has regularly expanded its business base. Considering the fact that Google does not work in China, as Zhuo has mentioned, according to a survey, more than

Challenges of language survival in digital perspectives

60% of Chinese people expect Google to return to the Chinese market (Si et al., 2022, p. 2170). It shows people's aspirations toward these big tech players; hence, the possibilities of their expansion in both directions, linearly and vertically, will always be high, at least in the current scenario. There were 700 million internet users in India, per data consumption in 2022, which was more than the number of users in the USA and China combined (PIB, 2023b). As a result, data consumption in India is projected to increase substantially, reaching 979.1k petabytes (Pb) in 2027, compared to 9.7 million Pb globally. This data consumption surge indicates the growing demand for online content and services among Indian consumers. Moreover, internet access in the country is expected to generate significant revenue, estimated at USD29.1 billion, around the same time (PWC, 2023, p, 4). These developments underscore the transformative impact of 5G technology on India's entertainment and media industry, facilitating enhanced user experiences and driving substantial growth opportunities. As data consumption continues to rise and internet accessibility expands, stakeholders in the industry are poised to capitalize on these trends and innovate to meet evolving consumer demands.

However, Google added 24 new languages to its MT module in 2023. It also includes eight languages from India: Sanskrit, Bhojpuri, Dogri, Assamese, Mizo, Konkani, Maithili and Manipuri, whereas Indian languages like Bengali, Gujarati, Hindi, Kannada, Malayalam, Marathi, Nepali, Oriya, Punjabi, Sindhi, Tamil, Telugu, and Urdu were already there before 2023. Thus, Google has made arrangements for two-direction machine translation for a total of 133 languages of the world. Further, a media report stated Google's promise – "We are helping to advance India's digital future, that includes our efforts to build a single, unified AI model that will be capable of handling over 100 Indian languages across speech and text – part of our global effort to bring the world's 1,000 most-spoken languages online and to help people access knowledge and information in their preferred language (ET, 2023)." Thus, Google Translate is like a bridge across the linguistic flow worldwide and is a significant achievement in overcoming global linguistic barriers, including the deep multilingual Indian linguistic landscape. Yes, the question of translation quality is always relevant, and it is here, too. However, despite all this, it has started translating well in many majority languages but needs more translation quality enhancement with minor languages. However, considering the new inclusion list of languages in the Google MT module, many encouraging conclusions can be drawn. First, Sanskrit, a representative language of the Indian knowledge tradition, did not yet have an equipped MT system. Second, a language like Bhojpuri, for which a parallel movement is going on for inclusion in the Eighth Schedule of the Indian constitution by accepting the importance of numerical strength, has been denied so far. There are also languages like Mizo and Konkani, whose numbers of speakers are comparatively low in the country. If this is taken superficially, then minority language speakers should expect Google to add their languages to its MT module. There is also a significant basis for such hope that the technology that Google is using in the current research process is the 'zero-shot' method, in which, based on AI, even from a monolingual corpus, the algorithm is being developed, while Google's early research was focused on parallel corpora, apparently, this linguistic data Google steals cleverly for free from people's creative activities as it is accepted in word such as – "We want you to understand the types of information we collect as you use our services. We collect information to provide better services to all our users – from figuring out basic stuff like which language you speak to more complex things like which ads you'll find most useful, the people who matter most to you online, or which YouTube videos you might like (Tripathi, 2022, p. 114)." The information Google collects and how that information is used depends on how you use our services and how you manage your privacy controls. Based on this, marginal language speakers should hope Google will include their languages in its digitalization process. However, the ultimate target of any company in the market is its own benefit.

More than 6000 languages are spoken in the global geography that the internet covers. Ninety percent of this population speaks only 300 languages. Still, the spread of information technology is limited to about 100 languages worldwide, while English remains dominant (Tripathi & Singh, 2021, p. 56). Global communication often fosters a homogenous culture, reflecting the economic and cultural influence of specific actors. A 2021 study revealed that 76.9% of online languages correspond to the world's top ten most spoken languages (UNESCO, 2023). The following table shows the actual scenario of multilingualism in digital space.

Thus, IT is not conducive to the linguistic diversity of information, which leads to the erosion of communication capabilities and is still secondary to a large part of the world's non-English speaking population. As a result, a new opportunity for corruption often emerges, and people may not be aware of it simply because of a lack of knowledge of English. Suppose a person from a low literacy background does not know basic English and is using a mobile banking application or ATM; in that case, his possibility of facing difficulties in operating the application will always be high; consequently, he may suffer from financial loss only because of lacking knowledge of English. The fact is that cybercrime is an emerging challenge for administrations in countries. As such, the NCRB reports that 65,893 cases were registered under cybercrimes, showing an increase of 24.4% over 2021 (NCRB, 2022a, p. xiv). Out of these, the registered cases under the Indian Panel Code (IPC) crimes (involving communication devices as medium/target) are remarkable, in which 1669 of ATM fraud, 6412 of online banking fraud, and 2819 cases of OTP-related cases in one year (NCRB, 2022b, p. 791). Since the focus on the banking system has been boosted in the last ten years to connect marginal people, the social environment in which having a bank account is essential is resulting in a threat of financial loss because of lacking technical awareness and knowledge of English or other prominent languages of one's digital surroundings. The other concern is about the neutrality of technology. The combination of the internet and English means they have strengthened each other, and the scope of struggle has become more significant for people living outside their circle. Hence, no neutrality should be expected from digital technologies. The digital infrastructure is not only an intermediary facility between users and companies but also an autonomous body that facilitates users per the interests of such companies. The scenario created by the advent of IT through the internet is based on the decentralized use of centralized resources in which there is an influence of English, and the expansion of alternative languages is discouraged at every level.

Table 11.2 Hierarchy of languages in digital space

Language	Percentage of websites
English	55.0%
Spanish	5.0%
Russian	4.9%
German	4.3%
French	4.2%
Japanese	3.7%
Portuguese	2.4%
Turkish	2.3%
Italian	1.9%
Persian	1.8%
Dutch, Flemish	1.5%
Chinese	1.4%

Source: ISF, 2023.

There have been issues in word processing itself for Indian languages as compared to English, the government accepts it as – "There is a serious problem in working in Hindi that the fonts used in different softwares are not compatible. Because of this, Hindi files cannot be easily exchanged from one computer to another as files in English are shared. There is also a problem merging Hindi text with other texts in other software (M.H.A., 2022, p. 64)." Further, Hindi has the highest number of speakers in the country, at more than 43.63% of the population (Census of India, 2011). This figure must have risen during the last decade, as vocal for local is a new campaign in India, and Hindi is being promoted in that sense through all feasible means. In that way, Hindi is the most representative language of India. Now, a question comes: If a language in the country, whose speaker's strength is 43.63% with figuring as more than 52 crores out of the total multilingual population (Census of India 2011, 2018, p. 7), what will the struggle level be for minority languages whose speaking strength is even less than 10,000, compared with Hindi? Hence, considering the minority languages, these could not stop being deprived of influence of dominance as IT has become a powerful medium of global uniformity sitting on the shoulders of English.

It is not a simple phenomenon that the information revolution is standardizing the form of English as well. Since the USA has been the regulator of this revolution, the British form of English, which was once a matter of loyalty and prestige for the monarchy in Britain, is today being changed according to American interests through Microsoft Office, Google Docs, and other related software. Thus, the American form of English is being used in most of the countries of the world through digital infrastructure. It can be correlated with Indian contexts. When the ordinary typewriter came into practice, it played a significant role in standardizing form of Devanagari. Which was a deviation from its handwritten form, and changed permanently as per the configuration of the typewriter or left out from the print industry. The form of Devnagari used in classical Sanskrit differs from that used today for various Indian languages. Even from the phase of TrueType fonts (TTFs) and Unicode, several forms of Devanagari letters have either been permanently changed or have gone extinct. The fundamental reasons are simplification of the form of letters and synchronization with computers. It is worth mentioning that the Devanagari script is used for writing major languages such as Hindi, Marathi, Sindhi, Nepali, Sanskrit, Konkani, and Maithili, while most marginal languages in the country do not have the script, and, consequently, the font is also lacking. Many of them use either Roman or the dominant script. The natural flow of speech is not limited to the script, but once a regional language uses a script like Roman, which is digitally rich but has limited sound symbols and is not generative, the challenges of all the regional sounds become more difficult, and communication competence accordingly becomes secondary in the digital world.

However, when a new product comes into society, it appears with a complete environment, which has its own direct or indirect conditions. For instance, it can be seen that the computer hardware called 'mouse' remains 'mouse' in every language. Whatever the logic behind its naming, it becomes secondary for cross-linguistic users. The name 'mouse' might have been kept because of its appearance being similar to that of a rat, but it remains the same in every language. Similarly, in the context of the use of phones, the word 'hello' can be considered, which is directly related to the invention of the telephone and was used for the first time in 1878 (Grimes, 1992). Later on, this remained the same with mobile phones, based on similar usage. Despite their different linguistic backgrounds, perhaps a large number of common people all over India use mobile phones and do not even know what is meant by the word 'hello,' as it is a non-native word, but it is connected naturally with the use of the telephone such that an illiterate person starts a conversation using 'hello,' irrespective their mother tongue and the language of the conversation. This means that neither the word 'mouse' nor 'hello' is translated in any context or linguistic environment of its use. Many examples of this can be seen in IT or any invention. As a result, the gap between societies increases based on class, and in a country like India, society divides into two classes, and of course, one represents as English class and it dominants the society. Non-native words like Gmail, Facebook, YouTube, WhatsApp, Tweet, app, website, GB, drive, RAM, e-mail, like, comment, forward, open, log in, log out, video, backup, charge, recharge, discharge, selfie, tag, hard disk, and tab have naturally reached all the languages of the country, while hundreds of words from Indian languages are constantly falling out of use, and thousands of words from languages have either gone out of existence or will disappear soon from society. A similar case occurred during the COVID pandemic and its post-effect, which borrowed and popularized many words in Indian contexts, such as community spread, COVID, enhanced community, isolation, lockdown, mass testing, outbreak, quarantine, screening, social distancing, super-spreader, vaccine, ventilator, work from home, and online classes. Hence, it is the compulsion of digital surroundings, if someone uses digital facilities, they will have to co-opt its conditions and also the linguistic compulsion.

However, if English colonialism is realized under the frame of Indianness as a thought process that expands the policies of colonialism and advances the goal of colonization, which deals with colonization of the mind through complete domination of the culture and worldview of the colonized society (Deepak, 2021, p. 49), the Indian situation may be an ideal example to analyze the reality of multilingualism and dominance of English because the nexus of English, IT, and globalization encapsulating not just the physical aspects of colonialism, such as power relations, political and economic control, but also the more profound influence on the culture, worldview, and identity of the societies. Thus, it is about the imposition of a dominant culture and information hegemony that often leads to the internalization of inferiority and the erasure or subjugation of indigenous cultures and perspectives. This process of colonization of the mind has long-lasting effects even after the physical presence of colonial powers has ended. However, with the tendency to reclaim an indigenous legacy, the Indian government has started naming 'Bharat' instead of 'India' (Times Now, 2024), even though both these terms were retained in the Indian constitution, vide Article 1 (Government of India, 2022a, p. 2) but were not in practice since implementation of the Constitution. It has taken about 75 years to use the indigenous form of the nation's name in official behaviors. On the other hand, the strategic challenge of the digitization process is that it is USA-centric, and most servers of social media websites and even Indian websites are hosted there, while the practical challenge is that the entire server environment is most compatible with English. On this basis, an American writer, Thomas L. Friedman, declared "the world is flat":

> Columbus reported to his king and queen that the world was round, and he went down in history as the man who first made this discovery. I returned home and shared my discovery only with my wife and only in a whisper. "Honey," I confided, "I think the world is flat."
>
> (2007, p. 5)

Interestingly, this conclusion was drawn from the corporate house of a leading IT company during his visit to Bengaluru, India. It is shocking that in a country like India, where the multilinguistic essence of society and multicultural sense of civilization still exists and is celebrated at the grassroots level, a scholar like Friedman visiting from the USA in a USA-based corporate house in India and denying the basic architecture of the globe, and narrating it as 'flat.' This flatness is actually the natural effect of globalization, of course, with the help of English, operating systems, and the internet. The visit of Mr. Thomas was at the start of the 20th century, and now, 20–25 later, this levelling has started to seem more natural from an Indian point of view, and people are now shying away from even considering how many societies, cultures, and languages have contributed to global homogeneity in the process of this flattening. It is generally said that technology expands human cognitive capacity, but it is also true that technology has its specific environment, and one cannot expect much neutrality from it and its ecosystem. On the other hand, the dominance of USA-based tech companies needs to be improved in accordance with the rules and regulations of business firms. The Competition Commission of India (CCI) imposed a monetary penalty of ₹1337.76 crore on Google for abusing its dominant position in multiple markets in the Android mobile device ecosystem, apart from issuing a cease-and-desist order and directing Google to modify its conduct within a defined timeline (CCI, 2023, p. XV). In another inquiry against Google, the commission imposed a penalty of ₹936.44 crore on Google for abusing its dominant position with respect to its Play store policies, apart from issuing a cease-and-desist order. The commission also directed Google to modify its conduct within a defined timeline (CCI, 2023, p. XV). Several cases are registered under Antitrust, Section 19 (1) (a) of the Competition Act, 2002, concerning unfair conduct by Google. Even though several penalties have been imposed in the USA, a Delaware federal jury has fined Google $15.1 million for infringing two patents related to audio software (Brittain, 2023). Also, Google agreed to a $391.5 million settlement over allegations by 40 US states that the tech titan illegally tracked users' locations (Barnett, 2022). Similar cases have been reported against other big tech companies in several countries for illegal, immoral data tracking. This means that these companies are working for their business and maximum profits, and hence, expecting them to improve marginal languages and cultures is just like asking a hungry monkey on the ground to return stolen bread.

Policy and practice

It is often said that only change is constant. The IT industry took shape after liberalization policies were adopted in India. Since then, changes have been made worldwide through computers, mobile phones, and the internet. There was a time when cash and cheques were the only way to transact money at the mass level. Then, with the help of computers, automated teller machines (ATMs) were installed in public places, but currently, the unified payments interface (UPI) has changed the entire dynamics of money transactions, enabling a cashless society with the help of mobile phones. The functional number of UPI platforms is 382, a tremendous rise, as it was 32 in 2016–17 when the UPI system was introduced (IPCIDE, 2023, p. 77). It is becoming an undeniable interface for money transactions in local markets, even in rural parts of the country. Consequently, the scenario of language and its speakers is being changed. The speed of the digitalization process at the grassroots level is faster than the requirement of common people, as they are skilled in the natural way, but digitalization is being imposed on them without considering their skills. It is necessary to note that GSMA conducted a survey on barriers to mobile internet use, in which the respondents who were aware of mobile internet but had not used it in the previous three months were asked what prevents them from using the internet on a mobile phone. For respondents from India, two of the most common barriers were handset cost and data cost in urban areas, whereas, for rural areas, the main barriers were affordability and reading and writing difficulties due to the non-availability of information in vernacular languages and digital skills (TRAI, 2023, p. 20).

Although it is also true that with the development of society, some words lose their existence, and new ones are added, this process is also necessary for language development. A "gradual change in language is natural, but the internet has accelerated the process of these changes" (Government of India, 2015). It has proved to be the indirect condition of joining 'Digital India' in the country, an ambitious initiative that was started by the government of India in 2015 and is now being implemented at the mass level. It aims to provide a much-needed boost to the nine pillars of growth areas, broadband highways, universal access to mobile connectivity, public internet access programs, e-governance: reforming government through technology, e-kranti – electronic delivery of services, information for all, electronics manufacturing, IT for jobs, and early harvest programs. Each area is a complex program that cuts across multiple ministries and departments (Government of India, 2015). Considering the comprehensive coverage of the Digital India scheme, it may be more dangerous to Indian linguistic ecology, as several grassroots facilities are being provided to its targeted beneficiary only in digital mode, and hence, suppressing marginal languages through English will be a common phenomenon in this procedure, if timely required multilingual digital infrastructure is not developed. It is noteworthy that the Indian government started a program called Technology Development for Indian Language (TDIL) in 1991 to build technology solutions and develop tools and other resources for Indian languages, focusing on (1) developing information processing tools and techniques, (2) facilitating human–machine interaction without a language barrier, (3) creating and accessing multilingual knowledge resources and integrating them to develop innovative user products and services (Jha, 2010, p. 983). Since then, the TDIL has been a nodal body that deals with computing for Indian languages. However, the language choice for the TDIL was mainly limited to the 22 languages of the Eighth Schedule of the Constitution. Later, the National Knowledge Commission (NKC) suggested that "Separate funding should be allocated to develop a new high-quality OCR software package so that new and old fonts in many different Indian languages can be converted into ISCI/ASCI code and open access (OA) portals and servers could be upgraded regularly (NKC, 2009, p. 94)," but not much was seen on the ground, especially with regard to minor languages and its digitalization. Several Indian groups are actively working to localize open source software (OSS) to Indian languages, including groups like Malayalam Linux and Tamil Linux. Other language computing technology development programs cover developing and providing software tools for text processing, spreadsheets, messaging, publishing, and text-to-speech and OCR to enable non-English speaking people to use computers in the Indian language effectively (Bist, 2007, p. 709). There was a time when the government of India recommended Google Translate. Google Translate performs all types of translations (Hindi, Bangla, Kannada, Tamil, Telugu, Urdu to English and vice-versa at a faster rate). When translating in Google, Google saves the translated sentences in memory to give a better translation when similar text is provided in the future (M.H.A., 2022, p. 64). In that sense, Google has become unavoidable for Indians. Most government departments have made YouTube channels for public orientation and for spreading relevant information. Interestingly, public broadcasting satellite channels have their own YouTube channels. Most government officials use either Gmail or its supported e-mail networks for interpersonal communication for official purposes. The government has accepted "many government departments, including DeitY and the prime minister's office, have uploaded their promotional video content on YouTube (DE & IT, n.d., p. 26)." Hence, the role of Google and its products is increasing daily in India's government(s).

Furthermore, India's competence in IT, combined with opportunities such as interoperability between multiple languages, provides a much-needed impetus for finding scalable solutions for problems that have global implications, such as natural language processing (NLP) (NITI Aayog, 2018, pp. 19–20). Several programs, such as public awareness, policy discussions, and academic events, are organized to deal with AI and Indian language computing using AI techniques under the efforts of the Indian government. Further, as such, the NEP-2020 states that efforts to preserve and promote all Indian languages, including classical, tribal, and endangered languages, will be taken on with new vigor. Technology and crowdsourcing, with extensive participation of the people, will play a crucial role in these efforts (Government of India, 2020, p. 55). In this spirit, the government has initiated the Bhashini program under the Digital India program, which aims to build a national public digital platform for languages to develop services and products for citizens by leveraging the power of AI and other emerging technologies. It also aims to substantially increase the content in Indian languages on the internet in the domains of public interest, particularly governance and policy and science and technology, thus encouraging citizens to use the internet in their language (Government of India, 2022c). Simultaneously, the Indian Institute of Science in Bengaluru and AI and Robotics Technology Park are partnering with Google to launch a large language model called Project Vaani (Shinde, 2024). Thus, not only private sector platforms but also governments in the country are focusing on Indian languages in the digital domains, as BHASHINI is being prepared for Indian linguistic digitization and has started research on MT afresh. The National Language Translation Mission (NLTM), Mission BHASHINI [BHASH A Interface for India], has been formulated to transcend the language barrier for digital access. The National Language Translation Mission started in March 2022 as a three-year mission with the vision of harnessing natural language technologies to create a diverse ecosystem of contributors, partnering entities, and citizens to transcend language barriers, thereby ensuring digital inclusion and digital empowerment in an AatmaNirbhar Bharat (Government of India, 2023, p. 34). BHASHINI is trying to stand in front of major players in the field. It has started becoming available to everyone through a website and mobile app in which translation is currently being arranged between English, Assamese, Oriya, Kannada, Gujarati, Tamil, Telugu, Punjabi, Bengali, Marathi, and Malayalam. Also, Bodo and Manipuri have been added to it, and the quality translation process continues. It will be the priority of researchers to add the languages of the Eighth Schedule of the Constitution to this AI-based system. In this system, people can speak their language and get it translated into their target language. Meaning-level translation is possible in both text-to-text as well as speech-to-text and text-to-speech forms. This is the only MT system developed in India by the government that can not only be compared with Google but is also the first MT system that has started moving beyond its laboratory and reaching society. Recently, a speech given by the prime minister in Hindi at a public program was broadcast in Tamil for the people of Tamil Nadu present there, and during the 18th G20 Summit held in September 2023, the JugalbandiBot, a product of BHASHINI, managed cross-lingual situations with the delegates and was also a curiosity point for foreign as well as Indian media professionals (Khedkar, 2023).

On the other hand, AI tools are being accepted rapidly by internet users. Time taken by Chat-GPT to reach up to 100 million customers is only two months, while for reaching same number of customers Twitter took five years and five months, Facebook took four years and six months, WhatsApp took three years and six months, Instagram took two years and six months, Google+ one year and two months, and TikTok nine months (PWC, 2023, p. 9). Considering the success of ChatGPT, Google has introduced the AI chatbot Gemini Pro, which is available in over 40 languages and covers nine Indian languages: Hindi, Tamil, Telugu, Bengali, Kannada, Malayalam, Marathi, Gujarati, and Urdu. This feature, extensively used in English, will now benefit users in multiple languages (Arora, 2024). In the latest development, QX Lab AI launched the world's first node-based, hybrid GenAI platform, Ask QX, which supports 100 languages, out of which 12 are Indian languages: Hindi, Bengali, Telugu, Marathi, Tamil, Urdu, Gujarati, Kannada, Malayalam, Odia, Punjabi, and Assamese (Times of India, 2024). In another move, Seetha Mahalaxmi (SML) India Private Limited and 3AI Holding Limited in Bengaluru on 10 May 2024 announced the launch of Hanooman, India's homegrown multilingual GenAI platform in 98 global languages, including 12 Indian languages, to build a GenAI ecosystem for India by leveraging the country's diverse linguistic and cultural heritage. The 12 Indian languages currently available on the web and app are Hindi, Marathi, Gujarati, Bengali, Kannada, Odia, Punjabi, Assamese, Tamil, Telugu, Malayalam, and Sindhi. The list of global languages includes English, Spanish, Italian, German, Japanese, and Korean. Along with its exceptional translation capabilities, Hanooman can handle everything from a casual chat to offering professional advice and perform complex technical tasks like coding and tutoring. The aim also caters to four sectors: healthcare, governance, financial services, and education (The New Indian Express, 2024). However, in another study, English is the most popular and represents 58.8% of web content as of January 2023. In contrast, the United States and India, the countries with the most internet users after China, are the world's biggest English-speaking markets (Shinde, 2024), but the sense of English supremacy is going down at the public level when the reach of AI tools is being proposed to wider society in the grassroots of India, which is basically a multilingual setting. Many such efforts have been made, but those have not been successful. There are many reasons for that, but one remains the same, and that is the dominance of English in the computing infrastructure. Simultaneously, English has attained its class in Indian society based on social parameters. This division takes shape as rich English speakers vs poor marginal linguistic communities (Tripathi, 2012, p. 89). Although the English class has no original roots in the country, it has no relation to the caste system. But as a symbol of richness, English attracts the lower middle class in society; consequently, guardians of this class are eager to have their children learn English. As a result, several online teaching learning applications have been introduced, institutionalizing English and discouraging the Indian languages on this front as well.

Conclusion

Naturally, multilingualism is an asset for nations where societies can enjoy life and routine tasks in their first language; hence, the high number of available language choices increases the degree of liberty in their natural habitats. The United Nations Charter, vide its article 1(3), had connected it with human rights: to achieve international cooperation in solving international problems of an economic, social, cultural, or humanitarian character and in promoting and encouraging respect for human rights and for fundamental freedoms for all without distinction as to race, sex, language, or religion (United Nations, 1945, p. 3). If any person from a dying linguistic community is trying to regain living, then his struggle for a healthy and natural life multiplies without his own language; in that case, a language acquires similar importance as water and food. Nowadays, digitalization is also aligning in the same row; hence, language with technology is becoming an essential ingredient in life, particularly if we look at the globe from a marginalized ethnic population's perspective. Indian youth have played a significant role in the IT revolution worldwide (Kumar, 2023). It is ironic that, despite this fact, English also maintains continued dominance in the digital space. Hence, Indian youth are becoming carriers of English. As far as Indian marginal language computing is concerned, it has never been an attractive area in the field of digital technologies, as it is a challenge for any company to develop a program or online interface first in English and then its replica in the rest of the marginal languages of the region. As noted, the fundamental reasons behind this are the strong links between English, the operating systems of computers and smartphones, and the internet. This juncture has unprecedentedly increased the dominance of English. A powerful or resourceful language becomes more powerful easily while overcoming the same distance for a lesser known language is the toughest task. This may be contextualized with regard to language computing, English, and marginal Indian languages.

However, COVID has been an eye-opener for policymakers because digitalization has emerged as an alternative for various domains of human activities in India. On the other hand, AI is emerging as a powerful tool for addressing several common issues in general and revolutionizing society in particular, where the interface between common people and digitalization is becoming essential. Consequently, the trend of switching over to digital facilities is attracting marginalized people to maintain e-citizenship for their basic needs. Therefore, the majority of non-English speakers in India are becoming a challenge to be addressed by governments, which are pressure groups in the Indian democracy and an emerging market as well. However, no one will take pain in preparing the compiler of a programming language other than in English as it is not an easy task, but extensive use of software developed with that compiler must be multilingual so that its reachability may assured up to wider Indian customers. The path for Indian languages in the digital space is being made smooth, but the ecosystem of technology is not adopting it at the same speed compared to English. Nevertheless, the fact is that the trend of using Indian language content on the internet is increasing gradually, and there will be days in the future when many marginal linguistic communities will get their language in digital space if they are interested; as has been said: when there is a will, there is a way. But sensitive efforts should be maintained by mainstream society toward marginal linguistic groups on the ground, while proactive action by state governments, as well as the central government at the policy level, concerning ethnic languages and cultures is expected so that a digital and just society may be created for the betterment of humanity and the world, provided marginal linguistic groups are keen to accept and continue with their languages in digital uses as well.

References

English references

Abbas, M. (2021, February 17). Now. Bharat domain available in 22 languages. *ET Telecom*. Retrieved February 12, 2024, from https://telecom.economictimes.indiatimes.com/news/now-bharat-domain-available-in-22-languages/81045889

Arora, S. (2024, February 11). Google's Gemini pro in bard now available in nine Indian languages. *AWBI*. Retrieved February 12, 2024, from https://awbi.in/googles-gemini-pro-in-bard-now-available-in-nine-indian-languages/

Barnett, K. (2022, November 15). Google's $400m penalty and impact of the 5 heftiest data privacy fines on 2023 ad plans. *The Drum*. Retrieved February 12, 2024, from www.thedrum.com/news/2022/11/15/googles-400m-penalty-the-impact-the-5-heftiest-data-privacy-fines-2023-ad-plans

Bigo, D., Isin, E. F., & Ruppert, E. (Eds.). (2019). *Data Politics: Worlds, Subjects, Rights*. Routledge.

Bist, R. S. (2007). ICT enabled development and digital divide: An Indian perspective. In *5th International CALIBER-2007, Panjab University, Chandigarh* (pp. 702–712). INFLIBNET Centre, Ahmedabad.

Brittain, B. (2023, June 21). Google hit with $15 mn penalty in US trial over two audio patents. *Company News. Business Standard*. Retrieved February 12, 2024, from www.business-standard.com/companies/news/google-hit-with-15-mn-penalty-in-us-trial-over-two-audio-patents-123062101325_1.html

CCI. (2023). *Annual Report 2022–23*. Competition Commission of India.

C-DAC. (2022, August 15). *C-DAC*. Retrieved January 15, 2024, from https://cdac.in/index.aspx

Census of India. (2011). C-17 population by bilingualism and trilingualism. *Census India*. Retrieved July 30, 2020, from https://censusindia.gov.in/2011census/C-17.html

Census of India 2011. (2018). Language: India, states, and union territories (Table 11. C-16). *Census of India 2011*. https://censusindia.gov.in

DE & IT. (n.d.). *Framework & Guidelines for Use of Social Media for Government Organisations*. Department of Electronics and Information Technology, Ministry of Communications & Information Technology, Government of India. Retrieved 2024, from www.meity.gov.in/writeaddata/files/Approved%20Social%20Media%20Framework%20and%20Guidelines%20_2_.pdf

Deepak, J. S. (2021). *India That Is Bharat: Coloniality, Civilisation, Constitution*. Bloomsbury.

Dolata, U. (2017). Apple, Amazon, Google, Facebook, Microsoft: Market concentration – competition – innovation strategies. In *SOI Discussion Paper, No. 2017–01* (pp. 1–33). University of Stuttgart, Institute for Social Sciences. http://hdl.handle.net/10419/152249

ET. (2023, October 1). Google's journey in India: From 5 employees in 2004 to largest employee base outside the US. *ET Government*. Retrieved January 27, 2024, from https://government.economictimes.indiatimes.com/news/technology/googles-journey-in-india-from-5-employees-in-2004-to-largest-employee-base-outside-the-us/104081349

Firstpost. (2006, October 12). Local search engine, Guruji.com, launched-technology news. *Firstpost*. Retrieved February 11, 2023, from www.firstpost.com/tech/news-analysis/local-search-engine-guruji-com-launched-3549413.html

Friedman, T. L. (2007). *The World Is Flat*. Picador.

Ghosh, A. (2022). Technical education in India: Role of the IITs. *Science Reporter*, 2022(July), pp. 14–21.

Government of India. (2015). *Digital India*. Retrieved January 19, 2024, from https://digitalindia.gov.in/programme-pillars/

Government of India. (2020). *National Education Policy 2020*. Ministry of Human Resource Development.

Government of India. (2022a). *The Constitution of India*. Government of India.

Government of India. (2022b, April 27). *Ministry of Education*. Retrieved January 15, 2024, from www.education.gov.in/institutions

Government of India. (2022c, August 26). *BHASHINI – National Language Translation Mission BHASHINI-BHASa INterface for India Digital India BHASHINI – India's AI-led l*. Retrieved January 19, 2024, from https://static.pib.gov.in/WriteReadData/specificdocs/documents/2022/aug/doc202282696201.pdf

Government of India. (2023). *Annual Report 2022–23*. Ministry of Electronics & Information Technology Government of India.

Grimes, W. (1992, March 5). Great 'Hello' mystery is solved. *The New York Times*. Retrieved March 6, 2024, from www.nytimes.com/1992/03/05/garden/great-hello-mystery-is-solved.html

IPCIDE. (2023). *State of India's Digital Economy*. Indian Council for Research on International Economic Relations (ICRIER), New Delhi.

ISF. (2023, May 15). What are the most used languages on the Internet? *Internet Society Foundation*. Retrieved January 27, 2024, from www.isocfoundation.org/2023/05/what-are-the-most-used-languages-on-the-internet/

Jha, G. N. (2010). The TDIL program and the Indian Language Corpora Initiative (ILCI). *European Language Resources Association (ELRA)*. www.lrec-conf.org/proceedings/

Karat, P. (1972, November). The role of the English-educated in Indian politics. *JSTOR, Social Scientist*, 1(4), pp. 25–46. www.jstor.org/stable/3516456

Khedkar, P. R. (2023, September 10). *Bhashini App: Bridging the Digital Divide with Language Diversity*. Retrieved May 8, 2024, from https://blogs.pib.gov.in/blogsdescr.aspx?feaaid=59

Kumar, S. R. A. (2023, July 5). The role of Indian youth in achieving the vision of dream India @2047. *Times of India*. https://timesofindia.indiatimes.com/readersblog/youthsparks/the-role-of-indian-youth-in-achieving-the-vision-of-dream-india-2047-56020/

M.H.A. (2022). *Compilation of Orders Regarding the Use of Hindi: Department of Official Language (Ministry of Home Affairs) for Official purposes of the Union (From July 2005 to December 2021)*. Ministry of Home Affairs, Government of India.

Mishra, V., Chapman, T., Sinha, R., Kedia, S., & Gutta, S. (2018). *Young India and Work: A Survey of Youth Aspirations*. The Observer Research Foundation, New Delhi.

NCRB. (2022a). *Crime in India-2022* (Vol. I). National Crime Records Bureau, Government of India.

NCRB. (2022b). *Crime in India-2022* (Vol. II). National Crime Records Bureau, Government of India.

The New Indian Express. (2024, May 11). India's GenAI platform now in 98 languages. *The New Indian Express*. www.newindianexpress.com/amp/story/states/karnataka/2024/May/11/indias-genai-platform-now-in-98-languages

NITI Aayog. (2018). *National Strategy for Artificial Intelligence*. Govt. of India.

NKC. (2009). *National Knowledge Commission: Report to the Nation 2006–2009*. Government of India.

PIB. (2023a, January 24). *Shri Dharmendra Pradhan with Shri Ashwini Vaishnaw Successfully Tests the 'BharOS,' a Made in India Mobile Operating System Developed by IIT Madras* [Press Release]. Press Information Bureau, Government of India, Delhi.

PIB. (2023b, July 14). *Press Information Bureau*. Retrieved February 8, 2024, from www.pib.gov.in/PressReleseDetailm.aspx?PRID=1939601

PTI. (2017, November 9). Internet domain names in Indian languages soon. *The Economic Times*. Retrieved February 12, 2024, from https://economictimes.indiatimes.com/tech/internet/internet-domain-names-in-indian-languages-soon/articleshow/65373345.cms

PWC. (2023). *Global Entertainment & Media Outlook 2023–2027: India Perspective*. PwC Network.

Rajaraman, V. (2012). *History of Computing in India (1955–2010)*. Supercomputer Education and Research Centre, Indian Institute of Science, Bangalore.

Sadagopan, S. (2007). Fifty years of Indian IT. *YOJANA*, November (2007), pp. 17–22.

Shinde, S. (2024, January 8). Can India create multi language AI like Chat GPT? *Rediff.com*. Retrieved January 22, 2024, from www.rediff.com/news/special/can-india-create-multi-language-ai-like-chat-gpt/20240108.htm

Si, M., Si, Z., & Ye, Y. (2022). Proceedings of the 2022 7th international conference on financial innovation and economic development (ICFIED 2022). *Advances in Economics, Business and Management Research*, 211, pp. 2168–2173.

Statcounter. (2024, September). Mobile operating system market share India – Sept 2023–Sept 2024. *StatCounter Global Stats*. Retrieved September 5, 2024, from https://gs.statcounter.com/os-market-share/mobile/india

Times of India. (2024, February 3). QX Lab AI launches world's first node-based, hybrid GenAI platform that supports Indian languages. *Times of India*. Retrieved February 12, 2024, from https://timesofindia.indiatimes.com/gadgets-news/qx-lab-ai-launches-worlds-first-nodebased-hybrid-genai-platform-supporting-indian-languages/articleshow/107383319.cms

Times Now. (2024, January 28). Supreme court terms union of India as Union of Bharat in new circular. *Times Now*. Retrieved May 7, 2024, from www.timesnownews.com/india/supreme-court-terms-union-of-india-as-union-of-bharat-in-new-circular-article-107203310

TRAI. (2023, September 14). *Consultation Paper on Digital Inclusion in the Era of Emerging Technologies*. Telecom Regulatory Authority of India, New Delhi.

Tripathi, A. K. (2022, June). Language revitalization: The NEP-2020. *Language and Language Teaching*, 11–2(22), pp. 96–104.

UNESCO. (2023, November 30). A digital future for indigenous languages: Insights from the Partnerships Forum. *UNESCO*. Retrieved February 13, 2024, from www.unesco.org/en/articles/digital-future-indigenous-languages-insights-partnerships-forum

United Nations. (1945). *Charter of the United Nations and Statute of the International Court of Justice*. United Nations, San Francisco.

Hindi references

Tripathi, A. K. (2012). *bhāṣā ke samakālīna saṃdarbha* (Contemporary Aspects of Language). Sahitya Sangam, Allahabad.

Tripathi, A. K. (2022). *sūcanā-praudyogikī kī sāmājikī* (Sociology of Information Technology). Prakrut Bharati Academy, Jaipur.

Tripathi, A. K., & Singh, P. (2021). *Bhāshāī varcasva evaṃ saṅkaṭa: saidhāntika evaṃ vyāvahārika paksha* (Linguistic Domination and Crisis: Theoretical and Practical Aspects). Prakrit Bharati Academy, Jaipur.

12
INDIGENOUS ARTIFICIAL INTELLIGENCE

Virtual and augmented reality as tools in the cultural preservation and education of endangered and extinct languages

Cringuta Irina Pelea

Introduction

I ka ʻōlelo nō ke ola; I ka ʻōlelo nō ka make.
In the language rests life, in the language rests death.
Traditional Hawaiian proverb

The present research aims to provide a systematic review of projects on virtual reality (VR) and augmented reality (AR) as tools in the cultural preservation, revitalization, and education of endangered or extinct languages. Whereas prior research has emphasized the efficiency of such tools in the usual language learning and acquisition process or their promising outlook in protecting cultural heritage, there is a scarcity of studies focused on examining the particular relationship between artificial intelligence (AI) from the Indigenous perspective and its potential in revitalizing and preserving the cultural heritage of endangered or extinct languages.

Linguists predict a bleak future for most of the world's Indigenous[1] languages: It is estimated that by the end of the twenty-first century, up to a staggering 90% of the languages spoken today are expected to disappear (Sherris & Peyton, 2020). Furthermore, according to Ethnologue reports, 3045 out of the 7164 reported living languages are labeled as "endangered" (Ethnologue, n.d.), and United Nations data warns that every two weeks, at least one Indigenous language is dying (United Nations Declaration on the Rights of Indigenous Peoples, 2007).

In a postcolonial and highly technologized context that emphasizes cultural diversity as a provisional and superficial remedy for the secular cultural genocide and forced assimilation of the Indigenous communities, we ponder the following question: Can AI, through VR and AR, overcome the dualistic and bipolar frame of Indigenous versus non-Indigenous cultures and increase to a sustainable level the vitality of Indigenous languages worldwide? As the linguist, philosopher, and cognitive scientist Noam Chomsky stated during an interview in the TV documentary *We Still Live Here – Âs Nutayuneân*: "A language is not just words. It is a culture, a tradition, a unification of a community, and a whole history that creates what a community is. It is all embodied in a language" (We Still Live Here – Âs Nutayuneân, 2010). Therefore, an Indigenous language

DOI: 10.4324/9781003439493-15

carries not only linguistic information but also ancient wisdom – history, traditions, myths, vibrant folklore, traditional and homeopathic medicine, and generationally passed nature-related secular knowledge (Piirainen & Sherris, 2015).

Considering this sensitive sociocultural background, the present chapter aims to examine the Indigenous character of AI serving as a language preservation tool and, therefore, to address the existing gap in the already-published academic research on this topic. Following multiple centuries of settler oppression and genocide, most Indigenous languages are now either endangered or have already become extinct (May, 2011). For this reason, the words "Indigenous," "endangered," and "extinct" will be used interchangeably throughout this chapter. On the one hand, the groundbreaking innovation of this research lies in its systematic approach to exploring VR and AR as pioneering technologies dedicated to the preservation, maintenance, or revitalization of (Indigenous) endangered or extinct languages. On the other hand, the present study is the first one to provide a global and comparative overview of the state-of-the-art Indigenous projects employing VR and AR for purposes of Indigenous language revitalization and, consequently, a catalyst of social justice and advocacy of Indigenous rights.

In what follows, we start by reviewing, in the theoretical section, the necessary framework, definitions, and the very few relevant research studies that focus specifically on how VR and AR are employed as Indigenous language endorsement agents. In the next section, we proceed by exploring the concept of Indigenous AI through the lenses of VR and AR and describe significant case studies in which such avant-garde technologies are employed with the specific purposes of Indigenous language preservation, revitalization, or teaching and education. A first relevant example is Indigenous AI, a project launched, developed, and currently maintained by Michael Running Wolf for revitalizing Cheyenne, his tribal language. Another noteworthy project is represented by the Kusunda film, an immersive and interactive production filmed with VR technology, which connects the audience with the extinct Kusunda language originating from Nepal. The analysis will continue by highlighting key issues, challenges, threats, and possibilities that arise from integrating immersive technologies in the field of Indigenous languages. The research concludes with a reflective discussion regarding potential avenues of further research while arguing for the need to approach immersive technologies from an interdisciplinary and cross-cultural perspective.

Literature review

The theoretical discussion is framed around three interconnected threads, which represent key starting points for the present empirical research. We will examine (1) brief accounts of scholarly definitions of VR, AR, and MR; (2) an overview of how immersive technologies are used particularly in the field of Indigenous languages; and (3) a critical perspective of Indigenous studies, with an emphasis on how specific instances of cultural genocide and aggressive assimilation and education policies endured by Indigenous communities located in North America and Australia lead to massive linguistic loss and to the extinction of many Indigenous languages.

Scholarly definitions

Despite the fact that such concepts are challenging to define, we propose the following working definitions. 'Virtual reality' is frequently referred to as "a simulation of a three-dimensional virtual environment (VE), generated by a computer, in which the person can interact with the said environment with, for example, a helmet with an integrated screen" (Peixoto et al., 2021).

An equally interactive type of immersive technology experiencing the same rapid increase in academic popularity and worldwide recognition is 'augmented reality,' which "allows users to see virtual elements superimposed upon or composited with the real world" (Stumpp et al, 2019; Azuma, 1997). Both technologies have been successfully employed in a wide variety of fields with significant social importance and impact: manufacturing, robotics, customer design, architecture, history (tangible and intangible cultural heritage), psychological and psychiatric treatment, medicine, and education (Peixoto et al., 2021).

Falling under the same umbrella of immersive technologies is the concept of 'mixed reality' (MR). According to an oft-cited definition, it is a "mix of real and virtual objects within a single display" (Milgram & Kishino, 1994). At the same time, other researchers note that, unlike AR, MR has the ability to manipulate a scene (Lopez et al., 2021). As such, based on the "reality-virtuality continuum" developed by Milgram and Kishino, the real world corresponds to the "fully real environment," whereas the fully virtual environment stands for VR. 'Augmented virtuality' (AV) is "either completely immersive, partially immersive, or otherwise, to which some amount of (video or texture mapped) 'reality' has been added" (Milgram & Kishino, 1994). MR, therefore, represents "everything in between" (Milgram & Kishino, 1994). In accordance with this perspective, VR is not a type of MR, while AR represents a subset of MR (when mostly real environments are augmented with some virtual fragments) (Milgram & Kishino, 1994).

Regardless of the vast majority of researchers who focused on the fruitful, practical applications of these emerging technologies among the fields mentioned previously or in the education process of second languages, exploring the applicability VR and AR in the preservation, revitalization, teaching, and education of endangered or extinct Indigenous languages remains scattered and very limited.

Previous research on VR, AR, and Indigenous languages

Although immersive technologies are becoming increasingly popular, the development, management, and cost reduction of VR and AR are still relatively recent. Thus, there is a dearth of research studies that have previously inquired into the state-of-the-art, impact, and critical challenges of VR and AR applications in the field of Indigenous languages.

Paul J. Meighan conducted a systematic and chronologically structured literature review of technology as a whole and its role in the revitalization process of Indigenous languages (Meighan, 2021). The author investigates the impact of different types, stages, and evolution of technology use over the preservation process of various endangered languages. The scholar's literature review of both academic and non-academic sources involves grouping technology into six categories predefined by the "dominant Western ideals of technological progress," thus underlining the idea that Western people created the "World Wide Web for a Western audience" (Meighan, 2021). In Meighan's perspective, the established categories that reflect the "dominant Western capitalistic worldview" are (1) facilitation technologies, (2) communication technologies, (3) web 1.0 digital and online technologies until the year 2005, (4) web 2.0 digital and online technologies until the year 2015, (5) web 3.0 digital and online technologies in the present, and (6) semantic technologies in the future (2021).

An interesting experiment in this field has been conducted by Hanna Outakoski, who examined the potential of VR as an online teaching solution among learners of North Saami, a severely endangered language spoken by Saami communities located in northern parts of Norway, Sweden, and Finland. The learning experiment performed by Outakoski – "Språkens hus ('House of Languages')" involved choosing the platform Second Life as a virtual teaching environment and developing the course with its teaching materials on the same platform. A fundamental conclusion of this empirical study is that virtual environments present an enormous potential in teaching endangered languages by granting learners the much-needed safety and comfort of ethnic anonymity (Outakoski, 2013).

The potential of the same 3D virtual environment – Second Life – in the revitalization of the Ainu language (one of Japan's most significant languages facing imminent threat of extinction) has been investigated as a promising research line by Tresi Nonno (2015). The independent scholar connects role-play and historical reconstruction with increasing the motivation and interest of non-Indigenous people toward culturally specific Ainu elements and argues for the importance of virtual environments in the acquisition of the Ainu language lexicon (Nonno, 2015).

With the objective of promoting proactive dissemination and awaken interest in the Náhuat language, Campos, Pina, and Rubio have designed the "Náhuat Language Interactive Kinect Application", which is now available for use in the anthropology museums in the capital city of El Salvador. Although the experiment had a very promising outlook in designing and developing the "Náhuat Augmented Reality Textbook", the impact of the application is in the process of being properly evaluated, given the suspension of museum activities during the COVID-19 pandemic (Campos et al., 2021).

Likewise, a brief 150-word section is dedicated to VR and AR by Patrick Littell et al., who briefly described the utilization of Indigenous language technologies in Canada. While acknowledging the growing amount of interest in integrating such technologies into the pedagogic process of Indigenous languages, the scholars admit that there are "very few implementations for Indigenous languages in Canada" (Littell et al., 2018). Furthermore, most apps of this type tend to concentrate more on spreading awareness and promoting the cultural heritage of Indigenous people without necessarily involving the linguistic component (Littell et al., 2018).

To some extent, there are similarities between the studies mentioned previously and our work; nevertheless, clear differences should be noted. Most of the already-published scholarly articles on this topic focus on a clearly delimited geographical and cultural area (Finland, Japan, Canada, and others), whereas this contribution aims to provide a worldwide perspective of the phenomenon. Albeit global in their approach, other scholars (see the work of Paul J. Meighan) dedicated only some very brief sections to the applications of VR and AR in the field of Indigenous language preservation. Moreover, unlike the present chapter, no academic source has sought to focus on key themes, similarities, and major challenges potentially faced by the tense intersection between Indigenous linguistic heritages regarded in this chapter as a component of the post-contemporary decolonization politics and the implementation of immersive technologies.

Indigenous studies: how past genocides have devastated the Indigenous linguistic heritage

Hillerdal, Karlström and Ojala emphasize the traumatic dimensions of Indigenous history and heritage by stating:

> Indigenous peoples in different parts of the world often share experiences of colonization, marginalization, and discrimination, which form individual and collective historical traumas. In this context, history and heritage often become contested and difficult. Furthermore, the colonialism experienced by indigenous groups is not only located in the past but in many ways also in the present (insensitive excavations and the plundering of graves and sacred sites) as a continuing colonial situation – which actually constitutes one of the defining traits of contemporary indigenous experiences.
>
> (Hillerdal et al., 2017)

Nonetheless, the devastating impact of cultural genocides has affected Indigenous languages as well (Hillerdal et al., 2017; Gabriel, 2019). Considered by UNESCO vehicles "of intangible cultural heritage," Indigenous languages represent "the very essences of [Indigenous] identity, including spirituality, traditional governance, medicines, health practices, well-being, and even sexuality" (UNESCO, 2003; Gabriel, 2019). However, this ancestral linguistic heritage that has endured centuries of colonial persecution is now either critically endangered or faces the imminent threat of extinction. In fact, the current situation represents

> the direct consequence of colonialism and colonial practices that resulted in the decimation of indigenous peoples, their cultures, and languages. Through policies of assimilation, dispossession of lands, discriminatory laws, and actions, indigenous languages in all regions face the threat of extinction. This is further exacerbated by globalization and the rise of a small number of culturally dominant languages. Increasingly, [Indigenous] languages are no longer transmitted by parents to their children.
>
> (Gabriel, 2019)

Therefore, Indigenous languages, cultures, and communities all over the world have experienced the long-standing and sometimes even irreversible effects of cultural genocide and settler mass destruction: Canada, the USA, Australia, New Zealand, Northern Europe, or Asia.

To close the theoretical section, we will provide two examples of how acts of genocide against Indigenous people directly affected not only the Indigenous identity and culture but also Indigenous linguistic heritages and, eventually, led to the endangering or extermination of Indigenous languages, a situation otherwise referred to as 'linguicide' (Griffith, 2017).

The first example is provided by the ideology "Kill the Indian and Save the Child,"[2] an expression first used by the general Richard Henry Pratt, who founded the first American government-sponsored Indian residential school in 1879 (Smith, 2011; Smiley-Marquez & Tompkins, 2011). The motto became central for the governing and educational policy of the Indian Residential School system (the USA and Canada, 1831–1996) (Gabriel, 2019). Through the weapon of cultural shaming, Indigenous children were forcibly removed from their homes, forbidden from speaking their mother tongue, and subjected to years of severe emotional, physical, and sexual abuse (Gabriel, 2019). Historical records testify that when Indigenous children attempted to speak their native languages, nuns and priests employed extreme physical and psychological punishment methods that included "whipping with a strap," locking the children in dark closets, shoving needles in their tongues, and even ripping their tongues from their throats (Ilyniak, 2015; Gantt, 2015; Hanson et al., 2020; Mabie, 2023). While acknowledging being ashamed and fearful of speaking his native language in public and with other people but his family, one of the surviving victims recalls: "Being hit for your language is a big thing, because that's who you are. That's part of you" (Ilyniak, 2015). Therefore, historically and academically speaking, residential schools are considered the most significant and largest contributor "to the loss of Indigenous languages in Canadian history" (Clare, 2022).

As the second example, "the Stolen Generations" is a metaphorical expression that refers to the forcible removal of Australia's aboriginal children from their families, only to "be placed or detained in religious missions that resembled prison-like institutions" (McGlade, 2020). The education policies were highly similar to the ones employed by the previous briefly described Canadian residential schools and focused on forbidding children to speak their native languages by employing inhuman punishments (McGlade, 2020). Marking a period of history that lasted from from 1900 to 1970, the cultural and linguistic genocide of Aboriginal and Torres Strait children was properly acknowledged and apologized for only in 2008 by the Australian parliament.

Figure 12.1 Photo: Thomas Moore, as he appeared when admitted to the Regina Indian Industrial School, and Thomas Moore, after tuition at the Regina Indian Industrial School. Image courtesy of the Library and Archives Canada/Annual report of the Department of Indian Affairs, 1896/OCLC 1771148

Figure 12.2 "Homes are sought for these children." Australian newspaper advertising Aboriginal children for adoption. Dated 1934. Image courtesy of the National Archives of Australia. NAA: A1, 1934/6800

Nonetheless, the full benefit of comprehensive reparations for the decades-long atrocities committed by the Australian government through its aggressive colonial policies is yet to be paid to the survivors and their descendants. However, such policies of "legalized systems of land dispossession, racial discrimination, state-sanctioned violence, and abuse exert their effect even nowadays" (McGlade, 2020). Widespread racism against Aboriginal people, who make up 3% of Australia's population yet speak up to 400 Indigenous languages, remains deeply embedded within Australian contemporary society, together with a blunt denial of institutional racism and former settler abuse (McGlade, 2020).

Case study: Indigenous AI in the decolonization process of the digital landscape

Methodology

Considering the chapter's objectives, as stated in the Introduction, we seek to answer the following five research questions:

1. How are immersive technologies such as VR and AR employed by Indigenous projects in preserving/revitalizing endangered/extinct languages?
2. Who are the main public segments/targeted users of the projects?
3. What are the overarching themes, specific features, differences, challenges, and current trends across the projects?
4. What are the major research/social contributions of the projects?
5. What future academic implications can be expected upon engaging in cutting-edge technologies to protect the linguistic heritage of Indigenous communities?

To address the previously mentioned research questions, we carried out a two-stage qualitative content analysis. The preference for this particular method is due to the fact that it allows a nuanced understanding of how VR and AR storytelling blends with language preservation and revitalization while giving insight into the discursive practices of Indigenous creators and artists. The first stage of the qualitative content analysis has an explorative-descriptive approach. It involves collecting and analyzing English-language media and online sources to identify and characterize a wide range of geographically and culturally diverse Indigenous projects that employ VR and AR for the preservation or revitalization of endangered or extinct languages. The second stage generates the overarching themes, similarities, and challenges presented by the Indigenous projects registered as distinctive units.

Search method, data collection, and selection

First, in order to identify and characterize relevant projects according to our initial objectives, we performed a Google search applying the following query string: ("virtual reality" OR "VR" OR "augmented reality" OR "AR") AND ("Indigenous language" OR "endangered language" OR "extinct language"). Table 12.1 provides an overview of the results. Second, we compiled a database of 389 web articles with *only* first-hand account content: media articles and sources that include testimonies, interviews, podcasts transcripts, blog posts, reports, opinions, and statements of the Indigenous creators and/or the projects' participants. This content was later

Table 12.1 Overview of findings Immersive technologies in the preservation and revitalization of Indigenous languages

Project name	Language	Geographical position	Status of language and characteristics
1. Michael Running Wolf	Cheyenne	USA, southeastern Montana and central Oklahoma	– critically endangered – complex agglutinative – polysynthetic morphology
2. Kusunda: Speak to Awaken	Kusunda	central western Nepal	– highly endangered – no words for "yes" or "no" – no words for direction
3. Biidaaban: First Light	Anishinaabemowin	southern Canada, northern Midwestern USA	– incorporates dialects with local writing systems – system of obviation – new consonant sounds (ch, sh, zh, and a glottal stop) – verb dominance
4. Last Whispers	Ahom	southeast China	– extinct – typical characteristics of Tai languages (SVO word order, lack of inflection, etc.) – Ahom script
	Ayoreo	Bolivia, Paraguay	– fusional and mood-prominent language
	Baṭfiari	Oman	– threat of extinction
	Lxcatec	southeastern Mexico, the village Santa María Ixcatlán	– highly endangered (400 speakers) – verb-initial constituent order – use of noun classifiers – complex phonology (contrastive phonation and contrastive tone)
	Dalabon	Australia	– severely endangered (fewer than ten speakers) – polysynthetic character
	Great Andamanese	India	– highly endangered (nine speakers) – head-marking polysynthetic and agglutinative – dependent and non-dependent nouns
	Ingrian	Russia	– Finnish alphabet – highly agglutinative

(*Continued*)

Table 12.1 (Continued)

Project name	Language	Geographical position	Status of language and characteristics
	Kotiria (Wanano)	Brazil, Colombia	– highly synthetic – agglutinative – nominative-accusative syntactic alignment – nasalization
	Koyukon (Denaakk'e)	western Alaska	– SOV order – large consonant inventory (40) – no gender distinction
	Ongota	southeast Ethiopia	– moribund – problematic classification – almost complete absence of nominal and inflectional verbal morphology
5. Thunder VR	Blackfoot	USA, Alberta and Montana	– specific syllabary – polysynthetic – fusional – flexible word order
6. Náhuat Language: The AR Textbook	Náhuat	central Mexico	– agglutinative – polysynthetic – reiterative
7. Nisga'a Language and Culture	Nisga'a (Nass-Gitxsan)	northwestern British Columbia, Canada	– syntactic ergativity – noun incorporation – reduplication
8. Jeju dialect. 99-Land (AR)	Jeju (Jejueo or Jejuan)	Jeju Island, South Korea	– classified as a dialect of Korean language – not mutually intelligible with standard Korean – lacking honorifics and formalities – lexical influence from Middle Mongolian – preservation of Middle Korean elements
9. Niwîchewâka: Cree Syllabics (VR)	Cree	Canada, USA (Montana)	– Cree syllabary – complex polysynthetic morphosyntax – non-regulated word order
10. Ogoki Learning (VR language app)	Ojibwen (Anishinaabemowin)	See entry no. 3	

Project name	Language	Geographical position	Status of language and characteristics
11. Hua Kiʻi (AR prototype app)	Crow (Apsáalooke), Hawaiian (Kanaka Maoli), Māori, Cheyenne Lakota, Gadigal/Dunghutti	Australia, Canada, Hawaii, New Zealand, USA	– specific features of each language
12. AbTec (Aboriginal Territories in Cyberspace – VR and AR)	Aboriginal languages of Canada and the USA	Canada, USA	– specific features of each language
13. Revitalization project of Secwepemctsin language (AR)	Secwepemctsin (Shuswap)	British Columbia, Canada	– Secwepemctsín alphabet – remarkable subject orientation in third-person contexts
14. Georgian College program for the acquisition of the Ojibwe language (VR)	Ojibwe (Anishinaabemowin)	See entry no. 3	
15. PARADISEC (VR)	Asian Pacific languages (700 collections incorporating over 1,370 languages)	Pacific region	– specific features of each language
16. Yalinguth (AR)	Aboriginal and Torres Strait Islander languages + English	Australia	– avoidance speech – ergative–absolutive case system – speech taboos have led to sign languages
17. Carriberrie (VR film)	Aboriginal and Torres Strait Islander languages	See entry no. 16	

(*Continued*)

Table 12.1 (*Continued*)

Project name	Language	Geographical position	Status of language and characteristics
18. Arctic Indigenous Digital Talent Hub (VR)	Arctic Indigenous Peoples Languages	Arctic region, Canada, and northern Europe	– polysynthetic ergativity
19. Indigenous San Community in Namibia, Africa (VR)	San	Namibia, Africa	– extensive use of click consonants
20. Teleport VR: ssForgotten Civilizations and Dying Languages	Jeru (Great Andamanese)	Andaman Islands	– five speakers
	Ainu	Hokkaido, Northern Japan	– 15 speakers
	Yuchi	Oklahoma, USA	– four speakers
	Oro Win	Brazil, bordering Bolivia	– five–six speakers
	Dumi	Nepal	– eight speakers
	Ter Sami	Kola Peninsula of Russia	– fewer than ten speakers
	N|uu	South Africa	– seven speakers

coded to generate general themes. The search and database compilation took place between 27 January and 18 April 2023.

The inclusion criteria for the first stage of the qualitative content analysis are as follows: the Indigenous projects *must* be related to VR/AR technology and *must be developed by* or at least *with* Indigenous people. Likewise, they should be dedicated to or at least make references to/address the linguistic-cultural heritage of endangered or extinct languages. In the second stage, the fundamental criterion was *the first-hand account nature* of the source.

The exclusion criteria were based either on the fact that the projects made no mention of VR/AR/the language component and focused solely on the Indigenous cultural heritage or on the absence of any form of Indigenous (creative) contribution from the development process of the project.

Findings

Case studies: VR and AR in the preservation and revitalization of Indigenous languages

1. Indigenous in AI

As the founder of the Indigenous in AI project, Michael Running Wolf is a Northern Cheyenne, Blackfeet, and Lakota researcher who has dedicated his efforts to "reclaiming Indigenous languages and culture by making use of immersive technologies and AI" (Internet Health Report, 2022). While exploring the mechanisms of Indigenous language revitalization through automatic speech recognition, the former software engineer of Amazon became a persistent advocate of "Indigenous data sovereignty," which is deemed necessary in order to reconsider the symbiosis of AI research and data governance (Internet Health Report, 2022).

2. Kusunda: Speak to Awaken

The multi-awarded "voice-driven virtual reality experience" directed by Felix Gaedtke and Gayatri Parameswaran and launched in 2019 is dedicated to revitalizing Kusunda, a dormant Indigenous language from western Nepal. The film production of 23 minutes is co-created by the elder shaman Lil Bahadur, who has long forgotten this language he once spoke and his granddaughter Hima, who strives to revive it: "If the Kusunda language disappears, then the existence of the Kusunda people in Nepal will also fade away. We will lose our identity. That is why I want to save our language" (Kusunda VR, 2019).

3. Biidaaban: First Light

Biidaban which can also be translated from the Anishinaabemowin language as "the moment of the first light of dawn," is the short title of the interactive, room-scale VR cinematic performance of Lisa Jackson, a multi-award-winning Anishinaabe director originating from Canada. Screened in the traditional languages of Wendat, Mohawk, and Ojibway, the production reimagines the urban landscape of a futuristic Toronto reclaimed by nature (Johnson, 2018).

4. Last Whispers

Metaphorically described as "a sound sculpture," Lena Herzog's audiovisual and immersive project entitled *Last Whispers: Oratorio for Vanishing Voices, Collapsing Universes, and a Falling Tree* celebrates the vocal diversity of a plethora of Indigenous endangered or extinct languages (Lena Herzog investigates the mass extinction of languages, 2020). After its much-acclaimed premiere at the Sundance Film Festival in 2019, this "immersive, experiential work dedicated to the extinction of languages" encompasses both spoken and sung recordings of individuals or groups in approximately 40 endangered or desiccated languages and dialects with a geographical global coverage and distribution (Last whispers, 2021; Globalization and the vanishing voices of the world, 2019).

5. Thunder VR

Designed as a virtual reality game by the Urban Society for Aboriginal Youth (USAY) in partnership with the VR/AR company MAMMOTH XR, this highly immersive Blackfoot language preservation and culture learning instrument draws inspiration from the Thunder Blackfoot graphic novel and similar folk legends (The experience: First of its kind, 2019; Virtual Reality, 2023). While the initiative is officially advertised as "first of its kind," dedicated to teaching but also empowering Indigenous youth to reconnect with their ancestral languages and traditions, the VR narrative "chronicles the journey of a man who must challenge the powerful spirit, Thunder, also known as Ksiistsikom" (The experience: First of its kind, 2019).

6. Náhuat language: the AR textbook

Another Indigenous language immersion project aiming to improve the acquisition of the Náhuat language has been developed by W. S. Campos, A. Pina, and G. Rubio and includes designing two Náhuat – Spanish dictionaries Android mobile applications and a Náhuat augmented reality textbook with marker images (Campos et al., 2021). The resources are to be employed in both public and private primary education facilities located in rural areas or the capital of El Salvador (Campos et al., 2021).

7. Nisga'a language and culture

Raising Nisga'a Language, Sovereignty and Land-Based Education Through Traditional Carving Knowledge has benefitted from the financial aid of Social Sciences Humanities Research Council's New Frontiers in Research Fund and encompasses a Nisga'a language revitalization module based on VR technology and two other culture-orientated modules ("the creation of an authentic house totem pole" and the repatriation of an original house totem pole from a museum located in Edinburgh, Scotland) (Project to use virtual reality technology to teach Nisga'a, 2021).

8. Jeju dialect. 99-Land

The AR project displayed in the Jeju Teddy Bear Museum presents bear-related folk and traditional fables of Jeju (*A Fable of 99 Valleys*) in the Jeju endangered dialect of South Korea and focuses on practicing particular speech sounds. As the authors of this initiative state: "Jeju dialect is a disappearing language that 99 percent of people do not use. The dialect reflects the environmental features, customs of the area, and its origin, so the value of preservation is very high in linguistic terms." (Shin et al., 2019; K design award – 99-land: AR project, 2019).

Indigenous artificial intelligence

9.   Niwîchewâka: Cree Syllabics Virtual Reality project (CSVR)

Officially acknowledged as the first practical attempt at using VR as a teaching tool for First Nations language, *Niwîchewâka* is a twenty-module VR game leading native elementary-school students in their journey to a "a land-based world where they follow Niipiish, a Cree girl, and her English-speaking dog Achimush," where they undertake "complete the word" and spelling activities in the Cree language (Using virtual reality to strengthen the Cree language, 2016).

10.   Other honorable mentions

Due to space constraints, the following projects are to be briefly named and described:

*   Ogoki Learning (VR language app);
*   Hua Ki'i (AR prototype app);
*   AbTec (VR and AR);
*   the initiative dedicated to revitalizing the Secwepemctsin language (AR app);
*   the Georgian College program for the acquisition of the Ojibwe language (VR);
*   PARADISEC (VR for the Pacific languages);
*   Yalinguth (AR app for Aboriginal Australian languages);
*   Carriberrie (VR film);
*   the Arctic Indigenous Digital Talent Hub for Indigenous communities and languages in the Arctic region, Northern Europe and Canada (VR);
*   A project undertaken in the Indigenous San Community in Namibia, Africa (VR; culture/language mix);
*   Teleport VR: Forgotten Civilizations and Dying Languages (a VR journey to various locations around the globe, which highlights various aspects regarding the endangered status of several languages and provides the viewer with basic lessons).

Overarching themes across the projects: new directions and critical issues

Following the qualitative content analysis and the subsequent coding procedure that involved identifying common concepts, ideas, and similar patterns, several overarching themes have been identified across the previously described case studies. The following categorization of the themes has been applied to highlight the state-of-art and the academic and social contributions, shared similarities, and future implications of such projects.

1.   Revitalization of Indigenous languages through formal education

Several of the aforementioned projects are specifically targeted towards the educational and pedagogical aspects as the main solutions to reverse the rapid decline of Indigenous languages and seek to improve language acquisition for Indigenous young(er) generations. Therefore, VR and AR are employed as innovative methodologies and venues that can enhance Indigenous language acquisition in various settings such as higher educational institutions, public spaces, and remote-learning environments.

Educational programs provided by institutions such as the Georgian College, the Cree School Board or the AR textbook of the Náhuat language can be interpreted not only as focusing primarily on the language acquisition process but also as an expression of Indigenous sovereignty and a tribal collective effort to elevate the socio-political position of that endangered language within the postcolonial context. Integrating the study of Indigenous languages into the formal teaching curricula is a significantly disrupting factor for the hegemonic position of the settler language, which usually represents the norm of instruction and examination in schools and universities. It comes as a counter-response to the former residential schools and their teaching practices, guided by the fundamental principle of "educating for integration (that is, educate to exterminate the Indigenous languages and cultures)" (Bojórquez, 2003).

Making use of advanced immersive technologies for formal educational purposes is more likely to maintain the interest of the younger generations, who experience various forms of social and inner pressure: From carrying on the heritage of the community to adjusting to modern times and circumstances that are highly likely to favor the reminiscences of the subversive colonial ideology (De Korne et al., 2024). Whereas the students might be enrolled in primary schools or college level, a shared similarity between these programs is that they provide a top-notch and attractive answer and alternative to the feeling of alienation of the young Indigenous people toward the modern education system.

2. Reinforcement of Indigenous languages as social justice: voicing narratives of resistance

The language remains a significant component of the healing process following centuries of cultural and linguistic genocide, marked by segregation, dispossession of their lands, resources, and cultural heritage, and forced assimilation policies. Survivors' testimonies reflect the depth of the intergenerational trauma:

> It was illegal to speak our language, and our culture was underground for a long time. . . It's typical for children of my generation, for our grandparents to restrict us from speaking our language because they didn't want us to suffer the humiliation of having the language ripped from our throats.
>
> (Mabie, 2023)

In this regard, the context of the historical injustice entailed by colonial powers is not perceived as diminishing in time. Therefore, reasserting one's linguistic heritage represents a counter-response and form of postcolonial/restorative social justice, which reflects a proactive engagement resonating with a certain sense of obligation of nowadays Indigenous populations toward their ancestors.

3. Empowerment, resilience and pride: VR and AR as decolonizing technologies

In the digital aftermath of colonial secular occupation, mixed reality technologies have become tools capable of decolonizing both the academic context and public spaces by emboldening and empowering Indigenous communities while fostering and nurturing a culture of Indigenous pride. As such, leading-edge technologies are breaking free from Western/colonial-centric discourse and settler philosophy. These technologies now serve to reinforce and reassert historically oppressed ethnic identities by revitalizing ancestral and traditional knowledge.

Indigenous artificial intelligence

4. Inner and outer awareness: connecting with the community

Another feature common among the previously mentioned case studies is the interconnectedness: a systemic negotiation process regarding the dynamics of traditions within immersive environments takes place between the younger generations and the elders. For instance, while describing the experience of working together with an elder on the first-ever Indigenous VR game – Thunder VR – the producer Shaun Crawford of MAMMOTH XR has stated:

> It can be intimidating working with an *elder*. . . . When recording voice-overs usually we'll give feedback but when you have an elder there, you're not going to give him any kind of direction because just being there to share that story is incredibly powerful. . . . It's all been very humbling. . . . This process gave us an opportunity to just listen. To listen and learn and be open and it has created this reverence for everyone at USAY whose partnership is the best thing to come out of this project. VR is an empathy machine. The experience itself is very compelling so the *youth* are really integrated into that process, it's extremely experiential [author's emphasis].
>
> (Condon, 2019)

5. Indigenous: virtual heritage, digital identity, and digital literacy

The VR/AR initiatives not only deliver language immersive experiences but also offer a sociocultural and historical mapping of Indigenous communities and explore marginalized historical discourses revolving around the communities' colonial past (see, for instance, the virtual reality films *Biidaban* or *Carriberrie*). Besides converting into resources through which one's attachment toward one's native community can be formed, nurtured, and strengthened, such projects have the potential to make Indigenous cultural heritage appealing to young (and not only) non-Indigenous audiences who otherwise might show little interest in the Aboriginal legacy. Hence, learning the language becomes more than an acquisition process, but one during which the participant also learns to navigate complex layers of folk stories, myths, perennial traditions, common local knowledge, and historical facts.

"Digital literacy" is another important concept worth discussing within this category. The definition and conceptualization of "digital and immersive literacy" within Indigenous studies represents a practical example of the way emerging technologies trouble and disrupt not only the negative stereotyping deeply embedded in the colonial discourses but also engage critical reflection regarding the inclusive character of academic terminology. First, it is important to acknowledge the conventional Western and predominant way of defining "digital literacy" as it follows: "the ability to understand information and – more importantly – to evaluate and integrate information in multiple formats that the computer can deliver" while emphasizing the high status of *written* practices" [author's emphasis] (Gilster, 1997). However, the mainstream definitions frequently employed within scholarship practices and discourses, reflect, as others have pointed out, "the exclusion of Indigenous epistemic and intellectual traditions," together with "the obstinate refusal of the academy to go beyond relatively shallow changes in the curriculum" (Kuokkanen, 2016). Indigenous languages are predominately characterized by *orality* and *usually lack writing systems* [author's emphasis]; therefore, achieving digital and immersive literacy in Indigenous languages while working with VR/AR should be interpreted and evaluated in a different manner than the regular L2 acquisition process.

The Routledge Handbook of Endangered and Minority Languages

6. Challenges, threats, and concerns in handling immersive technologies in the field of Indigenous languages

Regardless of the plethora of technological advances in VR and AR that undoubtedly play a decisive role in sustaining the revitalization of Indigenous languages, several significant challenges and concerns need to be highlighted.

A. LINGUISTIC DIFFICULTIES

One set of challenges involves the linguistic barriers that VR and AR might face when applied in the field of Indigenous languages, which is marked by nearly an unfathomable linguistic variety. Such languages usually have an extremely polysynthetic and/or agglutinative character and thus come in contrast with most European languages, for instance, renowned for being analytic. Until now, artificial intelligence has yet to solve the thorny issue posed by the highly polysynthetic nature typical of Indigenous languages, both in terms of software translation efficiency and automatic speech recognition technologies.

Another immediate linguistic concern is related to the authenticity of the Indigenous language used as a communication medium within virtual and augmented environments. Several questions arise: How much do VR and AR impact the (artificial) evolution and development of Indigenous languages? Is there a chance for such immersive technologies to replace an endangered/extinct language with its digital/cyber version, thus making it lose its authenticity and sociohistorical identity upon being removed from its traditional context?

B. EDUCATIONAL, PEDAGOGICAL, AND METHODOLOGICAL DIFFICULTIES

While referring to the traditional learning process, other researchers have already mentioned the crucial importance of "Indigenous pedagogies, methodologies, and research" in the sustenance of Indigenous language acquisition all over the globe (Jacob et al., 2015). Immersive learning makes no exception; thus, we consider it compulsory to develop Indigenous-appropriate pedagogies and learning materials relevant to the virtual and augmented environments and adjust them accordingly to the geographical space(s) and sociocultural and historical necessities of each Indigenous community.

Furthermore, the evaluation criteria and other necessary performance indicators related to program assessment should also be adjusted accordingly to match each Indigenous linguistic profile. Nonetheless, such an academic endeavor would be, from the beginning exceedingly difficult, given the extraordinary variety and linguistic nature of Indigenous languages.

A final challenge worth mentioning in this category is embedding Indigenous immersive technologies within future university curricula in order to provide an inclusive educational environment; obstacles such as implementation costs, teachers' digital/immersive literacy, skills, or additional technical issues can hinder the overall successful implementation of such educational projects.

C. TECHNICAL DIFFICULTIES

As Michael Running Wolf has synthesized: "The current [artificial intelligence] technology assumes all languages are a type of English. It's common . . . for voice AI to translate a French command into English, interpret the command in English, and then translate the response back to French. This process works for languages like Spanish, French, and German, which have similar morphologies to English, but [this] doesn't work for Indigenous languages" (Mabie, 2023). From this perspective, we can conclude the same pattern of technical difficulties can be observed in using immersive technologies.

D. SOCIAL CHALLENGES

The geographical distribution and location of the previously described Indigenous case studies reveal what we will refer to as an "immersive divide" within Indigenous studies (please see Table 12.1). Here, we will define the "immersive divide" as "the discrepancy of access to immersive technologies across different (Indigenous) populations at the local, regional, national, and global levels."[3] As such, there is a significantly higher number of creators, producers, researchers, and users in the Global North, whereas we have managed to identify very few and geographically disparate VR/AR projects in the Global South. It should be highlighted, nonetheless, that this degree of inequality and striking polarization, otherwise said, the existence of a "Global South" and "Global North" within Indigenous studies and between Indigenous populations, can be interpreted as the outcome of unequal access to immersive technologies, a situation prone to be systematically reinforced and perpetuated by the typical neoliberal and capitalist agenda.

E. ETHICAL CHALLENGES

Among the ethical issues that are most likely to arise from the employment of immersive technologies within the field of Indigenous languages, we have identified and will briefly examine the following ones.

- **Indigenous data sovereignty**
  By definition, "Indigenous data sovereignty affirms the rights of Indigenous Peoples to control the collection, access, analysis, interpretation, management, dissemination, and reuse of Indigenous data" (Kukutai & Taylor, 2016). Moreover, controlling the sharing of and restricting others' access to ancestral sacred knowledge (which should be read here as "Indigenous data") has proven to be a form of secular resistance and resilience. Regardless of the vibrant potential of immersive technologies to revitalize Indigenous languages, we cannot overlook the existing tension "between reigniting ancient knowledge and the nature of such mediums that is prone to allow uncontrollable exploitation of the sacred data" (Workshop: Sacred Assets: Data Sovereignty, 2020).
- **Colonial implications of VR and AR. ethical governance and Indigenous rights**
  Much of the serious concern regarding the intersection of Indigenous data/languages and VR/AR holds two facets. The first is a worry about the ownership and control of Indigenous data, while the second is associated with the possibility of political or governmental (occasional) intrusion. However, what this challenge highlights is the urgent necessity to develop an ethical protocol and guideline for mixed-reality research and educational projects on Indigenous languages.

Conclusions and future research directions

Far from being exhaustive, this study has attempted to present a state-of-art review of how cutting-edge technologies have been implemented in the revitalization and preservation of Indigenous languages while highlighting significant themes and contributions and raising a critical understanding of the challenges and obstacles pertaining to the uses of VR/AR in this particular field. Based on our knowledge and research, this work represents the first attempt to connect immersive technologies with Indigenous languages from a global and comparative perspective, thus integrating and analyzing multiple case studies across various geographical spaces. From this perspective, this work aimed to complement the existing literature on immersive technologies in Indigenous language preservation.

We will conclude the present chapter by sketching out what we consider as potential future scholarly directions of inquiry and prominent issues that derive from the themes discussed above and thus represent important considerations for the future advancement of immersive technologies within the field of Indigenous languages.

Future direction 1: Linguistics

A first critical suggestion for research is to investigate the potential for lexical innovation of Indigenous languages through their users within immersive environments and their pathways of diffusion outside such environments (if there are any). Nonetheless, such an attempt would require not only sufficient academic knowledge, scholarly experience and adequate time, but also linguistic proficiency of that specific language. Other questions that can enrich the research agenda in this field are as follows: What conception criteria and evaluation standards should be taken into consideration in the case of VR/AR Indigenous educational programs? What is the long-term effect of XR on Indigenous students' cognitive development and Indigenous language acquisition? However, to address such thorny issues, more interdisciplinary studies are required, incorporating perspectives not only from linguistics but also from education, second language acquisition and many other specializations as well.

Future direction 2: Cultural studies

The wide-ranging sociocultural, linguistic, technical, ethical and educational challenges described in the previous section and the expansion and consolidation of the colonial Artificial Intelligence hegemony are arguments that compel us to emphasize the necessity of developing Indigenous XR (research) methodology which will focus on advancing the decolonization process by balancing social goals and research objectives. Indigenous scholars such as Linda Tuhiwai Smith have already advocated for "Indigenous-centered research" without necessarily pleading for "total rejection of all theory or research or Western knowledge" (Smith, 2022). Moreover, the social construction of Indigenous identities, together with other significant concepts such as "Indigenous culture," "community", "knowledge/wisdom," and "leaders/elders," should be investigated through the lenses of immersive technologies.

Future direction 3: Communication sciences

Most theories, models and related epistemologies in communication sciences tend to be developed based on the Western, white, colonial worldview and mode of analysis, thus deliberately ignoring Indigenous cultures and their particular knowledge paradigms (see, for instance, the Shannon-Weaver model of communication or Lasswell's model of communication). In addition to being outdated and ignoring the widespread impact of immersive technologies, these communication models privilege Western epistemologies and bluntly deny the cultural viability of Indigenous knowledge and wisdom. As such, a major difference between the Western and Indigenous understanding of the communication process lies in the conceptualization and visualization of the *context* as a fundamental constituting element. In the latter perspective, the context is known as "the Land, with capital L" or "the nature," as a living being with conscience:

> Land is more than the diaphanousness of inhabited memories; Land is spiritual, emotional, and relational; Land *is* experiential, (re)membered, and storied; Land *is* consciousness – Land *is* sentient. . . . Land refers to the ways we honor and respect her as a sentient and conscious being.
>
> (Styres, 2019)

Therefore, as an Indigenous philosophical construct, the Land "expresses a [symbiotic] duality" that overpasses the Western conceptualization of "the context": "[it] refers not only to [the] place as a physical geographic space but also to the underlying conceptual principles, philosophies, and ontologies of that space" (Styres, 2019). Hence, inquiries worthy of further examination should address the reconceptualization and reframing of "the context" within the models of communication through the lenses of both immersive technologies and Indigenous languages, knowledge, epistemologies and modes of operating in the world.

Future direction 4: Futuristic Indigenous studies

Previous empirical studies on the subject of second language acquisition through cutting-edge technologies have already started to examine the effect and impact of integrating holographic technology and related mobile-based applications in the traditional learning process of second languages (Cerezo et al., 2019; Mukhallafi, 2023). However, the research revealed that no similar projects have made use of hologram technology or holographic tutors in developing Indigenous language communication skills. The absence of clear-cut data and conclusions regarding this specific intersection highlight the stringent necessity for further research. Within this future scholarly direction, a significant caveat could be the daunting ethical challenge of employing an Indigenous holographic tutor: making use of an elder's figure or portrait might give a sense of "belonging" and "inclusiveness" to the audience but might be deemed as an unacceptable practice from the perspective of Indigenous ethics. The next direction worth investigating is how Indigenous art, literature, and folklore interweave with immersive technologies and contribute to language education and preservation: studies and findings are still significantly under-represented in academia, making the future research in these particular subfields critically needed.

Final remarks

Notwithstanding the argument that even nowadays, Indigenous language speakers are subject to ongoing stereotypical representations and pejorative labeling while also facing long-term governmental pressures that privilege the colonial languages, it is only through cross-cultural understanding that we can liberate constructive criticism and expand the Indigenous interdisciplinary perspectives. It goes without saying that such cross-cultural understanding implies deconstructing the settler hegemonic discourses by decentering the West and the colonial self as the archetype of human cognition, development, and (artificially-constructed) philosophical superiority.

What remains indisputable is that the unceasing and unhindered progress of immersive technologies has also placed further impetus on Indigenous communities to express their secular resilience, community pride, and collective and self-identity – all intricately (inter-)connected with the

The Routledge Handbook of Endangered and Minority Languages

native language. Just like the old Hawaiian proverb states from the first lines of this chapter: "In the language rests life, in the language rests death" (Nāmāhoe, 2007), this poetic saying ('ōlelo no'eau) is one that the children of the [Hawaiian] land (kupa o ka 'āina) and all other Indigenous communities worldwide should bear in their minds and hearts.

Acknowledgment

My heartfelt thanks go to professor doctor and editor Chris Shei for encouraging the idea of this chapter in its initial stage.

Dedication

This chapter is dedicated to all the Indigenous populations in the world: The ones who have lived to endure centuries of colonial abominations, the ones who still are with us, living legacies of the Indigenous Spirit, and the ones who shall come to make all proud.

Notes

1 Throughout this chapter, the central concept of "indigenous" is written with a capital "I" to emphasize the significance of the Indigenous component as holding a fundamental role in the construction of the socio-cultural and historical identity of worldwide minority communities. Furthermore, we consider capitalizing "Indigenous" as "a sign of respect for the identities, governments, institutions and collective rights that have been historically considered illegitimate" (Capitalization and formatting of Indigenous terms, 2023).
2 On a side note, "the only good Indian is a dead Indian" is a similar expression. Tracing back to the 1860s, this stereotypical and slur phrase reveals the same settler-centric racist doctrine promoting Indian massacres on the territories of the USA (Gabriel, 2019).
3 The definition is suggested by the author of this chapter, based on the already-existing scholarly definition of "digital divide."

References

Azuma, R.T. (1997) 'A survey of augmented reality', *Presence: Teleoperators and Virtual Environments*, 6(4), pp. 355–385. doi:10.1162/pres.1997.6.4.355.
Bojórquez, F.S. (2003) *Pasado, presente y Futuro de la educación indígena: Memoria del Foro Permanente por la reorientación de la educación y el fortalecimiento de las lenguas y culturas indígenas*. México, México: Universidad Pedagógica Nacional.
Campos, W.S., Pina, A. and Rubio, G. (2021) 'Náhuat language Kinect application for the museum', *2021 International Symposium on Computers in Education (SIIE)* [Preprint]. doi:10.1109/siie53363.2021.9583657.
Cerezo, R., Calderón, V. and Romero, C. (2019) 'A holographic mobile-based application for practicing pronunciation of basic English vocabulary for Spanish speaking children', *International Journal of Human-Computer Studies*, 124, pp. 13–25. doi:10.1016/j.ijhcs.2018.11.009.
Clare, C. (2022) *Clara Clare: Loss of Language and Culture, Paths to Reconciliation*. Available at: https://pathstoreconciliation.canadiangeographic.ca/wp-content/uploads/2022/12/Lesson-1.pdf (Accessed: 24 February 2024).
Condon, O. (2019) *Calgary-made Virtual Reality Game Teaches Blackfoot Language, Culture, Calgary Herald*. Available at: https://calgaryherald.com/news/local-news/calgary-made-virtual-reality-game-teaches-blackfoot-language-culture (Accessed: 2 December 2023).
De Korne, H. *et al.* (2024) 'Youth in language endangerment and reclamation processes', in *The Routledge Handbook of Language and Youth Culture*. New York, NY: Routledge, pp. 108–121.
Gabriel, E. (2019) *Indigenous Languages: A Fundamental Right to Defend. Perspectives of a Mohawk Activist, Ellen Gabriel, Canadian Commission for UNESCO*. Available at: https://en.ccunesco.ca/-/media/Files/Unesco/Resources/2019/06/IndigenousLanguagesAFundamentalRightToDefend_EllenGabriel.pdf (Accessed: 1 December 2023).

Gantt, A.M. (2015) *Native Language Revitalization: Keeping the Languages Alive and Thriving*, Southeastern Oklahoma State University. Available at: www.se.edu/native-american/wp-content/uploads/sites/49/2019/09/AAA-NAS-2015-Proceedings-Gantt.pdf (Accessed: 24 February 2024).

Gilster, P. (1997) *Digital Literacy*. New York, USA: Wiley Computer.

'Globalization and the vanishing voices of the world' (2019) *Beyond Words Solutions – French and English Translation Services – Ohio, USA*. Available at: https://beyondwordssolutions.com/globalization-and-the-vanishing-voices-of-the-world/ (Accessed: 1 December 2023).

Griffith, J. (2017) 'Of linguicide and resistance: Children and English instruction in nineteenth-century Indian boarding schools in Canada', *Paedagogica Historica*, 53(6), pp. 763–782. doi:10.1080/00309230.2017.1293700.

Hanson, E., Gamez, D. and Manuel, A. (2020) *The Residential School System, Indigenous Foundations*. Available at: https://indigenousfoundations.arts.ubc.ca/residential-school-system-2020/ (Accessed: 24 February 2024).

Hillerdal, C., Karlström, A. and Ojala, C.-G. (2017) *Archaeologies of "Us" and "Them" Debating History, Heritage and Indigeneity*. New York, NY: Routledge.

'If not us, then who?' (2022) *The Internet Health Report 2022*. Available at: https://2022.internethealthreport.org/story/indigenous-in-ai-michael-running-wolf/ (Accessed: 1 December 2023).

Ilyniak, N. (2015) '"To rob the world of a people": Language removal as an instance of colonial genocide in the Fort Alexander Indian Residential School', *Genocide Studies and Prevention: An International Journal*, 9(2), pp. 76–97.

Jacob, W.J., Cheng, S.Y. and Porter, M.K. (2015) 'Global review of indigenous education: Issues of identity, culture, and language', in W.J. Jacob, S.Y.Y. Cheng, and M.K. Porter (eds.) *Indigenous Education: Language, Culture and Identity*. Springer.

Johnson, R. (2018) 'Anishinaabe artist's new VR experience takes an indigenous futurist look at Toronto', *CBC News*. Available at: https://www.cbc.ca/news/indigenous/lisa-jackson-biidaaban-vr-future-toronto-1.4619041 (Accessed: 1 December 2023).

'K design award – 99-land: AR project' (2019) *K DESIGN AWARD – 99-Land: AR Project*. Available at: https://kdesignaward.com/exhibition/191623 (Accessed: 1 December 2023).

Kukutai, T. and Taylor, J. (2016) *Indigenous Data Sovereignty: Toward an Agenda*. Canberra: ANU Press.

Kuokkanen, R. (2016) 'Reconciliation and mandatory indigenous content courses: What are the university's responsibilities?', *Rauna*. Available at: https://rauna.net/2016/03/21/reconciliation-and-mandatory-indigenous-content-courses-what-are-the-universitys-responsibilities/ (Accessed: 3 December 2023).

Kusunda VR (2018) *NowHere Media*. Available at: www.nowheremedia.net/kusundavr (Accessed: 1 December 2023).

Kusunda VR (2019) *Raindance Immersive*. Available at: www.raindanceimmersive.com/kusunda (Accessed: 1 December 2023).

'Last whispers' (2021) *Last Whispers*. Available at: www.lastwhispers.org/ (Accessed: 24 February 2024).

'Lena Herzog investigates the mass extinction of languages on Earth in "Last Whispers"' (2020) *The Diamondback*. Available at: https://dbknews.com/2019/02/27/last-whispers-lena-herzog-language-photography-vr-installation-kennedy- center/ (Accessed: 1 December 2023).

Littell, P. *et al.* (2018) 'Indigenous language technologies in Canada: Assessment, challenges, and successes', *ACL Anthology*. Available at: https://aclanthology.org/C18-1222 (Accessed: 4 December 2023).

Lopez, M.A. *et al.* (2021) 'Towards a solution to create, test and publish mixed reality experiences for Occupational Safety and Health Learning: Training-MR', *International Journal of Interactive Multimedia and Artificial Intelligence*, 7(2), p. 212. doi:10.9781/ijimai.2021.07.003.

Mabie, N. (2023) 'Meet Michael running wolf, the man using AI to reclaim native languages', *The Missoulian*. Available at: https://missoulian.com/news/local/meet-michael-running-wolf-the-man-using-ai-to-reclaim-native-languages/article_9cdd8db4–4074–5edb-9fa4–74773cdb9464.html (Accessed: 1 December 2023).

May, S. (2011) 'Indigenous language and education rights', in C. McKinney, P. Makoe, and V. Zavala (eds.) *Language and Minority Rights: Ethnicity, Nationalism and the Politics of Language*. London, UK: Routledge.

McGlade, H. (2020) 'Australia's treatment of Indigenous prisoners. The continuing nature of human rights violations in West Australian jail cells', in M. Berghs et al. (eds.) *The Routledge Handbook of Disability Activism*. New York, NY: Routledge, pp. 274–289.

Meighan, P.J. (2021) 'Decolonizing the digital landscape: The role of technology in indigenous language revitalization', *AlterNative: An International Journal of Indigenous Peoples*, 17(3), pp. 397–405. doi:10.1177/11771801211037672.

Milgram, P. and Kishino, F. (1994) 'A taxonomy of mixed reality visual displays', *IEICE Transactions on Information and Systems*, 77(12), pp. 1321–1329.

Ministry of Citizens' Services (2023) 'Capitalization and formatting of indigenous terms', *Province of British Columbia*. Available at: https://www2.gov.bc.ca/gov/content/governments/services-for-government/service-experience-digital-delivery/web-content-development-guides/web-style-guide/writing-guide-for-indigenous-content/capitalization-and-formatting-of-indigenous-terms (Accessed: 6 December 2023).

Mukhallafi, T.R.A. (2023) 'The effect of utilizing hologram technology on developing EFL communication skills and attitudes towards English among middle school students', *Studies in English Language Teaching*, 11(2).

Nāmāhoe, L. (2007) 'Aha Pūnana leo', *Cultural Survival*. Available at: www.culturalsurvival.org/publications/cultural-survival-quarterly/aha-punana-leo (Accessed: 6 December 2023).

(No date) *Ethnologue: Languages of the World*. Available at: www.ethnologue.com/ (Accessed: 10 March 2024).

Nonno, T. (2015) 'Second life as a possible platform for endangered languages revitalization (the case of Ainu language in particular): Problems and perspectives', *Cultural Anthropology and Ethnosemiotics*, 1(1), pp. 53–59.

Outakoski, H. (2013) 'Teaching an endangered language in virtual reality', *Keeping Languages Alive*, pp. 128–139. doi:10.1017/cbo9781139245890.013.

Peixoto, B. *et al.* (2021) 'Immersive virtual reality for foreign language education: A prisma systematic review', *IEEE Access*, 9, pp. 48952–48962. doi:10.1109/access.2021.3068858.

Piirainen, E. and Sherris, A. (eds.) (2015) *Language Endangerment: Disappearing Metaphors and Shifting Conceptualizations*. Amsterdam: John Benjamins.

'Project to use virtual reality technology to teach Nisga'a culture and language – CBC News' (2021) *CBC News*. Available at: www.cbc.ca/news/indigenous/nisga-a-vr-technology-language-culture-1.5846341 (Accessed: 1 December 2023).

Sherris, A. and Peyton, J.K. (2020) *Teaching Writing to Children in Indigenous Languages: Instructional Practices from Global Contexts*. New York: Routledge.

Shin, H.J., Lee, Y. and Park, S.J. (2019) '99LAND: Jeju dialect revitalization augmented reality', *Behance*. Available at: www.behance.net/gallery/82114645/99LANDJEJU-dialect-Revitalization-Augmented-Reality (Accessed: 24 February 2024).

Smiley-Marquez, C. and Tompkins, J.E. (2011) *Boarding School Healing Symposium*. Boulder: University of Colorado, School of Law.

Smith, A. (2011) 'Soul wound: The legacy of native American schools', in C. Smiley-Marquez and J.E. Tompkins (eds.) *Boarding School Healing Symposium*. Boulder, CO: University of Colorado, School of Law, p. 39.

Smith, L.T. (2022) *Decolonizing Methodologies: Research and Indigenous Peoples*. London, UK: Bloomsbury Academic.

Stumpp, S., Knopf, T. and Michelis, D. (2019) '14th European conference on innovation and entrepreneurship', in Kalamata, Greece.

Styres, S. (2019) 'Literacies of land: Decolonizing narratives, storying & literature', in L.T. Smith, E. Tuck, and K.W. Yang (eds.) *Indigenous and Decolonizing Studies in Education: Mapping the Long View*. New York, NY: Routledge, an imprint of the Taylor & Francis Group, pp. 24–37.

'The experience: First of its kind' (2019) *Thunder VR*. Available at: http://thundervr.usay.ca/ (Accessed: 1 December 2023).

'UNESCO – text of the convention for the safeguarding of the intangible cultural heritage' (2003) *Intangible Cultural Heritage*. Available at: https://ich.unesco.org/en/convention (Accessed: 1 December 2023).

'United Nations declaration on the rights of Indigenous peoples' (2007) *United Nations*. Available at: www.un.org/development/desa/indigenouspeoples/wp-content/uploads/sites/19/2018/11/UNDRIP_E_web.pdf (Accessed: 1 December 2023).

'Using virtual reality to strengthen the Cree language' (2016) *The Nation: Cree News*. Available at: http://formersite.nationnewsarchives.ca/using-virtual-reality-strengthen-cree-language/ (Accessed: 1 December 2023).

'Virtual reality' (2023) *USAY*. Available at: https://usay.ca/virtual-reality/ (Accessed: 7 December 2023).

We Still Live Here – Âs Nutayuneân (2010) Available at: https://www.pbs.org/independentlens/documentaries/we-still-live-here/ (Accessed: 8 December 2023).

Workshop: Sacred Assets: Data Sovereignty (2020) 'ILRN2020 6th international conference of the immersive learning research network'. Available at: https://ilrn2020.sched.com/event/chOy/workshop-sacred-assets-data-sovereignty-and-the-ethics-of-collecting-indigenous-data-for-new-media-development (Accessed: 1 December 2023).

SECTION III

Language policy, ideology, and multilingual education

13

"SPEAK STANDARD MANDARIN, WRITE STANDARD CHARACTERS"

Mandarin language promotion and its effect on minority languages in China

Britta Ingebretson

Introduction

China, the world's second most populous country, is home to over 300 languages across multiple language families (Eberhard et al. 2023). The largest language family is the Sino-Tibetan language family, which is divided into two main branches, the Sinitic and the Tibeto-Burman. The vast majority of the population (91%) speaks a Sinitic language as their native language (Chappell and Lan 2016; Eberhard et al. 2023). The Sinitic language family consists of hundreds of language varieties, which linguists have grouped into between seven and eleven language families, depending on the criteria used (Kurpaska 2010; Xiong and Zhang 2012; Wurm et al. 1988). In the PRC, these language varieties are referred to as dialects (*fangyan*), despite a wide degree of distinction and mutual unintelligibility. According to the *Linguistic Atlas of Chinese Dialects*, the Sinitic language families, listed in decreasing order of number of speakers, are: Mandarin, Min, Wu, Jin, Yue (Cantonese), Gan, Kejia (Hakka), Xiang, Pinghua, and Hui (Huizhou) (Cao 2008). Mandarin is the largest language family. Geographically it covers Northern and much of Western and Central China. Seventy percent of Chinese speakers speak a Mandarin language variety as their L1 (Norman 1988). The other language families are found in South and East China. Although they are spoken by fewer than a third of Chinese language speakers, Cantonese (Yue) and the Wu dialects have significant regional prestige (Liang 2015). Standard Mandarin, which I will refer to as Putonghua (lit. "common tongue") to distinguish it from other Mandarin varieties, was created as a lingua franca in the mid-20th century (Chen 1999; Weng 2018). It is based on but not reducible to Beijing Mandarin. As a construct it was initially no one's native language, although now it is increasingly learned as an L1, particularly among educated speakers. Putonghua is the official language of the PRC, and its use is mandated in institutional settings such as schools, government buildings, and broadcast media. The Sinitic languages are written using Chinese characters, many of which were simplified in the 1950s to promote literacy (Chen 1999). Although Chinese characters are not phonetic, modern written Chinese is based on Putonghua vernacular. Most Chinese language varieties do not have a script separate from written Modern Standard Chinese (MSC), although Cantonese is the exception (Liang 2015).

DOI: 10.4324/9781003439493-17

In addition to the majority Han population, China has fifty-five officially recognized ethnic minority groups. This number was established in the 1950s by Chinese social scientists working on the Soviet Nationality Model, which classified ethnic groups according to shared language, territory, customs, and economic mode of production (Mullaney 2010; Tsung 2009). Ethnic minorities make up 8.5% of the population and speak languages belonging to the Tungusic, Mongolian, Tibeto-Burman, Austroasiatic, Tai-Kadai, Hmong-Mien, Turkic, Burmese, Indo-European, and Koreanic language families. Of the 306 languages currently spoken in China, it is estimated that 170 are at risk (Eberhard et al. 2023). The Chinese government officially recognizes only fifty-four minority languages, one for all but one of the fifty-five officially recognized ethnic minorities (the Hui do not have a separate language). It is these languages that are eligible for protection as minority languages.

While Chinese language policy provides formal and legal support for preservation of linguistic diversity, this chapter shows that the situation in reality is quite different. Through a variety of direct and indirect means, Chinese language policy and planning promotes Putonghua at the expense of minority languages (Curdt-Christiansen and Gao 2021). Despite lip service paid to the importance of linguistic diversity, the end goal of Chinese language policy and planning is the "Putonghuaization" of the PRC (Li and Juffermans 2012; Hau 2022). The first half of this chapter provides a brief history of Chinese language policy, including in the domains of i) education, ii) media, and iii) urbanization and poverty elimination programs. In the second half, I examine the effects of these policies on language ideologies and attitudes. I first show how economic and social pressures have led to a preference for Putonghua even in the absence of state policy pressure. Finally, I examine how the metaphors of language as a "resource" in state planning documents, policies, and other linguistic materials may lead to a focus on language protection through documentation rather than through maintenance or revitalization. Data for this section is informed by twenty-two months of ethnographic fieldwork on the language attitudes and practices of native Huizhou language speaker in Huangshan, which I conducted between 2013 and 2015. My research methods included participant observation, interviews, focus groups, and elicitation sessions with a wide variety of speakers.

Language policy in the PRC

Chinese language policy during the PRC era has sought to balance maintenance of linguistic diversity with promotion of national unity through the universal use of Putonghua. Throughout Chinese history, the Imperial government needed a lingua franca to allow officials and bureaucrats to communicate with each other across the relatively far-flung Chinese empire. This form of Chinese was referred to as "Mandarin," a word borrowed into English from the Portuguese term for official in the 15th century to describe the language of the Imperial court (Chappell and Lan 2016). This "Mandarin" Chinese was only spoken by a small number of elites. The need for a common national tongue was relatively muted by the Chinese written language, a character-based system which was distinct from spoken Chinese vernaculars and which remained relatively stable for 2,000 years. Like Mandarin, literacy in written Chinese was confined to a small elite class of scholars and officials. It was not until the establishment of the Republic in the early 20th century that policy makers saw the need for a universally spoken lingua franca and a vernacular written language that would unite the Chinese people as a modern nation-state. Efforts to create a "common tongue" (*putonghua*) began in the 1910s when leading scholars, linguists, and writers gathered in Beijing to decide which language variety would be the basis for the standard vernacular. After much debate, the Conference decided that Putonghua would be based on the Beijing Dialect of Northern Mandarin with some minor variations, including less frequent use of *erhuayin*, or rhotic codas on certain words. Standard Modern Chinese, a written form that used the same characters but adopted the grammar and vocabulary of Putonghua, replaced literary or classical Chinese as the official written language. These efforts were not finalized until 1956, when the National Conference for Script Reform released an official dictionary of Putonghua. The dictionary also included simplified forms of 515 commonly used characters, later increased to 2,000 in the 1960s (Chen 1999; Norman 1988; Rohsenow 2004; Weng 2018). At that time, the State Council released a plan to promote the new official language in institutional settings such as schools and the military.

Mandarin promotion efforts continued until the start of the Cultural Revolution in 1966, when most state institutions were dismantled. It is important to note that although the state discontinued institutional efforts to promote Mandarin, this did not reflect support for multilingualism. Along with other cultural and religious customs, ethnic minority language usage was explicitly discouraged (Zhou 2019). It was not until the Opening and Reform period that official support for minority languages became reflected in policy. Support for minority languages was first explicitly enshrined in the 1982 Constitution, which granted the "freedom to use and develop" officially recognized minority languages (Grey 2021: 5). This official, explicit support for minority languages went hand in hand with the general liberalization and decrease of state intervention into daily life that marked the Reform and Opening period (Adamson and Feng 2009; Lam 2005). As Alexandra Grey notes, however, the "freedom" (*ziyou*) to use minority languages was a "negative right," as it only prevented governments from actively impeding language use, rather than a "positive right" that would mandate the government to provide active support for languages. This contrasts with other rights in the constitution that are enshrined as positive "rights" (*quanli*) and come with government enforcement mechanisms, such as state assistance for the disabled and elderly (Grey 2021: 69).

In 2000, the Law of the Nationally Used Language and Script of the PRC, which I will refer to as the Language Law, comprehensively defined language policy. The policy mandated the use of Putonghua in institutional settings such as government offices, schools, and broadcast media. It also required the use of Standard Modern Chinese script in institutional settings as well as in all published material, on commercial signs, business names, and packaging, with limited exceptions as necessary (Rohsenow 2004; Guo 2004). The Law also "encouraged" Putonghua use in the service industry and in public spaces more generally (Rohsenow 2004: 41). To enforce the use of Putonghua in institutions, the law stipulated that government bureaucrats, teachers, and media broadcasters demonstrate a certain level of Putonghua proficiency as required by the job. Applicants hoping for careers in civil service, education, or media must take the Putonghua Proficiency Test (*Putonghua shuiping ceshi*) and receive a minimum score, which ranges from 97% for CCTV news anchors to 60% for government bureaucrats. Chinese teachers in Northern China must score at least 92% and in Southern China at least 87%, while teachers of other subjects must score 80% or above (Zhou et al. 2013).

Formal protection for minority languages was also reaffirmed in the Language Law. Echoing the language of the constitution, Article 4 of the Language Law granted national minority groups "the freedom to use and develop their own languages and scripts" following guidance laid out in the constitution and the Law of Regional Ethnic Autonomy (Rohsenow 2004: 41), which I will call the Regional Autonomy Law. The Language Law also stipulated appropriate use of Chinese dialects. Article 16 states that dialects may be used when necessary in certain limited domains, including: for carrying out essential state business, in state-approved media broadcasts, in artistic productions, and in teaching and research (Rohsenow 2004: 41). The Language Law was the first official acknowledgment that dialects in addition to ethnic minority languages had a place, albeit limited, in Chinese institutional settings.

Since Xi Jinping's appointment as president in 2012, language rights for minority language speakers have been increasingly encroached upon as Chinese policy has promoted a more overtly assimilationist approach. Beginning in 2014, President Xi introduced "five identifications" for ethnic minorities: with the Chinese state, the unified Chinese nation, Chinese culture, the Party, and with socialism. These identifications, which were added to the constitution in 2018, demand that ethnic minorities "forge the awareness of the community of the unified Chinese nation" (Zhou 2021). Of these, identification with Chinese culture via learning Putonghua was considered the most important (Zhang and Pérez-Milans 2019; Zhou 2019). This constitutional amendment formally marks a longer process that represents a shift toward "mono-cultural centrism" (Bilik 2014, 78), which requires linguistic and cultural integration into a unified national identity defined by Han ethnicity and Putonghua (Bulag 2021). Although ethnically Han Chinese have not faced the same assimilationist pressure, those who speak non-Mandarin languages such as Cantonese still face significant pressure from the government's promotion of Putonghua.

Moreover, since they are lacking formal recognition as separate language varieties, they do not receive any formal protection for institutional use. Given the similar pressures on minority Sinitic and non-Sinitic languages, it makes sense to discuss them in tandem.

Overall, Putonghua promotion efforts have been successful. In 1950, only about 41% of Chinese were able to understand Putonghua, including 54% in Mandarin-speaking areas and 11% in other Sinitic language regions (Chen 1999; Gil 2021). By 1984, 90% of Chinese could understand Putonghua, and 53% could speak it (Chen 1999). By 2021, the Ministry of Education (MOE) estimates 80.72% can speak Putonghua, an increase from 53% in 2000 (MOE 2021). Similarly, literacy has also increased dramatically since 1950, particularly after the spread of universal compulsory education. In 1950, the literacy rate was only around 20% (and only 5% in rural areas), whereas by 2015 the literacy rate had reached approximately 97% (Ding 2019). By 2018, over 99.9% of children attended primary school (ibid).

In this section, I have discussed Chinese language policy in general. In the next sections, I will discuss Chinese language policy in the domains of education, media, and poverty elimination programs.

Education

Education has long been a site where national values are inculcated. In China, schools have been a major focus of Putonghua promotion efforts. Per the Language Law, all teachers are required to speak Putonghua in the classrooms and to receive a score of at least 80% on the Putonghua proficiency test, with Chinese teachers required to achieve a higher score (see previous section). Students are also expected to speak Putonghua during class, and some schools in Cantonese-speaking regions have gone so far as to try to mandate Putonghua usage among students even outside of class, although this has faced pushback from parents (Liang 2015). As a vehicle of Putonghua promotion, schools have been highly successful.

In keeping with the formal recognition of minority language rights in the early 1980s, in 1984 the Regional Autonomy Law granted the right to minority language education in regions in ethnic Autonomous Regions, provided the minority language was officially recognized by the Chinese government. Article 37 of the law states:

Schools (classes) and other educational organizations recruiting mostly ethnic minority students should, whenever possible, use textbooks in their own languages and use these languages as the media of instruction. Beginning in the lower or senior grades of primary school, Han language and literature courses should be taught to popularize the common language used throughout the country and the use of Han Chinese characters. Every local government should provide financial support for the production of teaching materials in the minority scripts and for publication and translation work.

(China 1984)

In theory, this grants the right to minority language education in minority-majority schools in Autonomous Regions and districts. In practice minority language education is rare to non-existent among China's largest ethnic groups, including the Zhuang (Grey 2021); the Hui, who do not have a unique language; and the Manchu, whose language is listed as "nearly extinct" (Eberhard et al. 2023). Importantly, this law does not grant the right to an education exclusively in a minority language, as minority language students are still expected to master Putonghua. Although this policy only includes protection for the seven official minority languages with standardized written scripts (Zhang and Tsung 2019), it was nevertheless a step at preserving multilingualism. Minority language schools did exist for Tibetans, Uyghurs, Mongolians, Kazakhs, and Koreans, with a majority of ethnic minority students living in autonomous regions attending primary school in their native languages into the 1990s (Atwood 2020; Ma 2014; Simayi 2014).

In the 21st century, language policy began to shift away from a model in which most instruction was in the ethnic minority language toward one where Putonghua was the primary medium of instruction for core academic subjects, and minority languages are taught as a separate subject (Bulag 2021). In 2010, Qinghai authorities introduced education reforms to phase out Tibetan as the primary medium of communication (Henry 2016). This was followed by similar programs in Inner Mongolia, Tibet, and Xinjiang (Byler 2019; Bulag 2020; Baioud 2020). Such policies set off widespread protests particularly in Qinghai and Inner Mongolia, though with little effect on policy. A similar shift in bilingual education has occurred in Yi autonomous prefectures as well (Zhang and Tsung 2019). By 2020, minority language schools in those areas were required to use Putonghua state language textbooks and provide the majority of instruction in Putonghua (Atwood 2020; Roche 2021). In 2023 and 2024, the Putonghuaization process continues. By September 2023, in Inner Mongolia, Mongolian language instruction has been further reduced from seven to three classes a week in high schools and banned from kindergartens. Mongolian will be removed from the high school entrance exam by 2025 and from the university entrance exam by 2028 (Gu 2023). In Tibet and Xinjiang, local schools, including private minority-language medium private schools, are being shut down and replaced by Mandarin language boarding schools, which are attended by children as young as four. In 2024, it is estimated that 80% of Tibetan children attend these boarding schools (Bristow 2024), while in Xinjiang, the number of children in boarding schools or Mandarin language orphanages has "exponentially increased" (UN OHCHR 2023).

Media

As stated previously, media is regulated under the Language Law, which mandates that most media programming be in Putonghua and that newscasters achieve the highest score (97% or above) on the Putonghua proficiency test. The use of other Chinese dialects in broadcast media must be approved by the Office of Radio and Television Broadcasting of the State Council (Rohsenow 2004: 41). In most non-Mandarin-speaking regions, programming in other Sinitic languages has been confined to a small number of shows, the exception being in Guangdong Province, which is allowed to operate TV channels in Cantonese (Zhang and Guo 2012; Liang 2015). The extensive dialect media programming in these provinces is an attempt to compete with broadcast media from Hong Kong and Taiwan, which are popular with mainland Chinese. In the early 2000s, dialect use in cultural programming was increasing in popularity, with viewers finding dialect use more authentic (Zhang and Guo 2012). In response, the government passed a series of regulations increasing restrictions on dialect programming. In 2004, the State Administration of Radio, Film, and Television (SARFT) mandated that foreign language programs must be dubbed into Putonghua and not dialects. In 2005, a requirement was added that programs should be in Putonghua, particularly ones that portrayed China's early Communist leaders. In 2009, SARFT announced a policy to limit the use of dialects in prime-time programming (Chan 2018). In 2011, the Guangdong regional government incited controversy when they suggested a switch away from Cantonese language programming during prime time in advance of the Asian Games athletic competition. The government backed down from this plan in the face of widespread protest in Guangzhou (Liang 2015; Gao 2012). The situation in Guangdong is somewhat unique given that Cantonese as a language is viewed as a source of prestige and Cantonese speakers also rely on Hong Kong as an alternate locus of linguistic cultural production and legitimacy. By contrast, the Wu language family, which includes Shanghainese and the dialects of the wealthy Jiangnan region (Zhejiang and Jiangsu province), does not receive the same level of institutional support in broadcast media. In Shanghai, all channels broadcast in Putonghua, with limited dialect programming at off hours (Shanghai Media Group n.d.).

Urbanization and poverty elimination programs

State poverty elimination campaigns have also made Putonghua promotion an explicit part of their policies. In 2016, the Ministry of Education and National Language Commission jointly published the Thirteenth Five Year Development Plan of National Language Works, which stated that:

> In accordance with national principles and strategies for taking targeted measures to help people lift themselves out of poverty, the popularisation of the national commonly used language and written script in minority regions needs to be accelerated, focusing on improving the language proficiency of teachers, local cadres, and young farmers and herdsmen.
>
> (as translated in Zhang and Pérez-Milans 2019: 43)

According to this logic, lack of Putonghua language skills are a direct cause of poverty and economic underdevelopment in ethnic minority communities. This Five-Year plan was translated into policy, first in the Southwest province of Yunnan in 2016 and then nationally in 2018. That year, the Office of Poverty Alleviation of the State Council, the State Language Commission, and the Ministry of Education jointly implemented the Action Plan to Promote Putonghua to Alleviate Deep Poverty (Zhou 2019). This program provides teacher training, free Putonghua classes, and vocational training programs with a focus on learning Putonghua in ethnic minority regions (ibid).

Effects of policies: language attitudes and ideologies

While the Chinese Constitution and the Language Law still formally preserves linguistic freedom for linguistic minorities, we can see a marked shift in government language ideologies and language policy since 2012. Behind government policy, Urdyn Bulag argues that this shift represents a change in ideological outlook. This new approach has been promoted by social scientists at China's most prestigious institutions, who claim that pluralistic ethnic minority policy based on the Soviet nationality model has led to ethnic violence and strife. The root cause of ethnic tensions has been the degree of freedom and autonomy granted to ethnic minority groups (Bulag 2021), which has led to a form of "plural monoculturalism," where ethnic minorities place ethnic membership above integrating into the nation (Postiglione 2014; Shen and Gao 2019). The current generation of scholars have proposed a "second generation ethnic policy" based on the idea that more overt assimilation into Han culture via language will lead to ethnic harmony (ibid). A similar approach has been taken toward Sinitic languages, particularly Cantonese. The result of this underlying change in language ideology has been the promotion of Putonghua use across all domains at the expense of other languages.

Yet it is not only, or perhaps even primarily, in policy where the influence of Putonghua promotion efforts is most felt. Equally important, if not more so, are the social and ideological effects. Even without policy, the increasing social, cultural, and economic dominance of Putonghua has led millions of Chinese to switch to Putonghua as their primary language or to encourage their children to do so. In non-Mandarin-speaking regions of China, the use of only Putonghua in educational settings further establishes Putonghua's cultural prestige and its social and economic value over minority languages. Putonghua language skills are seen as necessary for upward mobility, an "admission ticket" to higher education and white-collar employment (Xu 2019). Across China, parents believe that knowledge of Putonghua is necessary for children's academic success. Even before policy changes in bilingual education, ethnic minority parents increasingly chose to send their children to Putonghua schools (Schluessel 2009; Xu 2019). For example, in Tibet, by 2007 95% of Tibetan primary school children attended Putonghua dominant schools, up from only 5% in 2000 (Ma 2014). Parents who speak non-Putonghua dialects who might otherwise prefer to use the local language will often choose to speak to their children in Putonghua so as not to disadvantage them when they begin formal schooling. The result of this is that even parents who maintain positive attitudes towards their native language still prefer Putonghua for practical reasons, resulting in language shift or language loss despite positive speaker attitudes toward the home language (Zhang and Tsung 2019; Shen et al. 2021, Wang and Curdt-Christiansen 2021). Moreover, as Putonghua is the language of upward mobility, elites are more likely to have switched to Putonghua use in their daily life. This can result in the further loss of language prestige and indifferent attitudes towards language shift among those in power, as is the case with the Sibe language (Yin and Li 2021).

Economic pressures also have led millions of rural Chinese to perceive Putonghua language skills as more valuable than speaking a local language or dialect. As China urbanizes and as rural Chinese travel to cities to find work, Putonghua increasingly serves as a lingua franca in large cities. Even in non-Mandarin regions where the local Sinitic dialects carry significant prestige and regional cultural significance, migrants are increasingly turning to Putonghua rather than the local Sinitic language as the primary medium of communication. In Shanghai, migrants across the economic spectrum generally do not learn Shanghainese (Wu language family) (Xu 2021), and even in Guangdong migrants and their children increasingly use Putonghua over Cantonese (Liang 2015). Once rural Chinese are habituated to speaking Putonghua as migrant workers, they use Putonghua at higher rates even when they return to their home villages (Yan and Xu 2022). In addition to the practical need for communication, Putonghua is increasingly the language of urban areas due to its association with modernity and economic development, a link that has been promoted by state discourse on development. By linking civilizational development, economic development, and Putonghua, the state has created powerful "pull" factors towards Putonghua usage. Survey of migrant workers have found that 90% of migrant workers learned Putonghua either through schooling or in moving to cities to find work (Fu 2021).

My fieldwork, conducted in Huangshan, has revealed similar findings. Huangshan, a region in Southern Anhui province, is home to the Huizhou language family, the smallest of the Sinitic language families, with approximately 4–5 million speakers (Eberhard et al. 2023). While speakers across all generations had generally positive attitudes towards the local language and considered it a valuable part of local culture (see also Xu 2008), most parents admitted that they personally preferred that their children learn Putonghua in order to maximize chances of educational success. Even grandparents who did not speak Putonghua would attempt to speak "difang Putonghua," or Putonghua heavily influenced by regional dialects, instead of a local Huizhou language. The uneven consequences of speaking a fluent Huizhou dialect vs. speaking fluent Putonghua were put succinctly by a middle-aged vegetable seller: "Speaking Putonghua gets you a good job in the city. Speaking Tunxi dialect [a dialect in the Huizhou language family spoken in the municipal seat] gets you a few cents off the price of vegetables."

The unique nature of the Chinese language also contributes to less efforts on language maintenance than might otherwise be expected. As mentioned in an earlier section, all Sinitic languages are considered dialects of a single Chinese language, regardless of degree of difference. For Sinitic language speakers, then, there is often not an awareness of the local vernacular as a "language" worth protection in its own right. This is particularly the case in Mandarin-speaking regions, where local Mandarin dialects are simply seen as non-standard variations of Putonghua.

The unique qualities of written Chinese script similarly contribute to this, as, in theory, the nonphonetic Chinese script serves as a writing system for all dialects. In reality, Modern Standard Chinese is based on the grammar and lexicon of Beijing Mandarin vernacular (Weng 2018). Moreover, Sinitic languages like Cantonese also have their own writing system, including distinctive characters not found in MSC (Liang 2015). Yet language ideologies that view written Chinese as the cultural basis of the Chinese language make it easy to discount vernaculars as integral to Chinese culture or history. In Huangshan, I found a lack of linguistic awareness among older and more rural Huizhou dialect speakers who viewed their local way of speaking as simply a deviation from Putonghua rather than its own linguistic code. These speakers had little desire to preserve Huizhou dialects, nor did they see any value in doing so.

Multilingualism as a resource and language protection

In previous sections, I have demonstrated how the state overtly promotes Putonghua over minority language use both directly, through laws and policy, and indirectly, through shaping language attitudes and regimes of value. Yet, even given the move toward more overt Putonghua promotion in the past decade, the government still formally claims commitment to multilingualism, claiming to promote Putonghua alongside other languages to encourage bilingualism and bidialectism (Li 2014, 2015; Spolsky 2014). In this section, I show how even policies or language documents that on the surface seem designed to protect minority languages can contribute to language loss.

Multilingualism as a cultural resource

In this section, I analyze multilingual language policy as laid out in Chinese language planning and policy documents from the Chinese Language Commission (CLC), edited by Li Yuming and Li Wei and compiled into a nine-volume series, *Language Policies and Practices in China*, published in translation by DeGruyter Mouton. In these extensive language planning documents, the explicit overarching goal of Chinese language policy and planning is to promote "harmony" between

Putonghua and minority languages (including other Sinitic languages) in China. The "solution to the conflict between language communication and language maintenance" is bilingualism and bi-dialectalism, where all Chinese can speak Putonghua alongside a regional language or dialect (Li 2015: 135–136). Thus, formally, while Putonghua promotion is both the de facto and de jure reality of language policy, language planning documents are careful to never explicitly state that minority languages or dialects should be replaced by Putonghua. Instead, these documents praise linguistic diversity as an "invaluable treasure" of part of China's cultural heritage (Li 2015: 187). In these texts, the necessity to preserve linguistic diversity is well documented. For example, in *The Language Situation in China Vol 1*, a compilation of the CLC's annual reports from 2005 and 2006, Lü and Zou write,

> Numerous languages and multiple dialects are precious social, economic and cultural resources for a country rather than obstacles on the road to national unity and socioeconomic development. Therefore, linguistic harmony lies in the coexistence and common flourishing of all the languages and dialects, no matter how many people use them. Within a harmonious environment, they may have their own spaces to live and grow in, their own positions to occupy, and their own roles to play, so that a symphony of Chinese language will be played together.
>
> (Lü and Zou 2013: 247)

As this excerpt shows, linguistic diversity is explicitly celebrated as part of China's "social, economic, and cultural resources," a metaphor that is frequently used across this corpus of documents.

These language planning documents that promote linguistic diversity as part of China's "cultural resources" appear to be positively evaluating minority languages. Indeed, scholars of language planning have long noted that approaching multilingualism from a "resource model" can potentially create a system in which national unity can encompass linguistic diversity and in which linguistic and cultural diversity are valued (Ruíz 1984: Hult and Hornberger 2016). A potential pitfall of this approach, however, is that the concept of resource might be overly instrumentalized, valuing language as a resource only insofar is its intrinsic cultural value can be converted into extrinsic value or material wealth, for example, in economic or diplomatic spheres (Shen and Gao 2019; Wang and Gao 2023). Additionally, the resource model may become problematic if linguistic diversity is seen as valuable when it benefits the nation rather than the language community (Hult and Hornberger 2016; Ricento 2005). In these language planning documents, we see that this is precisely the case. Although language is frequently referred to as an "intangible cultural heritage" (*feiwuzhi wenhua yichan*), the specific benefits of language as a resource are almost all extrinsic. For example, protection of Chinese minority languages and dialects is valuable as these languages are shared across China's borders and widely spoken among overseas Chinese communities and thus important for "international economics and trade dealings, human exchanges, and security cooperation" (Tian 2022: 46). Domestically, protection of an

> abundant and diverse collection of language resources will make it possible to derive more and longer industrial chains, and produce a greater wealth of language and cultural products, offering vast prospects for the innovative development of our country's language and cultural industry.
>
> (Tian 2022: 47)

In other words, protection of minority languages is valuable insofar as it can contribute to China's economic and social development. Crucially, in the rhetoric of language planning, the benefits of language protection are framed solely in terms of national benefit, which Hult and Hornberger argue is "potentially morally and ethically problematic" (2016: 39).

As a result of this extrinsic framing, languages that no longer provide economic value or social prestige can quickly lose institutional and individual support. If spoken languages are only valuable insofar as they can contribute to economic development, either through international trade relations or through the promotion of a "culture industry" in rural and minority regions, then their value as the language of daily communication becomes unimportant. If linguistic value is framed in utilitarian terms, once speakers no longer see the utility in speaking a language in daily life, a shift to the dominant language is a natural next step.

Even more damaging, this resource metaphor of language places the value of linguistic diversity in language as a collection of data. Even when language resources are discussed in cultural terms, their value lies in their function as repositories of knowledge for China or the scholarly community more generally. For example, in a report on Language Endangerment, Xu Shixuan (2013) writes that,

[a]ll these endangered languages and dialects are of immense academic importance in that they preserve some unique features of ancient languages and embody precious cultural values. If these languages die out, it will be an irretrievable loss to both Chinese culture and human civilization.

(Xu 2013, 263)

Here, the focus is on languages as providing academic knowledge, which is of value to China and "human civilization." There is no mention of the cultural loss to the language or speech communities themselves.

Language protection programs (Yubao)

This highly instrumental view of the value of language diversity has several effects. First, as discussed, the importance of language protection or preservation does not lie in maintaining language use as a mode of daily communication, nor in revitalizing endangered languages. Instead, protection efforts take the form of Boasian "salvage linguistics" (Moore 2006), or the documentation of endangered languages before they die out in order to preserve knowledge of the language in its grammar, lexicon, and writing system. To the extent culture is preserved, it is preserved in written documents as collections of literature, folktales, Indigenous knowledge, and other verbal/written artistic forms. Once these scholarly documents are compiled and knowledge of "linguistic diversity" has been added to the catalogue of human knowledge, the existence of living speakers or a vibrant speech community is immaterial. We can see this ideology present in arguments for "preserving and exploiting linguistic resources" by setting up a "linguistic data bank" akin to a "gene bank," which preserves genetic diversity through the storage of DNA samples (Li 2015: 11).

It is then not surprising that recent state language protection efforts focus on language documentation over language maintenance or revitalization. In 2015, the Ministry of Education and the State Language Commission jointly implemented the *Project for the Protection of Language Resources of China*, or the Language Protection (*yubao*) project, which is a major initiative to "scientifically protect" endangered languages through documentation (Cao 2022; Shen and Gao 2019; Tian 2022). The core of the Language Protection project is a large-scale survey to document and record languages with a particular focus on those that are "critically endangered" (*binwei*). The vast majority of resources of the language protection program are focused on language preservation (*yuyan baocun*), which is the "recording the actual features of languages and dialects by means of comprehensive, detailed, scientific surveys, and engaging in long-term, effective preservation and exhibition" rather than language protection (*baohu*), which "refers to preserving the vitality of languages and dialects . . . and . . . preventing the decline of disadvantaged and critically endangered languages and dialects" (Cao 2022: 52). In other words, despite rhetoric, the choice to focus resources on language documentation over language revitalization reveals the preferences of the state, for whom "varieties of Chinese are not to be protected as live languages but to be preserved merely as cultural heritage" (Zhou 2019: 78).

Anachronization and preemptive eulogization

In the previous sections, I demonstrated how state rhetoric reveals a highly instrumental view of the value of linguistic diversity that does not value minority languages or dialects in themselves, nor does it value actual speaker communities. This is not surprising, given the state's placement of overwhelming importance on Putonghua as the language of national unity, modernization, and economic development. In this section, I demonstrate how language protection rhetoric may actually go a step further toward promoting language loss. This is carried out in two ways.

The first way is to portray a minority language as representing or belonging to "an ancient past," or to *anachronize* the language. Although this portrayal is ostensibly positive, it can also have the effect of making the language appear to be non-modern, or even to make its usage seem incompatible with being modern. Given the overwhelming importance placed on modernization in the PRC, portraying languages as non-modern means that they do not have a role in contemporary society. In other words, their value lies in their role as "heritage." We see this attitude present in Xu's statement previously, where the value of endangered languages lies in the fact that they "preserve some unique features of ancient languages" (2013: 263). This sort of portrayal is particularly common in characterizing other Sinitic language varieties, that is, Chinese dialects. For example, Li Yuming writes that "[f]rom a historical point of view, dialects are 'a warehouse of fossils' of ancient languages and cultures, preserving a large quantity of elements and essence of the ancient languages" (2015: 186). My research on the Huizhou language family in Huangshan has demonstrated a similar framing of Huizhou dialects as "living fossils," whose value lies in their similarity to ancient Chinese (Ingebretson 2022). By portraying other Sinitic languages as somehow more ancient, the state is anachronizing these dialects and making them appear stagnant and incapable of evolving to meet contemporary language needs. If they exist as remnants of the past, their loss is thus part of inevitable historical progress. This framing is not intuitive. Yue is the language of Hong Kong and Guangdong, two economic powerhouses associated with Chinese development and growth. The Min languages are similarly spoken in Fujian and Taiwan, also regions considered economically and culturally developed. There is nothing inherent in non-Putonghua Sinitic languages that make them incapable of adapting fully to modern life.

The second way can be through *preemptive eulogization*, which is the act of portraying a language as more moribund than it actually is in order make language loss appear inevitable and already well underway (Ingebretson 2022). Preemptive eulogization often follows from anachronization. Once a language is portrayed as anachronistic, its death appears to be a natural and unavoidable result. In my fieldwork in Huangshan, I demonstrated how local language experts

The Routledge Handbook of Endangered and Minority Languages

preemptively eulogize the local languages. For example, in the state-produced documentary, *The Charm of Huizhou Dialects* (*Huizhou fangyan de meili*), a local language expert discusses the future of the Huizhou dialects:

> Protecting the dialect is extremely important. Yet, my personal opinion is that given the speed of [current] language loss, the rate of loss will almost double within a decade. There-fore, we must prioritize Huizhou dialect research because if in the end Huizhou dialects completely assimilate into Mandarin, really, I can't imagine what meaning research into Huizhou culture will have.

As stated, the Huizhou languages have approximately 4–5 million speakers. While children in urban areas are more likely to learn Mandarin than the local dialect, Huizhou dialects are still the primary language in rural areas, which incorporate most of the region. This pattern of language use has been relatively stable for the past several decades, which means that it is unclear what factors would make the rate of language loss double within the decade. I have instead argued that the language expert's bleak prognosis is a performative act of encouraging language loss by implying that it is well under-way. In a less developed region like Huangshan where local officials view economic development as paramount, preemptive eulogization can be a way for local officials to encourage the switch to Putonghua without overtly appearing to do so. While my research focuses on Huangshan, this phe-nomenon is likely widespread, particularly in rural areas. Indeed, any time one encounters alarmist rhetorics about imminent language demise, it is worth paying attention to whether this pessimism is an act of preemptive eulogization rather than an objective description of fact.

Conclusion

Despite formal protection encoded into Chinese law, and despite language planning documents that promote "harmony" between Putonghua and other language varieties, the Chinese government overtly and covertly promotes a policy of Putonghuaization at the expense of other languages. In the past decade, the Chinese state has increasingly mandated the use of Putonghua in institutional settings. Ethnic minority languages, such as Mongolian, Tibetan, or Uyghur, are no longer the medium of instruction in bilingual schools. Other Sinitic languages, generally referred to as Chi-nese dialects, face increasing pressure not to be used in broadcast media or in the public sphere. These attempts to promote Putonghua at the expense of other language varieties are obvious. The Chinese state encourages Putonghuaization in more subtle ways as well. The highly instrumen-tal resource model of linguistic diversity means that languages are only valuable insofar as they provide extrinsic and material benefits. Their cultural value lies in their contribution to "cultural heritage" or general linguistic knowledge. Most importantly, their value is defined in terms of national benefit and not for speech communities. Additionally, minority languages, particularly other Sinitic languages, are frequently *anachronized* and *preemptively eulogized*, processes that frame languages as "living fossils" mired in the past whose demise is inevitable.

References

English references

Adamson, B. and Feng, A. (2009). 'A comparison of trilingual education policies for ethnic minorities in China'. *Compare: A Journal of Comparative and International Education.* 39(3): 321–333.
Atwood, C.P. (2020). 'Bilingual education in inner Mongolia: An explainer'. *Made in China Journal.* 30.

Baioud, G. (2020). 'Will education reform wipe out Mongolian language and culture?'. *Language on the Move*, August 30 [online]. Available at: www.languageonthemove.com/will-education-reform-wipe-out-mongolian-language-and-culture/ (Accessed: 3 January 2024).

Bilik, N. (2014). 'How do you say "China" in Mongolian? Toward a deeper understanding of multicultural education in China'. In J. Leibold and Y. Chen (eds), *Minority Education in China: Balancing Unity and Diversity in an Era of Critical Pluralism*. Hong Kong University Press.

Bristow, M. (2024). 'Tibet boarding schools: China accused of trying to silence language'. *BBC*, March 10 [online]. Available at: www.bbc.com/news/world-asia-china-68492043 (Accessed: 30 May 2024).

Bulag, U.E. (2020). 'Dying for the mother tongue: Why have people in inner Mongolia recently taken their lives?'. *Index on Censorship*. 49(4): 49–51.

Bulag, U.E. (2021). 'Minority nationalities as Frankenstein's monsters? Reshaping "the Chinese Nation" and China's quest to become a "Normal Country"'. *The China Journal*. 86(1): 46–67.

Byler, D. (2019). 'Preventative policing as community detention in northwest China'. *Made in China Journal*. 4(3): 88–94.

Cao, Z. (2022). 'Orientation, objectives, and tasks of the project for the protection of language resources of China'. In Y. Li and W. Li (eds), *The Language Situation in China Vol 7, 2016*. De Gruyter Mouton: 51–60.

Chan, L.T. (2018). 'The dialect(ic)s of control and resistance: Intralingual audiovisual translation in Chinese TV drama'. *International Journal of the Sociology of Language*. 2018(251): 89–109.

Chappell, H. and Lan, L. (2016). 'Mandarin and other Sinitic languages'. In S. Chan, F. Li Wing Yee, and J.W. Minett (eds), *The Routledge Encyclopedia of the Chinese Language*. Abingdon, Oxon; New York, NY: Routledge.

Chen, P. (1999). *Modern Chinese: History and Sociolinguistics*. Cambridge; New York: Cambridge University Press.

Curdt-Christiansen, X.L. and Gao, X. (2021). 'Family language policy and planning in China: The changing landscape'. *Current Issues in Language Planning*. 22(4): 353–361.

Eberhard, D.M., Simons, G.F. and Fennig, C.D. (eds) (2023). *Ethnologue*. Twenty-sixth ed. Dallas, TX: SIL International.

Fu, Y. (2021). 'Survey of the state of language among new and earlier rural migrant workers'. In Y. Li and W. Li (eds), *The Language Situation in China Vol. 6, 2015*. De Gruyter Mouton: 129–144.

Gao, X. (2012). '"Cantonese is not a dialect": Chinese netizens' defence of Cantonese as a regional lingua franca'. *Journal of Multilingual and Multicultural Development*. 33(5): 449–464.

Gil, J. (2021). 'Putonghua in the context of multilingual China and the world'. In B. Adamson and A. Feng (eds), *Multilingual China: National, Minority and Foreign Languages*. Routledge.

Grey, A. (2021). *Language Rights in a Changing China: A National Overview and Zhuang Case Study*. Walter de Gruyter GmbH & Co KG.

Gu, T. (2023). *China Bans Mongolian-medium Classes, Cuts Language Hours in Schools, Radio Free Asia* [online]. Available at: www.rfa.org/english/news/china/language-classes-10052023115908.html (Accessed: 30 May 2024).

Guo, L. (2004). 'The relationship between Putonghua and Chinese dialects'. In M. Zhou and H. Sun (eds), *Language Policy in the People's Republic of China: Theory and Practice since 1949*. Springer.

Hau, C.S. (2022). 'Ethnic-Chinese life-making, place-making, and claim-making in Southeast Asia' [online]. Available at: https://www.researchgate.net/publication/365013111_Ethnic-Chinese_Life-Making_Place-Making_and_Claim-Making_in_Southeast_Asia

Henry, C. (2016). 'The Chinese education system as a source of conflict in Tibetan areas'. In B. Hillman and G. Tuttle (eds), *Ethnic Conflict and Protest in Tibet and Xinjiang*. Columbia University Press: 97–121.

Hult, F.M. and Hornberger, N.H. (2016). 'Revisiting orientations in language planning: Problem, right, and resource as an analytical heuristic'. *The Bilingual Review/La Revista Bilingüe*. 33(3).

Ingebretson, B. (2022). '"Living Fossils": The politics of language preservation in Huangshan, China'. *Journal of Linguistic Anthropology*. 32(1): 116–138.

Kurpaska, M. (2010). *Chinese Language(s): A Look through the Prism of the Great dictionary of Modern Chinese Dialects*. Berlin; New York: De Gruyter Mouton (Trends in linguistics. Studies and monographs, 215).

Lam, A.S.L. (2005) *Language Education in China: Policy and Experience from 1949*. Hong Kong University Press.

Li, J. and Juffermans, K. (2012). 'Chinese complementary schooling in the Netherlands: Experiences and identities of final-year students'. In F. Grande, J.J. de Ruiter, and M. Spotti (eds), *Mother Tongue and Intercultural Valorization: Europe and Its Migrant Youth*. Milan: FrancoAngeli: 61–80.

Li, W. (2014). *The Language Situation in China*. Boston: De Gruyter Mouton (Language Policies and Practices in China [LPPC]).

Li, Y. (2015). *Language Planning in China, Language Planning in China*. De Gruyter Mouton.

Liang, S. (2015). *Language Attitudes and Identities in Multilingual China: A Linguistic Ethnography*. Cham: Springer International Publishing.

Lü, H. and Zou, H. (2013). 'Dialect craze'. In Y. Li (ed), *The Language Situation in China*. De Gruyter Mouton (Language Policies and Practices in China [LPPC]): 237–249.

Ma, R. (2014). 'Bilingual education and language policy in Tibet'. In J. Leibold and Y. Chen (eds), *Minority Education in China: Balancing Unity and Diversity in an Era of Critical Pluralism*. Hong Kong University Press.

Moore, R.E. (2006). 'Disappearing, Inc.: Glimpsing the sublime in the politics of access to endangered languages'. *Language & Communication*. 26(3–4): 296–315.

Mullaney, T. (2010). *Coming to Terms with the Nation: Ethnic Classification in Modern China*. Berkeley: University of California Press (Asia: Local Studies/Global Themes).

Norman, J. (1988). *Chinese*. Cambridge University Press.

Postiglione, G. (2014). 'Education and cultural diversity in multiethnic China'. In J. Leibold and Y. Chen (eds), *Minority Education in China: Balancing Unity and Diversity in an Era of Critical Pluralism*. Hong Kong: Hong Kong University Press (Education in China: Reform and Diversity): 27–43.

Ricento, T. (2005). 'Problems with the "language-as-resource" discourse in the promotion of heritage languages in the U.S.A.'. *Journal of Sociolinguistics*. 9(3): 348–368.

Roche, G. (2021). 'Tibetan language rights and civil society in the People's Republic of China: Challenges of and for rights'. *Asian Studies Review*. 45(1): 67–82.

Rohsenow, J. (2004). 'Fifty years of script and written language reform in the PRC: The genesis of the language law of 2001'. In M. Zhou and H. Sun (eds), *Language Policy in the People's Republic of China: Theory and Practice since 1949*. Springer.

Ruíz, R. (1984). 'Orientations in language planning'. *NABE Journal*. 8(2): 15–34.

Schluessel, E.T. (2009). 'History, identity, and mother-tongue education in Xinjiang'. *Central Asian Survey*. 28(4): 383–402.

Shen, Q. and Gao, X. (2019). 'Multilingualism and policy making in Greater China: Ideological and implementational spaces'. *Language Policy*. 18(1): 1–16.

Shen, Q., Wang, L. and Gao, X. (Andy). (2021). 'An ecological approach to family language policy research: The case of Miao families in China'. *Current Issues in Language Planning*. 22(4): 427–445.

Simayi, Z. (2014). 'The practice of ethnic policy in education: Xinjiang's bilingual education system'. In J. Leibold and Y. Chen (eds), *Minority Education in China: Balancing Unity and Diversity in an Era of Critical Pluralism*. Hong Kong University Press.

Spolsky, B. (2014). 'Language management in the People's Republic of China'. *Language: Journal of the Linguistic Society of America*. 90(4): 165–179.

Tian, L. (2022). 'Origin and significance of the project for the protection of language resources of China'. In Y. Li and W. Li (eds), *The Language Situation in China Vol. 7, 2016*. De Gruyter Mouton: 37–50.

Tsung, L.T.H. (2009). *Minority Languages, Education and Communities in China*. Basingstoke; New York: Palgrave Macmillan (Palgrave studies in minority languages and communities).

UN Commission for Human Rights Office of the High Commissioner. (2023). *China: Xinjiang's Forced Separations and Language Policies for Uyghur Children Carry Risk of Forced Assimilation, Say UN Experts*. September 26 [online]. Available at: www.ohchr.org/en/press-releases/2023/09/china-xinjiangs-forced-separations-and-language-policies-uyghur-children (Accessed: 30 May 2024).

Wang, S. and Gao, X. (Andy). (2023). 'A systematic review of research on language policy and planning for minority languages in China: What is next?'. *Journal of Multilingual and Multicultural Development*. 1–18.

Wang, W. and Curdt-Christiansen, X.L. (2021). 'Lost in translation: Parents as medium translators in intergenerational language transmission'. *Current Issues in Language Planning*. 22(4): 362–382.

Weng, J. (2018). 'What is mandarin? The social project of language standardization in early republican China'. *Journal of Asian Studies*. 77(3): 611–633.

Wurm, S.A. *et al.* (eds) (1988). *Language Atlas of China*. Hong Kong: Longman Group (Pacific linguistics, no. 102).

Xu, F. (2021). *Silencing Shanghai: Language and Identity in Urban China*. London: Rowman & Littlefield.

Xu, H. (2019). 'Putonghua as "admission ticket" to linguistic market in minority regions in China'. *Language Policy*. 18(1): 17–37.

Xu, S. (2013). 'Language endangerment'. In Y. Li and W. Li (eds), *The Language Situation in China Vol. 1, 2006–2007*. De Gruyter Mouton: 261–270.

Yan, Z. and Xu, X. (2022). 'Survey of the state of rural language use in Hubei Province'. In Y. Li and W. Li (eds), *The Language Situation in China Vol. 7, 2016*. De Gruyter Mouton: 83–98.

Yin, X. and Li, G. (2021). 'Language solidarity, vitality and status: Sibe family language attitudes in North-western China'. *Current Issues in Language Planning*. 22(4): 446–465.

Zhang, J. and Pérez-Milans, M. (2019). 'Structures of feeling in language policy: The case of Tibetan in China'. *Language Policy*. 18: 39–64.

Zhang, L. and Tsung, L.T.H. (2019). *Bilingual Education and Minority Language Maintenance in China: The Role of Schools in Saving the Yi Language*. Cham, Switzerland: Springer (Multilingual education, volume 31).

Zhang, X. and Guo, Z. (2012). 'Hegemony and counter-hegemony: The politics of dialects in TV programs in China'. *Chinese Journal of Communication*. 5(3): 300–315.

Zhou, M. (2019). *Language Ideology and Order in Rising China*. Singapore: Springer.

Zhou, M. (2021). 'Multiculturalism in China from melting pot to pressure cooker'. *East Asia Forum*, June 4 [online]. Available at: www.eastasiaforum.org/2021/06/04/multiculturalism-in-china-from-melting-pot-to-pressure-cooker/ (Accessed: 3 January 2024).

Zhou, Q., Wei, D. and Xie, J. (2013). 'Language policies and regulations in China: An overview'. In Y. Li (ed), *The Language Situation in China Volume 1, 2006–2007*. De Gruyter Mouton.

Chinese references

Cao, Zhiyun 曹志耘. (ed) (2008). 汉语方言地图集 *Linguistic Atlas of Chinese Dialects* (3 vols). Beijing: Commercial Press 北京: 商务印书馆.

China National People's Congress 中华人民共和国全国人民代表大会. (1984). *Regional Ethnic Autonomy Law of the People's Republic of China (Chinese and English Text)* 中华人民共和国民族区域自治法. May 31 [online]. Available at: www.cecc.gov/resources/legal-provisions/regional-ethnic-autonomy-law-of-the-peoples-republic-of-china-amended (Accessed: 27 January 2024).

Ding, Yasong 丁雅诵. (2019). 'Education after 70 years: From an 80% illiteracy rate to a compulsory education consolidation rate of 94.2%'. '教育事业 70 年: 从文盲率 80%到义务教育巩固率 94.2%. *CCTV News*, republished from People's Daily 人民日报. October 25 [online]. Available at: https://news.cctv.com/2019/10/25/ARTIHlay1cFV3VQaUqTaHjrM191025.shtml (Accessed: 27 January 2024).

Ministry of Education 教育部 (2021). 'National Putonghua level has reached 80.72%' 全国范围内普通话普及率达到 80.72%. *People's Republic of China Ministry of Education Webpage*. 中华人民共和国教育部政府门户网站. Republished from China News Net 中国新闻网. June 2 [online]. Available at: www.moe.gov.cn/fbh/live/2021/53486/mtbd/202106/t20210602_535129.html (Accessed: 27 January 2024).

Shanghai Media Group 上海广播电视台、上海文化广播影视集团有限公司. (n.d.). Shanghai Media Group Information 上海广播电视台简介 [online]. Available at: www.smg.cn/review/201406/0163874.html (Accessed: 30 January 2024).

Xiong, Zhenghui and Zhang, Zhenxing 熊正辉、张振兴 (eds) (2012). *Language Atlas of China*. 2nd ed. 中国语言地图集第 2 版. Beijing: Commercial Press 北京：商务印书馆

Xu, Ming 徐茗. (2008). 'Residents' perceptions to use and evolution of Huizhou dialect in she county' 歙县居民对徽州方言使用与演化的感知研究. *Resource Development & Market* 资源开发与市场. 24(6): 535–538.

i While Chinese characters themselves are not phonetic, a Romanized alphabet known as pinyin, based on Putonghua vernacular, was adopted in 1958 (Ramsey 1987). After initial debate, pinyin's purpose was meant to supplement rather than replace the character system.

ii I will use MSC to refer to standard written characters and Putonghua to refer to the spoken language.

iii 方言的保存也是非常必要的。而方言流失的速度我个人认为它几乎是以十年翻一倍的速度在流失。所以我们要重视徽州方言的研究，因为如果徽州方言都最后同化成普通话了，那么，我不可能想象了徽州文化的研究还有什么意义。也就是徽州方言的流失将会影响到徽州文化的流失

14

IDEOLOGICAL MONOLINGUALISM AND THE LANGUAGES CLASSROOM IN ENGLAND

Abigail Parrish

Introduction

Language learning in schools in England is in crisis, or so people would have us believe (Cannadine, 2019; Collen, 2020a; Haseldine, 2023; Kelly, 2019; Lanvers & Coleman, 2017; Lanvers & Graham, 2022; Lanvers et al., 2021). This situation is neither new (see, for example, Saunders, 1998) nor confined to the UK (Group of Eight, 2007; Levine, 2011) and as such, is something other, or perhaps more, than a crisis (Bowler, 2020; Brown et al., 2019).

Hay (1999) notes that the success of narratives of crisis

> relies not on their ability 'accurately' to reflect the complex webs of causation that interact to produce disparate effects, but on their ability to provide a simplified account sufficiently flexible to 'narrate' a great variety of morbid symptoms whilst unambiguously attributing causality and responsibility.
>
> (334)

Understood this way, the enduring nature of the narrative of a crisis in UK language learning is a function of its simplicity and its convenience – rather than considering *why* young people might be turning away from language learning, and attempting to understand their motivations and goals (Parrish, 2023; Parrish & Lanvers, 2019), the literature often focuses on the fact that they have been allowed to do so by so many policy decisions. This chapter does so too, but only in part, whilst also considering the bigger societal picture that has allowed this situation, and its associated narratives, to develop. It will offer the argument that it is against a complex socio-political backdrop that the education system has become one which is ideologically monolingual, despite the best efforts of languages teachers and the stubborn refusal of students to be, and remain, monolingual.

Crisis, permanent crisis, or just the way things are?

Whether or not 'crisis' is a suitable term, there is no question that language learning in schools faces challenges. One of these, and one which is often discussed, is the calamitous end of the policy known as 'languages for all' in 2004 (for discussion of this, see Dobson, 2018; Hagger-Vaughan,

DOI: 10.4324/9781003439493-18

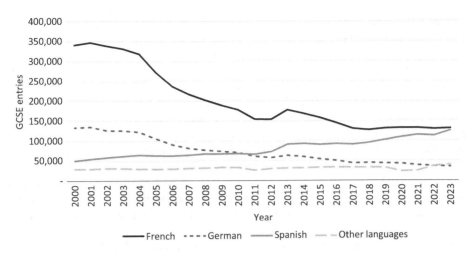

Figure 14.1 GCSE entries in modern foreign languages, 2000–2023. Data source: JCQ

2016). This policy change meant that it was no longer compulsory for students in England to study a language beyond the age of 14; it became an 'entitlement' – a subject which must be made available 'to any pupil wishing to study [it]' (Department for Education and Skills, 2002: 24), although some schools do continue to make the subject compulsory at a local level (Parrish & Lanvers, 2019). Between 1997 and this change in 2004, modern foreign languages (MFLs) had been part of the core national curriculum, theoretically making the study of a language compulsory until the age of 16. The argument made by the Department for Education and Skills at the time was that this was 'too constraining. For some students it is demotivating in the short term and has consequences for their eventual achievement of qualifications' (Department for Education and Skills, 2002: 24). Although this policy change demonstrably led to a dramatic drop in the number of students taking the subject (see Figure 14.1), only 75% of students had been entered for a GCSE exam during the 'languages for all' period (Lanvers, 2011). The subject had not been popular with students, and levels of competence were low (Macaro, 2008).

We can surmise two things from this data at this stage. First, that once students could opt out of studying a language, many did so immediately, and second, that this downward trajectory has continued more or less unabated (although we will return to this later) ever since. It is little wonder, then, that the term 'crisis' is so regularly deployed.

We must, however, consider first the aptness of the word 'crisis' to describe something ongoing – in general usage, the nature of a crisis tends to be that it is short term and acute rather than chronic, lasting in this instance two decades or more. There is certainly a decline, bringing with it problems for university-level language learning and skills in the workforce as a whole. And this is certainly something which should be considered cause for concern, with language skills being arguably valuable for a multitude of reasons beyond the scope of this chapter. But perhaps, as Bowler (2020) suggests, this is not something which can, or should, be meaningfully described as a crisis.

Fink (2002) suggests that a crisis exists in four stages: the prodromal stage (a medical term relating to the first onset of symptoms which signal an impending illness) during which initial problems might be recognised, for example, the lack of interest in language learning in the early

2000s; the acute stage, in which the crisis itself happens – the subject is made optional and students vote with their feet, for example; the chronic stage where lingering effects are felt; and the resolution stage, where normal service is resumed. Arguably, then, MFL remains in the chronic stage.

Hay (1999) notes that 'Etymologically, "crisis" refers to a moment of decisive intervention . . . a moment of rupture' (323). This decisiveness is what makes an intervention a crisis (rather than simply a tipping point; Hay, 1999: 325). The end of the policy of languages for all, might then be most accurately considered the 'crisis,' the acute stage, rather than the ensuing two decades. However, the 'moment of crisis' is not always recognised as a crisis when it first happens; a crisis is defined by its effects (Debray, 1973). In the context of school language learning, when the green paper which announced the end of languages for all was published in 2002 (Department for Education and Skills, 2002), although it was recognised as a critical moment by teachers and other stakeholders, it was not necessarily seen as a crisis, but the subsequent decline in numbers of students studying the subject has led to it being seen in this way; the dramatic effects it triggered represent the chronic post-crisis state.

The argument tends to be made that it was the end of languages for all that precipitated (the beginning of) the crisis. However, the policy change was itself precipitated by something in this prodromal stage, and the speed at which students opted out of the subject shows that there was no great warmth towards it (between 2004 and 2005, almost 65,000 fewer students took a languages GCSE and another 50,000 fewer were entered the following year). Why this might have been the case, and whether and how the change in policy resulted in a crisis, is the subject of this chapter. Whether the consequences made plain by Figure 14.1 were intentional or not is the question which dictates whether this was a crisis or a tipping point. Indeed, perhaps this is not a crisis so much as just 'the way things are,' something which had been temporarily masked by the implementation of languages for all. What were the conditions which allowed the government to decide that they could, or must, make that intervention (Hay, 1999)?

Background: languages in the curriculum

Before exploring the landscape within which this permanent crisis, this terminal decline, is enacting itself, we must get to grips with the basics. Language learning in schools in England[1] happens in the subject known as Modern Foreign Languages. It is currently taught to all young people from the ages of 7 to 14, with GCSE exams taken by those who opt to continue to age 16 and A-Levels taken at 18. As Figure 14.1 shows, the majority of language teaching has historically been in French, although Spanish has gained substantially in popularity in recent years. GCSE entries in German have been in marked decline since 2004 and have never recovered.

Although these three languages have historically made up the bulk of language teaching and continue to do so, other languages are available to be taught and examined (see Table 14.1) and are offered in some schools, although numbers are low: the largest number of students sit in Chinese (7,091 in 2023), and the lowest number sit Gujarati (312; JCQ, 2023). The question of which language(s) should be taught is a complex one in England and other Anglophone nations, much more so than in many countries where English is the first foreign language taught for geopolitical reasons.

School language learning has to fit into a tightly packed curriculum. One to two hours a week is common between the ages of 11 and 14, increasing to perhaps three hours in the GCSE years (Collen, 2023); between the ages of 7 and 11 the time allocated is around 45 minutes per week, generally delivered by non-specialists (Collen, 2022).

Having established the nuts and bolts of the matter, we come now to the key issues facing the subject and the arguments with which this chapter is concerned.

Everyone speaks English

One key problem facing any school languages teacher is the idea that 'everyone speaks English anyway.' This is the perennial excuse presented by generations of students in classrooms in England as to why learning a language is 'a waste of time' (see Gough, 2021; Jenkins, 2017). At the milder end, students might agree with the sixth former who reported that 'living in England, we may not feel we need to learn a language because English is so widely spoken' (Parrish, 2023: 105); at the more extreme end, they might argue that 'you *should* not learn other languages because everyone *should* learn English' (Parrish, 2023: 105, emphasis added). The idea that people 'should' learn English and we, as English speakers, 'should not' learn another language, is a clear problem for language teachers and for global socio-cultural understanding. It also highlights the way that language intersects with identity and how problematic this can be in adolescence (Taylor, 2013).

It is not only students who exemplify this 'English is enough' mentality. In 2008, then-Prime Minister Gordon Brown pronounced that 'if you have skills, educated in Britain, you can work almost anywhere in the world' (Brown 2008). In this assessment, made in a speech at the Specialist Schools and Academies Trust, the body responsible for the specialist schools programme which included Language Colleges, he made no mention of how language or cultural knowledge might play a part. This 'English is enough fallacy' (Lanvers et al, 2018: 778), perhaps most eloquently summed up by the student who wrote 'I AM HAPPY SPEAKING MY LANGUEDGE WHY WOULD I WANT TO LEARN ANY OTHER' (Parrish, 2023: 105; original emphasis and spelling) is not just played out in Anglophone nations. In Germany, Quetz asks whether the hegemony of English in school language learning and as a lingua franca means it acts as a 'killer language' (Skutnabb-Kangas, 2000), negatively impacting student motivation to learn other languages (Quetz, 2010: 183) and leading to a 'monoculture' of foreign language use. Could it be, then, that what Lanvers et al. (2018) refer to as linguaphobia, an aversion to learning foreign languages, is not actually that but rather part of a wider global discourse valorising English – could English really be enough?

It is certainly true that English is generally considered the global lingua franca, but this is a simplistic view which does not take into account the many local nuances of communication (see, for example, Kubota, 2013; McGroarty, 2006; Sharma, 2018). Indeed, the majority of the world's population do not, in fact, have a useful level of English (British Council, 2013), and misunderstandings may occur between users of English as a lingua franca from different linguistic backgrounds (Bayyurt, 2018; Deterding, 2013). All this suggests that although English may be the lingua franca of many commonly visited tourist destinations (the main contact points with speakers of languages other than English for students from England) and international diplomacy (the main contact points for politicians; Xhemaili, 2022), a need for language skills, even amongst L1 English speakers, remains (British Academy, 2019).

In spite of this, the UK remains the country with the poorest language skills in Europe (Eurostat, 2023). Coleman (2009) suggests that the poor language skills evidenced by Britons 'must be [attributable to] forces in the climate of public opinion, and in the public discourse' (116). And indeed, there is an ongoing anti-other – anti-European, anti-'foreign' – media discourse, chronicled by Coleman (2009) as well as Daddow (2006), Lanvers and Coleman (2017), and Lanvers et al. (2018). Language-related news reports often focus on bad news – declining student numbers, perceived poor-quality teaching, and so on – rarely do they report success stories. Liberal Democrat politician Nick Clegg was mocked in the left-leaning political magazine the New Statesman for conducting a meeting with a Flemish-speaking counterpart in Dutch: 'Irritated at No 10's snooping, Clever Cloggs conducted the entire session in Dutch, so the PM's cloth-eared spy was left fuming in the corner, listening but not understanding a double-Dutch conversation' (Maguire,

2012). The idea that the conversation was held in Dutch is presented here as an act of spite rather than an act of generous diplomacy, so unusual was it. When the media present language skills as unusual and 'other,' it is not surprising to find that they are not seen as desirable by young people.

England: a monolingual multilingual society?

It is, as a moment's thought would demonstrate, a fallacy to suggest that England is monolingual, despite the well-documented (or at least, oft-repeated) notion that 'the British do not learn languages' (Coleman, 2009) or are 'bad' at it (Milton & Meara, 1998). Indeed, around 9% of the population, or 5 million people, is estimated to speak a language other than English at home (ONS, 2022), including 18% of the secondary school population (DfE, 2023a). And around 90,000 people graduate each year with a degree including a modern language (HESA, 2023), as well as around 60,000 who take courses in university language centres alongside their degrees (AULC-UCML, 2018). This quite aside from the 13 million people who have downloaded language learning app Duolingo in the UK (Watkins, 2020). Even in areas of England where multilingualism, as commonly understood as the capability to use more than one language in everyday life (see Cenoz, 2013), is not the norm, it has been found that students may identify as multilingual by virtue of their school language learning experiences or cultural interests (Bailey et al., 2023).

England may be demonstrably not a monolingual nation, but the languages other than English which are used by its multilingual population are often not those taught in schools. Although GCSEs are available in heritage or so-called community languages (see Table 14.1), the numbers of students sitting them are low (a few hundred each year in some cases; JCQ, 2023) and the number of schools offering the languages as a curriculum subject substantially lower – around 150 schools offer Chinese, for example (see DfE, 2023c). In the prevailing school system, any languages which cannot be examined do not feature in the discussion at all (Parrish, 2023, 2024). All of this means that the multilingualism that is present in schools is undervalued, or even completely devalued, and at times even erased (Cunningham & Little, 2022; Cushing, 2020).

All this suggests, then, that the monolingualism that seems to be embedded within English schools is ideological, rather than factual. Multilingualism is there, untapped, unrecognised or unawakened, but the curriculum and the exam system do not support its development or recognition. The rest of this chapter will explore why this might be.

Systems and control

Policies and performance measures

As in many countries, schooling in England is beholden to an accountability system imposed on it by the government. There are two crucial measures which impact on MFL: the English Baccalaureate, or EBacc, and Progress 8. These measures are both concerned with GCSE exam performance, with the former being a set suite of subjects which students must pass, although they do not gain any additional certification for this – although initially conceived as a school leaving certificate, the EBacc soon became a performance measure only; something of value only to schools and 'the system' (Long, 2016). Table 14.1 shows the subjects which are currently included in the EBacc. It was the introduction of this measure in 2011 that led to the short-lived increases in GCSE MFL entries that can be seen in Figure 14.1 around 2012–13. At this time, schools were often minded to create EBacc and non-EBacc pathways for students, with those considered most likely to pass GCSEs in the requisite suite of subjects streamed onto the EBacc pathway (see Armitage & Lau,

2020; Hagger-Vaughan, 2020; Parrish & Lanvers, 2019). Despite this streaming, often students did not achieve a pass in a language, and so schools started to deprioritise the measure. In 2021, for example, only 38.7% of students passed GCSEs in all five elements, and for 87.6% of those who did not, it was MFL which was missing (Hallahan, 2021).

School performance must be measured somehow, or so the government believes, and although entry and pass rates for the EBacc continue to be reported, a more inclusive measure known as Progress 8 was also developed, based on student progress in eight subjects as measured against peers with the same prior attainment in English and maths. It is related to the EBacc by virtue of its structure, which draws on 'EBacc subjects' in creating a system of 'buckets' (see Table 14.2). The key feature of the measure in terms of MFL is the 'EBacc bucket,' which must include three subjects from one of the EBacc's five columns, which could be three languages. However, crucially,

Table 14.1 The structure of the EBacc

English Literature *and*	Maths	*and*	Combined Science	*and*	One of:	*and*	Geography
and			or three of:		Arabic		*or*
English Language			Biology		Bengali		History
			Chemistry		Biblical Hebrew		*or*
			Physics		Chinese		Ancient History
			Computer Science		Classical Greek		
					French		
					German		
					Greek		
					Gujarati		
					Italian		
					Japanese		
					Latin		
					Modern Hebrew		
					Panjabi		
					Persian		
					Polish		
					Portuguese		
					Russian		
					Spanish		
					Turkish		
					Urdu		

Table 14.2 Progress 8 'buckets'

English		Maths		EBacc		Other
English Literature *and*		Maths	*and*	Three of the science, languages and humanities subjects in Table 14.1.	*and*	Any three other subjects, which *may* include the lower of the two English qualifications *or* additional EBacc subjects
and						
English Language						
Higher grade double weighted; lower grade ignored		Double weighted				

it could also contain no languages and be filled by, for example, two sciences and humanities subject. It was this flexibility which made it more appealing to schools than the EBacc when it was introduced in 2016, and so, although the government set an 'ambition' that 75% of students would be entered for the EBacc by 2022 and 90% by 2025 (DfE, 2019), by 2023, the figure was 39% (Thomson, 2023), as it had been for the previous two years (FFTDatalab, 2022; Hallahan, 2021) as schools deprioritised it and rolled back their EBacc pathway systems. In addition, schools had no desire to see their students entered for subjects they were unlikely to pass (harsh grading in the subject being a perennial problem; Hagger-Vaughan, 2018; Parrish & Lanvers, 2019; Thomson, 2019). For their part, when given the autonomy to choose, students did not willingly opt for the subjects included in the EBacc, likely because they themselves would not actually get the benefit if they did; all they 'got' was a controlled lack of choice (see Parrish & Lanvers, 2019) and the inability to take the subjects which interested them or which might open the doors they wished to go through in the future. The government nevertheless doubled down on its 90% ambition towards the end of 2022 (Gibb, 2022) and indeed published its intention to make the percentage of pupils at each school entered for a GCSE in a language a 'headline measure . . . reported on the main school page in performance tables from autumn 2024' (DfE, 2023b).

As the two measures now exist alongside each other, a tension has been introduced (see Parrish, 2024). On the one hand, the government is promoting languages in schools, also promising additional funding through a newly-established National Consortium for Languages Education with a focus not only on MFL in general but on German specifically (Gibb, 2022; see www.ucl.ac.uk/ioe/departments-and-centres/centres/international-centre-intercultural-studies/national-consortium-languages-education-ncle). On the other hand, languages are not mandated in Progress 8, also a headline measure of school performance (DfE, 2023d). Ever since MFL was made optional at GCSE, a message has been communicated about the worth and status of language learning (Coleman et al., 2007; Fisher, 2011) which the non-inclusion of the subject in Progress 8 cements and its inclusion in the EBacc has not combatted. The EBacc as a measure is neither popular nor practicable; in 2017, 93% of secondary heads responding to a survey by their trade union believed that the measure should not be compulsory and 86% opposed the 90% target (NAHT, 2017). One concern raised in the survey was the recruitment of suitable teachers; indeed the number of additional teachers needed to meet even the lower 75% 'ambition' has been estimated at more than 3,000 (Allen, 2016). However, in 2023, the government reported a shortfall of around 33% of their recruitment target for trainee MFL teachers (Whittaker, 2023) suggesting that, on the basis of staffing alone, meeting the 90% ambition by 2025 is likely to be challenging.

What all this suggests is that if the crisis in language learning was the withdrawal of the policy of languages for all, the post-crisis recovery phase has not gone far enough. The government has not, even with its investment in language teaching hubs and development of the EBacc, managed to restore the status language learning had in the pre-2004 era. What Lanvers et al. (2018) refer to as 'overall weak policies and practices' (778) have certainly played their part in this.

EBACC AS A DOOMED POLICY

If policies in this chronic stage of the crisis have been weak, why might that have been? The EBacc, arguably the policy with the most hope of leading to a recovery from the crisis, was introduced by Michael Gove in 2010 (Long, 2016), only six years after the end of languages for all, almost single-handedly (Pring, 2013). As the architect of this policy, he is generally believed to have based it on memories of his own schooling (see The Observer, 2013), which he considered

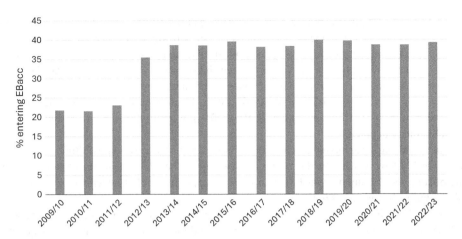

Figure 14.2 Percentage of students entered for the full EBacc, 2009–2022

to have been grounded in 'serious' academic knowledge (as contrasted with less serious creative subjects, or worse, skills; see Gibb, 2021) and on the list of 'facilitating subjects' published by the elite Russell Group of universities, which included languages on their list of eight subjects, designated as A-levels (not specifically GCSEs, although to enrol on an A-Level in those subjects, GCSEs would be prerequisite) 'that are required [for university entry] more often than others . . . sometimes referred to as facilitating subjects' (Russell Group, 2011: 20). The list was withdrawn in 2019, but the subjects persist within the EBacc. We can imagine his vision of a generation of pseudo-classically educated young people, leaving school with a working knowledge of languages ancient and modern, and their attendant big-C Cultural features (Gove, 2013; Vasagar, 2010). In the event, however, as Figure 14.2 shows clearly, this was not to transpire, and in asking why not, we turn first to the socio-political context mentioned previously.

Unlike in some other countries around the world, language learning is a socio-economic issue in England. As outlined, because of the dominance of English in commonly visited tourist destinations and amongst incoming visitors, it often requires a certain degree of cultural and economic capital for a student to imagine a situation whereby they might need a language – an extended sojourn or an experience which takes them off the beaten track, for example (Coffey, 2018; Netz & Finger, 2016). There are clear indications that socio-economic factors affect take-up of languages and the outcomes for those who do study the subject (Collen, 2020b; Lanvers, 2017). Although it has been made explicit that the EBacc ambitions are at a national rather than school level (Ofsted, 2023), given the socio-economic divide in language learning, it is likely that it will be schools in more deprived areas which have the lowest take-up. Gunter and Courtney (2023) argue that failure is the objective of some policies, 'premised on separating the school [we might substitute 'policy'] from the socio-economic, political and cultural context in which it is located and requiring it to improve and be judged effective as if that context did not exist' (358).

If the EBacc is to be characterised as an example of what we might call a 'doomed policy,' or what Gunter and Courtney (2023) characterise as 'policy mortality,' it is one set up to deflect blame. The government have proposed that up to 90% of students should study its 'academic core' of subjects; whose fault is it if this does not transpire? Surely not the government, who proposed the policy – surely the fault lies with the schools who failed to successfully enact it. The 'metrics and the narrative that gives meaning to the numbers [can be] selected in order to claim failure and who is responsible . . . so that the government can be seen to win' (Gunter & Courtney, 2023: 362). Although the EBacc features a lot in discussions around the take-up of MFL in schools, we must remember that its objective may never have been linked to recovery from the 'crisis' of the end of languages for all. Indeed, its introduction went hand in hand with the government's then focus on 'the soft bigotry of low expectations' (DfE, 2010: 4) and a move to equalise society through education, amongst other things (Bailey & Ball, 2016). Even in this, though, perhaps the policy was deliberately doomed.

With Gove long since moved to a less incendiary role, the EBacc remains, although with targets missed. In 2022, by which time the 'ambition' was to have had 75% of students 'studying' the full suite of subjects, the number was less than 40%, an upper limit it has never exceeded and around which it has stabilised (see Figure 14.2).

Nevertheless, the government persists with its ambition of 90% of pupils studying the subjects by 2025. This language used by the government in outlining this is instructive. They quote their 'ambition,' rather than their 'target,' and they specify that this is students 'studying' the subjects rather than passing them or even taking exams in them. This vagueness suggests that it was always seen as somewhat pie in the sky, a soft hope rather than a firm target – a doomed policy.

Targeted policy initiatives

Although in the two decades since MFL was made optional at GCSE, the government have shied away from reinstating it as a compulsory subject and there has been little impactful positive change, the inclusion of MFL in the EBacc does suggest that the government see some value in language learning. Indeed, when then–Parliamentary Under Secretary of State for Education and Childcare Liz Truss visited China in 2014, she came back inspired to emulate the education she had seen, setting up both maths hubs to share practice seen in China and Shanghai, and alongside this, a programme of Mandarin language learning for schools (Truss, 2014). As mentioned, in 2022, Minister of State at the Department for Education Nick Gibb announced a programme of funding to support the development of a programme of languages hub schools (Gibb, 2022), which followed his previous hub programme which had run from 2019 (Gibb, 2019). The original hub programme, which was built around the National Centre for Excellence for Language Pedagogy, estimates that its work reached around 50,000 students (Marsden et al., 2023) and evaluation of the Mandarin Excellence Programme suggests that it has had success with the small numbers of students enrolled (around 6000 by 2021; Nicoletti & Culligan, 2022). However, although increasing, numbers of students taking GCSEs in Chinese (which include Chinese L1 and heritage speakers) remain low, with only 7091 students entered in 2023, this represents a substantial increase on previous years for which data is available (see Figure 14.3).

Curriculum problems

The final area to which we turn is the MFL curriculum itself, which has been recently revised (see Coffey, 2022 for a summary). As in other subjects, what is taught is governed by what is examined, and in the case of MFL, bears little resemblance to the meaningful communication that is a feature of successful language use. As noted by Kubota (2013), 'the linguistic competence necessary for specific workplace communication might be quite different from what is typically taught in language classrooms which presumes ability of the complete spectrum of the standard variety of a language' (3), and in school classrooms, although workplace use might be a distant goal, it

Ideological monolingualism and the classroom in England

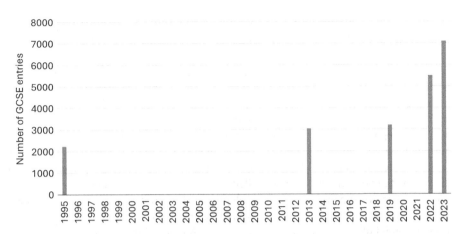

Figure 14.3 Number of entries for GCSE Chinese, 1995–2023. Data sources: www.jcq.org.uk/wp-content/uploads/2023/08/GCSE-Other-MFL-Entries-Summer-2023.pdf; www.britishcouncil.org/sites/default/files/alcantara_full_report_jun15.pdf

remains the case that when young people communicate naturally, whether in their own language(s) or another, they do so in ways which are meaningful to them – they talk to their friends about their common interests, or engage in interactions to achieve something specific. However, this is often not the goal of school language lessons or GCSE exams, which operate using pre-determined conversational scenarios, such as talking about your family in unnatural ways (I have a brother, he has brown hair and blue eyes) or describing a picture. The updated GCSE syllabus focuses on a list of 'most common' words, generated from an extensive published corpus, which by its very nature excludes much *genuinely* commonly used casual and conversational vocabulary (Blow & Myers, 2022). Culture is virtually excluded (see Scally et al., 2021) and traditionally the content has been exclusionary of many students, particularly those from lower socio-economic status backgrounds, focusing as it does on topics familiar only to the middle classes in many cases (for example, skiing holidays; see, for example, Determined Linguist, 2018; Panford, 2021).

Less than the sum of its parts: ideological multilingualism

As we have seen, languages teaching in England is in a tricky spot. It is not compulsory, and so it is perceived as low status. At the same time, it is part of the high-profile, supposedly highly valued EBacc measure – but there is little likelihood of this 'doomed policy' resulting in meaningful change, and its companion, or perhaps nemesis, Progress 8, acts as a barrier. Although the media and politicians at times discuss, even support, language skills, they do not do so in a way which supports improvement in the level of language learning or skill. The government may promise £15 million of investment in languages (Gibb, 2022) or £10 million for Mandarin (Nicoletti & Culligan, 2022), but the gains are small. The policies, arguably, are neither intended to address the 'crisis' nor to succeed – we might suggest that they are designed to fail to create ammunition for further curriculum reform.

Perhaps the previous suggestion is uncharitable, and we should consider the question posed by Wincott et al. (2021) regarding whether political actors 'understand that they are perpetuating ambiguity as their preferred outcome' (1535). In the context of MFL policy, we might question whether the government recognise the ambiguities and contradictions they are responsible for introducing into the system by creating two performance measures which act in tension with one another. They suggest that 'rather than failure, un(der)perceived ambiguities may have a 'constructive' or, perhaps better a constitutive character' (1535) – in other words, could it be that the government have introduced the contradiction between an academic performance measure which foregrounds MFL and a general one which does not, in a system which leaves decisions about the place of the subject in the curriculum up to individual schools, deliberately to serve their own ends? Are the tensions the desired end product? Having engendered the 'crisis' in language learning through the end of languages for all, whether intentionally or not; by failing to take decisive action at either a policy or curricular level; and perhaps in the belief that 'English is enough,' by creating policy tension and ambiguity, the unattainability of improved language skills becomes not the fault of the government (who after all, have introduced the EBacc and invested millions of pounds) but the fault of schools who have failed to translate that into results.

Policy, then, is not supportive of the development of multilingualism. Neither is the social or media climate, and this creates a background against which monolingualism is something approaching a point of pride – an ideological position. Although both classrooms and the population as a whole, when viewed at a macro level, are objectively not monolingual, education policy is not supportive of the development or sustaining of multilingualism. Without recognition, at a political and societal level, that multilingualism brings benefits including and beyond communication, this position will not change and school-level language learning will continue to decline. At present, neither the climate nor the curriculum supports it.

Note

1 The picture is different in Scotland, Wales, and Northern Ireland; this chapter focuses on England only.

References

Allen, R. (2016). *Revisiting how many language teachers we need to deliver the EBacc*. https://ffteducation-datalab.org.uk/2016/03/revisiting-how-many-language-teachers-we-need-to-deliver-the-ebacc/

Armitage, E., & Lau, C. (2020). Can the English Baccalaureate act as an educational equaliser? *Assessment in Education: Principles, Policy & Practice*, 27(1), 109–135. https://doi.org/10.1080/09695 94X.2019.1661222

AULC-UCML (2018). *AULC-UCML survey of institution-wide language provision in universities in the UK: 2017–2018*. https://university-council-modern-languages.org/wp-content/uploads/2019/08/ad65a-aulc_ucml_2017–2018.pdf

Bailey, E. G., Parrish, A., & Pierce, N. J. (2023). 'Having a decent understanding of more than one language': Exploring multilingualism with secondary school students in England. *Journal of Multilingual and Multicultural Development*, 1–13. https://doi.org/10.1080/01434632.2023.2216679

Bailey, P., & Ball, S. (2016). The coalition government, the general election and the policy ratchet in education: A reflection on the 'ghosts' of policy past, present and yet to come. In H. M. Bochel & M. A. Powell (Eds.), *The coalition government and social policy: Restructuring the welfare state* (pp. 127–151). Bristol: Polity Press.

Bayyurt, Y. (2018). Issues of intelligibility in world Englishes and EIL contexts. *World Englishes*, 37(3), 407–415. https://doi.org/10.1111/weng.12327

Blow, D., & Myers, H. (2022). Comparative analysis of the 2022 DfE GCSE Subject Content for French, German and Spanish and its implications for schools. *The Language Learning Journal*, 50(2), 238–248. https://doi.org/10.1080/09571736.2022.2045678

Bowler, M. (2020). A languages crisis? HEPI report 123. *HEPI*. www.hepi.ac.uk/wp-content/uploads/2020/01/HEPI_A-Languages-Crisis_Report-123-FINAL.pdf

British Academy (2019). *Languages in the UK: A call for action*. www.thebritishacademy.ac.uk/publications/languages-uk-academies-statement/

British Council (2013). *The English effect.* www.britishcouncil.org/sites/default/files/english-effect-report-v2.pdf

Brown, G. (2008). *12th annual lecture to the specialist schools & academies trust.* Specialist Schools & Academies Trust.

Brown, J., Caruso, M., Arvidsson, K., & Forsberg-Lundell, F. (2019). On 'Crisis' and the pessimism of disciplinary discourse in foreign languages: An Australian perspective. *Moderna Språk,* 113(2), 40–58. https://doi.org/10.58221/mosp.v113i2.7549

Cannadine, D. (2019). Brexit Britain cannot afford to be laissez-faire about its languages crisis. *The Guardian.* www.theguardian.com/commentisfree/2019/mar/01/britain-learning-languages-brexit – education

Cenoz, J. (2013). Defining multilingualism. *Annual Review of Applied Linguistics,* 33, 3–18. https://doi.org/10.1017/S026719051300007X

Coffey, S. (2018). Choosing to study modern foreign languages: Discourses of value as forms of cultural capital. *Applied Linguistics,* 39(4), 462–480. https://doi.org/10.1093/applin/amw019.

Coffey, S. (2022). 'Ambition for all'? Competing visions of 'ambition' and recognising language learning and teaching as a geo-historically situated social practice. *The Language Learning Journal,* 50(2), 142–145. https://doi.org/10.1080/09571736.2022.2045682

Coleman, J. (2009). Why the British do not learn languages: Myths and motivation in the United Kingdom. *The Language Learning Journal,* 37(1), 111–127.

Coleman, J., Galaczi, Á., & Astruc, L. (2007). Motivation of UK school pupils towards foreign languages: A large-scale survey at Key Stage 3. *The Language Learning Journal,* 35(2), 245–281. https://doi.org/10.1080/09571730701599252.

Collen, I. (2020a). *Language learning is still in decline in England's schools.* British Council. www.britishcouncil.org/voices-magazine/language-learning-decline-england-schools

Collen, I. (2020b). *Language trends 2020: Language teaching in primary and secondary schools in England.* London: British Council. www.britishcouncil.org/sites/default/files/language_trends_2020_0.pdf

Collen, I. (2022). *Language trends 2022: Language teaching in primary and secondary schools in England.* London: British Council. www.britishcouncil.org/research-insight/language-trends-2022

Collen, I. (2023). *Language trends 2023: Language teaching in primary and secondary schools in England.* London: British Council. www.britishcouncil.org/research-insight/language-trends-england-2023

Cunningham, C., & Little, S. (2022). 'Inert benevolence' towards languages beyond English in the discourses of English primary school teachers. *Linguistics and Education,* 101122. https://doi.org/10.1016/j.linged.2022.101122

Cushing, I. (2020). The policy and policing of language in schools. *Language in Society,* 49(3), 425–450. https://doi.org/10.1017/S0047404519000848

Daddow, O. J. (2006). Euroscepticism and the culture of the discipline of history. *Review of International Studies,* 32, 309–28.

Debray, R. (1973). *'Time and politics' in prison writings.* New York: Random House.

Department for Education and Skills (2002). *14–19: Extending opportunities, raising standards: Consultation document.* London: Her Majesty's Stationery Office.

Deterding, D. (2013). *Misunderstandings in English as a Lingua Franca: An analysis of ELF interactions in South-East Asia* (1st ed.). Berlin: De Gruyter, Inc.

Determined Linguist (2018). *Students are not picking MFL – and here's why I don't blame them.* https://transformmfl.wordpress.com/2018/07/08/students-are-not-picking-mfl-and-heres-why-i-dont-blame-them-2/

DfE (2010). *The importance of teaching: The schools white paper.* https://assets.publishing.service.gov.uk/media/5a7b4029ed915d3ed9063285/CM-7980.pdf

DfE (2019). *English Baccalaureate (EBacc) guidance.* www.gov.uk/government/publications/english-baccalaureate-ebacc/english-baccalaureate-ebacc

DfE (2023a). *Pupil characteristics – number of pupils by ethnicity and language.* https://explore-education-statistics.service.gov.uk/data-tables/fast-track/b0c47411-4f70-4a3e-85b8-14ce0bd6eb1f

DfE (2023b). *Secondary accountability measures guide for maintained secondary schools, academies and free schools.* DfE. https://assets.publishing.service.gov.uk/media/652fad41d0666200131b7c47/Secondary_accountability_measures_-_2023_guidance_for_maintained_secondary_schools__academies_and_free_schools.pdf

DfE (2023c). *Compare the performance of schools and colleges in England.* www.gov.uk/school-performance-tables

DfE (2023d). *Secondary accountability measures: Guide for maintained secondary schools, academies and free schools.* https://assets.publishing.service.gov.uk/media/652fad41d0666200131b7c47/Secondary_accountability_measures_-_2023_guidance_for_maintained_secondary_schools__academies_and_free_schools.pdf

Dobson, A. (2018). Towards 'MFL for all' in England: A historical perspective. *The Language Learning Journal*, 46(1), 71–85. https://doi.org/10.1080/09571736.2017.1382058

Eurostat (2023). *Number of foreign languages known.* https://ec.europa.eu/eurostat/databrowser/view/edat_aes_l21/default/bar?lang=en

FFTDatalab (2022). *Key stage 4 2022: The national picture.* https://ffteducationdatalab.org.uk/2022/10/key-stage-4-2022-the-national-picture/

Fink, S. (2002). *Crisis management: Planning for the inevitable* (Rev. ed.). New York: IUniverse.

Fisher, L. (2011). The impact of Specialist School status: The views of Specialist Language Colleges and other schools. *Educational Review* 63(3), 261–273. https://doi.org/10.1080/00131911.2011.553949.

Gibb, N. (2019). *New centre for excellence to boost modern foreign language skills.* www.gov.uk/government/news/new-centre-for-excellence-to-boost-modern-foreign-language-skills

Gibb, N. (2021). *The importance of a knowledge-rich curriculum.* www.gov.uk/government/speeches/the-importance-of-a-knowledge-rich-curriculum

Gibb, N. (2022). *Millions invested in language lessons.* www.gov.uk/government/news/millions-invested-in-language-lessons

Gough, V. (2021). *What do year 9 pupils think about learning languages?* www.britishcouncil.org/voices-magazine/what-do-year-9-pupils-think-about-learning-languages

Gove, M. (2013). *Michael Gove MP: Why traditional education is a work of social justice – one that I'm striving to deliver.* https://conservativehome.com/2013/09/08/michael-gove-mp-2/

Group of Eight (2007), *Languages in crisis: A rescue plan for Australia.* www.lcnau.org/resources/key-reports

Gunter, H., & Courtney, S. (2023). Policy mortality and UK government education policy for schools in England. *British Journal of Educational Studies*, 71(4), 353–371. https://doi.org/10.1080/00071005.2023.2193066

Hagger-Vaughan, L. (2016). Towards 'languages for all' in England: The state of the debate. *The Language Learning Journal*, 44(3), 358–375. https://doi.org/10.1080/09571736.2016.1199047

Hagger-Vaughan, L. (2018). *How schools in England understand and enact education policy: The case of modern languages at key stage 4* [Unpublished EdD thesis]. University of Nottingham.

Hagger-Vaughan, L. (2020). Is the English Baccalaureate (EBacc) helping participation in language learning in secondary schools in England? *The Language Learning Journal*, online only. https://doi.org/10.1080/09571736.2020.1752292

Hallahan, G. (2021). Why the government's EBacc targets will be missed. *TES.* www.tes.com/magazine/analysis/secondary/english-baccalaureate-gcse-why-long-standing-mfl-issues-mean-ebacc-targets-will-be-missed

Haseldine, L. (2023). The crisis in language teaching. *Spectator.* www.spectator.co.uk/article/the-crisis-in-language-teaching/

Hay, C. (1999). Crisis and the structural transformation of the state: Interrogating the process of change. *British Journal of Politics & International Relations*, 1(3), 317–344. https://doi.org/10.1111/1467-856X.00018

HESA (2023). *What do HE students study?* www.hesa.ac.uk/data-and-analysis/students/what-study

JCQ (2023). *GCSE other modern foreign languages entries summer 2019, 2022 and 2023.* www.jcq.org.uk/wp-content/uploads/2023/08/GCSE-Other-MFL-Entries-Summer-2023.pdf

Jenkins, S. (2017). Ignore the panic. There's little point learning languages at school. *The Guardian.* www.theguardian.com/commentisfree/2017/aug/25/languages-exams-test-league-tables-schools-fall-pupils

Kelly, M. (2019). *Is the UK in a language crisis?* London: British Council. www.britishcouncil.org/voices-magazine/uk-language-learning-crisis

Kubota, R. (2013). 'Language is only a tool': Japanese expatriates working in China and implications for language teaching. *Multilingual Education*, 3(1), 1. https://doi.org/10.1186/2191-5059-3-4

Lanvers, U. (2011). Language education policy in England. Is English the elephant in the room? *Apples-Journal of Applied Language Studies*, 5(3), 63–78.

Lanvers, U. (2017). Contradictory "Others" and the "Habitus" of languages: Surveying the L2 motivation landscape in the United Kingdom. *The Modern Language Journal*, 101(3), 517–532. https://doi.org/10.1111/modl.12410

Lanvers, U., & Coleman, J. A. (2017). The UK language learning crisis in the public media: A critical analysis. *The Language Learning Journal*, 45(1), 3–25. https://doi.org/10.1080/09571736.2013.830639

Lanvers, U., Doughty, H., & Thompson, A. S. (2018). Brexit as linguistic symptom of Britain retreating into its shell? Brexit-induced politicization of language learning. *The Modern Language Journal*, 102(4), 775–796. https://doi.org/10.1111/modl.12515

Lanvers, U., & Graham, S. (2022). Can we design language education policy and curricula for a motivated learner? Self-determination theory and the UK language crisis. *The Language Learning Journal*, 50(2), 223–237. https://doi.org/10.1080/09571736.2022.2046353

Lanvers, U., Thompson, A. S., & East, M. (2021). Introduction: Is language learning in anglophone countries in crisis? In U. Lanvers, A. S. Thompson, & M. East (Eds.), *Language learning in Anglophone countries* (pp. 1–15). Palgrave Macmillan.

Levine, G. S. (2011). Stability, crisis, and other reasons for optimism. *Arts and Humanities in Higher Education*, 10(2), 131–140. https://doi.org/10.1177/1474022211401861

Long, R. (2016). *English Baccalaureate: Briefing paper No. 06045*. London: House of Commons Library. https://dera.ioe.ac.uk/25366/2/SN06045_Redacted.pdf

Macaro, E. (2008). The decline in language learning in England: Getting the facts right and getting real. *The Language Learning Journal*, 36(10), 101–8.

Maguire, K. (2012). Clegg talks double Dutch. *New Statesman*, 141(5129), 17.

Marsden, E., Hawkes, R., Earnshaw, L., & Hobson, V. (2023). *NCELP final report*. https://eprints.whiterose. ac.uk/200637/1/NCELP_Final_Report_9_April_2023.pdf

McGroarty, M. (2006). Editor's introduction: Lingua Franca languages. *Annual Review of Applied Linguistics*, 26, vii–xi. https://doi.org/10.1017/S0267190506000018

Milton, J., & Meara, P. (1998). Are the British really bad at learning foreign languages? *The Language Learning Journal*, 18(1), 68–76. https://doi.org/10.1080/09571739885200291

NAHT (2017). *Limited choices: The NAHT secondary survey 2017*. www.naht.org.uk/Portals/0/PDF's/ Secondary%20survey%20report%20-%20Limited%20Choices.pdf?ver=2021-05-20-090106-430

Netz, N., & Finger, C. (2016). New horizontal inequalities in German higher education? Social selectivity of studying abroad between 1991 and 2012. *Sociology of Education*, 89(2), 79–98. https://doi. org/10.1177/0038040715627196

Nicoletti, R., & Culligan, K. (2022). *The Mandarin excellence programme: Evaluation of the first five years*. https://ci.ioe.ac.uk/wp-content/uploads/2022/05/MEP-Independent-Evaluation-Report-2016–2021.pdf

Ofsted (2023). *School inspection handbook*. www.gov.uk/government/publications/school-inspection-handbook-eif/school-inspection-handbook-for-september-2023

ONS (2022). *Language, England and Wales: Census 2021*. www.ons.gov.uk/peoplepopulationandcommunity/ culturalidentity/language/bulletins/languageenglandandwales/census2021

Panford, L. (2021). Race and racism in secondary modern foreign languages. *ReflectED: St Mary's Journal of Education*, 8(1), 1–12.

Parrish, A. (2023). Feminisation, masculinisation and the other: Re-evaluating the language learning decline in England. *The Language Learning Journal*, 51(1), 94–111. https://doi.org/10.1080/09571736.2021 .1989016

Parrish, A. (2024). Policy tug of war: EBacc, progress 8 and modern foreign languages in England. *Journal of Education Policy*, 39(5), 718–735. https://doi.org/10.1080/02680939.2024.2328625

Parrish, A., & Lanvers, U. (2019). Student motivation, school policy choices and modern language study in England. *The Language Learning Journal*, 47(3), 281–298. https://doi.org/10.1080/09571736.2018 .1508305

Pring, R. (2013). Another reform of qualifications-but qualifying for what? *The Political Quarterly*, 84(1), 139–143. https://doi.org/10.1111/j.1467-923X.2013.02429.x

Russell Group (2011). *Informed choices: A Russell Group guide to making decisions about post-16 education*. www.rsb.org.uk/images/Russell%20Group%20-%20Informed%20Choices.pdf

Saunders, K. (1998). Modern languages in crisis? *The Language Learning Journal*, 18(1), 63–67. https://doi. org/10.1080/09571739885200281

Scally, J., Parrish, A., & Montgomery, A. (2021). Intercultural competence and languages: Inextricably linked or linked inexplicably? *Compare*, 52(3), 492–510. https://doi.org/10.1080/03057925.2020.1851000

Sharma, B. K. (2018). Non-English lingua franca? Mobility, market and ideologies of the Chinese language in Nepal. *Global Chinese*, 4(1), 63–88. https://doi.org/10.1515/glochi-2018-0004

Skutnabb-Kangas, T. (2000). *Linguistic genocide in education – or worldwide diversity and human rights?* L. Erlbaum Associates.

Taylor, F. (2013). *Self and identity in adolescent foreign language learning*. Bristol: Multilingual Matters.

The Observer (2013). Michael Gove's reform agenda: Some good school work, but must do better. *The Observer*. www.theguardian.com/commentisfree/2013/feb/10/michael-gove-education-reforms-wrong

Thomson, D. (2019). Will anything ever be done about grading in modern foreign languages GCSEs? *Education DataLab*. https://ffteducationdatalab.org.uk/2019/09/will-anything-ever-be-done-about-grading-in-modern-foreignlanguages-gcses/.

Thomson, D. (2023). Making changes to the EBacc average point score measure: Some options. *Education DataLab*. https://ffteducationdatalab.org.uk/2023/11/making-changes-to-the-ebacc-average-point-score-measure-some-options/

Truss, E. (2014). *Education minister Elizabeth Truss speaks about increasing the number of children studying Mandarin*. www.gov.uk/government/speeches/elizabeth-truss-on-increasing-the-number-of-pupilsstudying-mandarin

Vasagar, J. (2010). Michael Gove: The teacher of the future. *The Guardian*. www.theguardian.com/education/2010/nov/02/teaching-awards-michael-gove#:~:text=%22My%20hunch%20is%20that%20there,more%20classical%2C%22%20Gove%20says.

Watkins, C. (2020). 2020 Duolingo language report: United Kingdom. *Duolingo*. https://blog.duolingo.com/uk-language-report-2020/

Whittaker, F. (2023). Just half of secondary teacher recruitment target met. *Schools Week*. https://schoolsweek.co.uk/just-half-of-secondary-teacher-recruitment-target-met/#:~:text=Overall%2C%20the%20total%20target%20for,missed%20by%2038%20per%20cent.&text=In%20total%20there%20were%2026%2C955,and%2040%2C377%20in%202020%2D21.

Wincott, D., Davies, G., & Wager, A. (2021). Crisis, what crisis? Conceptualizing crisis, UK pluri-constitutionalism and Brexit politics. *Regional Studies*, 55(9), 1528–1537. https://doi.org/10.1080/00343404.2020.1805423

Xhemaili, M. (2022). The importance of the English language in public diplomacy and international relations. *Journal of Liberty and International Affairs (Bitola)*, 8(1), 322–339. https://doi.org/10.47305/JLIA2281322x

German reference

Quetz, J. (2010). Toward a foreign language monoculture? Foreign languages in German schools [Auf dem Weg zur fremdsprachlichenMonokultur? Fremdsprachen an den Schulender Bundesrepublik Deutschland]. *Sociolinguistica*, 24, 170–186.

15

MULTILINGUALISM IN MINORITY SCHOOLS

New realities

Sabina Zorčič and Lara Sorgo

1. Introduction

Although referenced to the Slovene–Italian context, any ethnically mixed area could be perceived as a "natural laboratory" (Novak-Lukanovič 2011: 80), with numerous opportunities for observing the coexistence of different communities and cultures and building multicultural awareness and tolerance (Zudič Antonič 2012). Minority schools in particular can be seen as a true laboratory for the schools of the future, which are to be open to quality development of the educational process (Čok 2009: 21).

Recently, the various forms of minority education have been used by the wider community, not only by minorities and immigrants (and their descendants). For instance, in some minority schools for the Hungarian national community in Slovenia, we can find that already 30% of the students are from Hungary and migrate to school daily across the border (Kovács 2023), and in schools for the Italian community in Slovenia, there are also students from the majority population and immigrants from other countries (discussed in this chapter). Slovenian schools in Austria, which are intended for the Slovenian ethnic community, also enrol Slovenian immigrants and immigrants from other Slavic countries, as well as pupils from Slovenia (also discussed in this chapter). The current situation is a natural consequence of migration and globalisation, that is, the free movement of people, goods, and services. However, parents and their children are only using the available schooling alternatives, which are all in line with Europe's long standing inclusive and non-discriminatory policies. The motives for enrolment of speakers of majority languages in minority education programmes vary, ranging from the search for one's own roots to seizing the opportunity to increase one's cultural capital – with a view to possibly increasing economic capital through additional (linguistic) competences. Certainly, their presence in minority schools introduces a new dynamic that has both positive and negative consequences. The most obvious and far-reaching implications of the new realities in the minority schools are those affecting linguistic competence and multicultural awareness. Still, the topic of cross-border education and of the changing circumstances in minority schools following the enrolment of other nationalities in minority school programmes is relatively new, as this phenomenon has only become widespread in the last (in the Slovene context, two) decades (e.g., Grgič 2019; Kovács 2023, for cross-border education see also the European School Education Platform 2019). Of course, each geographical and temporal context must be considered separately.

DOI: 10.4324/9781003439493-19

Social dynamics in minority schools (co-)determine the success of language, culture, and knowledge transfer. A social group is defined as two or more people who interact with each other, share similar characteristics, and have a collective sense of community (Reicher 1982). Small groups in school classrooms are a common phenomenon, but in minority schools they are often defined by the means of communication, which leads us to the first problem. Language, in any of its geographical and social variations, can be a unifying or constraining element in the formation of class groups and class cohesion. The second problem concerns the heterogeneity of the students regarding their competence in the language of instruction. Since some students master the language of instruction as native speakers and others are still learning it (as a foreign language on different stages), these classes are very demanding from a didactic standpoint, since the need to adapt lessons to the speakers' level arises. Consequently, the students' linguistic competence in the minority language can be affected, both among members of linguistic minorities and members of linguistic majorities.

The chapter presents the data from our research exploring the Alps–Adria region, particularly two ethnically mixed areas, and focusing on: (1) Slovene minority secondary schools in Austria and (2) Italian minority schools from the coastal region of Slovene Istria in Slovenia.

What are the new realities in the presented minority schools, and what are their implications? Based on the presented data we will outline the positive and negative implications of such trends and also propose directions for further research which will allow for a deeper understanding of the phenomenon that is becoming increasingly widespread in minority education. In particular, the findings will benefit researchers in the field of educational and sociolinguistic sciences and serve as baselines for decision-makers designing language policy measures in (minority/language) education.

2. Case study 1: Slovene minority schools in Austria

2.1 Legal, historical, and social foundations for minority schools and cross-border education

In a defined area of Southern Carinthia, Austria bordering Slovenia, Slovene is protected as a minority language of the indigenous ethnic group. A complete overview of the Slovene language in education in Austria is described elsewhere (see, e.g., Doleschal 2023). In this section, we look at data collected by means of survey, semi-structured interviews, and focus groups in three different studies (Zorčič 2020a; Zorčič and Novak Lukanović 2023) carried out at the only three Slovene minority schools in Austria at the upper secondary level (age 15–19) where the language of instruction is Slovene. There are several reasons for not including also the pupils of lower age, but the main reason is that at this stage, the trend of cross-border schooling is the most noticeable. In all three schools, students from Slovenia have become an indispensable part of the Slovene minority classes in Austria, although the proportion varies depending on the school: the smallest number of students attends the Slovene Grammar School, a much higher number attends the Bilingual Commercial College, and the largest number is enrolled at the College for Commercial Vocations in St. Peter (cf. Zorčič 2020a, 2020b; Zorčič and Novak Lukanović 2023). The Slovene Grammar School (from K-5 to K-12) is historically the most important school for the Slovene minority in Austria. It was founded in 1957, on the basis of Article 7 of the Austrian State Treaty of 1955, to provide secondary education for young Slovenes, and it is the only school where the language of instruction is exclusively Slovene. The Bilingual Commercial College (from K-9 to K-13) in Klagenfurt was founded in 1990 as an additional secondary education option for the Slovene minority.

There, Slovene and German are equivalent languages of instruction and are exchanged monthly. The same language regime is also applied at the College for Commercial Vocations in St. Peter (from K-9 to K-13), a private Catholic school for gastronomic and commercial professions, which is almost 125 years old. The impact of students from Slovenia on Slovene minority schools in Austria is visible in two direct ways: (1) places are filled that would otherwise have remained unfilled or filled by students with a poorer knowledge of Slovene, and (2) with their presence, the Slovene language in all its variations is also much more present in the schools. In particular, it makes (colloquial) Slovene, and not the Slovene Carinthian dialect of the area, much more present (see also Lengar Verovnik 2023), as research shows that "the majority (86%) of students choose one of the non-Carinthian dialects of Slovene for communication with students from Slovenia, most often the standard colloquial language" (Zorčič 2020a: 145). As the choice of Slovene as a means of communication becomes more frequent, the students from Austria experience an increase in their communicative competence in Slovene, as the cause–effect relationship between language use and (active) language competence (i.e., speaking and writing) is well established and is also reflected in the self-assessment of their competence in this language (Zorčič 2020a).

Although originally founded to meet the needs of the Slovene ethnic community in Austria, today these schools could not survive with students from the minority base alone and therefore operate under the motto: "a school with a (supra-)regional focus" (see, for example, their online presentation (SLOGAT)). This is especially true for the public minority schools – the Bilingual Commercial College and the Slovene Grammar School – while the College for Commercial Vocations in St. Peter has always had a significant enrolment of students from Slovenia due to the fact that it is a private institution, which is located closer to the Slovene border.

The historical shifts that allowed cross-border education to flourish were gradual, but the main turning point was 1989 (the fall of the Berlin Wall) and the events that followed. In 1995, Austria became a member of the EU. Slovenia became a member nine years later, opening the way for closer links between border regions, towns, and people, and Slovene with about 2.5 million speakers (SURS 2015) became an official language of the EU. The possibility of students from Slovenia enrolling at these schools also depends on the vacancies in the schools and dormitories. In schools with Slovene or both Slovene and German as the language of instruction, students can be admitted as full-time students because they have mastered (one) language of instruction.

The attitude towards minority schools has always been socially and politically linked to the attitude towards the Slovene minority in Austria, which has certainly been more open and positive in recent times than it was in the last century. At the same time, the regional policy is much more economically oriented and promotes economic and social development. The minority schools (especially the two in Klagenfurt) have made good use of the niche that has emerged and have taken educational initiatives: they have become regional (language) schools that cover the social and economic needs of the Alps–Adria region. Enrolment of foreign nationals (especially from Slovenia) is on the rise at all the schools in question, and the number of students who enrolled because of their families moving to Austria is also rising. Table 15.1 shows the number of students from Slovenia enrolled in the last five school years, from which it is also clear that the COVID-19 pandemic of 2020–2022 has not had a major impact (at least in relative terms) on enrolment at the two schools in Klagenfurt. The situation is different at the College for Commercial Vocations in St. Peter, where the decline in enrolment was both nominal and relative (Table 15.1). The management of the school attributed this to the fact that the gastronomic industry (partly influenced by the pandemic) was experiencing a downward trend, which they believed was also reflected in the enrolment at other gastronomic schools in the region and beyond (Zorčič and Novak Lukanović 2023). It should also be noted that remote learning during the pandemic had an impact on class cohesion

Table 15.1 The number and share of students with permanent residence in Slovenia enrolled at Slovene minority schools at the upper secondary level in the last five school years

	Number of students from Slovenia (share) in 2018/19	Number of students from Slovenia (share) in 2019/20	Number of students from Slovenia (share) in 2020/21	Number of students from Slovenia (share) in 2021/22	Number of students from Slovenia (share) in 2022/23
Slovene Grammar School (upper level from K-9 to K-12)	26 (11.98%)	31 (14.42%)	31 (13.90%)	30 (14.15%)	26 (13.07%)
Bilingual Commercial College	121 (49%)	117 (50%)	110 (50%)	108 (51%)	107 (50%)
College for Commercial Vocations in St. Peter	110 (79.71%)	107 (74.31%)	106 (76.26%)	94 (67.63%)	76 (64.96%)
Total	257	255	247	232	209

Source: Zorčič and Novak Lukanović 2023: 96.

and the language skills of monolingual students, especially students from Slovenia whose German language input was lacking (Zorčič 2020b).

We should keep in mind that the proportion of students from the Slovene minority in Austria is constantly decreasing, owing to the lower birth rate and the migration of Carinthian Slovenes to larger cities that lead to a decline in the number of minority members, while immigration from Slovenia is increasing (e.g., OGM 2022). The fact is that the group of students who immigrate to Austria together with their parents is quite different from the group of students who live in Slovenia and migrate across the border daily or weekly. For the latter, attending a school in Austria is a personal (or family) decision, and therefore – also according to school management – there is a sense of "a certain relaxedness" (Zorčič and Novak Lukanović 2023), whereas those who have immigrated to Austria tend to be a group with less economic capital and fewer choices (similarly, Zorčič 2020a).

Here, we should also mention the increasing number of students from strictly German speaking families enrolled at these schools; their share at the secondary level is about 10% (Zorčič 2020a, 2020b). The increased enrolment of children with no prior knowledge of Slovene in bilingual classes is no longer a new phenomenon (cf. Domej 1999; Ogris 1995, 2014; Kern 2009) and is recorded to a greater extent at the primary level (from K-1 to K-4, Ger. *Volksschule*). Yearly assessments by primary bilingual teachers revealed that of the 643 children enrolled in bilingual classes on the primary level in the 2015/16 school year, only 15% showed good linguistic competence in Slovene; 22% had sufficient linguistic competence, while 62% had no linguistic competence in Slovene (Sandrieser et al. 2016: 65). For this reason, some researchers are convinced that "bilingual schools have more and more assumed the function of dual language (immersion) schools or enrichment programmes for children belonging to the linguistic majority" (Doleschal 2011: 164). Ogris (2014: 98) arrived at a similar conclusion, noting that German-speaking parents' motivation for enrolling their children in bilingual classes is "linguistic education and has nothing to do with the minority." As we will see later, a similar trend can be observed in Italian primary schools in Slovenia.

Multilingualism in minority schools

2.2 Motives

Students from Slovenia have various motives for enrolling at Slovene minority schools in Austrian Carinthia. Roughly speaking, they can be divided into two groups. In the first, there are students who have a rather elaborate idea of what their goals and interests are in the (long- or short-term) future, that is, students who have a rather elaborate identity capital (e.g., Côté and Levine 2016). The latter is the result of their personal characteristics, which are manifested in their individual search for different life alternatives and/or the result of strong family involvement in this identity constitution. These students choose Slovene minority schools in Austria because, among other reasons, there is better infrastructure in Klagenfurt for extracurricular intensive football coaching or studying music or because going to Austria is a kind of preparatory act for possible future studies abroad (Zorčič and Novak Lukanović 2023). For many students, the decision is based on prior recommendations from friends, and in some cases, all the children from one family attend school abroad. In all these cases, the influence of parents is usually very strong: they provide strong support or help their children in the decision for schooling abroad, while at the same time making it financially possible to do so. The second group of students are those whose decision to go to school in Austria was more influenced by circumstances. These are the children of parents working in Austria, who are sometimes in the process of moving or have already moved to Austria. For these students, the decision to go to a school where lessons are (also) taught in Slovene is understandable, because of the desire to reduce the language barrier and to integrate more easily into their new environment (e.g. Zorčič 2020a; Zorčič and Novak Lukanović 2023).

The students who return to Slovenia weekly and still have strong contacts and ties with friends and family in Slovenia are also exposed to constant comparisons between the Austrian and Slovene school systems, to which they also react critically. Owing to the different approaches and *modus operandi* in all three schools in question, the students' reactions are also different, although most of them are convinced that education in Austria is easier for them than it would be in Slovenia because there is less testing for grades. The schools are more student friendly, so they have more time to devote to themselves: to their various hobbies and self-reflection (Zorčič and Novak Lukanović 2023).

2.3 Exploring the implications on cross-border students in minority schools

2.3.1 Psychological: well-being and neuroticism

Students are convinced that studying abroad is not for everyone. One has to be an independent person, open to new things and ready to deal with new situations in life, which in turn makes one more independent and ready to face life. The students acknowledge that the bilingual environment and the possibility of living in a dormitory is a great help. They point out that it is easier because the (school) environment is very Slovene and they feel less immediate stress from not knowing the national language very well. However, they point out that sometimes the experience can be very tiring, and the constant adjustment to new circumstances can also be stressful. This feeling is especially strong at the beginning of school, but then, as they say, "you get used to it" (Zorčič and Novak Lukanović 2023). High levels of neuroticism found in previous research and reported in monolingual students of the same age and in the same circumstances (Zorčič 2019, 2020a) can therefore be interpreted as a habituated feeling or an internalised state of constant stress. Even in the later grades, some students report that the feeling of being a stranger persists. Students also have certain negative experiences when using Slovene and have sometimes been pejoratively labelled as Yugoslavian by the German-speaking majority when using Slovene in public (Zorčič and Novak Lukanović 2023).

2.3.2 Students' language proficiency

Learning foreign languages – and in particular the opportunity to learn German in the context of gaining an education in Austria – was one of the most significant motivations for enrolment as stated by students. One of the main findings among Slovene students seemed to be that most of them would have liked to have had a better knowledge of German at the end of their schooling but (now) realise that even though they are studying in Austria, a significant additional commitment is needed to master the language (Zorčič and Novak Lukanović 2023). This is especially true for the Grammar School, as Slovene is the only language of instruction, and the students really have to become active and find new sources of communication, preferably outside the school and the dormitory, as the possibility and temptation to use Slovene is too great in the context of minority institutions.

In the final two years, both vocational schools provide lessons in both languages; Slovene and German are exchanged monthly. However, these rules are not strictly followed (cf. Zorčič 2019, 2020a; Zorčič and Novak Lukanović 2023). It even seems that one could go through schooling (at least until the baccalaureate) with very poor or even no knowledge of German (Zorčič and Novak Lukanović 2023). However, at the College for Commercial Vocations in St. Peter, the compulsory work placement (praxis) in the gastronomic industry is strongly emphasised as a turning point in the knowledge and use of German.

On average, students who attend the grammar school and devote a significant amount of time and self-commitment to learning German rate their knowledge of German the highest. Students at both vocational schools rate their German language skills much lower (Zorčič 2020a; Zorčič and Novak Lukanović 2023); see Table 15.2. After four years of schooling in Austria, students from Slovenia did not feel themselves to be native speakers of German. Although some individuals admitted to speaking the language to some extent, even as well as native speakers: those were individuals who were very integrated into the German speaking environment and were forced to

Table 15.2 Self-assessment of language proficiency in students from Slovenia in minority schools in Austria

	Self-assessed language proficiency in German (10 = excellent). Average +/- SD	*Self-assessed language proficiency in English (10 = excellent). Average +/- SD*	*Self-assessed language proficiency in Slovene (10 = excellent). Average +/- SD*
Slovene Grammar School (upper level from K-9 to K-12)	7.8438 +/–0.865	9.3438 +/–0.544	9.8750 +/–0.331
Bilingual Commercial College	6.5192 +/–1.877	8.4231 +/–1.007	9.6346 +/–0.677
College for Commercial Vocations in St. Peter	6.1324 +/–1.348	8.5147 +/–1.016	9.6618 +/–0.594
	ANOVA: 3.419 ($p = 0.044$, $N = 38$)	ANOVA: 2.553 ($p = 0.092$, $N = 38$)	ANOVA: 0.444 ($p = 0.645$, $N = 38$)

Source: Composed of data in Zorčič and Novak Lukanović 2023: 101–106.

use the language to the fullest extent (Zorčič and Novak Lukanović 2023). Still, there is an obvious discrepancy between how the students imagined learning German in Austria when they enrolled at school and the results after four years. The data show that a lot of commitment was required for quality and quantity language input in the German language.

The students from Slovenia are much more confident about their English than their German peers (Table 15.2), although most of them are not sure that their English proficiency is equal to the proficiency they attribute to native speakers; they think of it more as very good working proficiency (Zorčič and Novak Lukanović 2023). Students are fully aware of their immersion in the English language, and they also analyse the difference in their English knowledge compared to their Austrian classmates (earlier language introduction, different curricula, non-dubbed video content on television, etc.) (Ibid.). Although there was also one reported case of communication in English between students from Slovenia and Austria (Zorčič 2019), that is non-standard practice.

Regarding their first language, Slovene, the students are aware of the fact that Slovene as a language of instruction is different in Austria than it is in Slovenia. According to the students, there is "a lot of literal translation and incorrect terminology," and the level of the language is "lower than . . . in school in Slovenia" (Zorčič and Lukanović 2023: 103). Some students are quite lenient on this issue, while others are quite critical, as they feel that no one is progressing because of the language situation in the classroom (Slovene adapted for Austrians, German adapted for Slovenes), or, as one student pointed out in one of the studies: "but now we are learning Slovene from someone whose Slovene is probably worse than mine, so sometimes I wonder a little bit how much sense it makes" (Zorčič and Novak Lukanović 2023: 103). Teaching materials in Slovene also present a problem, as there are not many textbooks published in Slovene (Zorčič 2019, 2020b; Zorčič and Novak Lukanović 2023).

2.3.3 Multicultural and European awareness

Because of their cross-border schooling experience, these students have a certain advantage over their peers when it comes to visualising their future path. Individuals who have not had a positive experience of schooling in their current environment state that they will not continue their education in Austria. Some of them will not even continue it in another German-speaking country, as after all their time in Austria, many still do not feel confident about their knowledge of German, and some have even developed a dislike for the German language. There are even a few who want to return to Slovenia and continue their educational path in a more Slovene environment (Zorčič and Novak Lukanović 2023). However, most would like to benefit from the (linguistic) knowledge and cultural experience they have gained during their studies in Austria and would like to study abroad.

Given that their schooling in the neighbouring country is also largely possible because of Slovenia's membership in the European Union, Europeanisation and the students' sense of belonging or their otherwise expressed identity are topics of interest also for the students (see Zorčič and Novak Lukanović 2023). The discussion about what being European even means, with the generations who grew up when Slovenia was already part of the EU, showed that the students take most of the privileges of EU membership for granted. As expected, the students who were already discovering the benefits of living without the borders expressed very high values of belonging to Europe, but many other identities also came to the fore, since the group of students from Slovenia is not entirely homogeneous in terms of their first language or first ethnic self-definition. Beside Slovene citizenship, the group was united on two linguistic issues: on the one hand, their knowledge of the Slovene standard language and, on the other, their lack of knowing the local Slovene Carinthian dialect (and consequently not being part of the Slovene minority community in Austria).

2.4 Social consequences: new realities in Slovene minority schools in Austria

Students from Slovenia come to Austria not only with better proficiency in Slovene but also from a higher socio-economic background and, as far as their academic career is concerned, from a slightly different school culture and, above all, from schools where the only language of instruction had the status of national language. Collected data in the presented research (Zorčič 2020a, 2020b; Zorčič and Novak Lukanović 2023) were in line with this difference and confirmed the existence of a new dynamic that these students bring with them to the Slovene minority schools in Austria. This is not only observed by researchers (Kolb 2018; Vavti 2012; Zorčič 2020a, 2020b; Zorčič and Novak Lukanović 2023); school management has been dealing with this issue since the very beginning of the admission and enrolment of Slovene students at schools in Austria.

Research confirms (Kolb 2018; Zorčič 2019, 2020a, 2020b; Zorčič and Novak Lukanović 2023) that groups in classes are usually formed on the basis of the language of communication and previous acquaintances. This means that students from Slovenia are less likely to bond with groups of students from Austria, which is due to at least two reasons: (1) many students from Slovenia come to Austria at later stages of their schooling and enter a (sometimes already quite) pre-grouped school environment (especially in the grammar school, where certain friendships are already made at the lower level, and groups are also formed on the basis of a common living environment, which presupposes the use of a shared Carinthian dialect) and (2) knowledge of German, especially the locally spoken version, is very low among students from Slovenia, which makes genuine and spontaneous communication between adolescents difficult.

School management plays a particularly important role in classroom dynamics when forming the classes, as class cohesion is largely determined by the size of the class and the number of students from Slovenia it contains. Larger classes are always linguistically differentiated into Slovene and German groups, while smaller classes tend to have more coherence (and consequently more communication in both languages). Another special case is the almost "all-Slovene sections" in which, owing to the large number of Slovenes, the majority language, German, is practically unheard. Once this situation is established, it will persist for the rest of schooling without reforming the classes. Class formation must therefore be given great attention if schools are to give all students the best possible chance of communicating in as linguistically diverse a manner as possible. Although the other two groups of students from Austria, the Slovene minority and the German speakers, almost always speak German to each other, it is obvious that there is very little communication in German at school with the students from Slovenia: students from the Slovene minority use Slovene, and so do the students from German-speaking families, and even teachers adapt and use more Slovene (Zorčič 2020a; Zorčič and Novak Lukanović 2023).

Therefore, if we look at the consequences of the enrolment of students from Slovenia at minority schools in Austria from a different perspective, that is, not from the point of view of students from Slovenia, but from the point of view of the Slovene minority, it is necessary to stress the good aspects of this practice, which has become widespread since Slovenia's accession to the European Union. The presence of students from Slovenia in these schools has led to a much greater presence of the Slovene language. In this way, students from the Slovene minority, as well as monolingual students from German families, are exposed to a version of the Slovene language that they rarely hear otherwise, since in Carinthia, they are mostly exposed to the dialect (especially at home but also in schools) and in more formal speaking positions to the supra-regional Carinthian version of Slovene (also in local media, the mainstream Slovene media are usually not in use). The Slovene colloquial language that their classmates from Slovenia bring with them, and which they

Multilingualism in minority schools

undoubtedly use when communicating with their Austrian classmates, thus brings new speaking experiences to the speakers of Slovene in Austrian Carinthia and, as a consequence, better speaking competence in the social variety of Slovene, which is very important for the expansion of their linguistic repertoire. The latter enables better linguistic proficiency and greater confidence in feeling better able to communicate in Slovene.

3. Case study 2: Italian minority schools in Slovenia

3.1 The educational model

The ethnically mixed area of Slovene Istria, the coastal border region between Italy and Croatia, is a heterogeneous territory, a meeting point for different cultures and languages where individuals from different ethnic groups coexist. Slovene Istria has historically been home to the Italian national community, which is one of the two constitutionally recognised autochthonous minorities in Slovenia. The Constitution of the Republic of Slovenia (Constitution of RS 1991, art. 11; art. 64), various laws (especially the Act Regulating Special Rights of Members of the Italian and Hungarian Ethnic Communities in the Field of Education, 2001), and the national language policy provide the conditions for the use of the minority language – Italian – which in Slovene Istria is an official language alongside Slovene. This means that the Italian national community is guaranteed equal status, which is particularly important for maintaining its vitality. Thus, the model of education is designed to meet the specific needs of the environment, take into account the cultural and educational traditions of the ethnic group, and reflect the political status of the minority population (Novak-Lukanovič et al. 2011: 350; also Zorman 2021).

Schools with Italian as the language of instruction play a key role for both the Italian minority and the majority population, as they attach great importance to language learning and to the development of multilingualism and multiculturalism. As Zudič Antonič (2009: 79–80) points out, Italian minority schooling has a broader role, which is expressed not only in the implementation of the learning process but also in the achievement of numerous educational objectives. The school creates conditions for the preservation of cultural heritage in the ethnically mixed area, while strongly emphasising the development of intercultural communication and positive attitudes towards diversity.

In the ethnically mixed area of Slovene Istria, there are three primary schools with Italian as the language of instruction (Pier Paolo Vergerio il Vecchio in Koper, Dante Alighieri in Izola, and Vincenzo e Diego de Castro in Piran), two general secondary education schools (the Gian Rinaldo Carli Grammar School in Koper and the Antonio Sema Grammar School in Portorož), and one upper secondary vocational school (Pietro Coppo in Izola) (Zudič Antonič and Zorman 2023). Their specific task in this context is to preserve and promote the importance of the historical presence of the language, culture, and identity of the Italian national community. The curriculum and syllabus of schools with Italian as the language of instruction contain, in addition to the objectives laid down by educational regulations, specific socialisation objectives aimed at familiarisation with the culture and history of the ethnic community present in the local environment, as well as at transmitting different values and shaping students' attitudes towards the linguistic and cultural diversity in their environment (Nečak Lük 2009: 115). Schools are attended by children of the Italian national community but are also open to other students, regardless of their ethnicity and nationality, who perceive contact with Italian culture and language as a positive value (Novak Lukanovič et al. 2011: 351). For the latter group, in particular, the motivation to learn Italian in the school context and use it outside of school or in everyday communication is very important.

251

As contemporary societies are becoming increasingly plural, multi-ethnic, and characterised by superdiversity (Vertovec 2007, 2023; Crul 2016), even in the classes of the schools with Italian as the language of instruction there is an increasing presence of students of different nationalities, children of immigrants from the Republics of the former Yugoslavia, or students from abroad, especially from Eastern European countries (Sorgo et al. 2022).

In this section, we present some of the insights drawn from the three studies conducted in 2019 (Sorgo et al. 2022), 2020 (Sorgo 2023), and 2023 at Italian minority primary schools in Slovene Istria. The perspectives of students (12–15 years old), their parents, and teachers were investigated using questionnaires and semi-structured interviews.

3.2 The importance of (minority) language knowledge

The research in 2019 (Sorgo et al. 2022) was conducted by using a questionnaire in Italian, because the Italian language is the language of instruction at school. Students were asked to assess their Italian language skills. They reported the highest ratings in understanding: 62.5% have very good, 27.5% good, and 10% neither good nor poor understanding of Italian. No student chose the answer poor or very poor. In speaking, 41% of the students chose very good and 42.3% good. The ratings were relatively low in writing, which also presents the highest coefficient of variability, since 28.2% of students assessed their writing in Italian as very good, 34.6% as good, 30.8% as neither good nor poor, and 6.4% as poor. The most incomplete data were obtained for reading. Six students did not answer the question; 44.2% of those who answered assessed their reading in Italian as very good, 28.6% as good, 24.7% as neither good nor poor, and 2.6% as poor. These results are aggregated in Table 15.3: the answers indicate that students assess their linguistic competence the highest in understanding ($\bar{x} = 4.52$) and the lowest in writing ($\bar{x} = 3.85$).

Although Slovene language has been studied since the beginning of primary school by the students involved in the research, and for many it is also the first language spoken in the family, students rated their knowledge of Slovene language as rather low in all skills. On average, understanding (51.8% very good, 25.3% good) was ranked the highest, while writing claimed the lowest scores. In fact, only 23.5% of students rated their writing skills in Slovene as very good and 33.3% as good, while 22.2% of students assessed their writing as neither good nor poor, 19.8% as poor, and 1.2% as very poor (Sorgo et al. 2022).

In the context of Italian minority primary schools, the explanation of such results is most likely to be found in the educational system itself. Students are more exposed to the Italian language since the whole educational process takes place in Italian, and they also speak Italian with their classmates. As they confirmed, communication with their classmates outside school was also mainly in Italian (Sorgo et al. 2022).

Table 15.3 Self-assessment of Italian language skills

	Very bad	Bad	Neither good nor bad	Good	Very good	Arithmet. mean	SD
Understanding	0%	0%	10%	27.5%	62.5%	4.52	.675
Speaking	0%	3.8%	12.8%	42.3%	41%	4.21	.812
Reading	0%	2.6%	24.7%	28.6%	44.2%	4.14	.884
Writing	0%	6.4%	30.8%	34.6%	28.2%	3.85	.913

Source: Sorgo et al. 2022: 80.

Multilingualism in minority schools

In the research conducted in 2023 through interviews with students, we asked them to indicate how they felt when speaking or writing the two languages – Italian and Slovene – in various informal or formal situations, and again most of them said they felt less comfortable using Slovene, especially when they had to produce a written text such as an essay. One of the reasons for the different ratings lies in how critical they are of their language knowledge. In fact, a subjective assessment of language skills does not always reflect actual knowledge, as students – when self-assessing – had the school curricula and the lessons in mind rather than merely their language knowledge.

However, bearing in mind that for most of them Italian is not their native language, when asked about the importance of knowing the Italian (minority) language and about the educational model, students agreed that it was important to learn the language, because it would enable them to continue their education in Italy. Although the collected data are from primary school and we do not have the data on how many of the students actually continue their secondary education in Italy, we can conclude that they rate the knowledge of Italian they acquire at school as important. Their strong agreement with this fact also offers insight into the effectiveness of the educational model in schools with Italian as the language of instruction, that is, that the model enables the development of language and communicative competence and the transfer of knowledge useful for students' further education. Besides, knowing Italian brings more job opportunities, which is consistent with the economic factors of the language. Knowledge of Italian is therefore important from a practical point of view and is seen as a form of capital. Previous research (Novak-Lukanovič 2006) presented some indicators of the specific role of Italian in Slovenia: economic cooperation with Italy, the presence of the Italian language in the ethnically mixed area, and the usefulness and spread of the language in the world. In line with this, parents considered it important that knowledge of Italian would enable their children to continue their education in Italy and would open up more job opportunities (Sorgo et al. 2022).

During research conducted in 2019, parents were asked to compile a questionnaire with some similar questions as the ones for students. Parents mostly agreed that in the ethnically mixed area, there should be schools with both languages, Italian and Slovene, as the languages of instruction. This result suggests that the respondents were aware of the importance of a multilingual and multicultural environment in which they live and in which Italian language has the same status as Slovene. Therefore, they were aware that the implementation of bilingualism requires that both members of the majority population as well as members of the minority population master (at least to some extent) both languages, Italian and Slovene (Sorgo et al. 2022).

Given that the school system in the ethnically mixed area is adapted and suited to the specific needs of the bilingual context, we also explored whether parents consider the current form of schooling in Slovene Istria suitable and of good quality. Parents were asked to justify why they thought the current model of education was of good quality and suitable or why they thought it was not. Parents who thought that the form of schooling in the Italian minority schools in the ethnically mixed area of Slovene Istria was suitable and of good quality (53.5%) justified their answer by arguing that the level of Slovene and Italian knowledge was suitable and enabled minority children to be educated in their mother tongue. Parents who felt that the current form of schooling was not suitable (23.3%) made other arguments, for example, that students do not have enough knowledge at the end of school, that teachers are not sufficiently prepared and that the school with Italian as the language of instruction is not sufficiently ambitious and does not know how to take advantage of the opportunities offered in the educational process. The data also show that parents were not sufficiently familiar (20.9%) with the educational system in the ethnically mixed area of Slovene Istria (Sorgo et al. 2022).

The Routledge Handbook of Endangered and Minority Languages

Table 15.4 Students' mother tongues

Italian	20.5%
Slovene	27.7%
Italian and Slovene	28.9%
Other	22.9%
Total	100%

Source: Sorgo et al. 2022: 78.

3.3 The classroom as a multicultural and multilingual environment

Schools in Slovenia are today increasingly culturally and linguistically diverse, and the situation in Italian minority schools is no different. This fact is confirmed by our study from 2019 (Sorgo et al. 2022) when students were asked to indicate their mother tongue or L1.

As indicated in Table 15.4, 28.9% of students answered that they had two mother tongues or L1s, Slovene and Italian; 27.7% reported Slovene to be their L1; and 20.5% reported Italian to be their L1. For 22.9% of students, their mother tongue was a different language, such as Macedonian, Albanian, Serbian, Bosnian, Croatian, or Russian (Sorgo et al. 2022).

On account of this increasingly culturally and linguistically heterogeneous situation, teachers have a very demanding job in the classroom, especially when most students starting school do not have sufficient knowledge of the Italian language for a variety of reasons, such as not speaking Italian language at home or not having studied it since first grade. This fact is confirmed by our research conducted in 2020 (Sorgo 2023) when we conducted semi-structured interviews with teachers. Although most teachers agree that the students' language abilities are generally good, it is important to bear in mind that schools are also attended by students who speak Slovene at home with their parents and by students of other nationalities for whom even Slovene is not their mother tongue or L1. According to teachers' experiences, there are fewer and fewer students whose mother tongue is Italian, and in some cases the class is composed only of students of other nationalities (e.g., Albanian, Czech, Macedonian, Russian). For these students, the biggest deficiencies in Italian are caused by them having no interactions in the Italian language outside the school environment, except communication with their schoolmates. In order to meet their needs and facilitate comprehension, teachers reported that they use various methods to help students, but in most cases, they are forced to simplify vocabulary, sometimes to the detriment of students with advanced language skills or those who speak Italian at home, who are unlikely to improve unless they engage with the language on their own. Also, because the classes are multicultural and therefore linguistically diverse, Italian is barely taught at the level of mother tongue or L1, even though this is foreseen in the curriculum of the subject. However, all teachers make themselves fully available to these students and do their best to make sure that they can reach the planned objectives, despite their language knowledge not being at a sufficient level. Regarding the educational model, teachers' opinions are that minority schooling is of great quality, arguing that it not only enables children of the Italian national community to be educated in their own language, but it is also competitive with the majority schools. Better teaching conditions, fewer students in the classroom, consequently more attention for the individual students, and the fact that after mandatory primary schooling, students master at least three languages are some of the arguments in favour of the schools with Italian as the language of instruction in Slovenia (Sorgo 2023).

3.4 The role of English and the students' language awareness

Almost all the students are bilingual (or even trilingual), and at school they study one or two foreign languages. Since they know and use so many different languages daily, they all stated that they mix languages when speaking. Code-mixing and code-switching are natural occurrences, but sometimes they feel embarrassed, especially when talking to parents or relatives, because they feel that this way of communicating is wrong. For students who speak Slovene or another language at home that is not Italian, the transfer from the minority language they learn at school, in this case Italian, and also transfer from global English, is very common.

English, seen as the language of the globalised world, is declared a useful language by almost all students, who also proudly emphasise their English language knowledge. English is also the main language in which students consume digital content (e.g. watching movies or TV series, and listening to music). When asked why they use mainly English in their free time activities, the answers differ, but most of them say that it is a good way to improve their language skills. Besides that, in their opinion English is also useful for global communication, especially when travelling and as a means of communication in lingua franca.

However, as most of the students involved in the research told us, if everyone were to speak English in the future, this would lead to the loss of linguistic diversity, and most of the students do not want to have more hours of English instead of Italian and Slovene. Even though the students who participated in the study were young, between 12 and 14 years old, they were aware of the importance of preserving all the languages of their repertoire, especially their mother tongue or L1, as a sign of respect for their origins but also as the languages of their environment. Language and identity are closely linked, and language is considered one of the most important symbols of an individual, passed on from generation to generation along with culture. Students are aware of the connection between language and identity, which for most of them is also of the local type or subjective, connected to the territory where they live. Above all, solid knowledge of one's own language makes people more self-confident. The latter is also a common trait in mixed marriages, where children are brought up speaking two different languages.

It can be concluded that the students show positive attitudes toward linguistic diversity and that schooling in a minority institution and in an ethnically mixed territory adds value to their education and life experience.

4. Conclusion

The chapter addressed the recent issue of students with different linguistic and ethnic backgrounds attending Slovene-minority schools in Austria and Italian-minority schools in Slovenia. Although the specific task of minority schools is education of the minority, along with preservation and promotion of the importance of the historical presence of the language, culture, and identity of the ethnic communities, the described new reality is a natural consequence of globalisation, migration, and the concurrent decline of indigenous minority ethnic populations in border areas (the typical Western demography of ageing populations and urbanisation). Still, these students bring a new dynamic into the education of (linguistic and/or ethnic) minorities, which has both positive and negative implications. The two case studies presented show the impact on the linguistic homogeneity of the classes, which make the teachers' work more didactically demanding and, as a result, the teachers' expectations of the competence and knowledge of the language of instruction for non-native students are not always very rigorous. Conversely, the students attending minority schools have very high linguistic and cultural awareness. Despite addressing different educational levels, both cases stressed the importance of openness to solutions for minority education preservation (despite the declining number of people belonging to a minority), although not at the expense of quality. Hence, the quality of the curricula, teacher training, and teaching materials must be constantly monitored throughout the entire age span of education in the minority language, from kindergarten to secondary school.

Still, students from Slovenia in Slovene-minority secondary schools in Austria can be considered a success story. The outcome seems to be particularly favourable for the Slovene minority in Austrian Carinthia, which in this way not only maintains minority education at the upper secondary level but even contributes to its quality by increasing the quantity and quality of the Slovene language input. These schools would otherwise have had difficulties in securing an influx of students due to the decline of the ethnic community over the last century (assimilation) and decades (poorer demographics and urbanisation). However, thanks to the cross-border economy, these schools have been able to exploit their niche and not only survive but also become language-education centres for the wider region. The context also has beneficial consequences for the members of the Slovene minority who are educated at these schools: their classmates from Slovenia expose them to the Slovene language to a much greater extent, especially the colloquial version, with which they have less direct contact. Students from Slovenia also largely confirm their expectations of the experience of schooling abroad, especially individuals who have a very elaborate self-image or clear plans for the future, so that they are able to neutralise any shortcomings in this mode of schooling in advance by themselves.

Conversely, when dealing with younger children, as is the case in the presented primary schools with Italian as the language of instruction, the curricula require continuous monitoring, not only in the narrow circle of stakeholders involved in education but also in the wider environment in which the schools operate. The benefits of this type of education, or the knowledge of several languages, are sometimes not as obvious or straightforward, and therefore we should strive to raise parents' awareness and, consequently, to achieve a high quality of professional staff in schools. The situation could be improved by providing parents with additional information, as they have an important influence on the students' views, their perception of the educational model, and their general language attitude. A positive attitude towards languages and bilingualism in an ethnically mixed area promotes the possibility of using the Italian (minority) language in all domains, including outside the school environment, thus contributing to the vitality of the Italian national community. Furthermore, it is important that teachers at all minority schools receive adequate training, especially in intercultural education.

The new realities of minority schools described previously will only become more evident in the future. Accepting the new situation, with constant, research-based monitoring, is the only effective way to achieve a multilingual and multicultural future.

References

Čok, L. (2009). 'Izobraževanje za dvojezičnost v kontekstu družbenega sobivanja in raziskovanja'. In L. Čok (Ed.), *Izobraževanje za dvojezičnost v kontekstu evropskih integracijskih procesov* (pp. 11–26). Koper: Založba Annales.

Constitution of the Republic of Slovenia. (1991). *Official Gazette of the Republic of Slovenia 33.*

Côté, J. E. and Levine, C. G. (2016). *Identity Formation, Youth, and Development: A Simplified Approach.* New York: Psychology Press.

Crul, M. (2016). 'Super-Diversity vs. Assimilation: How Complex Diversity in Majority – Minority Cities Challenges the Assumptions of Assimilation'. *Journal of Ethnic and Migration Studies* 42(1): 54–68. https://doi.org/10.1080/1369183x.2015.1061425.

Doleschal, U. (2011). 'Bilingual Education in Austria: The Case of Slovene in Carinthia'. In S. Novak Lukanovič and V. Mikolič (Eds.), *Slovenski jezik v stiku – sodobne usmeritve večjezičnega in manjšinskega izobraževanja* (pp. 158–175). Ljubljana: Slovene Association of Applied Linguistics.

Doleschal, U. (2023). *The Slovene Language in Education in Austria/Regional Dossiers Series*. Leeuwarden: Mercator, European Research Centre on Multilingualism and Language Learning. https://www. mercator-research.eu/fileadmin/mercator/documents/regional_dossiers/slovene_in_austria_3rd_2023.pdf (accessed 27 November 2023).

Domej, T. (1999). *Položaj manjšinskega jezika v izobraževanju na Koroškem, Materni jezik na pragu 21. stoletja = The Mother Tongue on the Door of 21st Century 1999*. Portorož: Zavod Republike Slovenije za šolstvo, 2–4 Decembra.

European School Education Platform. (2019). *Cross-Border Schools: Transcending Borders in Education*, 16 November. https://school-education.ec.europa.eu/en/insights/practices/cross-border-schools-transc ending-borders-education (accessed 14 November 2023).

Grgič, M. (2019). 'Manjšinski jeziki med Italijo in Slovenijo – zakaj potrebujemo čezmejno šolstvo?'. *Treatises and Documents, Journal of Ethnic Studies* 83: 35–50. https://doi.org/10.36144/RiG83. dec19.35-50.

Kern, D. (2009). 'Slovenski jezik v vzgojno-izobraževalnih ustanovah v manjšinskem prostoru'. In M. Stabej (Ed.), *Infrastruktura slovenščine in slovenistike* (pp. 191–196). Ljubljana: Znanstvena založba Filozofske fakultete.

Kolb, J. (2018). *Präsenz durch Verschwinden: Sprache und Ethnizität in der Alltagspraxis junger Kärntner Slowen_innen*. Bielefeld: Transcript Verlag.

Kovács, A. (2023). 'Šola onkraj meje: Učenci iz Madžarske, ki se šolajo na dvojezičnih osnovnih šolah v Sloveniji'. In B. Riman and S. Novak Lukanović (Eds.), *Raznolikost v raziskovanju etničnosti: Izbrani pogledi III* (pp. 169–192). Ljubljana: Institute for Ethnic Studies. https://doi.org/10.69070/2024_7.

Lengar Verovnik, T. (2023). 'Različice govorjene slovenščine na avstrijskem Koroškem in govorne prakse mladih pripadnikov manjšine'. *Slovenski jezik/Slovene Linguistic Studies* 13. https://doi.org/10.3986/ sjsls.13.1.06.

Nećak Lük, A. (2009). 'Učenci o svojem jeziku in o jeziku drugega'. In L. Čok (Ed.), *Izobraževanje za dvojezičnost v kontekstu evropskih integracijskih procesov* (pp. 105–116). Koper: Založba Annales.

Novak-Lukanovič, S. (2006). 'Percepcija učenja jezika večine in manjšine na narodnostno mešanih območjih v Sloveniji'. *Sodobna pedagogika* 57(1): 36–55.

Novak-Lukanovič, S. (2011). 'Language Diversity in Border Regions: Some Research Data on the Perception Among the Pupils of Two Secondary Schools'. *Annales, Series historia et Sociologia* 21(1): 79–92.

Novak-Lukanovič, S., Zudič Antonič, N. and Varga, Š. I. (2011). 'Vzgoja in izobraževanje na narodno mešanih območjih v Sloveniji'. In J. Krek and M. Metljak (Eds.), *Bela knjiga o vzgoji in izobraževanju v Republiki Sloveniji* (pp. 347–367). Ljubljana: Ministrstvo za šolstvo in šport.

OGM. (2022). *Položaj, raba jezika in perspektive slovenske narodne skupnosti na Koroškem*. O. r. Communication. https://www.ogm.at/wp-content/uploads/2022/09/OGM_Endbericht_Volksgruppe_130922_ slowenisch.pdf.

Ogris, K. (2014). *Schule = šola? Zur Gleichwertigkeit der Unterrichtssprachen Deutsch und Slowenisch an Kärntner Volksschulen*. Klagenfurt/Celovec: Drava Verlag/Založba Drava.

Ogris, T. (1995). 'Slovenščina – dvojezični pouk v južnokoroških šolah'. In D. Sedmak (Ed.), *Podoba našega otroka na Koroškem* (pp. 27–38). Trst: SLORI.

Reicher, S. D. (1982). 'The Determination of Collective Behaviour'. In H. Tajfel (Ed.), *Social Identity and Intergroup Relations* (pp. 41–83). Cambridge: Cambridge University Press.

Sandrieser, S., Vrbinc, M. and Weinfurter, M. (2016). 'Jahresbericht über das Schuljahr 2015/16'. In *Klagenfurt am Wörthersee: Landesschulrat für Kärnten, Ableitung VII*. Minderheitenschulwesen.

SLOGAT – Slovenska gimnazija/Slowenisches Gymnasium. www.slog.at/sola/detajl/C16/das-slowenische-gymnasium (accessed 5 December 2023).

Sorgo, L. (2023). 'Pregled raziskav Inštituta za narodnostna vprašanja v sklopu strokovno-razvojnih nalog na področju izobraževanja v slovenski Istri'. In B. Riman and S. Novak Lukanović (Eds.), *Raznolikost v raziskovanju etničnosti: Izbrani pogledi III* (pp. 345–372). Ljubljana: Institute for Ethnic Studies. https:// doi.org/10.69070/2024_12.

Sorgo, L., Novak Lukanović, S. and Zudič Antonič, N. (2022). 'Pupils' and Parents' Opinions on Schools with Italian as the Language of Instruction'. *Treatises and Documents, Journal for Ethnic Studies* 89: 73–90. https://doi.org/10.36144/RiG89.dec22.73-90.

SURS. (2015). *Slovene: A South Slavic Language Spoken by About 2.5 Million Speakers in the World.* www. stat.si/StatWeb/en/News/Index/5004 (accessed 4 March 2024).

Vavti, Š. (2012). *"Včasih ti zmanjka besed . . . " Etnične identifikacije pri mladih Slovenkah in Slovencih na dvojezičnem avstrijskem Koroškem.* Klagenfurt/Celovec: Drava Verlag/Založba Drava.

Vertovec, S. (2007). 'Super-Diversity and Its Implications'. *Ethnic and Racial Studies* 30(6): 1024–1054. https://doi.org/10.1080/01419870701599465.

Vertovec, S. (2023). *Superdiversity: Migration and Social Complexity.* London and New York: Routledge.

Zorčič, S. (2019). 'Linguistic Habitus, Different Capitals and the Identity of Bilingual Youth: The Case of Austrian Carinthia'. *Journal of Multilingual and Multicultural Development* 40(9): 787–800. https://doi.org/10.1080/01434632.2019.1568442.

Zorčič, S. (2020a). *Habitus, kapitali in identitete v sporazumevalnih praksah na avstrijskem Koroškem.* Ljubljana: University of Ljubljana.

Zorčič, S. (2020b). 'Dimensions of Remote Learning During the Covid-19 Pandemic in Minority Language Schools (The Case of Austrian Carinthia)'. *Treatises and Documents, Journal of Ethnic Studies* 85: 223−252. https://doi.org/10.36144/rig85.dec20.223-252.

Zorčič, S. and Novak Lukanović, S. (2023). 'Cross-Border Education: Students from Slovenia in Austrian Minority Schools'. *Treatises and Documents, Journal of Ethnic Studies* 91: 91–114. https://doi.org/10.2478/tdjes-2023-0016.

Zorman, A. (2021). 'Bilingual Education as an Instrument of Ethnic Minority Protection: The Case of Italian L2 in the Slovene Littoral'. *Treatises and Documents, Journal of Ethnic Studies* 87: 195–209. https://doi.org/10.36144/rig87.dec21.195-209.

Zudič Antonič, N. (2009). 'Italijanščina kot prvi jezik v manjšinskih šolah Slovenske Istre'. In L. Čok (Ed.), *Izobraževanje za dvojezičnost v kontekstu evropskih integracijskih procesov* (pp. 75–88). Koper: Založba Annales.

Zudič Antonič, N. (2012). 'Insegnare letteratura a scuola nell'ambito dell'italiano come L2'. *Annales, Series historia et sociologia* 22(1): 141–156.

Zudič Antonič, N. and Zorman, A. (2023). *The Italian Language in Education in Slovenia.* Leeuwarden: Mercator European Research Centre on Multilingualism and Language Learning.

Funding:

Research program Minority and Ethnic Studies and the Slovenian National Question (P5–0081), funded by ARIS, Slovenian Research and Innovation Agency.

16

LEARNING THE NEIGHBOR'S LANGUAGE

Regional and minoritized languages as a resource in the European educational context

Marija Mandić

Introduction

Learning regional, minoritized and migrant languages has been marginalized, framed as a problem or just a matter of heritage that is neither related to modernity nor seen as a useful form of knowledge. Overall, bi/multilingualism as a resource is valued for the "'world" standard languages which one is expected to learn in school for personal enrichment or international understanding or foreign service' (Ruiz 1984: 27), but not for non-dominant languages. The nature of contemporary multilingualism has been accordingly shaped by the distinction between elite and folk multilingualism (de Mejía 2002), on the one hand, and, on the other hand, by the social hierarchy of majority vs. minority, 'which derives from the size of the population and/or extent of the power of the speakers of the languages' (Annamalai 2003: 115). The majority hence tends to live with one language, while the minority speakers generally speak two or more languages on a daily basis, which for them is a matter of survival.

Since the majority standard is considered 'the most natural default for human communication,' the contemporary education and knowledge production consequently suffer from monolingual bias (Ortega 2014: 48). Likewise, the multilingual education is primarily focused on either elite or minority bi/multilingualism – conceived as 'a set of parallel monolingualisms' (Heller 1999: 5) – which means that a language is seen as an entity that conforms to certain prescriptive norms and that it must be kept 'uncorrupted' by the influence of other languages in the speaker's repertoire.

An emerging research paradigm called 'multilingual turn' instead understands languages as social practice and approaches them as resources for the whole community (Cummins et al. 2006; May 2014). Within this paradigm, a question arose: 'How can a minority language gain sufficient support from majority language speakers for it to be accepted (and spoken regularly) as a state language?' (May 2000: 101). Along the same lines, Skutnabb-Kangas and García (1995) argued that one of the important educational tasks in multilingual settings would be to overcome one-sided societal multilingualism by making the majority multilingual together with the minority. However, educational programs with minoritized languages for L2 speakers in multilingual contexts are still underdeveloped and subject to ongoing debates (Genesse 2004; Cenoz and Gorter 2023), while many grassroots initiatives at the local level call for their inclusion in the curriculum.

DOI: 10.4324/9781003439493-20

This chapter examines how European regional and minoritized languages are institutionalized as a resource for the wider community, in the light of historical and current language educational policies. The following questions are posed, each corresponding to a different level of analysis: What are the main orientations in the current European language policy on multilingualism, on the one hand, and, on the other hand, what were multilingual educational strategies in the states that preceded or paralleled the nation-state? How regional and minoritized languages are employed in education for L2 speakers across Europe? It is argued that school curricula that include regional and minoritized languages for L2 speakers reinforce the already existing emic view of local languages as resources and contribute to a balanced social hierarchy among local communities, but they are still underdeveloped, constantly challenged and in decline, facing English as a global *lingua franca*.

The first part of the chapter presents Ruiz's (1984) language orientations to language policy as a theoretical framework for approaching regional and minoritized languages in educational context. In light of this theory, current European language policy on multilingualism, as well as multilingual educational strategies in the modern European empires and socialist federations, are (re)examined. The second part provides a selective critical overview of the present European educational models which assess regional and minoritized languages as a resource for the wider community and include them in school curriculum for L2 speakers.

Minoritized language as a resource

Minoritized languages have been largely studied within Ruiz's (1984) paradigm of tripartite orientation to language policy: language as problem, right and resource, which then stands for a more general outlook on cultural and social diversity. Unlike the 'language as problem' orientation, which approaches minoritized languages as a threat to national unity and a problem to be overcome, while monolingualism is regarded as a way to emancipation from a subordinate social position via transitional bilingual educational programs, 'language as right' and 'language as resource' are complementary in nature, in the sense that they both support societal and institutional multilingualism, although they assess it in different ways (Ruiz 2010). 'Language as right' approaches language as a basic human right which entails its use in the communal life and education, including the right not to be discriminated against on the basis of it. In the larger context, ethnic languages are considered 'both a legal entitlement and a natural endowment' (Ruiz 1984: 23). However, this orientation still positions majoritized/minoritized languages against each other, with multilingualism being conceived differently depending on whether the speaker belongs to the majority or the minority. In contrast to it, the 'language as resource' orientation approaches minoritized languages as resource for the whole community – majority and minority. Minoritized languages are hence recognized as resource with intellectual, cultural, economic and social manifestations (Lo Bianco 2001).

The 'language as resource' orientation to language policy nevertheless drew criticism raising important questions: A resource for whom? For what purpose or end? (Ricento 2005; Petrovic 2005). Given the fact that groups in a dominant position shape social relations, define the value of resources and set rules for their distribution, the 'resource orientation' may bring a potential risk of putting minoritized languages in the service of the dominant majority, thereby maintaining a power imbalance between majority and minority speakers. However, Hult and Hornberger (2016) remind that Ruiz (1984, 2010) advocated cooperative language planning and tempering extrinsic rationales of top-down language policy with intrinsic values ascribed to local languages by the speakers themselves. Hence, as a resource, minoritized language 'may have intrinsic value in relation to cultural reproduction, community relations, inter-generational communication, identity construction, building self-esteem, and intellectual engagement, among other possibilities,' while extrinsic value include national security, diplomacy, military action, business or media (Hult and Hornberger 2016: 39). Eventually, de Jong et al. (2016) propose that Ruiz's framework should be expanded to 'bi/multilingualism as a resource.' The contemporary European language policy, which is discussed in the next section, approaches language as a resource in two cases: if it is a world *lingua franca* or if it is considered as European cultural heritage.

Contemporary European language policy on multilingualism

From the 18th century onwards, European countries began to establish a political pattern based upon the Enlightenment and the Romantic notions of the (ideal) overlap of language, ethnicity and territory (Anderson 1991). In post-Versailles (1919) Europe, the minority/majority dichotomy developed as a legal and political category within the peace treaties that dissolved the multiethnic empires and established nation-states. Two principles appeared to be pertinent in defining ethnic, religious or linguistic minorities: numerical ('a group numerically inferior to the rest of the population') and 'non-dominant position' (Capotorti 1979). Heller (2006: 7) thus puts it pointedly: 'Linguistic minorities are created by nationalisms which exclude them.' The nation-state building has likewise rendered minoritized varieties a problem that hinders political unity in contrast to the unifying and homogenizing national standard variety. Hence, they have been marginalized or assimilated in the process, which eventually fashioned the European ethno-linguistic nationalism (Kamusella 2009) and standard language ideology (Milroy 2001).

Considering that 'minority' is a historically recent and contingent term created in the process of Othering and hierarchization, Costa et al. (2018: 8) instead propose the term 'minoritized,' which 'implies not only that "minorities" are forged out of "majorities"' but also entails 'the creation of a marginalized collective "Other".' Busch (2022: 58) likewise points out that the majority/minority relationship is scalar, depending on the spatial-temporal frame of reference: one and the same community can be the majority in one historical, geopolitical or social framework and the minority in another.

Safeguarding minoritized languages in a systematic way took place in the 1990s, when under the auspices of the Council of Europe, two conventions were adopted: the European Charter for Regional or Minority Languages (ECRML 1992) and the Framework Convention for the Protection of National Minorities (FCNM 1995), which included the establishment of committees for monitoring their implementation.

ECRML defines regional or minority languages as:

i) traditionally used within a given territory of a State by nationals of that State who form a group numerically smaller than the rest of the State's population;
ii) different from the official language(s) of that State.

The minoritized languages protected under ECRML (presently more than 80) are considered inherited European cultural assets that contribute to language diversity, but dialectal varieties of the official language(s) and immigrant languages are not included. Both ECRML and FCNM indorse the right to learn a minority language or to be taught as such. The Explanatory Report FCNM (1995: 22) states that that bilingual instruction may be one of the means of achieving this goal. The Advisory Committee of FCNM called on 'member states with more than one official language to provide sufficient opportunities for students to learn the respective other language'; it also encouraged 'the development of bi- or multilingual teaching models as part of the mandatory school curriculum,' which 'attract children from minority and majority backgrounds and cater for children who grow up bilingually, or in "mixed" families' (Busch 2018: 264–265).

In the 1990s, a European educational program for foreign languages called Content and Language Integrated Learning (CLIL) was likewise developed. CLIL drew on the bilingual immersion programs implemented in the US and Canada since the 1960s. It has been argued that CLIL differs from the dual language immersion programs in that the second language is mostly international *linguae francae* (English, French, Spanish, German) rather than the L2 spoken locally (Dalton-Puffer et al. 2014: 215). However, the Eurydice Report (2023: 66) finds that CLIL is used in almost all European countries as a generic term to describe all types of teaching L2, such as a foreign, regional or minority language and/or another official state language.

The European policy on multilingualism was eventually profiled in the 2000s, placing it so high on the agenda that some qualify it as a 'new dominant ideology' (Garcia 2015: 44). The Maalouf Report, one of the key policy documents, envisions an ideal European as a speaker of 'native language + 2,' whereby one foreign language is intended for business and another for pleasure (European Commission 2008). The latter is meant to be a 'personal adoptive language,' the learning of which should be guided by personal reasons, 'stemming from individual or family background, emotional ties, professional interest, cultural preferences, intellectual curiosity, to name but a few' (Ibid.: 11). The Maalouf Report states that there is a need to develop 'bilateral relations between the peoples of the European countries' by means of 'powerful ties based on the knowledge of the language of the other,' which aims to prevent further 'erosion [*effritement*] of the level of knowledge of the neighbor's language in favor of a language of international communication' and tend to 'restore a powerful motivation to learn every European language' (Ibid.: 16–17). The similar urge was stressed in the series of the Europe's policy documents (cf. Busch 2011; Cavaion 2022). As for immigrants, the Maalouf Report considers that 'the personal adoptive language should in the normal run of events [*en règle générale*] be that of the country in which they have chosen to live in' (European Commission 2008: 19).

Yet the European multilingual policy has received serious criticism. Garcia (2015: 52) maintains that it is characterized by the tension between the utilitarian and the cultural dimension, whereby minoritized languages 'have little space in the "mother tongue plus two" language model,' and they always rank lower than the national majority and foreign languages. Gal (2006) points out that the European policy embodies the standard language ideology, as it relies on the idea of the cooperation of different nation-states that have their own codified official languages. Moore (2015: 28) argues that the European main supranational bodies conceive languages as 'emblems of culture and tradition, but [have] very little to say about the actual use of language in actual communicative practices.' Moreover, he sees the EU policy as reactionary to the 'threats' that destabilize an idealized image of 'European multilingual orderliness,' which come from outside, in three forms: (1) English as a *lingua franca*, (2) non-EU immigrant languages and (3) languages that overflow the territorial boundaries of EU member states (e.g., Basque; Russian in parts of Eastern Europe) (Ibid.: 29). However, a critical look at the multilingual educational strategies in the states that preceded or paralleled the nation-state can inform the new multilingual paradigm and mitigate the current European controversies caught in-between 'authenticity' and 'instrumentality,' as the next section shows.

Multilingual educational strategies in the modern past

Contemporary social theory and sociolinguistics often observe linguistic diversity in modern urban centers as a phenomenon unparalleled in history calling it 'superdiversity' (Blommaert

Learning the neighbor's language

2015). Pavlenko (2023) considers these views 'historical amnesia' and points to numerous examples of multilingual policies, strategies and practices from antiquity onwards. A selective and critical examination of multilingual educational strategies in the Habsburg Monarchy, Imperial Russia and the socialist federations of the Soviet Union and Yugoslavia shows that linguistic diversity was often viewed as a resource that facilitates strategic inclusion, cohesion, administrative management and multilingual coexistence of the diverse population. Moreover, in the imperial states, more or less developed competence in local languages was considered a marker of authenticity for an individual living in a multilingual region.

In the Habsburg Empire, locally and regionally oriented polyglossia was part of everyday life, as it provided more opportunities for vertical mobility and trade, with citizens constantly crossing the alleged local linguistic and ethnic boundaries. It is the (post)Habsburg 'folk multilingualism' for which sociolinguists coined various terms – *lived multilingualism* (Schjerve-Rindler and Vetter 2007), *polyglot nationalism, imperial linguistics* (Gal 2011, 2015), *multilingual habitus* (Krel and Mandić 2016), *bilateral bi/multilingualism* (Mikeš 1974) – yet all refer to the same: a community-based instrumental polyglossia. The imperial multilingualism, however, was not located just in individuals, but it was likewise institutionalized through administration, education, church and military (Prokopovych et al. 2019).

Unlike the Habsburg Monarchy, Tsarist Russia did not pay due attention to the systematic education of peasants but focused on the elite, who were educated in Russian and the world languages, such as German and French (Pavlenko 2011). In the period from the 17th until the Russification reforms in the late 19th century, a territorial approach to language management was adopted in the Western part of the Empire: Baltic provinces were administered in German, Finland in Swedish and Poland in Polish (Ibid.). During the 19th century, bilingual education was established in the Eastern part – the Volga region, Siberia and central Asia, which facilitated acquisition of the Russian language and accelerated 'the intellectual and moral development of non-Russians' (Dowler 1995: 526).

The main educational institutions that fostered regional multilingualism were utraquist schools, in which teaching was carried out in at least two and at most four regional languages, whereby it entailed 'ceaseless switching between the various languages . . . [as a] daily routine for both teachers and students' (Wolf 2015: 58). Such utraquist schools existed alongside one-language schools in the Habsburg Monarchy, Kingdom of Prussia, Kingdom of Poland and the Grand Duchy of Lithuania, Tsarist Russia (Burger 1995; Snyder 2003; Knabe 2000).

Nevertheless, during the 18th and 19th centuries, two main European language ideologies competed over primacy in defining national identity – monoglot and polyglot nationalism (Gal 2011). In contrast to monoglot nationalism, which equated the nation with a single language, polyglot nationalism indorsed learning, speaking and interchangeable use of regional languages, which was considered as being in agreement with a national identity. Invigorated by the French Revolution and German Romanticism, the monoglot nationalism eventually triumphed, which led to national homogenization and nationalization of curriculum. The attachment to one language began to serve as an index of national loyalty, while locally oriented bi/multilingualism was seen as a potential danger to the national cause. Hence, in the Austrian half of the Austro-Hungarian Monarchy, the Constitution 1867, which remained in force until 1918, secured each group's right to education in its language, while it abolished bi/multilingual utraquist education that embodied the resource orientation to local languages (Wolf 2015: 42).

The spontaneous language acquisition, nevertheless, continued to be negotiated outside of institutional conditions and premises. Although parents who persisted in demands for bilingual education 'became increasingly stigmatized' (Judson and Zahra 2012: 25), they continued sending their children to study in different language environments or practiced temporary (from one month to one year) 'exchange of children' between neighboring families speaking different languages (e.g. Hun. *gyerekcsere*/Ger. *Kindertausch*) (Gal 2011: 43–48). In addition, 'the second or third language was generally acquired on the "uncontrolled" pattern: the learners, usually migrant workers, gained their knowledge of the language or languages chiefly through daily communication,' as it was the only way for them to communicate in a new environment (Wolf 2015: 50). Pavlenko (2011: 346) notes that in the acquisition of the languages in the Russian Empire, bottom-up processes were much more effective than top-down policies, as a result of the desire of members of various ethnic groups for a greater social mobility.

The multilingual educational policy was systematically implemented in the socialist federations. The Soviet Union 'pursued a dual course supporting the spread of Russian and the maintenance of titular and some minority languages' (Pavlenko 2013: 665), with three types of schools: (1) titular language is language of instruction, Russian is school subject; (2) Russian is language of instruction, titular language is school subject; and (3) bilingual schools (Ibid.: 25). In addition, the teaching in minority languages was carried out in some republics, but the number of these schools decreased over time, while the offer of minority languages as subjects increased at all levels of education. The choice of educational type varied significantly across republics. This means that Russian was viewed as a resource at the state federal level, titular languages at the republic national level, and minority languages were approached within the 'language as right' paradigm. Pavlenko (2013: 666) concludes that the 'Soviet language management efforts led to high levels of monolingualism among native speakers of Russian, high levels of native language maintenance and bilingualism among the titulars and language shift among minority language speakers.'

In Socialist Yugoslavia, an orientation towards a decentralized language policy was developed with no official language on the federal level; each constitutive republic and province determined which language(s) were to be recognized for administrative and educational purposes. The Yugoslav language policy in multilingual regions sustained, on the one hand, 'language as right' for a national community and, on the other hand, 'language as resource' for the wider community. Thus, four education models were offered: (1) minority language (L1) for instruction, state language (L2) as school subject; (2) bilingual education; (3) state language (L2) for instruction, minority language (L1) as school subject; (4) state language (L1) for instruction, local minority language (L2) as school subject (Novak-Lukanovič 1988). In multilingual regions where minoritized languages were spoken as L1 by more than one third of the local population, type (4) was realized as an obligatory school subject language of social environment (LSE) for the students belonging to the national majority (Mikeš 1974). Yugoslav sociolinguists highlighted the role of the school subject LSE in securing equal legal status to both majority and minority languages, which contributed to balanced social hierarchies at the local level (Novak-Lukanovič 1988; Mandić and Rácz 2023). In the light of the 'language as resource' orientation, the following section provides a critical and selective overview of the contemporary European curricula which include regional and minoritized languages for L2 speakers.

Regional and minoritized languages in education for L2 speakers

The ideology of monoglot standard in the late modern period has been central to the legitimization of the nation-state, but it became confronted with supranational policies and migration, resulting in the paradox of modern linguistic diversity which locates 'multilingualism in the individual (as "skills") or in international communication, while it zones off the national territory as monolingual' (Jaspers 2015: 110). In this discursive order, the value of ethnic languages is structured, as

Learning the neighbor's language

Heller and Duchêne (2012) metaphorically put it, between 'pride' and 'profit.' In most European countries, only one language is recognized as a state language, although in the European Union almost quarter of adolescents speak a different language at home from the language of schooling (Eurydice 2023: 29–32).

Due to the (legal) status granted to languages, it can be distinguished between states with linguistic federalism (e.g. Switzerland, Belgium), institutionalized multilingualism (e.g. Finland, Luxembourg, Ireland); the special status given to regional languages in certain countries and regions, usually associated with a specific political status (e.g. Wales, South Tyrol, Basque Country, Prekmurje, etc.); and so on. The overview generally follows the geographical distribution of countries from the north, via the west and the center to the south and the east.

In Finland the official bilingualism includes two constitutional languages: Finnish and Swedish. However, Swedish with around 5% L1 speakers has an ambivalent position, being considered both a national and a minority language that needs to be protected. The curriculum is based on a single language of instruction (Finnish or Swedish as L1) with the other national language as L2 and one foreign language as compulsory school subjects, except for matriculation exams, where L2 is optional (Pöyhönen and Saarinen 2015). The special status of Swedish derives from its historical role as the main language from the 12th to the 19th century and its role in strengthening Finland's Nordic ties (Ibid.). On the one hand, this special status has been recently opposed by some right-wing parties and citizens' initiatives, which aim to make Swedish a facultative school subject, while, on the other hand, there is an increasing demand for bilingual education from families with mixed and migrant background (Pöyhönen and Saarinen 2015; From 2023). Although Swedish is approached as a resource 'with an aim of integrating multilingual perspectives into the whole curriculum' (Paulsrud et al. 2020), the monoglot national ideology still prevails, as the Finnish legislation does not allow bilingual Finnish–Swedish schools and permits speakers to register officially just one mother tongue (Ibid.). As for migrant languages whose number of speakers has exceeded Swedish speakers in the last decades, there is still no place for them in the curriculum.

In Friesland in the Netherlands, Frisian is an officially recognized minority language and approached as a resource for the regional community. Thus, students in primary and lower secondary education have to study it as obligatory school subject alongside Dutch and foreign language (Eurydice 2023: 58). Nevertheless, Dutch L1 speakers and new migrants consider Dutch and English far more useful than Frisian (Debreczeni et al. 2023).

The re-emergence of Welsh in Wales, in the United Kingdom, after centuries of complete dominance by English, began as the grass-root initiative of Welsh-speaking parents already in the 1930s (May 2000: 103–106). Welsh was eventually recognized as a principal language of instruction within Welsh-medium schools in 1988, while Welsh language was introduced as a compulsory subject in all schools in Wales. Still, Welsh language retains an ambivalent position as a co-official national and minoritized language at the same time, since the Welsh-speaking population, according to the 2021 census, makes up 17.8% in Wales, and nearly three quarters of the population said they had no Welsh language skills.[1] Although there is generally a very positive attitude to Welsh-medium education and although it is seen as a resource for employment and social cohesion (Wilson 2023), the debates about whether it should be compulsory for everybody continue.

In Ireland, since its independence in 1922, the educational policy has had a dual aim: to increase the number of Irish medium schools and to introduce Irish as L2 in English medium schools, which still make up 90% of all schools (Ó Duibhir and Harris 2023). While Irish is a co-official language alongside English and a compulsory subject in all English medium schools, it is not a language that is actively used outside the classroom and the Gaeltacht (May 2000). The case of Irish shows that the official recognition, legal protection and obligatory status of the language in schools are just not enough, if it is not a resource in employment, social relations or other social domains (Ó Duibhir and Harris 2023: 51).

Through a comparison of France and Germany, Garcia (2015: 43) finds that 'the education systems of the two countries favor the teaching of 'useful' European standard languages, particularly English, over that of minority and migrant languages that are conceived in merely cultural terms.' In Germany, regional and minoritized languages – such as Sorbian, Danish, Frisian – can be used for instruction in bilingual schools, taught as elective school subjects or L3 (Dołowy-Rybińska and Ratajczak 2019). As more German L1 speakers are attending these programs, debates flare up about how to reconcile the strategy of maintaining a minority language with the strategy of creating 'new speakers' and cohesive local communities (Ibid.). Still, migrant languages are approached as cultural heritage of migrants and as such remain marginalized in public education or outside regular classes. Recently, awareness has grown that migrant languages, such as Turkish, can be a resource in the German transmigration society, resulting in the establishment of bilingual schools and programs that are open not only to speakers of the heritage languages, but these schools are still very few (Küppers et al. 2015).

In France, the exclusion of regional and minoritized languages from the education dates back to the French Revolution. Thus, their teaching was framed as matter of cultural heritage and generally restricted to elective school subject (Garcia 2015: 51). Furthermore, France has not ratified ECRML as incompatible with the French constitution, but at the regional and local level minoritized languages have been gradually introduced in curriculum through local charters within ECRML (Popović 2024). Due to the dramatic decline of speakers of regional and minoritized languages, France is considering for the first time the introduction of regional language immersion programs within the state education system, such as for Breton (Wilson 2023). However, the German language in France still holds a better status in the curriculum as a foreign than as a regional language (Liddicoat and Curnow 2014: 286).

Belgium consists of three regional national communities, whose languages are recognized as official: in Flanders Dutch is official, Brussels is French–Dutch bilingual and in Wallonia it is French with a small German minority and the official German language. The curriculum is based on a single language of instruction (L1), but students are given the opportunity to learn Dutch, French or German as L2 in the form of facultative or obligatory school subject, in addition to English or other foreign language (Mettewie and Van Mensel 2023). The choice of L1 and L2 depends on the region, but there are also differences conditioned by socio-historical factors, such as the historical prestige of French, which influenced its learning as a compulsory L2 school subject in German and Dutch medium schools. In French-medium schools in Wallonia, students can choose L2 depending on what their school offers, while in Brussels, Dutch is compulsory L2. There are public debates, however, whether English instead of French should be compulsory in Dutch schools, as well as if Dutch should be compulsory in French schools, bearing in mind that it brings great benefits in the national labor market (Ibid.). As a result, students who attend Dutch and German medium schools are often bilingual, unlike most French students, but all students have better competence in English as L2 than in the national languages. In response to many bottom-up initiatives for including national languages in the curriculum, top-down policies implement CLIL programs which introduce bi/multilingual education through back door (Mettewie and Van Mensel 2023; Jaspers 2015). Finally, in the Belgian schools, there is almost no space for migrant languages, although they are widely used in informal settings.

In Luxembourg, three languages are recognized as official: Luxembourgish (Lëtzebuergesch), French and German (Horner and Weber 2008). The majority uses multiple languages on a daily basis, while a trilingual educational model is maintained, but it is directed towards elite multilingualism: the main teaching languages are standard varieties of German (in lower grades) and French (in higher grades), whereas non-standardized Luxembourgish is used as an auxiliary teaching language and studied as school subject. In addition, students also learn English, while migrant languages are excluded. In fact, it is the elite multilingualism that 'creates opportunities in various spheres of employment, while knowledge of Luxembourgish continues to serve as a gate-keeping device with regard to civil service positions,' in addition to its affective value, as a marker of solidarity and group membership (Ibid.: 119).

Switzerland has four official languages, but it applies the principle of linguistic territoriality with most of its cantons being monolingual – German is the only official language in 17 cantons, French in 4 and Italian in 1, while 3 cantons are German-French bilingual and 1 is German, Italian and Romansh trilingual. Learning the second national language – called *langue partenaire* – is compulsory, as it is believed to contribute to a balanced social hierarchy and signals that language communities respect each other's culture (Stotz 2006). Still, Switzerland has been 'caught in the midst of a discursive struggle' about languages in education which involved the issues of power and resources (Ibid.: 261–262). On the one hand, the 'confederate discourse on multilingualism' sees formal education as the 'major site for the creation of multilingual citizen' and English as a potential threat to the Swiss regional multilingualism. On the other hand, 'globalization discourses' demand that English becomes L2 instead of a *langue partenaire* as a more useful one (Ibid.). The response varies by region and canton: the further away from the German–French language border, the louder the call for English (Ibid.: 263). Finally, minority, immigrant and heritage languages still remain out of the official language policy (Giudici 2019).

The Slovenian education in Carinthia in Austria was based on subtractive bilingualism aimed at language shift from Slovenian to German. In the 1990s, however, a monolingual paradigm began to shift on the European level, which led to the creation of dual-medium Slovene–German programs with additional foreign language learning (Purkarthofer and Mossakowski 2011). These curricula raised interest among non-Slovene, mainly L1 German, speakers who either wanted to learn Slovenian as heritage or neighboring language.

In Slovenia, two different regional educational models have been developed with the linguistic goal of achieving functional bilingualism. In Prekmurje, a bi-directional bilingualism in schools promotes the equality of Slovene and Hungarian as languages of instruction from kindergarten (Novak Lukanovič and Limon 2014: 429–431). In Istria, however, schools use either Slovene or Italian as L1, while L2 – the language of the social environment – is taught as compulsory. In addition, 'all pupils learn about the culture and history of the other nation or ethnic group living on the same territory' (Ibid.: 429). The research has shown that the knowledge of the regional L2 has been decreasing, while many students see English as more important than the language used in the local environment (Ibid.: 435).

There are civil initiatives and projects focused on learning the language of the social environment in the Italian mainstream primary and secondary schools located along the Italian-Slovenian border, where Slovenian is not considered a foreign but a neighboring language, used in everyday life and known through friends and relatives (Cavaion 2018, 2022). Therefore, the method Contact Based Language Learning and Teaching (CoBLaLT) was developed (Cavaion 2022). The proponents of this initiative claim that learning Slovenian in the Italian borderland schools contributes to a revival of the minoritized Slovenian language, encourages Slovenian participation in social life, and improves relations between the minority and majority communities (Cavaion 2018: 106). The initiatives resulted in the introduction of Slovenian as a school subject at various schools, such as in the provinces of Trieste and Gorica, but the decision on its status was left to the discretion of the school (Ibid.).

In the Italian Autonomous province of South Tyrol, three main language communities – German (regional majority which makes up around 70%), Italian and a very small Ladin community – have enjoyed cultural autonomy since the 1970s, with the right to use their L1 in administration and education, while the regional languages are compulsory L2 school subjects in primary and secondary education; in Italian schools it is German and vice versa, and in Ladin schools, both Italian and German are learnt (Cavagnoli and Nardin 1999). Although bilingualism is a prerequisite for employment in the public sector and judicial services in the region, only Ladins are predominantly balanced multilingual speakers, while the other two communities remain mainly monolingual (Ibid.: 20). The research on speakers' attitudes shows the regional L2 is viewed as economic resource but not as cultural, social or personal one, which is a consequence of the institutional setting (Abel et al. 2012). Meanwhile, the parents launched many initiatives demanding bilingual immersion education for their children which would improve their chances for employment.

In the Basque Autonomous Community in Spain, Basque has gained important value over the last thirty years, since it has been required for many jobs, the state administration and private sphere. Hence, three schooling models were established: A-model – with Spanish as language of instruction and Basque as an obligatory school subject; B-model – with both Basque and Spanish as equally used languages of instruction; D-model – Basque is the language of instruction, and Spanish is an obligatory school subject (Gorter and Cenoz 2011: 657). The first two models are intended for speakers of Spanish as L1, but the D-model, although intended of L1 Basque speakers, also includes a large number of Spanish L1 speakers. The least successful in achieving functional additional bilingualism appeared to be the A-model, contrary to the most popular D-model, given the intensive use of Basque in the school and the dominant position of Spanish in society, which leads to high levels of proficiency in both languages.

The autonomous communities of Spain, Catalonia and Valencia have developed a 'linguistic conjunction model' of schooling in which both regional (Catalan or Valencian) and the state Spanish language are used as the media of instruction in different proportions while being at the same time compulsory subjects at all levels. According to the legislation, at least 25% of teaching must be delivered in Spanish/Castilian in all schools (Branchadell 2023). The 'linguistic conjunction model' prohibits the separation of students into different schools by language, and all children are expected to be balanced bilinguals by the end of their compulsory education (Ibid.). The curriculum also regulated the proportion of English at around 15%. There are debates whether the share of Spanish in teaching should be strictly regulated or left to the schools to adjust it 'according to need, on the road to full Catalan-Spanish bilingualism' (Ibid.: 242).

In Cyprus, the two major language communities – Greek and Turkish – have separate education systems – a tradition dating back to the Ottoman period (1571–1878) and the British rule (1878–1960) (Hadjioannou et al. 2011). The Cyprus Constitution (1960) recognized Greek and Turkish as official languages but established two educational systems in which standard varieties of Greek or Turkish are the sole languages of instruction and the foreign prestigious languages are school subjects (Ibid.: 508). However, until the inter-communal conflicts in 1963, Greek–Turkish folk bilingualism was common, while Greek served as *lingua franca*. The Turkish language was introduced in formal education for the first time for Greek L1 speakers only in 2003, when Cyprus signed the EU Accession Treaty. Turkish was then introduced as an optional school subject at secondary school, among other foreign languages, while free courses in the Greek and Turkish languages were offered for adults in public education institutes (Charalambous et al. 2017; Charalambous 2019). Because of the long-standing ethno-political conflict, these courses, however, often involve issues of national loyalty, securitization and conflicted heritage. In order to avoid Turkish and Greek being framed as 'the language of the enemy,' the teaching of these languages to L2

Learning the neighbor's language

speakers was reframed in public discourse as part of the European supranational multilingual ideology (Charalambous 2019).

Though the 15 post-Soviet successor states tended to distance themselves from Russian, the language policy in each of them unfolded differently, ranging from predominant national mono-lingualism to societal bilingualism. Many post-Soviet countries opted for trilingual competence in education: in the national language, Russian as obligatory foreign language and another foreign language (Pavlenko 2013: 668–673). While Russian has been significantly reduced in all countries and relegated to minority or foreign language, it remained an important resource for administration, interethnic communication, information access and labor migration alongside English as a global *lingua franca*.

Conclusion

The use of regional and minoritized languages in education of L2 speakers is broadly concerned with issues of hegemony and minoritization. In European countries, societal bilingualism is primarily constructed through *de facto* 'parallel monolingualisms,' which does not entail individual bilingualism. Moreover, individual multilingualism is largely ideologically impossible, as state institutions allow speakers to register only one language as their main language, while bilingual schools that include local languages are not common or even permitted. This conflicts with the principle of plurilingualism, to which Council of Europe policy attaches particular value as 'need to ensure the harmonious development of learners' plurilingual competence through a coherent, transversal and integrated approach that takes into account all the languages in learners' plurilin-gual repertoire and their respective functions' (Liddicoat and Kerry Taylor-Leech 2015: 3).

In an effort to conceptualize an integrative and responsible language education policy in multi-lingual environments, Ruiz (1984: 15) advocated a 'language as a resource' orientation to language policy, which is informed by community-based initiatives and aims to harmonize the extrinsic principles of a top-down language policy with the intrinsic values ascribed to local languages by the speakers themselves. In a similar vein, Ricento (2005: 364) asks how far we can develop the principle that national unity includes diversity; that is, can we produce alternative discourses that consider languages other than that of the national majority as intrinsically 'ours' rather than 'for-eign'? Busch (2011: 544) argues that the use of non-dominant languages in multilingual education 'represents a resource on the individual and the societal level encompassing intellectual, cultural, economic, social, civic and human rights dimensions.'

The brief overview of approaches to multilingual education in the European modern imperial and the socialist countries has shown that the practices and experiences of the past can be used as a legacy that informs the new multilingual paradigm. A look through a post-imperial lens, how-ever, proves that the process of ethnic and linguistic unmixing has taken place over the last two centuries (Brubaker 1998), leading to a general decline in regional multilingualism. The influx of new migrants to the European centers brought, on the one hand, a dynamic ethnic and linguistic diversification. On the other hand, the rise of English as a global *lingua franca* has led to a new linguistic hegemony and homogenization.

Regional and minoritized languages certainly play an ambivalent role in the European states. On the one hand, they are not considered foreign but 'authentic' languages of the social environment, being institutionally protected as part of the European cultural heritage and located within the 'language as right' paradigm which is related to L1 speakers. On the other hand, they are also approached as a resource for the wider community, primarily associated with the cultural sphere; they are taught to L2 speakers in public schools, but to a limited extent, so as not to disrupt the established ideological matrix of monolingual nationalism. Instrumental value is mainly attributed to standard majority and 'world' standard languages. Migrant languages are generally denied institutional protection, as they are considered the cultural heritage of their language communities and native speakers but not of Europe in general and as such remain largely outside formal education.

The teaching of regional and minoritized languages to L2 speakers in public schools is still underdeveloped and the subject of much debate. On the one hand, many initiatives are in favor of removing them from the curricula in order to give more space to English and other prestige foreign languages, and on the other hand, there are numerous grass root initiatives that call for their greater inclusion in the curricula, as they are viewed as a resource in the local labor market and in intergroup cohesion. Still, if regional and minoritized languages are approached as a resource only in the classroom and not in employment, intellectual life and social relations, they are destined for decline and social marginalization.

Acknowledgment

I am very grateful to Brigitta Busch and Judith Purkarthofer for their valuable comments and suggestions.

Funding

This research was supported by the Science Fund of the Republic of Serbia. #7422, Imagining a Nation: The Contesting Serbian National Narratives (XX-XXI century) – IMAGINATION and the Ministry of Education, Science and Technological Development of the Republic of Serbia, according to the Agreement on the realization and financing of scientific research.

Note

1 Office for National Statistics, www.ons.gov.uk/census (accessed February 10, 2024).

References

Abel, A., Vettori, C. and Forer, D. (2012). 'Learning the Neighbour's Language: The Many Challenges in Achieving a Real Multilingual Society. The Case of Second Language Acquisition in the Minority-Majority Context of South Tyrol'. *European Yearbook of Minority Issues*. 9(1): 271–304.

Anderson, B. (1991). *Imagined Communities: Reflections on the Origin and Spread of Nationalism*. London, New York: Verso.

Annamalai, E. (2003). 'Reflections on a Language Policy for Multilingualism'. *Language Policy*. 2(2): 113–132.

Blommaert, J. (2015). 'Commentary: Superdiversity Old and New'. *Language & Communication*. 44: 82–88.

Branchadell, A. (2023). 'Education in a Regional or Minority Language: The Case of Catalan in Spain'. *Revista de Llengua i Dret, Journal of Language and Law*. 79: 227–243.

Brubaker, R. (1998). 'Migrations of Ethnic Unmixing in the "New Europe"'. *International Migration Review*. 32(4): 1047–1065.

Burger, H. (1995). *Sprachenrecht und Sprachgerechtigkeit im österreichischen Unterrichtswesen 1867–1918*. Verlag der Österreichischen Akademie der Wissenschaften.

Busch, B. (2011). 'Trends and Innovative Practices in Multilingual Education in Europe: An Overview'. *International Review of Education*. 57: 541–549.

Busch, B. (2018). 'Article 14'. In R. Hofmann, T. H. Malloy and D. Rein (Eds.), *The Framework Convention for the Protection of National Minorities* (pp. 254–268). Leiden, Boston: Brill Nijhoff.

Busch, B. (2022). 'Minderheitensprachen'. In C. Fölbes and T. Roelcke (Eds.), *Handbuch Mehrsprachigkeit* (pp. 57–82). Berlin: De Gruyter.

Capotorti, F. (1979). *Study on the Rights of Persons Belonging to Ethnic, Religious and Linguistic Minorities.* UN Doc. E/CN4/Sub2/384/Rev. 1.

Cavagnoli, S. and Nardin, F. (1999). 'Second Language Acquisition in South Tyrol: Difficulties, Motivations, Expectations'. *Multilingua*. 18(1): 17–45.

Cavaion, I. (2018). 'Promoting Minority Language Learning Within Mainstream Primary Schools: Five-Step Constructivists and IT-Enhanced Model'. In J. Filipović and J. Vučo (Eds.), *Minority Languages in Education and Language Learning: Challenges and New Perspectives* (pp. 105–122). Belgrade: Faculty of Philology University of Belgrade.

Cavaion, I. (2022). 'Teaching and Learning the Language of the Neighbour Country: Tools for Mainstream Primary Education in the Slovenian-Italian Border Area'. *Zeitschrift für interkulturellen Fremdsprachenunterricht*. 27(1): 81–103.

Cenoz, J. and Gorter, D. (2023). 'Second Language Acquisition and Minority Languages: An Introduction'. In J. Cenoz and D. Gorter (Eds.), *The Minority Language as a Second Language: Challenges and Achievements* (pp. 1–15). New York: Routledge.

Costa, J., Lane, P. and De Korne, H. (2018). 'Standardising Minority Languages: Reinventing Peripheral Languages in the 21st Century.' In P. Lane, J. Costa and H. De Korne (Eds.), *Standardizing Minority Languages: Competing Ideologies of Authority and Authenticity in the Global Periphery* (pp. 1–23). New York: Routledge.

Charalambous, C. (2019). 'Language Education and "Conflicted Heritage": Implications for Teaching and Learning'. *The Modern Language Journal*. 103(4): 874–891.

Charalambous, P., Charalambous, C. and Rampton, B. (2017). 'De-Securitizing Turkish: Teaching the Language of a Former Enemy, and Intercultural Language Education'. *Applied Linguistics*. 38: 800–823.

Cummins, J., Chow, P. and Schecter, S. R. (2006). 'Community as Curriculum'. *Language Arts*. 83(4): 297–307.

Dalton-Puffer, C., Llinares, A., Lorenzo, F. and Nikula, T. (2014). '"You Can Stand Under My Umbrella": Immersion, CLIL and Bilingual Education. A Response to Cenoz, Genesee & Gorter (2013)'. *Applied Linguistics*. 35(2): 213–218.

Debreczeni, S., Duarte, J. and van der Mei, M. G. (2023). 'Potential New Speakers of Frisian in Educational Settings – Implicit and Explicit Attitudes in Learning a Minority Language'. In J. Cenoz and D. Gorter (Eds.), *The Minority Language as a Second Language: Challenges and Achievements* (pp. 159–189). New York: Routledge.

de Jong, E., Li, Z., Zafar, A. and Wu, C. H. (2016). 'Language Policy in Multilingual Contexts: Revisiting Ruiz's "Language-as-Resource" Orientation'. *Bilingual Research Journal*. 39(3–4): 200–212.

de Mejía, A. (2002). *Power, Prestige and Bilingualism: International Perspectives on Elite Bilingual Education*. Multilingual Matters.

Dołowy-Rybińska, N. and Ratajczak, C. (2019). 'Upper Sorbian Language Education: When Community Language Maintenance Practices Disregard Top-Down Revitalisation Strategies'. *Language, Culture and Curriculum*. DOI: 10.1080/07908318.2019.1630424

Dowler, W. (1995). 'The Politics of Language in Non-Russian Elementary Schools in the Eastern Empire, 1865–1914'. *Russian Review*. 54(4): 516–538.

ECRML (1992). *European Charter for Regional or Minority Languages*. Strasbourg: Council of Europe Publishing. Accessed September 20, 2023. www.coe.int/en/web/european-charter-regional-orminority-languages/text-of-the-charter.

European Commission (2008). *A Rewarding Challenge. How the Multiplicity of Languages Could Strengthen Europe: Proposals from the Group of Intellectuals for Intercultural Dialogue Set up at the Initiative of the European Commission (Report)*. Luxembourg: Office for Official Publications of the European Communities. Accessed September 20, 2023. http://ec.europa.eu/education/languages/pdf/doc1646_en.pdf.

Eurydice Report (2023). *Key Data on Teaching Languages at School in Europe*. Eurydice Report. Brussels: European Education and Culture Executive Agency.

FCNM (1995). *Framework Convention for the Protection of National Minorities and Explanatory Report*. Strasbourg: Council of Europe. Accessed September 20, 2023. chrome-extension://efaidnbmnnnibpcajpcglclefindmkaj/https://rm.coe.int/16800c10cf.

From, T. (2023). 'Rethinking Finland's Official Bilingualism in Education'. In M. Thrupp, P. Seppänen, J. Kauko and S. Kosunen (Eds.), *Finland's Famous Education System* (pp. 369–384). Singapore: Springer.

Gal, S. (2006). 'Contradictions of Standard Language in Europe. Implications for the Study of Practices and Publics'. *Social Anthropology*. 14(2): 163–181.

Gal, S. (2011). 'Polyglot Nationalism: Alternative Perspectives on Language in 19th Century Hungary'. *Langage et société*. 136(2): 31–54.

Gal, S. (2015). 'Imperial Linguistics and Polyglot Nationalisms in Austria-Hungary: Hunfalvy, Gumplowitz and Schuchardt'. *Balkanistica*. 28: 151–173.

Garcia, N. (2015). 'Tensions Between Cultural and Utilitarian Dimensions of Language: A Comparative Analysis of "Multilingual" Education Policies in France and Germany'. *Current Issues in Language Planning*. 16(1–2): 43–59.

Genesse, F. (2004). 'What Do We Know About Bilingual Education for Majority-Language Students?' In T. K. Bhatia and W. C. Ritchie (Eds.), *The Handbook of Bilingualism* (pp. 547–576). Blackwell Publishing.

Giudici, A. (2019). 'Explaining Swiss Language Education Policy'. Doctoral Thesis. University of Zurich.

Gorter, D. and Cenoz, J. (2011). 'Multilingual Education for European Minority Languages: The Basque Country and Friesland'. *International Review of Education*. 57: 651–666.

Hadjioannou, X., Tsiplakou, S. and Kappler, M. (2011). 'Language Policy and Language Planning in Cyprus'. *Current Issues in Language Planning*. 12(4): 503–569.

Heller, M. (1999). *Linguistic Minorities and Modernity: A Sociolinguistic Ethnography*. London: Longman.

Heller, M. (2006). *Linguistic Minorities and Modernity: A Sociolinguistic Ethnography*. London: Bloomsbury Publishing.

Heller, M. and Duchêne, A. (2012). 'Pride and Profit Changing Discourses of Language, Capital and Nation-State'. In M. Heller and A. Duchêne (Eds.), *Language in Late Capitalism: Pride and Profit* (pp. 1–21). New York: Routledge.

Horner, K. and Weber, J. J. (2008). 'The Language Situation in Luxembourg'. *Current Issues in Language Planning*. 9(1): 69–128.

Hult, F. M. and Hornberger, N. H. (2016). 'Revisiting Orientations in Language Planning: Problem, Right, and Resource as an Analytical Heuristic'. *The Bilingual Review/La Revista Bilingüe*. 33(3): 30–49.

Jaspers, J. (2015). 'Modelling Linguistic Diversity at School: The Excluding Impact of Inclusive Multilingualism'. *Language Policy*. 14: 109–129.

Judson, P. and Zahra, T. (2012). 'Introduction: Sites of Indifference to Nationhood'. *Austrian History Yearbook*. 43: 21–27.

Kamusella, T. (2009). *The Politics of Language and Nationalism in Modern Central Europe*. Palgrave Macmillan.

Knabe, F. (2000). *Sprachliche Minderheiten und nationale Schule in Preußen zwischen 1871 und 1933: Eine bildungspolitische Analyse*. Münster: Waxmann.

Krel, A. and Mandić, M. (2016). 'Višejezičnost kao habitus: Diskurs banatskih Nemaca o periodu između dva svetska rata'. *Etnoantropološki problemi*. 11(2): 583–600.

Küppers, A., Şimşek, Y. and Schroeder, C. (2015). 'Turkish as a Minority Language in Germany: Aspects of Language Development and Language Instruction'. *Zeitschrift für Fremdsprachenforschung*. 26(1): 29–51.

Liddicoat, A. and Curnow, T. (2014). 'Students' Home Languages and the Struggle for Space in the Curriculum'. *International Journal of Multilingualism*. 11(3): 273–288.

Liddicoat, A. and Taylor-Leech, K. (2015). 'Multilingual Education: The Role of Language Ideologies and Attitudes'. *Current Issues in Language Planning*. 16(1–2): 1–7.

Lo Bianco, J. (2001). *Language and Literacy Policy in Scotland*. Stirling: Scottish CILT.

Mandić, M. and Rácz, K. (2023). 'Learning the Language of Social Environment: The Case of Hungarian in Vojvodina (Serbia)'. *Current Issues in Language Planning*. 24(4): 460–480.

May, S. (2000). 'Accommodating and Resisting Minority Language Policy: The Case of Wales'. *International Journal of Bilingual Education and Bilingualism*. 3(2): 101–128.

May, S. (Ed.) (2014). *The Multilingual Turn: Implications for SLA, TESOL and Bilingual Education*. New York: Routledge.

Mettewie, L. and Van Mensel, L. (2023). 'Understanding Foreign Language Education and Bilingual Education in Belgium: A (Surreal) Piece of Cake'. *International Journal of Bilingual Education and Bilingualism*. 26(5): 639–657.

Milroy, J. (2001). 'Language Ideologies and the Consequences of Standardization'. *Journal of Sociolinguistics*. 5(4): 530–555.

Mikeš, M. (1974). 'Tipologija dvojezičnosti u vaspitnoobrazovnom sistemu Vojvodine'. *Kultura*. 25: 147–167.

Moore, R. (2015). 'From Revolutionary Monolingualism to Reactionary Multilingualism: Top-Down Discourses of Linguistic Diversity in Europe, 1794-Present'. *Language & Communication*. 44: 19–30.

Novak-Lukanovič, S. (1988). 'Bilingual Education in Yugoslavia: Some Experiences in the Field of Education for National Minorities/Nationalities in Yugoslavia'. *Journal of Multilingual and Multicultural Development*. 9(1–2): 169–176.

Novak Lukanovič, S. and Limon, D. (2014). 'Attitudes to Bilingual Education in Slovenia'. *Current Issues in Language Planning*. 15(4): 426–442.

Ó Duibhir, P. and Harris, J. (2023). 'The Acquisition and Use of Irish as a Minority Language'. In J. Cenoz and D. Gorter (Eds.), *The Minority Language as a Second Language: Challenges and Achievements* (pp. 35–59). New York: Routledge.

Ortega, L. (2014). 'Ways Forward for a Bi/Multilingual Turn in SLA'. In S. May (Ed.), *The Multilingual Turn: Implications for SLA, TESOL, and Bilingual Education* (pp. 32–53). New York: Routledge.

Paulsrud, B., Zilliacus, H. and Ekberg, L. (2020). 'Spaces for Multilingual Education: Language Orientations in the National Curricula of Sweden and Finland'. *International Multilingual Research Journal*. DOI: 10.1080/19313152.2020.1714158

Pavlenko, A. (2011). 'Linguistic Russification in the Russian Empire: Peasants into Russians?' *Russian Linguistics*. 35: 331–350.

Pavlenko, A. (2013). 'Language Management in the Russian Empire, Soviet Union, and Post-Soviet Countries'. In R. Bayley, R. Cameron and C. Lucas (Eds.), *The Oxford Handbook of Sociolinguistics* (pp. 651–679). Oxford: Oxford University Press.

Pavlenko, A. (2023). 'Multilingualism and Historical Amnesia: An Introduction'. In A. Pavlenko (Ed.), *Multilingualism and History*. Cambridge: Cambridge University Press.

Petrovic, J. E. (2005). 'The Conservative Restoration and Neoliberal Defenses of Bilingual Education'. *Language Policy*. 4(4): 395–416.

Popović, L. (2024). 'Lokalne povelje o regionalnim ili manjinskim jezicima'. In M. Mandić (Ed.), *Manjinski jezici u Vojvodini: Jezička obrazovna politika, ideologija i praksa* (pp. 81–118). Novi Sad: Akademska knjiga.

Pöyhönen, S. and Saarinen, T. (2015). 'Constructions of Bilingualism in Finnish Government Programmes and a Newspaper Discussion Site Debate'. *Current Issues in Language Planning*. 16(4): 392–408.

Prokopovych, M., Bethke, C. and Scheer, T. (Eds.) (2019). *Language Diversity in the Late Habsburg Empire*. Leiden, Boston: Brill.

Purkarthofer, J. and Mossakowski, J. (2011). 'Bilingual Teaching for Multilingual Students? Innovative Dual-Medium Models in Slovene-German Schools in Austria'. *International Review of Education*. 57: 551–565.

Ricento, T. (2005). 'Problems with the "Language-as-Resource" Discourse in the Promotion of Heritage Languages in the U.S.A.'. *Journal of Sociolinguistics*. 9(3): 348–368.

Ruiz, R. (1984). 'Orientations in Language Planning'. *NABE Journal*. 8(2): 15–34.

Ruiz, R. (2010). 'Reorienting Language-as-Resource'. In J. E. Petrovic (Ed.), *International Perspectives on Bilingual Education: Policy, Practice, and Controversy* (pp. 155–172). Information Age.

Schjerve-Rindler, R. and Vetter, E. (2007). 'Linguistic Diversity in Habsburg Austria as a Model for Modern European Language Policy'. In L. Zeevaert and J. D. Ten Thije (Eds.), *Receptive Multilingualism: Linguistic Analyses, Language Policies, and Didactic Concept* (pp. 49–70). John Benjamins.

Skutnabb-Kangas, T. and García, O. (1995). 'Multilingualism for All – General Principles?' In T. Skutnabb-Kangas (Ed.), *Multilingualism for All* (pp. 221–225). Lisse: Swets & Zeitlinger.

Snyder, T. (2003). *The Reconstruction of Nations Poland, Ukraine, Lithuania, Belarus, 1569–1999*. Yale University Press.

Stotz, D. (2006). 'Breaching the Peace: Struggles Around Multilingualism in Switzerland'. *Language Policy*. 5: 247–265.

Wilson, G. (2023). 'A Comparative Study of Regional-Language Immersion Education in Brittany and Wales'. *Current Issues in Language Planning*. 24(4): 418–439.

Wolf, M. (2015). *The Habsburg Monarchy's Many-Languaged Soul: Translating and Interpreting, 1848–1918*. John Benjamins.

17

CHALLENGING STANDARD LANGUAGE IDEOLOGY IN L2 LEARNING CONTEXTS FOR ENDANGERED AND MINORITY LANGUAGES

Katharine E. Burns

Introduction

If you are hoping to learn a language this year, you might browse the course offerings at your local institutions of learning, or take a look at the options available on language-learning software or apps. You will likely find a list that includes choices such as Arabic, Spanish, French, Japanese, Russian, Korean, and Mandarin. This may seem straightforward, but is it? For example, what variety of your chosen language will be taught in the course? Much of the work of language education has relied on the notion that there is a standard form of a language, and this belief is not limited to language educators – in fact, as L. Milroy (2002) argues, it is pervasive in society. Despite the fact that many world languages exhibit considerable diversity while also being in a state of ongoing change, we do not always see this reality reflected in language learning contexts. This behavior is rooted in standard language ideology (SLI), or the notion that a mostly uniform, largely unvarying, and canonical form of a language exists and is the preferred, correct, and most prestigious variety. As J. Milroy (2001) points out, the designation of 'standard' variety would suggest that such forms of the language are characterized by higher degrees of regularity or uniformity than other forms. However, as J. Milroy (2001) argues, so-called 'standard' varieties are actually those that have the most historical and/or current social prestige. Some scholars have maintained that standard languages are, in fact, abstract ideological constructs. Lippi-Green (2012), for example, defines SLI as

> a bias toward an abstracted, idealized, homogenous spoken language which is imposed and maintained by dominant bloc institutions and which names as its model the written language, but which is drawn primarily from the spoken language of the upper middle class.
>
> (p. 67)

If this is the case, how does a particular language variety come to be considered a standard?

Bourdieu (1991) describes this process as taking place over long periods of time, and as being at the intersection of political, economic, and educational spheres. He roots language standardization

DOI: 10.4324/9781003439493-21

in the milieu of the formation of the nation-state, which involves unifying disparate groups under a common system:

> only when the making of the "nation," an entirely abstract group based on law, creates new usages and functions does it become indispensable to forge a *standard* language, impersonal and anonymous like the official uses it has to serve, and by the same token to undertake the work of normalizing the products of the linguistic habitus.
>
> (p. 48)

The two main forces that Bourdieu (1991) recognizes in forming, reproducing, and reinforcing a standard language are the education system and the labor market, which are in a dialectical relationship: the education system prepares workers for the labor market, including for the civil and administrative roles required in the nation-state. In this capacity, the schools teach the state-approved, standard language directly at the expense of language variation, in particular spoken varieties, which are often devalued and dismissed as "slang and gibberish" (Bourdieu 1991: 49).

In this system, access to, and command of, the standard language provides access to Bourdieu's well-known concepts of cultural, social, economic, and symbolic capital. The power of this variety or varieties is therefore continually reproduced and reinforced by dominant societal institutions such as the education system, the labor market, the government, and the media, while any non-standard varieties or minority languages are continually relegated to the margins and endowed with less and less cultural, social, economic, and symbolic capital from the perspective of the powerful mainstream. As Bourdieu puts it, they are

> found wanting and cast into the outer darkness of *regionalisms*, the "corrupt expressions and mispronunciations" which school masters decry. Reduced to the status of quaint or vulgar jargons, in either case unsuitable for formal occasions, popular uses of the official language undergo a systematic devaluation.
>
> (1991: 54)

Ferguson (1959) also addresses the issue of standard languages, language variation, and power dynamics in his conceptualization of diglossia: the co-existence of multiple varieties or dialects of the same language in a society with different, hierarchically stratified purposes. For example, a prestigious standard used for writing and in education (what Ferguson calls the "high" variety) and one or more less prestigious varieties used primarily for speaking in everyday conversations (what Ferguson calls the "low" variety or varieties). Over the years, many scholars have challenged Ferguson's original notion of diglossia for a variety of reasons; for example, that it reinforces SLI and does not adequately allow for the complexity of the relationship among multiple language varieties in many societies (for a more detailed description of the challenges to Ferguson, see Al Masaeed 2022).

Fuller and Leeman (2020), invoking the work of Irvine (1989), point out that SLI has a moral and political component. This means that speakers of standard varieties are portrayed as "intellectually and morally superior to speakers of nonstandard varieties – who are portrayed as ignorant or lazy – and they are offered more educational and professional opportunities" (Fuller and Leeman 2020: 65). Therefore, they argue, language ideologies, including SLI, have a bi-directional and co-constitutive relationship with social norms.

Additionally, according to Walsh (2021), many conceptualizations of language standardization come from a fundamentally monolingual perspective, ignoring or paying only cursory attention to

The Routledge Handbook of Endangered and Minority Languages

other languages and language varieties that may co-exist with a standard language. Therefore, language standardization explicitly disadvantages endangered and minority languages and language varieties, and likely has contributed to the reasons they are endangered and/or minoritized in the first place. Despite the power of language standardization, language diversity and language variation persist, and nonstandard varieties are ubiquitous, particularly in spoken communication. In the next section, the ways in which this reality manifests in the additional language (L2) classroom are discussed.

SLI in heritage and L2 language instructional contexts

SLI and linguistic prescriptivism have been well documented in L2 and heritage language (HL) textbooks and pedagogical materials, even when the authors of these textbooks purport to take an inclusive and communicative approach (Burns 2018; Burns and Waugh 2018; Heinrich 2005; Brown 2010). Research has further revealed that SLI is foundational to the ways in which languages are conceptualized and taught in many U.S. universities (Valdés, González, López García, and Márquez 2003; Leeman 2012). Valdés, González, López García, and Márquez (2003) found in interviews with university Spanish instructors that the majority believed "the 'best' Spanish [is] defined as pure, formal, and error-free" (p. 16). In cases where language academies exist (e.g., *La Real Academia Española*; *L'Académie française*), various scholars have found their influence over what varieties of a language should be taught in L2 and HL contexts profound, despite their tendency toward a hierarchical view of language variation and a prescriptivist attitude that is conservative regarding language variation and change. Additionally, many studies have discovered that L2 and HL pedagogical materials devalue, dismiss, or give perfunctory attention to language variation (Burns 2020; Ducar 2009). As Burns (2020) points out, reproduction of SLI in these instructional materials and contexts gives L2 and HL students an inaccurate picture of the sociolinguistic reality of target language communities of practice and leaves them ill-prepared to participate in those communities when they leave the classroom, especially when it comes to speaking. Additionally, in disregarding or erasing language varieties, the cultures and experiences of their users are effectively marginalized as well (Bourdieu 1991), and while this constitutes a detriment to all learners, it can be particularly devastating for heritage language learners (HLLs) if they see themselves and/or their loved ones marginalized or erased in the very courses for which they have registered to gain a deeper connection to, and understanding of, their HL. Textbooks and other pedagogical materials are seminal components of most L2 and HL courses, but they do not tell the whole story. Instructor and student perspectives on SLI in these contexts are also key pieces of the overall picture.

Research has found that there can be a disconnect between instructor beliefs and classroom practices regarding SLI. Lowther Pereira (2010) found that despite the fact that HL instructors explicitly stated that they were in favor of their students' home language varieties and that they had the goal of validating their HL students' diverse linguistic repertoires, their practices in the classroom often served to uphold an SLI-infused prescriptivist outlook on Spanish, both implicitly and explicitly. Similarly, Kawafha and Al Masaeed (2023) found that although L2 Arabic instructors claimed to encourage the use of multiple Arabic varieties, classroom observations revealed that instructors routinely objected to students' use of nonstandard Arabic varieties, despite the fact that they often posed questions and provided feedback to students in a nonstandard variety themselves. Del Carpio and Ochoa (2022) echo these findings in their study of a HL program explicitly focused on critical language awareness (CLA), finding that SLI was pervasive among instructors – and at times they were aware of this orientation – despite their competing ideology of upholding CLA. Similarly, Burns and Waugh (2018) conducted focus groups with HL instructors who recognized a mismatch between the stated ideology of the department and program (to validate HL student language varieties) and its reality, in which SLI is dominant in the textbook and syllabi, and student varieties are at times devalued. In addition to textbooks and instructor beliefs and practices, department/program-written exams were identified by instructors in Burns (2018) as a strong source of SLI and of a significant washback effect in the L2 classroom. Efforts to incorporate language variation were in conflict with urgent demands from students to help them prepare for high-stakes exams.

Because SLI is so pervasive in society, students often come to their L2 and HL courses with deeply held language ideologies, whether conscious or not. Coryell, Clark, and Pomerantz (2010) found that SHL learners held strong convictions about the need to speak "proper Spanish," as opposed to their own home variety. Consequently, they expressed a desire to model their Spanish learning after more prestigious varieties of Spanish spoken by monolingual communities, eschewing their own bilingual communities and language practices in the U.S. Southwest. However, there is also evidence in the literature (e.g., Magaña 2015; Ducar 2008; Schwarzer and Petrón 2005) that HL students are not held hostage by SLI and that they in fact prioritize the ability to improve their use of the HL with family and friends over the development of academic or professional registers. Thus, these students favor an approach in their HL courses that privileges practical, authentic, hands-on activities and is not overly concerned with standard varieties.

On the other hand, recent studies have also noted instances in which instructors are successfully challenging SLI in L2 and HL classrooms, often with mixed results. For example, Loza (2017) found that the HL instructors in his study were able to encourage students to think critically about SLI and standard Spanish and that they were to some degree successful in aligning their classroom practices with their beliefs about validating non-standard varieties. Del Carpio and Ochoa's (2022) study indicated that students in a HL program exposed to CLA were increasingly less likely to display SLI as they moved through the program. This indicates that the program and its instructors were having some success at countering SLI, despite the instructors' mixed ideological messages regarding language (described previously). Gasca Jiménez and Adrada-Rafael (2021) corroborate this finding in a study of SHL learners who seemed to hold on to their alignment with SLI despite displaying some progress toward a positive orientation to other aspects of CLA such as language diversity and bilingualism. Similarly, Milojičić (2023), in her study of SLI in an L2 German university program, found that instructors actively attempted to challenge students' preconceived notions of standard German as superior, though students tended maintain their alignment with SLI despite their instructors' stance. Showstack (2017) demonstrates that SLI is both reproduced and challenged in her study of an SHL classroom and that this is related to the ways in which students take on both expert and novice roles in turn.

Overall, then, research shows that SLI is deeply entrenched in HL and L2 instructional contexts, including in pedagogical materials and in instructor and student beliefs and practices. Recent work indicates some progress toward countering SLI in these contexts, but often there emerges a complex picture in which SLI may be challenged on the one hand, especially in textbook prefaces or program mission statements, but then upheld more often than not, both implicitly, and explicitly in pedagogical materials as well as in instructor and student beliefs and practices. In many cases, HLs are immigrant languages, and while they may be minority languages in the context of a given society (i.e., Spanish in the U.S.), in many cases they are not endangered or minoritized when viewed from a global perspective. Of course, there are also cases in which HLs are endangered languages, such as in the case of Indigenous languages. Endangered and minority language (EML) situations, of course, have some overlap with general HLs in instructional contexts but are also unique in some ways. In the next section, we examine the role of SLI in EML instructional contexts.

SLI in endangered and minority language instructional contexts

In cases of some Indigenous EMLs, particularly those with non-Western epistemological and onto-logical orientations, it can be crucial to understand the role language plays in culture, spirituality, and overall worldview. In their work on Indigenous language rights, Nicholas and McCarty (2022) offer a "relational approach" to understanding language, language rights, and the epistemological landscape of many Native American communities. They contend that a relational approach is use-ful because it "foregrounds Indigenous notions and practices of mutuality and responsibility to generations past, present, and future" (Nicholas and McCarty 2022: 229). The relational approach helps us to understand that, in the worldview of many Native American communities, relation-ship is the fundamental lens through which they view themselves and the world. Relationship or kinship ties may be with physical or metaphysical entities, and may occur on various axes of animacy, time, and space. For example, one might be in relationship with humans, animals, plants, other dwellers of the natural world, the land itself, ancestors, future generations, the Creator, and so on. Nicholas and McCarty (2022) point us to the words of Shawn Wilson, an Opsakwayak Cree scholar, who states "relationships do not merely shape reality, they *are* reality" (2008:7). Language is considered a gift from the Creator, and it is the means by which such relationships are conducted, and therefore, the means by which reality is experienced. Native American epistemolo-gies tend to conceptualize time as non-linear, which means that all time periods are experienced concurrently. Consequently, intergenerational transmission of language is not an endeavor focused on a discrete notion of "the future" as it might be for Westerners. Stewardship of language is also a sacred responsibility. With some sensed of the stakes, then, we can turn to a discussion of the role of standardization for EMLs.

In the case of EMLs where language preservation and revitalization are a concern, language standardization can be a double-edged sword, as Lane, Costa, and De Korne (2018) point out: "On the one hand, standardisation remains a potent way of doing or inventing language, of producing languages as bounded, discrete entitles and as social institutions and subsequently increasing the social status of those who use them. On the other hand, standardisation is inherently a limitation of diversity" (p. 2). Identifying, curating, and promoting a standard form of an EML can be a means of advocating for the existence and rights of an Indigenous or minority group, as well the for protection and transmission of the EML to subsequent generations, such as access to mother tongue instruction or status as an official language. Standardization can also provide the basis upon which, for example, a written form of an EML is created and thus items such as diction-aries and pedagogical materials, which can be vital tools for preservation and intergenerational transmission. However, as pointed out in the discussion of language standardization previously (e.g., Bourdieu 1991), language standardization demands that variation be limited, and typically involves selecting and elevating one language variety at the expense of others, especially when literacy and institutionalized education are involved. As Gal (2006) points out, this often creates a complex, contradictory situation in which some EML speakers are doubly stigmatized: those who speak a variety other than the chosen standard may be positioned as speaking a different dialect or language. Situated at the linguistic periphery, their ways of using the language may become stigmatized and even portrayed as 'inauthentic' when measured against the constructed standard. Of course, marginalization of speakers is direct opposition to the purported reason for EML stand-ardization in the first place: maintenance of the EML among as many speakers as possible. This is what Gal (2006) has called "killing a language in order to save it" (p. 171). It is also an example of what Irvine and Gal (2000) referred to as "fractal recursivity," which they define as "the projection of an opposition, salient at one level of relationship onto some other level" (p. 38). In mathematics, fractals are geometric shapes or structures that occur periodically and repeatedly (i.e., "recur") on a progressively smaller scale. Fuller and Leeman (2020) clarify the fractal recursivity metaphor in a language ideologies context by pointing out that "ideological features that are used to differentiate *between* groups are often also used to differentiate *within* groups" (p. 70). In the case of EMLs and standardization, one way in which fractal recursivity may manifest is in dichotomizing a standardized form of the EML against all other varieties in the same way that this is done with a national or non-EML language in that society.

Important as well in the ideological discussion of standardization among EMLs has been the question of the relationship between standard and nonstandard languages and varieties, and the point that "it is (only) in contrast to minority languages (or patois, dialects, Indigenous practices – whatever is relevant to the historical situation) – that standards gain their values." (Gal 2018: 233). In addition, Gal (2006) has argued that two ideologies underpin the authority of standard languages in modernity: authenticity and universality. Authenticity is the belief that the standard variety is a truer representation of its speakers than any other. Universality is the belief that the standard language is the patrimony of an entire entity (nation, tribe, ethnic group, etc.) and thus is "unbiased because it is no one's in particular, and hence represents a socially neutral, supposedly anonymous voice" (Gal 2006: 166). In their work on Aragonese, an EML in northern Spain, Gimeno-Monterde and Sorolla (2022) examine the interplay of arguments related to authenticity vs. authority for new speakers of the language, who are positioned as supplanters of the traditional varieties of Aragonese. The two groups seem unable to agree on a standard variety of the language, and there are arguments over which group has the authority to carry the language forward into the new generation. The authors posit that, in the absence of an agreed-upon standard and the anonymity typically associated with standard languages, the traditional varieties will likely be replaced by what they call an "unrecognized standard." Therefore, the authors conclude, if Aragonese is to continue, new speakers must be incorporated and conflicts must be resolved collaboratively.

Often, in the process of revitalizing or conserving an EML, the issue of language attitudes, in particular those of linguistic purism, can be at play in the standardization process. As Walsh (2021) points out, there is some overlap between the concepts of language attitudes and language ideologies, though she argues that ideologies exist at the societal level, while attitudes are found at the personal level. SLI, then may give rise to puristic attitudes in some speakers. In her work on the revival of Australian Aboriginal languages with no living speakers, Bell notes, "A puristic attitude takes the view that the language being revived should be as close as possible to how it was once spoken many generations ago, or as it is represented in the available historical documents" (2013: 403–404). Those holding such attitudes are typically opposed to code-switching, translanguaging, or any kind of language mixing, as well as the kinds of hybrid languages that have been useful in some revitalization scenarios. Referring to puristic attitudes as "unrealistic," Bell, an Aboriginal linguist, argues that perhaps intermediate levels of revival in which Aboriginal languages are spoken alongside English, Aboriginal English, or other languages should be supported and respected as either stepping stones toward a more robust revival or, in some cases, the furthest some revival efforts may ever advance. Arguing for positive language attitudes over negative ones, Bell points out that some level of survival is key to Aboriginal culture and identity.

In the somewhat complex and contradictory landscape of language standardization for EMLs, and in light of the presence of SLI and puristic language attitudes, what are some best practices to support the revitalization and maintenance of EMLs? How can we attempt to counteract SLI and related language attitudes, especially in instructional contexts?

Models for counteracting SLI in instructional contexts

Identifying and counteracting deeply embedded ideologies, such as SLI, in our instructional contexts can seem daunting. The good news is that we can look to many promising models that have been proposed for challenging SLI and introducing more evidence-based sociolinguistic information into instructional contexts.

Critical language awareness, second dialect acquisition, translanguaging, and heteroglossia

In the context of HL instruction, researchers in the past several decades have called for a turn toward CLA in the HL classroom as a way to explicitly address and challenge various language ideologies in the classroom, including SLI. A CLA approach provides a theoretical and pedagogical orientation in which students are encouraged to learn about the diverse ways in which a particular language or languages are used and to understand that diversity in the context of societal power dynamics (Clark, Fairclough, Ivanič, and Martin-Jones 1990). The goal of CLA is to empower students to exercise their sociolinguistic agency as they negotiate the linguistic component of their L2 or HLL identities. For more information on CLA in the HL classroom, see the special issue of the journal *Languages* edited by Beaudrie (2023). Similar to CLA, Fairclough (2016) proposes second dialect acquisition (SDA) for HLL contexts. SDA is a model that promotes an additive, rather than a subtractive, approach to multiple varieties. The students' home varieties, rather than being stigmatized as in some HL contexts, are treated as a useful first dialect, to which students may add additional varieties or dialects, such as the standard. This process is contextualized using explicit information about language ideologies, the process of language standardization, and the relationship between language and power in society.

Both CLA and SDA share a spirit with translanguaging, an approach with roots in the EML context of Wales (originally coined as *trawsieithu* by Cen Williams 1994, 2000). More recently, translanguaging has been conceptualized in various ways (pedagogical, multilingual, sociopolitical, etc.) and has gained a fair amount of popularity in the field of applied linguistics while also generating some controversy. Ofelia García (2011)'s work with translanguaging among Spanish-English bilingual children in the USA (see also Seltzer, Ascenzi-Moreno, and Aponte, 2020) is well known, and bilingual education contexts, especially those in which students speak an EML, are considered the roots of modern translanguaging approaches. Translanguaging proponents claim to adopt the perspective of a bilingual language user rather than a monolingual one and promote additive bilingualism, in which speakers deploy and expand their full linguistic repertoires rather than suppressing their minority language(s) in order to focus solely on acquiring a majority language (e.g., García and Otheguy, 2016). Translanguaging may be used to combat SLI because it encourages students to draw on all of their existing linguistic resources, including multiple languages and language varieties, in order to communicate effectively and construct knowledge, depending on the situation and interlocutor(s). Hierarchical distinctions between language resources (including languages and language varieties) are avoided. For example, Al Masaeed (2020) has shown how translanguaging can be a resource for L2 learners of Arabic, who harness the breadth of their linguistic repertoires in conversations with their Arabic native speaker peers, deploying multilingual and multidialectal practices despite the monolingual and monodialectal policies of their institution.

Translanguaging approaches also represent a strong challenge to SLI in that many of them question whether standard languages, or, indeed, discrete, so-called 'named languages' exist at all, arguing instead that they are sociopolitical constructs tied to nation-states (García and Li Wei 2014). This is referred to by MacSwan (2017, 2022) as the "deconstructivist turn," of which he is critical, arguing that if named languages are not real, then bi/multilingualism cannot be real either and that the ability of EML communities to advocate for themselves on the basis of their unique languages is also rendered nonexistent. Indeed, Nicholas and McCarty (2022) underscore how fundamental and vital the existence and recognition of separate, named languages are to Indigenous peoples in a myriad of ways: from epistemology and spirituality to fundamental linguistic and human rights, including the right to self-determination. In addition, as McPake and Tedick (2022) point out, those critical of translanguaging approaches for EML immersion programs worry that allowing the use of multiple languages, especially the dominant language(s) of the wider society, may threaten the purpose of having a dedicated, protected forum in which to use, revitalize, and preserve the EML. These concerns do not appear to be limited to EML users and are echoed in a mother tongue instruction context in South African primary schools by Bloch, Guzula, and Nkence (2010: 102): "it will take some effort and time for teachers to stop using code-mixing as it has become common practice with many. The need to code-mix will only fade once all significant aspects of teaching are delivered as a matter of course in isiXhosa" They are critical of students and teachers engaging in multilingual practices, and strongly advocate for the mother tongue, isiXhosa (not an EML), and English to be treated as separate languages. Therefore, it seems that anxieties around the use of multilingual practices (translanguaging, code-switching, code-mixing, etc.) are not limited to EML contexts, though of course they may be more heightened in cases where language survival is at stake.

In response to the deconstructivist turn, MacSwan advocates for a multilingual perspective on translanguaging, which treats bi/multilingualism as "psychologically real and socially significant" (2022: xvii) and embraces the many decades of bilingualism, code-switching, and psycholinguistic research upon which modern conceptualizations of translanguaging are built. While the multilingual perspective on translanguaging rejects the idea of a unitary linguistic repertoire without boundaries between discrete, 'named' languages, it recognizes and affirms the pedagogical benefits for learners of validating and encouraging the use of all their semiotic resources, especially for bi/multilingual learners, EML users, and HLLs. In this way, most translanguaging approaches share a desire to challenge monolingual ideologies and SLI, which both stigmatize bilingual language practices.

Translanguaging, especially in EML contexts, has also often adopted a critical, social justice-oriented perspective for the purposes of supporting and empowering EML-speaking bilingual students. However, operationalizations of translanguaging in more traditional instructed L2 contexts, especially for adolescent or adult learners, have been criticized for lacking the social justice component of translanguaging that seeks the "disruption of language hierarchies" (Turner and Lin 2017: 423). Such criticism has been primarily directed at contexts in which there is a perceived power imbalance between students' L1 (higher overall global economic, social, and/or cultural capital) and the language they are seeking to learn (lower overall global capital). In other words, can students who are not operating from linguistically minoritized positions rightfully participate in translanguaging? In contrast, some researchers have argued that translanguaging can occur alongside the existence of named languages and that the desire of many language learners to study so-called named languages is not in conflict with the idea of expanding their linguistic repertoires. Al Masaeed (2020) advocates for the validation of "speakers' linguistic repertoires as their own idiolects without ignoring their desire to enrich their repertoires in the target language or variety they are pursuing" (p. 2).

In a similar vein, but in an L1 context, Huang (2016) employs both Bakhtin's concept of heteroglossia and critical discourse studies to explore the relationship between the SLI at the national level in China (the Putonghua Promotion Policy) and teachers' local language ideologies. Heteroglossia, as defined by Bakhtin, reflects the diversity and multiplicity within standard/national languages:

> The internal stratification of any single national language into social dialects, characteristic group behavior, professional jargons, generic languages, languages of generations and age groups, tendentious languages, languages of the authorities, of various circles and of passing fashions, languages that serve the specific sociopolitical purposes of the day, even of the hour.
>
> (Bakhtin 1981: 262–263)

Acknowledging this multiplicity of voices within the unity of a national language, in this case, Putonghua (or Standard Mandarin), Huang (2016) investigates teachers' discursive practices and discovers the ways they negotiate, reproduce, or resist national language policies aligned with SLI, and further advocates for classroom policies that explicitly acknowledge and promote languages as inherently heteroglossic.

Ideological clarification and the polynomic model

Turning now to some models for counteracting SLI that have specifically been implemented for EML contexts, Roche (2019) has explored whether ideological clarification might be of use in the context of Manegacha, a Tibetan minority language. Ideological clarification (Fishman 1991) calls for a community to directly address, and attempt to resolve, contradictory or conflicting language ideologies in order to move forward with revitalization and maintenance efforts. Kroskrity (2009) points out that this process should involve confronting attitudes and ideologies that are both Indigenous to the community and those that have been imposed or introduced by out-group members. Roche (2019), invoking a variety of theoretical principles such as "heteroglossia, discursive polyphasia, cognitive polyphasia, the compartmentalization principle, and nonoverlapping magisteria" (p. 127), argues that perhaps ideological contradictions are not inherently negative, may not need to be resolved and may be able to exist in a functional and normal way that is not necessarily in opposition to language maintenance. In his case study of two Manegacha-speaking communities, contradictory attitudes toward language maintenance were found, regardless of the degree to which Manegacha was being successfully maintained in each community. Therefore, it is possible, argues Roche (2019), that ideological clarification is not necessary for maintenance efforts. We can extrapolate, then, that there might not be a need to completely eradicate ideologies such as SLI for EML revitalization and maintenance efforts to succeed.

Also promising in challenging SLI is the polynomic model, originally described by Corsican linguist Jean-Baptiste Marcellesi, in which a community of speakers mutually agrees upon which linguistic forms will be recognized as constituting their language and does not place hierarchical distinctions on these forms. Therefore, as there is no variety more prestigious than any other, the polynomic model directly contradicts SLI (van der Lubbe 2023). Advocating for the application

Challenging standard language ideology

of a polynomic model to the maintenance and revitalization of the Ryukyuan languages (EMLs in Okinawa, Japan), van der Lubbe (2023) argues that the application of such a model could circumvent the 'double stigma' issue discussed previously. Declining to identify and promote a standard version of the EML would protect its speakers from the further minoritization and marginalization that can occur for those who do not speak a newly identified standard. In addition, the community avoids what van der Lubbe calls "the colonialist attitudes that led to the endangerment of Okinawan and the other Ryukyuan languages in the first place: hierarchisation and discrimination of variation" (2023: 11).

Finally, it is important to note that academic theories, empirical research, and the support of professional linguists may not be the solution for EML revitalization and maintenance. There have long been calls in the field for community members, whether or not they have academic training, to lead any efforts to reverse language shift in EML communities. Academic endeavors, including this chapter, should not assume they understand the priorities of the communities, who, for example, may not even count SLI among issues of importance to them. As Bell put it, "Many community language activists today are keen to reclaim the language back from academics and missionaries and to put their own brand on it, generally with the backing of their community" (Bell 2013: 405).

Conclusions and future directions

This chapter has focused on the issue of SLI when it comes to instructional contexts for L2, HL, and EML speakers and learners. This includes pedagogical materials, instructor perspectives, and student perspectives. Theoretical and empirical work has argued that SLI is pervasive in society, limits linguistic diversity, and can disadvantage speakers of nonstandard language varieties. Educational institutions are key sites of the reproduction of SLI, and its impacts can be complex. In cases of Indigenous communities, such as the North American ones discussed previously, relational approaches to language have been proposed as a way of expressing the foundational importance of language as a mediational tool in the epistemological and ontological orientations of such communities. In light of this relational perspective, the importance of revitalization and maintenance of Indigenous EMLs is made clear, which sets the stage for us to question the role standardization might play in these efforts. Though much of the applied linguistics literature is critical of SLI because of its negative implications for language diversity, there are voices who point out some potential benefits of language standardization for EML-speaking communities who have the goal of language revitalization and/or maintenance. For instance, standardized, discrete forms of an EML may provide an important basis from which to conduct advocacy for EML communities, argue for their self-determination, and contribute to a sense of identity (cultural, political, national, etc.). Additionally, a standard form of the EML may be helpful in creating a written form of the language, if necessary, which is useful for documenting the EML and designing pedagogical materials to be used for revitalization, maintenance, and intergenerational transmission efforts.

Some approaches to counteracting SLI in instructional contexts have been highlighted in this chapter as well. Critical language awareness and second dialect acquisition provide theoretical and pedagogical frameworks to challenge SLI by embracing multilingual and multidialectal practices and de-stigmatizing language diversity (both between and within languages). Students are encouraged to examine the relationship between sociolinguistic variation, language ideologies, bilingualism, and power explicitly and critically. The hope is that, armed with this information as well as an ever-expanding set of semiotic resources, they will be able to exercise sociolinguistic agency and decide which language(s) and varieties they prefer to use (including standard varieties), depending on factors such as the context and their desired positioning as they dynamically negotiate their linguistic identities. Translanguaging and heteroglossic approaches, which also embrace linguistic diversity and challenge SLI, have been examined here as well, along with some criticism of translanguaging's contention that so-called 'named languages' are not real, which has been called deconstructivist and thus damaging to language diversity, EMLs, and Indigenous and language minority communities. In EML-specific contexts in which language revitalization and maintenance are of concern, scholars have evaluated the benefits and drawbacks of approaches such as ideological clarification and the polynomic model.

SLI is unlikely to disappear, and many of the approaches to counteracting SLI discussed in this chapter are aimed at creating a more equitable balance of power in instructional contexts between SLI and various ideologies promoting language diversity and multilingual and multidialectal practices, especially for EML-related situations. While there are some, such as Villa (1996), who contend that standard languages are abstract, idealized fabrications that should no longer be taught or perpetuated, most acknowledge at least some role for standard varieties in the classroom, often in the domain of writing. However, scholars such as Lippi-Green (2012) have cautioned that this can be a slippery slope, because one main source of power for SLI is in portraying the standard form of a language as aligned with, or identical to, the written form(s) of language. Additionally, educational institutions (language departments in particular) have been identified as overly preoccupied with literature and written language and as typically dismissive of spoken language varieties, which contributes to the reproduction of SLI and the suppression of variety (Ortega 1999). On the other hand, it maybe be prudent to take a measured approach to critical perspectives in the classroom and avoid leaving learners with the impression that they do not need to have a strong command of the standard language(s) that are pertinent to their lives and futures.

Future work, then, might seek to find ways in which to recognize and challenge SLI while avoiding the some of the potential pitfalls of deconstructivism. Needed as well are more empirical studies that provide detailed evidence of the specific ways in which translanguaging contributes to the learning progress and outcomes of L2, HL, and EML learners. In the context of translanguaging for EML instructional contexts, for example, McPake and Tedick (2022) point out the lack of research aimed at measuring students' progress – is translanguaging contributing to, or detracting from, their language progress? They further underscore the need to approach such assessments from the perspective of assessing students' bilingualism rather than assessing them against monolingual speakers of the L1, and, in turn, the L2. They also call for more studies tracking outcomes of the graduates of translanguaging-focused EML immersion programs in order to ascertain to what extent the alumni live as bilingual people and to have a longitudinal perspective. There have also been calls for language instructors to have more teacher training and preparation not only in some of the approaches and models discussed in this chapter but also about the basic linguistic profiles and pedagogical needs of HL and EML speakers, who are not always included in pre-service education for L2 and World Language teachers (see Ducar 2022; McPake and Tedick 2022). In keeping with the principles of CLA and SDA, future work could also seek to further and to solidify our understanding of the effects of including evidence-based sociolinguistic information and measured critical perspectives in L2 learning, with the aim of empowering learners as (emergent) bilinguals, particularly for EML users, for whom the stakes can be quite high. Nicholas (a Hopi scholar) and McCarty (2022: 242) remind us: "Names and naming – myaamia, Hopilavayi, Kanienke:ha – are vitally important connectors to distinct lands/waters, people, and home place."

Challenging standard language ideology

References

Al Masaeed, K. (2020). 'Translanguaging in L2 Arabic Study Abroad: Beyond Monolingual Practices in Institutional Talk.' *The Modern Language Journal*. 104(1): 250–266.

Al Masaeed, K. (2022). 'Sociolinguistic Research vs. Language Ideology in L2 Arabic.' In K. Geeslin (Ed.), *The Routledge Handbook of Second Language Acquisition and Sociolinguistics* (pp. 359–370). New York, NY: Routledge.

Bakhtin, M. M. (1981) *The Dialogic Imagination: Four Essays* (C. Emerson and M. Holquist, Trans.). Austin, TX: University of Texas Press.

Beaudrie, S. M. (Ed.) (2023). 'Developing Heritage Language Learners' Critical Language Awareness [Special Issue].' *Languages*. 8(1). https://doi.org/10.3390/languages8010081

Bell, J. (2013). 'Language Attitudes and Language Revival/Survival.' *Journal of Multilingual and Multicultural Development*. 34(4): 399–410. https://doi.org/10.1080/01434632.2013.794812

Bloch, C., Guzula, X., and Nkence, N. (2010). 'Towards Normalizing South African Classroom Life: The Ongoing Struggle to Implement Mother-Tongue Based Bilingual Education.' In K. Menken and O. García (Eds.), *Negotiating Language Policies in Schools* (pp. 88–106). Abingdon: Routledge.

Bourdieu, P. (1991). *Language and Symbolic Power*. Cambridge, MA: Harvard University Press.

Brown, L. (2010). 'Questions of Appropriateness and Authenticity in the Representation of Korean Honorifics in Textbooks for Second Language Learners.' *Language, Culture and Curriculum*. 23(1): 35–50.

Burns, K. E. (2018). 'Marginalization of Local Varieties in the L2 Classroom: The Case of U.S. Spanish.' *L2 Journal*. 10(1): 20–38. https://doi.org/10.5070/L210135863

Burns, K. E. (2020). 'Beyond the Idealized Native Speaker in L2 Spanish Contexts: Standard Language Ideology, Authenticity, and Consequences for Learner Identity Construction.' In B. Dupuy and K. Michelson (Eds.), *Pathways to Paradigm Change: Critical Examinations of Prevailing Discourses and Ideologies in Second Language Education* (pp. 32–52). Boston, MA: Cengage.

Burns, K. E., and Waugh, L. R. (2018). 'Mixed Messages in the SHL Classroom: Insights from CDA of Textbooks and Instructor Focus Group Discussions.' *Heritage Language Journal*. 15(1): 1–24. https://doi.org/10.46538/hlj.15.1.2

Clark, R., Fairclough, N., Ivanič, R., and Martin-Jones, M. (1990). 'Critical Language Awareness Part I: A Critical Review of Three Current Approaches to Language Awareness.' *Language and Education*. 4(4): 249–260. https://doi.org/10.1080/09500789009541291

Coryell, J. E., Clark, M. C., and Pomerantz, A. (2010). 'Cultural Fantasy Narratives and Heritage Language Learning: A Case Study of Adult Heritage Learners of Spanish.' *Modern Language Journal*. 94(3): 453–469.

Del Carpio, L., and Ochoa, V. (2022). 'Language Ideologies in the Spanish Heritage Language Classroom: (Mis)alignment between Instructor and Students' Beliefs.' *Languages*. 7(3): 187. https://doi.org/10.3390/languages7030187

Ducar, C. M. (2008). 'Student Voices: The Missing Link in the Spanish Heritage Language Debate.' *Foreign Language Annals*. 41(3): 415–433.

Ducar, C. M. (2009). 'The Sound of Silence: Spanish Heritage Textbooks' Treatment of Language Variation.' In M. Lacorte and J. Leeman (Eds.), *Español en Estados Unidos y otros contextos de contacto: Sociolingüística, ideología y pedagogía/Spanish in the United States and Other Contact Environments: Sociolinguistics, Ideology and Pedagogy* (pp. 347–367). Madrid, Spain: Iberoamericana/Vervuert.

Ducar, C. M. (2022). 'SHL Teacher Development and Critical Language Awareness: From Engaño to Understanding.' *Languages*. 7(3): 182. https://doi.org/10.3390/languages7030182

Fairclough, M. (2016). 'Incorporating Additional Varieties to the Linguistic Repertoires of Heritage Language Learners: A Multidialectal Model.' In M. Fairclough and S. M. Beaudrie (Eds.), *Innovative Strategies for Heritage Language Teaching: A Practical Guide for the Classroom* (pp. 143–165). Washington, DC: Georgetown University Press.

Ferguson, C. A. (1959). 'Diglossia.' *Word*. 15(2): 325–340. https://doi.org/10.1080/00437956.1959.11659702

Fishman, J. (1991). *Reversing Language Shift: Theoretical and Empirical Foundations of Assistance to Threatened Languages*. Clevedon: Multilingual Matters.

Fuller, J. M., and Leeman, J. (2020). *Speaking Spanish and the US: The Sociopolitics of Language*. 2nd Edition. Bristol, UK: Multilingual Matters.

Gal, S. (2006). 'Contradictions of Standard Language in Europe: Implications for the Study of Practices and Publics.' *Social Anthropology*. 14(2): 163–181.

Gal, S. (2018). 'Visions and Revisions of Minority Languages: Standardization and Its Dilemmas.' In P. Lane, J. Costa, and H. De Korne (Eds.), *Standardizing Minority Languages: Competing Ideologies of Authority and Authenticity in the Global Periphery* (pp. 222–242). Taylor & Francis. https://doi.org/10.4324/9781315647722

García, O. (2011). 'The Translanguaging of Latino Kindergarteners.' In K. Potowski and J. Rothman (Eds.), *Bilingual Youth: Spanish in English-Speaking Societies* (pp. 33–55). Amsterdam: Johns Benjamins.

García, O., and Li, W. (2014). *Translanguaging: Language, Bilingualism and Education*. New York, NY: Palgrave Macmillan.

García, O., and Otheguy, R. (2016). 'Interrogating the Language Gap of Young Bilingual and Bidialectal Students.' *International Multilingual Research Journal*. 11(1): 52–65.

Gasca Jiménez, L., and Adrada-Rafael, S. (2021). 'Understanding Heritage Language Learners' Critical Language Awareness (CLA) in Mixed Language Programs'. *Languages*. 6(37). https://doi.org/10.3390/languages6010037

Gimeno-Monterde, C., and Sorolla, N. (2022). '"To Die with Dignity or to Be Supplanted by the Standard": Empowerment and Inclusive Practices of Urban New Speakers of Aragonese.' *Journal of Multilingual and Multicultural Development*. 43(1): 8–20. https://doi.org/10.1080/01434632.2021.1963268

Heinrich, P. (2005). 'Language Ideology in JFL Textbooks.' *International Journal of the Sociology of Language*. 175–176: 213–232.

Huang, J. (2016). 'Heteroglossic Practices and Language Ideologies: Combining Heteroglossia with Critical Discourse Studies to Investigate Digital Multilingual Discourses on Language Policies.' In E. Barakos and J. W. Unger (Eds.), *Discursive Approaches to Language Policy* (pp. 129–149). London: Palgrave Macmillan. https://doi.org/10.1057/978-1-137-53134-6_6

Irvine, J. T. (1989). 'When Talk Isn't Cheap: Language and Political Economy.' *American Ethnologist*. 16(2): 248–267.

Irvine, J. T., and Gal, S. (2000). 'Language Ideology and Linguistic Differentiation.' In P. Kroskrity (Ed.), *Regimes of Language* (pp. 35–84). Santa Fe: School of American Research Press.

Kawafha, H., and Al Masaeed, K. (2023). 'Bilingual and Multidialectal Practices in L2 Arabic Classrooms: Teachers' Beliefs vs. Actual Practices.' *Frontiers in Education*. 8: 1060196. https://doi.org/10.3389/feduc.2023.1060196

Kroskrity, P. (2009). 'Language Renewal as Sites of Language Ideological Struggle: The Need for "Ideological Clarification".' In J. Reyhner and L. Lockhard (Eds.), *Indigenous Language Revitalization: Encouragement, Guidance and Lessons Learned* (pp. 71–83). Flagstaff, AZ: Northern Arizona University.

Lane, P., Costa, J., and De Korne, H. (2018). 'Standardising Minority Languages: Reinventing Peripheral Languages in the 21st Century.' In P. Lane, J. Costa, and H. De Korne (Eds.), *Standardizing Minority Languages: Competing Ideologies of Authority and Authenticity in the Global Periphery* (pp. 1–23). London: Taylor & Francis. https://doi.org/10.4324/9781315647722

Leeman, J. (2012). 'Investigating Language Ideologies in Spanish as a Heritage Language.' In S. M. Beaudrie and M. Fairclough (Eds.), *Spanish as a Heritage Language in the United States: The State of the Field* (pp. 43–59). Washington, DC: Georgetown University Press.

Lippi-Green, R. (2012). *English with an Accent: Language, Ideology, and Discrimination in the United States*. New York, NY: Routledge.

Lowther Pereira, K. (2010). 'Identity and Language Ideology in the Intermediate Spanish Heritage Language Classroom.' Unpublished Doctoral Dissertation (University of Arizona, Tucson, AZ).

Loza, S. (2017). 'Transgressing Standard Language Ideologies in the Spanish Heritage Language (SHL) Classroom.' *Chiricú Journal*. 1(2): 56–77. https://doi.org/10.2979/chiricu.1.2.06

MacSwan, J. (2017). 'A Multilingual Perspective on Translanguaging.' *American Educational Research Journal*. 54(1): 167–201. https://doi.org/10.3102/0002831216683935

MacSwan, J. (Ed.) (2022). *Multilingual Perspectives on Translanguaging*. Bristol, UK: Multilingual Matters.

Magaña, D. (2015). 'From Pedagogy to Communities: Issues Within and Beyond the Spanish Heritage Language Classroom.' *Studies in Hispanic and Lusophone Linguistics*. 8(2): 375–388.

McPake, J., and Tedick, D. J. (2022). 'Translanguaging and Immersion Programs for Minoritized Languages at Risk of Disappearance: Developing a Research Agenda.' In J. MacSwan (Ed.), *Multilingual Perspectives on Translanguaging* (pp. 295–320). Bristol, UK: Multilingual Matters.

Milojičić, V. (2023). 'Deconstructing the Myth of Standard German: Navigating Language Ideologies in the L2 German University Classroom.' *Foreign Language Annals*. 56: 453–479. https://doi.org/10.1111/flan.12665

Milroy, J. (2001). 'Language Ideologies and the Consequences of Standardization.' *Journal of Sociolinguistics*. 5(4): 530–555.

Milroy, L. (2002). *Standard English and Language Ideology in Britain and the United States*. New York, NY: Routledge.

Nicholas, S. E., and McCarty, T. L. (2022). 'To "Think in a Different Way" – A Relational Paradigm for Indigenous Language Rights.' In J. MacSwan (Ed.), *Multilingual Perspectives on Translanguaging* (pp. 227–247). Bristol, UK: Multilingual Matters.

Ortega, L. (1999). 'Language and Equality: Ideological and Structural Constraints in Foreign Language Education in the U.S.' In T. Huebner and K. Davis (Eds.), *Sociopolitical Perspectives on Language Policy and Planning in the USA* (pp. 243–266). Amsterdam: Johns Benjamins.

Roche, G. (2019). 'Does Ideological Clarification Help Language Maintenance? Exploring the Revitalization Paradox Through the Case of Manegacha, a Tibetan Minority Language.' *Anthropological Linguistics*. 61(1): 114–134. www.jstor.org/stable/26907073

Schwarzer, D., and Petrón, M. (2005). 'Heritage Language Instruction at the College Level: Reality and Possibilities.' *Foreign Language Annals*. 38(4): 568–578.

Seltzer, K., Ascenzi-Moreno, L., and Aponte, G. Y. (2020). 'Translanguaging and Early Childhood Education in the USA: Insights from the CUNY-NYSIEB Project.' In J. Panagiotopoulou, L. Rosen, and J. Strzykala (Eds.), *Inclusion, Education and Translanguaging* (pp. 23–39). Wiesbaden: Springer.

Showstack, R. E. (2017). 'Stancetaking and Language Ideologies in Heritage Language Learner Classroom Discourse.' *Journal of Language, Identity and Education.* 16(5): 271–284.

Turner, M., and Lin, A. M. Y. (2017). 'Translanguaging and Named Languages: Productive Tension and Desire.' *International Journal of Bilingual Education and Bilingualism*. 23(4): 423–433.

Valdés, G., González, S. V., López García, D., and Márquez, P. (2003). 'Language Ideology: The Case of Spanish in Departments of Foreign Languages.' *Anthropology & Education Quarterly*. 34(1): 3–26.

Walsh, O. (2021). 'Introduction: In the Shadow of the Standard. Standard Language Ideology and Attitudes Towards "Non-Standard" Varieties and Usages.' *Journal of Multilingual and Multicultural Development*. 42(9): 773–782. https://doi.org/10.1080/01434632.2020.1813146

Wilson, S. (2008). *Research Is Ceremony: Indigenous Research Methods*. Halifax, NS and Winnipeg, MB: Fernwood Publishing.

Williams, C. (1994). 'Arfarniad o Ddulliau Dysgu ac Addysgu yng Nghyd-destun Addysg Uwchradd Ddwyieithog [An Evaluation of Teaching and Learning Methods in the Context of Bilingual Secondary Education].' Unpublished Doctoral Thesis (University of Wales, Bangor).

Williams, C. (2000). 'Bilingual Teaching and Language Distribution at 16+.' *International Journal of Bilingual Education and Bilingualism*. 3(2): 129–148. https://doi.org/10.1080/13670050008667703

Van der Lubbe, G. (2023). 'Introducing a Polynomic Approach in Ryukyuan Language Learning.' *Languages (Basel).* 8(1). https://doi.org/10.3390/languages8010011

Villa, D. J. (1996). 'Choosing a "Standard" Variety of Spanish for the Instruction of Native Spanish Speakers in the U.S.' *Foreign Language Annals*. 29(2): 191–200.

18
TURNING TOWARD PLURILINGUALISM THROUGH A FOCUS ON PLACE

Kellie Rolstad

Introduction

The inclusion of this chapter in *The Routledge Handbook of Endangered and Minority Languages* provides an opportunity to consider both the endangered and precarious condition of languages such as Hawaiian, Navajo, and Welsh and also the endangered and precarious condition of whole groups of people who speak minoritized languages and dialects, including African American people, whose languages and dialects have survived despite ongoing and systematic social oppression (Rickford and Rickford 2000). African American Language (AAL) has been historically denigrated and widely considered 'slang' or 'not a real language' and is often expressly forbidden for use in schools (Pullum 1999; Reaser et al. 2017). While Hawaiian, Navajo, and Welsh are spoken and also written, and speakers of these languages are encouraged to develop oral and literate proficiency in those languages, speakers of AAL are typically permitted to use only General American English (GAE) in schools, are discouraged from maintaining their oral proficiency in AAL, and typically receive no instruction in AAL literacy traditions; learning literacy in GAE, a dialect unfamiliar to many young African American children, complicates the process (Baugh 2000). Why should AAL speakers not be permitted to learn literacy in their own language? As Noam Chomsky has said,

> A language is not just words. It's a culture, a tradition, a unification of a community, a whole history that creates what a community is. It's all embodied in a language.
>
> (as quoted in Makepeace 2010)

Understanding that *all* dialects and languages of *all* speech communities are legitimate and worthy of respect can help teachers create classrooms that celebrate linguistic proficiencies rather than discourage them.

In this chapter, I discuss the contributions of several terms and theoretical frameworks used in education for examining language policies and practices. I propose using the term *linguaphobia* to describe the irrational fear of and reactions, both personal and societal, against languages and accents other than the standard dialect selected and used by powerful members of a society. I also seek to promote the use of the terms *plurilingualism* and *plurilanguaging* in place of

DOI: 10.4324/9781003439493-22

translanguaging in line with current global research and policy (Mendoza 2023; MacSwan and Rolstad 2024). Last, I propose incorporating pedagogies of place into teacher education as a way of raising language awareness by bridging between classrooms and authentic speech communities. It is my hope that by weaving together theoretical concerns and proposals, practical problems, history, critique, and some evidence of program improvements, this chapter will illustrate the importance of bringing linguistic theory into education in a way that informs research, policy, and practice.

Linguaphobia around the world

Responsible people in societies around the world know that expressing racist, ethnocentric, and xenophobic ideas is unacceptable; as of 2020, the United Nations has again affirmed that 'any doctrine of racial superiority is scientifically false, morally condemnable, socially unjust and dangerous and must be rejected' (United Nations General Assembly 2020: 2) and has issued a global call for 'concrete action for the elimination of racism, racial discrimination, xenophobia and related intolerance' (United Nations General Assembly 2020: 1). We know racism and xenophobia are deplorable, yet disparaging the *language* used by marginalized, 'outsider' groups continues to be considered acceptable in schools and other mainstream settings; the disrespect shown toward these languages and dialects can be considered covert racism, or 'racism by proxy' (Lippi-Green 2012). In 2001, the Common European Framework of Reference for Languages (CEFR) began promoting the term *plurilingualism* to denote the extra, value-added aspect of appreciating multilingualism as language diversity (Piccardo 2017), and yet nearly two decades passed before France passed legislation forbidding accent discrimination, including against speakers of France's regional varieties and against international speakers (Assemblée Nationale 2019). The new law made France the first and thus far only country to illegalize 'la glottophobie' – language/accent phobia. According to Nguyen and Hajek (2022: 188), 'To the best of our knowledge . . . linguistic discrimination has not been officially made unlawful in many other polities in the world.' In their review of terms used to explore linguistic discrimination, Nguyen and Hajek (2022) decide in favor of *linguicism*, a term coined by Tove Skutnabb-Kangas (1988). Nguyen and Hajek do not, quite understandably, consider *glottophobia* as an appropriate English term; however, the *phobia* aspect warrants consideration. In terms ending in *-ism*, such as *racism, sexism, ageism, ableism*, and so forth, the subject rather than target of discrimination is specified. In terms such as *homophobia, transphobia, xenophobia* and *Islamophobia*, the targeted group is explicitly named. Into which category, then, does discrimination against language and accent fall? Attaching *phobia* to *lingua* creates *linguaphobia*, the irrational fear of languages, capturing the idea that language itself is the object of suspicion and contempt. I will thus use *linguaphobia*[1] here.

Linguaphobia remains prevalent, yet mostly unnoticed, even in otherwise progressive societies, with schools and curricula implicitly or explicitly disparaging languages and dialects other than the standard dialect (Baker-Bell et al. 2020). This is the case not only in U.S. K–12 schools but also at the college level (Savini 2021). Dubinsky and Starr (2022) document 'ways in which the oppression of language use on the part of a dominant language/ethnic group is instrumentalized as a tool to inflict gratuitous societal pain and punishment upon nondominant ethnolinguistic groups and their individual members' (2022: 1) and cite the cases of Uyghurs in China, Kurds in Turkey, and Hungarians in Slovakia. In places like these, standard language policies routinely serve to indoctrinate children to believe that some languages are better than others, pushing standard language use and denouncing linguistic diversity (Dubinsky and Starr 2022). Standard language ideology often leads to the mistreatment of students whose home language differs from the standard variety, which occurs routinely in schools despite legal precedents such as *Lau v. Nichols* in 1974 and the 1979 Ann Arbor Decision, where children who speak Cantonese and children who speak African American Language, respectively, were found to have been wrongly treated as deficient (MacSwan 2020). Standard language hegemony is especially insidious given the prevalence of anti-Blackness; Wun argues that "school discipline policies position Black girls as 'captive objects.' The girls are under constant surveillance while they are refused access to agency, autonomy, and self-defense against multiple forms of violence including gratuitous punishment inflicted by school faculty" (2016). Racism influences all aspects of instruction; as some have argued (Baker-Bell 2020; Hankerson 2022; Reagan 2019), language arts lessons in U.S. schools are in many ways unwittingly based on White supremacy–driven curricula and practices, privileging dominant English over socially stigmatized varieties. Indeed, anti-Blackness is a global problem that involves language supremacy as well as racial supremacy (Carr Center for Human Rights Policy 2024). In the U.S., concepts of race and racialization have played an outsize role in discrimination. In other contexts, such as Great Britain, social class may play the main role, and accent discrimination creates unjust systems that oppress English speakers whose accents reveal less privilege and often lower socioeconomic status (Levon et al. 2022). In both cases, these linguaphobic policies and practices reify racist and classist social divisions and perpetuate prejudice and discrimination (Alim 2016).

It is astounding to anyone familiar with the beauty and intricacies of AAL that anyone, least of all the teachers of children in schools, should denigrate and deny children the use of their powerful language ways. Baker-Bell and colleagues demand change, stating,

> As language and literacy researchers and educators, we acknowledge that the same anti-Black violence toward Black people in the streets across the United States mirrors the anti-Black violence that is going down in these academic streets (Baker-Bell et al. 2017). In this current sociopolitical context, we ask: How has Black Lives Mattered in the context of language education?
>
> (Baker-Bell et al. 2020)

Linguaphobia in policy and in practice: the language gap

Linguaphobia, which stems from misguided assumptions about the relative value of languages and dialects, has long held sway in education, both in language arts, as students learn about the standard dialect, and in the study of other languages. Rather than nondominant varieties being considered merely different, difference tends to turn into deficit views: 'In terms of language, proponents of the deficit position believed that speakers of dialects with non-standard forms have a handicap – socially and cognitively – because the dialects are illogical, or sloppy, or just bad grammar' (Wolfram et al. 1999: 20). At the heart of linguaphobia lie both ignorance and deep disrespect for entire cultural and ethnic groups, though the prejudice often goes unrecognized as such; instead, the language used by racialized, minoritized cultural and ethnic groups is assumed to be 'the problem' that causes the socioeconomic and educational failure of linguistically minoritized groups. The pre-eminent study outlining this sort of blame-the-victim deficit theory which continues to drive U.S. policy and practice is Hart and Risley (1995). In their study, the researchers observed a very small number of families and counted up the number of words directed to very young children, who ranged from seven months to three years of age. Professional parents (12/13 of whom were from White families) were documented as speaking more to their children than did middle-class or working-class parents or parents living in poverty (6/6 families in the study living in poverty were Black). The researchers reported, based on their observations, that the children in professional families had heard over 1000 words over the course of the study, while the children in the six Black, low-income families had heard about 500 words. There are many reasons to question this finding, including 'an ethnocentric bias that takes for granted the normative status of the linguistic and cultural practices of the middle- and upper-income families in their sample: the failure to make explicit the theory of language and culture that frames their analysis' (Dudley-Marling and Lucas 2009) and the failure to count words that the researchers did not know (words that were not in 'the dictionary' of standard English, according to the researchers). These are just a few of the many severe methodological flaws of Hart and Risley (1995).

However, Hart and Risley (1995) further claimed that if they extrapolated based on the 500-vs. 1000-word difference, then eventually the children in the professional families would have heard 30 million more words than the children in the Black, low-income families. Thirty million words signifies a tremendous gap, likely to be insurmountable, and this 'language gap' problem has led to many, many federally funded studies and programs designed to address this linguistic deficit (HRSA 2021). Unfortunately, despite criticism (for example, Dudley-Marling and Lucas 2009; Avineri et al. 2015), Hart and Risley's deficit perspective continues to drive much of U.S. education and practice (see Rolstad 2014 for further concerns with their work); however, the issue I would like to highlight here is that many readers assume that the researchers meant that the children would hear 30 million *different* words. When I assign Hart and Risley (1995) to my graduate students to read, their most common reaction is concern over how to teach 20 million more words to low-income children of color or how to get their parents to talk to them more and earlier. I then press my students to think about how many words there are in the English language. The average vocabulary size of a college-educated American adult is estimated to be less than 20,000 words, and the entire vocabulary of English tops out somewhere around 1 million (Hashimoto 2021); out of those 1 million words, however, Merriam-Webster currently maintains only 470,000 words in its online dictionary, with others considered too archaic or otherwise unworthy of inclusion (Merriam-Webster 2024).

What then is the actual significance of this 30-million-word-gap finding? Due in part to research in linguistic anthropology, we know that whether or not adults speak directly to children is irrelevant to children's successful acquisition of language, as long as the children are exposed to language interactions in their environment (Ochs 1982). What the 'language gap' line of research does show is that racism and classism are very much alive in the linguaphobic U.S. domains of research and teaching, still driving studies and leading to funding that seeks to support low-income children of color because of their supposed linguistic deficits (Rolstad 2014). These children need and deserve full support of all their educational needs, but their linguistic needs are drastically misunderstood. Instead of 'correcting' or 'improving' their language development by pushing standard English only, educators and education researchers can learn to recognize that all children's languages and dialects are inherently good and valuable and worthy of development in and of themselves rather than something faulty to eradicate and replace with standard English. Learners can maintain their home languages and dialects while also learning the standard variety.

Critical language awareness as an antidote to linguaphobia

Current anti-bias education policies are necessary and laudable; however, even in well-established anti-bias education programs, linguaphobia is rarely discussed. The dearth of either curriculum or policies to promote equitable dialect use leads to the denigration of minoritized dialects, and of the children and families who speak them (Lippi-Green 2012). Where anti-bias approaches are encouraged and used, a 'good' education remains predicated on students' willingness to relinquish or even to repudiate their stigmatized or marginalized dialect in favor of a standard variety (Bacon 2017). In the absence of appropriate policies and curriculum, it falls on individual educators to promote language variation, but this is only possible once the educators have come to recognize the linguaphobia that holds sway in so many schools.

Critical language awareness (CLA) captures the understanding that all human languages and dialects are equally valid and deserving of respect, as are the people who speak them. Linguists refer to 'a language' as an umbrella term that includes various 'dialects' that are mutually intelligible; speakers of different languages struggle to understand each other, while speakers of different dialects of a language can generally understand each other fairly easily (Linguistic Society of America 2017).[2] All dialects, like all human languages, are equally expressive, systematic, logical, and grammatical, and the question of which dialect serves as the standard is a matter only of determining who has the sociopolitical power to choose their own dialect and force others to use it (Lippi-Green 2012).

The origins of linguaphobia: standard language ideology

In U.S. society, and in education settings more specifically, SLI holds that one way of speaking and writing is superior to all others and that it is the inherent superiority of that particular dialect that has led to its selection as 'the standard' language (Baugh 2000; Charity-Hudley and Mallinson 2010; MacSwan 2020). Linguistics research showing the baselessness of SLI has had very little impact on the U.S. K–12 curriculum. Children whose language use differs are often labeled not only as unfamiliar with the standard variety, but as ignorant, lazy, incapable of learning. It is in this way that standard language use is falsely and harmfully equated with intelligence. Promoting CLA in teacher education programs can help pre-service and in-service teachers to think explicitly and critically about the nature of language and its role in the classroom (Godley et al. 2015; Krulatz et al. 2018; Leeman 2018; Reaser et al. 2017).

Monolingualism and multilingualism

Despite the fact that the U.S. has no official language, 'standard English' is widely regarded as the premier language of mass communication, and monolingualism in standard English is considered normal and desirable (Wiley and Lukes 1996); further, the 'standard' is defined as the variety used by the White middle and upper classes, and it is widely believed that 'standard English is singularly correct and that all other languages and social dialects are inferior' (Kroskrity 2021: 183). However, even when considering standard English, there is no single 'standard American English'; rather, there are multiple standard varieties that vary by region. Monolingualism in English remains the norm for the majority of Americans, despite research support for, and popular movements to promote, bilingual or dual language education in elementary education, and where multilingual programs are popular, they are often promulgated by and for more privileged White families (Bacon 2017; Chang-Bacon 2021).

While decades of research in child bilingualism have shown that children can learn multiple languages given adequate support, it remains commonplace for teachers, pediatricians, speech therapists, and many other people who work with children to tell linguistically minoritized parents to avoid speaking their stigmatized or nonstandard language or dialect with their own children, under the assumption that more than one language confuses children (National Academies of Sciences, Engineering, and Medicine 2017). Language acquisition research, by contrast, shows that no such confusion occurs, even among children with developmental delays (Kay-Raining Bird et al. 2016). Language of instruction program evaluation shows that children learn both content and language best when instruction is delivered bilingually and is more effective the more the first language is included (MacSwan et al. 2017; McField 2014; Rolstad et al. 2005).

Language arts vs. language science

Language and literacy instruction, typically called 'language arts' in schools is based on classist and racist tradition, not on language science, and because teachers themselves typically do not understand precisely why the language they must teach to children may feel inauthentic and unnatural, children are frequently left confused. As evidence, consider this: In many dialects of English, speakers are comfortable using 'Me and [someone]' as the subject of a sentence. For example, 'Me and my friend walk home together after school,' or 'Me and him are collaborating on that project.' In standard English(es), the subject requires the nominative case, so that would translate to 'My friend and I walk home' and 'He and I are collaborating on that project.' This is because in standard English, conjoining two or more subjects requires that the other person take the lead position in the sentence, and the self comes last in the conjoined subject phrase. At the same time, when two people are conjoined in an object phrase, 'me' is correct, and the order does not matter. In standard English as in many English dialects, it is grammatical to say, 'This present is from Bobby and me.' There is no other way to express that. Many readers are probably arguing back at this moment, thinking, that's not right, it should be 'This present is from Bobby and I!' The grammaticality test, however, is to separate the conjoined phrase, as follows: 'The present is from Bobby. The present is from me.' Recombining them, it can only be – 'The present is from Bobby and me.' If you wonder, as I do, why English speakers are so confused about this, I suspect it is because most of us were told as children that it is incorrect to say 'Me and Bobby are walking home'; this construction is ungrammatical *only* in standard English, not in most other English dialects. Children may even be punished for violating this standard English rule. But no matter how severe the punishment or how frequent the reminders, if the child does not understand why 'me and Bobby' is incorrect as a subject phrase, the child will assume that it is simply *always* incorrect to say 'me and Bobby', even when it is not.

An appropriate education includes the study of arts of all kinds but must also include the study of science. The previous pronoun confusion example is just one example of language arts instruction leading to widespread confusion, highlighting the importance of incorporating language science/linguistic theory in education, but there are many other misunderstandings related to language and language learning.

From multilingualism to plurilingualism

Historically, it was widely believed that while elite families do well to encourage multilingualism in their children, families living in poverty or in any sort of less advantaged conditions should speak only English to their children and insist that the children focus solely on English language development (Hakuta 1986). This double standard of 'multilingualism for elites only' has shifted in recent decades to 'multilingualism for all,' more slowly perhaps in the U.S. (American Academy of Arts and Sciences 2016) but more quickly elsewhere (Piccardo 2018). Elite families were largely responsible for driving interest in language immersion programs in Quebec and Florida in the 1960s, first one-way and then two-way immersion, which led to a burgeoning interest among teachers and parents in promoting bilingualism in early childhood (Lindholm-Leary 2012). However, language-minoritized communities soon joined the language immersion movement as a way of bringing their endangered languages back and allowing their children to learn and develop those heritage languages; by the 1990s, ground-breaking language revitalization programs were reversing language loss in places like Hawaii (Kawai'ae'a et al. 2007), in the Navajo Nation (Lockard and De Groat 2010), and in Wales (Williams 2014).

The utility of translanguaging

The turn away from monolingualism to multilingualism reflected a shift in cultural values, which in turn promoted a shift in pedagogy. Languages had long been taught in isolation, and students were often not permitted to use the 'wrong' language during language instruction, but in the 1980s, Cen Williams promoted the planful use of two languages in the same lesson and coined the term 'translanguaging' for this bilingual pedagogical practice (Lewis et al. 2012). García (2009) popularized 'translanguaging' in the U.S., then later turned to postmodernism to repudiate the basis of translanguaging, claiming that postmodernism does not allow the existence of 'named' languages and that, therefore, bilingualism, first languages (L1) and second languages (L2) do not exist (Garcia et al. 2021). This postmodernist stance has rendered the term 'translanguaging' useless in discussing or defending bi/multilingualism and bi/multilingual education. (See MacSwan and Rolstad 2024 for further discussion.)

Monolingualism has begun to lose value in favor of multilingualism in many societies today, and newer pro-multilingual policies reflect that shift. Multilingualism is often widely valued primarily as a tool for economic gain; however, multilingualism embedded within multiculturalism can promote appreciation of diversity, not merely tolerance of it. Diversity of many types has become more established as a positive value in education. Still, while the term 'multilingualism' captures the ability to use more than one language, the term is otherwise value neutral and hence does not convey much meaning when it comes to promoting attitudes toward diversity and difference (Piccardo and Capron 2015). While CEFR has been promoting plurilingualism in Europe since 2001, during the time that translanguaging has influenced educators in the U.S., the term *plurilingualism* has caught on in the rest of the world (Piccardo 2017), without any of the confusion introduced by translanguaging's deconstructivist pitfalls. What can be done to promote plurilingualism, especially among monolingual teachers?

Promoting plurilingualism in teacher preparation programs: the plurilingual turn

In an attempt to combat this rampant and widely accepted linguistic racism and classism, teacher preparation programs can incorporate materials and activities that show that all languages and dialects are linguistically valid and valuable (Alim 2007; Baker-Bell 2013; Cushing 2023; Godley et al. 2015; Reaser et al. 2017; Shi and Rolstad 2022; Chi and Rolstad 2024). Robust, overlapping theoretical frameworks taken up recently to support these pedagogical practices include critical language awareness (e.g., Metz 2022), pedagogical translanguaging (e.g., Cenoz and Gorter 2022), and plurilingualism (e.g., Wichser-Krajcik 2021).

Teachers can help students understand the basics of linguistics and model for them how to listen to and show respect for all dialects and languages. Classrooms and teachers that engage CLA can create welcoming, supportive environments where all students can learn and thrive, not only by witnessing positive treatment of their own language variety but also those of others (Alim 2010; Baker-Bell 2020; Hankerson 2022). In other words, linguistic representation is extremely important, especially for those who face a long history of linguistic denigration, but representation is only the first, crucial step in fostering authentic anti-bias beliefs and attitudes. Instead of focusing solely on monolingual development, instruction can be provided to all children in ways that promote more equitable access to education and goals of valuing linguistic diversity, often with little more than a change in teacher understanding of, and attitude toward, plurilingualism (Chi and Rolstad 2024). Plurilingualism added to an anti-bias curriculum can serve as a strong foundation for linguistic justice in schools and beyond. It is long past time for educators and education researchers to stop the widespread practice of denigrating dialects and languages that happen to differ from whatever the regional standard may be and to begin celebrating the linguistic repertoires of all children and their families and communities, providing culturally sustaining pedagogy and keeping their precious language heritages intact (Smitherman 1986; Paris 2012). Taking a plurilingual turn in teacher education is the crucial next step in promoting truly anti-bias education (Rolstad 2023).

While access to information can help, developing relationships across linguistic and cultural boundaries is key to increasing teachers' respect for stigmatized languages and their speakers (Nieto 2006; Leeman 2018; Chi and Rolstad 2024; Shi and Rolstad 2022). Who are these speakers of stigmatized languages? In the U.S., many people who speak stigmatized languages and dialects live in urban settings; African American Language is well represented in U.S. cities, including many regional dialects of AAL (Wolfram and Thomas 2002). Cities also are often home to immigrant families who have come from many different areas of the world, and while some immigrants speak world languages generally viewed as prestigious, such as French, Russian, and Japanese, others speak languages that are generally stigmatized in the U.S. The combination of social, economic, and linguistic factors affecting language status can be called *sociolinguistic status* (Rolstad 1997). If a local speech community is wealthy and/or holds high status in mainstream community, its language will generally be considered valuable, and children are likely to be encouraged toward bilingualism; however, if the speech community is not wealthy and/or lacks high status in the mainstream community, its language will probably be stigmatized, and children from the community may be pushed to speak only standard English in school. It is crucial that educators become aware of their local linguistic context and prepare appropriate relevant lessons to counter whatever negative perceptions are present in their school population and in the wider community.

Knowing the social and linguistic context of their school is teachers' first step; the second step is getting to know adult speakers who are willing to work with teachers. Sometimes parents are available who can connect with teachers, though many parents find it difficult to arrange time to visit the school site. Parents can be a tremendous language resource, often able to share stories in their language/dialect, either by reading published children's books or by telling stories from their own lives. In cases where the language is not easily understood by students, storytelling aids such as drawings, photographs, realia, and dramatic gestures can help students follow the story. However, when parents are not available, there may be community resources; the more students who speak a given language are present in a school, the greater the likelihood that there is a population of adult speakers in the neighborhood as well, and these are the people who can be invited to share their experiences and stories with students. How might teachers form relationships with speakers of stigmatized languages and dialects in the community in ways that inform and support their teaching? In the next section, I describe one approach to establishing relationships in the community around the school.

Place-based education

Principles drawn from place-based education (PBE) can help teachers connect with the greater community. In the PBE curriculum approach, learning first begins at the most local level; the younger the student, the more local the learning context (Anderson 2017; Sobel 2005). Place-based education incorporates two important features: (1) *place* (where the students are) provides the focus of instruction, and (2) *projects*, because projects involve concrete learning. Once students are involved in concrete learning, abstract concepts become more relevant and easier to learn. Projects are designed to be useful to the students and/or to their community, and students collaborating first to conduct a critical analysis helps provide the basis for choosing projects to do (Yemini et al. 2023). The goal is not to teach subject matter for its own sake; instead, subject matter knowledge provides *tools* for authentic learning. When the focus is on place and projects, there are no rigid subject area boundaries; creating something is never about *only* math or *only* physics or *only* writing (Dewey 1899; Krajcik et al. 2022). Place shifts over time; in kindergarten, children focus on their classroom and playground, then each year, the focus expands – from the school, to the town, region, the nation, and so on, from local to global (Sobel 2005).

Critical engagement in the community means considering the social and ecological exploitation of people and places, doing something to improve or even rehabilitate places and processes, and helping the people who are affected (Gruenewald 2003). Teacher interns can learn about plurilingualism and how to create and share their own locally inspired linguistic justice lessons with children. They can help children adopt a more open-minded, egalitarian approach to languages and language diversity. PBE can engage students in learning all of the subject areas required in children's education through a focus on community, but such place-based programs are still rare in public education settings. Modeling a place-based approach with teacher interns is an important step. Reaching out to the local community provides several important additional benefits. It is not uncommon for teachers to be hired to work in schools where they do not share the cultural backgrounds of their students, which often creates a disconnect between teachers and their students and the students' families. PBE provides a framework for contextualizing the curriculum and lessons within the students' daily lives, which is powerful for engaged learning, and can also benefit the community, as the school becomes more integrated into the community, and school/community partnerships can more easily be developed.

First, PBE helps teachers develop community relationships and local knowledge. Second, teachers and students familiarize themselves with the community, the most local community early on, and then gradually expanding the circle of 'community' each year. By reaching out and involving participants beyond the school, important and valuable connections are made with community members. Third, a place-based approach can enable teachers and their students to become activists in the community who can support wider awareness of the issues under study.

Fourth and finally, building on these community connections, the community and school may be able to adopt additional aspects of place-based education, being open to considering and engage further issues and problems faced by the community, whether in terms of resource distribution, pollution, transit, civic engagement, climate change, and other elements of social and environmental justice. PBE thus allows students to engage in contextualized, project-based learning and skills development in ways that simultaneously serve and support the community.

Incorporating a focus on language in place-based education

Teacher educators can show intern teachers the importance of developing lessons based not only on the culture but also the languages of people in the local community. This plurilingual approach can help intern teachers contextualize lessons and forge connections with local language speakers and their language practices. The interns learn about plurilingualism and in turn create and share their own locally inspired linguistic justice lessons with children and teens, inviting students to adopt a more open-minded approach to languages and dialects – first to those of their community and, expanding outward to those of their region, of their society and of the larger world. We can now augment PBE to place-based plurilingual education (PBPE).

The first step in implementing PBPE can be, quite literally, to take a walk in the community (Gorter et al. 2021). With teachers as guides to view the linguistic landscape, students can see for themselves the various languages on display, used in signage, murals, and so on. These public language and literacy displays present rich opportunities for teaching multiliteracy and language awareness. In addition to the visual element, El Ayadi (2021) points out the importance of the linguistic soundscape; 'soundwalking' allows students to hear the sounds of the languages so that they are not only seen but heard. This way, students can personally and directly experience the languages around them, bringing their thoughts and experiences into deep discussions of language diversity in different times and spaces. 'Through urban walks, the linguistic soundscape is a source of constantly negotiating the present with past experiences and more broad ideas about places, people and languages' (El Ayadi 2021). In cases where mobility is an issue, students can settle into a suitable area to experience what Bruce (2023) calls 'soundsitting.' As humanistic geographers, Mamadouh and El Ayadi (2022) highlight the ways in which exploration of urban multilingualism 'foregrounds the perceptions and representations of languages in relation to a sense of place and a sense of belonging'. This sort of linguistic place-based experiential learning can increase linguistic sensitivity and awareness for anti-bias education, helping students acknowledge and appreciate not only the functions of multilingualism but the beauty of plurilingual people and places.

> The importance of language in socio-spatial relations is . . . likely to become progressively more apparent as contemporary processes of globalization are intensifying cultural contact, such that linguistic diversity increasingly characterises both local and global context. This is both challenging traditional assumptions about the relationships between linguistic uniformity, cultural homogeneity and national identities as well as impacting on self-identities.
>
> (Valentine et al. 2008: 385)

PBPE is interdisciplinary and grounded in places and systems; the boundaries set by the curriculum for any given period of time are geographic, with the selected area of study serving as a touchstone of sorts. In considering any particular focus, for example, geography – the teacher can ask, Who has lived or passed through these places, and what languages did they speak? Of economics, What languages and dialects are financially more viable? Of mass incarceration, Are the languages and dialects of incarcerated people representative of the population as a whole, or does there seem to be any linguaphobia influencing incarceration?, and so forth. Regardless of the issue, there is always a linguistic connection to be drawn. Layering in plurilingualism exposes many unexpected disparities and inequities and enriches the understanding of complex phenomena. In extending the PBPE approach to matters of linguaphobia and linguistic justice, a unit on critical language awareness can lay the foundation for subsequent community engagement; once students understand the basics of language variation and multilingualism, they are better able to interact respectfully and profoundly with people whose language use differs from theirs and/or from the standard variety commonly found in a school curriculum.

Plurilingualism and plurilanguaging

Making the shift from U.S.-centric deconstructivist translanguaging to the broader global focus on plurilingualism invites fresh perspectives grounded in firm theoretical footing (MacSwan and Rolstad, in press 2024; Piccardo 2017; Piccardo et al. 2021). Research in languaging can be conducted worldwide, with shared understandings, theoretical frameworks, methods, and data. I use the term 'languaging' following Jørgensen (2004), who says, 'what we do when we use the uniquely human phenomenon of language to grasp the world, change the world, and shape the world is languaging' (2004: 13). Languaging means that each person plays a part in shaping the world through their use of language(s) and in doing so shapes the language(s) in turn (Becker 1991). Plurilingualism brings creativity to the fore, leading to a synergy between language and creativity that often results in hybridity and innovation (Piccardo 2017). What plurilingualism adds to languaging is the high valuing of all the languages and dialects in a person's existing and growing repertoire, beyond the mere fact of their repertoire; plurilanguaging highlights the love of languaging, creativity, and the continual recognition of the power and joy of languaging. In other words, a multilingual speaker may be observed utilizing a mix of languages and/or dialects to achieve an end, but a plurilingual person who is employing their languages joyfully, powerfully, lovingly, or in any way going above and beyond the minimum can be said to be plurilanguaging. Plurilanguaging is how we 'do plurilingualism' or use our languages creatively, and creating environments where all children feel comfortable and encouraged to bring their talents, their joy, and their creativity into their language use should be the primary goal of education.

This chapter explores the blending of these critical linguistic approaches with place-based learning strategies to propose ways in which linguistic social justice pedagogies can inject plurilingualism into anti-bias pedagogy. With or without plurilingual policies and linguistically informed curricula, teachers must assume responsibility for learning and spreading the truth about language and language diversity and should no longer participate in inflicting linguistic trauma. It is not difficult to teach standard language varieties while also maintaining home languages and dialects; educators need only normalize plurilingualism rather than monolingualism and standard language ideology. Teachers taking the lead to create a sense of community – based in place – is a simple and satisfying way to promote plurilingualism as one of the crucial foundations of the acceptance and celebration of diversity of all kinds in our fantastically diverse world.

Notes

1 In 1958, Furness proposed the term *linguaphobia*, but in her definition, she included the fear of *the study of* languages, including one's own language. I propose using *linguaphobia* without the added element of *study*.
2 According to the Linguistic Society of America (2017, section b), 'the distinction between "languages" and "dialects" is usually made more on social and political grounds than on purely linguistic ones" and for the purposes of this chapter, both 'language' and 'dialect' will be used interchangeably.

References

Alim, H. S. (2007). 'Critical hip-hop language pedagogies: combat, consciousness, and the cultural politics of communication.' *Journal of Language, Identity, and Education, 6*(2): 161–176.
Alim, H. S. (2010). 'Critical language awareness.' In Hornberger, N. H. & McKay, S. L. (eds.), *Sociolinguistics and language education* (pp. 205–231). Multilingual Matters.
Alim, H. S. (2016). 'Introducing raciolinguistics: racing language and languaging race in hyperracial times.' In Alim, H. S., Rickford, J. R. & Ball, A. F. (eds.), *Raciolinguistics: how language shapes our ideas about race* (pp. 1–30). Oxford University Press. https://doi.org/10.1093/acprof:oso/9780190625696.003.0001

American Academy of Arts and Sciences. (2016). *The state of languages in the U.S.: a statistical portrait*. Retrieved January 29, 2024 from www.amacad.org/publication/state-languages-us-statistical-portrait

Anderson, S. K. (2017). *Bringing school to life: place-based education across the curriculum*. Rowman & Littlefield.

Assemblée Nationale/National Assembly. (2019, December 3). *Proposition de loi visant à promouvoir la France des accents/Legal proposition to promote accents in France. N° 2473*. Retrieved February 9, 2024 from www.assemblee-nationale.fr/dyn/15/textes/l15b2473_proposition-loi

Avineri, N., Johnson, E., Brice Heath, S., McCarty, T., Ochs, E., Kremer-Sadlik, T., Blum, S., Zentella, A. C., Rosa, J., Flores, N., Alim, H. S. & Paris, D. (2015). 'Invited forum: bridging the "language gap".' *Journal of Linguistic Anthropology, 25*(1): 66–86.

Bacon, C. K. (2017). 'Dichotomies, dialects, and deficits: confronting the "Standard English" myth in literacy and teacher education.' *Literacy Research: Theory, Method, and Practice, 66*(1).

Baker-Bell, A. (2013). '"I never really knew the history behind African American language": critical language pedagogy in an advanced placement English language arts class.' *Equity & Excellence in Education, 46*(3): 355–370. https://doi.org/10.1080/10665684.2013.806848

Baker-Bell, A. (2020). *Linguistic justice: Black language, literacy, identity, and pedagogy*. Routledge.

Baker-Bell, A., Stanbrough, R. J. & Everett, S. (2017). 'The stories they tell: mainstream media, pedagogies of healing, and critical media literacy.' *English Education, 49*(2): 130–152.

Baker-Bell, A., Williams-Farrier, B. J., Jackson, D., Johnson, L., Kynard, C. & McMurtry, T. (2020). *This ain't another statement! This is a DEMAND for Black linguistic justice! Statement on anti-Black racism and Black linguistic justice, or, why we cain't breathe!* Conference on College Composition and Communication. Retrieved May 29, 2024 from https://cccc.ncte.org/cccc/demand-for-black-linguistic-justice

Baugh, J. (2000). *Beyond ebonics: linguistic pride and racial prejudice*. Oxford University Press.

Becker, A. L. (1991). 'Language and languaging.' *Language & Communication, 11*(1–2): 33–35. https://doi.org/10.1016/0271-5309(91)90013-L

Bruce, N. S. (2023). 'Extending soundwalking practice: soundsitting as an inclusive and complementary method to soundwalking.' *Acoustics, 5*(3): 788–793.

Carr Center for Human Rights Policy. (2024, April 10). *Global anti-Blackness and the legacy of the transatlantic slave trade*. Symposium Report. Harvard Kennedy School. Retrieved May 29, 2024 from www.hks.harvard.edu/centers/carr/publications/global-anti-blackness-and-legacy-transatlantic-slave-trade

Cenoz, J. & Gorter, D. (2022). 'Pedagogical translanguaging and its application to language classes.' *The RELC Journal, Singapore, 53*: 342–354.

Chang-Bacon, C. K. (2021, January). 'Monolingual language ideologies and the idealized speaker: the "new bilingualism" meets the "old" educational inequities.' *Teachers College Record, 123*(010306).

Charity-Hudley, A. H. & Mallinson, C. (2010). *Understanding English language variation in U.S. schools*. Teachers College Press.

Chi, J. & Rolstad, K. (2024). 'Challenging standard language ideology and promoting critical language awareness in teacher education.' In Kocaman, C. & Selvi, A. F. (eds.), *International perspectives on critical English language teacher education: theory and practice* (pp. 27–32). Bloomsbury.

Cushing, I. (2023). 'A raciolinguistic perspective from the United Kingdom.' *Journal of Sociolinguistics, 27*(5): 473–477.

Dewey, J. (1899). *The school and society: Being three lectures*. The University of Chicago Press.

Dubinsky, S. & Starr, H. (2022, April). 'Weaponizing language: Linguistic vectors of ethnic oppression.' *Global Studies Quarterly, 2*(2): 1–13.

Dudley-Marling, C. & Lucas, K. (2009). 'Pathologizing the language and culture of poor children.' *Language Arts, 86*(5): 362–370.

El Ayadi, N. (2021). 'Linguistic sound walks: setting out ways to explore the relationship between linguistic soundscapes and experiences of social diversity.' *Social & Cultural Geography, 23*(2): 227–249.

Furness, E. L. (1958, January). 'Are we victims of linguaphobia?' *The Modern Language Journal, 42*(1): 20–22.

García, O. (2009). 'Education, multilingualism and translanguaging in the 21st century.' In Skutnabb-Kangas, T., Phillipson, R., Mohanty, A. K. & Panda, M. (eds.), *Social justice through multilingual education* (pp. 140–158). Multilingual Matters.

Garcia, O., Flores, N., Seltzer, K., Wei, L., Otheguy, R. & Rosa, J. (2021). 'Rejecting abyssal thinking in the language and education of racialized bilinguals: a manifesto.' *Critical Inquiry in Language Studies, 18*(3): 203–228.

Godley, A. J., Reaser, J. & Moore, K. G. (2015). 'Pre-service English language arts teachers' development of critical language awareness for teaching.' *Linguistics and Education*, *32*(Part A): 41–54. https://doi.org/10.1016/j.linged.2015.03.015

Gorter, D., Cenoz, J. & van der Worp, K. (2021). 'The linguistic landscape as a resource for language learning and raising language awareness.' *Journal of Spanish Language Teaching*, *8*(2): 161–181.

Gruenewald, D. A. (2003). 'The best of both worlds: a critical pedagogy of place.' *Educational Researcher*, *32*(4): 3–12. https://doi.org/10.3102/0013189X032004003

Hakuta, K. (1986). *Mirror of language: the debate on bilingualism*. Basic Books.

Hankerson, S. (2022). '"Why can't writing courses be taught like this fo real": Leveraging critical language awareness to promote African American Language speakers' writing skills.' *Journal of Second Language Writing*, *58*: 1–14. https://doi.org/10.1016/j.jslw.2022.100919

Hart, B. & Risley, T. R. (1995). *Meaningful differences in the everyday experience of young American children*. Paul H Brookes Publishing.

Hashimoto, B. J. (2021). 'Is frequency enough? The frequency model in vocabulary size testing.' *Language Assessment Quarterly*, *18*(2): 171–187. https://doi.org/10.1080/15434303.2020.1860058

Health Resources and Services Administration. (2021). *Bridging the word gap research network*. Maternal and Child Health Bureau. Retrieved January 28, 2024 from www.hrsa.gov/grants/find-funding/HRSA-21-040

Jørgensen, J. N. (2004). 'Languaging and languagers.' *Languaging and Language Practices*, *5*(23).

Kay-Raining Bird, E., Genesee, F. & Verhoeven, L. (2016). 'Bilingualism in children with developmental disorders: a narrative review.' *Journal of Communication Disorders*, *63*(1): 1–14.

Kawai'ae'a, K. K. C., Housman, A. K. & Alencastre, M. (2007). 'Pü'ä i ka Ölelo, Ola ka 'Ohana: Three generations of Hawaiian language revitalization.' *Hūlili: Multidisciplinary Research on Hawaiian Well-Being*, *4*(1): 183–237.

Krajcik, J., Schneider, B. L., Miller, E. A., Chen, I.-C., Bradford, L., Baker, Q., Bartz, K., Miller, C., Li, T., Codere, S. & Peek-Brown, D. (2022). 'Assessing the effect of project-based learning on science learning in elementary schools.' *American Educational Research Journal*, *60*(1): 1–33. https://doi.org/10.3102/00028312221129247

Kroskrity, P. V. (2021, August). 'Covert linguistic racisms and the (re-)production of White supremacy.' *Linguistic Anthropology*, *31*(2): 180–193.

Krulatz, A., Steen-Olsen, T. & Torgersen, E. (2018). 'Towards critical cultural and linguistic awareness in language classrooms in Norway: fostering respect for diversity through identity texts.' *Language Teaching Research*, *22*(5): 552–569. https://doi.org/10.1177/1362168817718572

Leeman, J. (2018). 'Critical language awareness and Spanish as a heritage language: challenging the linguistic subordination of US Latinxs.' In Potowski, K. (ed.), *Handbook of Spanish as a minority/heritage language* (pp. 345–358). Routledge.

Levon, E. Sharma, D. & Ilbury, C. (2022, November). *Speaking up: Accents and social mobility*. The Sutton Trust.

Lewis, G., Jones, B. & Baker, C. (2012). 'Translanguaging: origins and development from school to street and beyond.' *Educational Research and Evaluation: An International Journal on Theory and Practice*, *18*(7): 641–654.

Lindholm-Leary, K. (2012). 'Success and challenges in dual language education.' *Theory into Practice*, *51*(4): 256–262.

Linguistic Society of America. (2017). *LSA resolution on the Oakland "ebonics" issue*. Retrieved January 29, 2024 from www.linguisticsociety.org/resource/lsa-resolution-oakland-ebonics-issue

Lippi-Green, R. (2012). *English with an accent: language, ideology, and discrimination in the United States*. Routledge.

Lockard, L. & De Groat, J. (2010). '"He said it all in Navajo!": indigenous language immersion in early childhood classrooms.' *International Journal of Multicultural Education*, *12*(2): 1–14.

MacSwan, J. (2020). 'Academic English as standard language ideology: a renewed research agenda for asset-based language education.' *Language Teaching Research*, *24*(1): 28–36.

MacSwan, J. & Rolstad, K. (2024). '(Un)grounded language ideologies: a brief history of translanguaging theory.' *International Journal of Bilingualism*, *28*(4): 719–743. https://doi.org/10.1177/13670069241236703

MacSwan, J., Thompson, M., Rolstad, K., McAlister, K. & Lobo, G. (2017). 'Three theories of the effects of language education programs: an empirical evaluation of bilingual and English-only policies.' *Annual Review of Applied Linguistics*, *37*: 218–240. https://doi.org/10.1017/S0267190517000137

Makepeace, A. (Director). (2010). *We still live here (Âs Nutayuneân)* [Film]. Bullfrog Films.

Mamadouh, V. & El Ayadi, N. (2022). 'Urban multilingualism: place-making, mobility and sense of belonging in European cities.' In Grin, F., Marácz, L. & Pokorn, N. K. (eds.), *Advances in interdisciplinary language policy* (pp. 151–170). John Benjamins.

McField, G. P. (ed.) (2014). *The miseducation of English learners: a tale of three states and lessons learned.* Information Age Publishing.

Mendoza, A. (2023). *Translanguaging and English as a lingua franca in the plurilingual classroom.* Channel View Publications.

Merriam-Webster. (2024). Retrieved January 28, 2024 from www.merriam-webster.com/help/faq-how-many-english-words

Metz, M. (2022). 'Applying a critical language lens: analyzing language use in everyday video texts.' *Journal of Adolescent & Adult Literacy, 65*(5): 409–417.

National Academies of Sciences, Engineering, and Medicine. (2017). *Promoting the educational success of children and youth learning English: promising futures.* National Academies Press.

Nguyen, T. T. T. & Hajek, J. (2022). 'Making the case for linguicism: revisiting theoretical concepts and terminologies in linguistic discrimination research.' *International Journal of the Sociology of Language, 2022*(275).

Nieto, S. (2006). 'Affirmation, solidarity and critique: moving beyond tolerance in education.' In Lee, E., Menkart, D. & Okazawa-Rey, M. (eds.), *Beyond heroes and holidays: A practical guide to K-12 anti-racist, multicultural education and staff development* (pp. 18–29). Teaching for Change.

Ochs, E. (1982, April). 'Talking to children in Western Samoa.' *Language in Society, 11*(1): 77–104.

Paris, D. (2012). 'Culturally sustaining pedagogy: a needed change in stance, terminology, and practice.' *Educational Researcher, 41*(3): 93–97. https://doi.org/10.3102/0013189X12441244

Piccardo, E. (2017). 'Plurilingualism as a catalyst for creativity in superdiverse societies: a systemic analysis.' *Frontiers in Psychology, 8*(2169).

Piccardo, E. (2018). 'Plurilingualism: vision, conceptualization, and practices.' In Trifonas, P. & Aravossitas, T. (eds.), *Springer international handbook of research and practice in heritage language education* (pp. 207–226). Springer International Publishing.

Piccardo, E. & Capron, P. I. (2015). 'Introduction. From second language pedagogy to the pedagogy of 'plurilingualism': a possible paradigm shift?/De la didactique des langues à la didactique du plurilinguisme: un changement de paradigme possible?' *The Canadian Modern Language Review/La revue canadienne des langues vivantes, 71*(4): 317–323.

Piccardo, E., Germain-Rutherford, A. & Lawrence, G. (Eds.). (2021). *The Routledge handbook of plurilingual language education.* Routledge.

Pullum, G. K. (1999). 'African-American vernacular English is not standard English with mistakes.' In Wheeler, R. S. (ed.), *The workings of language.* Praeger.

Reagan, T. (2019). 'Linguistic hegemony and "official languages".' In Canestrari, A. S. & Marlowe, B. A. (eds.), *The Wiley international handbook of educational foundations.* John Wiley & Sons, Inc.

Reaser, J., Adger, C. T., Wolfram, W. & Christian, D. (2017). *Dialects at school: educating linguistically diverse students.* Routledge.

Rickford, J. R. & Rickford, R. J. (2000). *Spoken soul: the story of Black English.* Trade Paper Press.

Rolstad, K. (1997). 'Effects of two-way immersion on the ethnic identification of third language students: an exploratory study.' *Bilingual Research Journal: The Journal of the National Association for Bilingual Education, 21*(1): 43–63. https://doi.org/10.1080/15235882.1997.10815601

Rolstad, K. (2014). 'Rethinking language in school.' *International Multilingual Research Journal, 8*(1): 1–8.

Rolstad, K. (2023, July 11). *The plurilingual turn* [PowerPoint presentation]. International Symposium on Language Use in Education, Akademi Pengajian Bahasa, Shah Alam, Selangor, Malaysia.

Rolstad, K., Mahoney, K. & Glass, G. V. (2005). 'The big picture: a meta-analysis of program effectiveness research on English language learners.' *Educational Policy, 19*: 572–594.

Savini, C. (2021, January 26). 'Ten ways to tackle linguistic bias in our classrooms.' *Inside Higher Ed.* Retrieved May 29, 2024 from www.insidehighered.com/advice/2021/01/27/how-professors-can-and-should-combat-linguistic-prejudice-their-classes-opinion

Shi, L. & Rolstad, K. (2022). '"A good start": a new approach to gauging preservice teachers' critical language awareness.' *Journal of Language, Identity & Education, 21*(6): 408–422. https://doi.org/10.1080/15348458.2020.1810045

Skutnabb-Kangas, T. (1988). 'Multilingualism and the education of minority children.' In Skutnabb-Kangas, T. & Cummins, J. (eds.), *Minority education: from shame to struggle* (pp. 9–44). Clevedon, Avon: Multilingual Matters (revised version of Skutnabb-Kangas, T. (1986). 'Multilingualism and the education of minority children.' In Phillipson, R. & Skutnabb-Kangas, T. (eds.), *Linguicism rules in education, Parts 1–3* (pp. 42–72). Roskilde University Centre, Institute; republished 1995 in García, O. & Baker, C. (eds.), *Policy and practice in bilingual education: a reader extending the foundations* (pp. 40–59). Multilingual Matters; questions added, pp. 59–62).

Smitherman, G. (1986). *Talkin and testifyin: the language of Black America*. Wayne State University.

Sobel, D. (2005). *Place-based education: connecting classroom and community*. The Orion Society and the Myrin Institute.

United Nations General Assembly. (2020, January 27). *Elimination of racism, racial discrimination, xenophobia and related intolerance*, G.A. Res. 74/137, U.N. Doc. A/RES/74/137. Retrieved January 28, 2024 from https://undocs.org/Home/Mobile?FinalSymbol=a%2Fres%2F74%2F137&Language=E&DeviceType=Desktop&LangRequested=False

Valentine, G., Sporton, D. & Bang Nielsen, K. (2008). 'Language use on the move: sites of encounter, identities and belonging.' *Transactions of the Institute of British Geographers*, 33(3): 376–387.

Wichser-Krajcik, E. (2021). *A teacher's guide to plurilingual pedagogy*. MA TESOL Collection. 756. https://digitalcollections.sit.edu/ipp_collection/756

Wiley, T. G. & Lukes, M. (1996, Autumn). 'English-only and standard English ideologies in the U.S.' *TESOL Quarterly*, 30(3): 511–535. Language Planning and Policy.

Williams, C. H. (2014). 'The lightening veil: language revitalization in Wales.' *Review of Research in Education*, 38: 242–272. Language Policy, Politics, and Diversity in Education.

Wolfram, W., Adger, C. T. & Christian, D. (1999). *Dialects in schools and communities*. Routledge.

Wolfram, W. & Thomas, E. R. (2002). *The development of African American English*. Wiley.

Wun, C. (2016). 'Against captivity: Black girls and school discipline policies in the afterlife of slavery.' *Educational Policy*, 30(1): 171–196.

Yemini, M., Engel, L. & Ben Simon, A. (2023). 'Place-based education – a systematic review of literature.' *Educational Review*: 1–21. https://doi.org/10.1080/00131911.2023.2177260

19

BORDER CULTURE IDENTITY

Iván A. Sanchís

One hand washes the other.

(Seneca the Younger, 5 B.C.–65 A.C.).

Introduction

If there is something that could be called border culture, we surely can find plenty of it all along the Guadalupe–Hidalgo line (which defines the Mexico–United States border), from Tijuana to Matamoros or from San Diego to Brownsville as counter border cities. Let me bring up some quick numbers to summarize the whole situation. The current population of Mexico is 126,014,024 people,[1] and 6 out of the 32 Mexican federal entities (Baja California, Sonora, Chihuahua, Coahuila, Nuevo León and Tamaulipas) share a border with their four counterparts in the United States (California, Arizona, New Mexico and Texas). Hence, we are talking about the Hispanic nation with the most contact and interaction with its (predominantly English-speaking) northern neighbors, which accumulated a total of 335,805,639 inhabitants by December 3, 2023.[2] In relation to this, according to US Census Bureau (2011), California and Texas are the most populated states of the US, and the Hispanics living in the US (19% of the country's population) are largely concentrated in these two states, most of them being of Mexican origin. This interaction has generated a wide range of economic, cultural and social synergies, bringing out inherent problems, among which language is a main concern. One could think that the movement of people is mainly northwards, but this border buffer[3] sees a variety of movements motivated by different reasons that affect the identities and languages of the social groups involved in these tidal travels. In fact, frontier activity was not been under strict control, as we see it nowadays, until the 1980s. The first Cross Border Patrol check point was installed in 1924 by the US and Mexican authorities due to the growth of immigrational movement of Mexican, Chinese and other groups motivated by the lack of work after the end of the railway construction, but the Cross Border Patrol was quite relaxed at the beginning. The 1929 stock market crash also provoked a drop in labor, which led the US government to reinforce the control of migration with less flexibility until the current situation. Deportation and immigrational control have grown gradually until today, reaching, in the last two decades, high levels of complex restrictions for the inhabitants who suffer the consequences of living in the border line with higher transit of the entire world.[4]

DOI: 10.4324/9781003439493-23

People living in the north of Mexico have more in common with California, Arizona, New Mexico and Texas inhabitants than with their fellow citizens in Mexico. The Guadalupe–Hidalgo border divide tribes, towns, families and their activity in their region. Part of the population affected by this separation was split into two nationalities, and this influenced every aspect of their lives. But this division became a common feature of their identity as binationals, borderliners, borderlanders or just individuals who live amongst cultures and languages moving from one side to the other of the border between two countries. These nuances are basic features of their complex social identity. There are stereotypes that shape the identity of the borderlander, for example, the one called *Coyote*. This term is often used to refer to people (predominantly male) who traditionally dedicate themselves to smuggling drugs, people or any kind of goods across the border area, resembling animal movement in the desert lands between the countries, free of laws or human restrictions except random pieces of a wall. Life around the border is fraught for a varied group of people.

Activism around these issues has its echo in the academic literature. For example, a recent contribution by Edward J. McCaughan (2020) offers a brief, yet very accurate, overview of the activism involved in the Hispanics' situation in the Southwest of the US. McCaughan uses artistic images to support the evolution of the identities of the southwestern area of the United States. His contribution provides a good summary of the social and historic evolution of this land and its people. His conclusions are that contemporary artists are expanding and enriching their exploration of immigration and the border with joyful butterflies that boldly traverse boundaries, unapologetic UndocuQueer activists, assertive expressions of dual belonging ('de aquí y de allá'), deeper engagements with Indigenous communities and spiritual appeals to reclaim our shared humanity. In his opinion, time will determine the impact of these artistic representations in confronting and potentially reversing the current wave of intense racism and xenophobia in the United States.

With a different tone, Juan Manuel Lope Blanch, in his 1994 article, 'El concepto de frontera lingüística' (The Concept of Linguistic Frontier), depicted a deep review of the linguistic border concept – when there was still no physical fencing – basing the reasoning on the historic–linguistic situation of the US–Mexican border. Among other reflections, Lope Blanch analyzes the difference between the concepts of the geographic border and linguistic border along with boundaries between languages and dialects and the relation of dependence or collaboration between the groups divided by the line. His reasoning is grounded in the ways native languages came under external influence through invasions, like what happened to the Spanish language (Castilian at that time) when the Arabic language and culture occupied the Iberian Peninsula. He uses this example to compare the relation of Spanish and Nahuatl after the Spanish occupation of America and the work of the missionaries on Native languages, which brought a significant amount of Nahuatl lexicon, among other Native languages, into the Spanish language.[5]

Since the 16th century, the Spanish, Portuguese and, not much later, English languages have blatantly dominated the continent, becoming the most-used languages in the social and political spheres. The American continent has become the place of development and growth of these languages with their inherent cultures. The US Southwest has been of Spanish tradition longer than other regions of the current US's territory. The radical change of location of the border after the Mexican–United States war generated a clear situation of difference between linguistic and geographical border (Lope Blanch 1994). Despite the tensions between both languages (English and Spanish) in this area of predominance, different social uses are assigned to each of them. Spanish was used in domestic and familiar environments, along with all the cultural charge which is present in many aspects of life in the Southwest, whereas English was used for commercial and institutional purposes. Spanish is largely more spoken in the United States than English is spoken in Mexico, and this is mainly due to the presence of traditional heritage speakers remaining in the area between the Guadalupe–Hidalgo line since 1848 and the pre-war border (Stegmaier & McCulley 2009).[6]

The importance of the lost Mexico (México perdido/Hispania Perdida) is still more present in the minds of the inhabitants of the Treaty land than in the minds of Mexicans from the current territory. These Mexicans seem to have completely forgotten that their country used to be 55% bigger, and, in fact, they have generated a sense of rejection towards their former compatriots from those lost lands. As McCaughan's (2020) article says in the title: 'We didn't cross the border, the border crossed us'; the situation of this territory is very special due to its cultural composition. Many Hispanic and Indigenous people claim this land as theirs. They woke up one day in February 1848 to find out that they were not Mexicans anymore, to realize that they, their family members and relatives (living two blocks away) were *de facto* in another country. A few years later, as the southern migration movements towards the US started, they also were to be called immigrants because of the common cultural and former 'national' origin; immigrants in their own land. Nowadays, settlers of the old tradition speakers of Castilian/Spanish and newcomers as real immigrants compose the majority of the population of the states included in the new territories after the Mexican–US war. A lot of immigrants entering the US are from original Native cultures and speak Indigenous languages, or, at least, they identify with these languages and cultures. They come from the center and south of Mexico and belong to mainly Mixtec and Zapotec. Other Native groups from those areas also claim the land and the right to cross the border freely inside their territory limits. Central and South American groups join this potluck. They, along with other immigrants, form random places around the world[7] in pursuit of an opportunity to enter the United States along the 'Baja-Cali' border buffer, come to complete the group of languages, cultures and identities establishing new roots in the borderlands. These groups feature their new location as the common bond between them as no land people carrying all the power of their cultures with them and melting along and around the line. The problems involved in the border come together to define the border cultural identity.

What this chapter provides, despite the complexity of the matter, is a brief overview of the social, academic and institutional/governmental state of the art, which reflects the evolution of the linguistic situation on this border and the effects of this on the population intersected by this political line. Furthermore, it seems that the major possible measures are to be taken in schools, where the new generations of different cultural groups interact in a multilinguistic environment. Some proposals are provided in the conclusion.

Border living: cultures and identities

The principal situation that brings these border-living groups together is the not-belonging feeling. This estrangement; this feeling of being an outsider; this lack of acceptance, affinity, association, attachment or inclusion to any of the countries on both sides has become their common bond as a multicultural diaspora. Hence, is not only about two cultures and languages. It turns into something more complex. Minority endangered languages and their cultures need to adapt or die in search of better living conditions. What makes this region unique from a global sociolinguistic perspective is not only the controversial interaction of the English and Spanish languages but the diminishing presence of the Indigenous cultures and their role in local cultural life and social interaction. There are several languages involved. Despite the fact that this situation is slowly changing, these cultural groups are still bound to go slipstreaming any of the dominant languages in a last attempt to survive the futile attention from institutions on both sides of the border. Therefore, the term 'heritage language' see a wider interpretation in the case of these minorities. Their linguistic identity drops into limbo due to the combination of many factors, resulting in the lack of adaptation of these groups to the global environment. They regularly end up adapting to their new common culture of bond, which tends to be the Hispanic or English culture in North America. Here is when the minor cultures decide, having no other choice, to survive attached to one of the two dominant cultures and their languages. That is the reason Mixtec and Zapotec groups embraced the Hispanic culture and blended their identity. But, once they cross the border, they have to embrace the Anglo-speaking culture to be able to survive in the new location.

This is the case of the *Chicanos*, which involve a mixture of Indigenous, Hispanic and Anglo-American features of identity with a recent return to their Indigenous roots in their search for *Aztlan* (a magical/mystical civilization of the Aztec ancestors). If one ever visits Chicano Park in San Diego, California, or any Chicano neighborhood in East Los Angeles, one can witness this cultural blending and how this phenomenon has been changing and developing over time. There are plenty of references to this famous Aztlan in their murals that are produced to convey, as a permanent discourse, what these peoples represent for every person passing by to remind them of their identity and claims. So, on the border, we find the Native–Hispanic tradition of the settlers[8] of the Treaty land co-living with the immigrants of south and central Mexican origin in a similar identity status and the group of people (with different origins) stuck mainly on the Mexican side wanting to cross to the United States while they wait for the Migrant Protection Protocol[9] to be enforced. But some are just trying to cross illegally, having to go through an ordeal to survive in the host country or ending up deported back to Mexico (swelling the rank of people waiting to cross the border). Also, on the Mexican side (with a focus on the Tijuana area), we find the previously mentioned immigrants co-living with the *Tijuanenses*, US expats who live in Tijuana[10] and Mexicans with United States nationality who also travel or spend long terms in Mexico (either in Tijuana or nearby areas). On the US side, we also find these Mexicans with United States nationality (usually called Mexican Americans), the Hispanics who settled in the Southwest before the Treaty, the illegal immigrants and the Anglo-American majority of Protestant/Puritan tradition. This group interacts with the binational identity overshadowing the border buffer.

The members of the tribes crossed by the borderline[11] may be less included in the social systems of both countries. Their identity has been preserved by their strong efforts to keep alive traditions from their ancestors. This has helped to maintain their existence despite the border. The Kumeyaay, the Cocopah, the Quechan, The Yaqui, the Tiguan, the Kickapoo and the Tohono O'odham tribes (as the biggest group) are concentrated along the Guadalupe–Hidalgo line, having no other choice but to get used to an almost everyday border crossing. These are the most representative diminished Native groups of the border buffer. Yaqui Natives are from southern lands, too, and have different locations due to their continuous displacements (Rivera 2022). The organization can only attend to the main tribes or Indigenous groups with a long tradition of occupation in his area, but there are a few more, and we cannot forget the great exodus of Mixtec or Zapotec groups that have been settling along the border, creating their own spaces of cultural interaction with these tribal groups and the two dominant languages. The introduction of the *Handbook on Indigenous Peoples' Border Crossing Rights Between the United States and Mexico* (Leza *et al.* 2019: 2) summarizes this complex situation. They claim that the native peoples inhabiting the lands affected by these international agreements were not sufficiently taken into account during the negotiations between Mexico and the United States that led to the establishment of the current US–Mexico international border. Just to have a general view, the Yaqui people are represented by the Pascua Yaqui Tribe of Arizona in the United States and traditional pueblo communities in Sonora, Mexico, within the Yaqui Indigenous Zone, a federally recognized land reserved as Yaqui

Border culture identity

territory by the Mexican government. The Tohono O'odham (Desert People), Akimel O'odham (River People) and Hia-Ced O'odham (Sand People) are gathered within the Tohono O'odham group and others, which are called nations or communities. 'There are approximately nine Tohono O'odham communities in Sonora, Mexico, along the border of the Tohono O'odham reservation,' with a few thousand members. These are spread over Sonora and Chihuahua states in Mexico. The Yuman groups are collectively identified as the Pai (or Pa'a) and are also spread over both sides of the fence. The Cocopah (or Cucapá) live near the Colorado River and some areas of southern California and Baja California, Mexico. 'The Cucapá community in Mexico locates in Baja California. Besides, the Apache peoples are represented by nine federally-recognized tribal nations in the US, with five located in Arizona' and another two in Texas. The Kickapoo, or Kikapú, are also represented in Texas, Oklahoma and Kansas in the US, with a smaller community in Coahuila and Sonora, Mexico.

The enforcement and militarization of the US–Mexico border have significant impacts on Indigenous peoples, including ecological destruction of their territories due to border barrier construction and Border Patrol operations, threats to sacred areas, restricted access to traditional spiritual and cultural sites and obstacles to movement across Indigenous lands. Many Indigenous communities along the US–Mexico border are concerned about the impact of border enforcement policies on their ability to maintain social and cultural connections with members across the international border. International legal instruments from the United Nations confirm the rights of Indigenous peoples, which are currently violated by US–Mexico border enforcement (Leza *et al.* 2019: 2–3).

The cultures, rituals, languages and communication among members of the cultures interacting along the border have been steadily threatened as the crossing border patrol started to increase enforcement and to become more and more exhaustive. Their identity has also been jeopardized due to the reasons mentioned previously and widely exposed in this *Handbook*.[12] The situation of the border devours these *pueblos*, making them become part of the multiracial and multicultural mass, so they end up being treated in the same way, not taking them into account as minority local cultures. Their locality is likewise unclear, as they live as borderliners; the border crossed them, and equilibrium on the line is not an easy task, especially to those who have no middle or upper education and have to reluctantly accept what the authorities impose on both sides of this division. It is hard to put yourself in these people's shoes. It is a dilemma; their culture has been attacked, and they do not feel complete on either side.

Leza *et al.* (2019: 3) also assert that several international legal instruments from the United Nations affirm the rights of Indigenous peoples, rights which are currently violated by US–Mexico border enforcement. Some Indigenous groups have taken legal action to address these violations through the United Nations reporting system, but international human rights law, including recent rights outlined in the United Nations Declaration on the Rights of Indigenous Peoples, is not currently acknowledged as a standard regulatory code for decision-making in US domestic courts. Nonetheless, the US Department of Homeland Security has established some protocols to facilitate border crossing for these Indigenous peoples. This handbook, created by Indigenous Alliance Without Borders, focuses on assisting Indigenous peoples in maintaining community across the international border and preserving traditional cultural knowledge and practices through such interactions.

There is not much action taken to protect the tribal boundaries, culture, art, language, self-living and identities of these groups. Given the lack of institutional attention, these border inhabitants are joining forces to keep their lifestyles as cultural patrimony of the Americas. As a result, a binational Indigenous community is being created. Only the Kickapoo have this legal status, recognized first by the US and later Mexican governments. This status was granted by the US

Immigration and Naturalization Service (INS), but this institution does not exist anymore, because it was absorbed by the Department of Homeland Security. Then, the Enhanced Tribal Identification Card (ETC) – previously Form I-872's title, 'American Indian Card' – was issued for the Indigenous to be able to use it as a passport to (supposedly) move freely for a certain number of activities like family gatherings, social events, religious rites or practices, artistic development and emergency situations. There is a whole policy to get the concession of these ETCs, which are backed by the federal recognized US tribal nation and the Cross Border Patrol (CBP). This rule is gathered in a Memorandum of Agreement (MOA). For example, 'The Pascua Yaqui Tribe was the first tribal nation to develop and issue an ETC in 2010. The Kootenai Tribe of Idaho began issuing its ETC in 2011. At least seventeen additional tribes are now in the process of developing their own ETCs' (Leza *et al.* 2019: 5). These permits are permanent or temporary/non-renewable, depending on the use proposed in the application. The requirements are basically to show economic solvency proof and letters of invitation by leaders of the tribe from both sides of the border. The *Instituto Nacional Indigenista* (INI), from the Mexican side, provides help and guidance to applicants. But as Leza et al. indicate (2019: 9):

> approval of 'paroled' entries into the US for Indigenous cultural reasons remains at the discretion of CBP officials at the time of entry. Letters of invitation to Mexican Indigenous community members applying for a border crossing permit should be written by a tribal official or otherwise certified as coming from a US tribal nation and should include a few requirements.

Hitherto, one may infer that the whole procedure to get a permit to cross the border is only requested by authorities on the way up north and not on the other direction. This is a common feature in all ports of entry along the border. The waiting line to cross northwards can take up to six or seven hours, especially in holiday seasons, due to the exhaustive inspection of moving people and the number of people crossing every day. On the contrary, crossing southwards goes easily and is hardly ever delayed by inspections, verifications, document checking or interviews from any of the Mexican CBP officers. In contrast, it is surprising how the Mexican military force only detains loaded trucks or random vehicles for quick inspections or short interviews with travelers. They do not even stamp passports of visitors (as is the case in international airports) if one does not specifically ask it of authorities. These Indigenous people, who are permitted to pass and not necessarily through the ports, do not escape these procedures that can turn into what Leza et al. explain in their Handbook as follows (2019: 9): 'Title 8 US Code §1357 gives CBP officers significant powers to interrogate, search, seize, and arrest individuals without warrant at the US–Mexico border.' Sometimes, these inspections turn into long detainments, denials of entry or uncomfortable interrogatories and accusations as a consequence of the tensions generated by the illegal activities of the border.

This is a controversial matter because not all CBP or port of entry officers agree with the amnesty provided to the Indigenous tribal members fulfilling this binational condition for different reasons, but especially since the September 11, 2001, attacks. The main reasons can be the fear that other Mexican immigrants with Native appearance can falsify forms to take advantage of the cultural amnesty granted to these group members or fear that they could be drug traffickers and the fear of further terrorist attacks. They have to pay the consequences of the people who try to cross the US–Mexican border illegally at any cost. The barrier cut old trails of tribes' territories, and the inhabitants are always under surveillance.

Border culture identity

The history of these tribes has a dramatic origin. Some, like the Navajo, come from a long journey of historical removals from their original lands towards the Southwest. This is basically the scenario, and the 'crossed tribes' are paying the dues of this ongoing situation. Hopefully, the initiatives taken to protect these Native cultures are increasing, but their languages are dying because, as within other minority languages in the US, new generations, despite identifying themselves as Natives, do not speak the language. This fact, added to the lack of written records, alphabet or a writing corpus, leads to the loss of original languages. The inclusion of kids in the Native boarding schools, under the national program of assimilation in which the maxim was 'Kill the Indian in him, and save the man' (Little 2017), contributed to the gradual removal of their languages. This is part of the unspoken history of America. During the previous decades of the establishment of the new political border after the war, the Native groups absorbed the Hispanic tradition. In the current situation, they have to continuously negotiate their identity in their everyday lives because of their race, appearance, social status and place of living.

As mentioned earlier, they embrace Hispanic culture by blending their traditions, and, more importantly, part of their lexicon is also kept alive within their use of Spanish language. This is a constant feature among these American Native cultures. We find examples of it mainly in rituals and religious celebrations. Many linguistic features of their languages are preserved in their rituals as one of the major expressions of their identity. The Pascua Yaqui and Tohono O'Dham tribes have a strong bond with the *Virgen de Guadalupe*, and one can find its image in many celebrations, ornament and artistic expressions as one of the most important symbols of *mestizaje* (fussion). The *Altar de Muertos* tradition is also blended with their ancestral practices, turning into a new concept on the religious/pagan continuum, like Mixtec's celebrations involved in this festivity. This could happen because missionaries may have embraced the peoples' lifestyle, leaving a record of it instead of removing their customs, rituals and cultural identity in general, and also because of a longer tradition of interaction between Natives and Christian settlers (Lope Blanch 1994).

English, Spanish and Indigenous languages' 'potluck'

These are the foundations of the cultural-linguistic identity on the border buffer. Language is the major sign of identity of a culture. It has been proven that when a civilization is deprived of its language, that civilization tends to disappear with it. Language manipulation is a recurrent issue in politics. The beginning of the decay of civilizations starts with the linguistic and cultural life. On this note, as Francis George Steiner said, 'when a language dies, a way of understanding the world dies with it, a way of looking at the world.' Globalization is absorbing cultures and identities into a universal way of buying, making business, interacting on social networks and speaking. Most spoken languages are erasing the differences between their dialects and varieties. The way of speaking of an Australian is less and less different from the way of speaking of a British person or an American. In the same way, Mexican Spanish is becoming more and more similar to Spanish from Spain, Argentina or Venezuela in terms of lexicon and expressions. Big languages are getting globalized, and, in the case of Spanish, US Spanish has a lot to do with this tendency.

Oral tradition is the base of Indigenous cultures, and their members find no other way to keep spreading their stories and legends better than by mixing with Spanish in their music, poetry and storytelling. The *corrido*, for example, is a music genre which has been included in everyday life and celebrations. The relation of new Native generations to their languages follows the pattern of most of the languages (other than English) in the US, which is one of disappearing. Only the lexicon involved in their rituals, celebrations and the words of most common use are surviving.

As Ludwig Wittgenstein states in his *Tractatus Logico-Philosophicus* (1921): 'The limits of my language mean the limits of my world.' The contact between the border Native languages and the dominant ones around them in growing social globalization may be affecting their survival. It is just the will of people that keeps them alive.

The Spanish spoken in the United States by speakers of different origins and nationalities is shaping its own characteristics, and it is the most globalized variety (Betti 2016). Also, the Spanish spoken in Mexico is increasingly influenced by US Spanish due to digital globalization. We cannot forget that most of the Spanish speakers in the United States are of Mexican origin. The Pew Research Center (2021) identifies that 'the five largest Hispanic populations in the US by origin group were Mexicans (37.2 million), Puerto Ricans (5.8), Salvadorans (2.5), Dominicans (2.4) and Cubans (2.4).' The Instituto Cervantes publishes a yearly report about the situation of the Spanish language in the world, and much of its influence concentrates in the United States and Mexico, as stated in the following extract (Fernández Vítores 2023): 'In 2060, the United States will be the second Spanish-speaking country in the world, after Mexico. 27.5% of the US population will be of Hispanic origin.'[13]

As previously mentioned, Native languages and identities are incessantly blending with Spanish. Most of the changes introduced into languages in contact have traditionally been of a lexical nature, but recently, and especially in the US Spanish diglossia, more English structures like 'It makes the difference/Esto hace la differencia' or 'This is not my point/Este no es mi punto' are incorporated in the Spanish spoken in these areas. Can it be considered bilingualism or lexical insecurity? The immigrants' and Treaty land peoples' way of speaking Spanish is different. Literacy is sometimes a matter of social status, and it is the most common problem. It continuously emerges in bilingual and dual immersion schools which base their communication skills in the English and Spanish languages, removing any trace of Indigenous languages if that is the case of some students. It is important to point out that English and Spanish do not have the official status in these two countries (the US and Mexican constitutions do not specify any official language), but their officiality is assumed by population and given for granted by governments. Official or not, one's language and linguistic identity determine a certain status in United States society, and the border with México area is not an exception (Valdés 2006). The term 'Language other than English' (LOTE) used by the US government gives the impression of implied otherness towards people who do not speak English as their first/mother tongue. The reality of this linguistic otherness in the US has recently been updated by Census Bureau American Community Survey information (What Languages Do We Speak in the United States? 2022), and the most spoken other than English are Spanish or Spanish creole, Chinese, Tagalog, Vietnamese and Arabic. It would be interesting to find out how much of the border tribes' culture, language and identity have been absorbed by the Spanish-speaking (Hispanic) communities represented in this group. The US Census Bureau categorization of Race and Ethnicity (2020) is subtly introducing Indigenous in the last entry of the following list. The following groups are used in diversity calculations:

- Hispanic or Latino.
- White alone non-Hispanic.
- Black or African American alone non-Hispanic.
- American Indian and Alaska Native alone non-Hispanic.
- Asian alone non-Hispanic.
- Native Hawaiian and Other Pacific Islander alone non-Hispanic.
- Some Other Race alone non-Hispanic.
- Multiracial non-Hispanic.

The Census also states that 'Hispanic origin can be viewed as the heritage, nationality, lineage, or country of birth of the person or the person's parents or ancestors before arriving in the United States. People who identify as Hispanic, Latino, or Spanish may be any race' (US Census Bureau 2024). Hence, all people from Spanish-speaking countries, regardless of their ethnic or cultural identity, are categorized as Hispanic. This government categorization, at least in the case of Hispanics (due to the data provided previously), can turn into a rather inconsistent conceptualization. All in all, these Indigenous groups crossed by the border still have to continuously negotiate their origin, identity, territory, language and all that is central for their cultural development, which is going to be endlessly questioned by the Border Patrol on their northward movements inside their territory. This terminology is spread among US citizens by migration institutions and affects the problems exposed here, but this is a further topic, just mentioned to be taken into account.

There are a number of governmental and non-governmental institutions created for the purpose of attending to the needs and problems of the border. Also, there is a lot of academic literature on the matter of border multicultural environments. Ruben G. Rumbaut, a distinguished professor of sociology at the University of California, Irvine, has much to say about immigration in the US, as he clearly explains in his *Jane Menken Distinguished Lecture in Population Studies* at the Institute of Behavioral Sciences last January 2021. In this lecture, he offers a review of the evolution of immigration to the US in general terms and points out that the wall dividing the Mexico and US border is a recent issue (started its first 14 kilometers in 1994), and its social consequences are a matter of current discussion. Manuel Sánchez-Fernández (2022) provides a more profound review of the literature about what has been done by academics on both sides of the border concerning the issue of linguistic identity. Also, a recent publication of the Colegio de la Frontera Norte[14] entitled *Antropología del norte de México y el suroeste de los Estados Unidos. Entrecruce de caminos y derroteros disciplinarios* (Leyva 2021) provides a very complete overview of the border situation from different perspectives. The chapter titled 'Enredos fronterizos: Las lenguas nativas de Baja California' by Ana Daniela Leyva (2021) contributes to our understanding of the Indigenous linguistic limbo of the frontier. This 'idea of in-betweenness includes a process of redefinition of culture' (Bhabha *apud*. Rivera 2022), which is, by and large, too hard to handle by the affected cultures. Most of these contributions agree that aid and guidance are mandatory to keep the Indigenous cultural paradigm alive before it gets totally lost, as recently happened to other cultures in the area like the Yana, the Tunica or the Tillamook from the Midwest and Northwest lands of North America.

Official institutional support

The general action taken in the United States in relation to languages and identity is represented by a few official institutions and a large group of non-governmental organizations. California is the state with the most linguistic accessibility for displaced people, with measures like Medi-Cal threshold languages and in-home supportive services threshold languages for disabled people (Hernández Nieto 2017: 68). Along with these services in the education sector, the California Association for Bilingual Education (2024) was founded with the mission of supporting 'the vision of biliteracy, multicultural competency, and educational equity for all students.' It joins forces with the California Department of Education, which takes action in relation to these issues for students, parents and teachers. The State Seal of Biliteracy (2024), which is 'marked by a gold seal on the diploma or transcript, recognizes high school graduates who have attained a high level of proficiency in speaking, reading, and writing one or more languages in addition to English' through the Multilingual Education Chapter that timidly includes some attention towards

Indigenous speakers in the following program (California Department of Education 2024; Multilingual Education 2024):

Heritage Language or Indigenous Language provides instruction in English and another language for non-English speakers or students with limited literacy skills in their first language. Indigenous language programs support endangered minority languages in which students may have limited receptive and no productive skills. Both programs often serve American Indian students. This program is typically found in kindergarten through grade twelve.

These groups are treated collectively, not individually, weakening their identities and melting them together in the aforementioned 'Otherness,' mostly expressed through language. In the same line of multilingualism in California, the English Learner Advisory Committee (California Department of Education 2024), defined as 'A school-level committee comprised of parents, staff, and community members designated to advise school officials on English learner programs and services,' is taking some action over the linguistic identity matter in California. Nonetheless, the efforts of these institutions are more oriented towards facilitating knowledge and training in English rather than the maintenance of minority languages and their speakers' cultural identity. The bilingual policy is not complete; it is just a way of enabling social inclusion for speakers of LOTE to achieve more proficiency in the English language.

On the Mexican side, things are not much different, but there are more defined policies. The *Secretaría de Educación Pública* (SEP) and the *Secretaría de Relaciones Exteriores* (SRE) have many chapters and offices related to the identity of the *pueblos indígenas* and the border issues. There are portals for citizens of Indigenous origin which are supposedly ready with information for these groups in their languages, like the *Portal Ciudadano en Lenguas Indígenas* (2024), but the links do not work yet. The major issue here is that these languages are of oral tradition, and two obstacles come together; one is that most of the speakers are illiterate, and the second is that there is a lack of translators to these languages. On the academic side, Mexico has the *Instituto Nacional de Lenguas Indígenas* (2024) (INALI), and many departments of different universities around the country which are active in the field of Indigenous language research, like *El Colegio de la Frontera Norte* (COLEF) in Tijuana, which implements collaboration programs with the University of California, University of Arizona and some of the aforementioned institutions. *Universidad Autónoma de Baja California* (UABC) has recently started some activity in relation to border issues and original languages, but more effort is directed towards the international community stuck along the border, which is seen as a principal problem for the state and the country.

Apparently, one of the most active governmental institutions on border issues in both directions, which collaborates with the US institutions, is a chapter office that belongs to the SEP and the *Instituto de Mexicanos en el Exterior* (IME) under the name *Programa Binacional de Educación Migrante* (PROBEM 2024), situated in Tijuana. Yara Amparo López has been coordinating this program for the last two decades, envisioning the realities of the border. She has contributed not only with governmental action but also with research on transnational migration (Sierra & López 2013) and with the elaboration of multiple reports which have helped clarify the situation of the binational population and the migrant groups. Collaboration is established between PROBEM and UABC through the creation of a Social Service Program carried out by our students to address the literacy problems of the heritage language students stuck in the border, whatever their cultural language is. Some of these students belong to Indigenous border cultures, know the languages and are getting training to teach their languages to people that are not completely competent in any of the languages they identify with.[15] One of the greatest assets of PROBEM has been the recent formation of a primary school exclusively devoted to Mixtec kids in Tijuana. They have the possibility of sharing their bonds while learning Spanish, English and other disciplines, but there is a great lack of teachers of Indigenous languages. This shortage of qualified teachers is also present on the US side. That is why PROBEM established an agreement of collaboration with International Alliance Group and UABC to create the *Programa de intercambio de maestros México-EEUU* (US–Mexico Teachers' Exchange Program) in 2023, through which teachers from both sides have the opportunity of working during a period of time in schools on both sides of the border. This initiative has been developed to learn about the shortcomings of their students when they arrive. Teacher training is one of the first measures to be taken for them to address the problems effectively.

Conclusions

Language is the major carrier of culture and the most powerful feature of human identity. After this brief review of the US–Mexican border problems triggered by the circumstances in which populations are involved, I would like to conclude with some proposals for improving cultural communication in the border buffer. More focus should be put on the schools. The classroom can be used as a safe space where the students should feel at ease. Attending to diversity at the emotional and academic levels is very important in these kinds of environments. There are common features between immigrant communities and the Indigenous people. Both groups belong to a lower social status and come from illiterate environments. Also, as these are small communities, they tend to be grouped together in the classroom, and this creates the impossibility of fully attending to either cultural group, and the cultural identity of these groups gets absorbed by the *lingua franca* (Spanish or English) between them. This means that profound specialization of teachers on plurilingual approaches should take place.

> In order to be effective and efficient, the design and development of an assessment test for an endangered oral language must take into consideration the sociolinguistic particulars of the language and its speakers: the existence or not of a writing system, the (advanced) stage of language shift, and the endangered position of the language.
>
> (Karyolemou 2022: 404)

Teachers must learn from their students' culture, and their teaching practice must be improved with correct training adapted to the needs of these students. New approaches must be driven towards more accurate teaching practice supported by sociolinguistic and affective components. This helps to maintain the students' cultural identity and level of knowledge of their origin languages. Working with these kinds of students is not an easy task, and many problems can arise. These problems are mostly related to students' emotional state rather than their academic performance. Training teachers seems crucial to build a solid linguistic and cultural foundation from primary school to university levels. CABE and PROBEM seem to have started this training and also contribute with congresses and binational forums (CABE Annual Conference already has a long tradition of participation) to gather teachers from both sides of the border with the intention to find solutions to these matters.

In order to carry out these important measures, governmental policies and implementation of resources are a basic departure point. The problem here is that there is a lack of both, and we do not know whether policies are not implemented because there are no resources or, on the contrary, these are just not implemented by political institutions yet. The border culture identities as new phenomena in the global environment have to be accepted and addressed as an important social concern. The relation of collaboration or dependence between the Mexican and United States governments must focus on these social and educational issues more than the economic ones in a region which is growing together despite the existing border. The *maquiladora* and the ranch come to form the landscape of a binational growing society which demands more attention due to the impact that this new cultural influence is having on both countries. The rise of the binational figure will surely reshape the meaning of the words *Mexican* and *American* in the near future.

Notes

1 Data extracted from INEGI April 2023. www.inegi.org.mx/app/areasgeograficas/
2 Data extracted from US Census Bureau. www.census.gov/popclock/
3 The border buffer zone can be delimited by 100 km up and down the border line, where nearly all the border activity takes place and the majority of cultural interaction happens.
4 Data extracted from Smart Border Coalition. https://smartbordercoalition.com/about-the-border#:~:text= The%20San%20Ysidro%20and%20El,and%20trucks%20cross%20each%20year
5 It is important to point out that the second grammar published in the world was the one dedicated to *Nahuatl* by Alonso de Molina: *Arte de la lengua mexicana y castellana.* Mexico: Pedro Ocharte, 1571. These kinds of texts came to improve the use and maintenance of these languages.
6 See map at www.docsteach.org/documents/document/western-territories-map
7 Most of these immigrants are concentrated in Tijuana and San Diego and are from Haiti, China, Korea, Ukraine, Russia, India, Senegal and various parts of Africa.
8 These are called *Paisanos* in Steinbeck's literary work *Tortilla Flat* (1935), and they extended to the central and northern lands of what is today California.
9 The Homeland Security office of the United States in collaboration with the Mexican authorities agree on the following terms: 'The Migrant Protection Protocols (MPP) are a US Government action whereby certain foreign individuals entering or seeking admission to the US from Mexico – illegally or without proper documentation – may be returned to Mexico and wait outside of the US for the duration of their immigration proceedings, where Mexico will provide them with all appropriate humanitarian protections for the duration of their stay' (www.dhs.gov/news/2019/01/24/migrant-protection-protocols#:~:text=The%20Migrant%20 Protection%20Protocols%20(MPP,of%20their%20immigration%20proceedings%2C%20where).
10 These are US retired or workers commuting across the border every day due to the growing differences in the cost of living.
11 See non-governmental organization (NGO) Alianza Indígena sin Fronteras (Indigenous Alliance Without Borders). This organization provides more information on the situation, along with maps. https://alian-zaindigenasinfronteras.org/land-acknowledgement/
12 See https://indigenousalliance.org/
13 Translation by myself.
14 The *Colegio de la Frontera Norte* may be the research center with more activity in this field in Mexico.
15 It is important to remember that not all people who identify with a Native cultural ethnicity are able to speak the language or do it on a completely competent level.

References

Alianza Indígena Sin Fronteras (2024). https://alianzaindigenasinfronteras.org/land-acknowledgement/
Betti, Silvia (2016). 'Una cuestión de identidad . . . español y "spanglish" en los Estados Unidos.' *Camino real: Estudios de las hispanidades norteamericanas*, vol. 8, no. 11, pp. 61–76. ISSN 1889-5611.
California Association for Bilingual Education (2024). www.gocabe.org/
California Department of Education (2024). *District English Learner Advisory Committee.* https://www.cde. ca.gov/ta/cr/delac.asp
California State Seal of Biliteracy (2024). www.cde.ca.gov/sp/el/er/sealofbiliteracy.asp
de Molina, Alonso (1571). *Arte de la lengua mexicana y castellana.* México: Pedro Ocharte.
Fernández Vítores, David (2023). *El español, una lengua viva. Informe 2023.* Instituto Cervantes. https://cvc. cervantes.es/lengua/anuario/anuario_23/informes_ic/p01.htm

Hernández Nieto, Rosana (2017). *La legislación lingüística en los EEUU*. Observatorio de la lengua española en Harvard. https://cervantesobservatorio.fas.harvard.edu/sites/default/files/legislacion_linguistica_eeuu.pdf

International Alliance Group (2024). www.iagusa.org

Instituto de los mexicanos en el exterior (2024). https://ime.gob.mx/

Instituto Matías Romero. www.gob.mx/imr/que-hacemos

Instituto Nacional de Lenguas Indígenas (2024). www.gob.mx/inali

Karyolemou, Marilena (2022, April). 'Teaching Endangered Languages of Oral Tradition: How and What to Assess?' *Applied Linguistics*, vol. 43, no. 2, pp. 389–411. https://doi.org/10.1093/applin/amab045

Language Magazine (2024). www.languagemagazine.com/census-shows-Native-languages-count/#:~:text=The%20American%20Communities%20Survey%20currently,using%20the%20language%20at%20home

Latino Data Hub (2024). https://latinodatahub.org/?mc_cid=6a23aaa56d&mc_eid=5c1bf81d98

Leyva, Ana Daniela (2021). 'Enredos fronterizos: Las lenguas nativas de Baja California.' In Matus & Olmos Coords (Eds.), *Antropología del norte de México y el suroeste de los Estados Unidos. Entrecruce de caminos y derroteros disciplinarios*. México: El Colegio de la Frontera Norte.

Leza, Christina; Alianza Indígena Sin Fronteras; Indigenous Alliance Without Borders (2019). *Handbook on Indigenous Peoples' Border Crossing Rights Between the United States and Mexico*. www.ohchr.org/sites/default/files/Documents/Issues/IPeoples/EMRIP/Call/IndigenousAllianceWithoutBorders.pdf

Little, Becky (2017). 'How Boarding Schools Tried to "Kill the Indian" Through Assimilation.' *History. com.* www.history.com/news/how-boarding-schools-tried-to-kill-the-indian-through-assimilation

Lope Blanch, Juan Manuel (1994, julio). 'El concepto de frontera lingüística.' *Revista de la Universidad de México*, vol. 49, no. 522, pp. 16–21.

McCaughan, Edward J. (2020). '"We Didn't Cross the Border, the Border Crossed Us" Artists' Images of the US–Mexico Border and Immigration.' *Latin American and Latinx Visual Culture*, vol. 2, no. 1, pp. 6–31. https://doi.org/10.1525/lavc.2020.210003

Migrant Protection Protocol (2024). www.dhs.gov/news/2019/01/24/migrant-protection-protocols#:~:text=The%20Migrant%20Protection%20Protocols%20(MPP,of%20their%20immigration%20proceedings%2C%20where

Multilingual Education (2024). www.cde.ca.gov/sp/el/er/multilingualedu.asp

National Association for Bilingual Education (2024). https://nabe.org/

Pew Research Center (2021). *11 Facts About Hispanic Origin Groups in the US* www.pewresearch.org/short-reads/2023/08/16/11-facts-about-hispanic-origin-groups-in-the-us/

Portal Ciudadano en Lenguas Indígenas (2024). http://comunidades.edomex.gob.mx/

PROBEM (2024). https://ime.gob.mx/educacion/programa/probem

Programa de intercambio de maestros México-EEUU. PROBEM https://dgpempyc.sep.gob.mx/probem.html

Rivera Cohen, Aracely (2022). 'Yaquis of Southern California in-Between the US–Mexico Border.' *E-rea.* https://doi.org/10.4000/erea.15008

Rumbaut, Ruben G. (2020). *The Wall: American Nativism, Immigration Policy, and the Great Exclusion of 2017–2020*. www.youtube.com/watch?v=OcZL_lxSe-o

Sánchez-Fernández, M. A. (2022). 'La investigación lingüística de las lenguas yumanas en México (LYUM), Expedicionario.' *Revista de estudios en Antropología (ENAH-Chihuahua)*, no. 4.

Schwaller, John Frederick (1973). *A Catalogue of Pre-1840 Nahuatl Works Held by the Lilly Library: A Machine-Readable Transcription*. Transcribed from: The Indiana University Bookman, no. 11, pp. 69–88. https://liblilly.sitehost.iu.edu/etexts/nahuatl/index.shtml

Sierra, P. S. E.; López, L. Y. A. (2013). 'Infancia migrante y educación trasnacional en la frontera de México-Estados Unidos.' *Revista Sobre La Infancia Y La Adolescencia*, no. 4, pp. 28–54. https://doi.org/10.4995/reinad.2013.1461

Stegmaier, Mark J.; McCulley, Richard T. (2009). 'Ephraim Gilman's 1848 Map of the United States, Now Expanded Coast to Coast.' *Cartography, Politics and Mischief*, vol. 41, no. 4.

Unidad de Política Migratoria, Registro e Identidad de Personas (2024). https://portales.segob.gob.mx/es/PoliticaMigratoria/UnidadDePoliticaMigratoria

US Census Bureau (2011). *Native North American Languages Spoken at Home in the United States: 2006–2010*. https://www2.census.gov/library/publications/2011/acs/acsbr10-10.pdf

US Census Bureau (2020). *Race and Ethnicity*. www.census.gov/library/stories/2021/08/2020-united-states-population-more-racially-ethnically-diverse-than-2010.html

The Routledge Handbook of Endangered and Minority Languages

US Census Bureau (2022). *What Languages Do We Speak in the United States?* www.census.gov/library/stories/2022/12/languages-we-speak-in-united-states.html#:~:text=Nearly%2068%20Million%20People%20Spoke,English%20at%20Home%20in%202019&text=The%20number%20of%20people%20in,recent%20U.S.%20Census%20Bureau%20report

US Census Bureau (2024). *Hispanic Origin.* www.census.gov/topics/population/hispanic-origin.html

Valdés, Guadalupe (2006). *Developing Minority Language Resources: The Case of Spanish in California.* Prof. Guadalupe Valdés; Prof. Joshua A. Fishman; Rebecca Chávez; William Pérez. Series: Bilingual Education and Bilingualism, Vol. 58. 1st ed. Buffalo: Multilingual Matters. e-book.

Wittgenstein, Ludwig (1921). 'Logisch-Philosophische Abhandlung.' In Wilhelm Ostwald (Ed.), *Annalen der Naturphilosophie*, Vol. 14. Leipzig.

20
TEXTUAL PHENOMENA ADDRESSING YOUTH

Orthographic, typographic, and ideological aspects of the Cypriot-Greek dialect

Aspasia Papadima

Cypriot-Greek: A living dialect

Imagine being told that writing in one's native language variant is discouraged, even taboo. Picture a student being reprimanded for using their mother tongue in written expression. Strange as it may sound, this is not a hypothetical scenario but part of a reality that can be explained by addressing the following questions: Is it possible to write without adhering to established or widely acknowledged orthographic conventions? And if there is a certain level of intricacy, what motivates individuals to persist in writing and publishing literary works in this vernacular? Does one's political ideology intersect with the linguistic variety employed in written communication? How many versions could be found for rendering a fundamental three-lettered word while ensuring it remains readable? In what ways has Cypriot-Greek been transcribed on paper? And most interestingly, what are the codes and modes used in contemporary online interactions of today's youth? These are some of the intriguing questions addressed in this chapter, which explores the linguistic landscape in Cyprus, delving into the evolution of the Cypriot-Greek dialect and its current use in written discourse by the younger generation.

Occupying a geopolitically interesting location in the Mediterranean, Cyprus has developed distinct political, cultural, and linguistic characteristics shaped by the influence of its successive conquerors from ancient times to present day. Since the island's first evidence of human habitation, at least 11 groups of settlers governed it, contributing to the island's complex history and culture (Terkourafi 2007). The arrival of populations from Asia Minor and the Aegean around 1900 BC was followed by Mycenaean settlement around 1200 BC, marking the island's Hellenization. Cyprus was then successively occupied and ruled by Phoenicians, Assyrians, Persians, Ptolemaic Egyptians, Romans, Byzantines (with Arabs in common rule), Franks, Venetians, and Ottomans. The British colonized Cyprus in 1878 until the proclamation of the first independent Republic of Cyprus in 1960 (Terkourafi 2007). Since the Turkish invasion and occupation of the northern part of Cyprus in 1974, the island remains divided. By joining the European Union in 2004 and the Eurozone in 2008, the Republic of Cyprus has strengthened its ties with the West, promoting a free and open market through its service sector, including banking, tourism, construction, and trade.

In Cyprus, *diglossia*[1] is prevalent, with two equally dominant varieties of Greek coexisting and used for communication in daily life. These varieties have distinct communicative functions

DOI: 10.4324/9781003439493-24

and suggest different social statuses. Standard Modern Greek (SMG) serves as the state's official language and is utilized for all official and formal communications. Meanwhile, Cypriot-Greek (CG), the native language variety of Greek–Cypriots, is used in everyday oral communication. It is characterized by familiarity and informality (Karyolemou 2000: 204); other than in everyday speech, it is also employed in folk literary and cultural production, including prose, poetry, and satire (Sophocleous 2006). The current language policy in Cyprus reflects a compromise between linguistic liberalism, that is, the freedom of individuals to use the linguistic variety of their choice and legal regulation aimed at codifying language use and promoting the use of SMG 'as a means of maintaining an unaltered Greek national identity' (Karyolemou 2001). In the process of language acquisition, children typically acquire CG at home, while SMG is generally learned through formal education. In the public education system, SMG is used as the language of instruction, with only a limited amount of CG literature included in the Modern Greek curriculum (Themistocleous 2015). In recent years, CG has been used more frequently both in spoken and written communication, even in circumstances previously considered inappropriate, such as in public speeches, broadcasted discussions and political debates, advertising, etc. The linguistic landscape in Cyprus can thus be characterized as a 'dialect continuum' between CG and SMG (Katsoyannou et al. 2006; Tsiplakou et al. 2006), with CG considered a dialect rather than a language, primarily for political reasons (Papapavlou 2011). Thus, the choice of linguistic variety used in oral or written communication in this diglossic setting reveals hidden semiotic traits that reflect national and linguistic ideology, as outlined by Terkourafi (2007). These linguistic decisions act as markers of 'language's territoriality' (Terkourafi 2007).

The rapid process of homogenization within contemporary CG has led to the formation of a pan-Cypriot *Koine*, 'which has shed features from the reported eighteen regional idioms and has undergone heavy lexical influence from Standard Greek' (Tsiplakou 2006). The aforementioned homogenization has been expedited by forced population movements and significant demographic changes following the 1974 war, resulting in the relocation of individuals from the northern parts of the island to the south. This sudden homogenization occurred within a single generation due to heightened interaction among populations from different regions, necessitating the abandonment of distinct local dialectal forms in favor of enhanced mutual intelligibility. Moreover, various factors such as economic and infrastructural developments, urbanization, improved transportation and communication, higher literacy rates, and exposure to SMG media likely contributed not only to the homogenization process, but also to the emergence of a pan-Cypriot variety devoid of local features (Tsiplakou 2006).

Cypriot-Greek is distinctive among Greek dialects as it developed and evolved at the periphery of the Grecophone world, and remains the mother tongue of the majority of a separate state's population (Terkourafi 2007). Moreover, it is the only living Greek dialect that largely preserves the grammar of medieval Greek (Kontosopoulos 2008). The CG dialect emerged between the 7th and 14th centuries AD, preceding other Modern Greek dialects, and is phonologically a South-Eastern variety (Horrocks 2010; Kontosopoulos 2008). The earliest written evidence of the dialect dates back to the Middle Ages, as seen in the 14th-century legal text of Assizes, as well as in the Chronicle of Leontios Machairas in the 15th century, which represents an early example of 'extended vernacular writing in prose' (Horrocks 2010: 362), and in the Chronicle of Georgios Voustronios in the 16th century.

With its 'rich and varied consonantal inventory' (Arvaniti 2010), CG also possesses several unique features, including its diverse local variants, the retention of the ancient final /n/ at the end of words, the preservation of *geminate* consonants, the pronunciation of the four *palato-alveolar* consonants ([tʃ], [dʒ], [ʃ], [ʒ]), and the phenomenon of *tsitakism*, in which the sound /k/ is pronounced as [tʃ] when preceding the vowels /e/ and /i/ (Kontosopoulos 2008). Furthermore, the dialect's grammar is distinctive, as is its rich local vocabulary and expressions.

The limitations of the Greek alphabet in accurately representing the phonological intricacies of CG, 'two *fricative palatal sounds* (one voiced /ʒ/ and one voiceless /ʃ/) and two *affricate palatal sounds* (one voiced /dʒ/ and one voiceless /tʃ/)' (Papapavlou 2010), pose a complex challenge in written representation. This issue encompasses the unique characteristics of the dialect, as well as its cultural and linguistic context. While some scholars advocate for the implementation of a standardized spelling system, others argue in favor of a more adaptable approach that respects the dialect's oral traditions and allows for variation. Various phonetic analyses of the dialect's sounds have led scholars to propose different spelling systems, such as the utilization various diacritical marks to indicate consonant palatalization, or the inclusion of additional letters in a modified Greek alphabet to more accurately represent the dialect's sounds. CG writing and its systematization is intricate due to a variety of factors, including its phonetics, phonology, morphology, and etymology, practical considerations, as well as the preferences and the needs of native speakers and established editorial practices (Armostis et al. 2014, 2016).

The absence of a widely accepted or official orthographic system for CG is clearly intertwined with social and geographic issues, political positions, and conflicting ideologies. Constitutionally, only the Council of Ministers can suggest and implement alterations to language policy (Papapavlou 2010). Yet the politically charged and contentious debate surrounding the linguistic status of CG has effectively precluded any substantial discourse on the matter. This has resulted in an irregular and idiosyncratic collection of typographic conventions that rarely host characters from the Roman script (Papadima et al. 2013, 2014; Papadima and Kyriacou 2014). These conventions are subject to personal preferences, underlying ideologies, the medium used (i.e. writing on paper or typing on a keyboard or personal device), or even practical inventions in print production.

Electronic communication has facilitated both the written dissemination of CG and the destigmatization of its writing, as discussed further subsequently. Nowadays, CG writing is flourishing, manifesting itself in numerous and diverse forms across media, genres, contexts, as well as the purpose or the ideological approach of the writer.

Cypriot-Greek in education: language ideology and semiotic traits

In October 2022, the Cyprus University of Technology organized an experiential workshop on gender discrimination for its students. The workshop was titled 'What do you know about gender discrimination? Come and learn more!' ('Εσύ νάμπου ξέρεις για τες διακρίσεις του φύλου; Κόπιασε να μάθεις τζ' άλλα' [e̞'si 'nɐmbu 'kse̞riz jɐ ˍte̞z ˍðiɐ'krisis ˍtu 'filu? 'kopce̞se̞ nɐ ˍ'me̞θis tʃ ˍ'ɐl:ɐ]). Written in CG and incorporating elements of contemporary youth slang, the title aimed to be playful and appealing to the student audience, so as to encourage wide participation. However, the use of CG in written form, particularly in a post on the university's website and social network accounts, proved to be controversial.

A few weeks later, in a newspaper article from a right-leaning publication (Georgiadou 2022), titled 'Our language quirks: What do you think?' ('Οι γλωσσικές μας φαιδρότητες: Νάμπου λαλείτε;' [i ˍɣlo̞sːi'ce̞z ˍmɐs fe̞'ðro̞tite̞s | 'nɐmbu lɐ'lite̞?]) – imitating and mocking the choice of slang used in the original title of the event – a philologist and advisor to the Ministry of Education on literature courses criticized the use of the Cypriot dialect in the workshop's title. Georgiadou claimed that 'the Cypriot dialect . . . as an integral part of the Greek language cannot be written, except in the context of its use in literature'. She described the use of the Cypriot dialect in an announcement by a state university as unprecedented. The author argued that the slangy title was historically, etymologically, and orthographically inaccurate and expressed concerns about the coherence of written language that employs local dialect. She also expressed disapproval around the 'increasing promotion, nowadays, of the dialect', characterizing it as part of a broader plan for the 'de-Hellenization of Cyprus' and an attack on the 'Greekness of our people'.[2]

'Prescriptivism', a term that could well describe this position, is based on the belief that certain forms of language possess inherent value superior to other varieties. As Crystal (2006: 67) explains, this ideal is expected to be imposed upon the entire speech community. The approach thus carries authoritarian tendencies, which involve enforcing a particular normative standard on linguistic expression. Typically, the favored mode of writing under this paradigm is one that closely approximates the stylistic conventions of literary language.

The incident described previously highlights the significant ideological burden placed on dialects, especially in contexts around written communication. While the workshop's organizers may have intended to use the dialect as a friendly and accessible means of engaging young people, its use was met with hostility by more conservative members of the academic community. The article's strident tone and nationalistic rhetoric illustrate the complexity of language politics and the deep-seated attitudes that can be triggered by the use of non-standard varieties in written communication.

Promotion of language purity and superiority carries significant ideological implications. Moschonas (2005: 20) contends that linguistic ideology is primarily concerned with establishing a standard or standardized form of language and that such ideologies – as metalinguistic systems – are inherently connected to the standards and values associated with language. In relation to the CG dialect, Karyolemou (2010) argues that despite its systematic usage and the existence of a local political entity that could provide support for standardization attempts, two prominent factors challenge and impede CG's progress towards recognition as a standardized variant of Modern Greek: the entrenched link between language and national identity and the feeling of uncertainty among dialect speakers, which further undermines efforts towards standardization.

Education plays a significant role in constructing children's national identities – it draws upon two distinct ideologies or discourses: Hellenocentrism and Cypriocentrism. The former emphasizes the Greekness of Greek–Cypriots, while the latter highlights the Cypriot identity that all communities in Cyprus share. In school settings, a nationalist-Hellenocentric discourse prevails that essentializes identity by placing emphasis on shared attributes such as the Greek language, religion, and history (Spyrou 2000; Stavrinides and Georgiou 2011). The educational system often subverts CG in classrooms, denying the fact that the dialect already operates (Kostoula-Makraki 2001) as the mother tongue of Greek–Cypriot students.

As further pointed out by Pavlou (2009), CG is the mother dialect for both teachers and students. Although it is commonly used outside the classroom by both teachers and students, it is corrected by teachers, particularly in written assignments, with SMG reinforced as the preferred form (Pavlou and Papapavlou 2004). However, CG may be allowed for informal discussions in class or when explaining complex concepts, and it seems that teachers are more tolerant to the use of CG by students if it is limited to oral speech (Pavlou 2009). Teachers may also switch to the local dialect to assert authority or scold students (Themistocleous 2015). More formally, though, the educational reform introduced by the relevant ministry in 2010, which included provisions for the comparative-contrastive utilization of CG and SMG (Armostis et al. 2012), was ultimately abandoned.

Cyprus's linguistic landscape has also been affected by the growing influence of the English language, which can be traced back to British colonization that lasted until 1960 (Kontosopoulos 2008) and is amplified by the broader forces of globalization, digital media, emigration, and immigration. Karyolemou (2001) has highlighted that the extensive influence of English has negative effects on the competent use of Greek, while the adoption of English linguistic patterns displaces traditional Greek language usage. She posits that the prominence of English in Cyprus is attributed not only to English-language instruction but also to the nature of the Cypriot economy, which heavily relies on the tertiary sector of services, as well as tourism. The adverse consequences of extensive contact with English on Greek language skills manifest in perceived deficiencies in technical or professional vocabulary, limited expression, excessive borrowing of English words, and frequent code-switching (Karyolemou 2001).

Meanwhile, English continues to gain popularity among young people, who encounter it as a *lingua franca* in mass media texts and incorporate it into their daily language, resulting in frequent code-switching between CG and English in both spoken and written communication, specifically in computer-mediated communication, as explored further in the following.

Textual phenomena in computer-mediated communication

Computer-mediated communication (CMC) is a contested term due to the diverse range of devices and rapidly evolving technologies used for communication. It encompasses various concepts related to media, written and spoken language, language repertoires, the expression of paralinguistic and non-verbal cues, communication connotations, contextual factors, perception, and the local and global impact and evolution of individual languages (Herring et al. 2013). Gnanadesikan (2009) underlines that the use of text messaging has brought about a revolutionary transformation in communication as it emulates real-time conversation. Nevertheless, she posits that the consequent assumption of a genuine conversation would be erroneous, as vital communicative cues, such as facial expressions, pauses, and intonation that are typical in face-to-face interactions, are absent. Typing, which replaces spoken language and handwriting, thus fails to encapsulate much informative content that would otherwise be conveyed through speech.

Nevertheless, CMC imitates the immediacy, speed, and expressive range of spoken language by incorporating multimodal features and inventive orthographic and typographical combinations of characters, symbols, and punctuation. Within the realm of written communication, Crystal (2006) describes this phenomenon as 'Netspeak', while Turner et al. (2014) characterize the innovative form of digital writing employed by adolescents in CMC as 'digitalk'. This unique style encompasses a captivating amalgamation of written and conversational languages, resulting in a complex and intriguing linguistic phenomenon (Turner et al. 2014). The creative linguistic and typographic features to an extent compensate for the lack of paralinguistic expression in written communication, resulting in the emergence of a new language known in contemporary literature as 'Textese'.

An informal and concise linguistic code that is a hybrid of writing and speech, Textese is nevertheless distinct from writing and speech norms, as it possesses unique characteristics that differentiate it from both modes of communication (Crystal 2006; Kemp et al. 2021; Thurlow and Brown 2003). This linguistic style encompasses various related practices, including abbreviations, inventive respellings, and the utilization of additional semiotic features such as non-alphabetical glyphs, and emojis. Scholars have coined the term 'textisms' to encompass practices associated with the abbreviated and creative nature of digital communication (Kemp et al. 2021). Moreover, Lyddy et al. (2014) identify the consistent occurrence of region-specific textisms and emphasize the imperative of considering these localized variations. This observation highlights the significance of investigating local dialects within the realm of textism research.

While there is limited research on CMC utilizing CG, Themistocleous (2009, 2010) has found evidence of its extensive usage among young Greek–Cypriots. Notably, in online interactions, these individuals favor the Roman over the Greek script. Teenagers and young adults, regardless of gender, display a preference for CG in online chat due to its capacity to foster a sense of solidarity and enable the expression of their national and language identity. Themistocleous's (2010) study reveals the significant impact of the internet on sociolinguistic environments, highlights the transformative role of the internet in shaping linguistic dynamics, and introduces the need for further examination of the potential diffusion of these orthographic practices beyond the digital realm.

The predominance of English in online communication was originally driven by practical considerations. Yet, gradually, the online environment has transitioned from monolingual to multilingual (Danet and Herring 2007). Danet and Herring (2003) discuss CMC in languages other than English, including instances where English is used as a *lingua franca* in non-native contexts. They address practical and scholarly questions related to the multilingual internet and its effects on language structures, meanings, and usage. Nevertheless, apart from its global imposition as *lingua franca*, English continues to hold a significant position in post-colonial Cyprus, functioning as a prominent foreign language within the society.

The influence of the English language is evident in the use of *Greeklish*, which involves transcribing the Greek language into the Roman script – a practice widely employed in other languages in online communication. Greeklish originated from the ASCII character encoding used in the early internet and has gained popularity due to its symbolic value in relation to the medium and its perceived ease of processing (Androutsopoulos 2016). Androutsopoulos notes that Greeklish exhibits a notable lack of uniformity, primarily characterized by spelling variations. This is attributed to its acquisition process, which does not adhere to the normative mechanisms of formal education and has not undergone regulation by authoritative bodies. And yet, Greeklish is widely recognized and understood among the younger generation (Androutsopoulos 2016). The same applies for *Cyprenglish* – a term introduced by the author (Papadima and Kourdis 2016), which is akin to the previously established Greeklish. It is formed by combining the words Cypriot and English and serves to designate the practice of transcribing CG text using the Roman script. Essentially, Cyprenglish refers to informal and spontaneous conventions that emerge within the domain of CMC among young Greek–Cypriots. These conventions alleviate the stress of 'correct' writing in CG, while accommodating the distinct sounds of the dialect (Armostis 2022). Notably, they also diverge from orthographic norms and established typographic standards.

Cyprenglish is utilized in CMC to allow online users to demonstrate unity and celebrate their linguistic and cultural heritage in the worldwide web, and involves creatively representing the unique phonetic qualities of CG using a variety of methods such as phonetic, orthographic, and combined transcriptions (Themistocleous 2010). Unconventional orthographic representations in Cyprenglish serve to convey Cypriot culture and the linguistic intricacies of Greek–Cypriots' spoken language. These alternative spellings also imply an act of defiance against the prevailing standard orthography and the dominance of SMG in Cyprus (Themistocleous 2010).

At the same time, *trans-scripting* – a respelling process that develops alternative spellings through creative manipulation of English and Greek – is utilized to cater to and engage multiple interconnected audiences across the two languages (Spilioti 2019). Spilioti (2019) argues that this 'phenomenon of reversed Romanization' involves creative respellings 'as transformative act[s] performed at specific – often transient – moments' that acknowledge the presence of digital orality exhibiting characteristics similar to oral communication. This has been classified as Greek-Alphabet English (GAE) (Spilioti 2012, 2019) and is also commonly known as *Engreek* ('engreek' n.d.a, n.d.b). All these textual phenomena and conscious practices are used, addressed to, and performed by young Greek–Cypriots in digital communication, as will be exemplified in the following section.

Textual phenomena addressing youth

Behind the screen of social networking: CG in written discourse

In order to understand the written modes of communication and prevalent textual phenomena in contemporary social networking among young Greek–Cypriots, this chapter uses an ethnographic methodology, involving the collection, observation, recording, and analysis of existing secondary data from online platforms. Participant observation and code registration techniques were utilized to gather and classify the findings.

The discourse found on social platforms – discussed in the following – has the use of CG in written form as a common feature. Specifically tailored for and by Cypriot youth, these texts serve as cultural artifacts with communication and entertainment purposes, targeting a younger audience. Fiske (2005, 2010) underlines the pivotal role of texts in popular culture, contributing to the construction of meaning and signification in everyday life. Through observation, documentation, and analysis of examples of this discourse, the study aims to illuminate how CG is expressed in written form, enhancing our understanding of the textual and visual communication strategies employed on social media platforms. This sheds light on the latter's role in constructing and promoting cultural identity.

The research examines two social platforms frequently used by young Greek–Cypriots. This approach yields a comprehensive categorization of diverse expressions of CG in written discourse based on predetermined codes. The selection of these examples is intentional, aiming to provide insights into the various ways in which CG is manifested within interactive and informal written communication among peers in social networking.

More specifically, the study looks at communication platforms used by students at the Cyprus University of Technology (CUT). Data was collected from two sources: the public Facebook page 'Cyprus University of Technology Secrets' ('Ανομολόγητα Τεχνολογικού Πανεπιστημίου Κύπρου') and the community text channel 'CUTchat' on the Discord social platform. The platforms were selected based on the participants' demographic data, the number of participants, and the ease of access for non-participatory observation and recording. The text genre of this study is based on written exchanges that occurred between individuals in social networking platforms, characterized by a casual and conversational tone. It includes interactions such as comments, messages, and posts shared among friends or acquaintances within social networks. To protect participants' privacy and ensure anonymity, complete posts, discussions, and users' nicknames were not recorded. Instead, the study focused on isolating items of research interest and documented the researcher's observations. The researcher did not interact with any participants on either platform.

Discord channels offer real-time communication, while Facebook pages are characterized by asynchronous communication. However, the platforms share other key features, such as social connection, community building, anonymity supported by the use of nicknames and/or anonymous posting, and personalization. In addition, it is evident from both posts and comments that many members follow and participate in both platforms. Therefore, the two platforms were studied synergetically so as to render the case study both seamless and comprehensive, while also highlighting individual features and findings.

Users can post anonymously on 'Cyprus University of Technology Secrets', a Facebook page classified as 'for fun'. The study recorded all the posts from the time period September 1, 2022, to March 31, 2023. Once posts devoid of text (i.e. those containing only a hyperlink) were discarded, 873 remaining posts from this page were coded and analyzed. In the period of recording (March to April 2023), the page had 1,985 followers. Out of the recorded posts, 350 were written in Cyprenglish (CG with Roman characters), 254 in mixed codes (such as CG and English, CG and English with Greek characters, etc.), 177 in CG with Greek characters, 77 in SMG and 15

323

in English. Most posts were casual, informal, and/or humorous in nature. These posts included inquiries and requests for advice, personal announcements, expressions of love interest in others, requests for further information, comments on previous posts, and announcements of student political unions, along with informative posts related to events, studies and student life, food, accommodation issues, socio-political discussions, and reflections and commentaries on news and sports. Asynchronous communication allows for time to reflect, shape, and edit messages before posting, resulting in posts that appear more refined in content and style, compared to those of the CUTchat Discord channel, regardless of the language and spelling choices. Moreover, the anonymity of posts allows for free personal expression, hyperbole, intimate disclosures, inappropriate language, and profanity. Despite the prevalent anonymity of the participants, we take the diversity of styles and language/spelling preferences to suggest that numerous individuals participate in this forum.

The real-time communication feature of Discord promotes more spontaneous, casual, and unfiltered messages. During the study period, CUTchat had 423 members. The study covers a period of three months, from January 1 to March 31, 2023, and includes 2,684 messages. Although the group has many members, the same few individuals predominantly writing in Cyprenglish account for the majority of messages. Comparatively few messages are written in CG in Greek characters. A closer inspection of the content posted by participants, clearly identified by their nicknames on this platform, allows us to better understand the participants' language preferences, local dialectal nuances, and the typographical and spelling patterns that they apply when writing in CG. For example, in certain instances, CG Textese consciously aims to visually represent the distinct tonal qualities of subdialects, as exemplified by the words 'payia' and 'etegiwsan'. As Arvaniti (2010) explains, some subdialects do not differentiate between [j] and [ʎ], instead utilizing [j] for both. In these instances, 'the voiced palatal fricative [j] . . . that substitute[s] the lateral palatal [ʎ]' (Arvaniti 2010) is visually depicted in Cyprenglish through the use of different characters in lieu of 'l', such as 'y' and 'g'.

The messages on Discord are often fragmented, with complete sentences spanning several consecutive messages. Furthermore, many messages lack text and only contain gifs, stickers, or emojis. Therefore, a quantitative classification of messages was not deemed suitable for the purposes of this study, which focuses solely on text-containing messages.

The findings of the study from both platforms provide an indicative picture of how young people write the Cypriot dialect, as demonstrated in Tables 20.1 and 20.2. In this study, the classification system employed for the analysis of Textese is based on *a priori* codes, adapted from Ong's (2017) typology of Textese to the specificities of the glocal CG Textese.

The following tables document representative, noteworthy examples sourced from the corpus collected for this particular study.

CUT students employ diverse conventions to transcribe CG into writing, with a prominent inclination towards the Roman script. Cypriot-Greek Textese (CG Textese) is forming a rich and creative vernacular orthography full of personalized spelling choices that allows for the simulation of spoken communication (Shortis 2007a) and incorporates a range of linguistic features, such as:

a. Predominance of Cyprenglish with the Roman script as a preferred code
b. Word shortenings with omission of letters (<brkm>, <ενξρ>)
c. Phonetic spellings (<eshi>, <enjen>)
d. Orthographic transliterations (<e3iasamen>, <σπ@σμα>)
e. Simulated sub-regional accents (<payia>, <pohen>)
f. Spelling variations (<s3ξ>, <s3x>, <σЄξ>)

Table 20.1 Textism findings from the 'CUTchat' Discord channel

Textism type	Roman script	Greek script
Omission of vowels or partial vowel/consonant truncation	m [mu] 'my' vrkme/brkm [ve'rkumɐ] 'I'm bored' vska [vesi'kɐ] 'basically' gt/gti [ʝe'ʝi] 'why' kltrs [kɐ'l:iʧʰːɐɾɔs] 'better (masculine-singular-nominative)'	λλεις [lɐ'lis] 'you say'
Respellings by analogy to other words or coinages with sound-spelling correspondences	jenurka [ʧɐ'nuɾkɐ] 'new (neuter-plural)' pastin kelemu ['pɐ sʈḭ__cʰːeˈl:ɐ_mːu] 'on my head' jegw [ʧ__ɐ'ɣo] 'and I' eshi ['ɛʃi] 'there is' mpi ['mbiʝ] 'to enter (3rd singular)'	πλς ['pʰːlis] 'please' εβριθινκ ['ɛvɾiθiŋk] 'everything' Εισεν βετζμπερκερ ['iʃɐ 'vɐ̤ʧ̃i pɐ̤ɾçɐɾ] 'there was veggie burger' να πκτιο [nɐ__'pcɔ] 'to drink (1st singular)'
Semiotic features to indicate para-linguistic details such as volume or emphasis	NAIII [n:ɐ̤:] 'yessss!' Mpravwww ['mbɾɐvɔː] 'bravoooo!' Gtiii? [ʧjɐↄↄ'ʧi:] 'whyyyy?' Eee [e:] 'errrr. . .' tststststs [k̩ k̩ k̩ k̩ k̩] 'tsk tsk tsk tsk tsk!'	Αμαναμουου ['ɐ mɐnɐ_mu:] 'oh, wowwww!' Γοουότ γιου ντοόουουουν; [yuↄ ɒʈˌju ↄ'ndu:ↄin] 'What (are) you dooooin'?'
Orthographic transliterations including leetspeak and semiotic words	8oreis [θɒ'ris] 'you see' 4ema ['psɐmen] 'lie (noun)' e3iasamen [ɐksi'ɐsmɐn] 'we forgot' sk@t@ [skɐ'ʈɐ] 'sh!t' k@r!0l! [kɐr'jɒli] 'motherf@cker!'	
Eye dialect or non-contractive/non-economical respellings/accent simulation	oxsa [ɒ'ksɐ] 'or maybe' ta payia ccartoo [tɐ__pɐ'jːɐ kʰːɐ'ʈun] 'the old cartoons' 3 plazmata ['tɾiɐ 'plɐzmɐʈɐ] 'three people' mxx [mu] 'my' etci ['ɛtsʰːi] 'thus' kaxolou [kɐ'xɒlu] 'at all'	Να μπου λλεις [ↄ'nembu lɐↄↄ'lis] 'Whatcha say?'

Table 20.2 Textism findings from the 'Cyprus University of Technology Secrets' Facebook page

Textism type	Roman script	Greek script
Omission of vowels or partial vowel/consonant truncation	jj/j / k/tz [ʧe] 'and' smra ['simːɛɾɛ] 'today' r/rr ['rɛ] '(vocative interjection)' tpt/tpte ['ʧipoʧɛ] 'nothing' mlkies [mɐlɛ'ʨɛs] 'bullshit' thls ['θɛlis] 'you want'	τζ [ʧe] 'and' τ [ʧo] 'the (neuter singular/it)' τρ [ʧoˈɾɛ] 'now' ττο [ˈʧuʧon] 'this (neuter)' επδ [ɛpiˈði] 'because' νμζω [nɔˈmizːɔ] 'I think' μεστα ['mɛ stɛ] 'in the (neuter plural)' μεστο ['mɛ stɔ] 'in the (neuter singular)'
Respellings by analogy to other words or coinages with sound-spelling correspondences	jinin [ʧinin] 'that (feminine accusative)' mestes ['mɛ stɛs] 'in the (feminine plural)' pase ['pɛ sɛ] 'on top of' enjen [ɛnʤ‿ɛn] 'it's not the case that it is'	ρρ ['rɛ] '(vocative interjection)' ρρρ ['rɛ] '(vocative interjection)' πλσσος ['pʰːlis] 'please!' ΑΓΑΠΠΗΜΟΥΥ [ɐˈɣɐpi‿mu] 'my love!' Θελω γλυκοοοοοοοο 🍩🍫🍬🍭🍪 [θelo] yliˈkon] 'I want something sweet!' τοππππ 🔝!!!!! [ʧʰːɔp] 'top!'
Semiotic features to indicate paralinguistic details such as volume or emphasis	vrkmeeeee [vɐˈʃkumɛ] 'I'm booored' POTTTE [pɔˈʧʰːɛ] 'never!' TZ OMWWSS [ʧ‿ˈɔmɔs] 'and yet' allaa [ɐˈlːɐ] 'but' kaniiiii [kɐˈniː] 'enough!' Eshi 🍃 ['ɛʃi ɐ'ɛɾɛn] 'it's windy'	σΈξ ['sɛks] 'sex'
Orthographic transliterations including leetspeak and semiotic words	s3x/s3ξ ['sɛks] 'sex' 4ili [psi'li] 'cannabis joint' 8elo ['θelo] 'I want' thki@ole ['θcɐɔlɛ] 'damn!' 3ekathara [ksɛˈkɐθɐɾɐ] 'clearly' sh1st0 ['ʃːistɔn] 'cunt (accusative)'	σπ@σμα ['spɐzmɐn] 'nerd' έκτρ.σ1 ['ɛxtrɔsi] 'abortion' κοτσιρ@κι@ [kɔʦʰːiˈɾɐcɐ] 'doodies' α****θκια [ɐ'ʧʰːθcɐ] 'testicles'
Eye dialect or non-contractive/non-economical respellings/accent simulation	sxx [su] 'your (singular)' ggrizo ['ngrizːɔn] 'grey' toy [ʧu] 'his' toys [ʧus] 'their' janthes [ksɐˈθːɛs] 'blond (female plural)' mitcis [miˈtsʰːis] 'small (masculine singular nominative)'	απ [ɐp] 'app' ταγκ ['ʧʰːɐk] 'tag' ΚρισμάΚκει ['kʰːɾizmɐs ˌcʰːɛik] 'Christmas Cake' ασπουμε [ɐ'spumɛn] 'for example' δισκορτ ['ndiskoɾʧ] 'discord' κσεροουμε ['ksɛɾumɛn] 'we know'

Textual phenomena addressing youth

g. Diverse semiotic elements, such as microtypographic manipulations (i.e. capitalization, letter replacements with non-alphabetical glyphs), and paralinguistic details (i.e. emojis, repeated punctuation) that form multimodal messages, all geared towards facilitating the reader's comprehension of the intended tone and emphasis of a sentence (<OULLAAA>, <Εγαμ*ς@ ν>, <Θελω γλυκοοοοοοοο 🔪 🍩 🐿 🍦 🎁 🔍 😊>, <ΑΓΑΠΩΣΕ ΡΕ ΘΚ1@ΟΛΕ, ΓΙΑΤΙ ΜΕ ΖΑΟΘΩΡΕΙΣ???>).

The resulting visual language is based on creative and evolving repertoires and characterized by heterogeneous typographical elements and spelling choices that are both expressive and obscure. Despite the frequent presence of certain expressive tendencies, these individualized modes of written expression are marked by spelling variations and distinctive deviations from standard and/or prevalent spelling and stylistic conventions, which form a vernacular system of a glocal 'deviant orthography'. For instance, word stress, a fundamental feature of lowercase Greek writing, is rare even when the Greek script is employed.

The complexity associated with the representation of CG in written form is exemplified in the usage of the compound conjunction 'και' [ce] (=and). This frequently used word exhibits various conventions, which have been documented through the analysis of our example text. Table 20.3 presents a compilation of 16 distinct modes recorded in this study of writing this word. Among these modes, 11 use letter combinations from the Roman script, while 5 employ letter combinations from the Greek alphabet. Transliterations represent various orthographic conventions influenced both by English and Greek languages and can be orthographic, phonetic, or a combination of the two.

Glocal CG Textese: vernacular orthography and typography in identity formation

The orthographic choices utilized by young Greek–Cypriots in their CMC use various linguistic codes that tend to deviate from the norms of acceptable writing and established orthographic rules and conventions (usually SMG). This is because 'typography and orthography take over the functions of sound' in CMC's e-grammar (Herring 2022). These instances of deviant orthography align with Frank Nuessel's original definition – they intentionally imitate spoken language or reveal a lack of familiarity with traditional orthographic norms (Nuessel 2015: 292). As previous studies have shown (Papadima and Photiadis 2019), deviant orthography can result from a disregard of orthography, adjustment for pragmatic reasons dictated by social dynamics, a lack of widely accepted orthographic conventions in the case of CG, and a range of restrictions, options, and auxiliary tools—often technological—that are employed by users in online written communication.

Table 20.3 Written conventions found in CG Textese of the 'and' conjunction

SMG	Transliteration of the SMG [ce] conjunction in CG Textese	Transliteration of the CG [ʧe] conjunction in CG Textese					
και	k	tse	τσε	ge	j	tz	τζ
					jj	tzai	τζαι
					jai	tziai	τζε
					je		τζιε
					jie		

327

Nevertheless, Turner et al. (2014) challenge the notion that digitalk is lacking in conventions by arguing that the development of digitalk is neither solely dependent on technological advancements nor driven by laziness; additionally, it reflects choices made by youngsters based on their identities and social and communicative aims, which are strongly motivated by the desire for effective communication, community membership, and personal expression.

Shortis (2007b) discusses the 'orthographic intertextuality' in spelling practices that stem from specific contexts, software limitations, audience expectations, social attitudes, communication conventions, and respelling and recycling of orthographic practices in text messaging. Such creative orthographic attitudes, identified as 'vernacular orthography' (Shortis 2007b), are observed in the body of CG Textese used by Greek–Cypriot youth. The motivation behind the need to accelerate typing in order to provide quick and direct responses in CMC communication, as well as to create short and condensed messages by reducing the number of glyphs, is grounded in the principles of economy (Shortis 2007b) and least effort. This leads to the use of enregistered features such as respellings, abbreviations, vowel omissions, substitution with alternative typographical symbols, and omission of the word stress diacritic. Nevertheless, Kemp (2010) highlights a noteworthy finding: While messages incorporating textisms exhibit increased writing speed, they require nearly twice the time to read and are associated with a heightened frequency of reading errors. Irrespective of these concerns, spelling approximations often observed in Textese – serving a similar purpose as phonological approximation in spoken discourse (Thurlow and Brown 2003) – aim to bridge the gap between unfamiliar linguistic elements, that is, the representation of non-standard or dialectal pronunciations in written form, and the writer's linguistic repertoire. Local CG textisms often attempt to visually represent the distinct sounds of the dialect through a variety of glyphs, which can conflict with the principle of economy by requiring additional characters for accurate rendering, resulting in eye dialect or non-contractive and non-economical respellings.

The plethora of typographic practices, conventions, and innovations evident in CG Textese reflects the pragmatic approach to written communication embraced by young Greek–Cypriots. Social, pragmatic, and technological conventions, as discussed by Shortis (2016), disrupt ideologically driven and authoritative spelling norms, fostering a sense of localized community cohesion and underscoring the importance of localized textisms in CG Textese. These disruptions highlight the nuanced interplay of societal, communicative, and technological factors in shaping novel language and typographic practices within this context. According to Luna (2018), language can be reconfigured as a means of expressing self-conception to others, establishing connections with readership, and communicating identity. Effective written communication occurs within a community that shares a mutual understanding of the world conveyed through language. Typography plays a crucial role in achieving this objective by facilitating the intended purpose of the written work for the target audience. Various typographic markers commonly associated with digitalk, such as unconventional punctuation, repeated symbols, phonetic spellings, and glyphic or lexical substitutions, frequently convey socio-emotional nuances. These markers serve to transform non-verbal cues inherent in face-to-face interactions into textual form (Vandergriff 2013). However, typography should not be perceived solely as an abstract system of signs but rather as a deliberate choice of codes extending beyond the representation of spoken language features (Androutsopoulos 2004). Consequently, an author's choices in composition, morphology, and typographic manipulation can yield a distinct stylistic quality, as observed in the case of CG Textese.

Just as fonts convey non-verbal information and influence our reading and perception of text (Hyndman 2016), character replacements within words also serve various functions while trying to maintain the visual analogies of the words and some orthographic clarity in order to preserve a certain level of legibility. In *leetspeak*, for example, some or all letters within a word are substituted with non-alphabetic characters (numerals, punctuation, special glyphs) chosen for their visual similarity (Herring 2022). However, the use of unexpected glyphs and character combinations – for example, in the word <k@r!0l!> shown in Table 20.1 – deconstructs the visual representation of words, sometimes to the extent of rendering them illegible to untrained or inexperienced readers. These readers may have to 'look' and 'interpret' rather than 'read' (Unger 2007) in a conscious effort to decipher the text. This deliberate application of deviant yet playful orthography is targeted at a specific and knowledgeable reading audience. Its purpose is to primarily disguise profanities and vulgar language – thus avoiding reporting and censorship in online postings and CMC – as well as to emphasize, attract attention, and generate interest. Inappropriate language necessitates unconventional typesetting, alongside the inclusion of specific emojis used as visual metaphors to express illicit or sexual content, a common feature in CG Textese used by young people. In contemporary communication, emojis – modern pictograms predominantly used by younger generations – exhibit a dual nature by combining both pictographic and ideographic elements. They function as a universal and culturally adaptable system of visual communication, offering an efficient means of swift interaction. Emojis possess semantic structure and carry implicit nuances within their manufactured symbols. Furthermore, they encompass both literal and associative meanings, infused with significance through symbolic representations that serve communicative intentions (Danesi 2016). Acquiring the skill of strategically employing emojis involves developing pragmatic competence, which necessitates the ability to switch between varied writing systems (Danesi 2016), an ability that Greek–Cypriot youth seem to possess.

Individualism, exploration, and expansion: A renaissance of Cypriot-Greek?

Ideological disparities, political stances, and the intricate nature of the linguistic matter in Cyprus frequently result in polarization and entrenched viewpoints that range from prescriptivism to the complete destigmatization of the widespread use of the dialect. The apprehension of the older generation regarding the 'contamination' of the language is further intensified by imported linguistic trends, the incorporation of multimodality and e-grammar into written communication, and the prevalence of Cyprenglish in written communication among the younger generation. All these factors ultimately widen the intergenerational schism pertaining to language. Nevertheless, CG continues to evolve, adapt, modernize, and gain increasing popularity through the utilization of CG Textese.

Glocal CG Textese encompasses a diverse range of culturally significant components, borrowed practices, multimodal elements, and frequent code-switching. These elements contribute to the expression of the different linguistic varieties used, imbued with a multitude of semantic and pragmatic nuances. The recent tendency to 'decolonize' the use of CG in public discourse has led to a notable increase in its written form. This shift can be attributed to the freedom of expression facilitated by modern communication platforms, the proliferation of networking media, and the anonymity afforded to users. These factors have created an environment conducive to the use of the dialect.

The absence of fixed rules and a standardized framework for CG's written representation further encourages unrestricted creativity in written expression, resulting in many different spellings, conventions, and individual styles. The diverse range of spelling conventions is also influenced by current writing trends in CMC, youth's exposure to popular culture texts in their native language, the dynamic influence of the English language, and the application of multimodal elements to written texts that has resulted in a new approach to writing the dialect, with a prevailing emphasis on phonetic representation. Furthermore, writing choices reflect young people's attitudes and beliefs, as well as their overall identities.

The complexities involved in accurately representing the phonological intricacies of CG highlight the broader social and political dynamics at play. Within the context of the CG dialect, the intricate relationship between language, culture, and identity illuminates various dimensions of CG Textese, including orthographic, typographic, and ideological aspects. The prevalent textual phenomena used by young Greek–Cypriots provide valuable insights into the dynamic shaping and negotiation of language within contemporary media and social networks. Moreover, the evolution of the dialect within a multicultural and European framework reflects the ongoing tensions between tradition and modernity, as well as the interplay between local identity and global influences. Young people are actively developing, enriching, and mastering the modern written form of their dialect, thereby contributing to its widespread adoption. In contrast to past purist perspectives on the language, the debates surrounding its written representation, and the dogmatic biases against its use, Cypriot youth is paving the way for a more liberal and inclusive approach to writing CG and embracing its extensive usage in all forms of communication.

Acknowledgments

The author extends heartfelt appreciation to Spyros Armostis, a lecturer in linguistics in the Department of English Studies at the University of Cyprus. His invaluable support in offering the phonetic transliteration in the International Phonetic Alphabet (IPA) and translating/interpreting the original CG spellings into English significantly enhanced the precision and clarity of this research project. His expertise and careful attention to detail have been highly treasured.

Notes

1 *Diglossia* refers to the phenomenon where multiple varieties of the same language are used by speakers in different contexts, typically involving the coexistence of a standard language and regional dialects (Ferguson 1959).
2 All translated quotes in this chapter are provided by the author of the chapter.

English references

Androutsopoulos, J. (2004). 'Typography as a resource of media style: Cases from music youth culture'. In *Proceedings of the 1st International Conference on Typography and Visual Communication*. Thessaloniki: University of Macedonia Press.
Androutsopoulos, J. (2016). '"Greeklish": Transliteration practice and discourse in the context of computer-mediated digraphia'. In A. Georgakopoulou and M. Silk (Eds), *Standard Languages and Language Standards – Greek, Past and Present* (pp. 249–278). London: Routledge.
Armostis, S., Christodoulou, K., Katsoyannou, M. and Themistokleous, C. (2014). *Addressing Writing System Issues in Dialectal Lexicography: The Case of Cypriot Greek*. Cambridge: Cambridge Scholars Publishing.
Arvaniti, A. (2010). 'A (brief) overview of the phonetics and phonology of Cypriot Greek'. In A. Voskos, D. Goutsos and A. Mozer (Eds), *The Greek Language in Cyprus from Antiquity to Today* (pp. 107–124). University of Athens Press.
Crystal, D. (2006). *Language and the Internet*. Cambridge: Cambridge University Press.
Danesi, M. (2016). *The Semiotics of Emoji*. London: Bloomsbury Publishing.
Danet, B. and Herring, S. C. (2003). 'Introduction: The Multilingual Internet'. *Journal of Computer-Mediated Communication*, 9(1), JCMC9110. https://doi.org/10.1111/j.1083-6101.2003.tb00354.x
Danet, B. and Herring, S. C. (2007). *The Multilingual Internet*. Oxford: Oxford University Press.
engreek. (n.d.-a). Retrieved May 22, 2023, from urbandictionary.com: www.urbandictionary.com/define.php?term=engreek

engreek. (n.d.-b). Retrieved May 22, 2023, from slang.gr: www.slang.gr/lemma/5869-engreek

Ferguson, C. A. (1959). 'Diglossia'. *Word*, 15(2), 325–340. https://doi.org/10.1080/00437956.1959.11659702

Fiske, J. (2005). *Reading the Popular*. New York: Routledge.

Fiske, J. (2010). *Understanding Popular Culture*. London: Routledge.

Gnanadesikan, A. E. (2009). *The Writing Revolution: Cuneiform to the Internet*. Hoboken, NJ: Wiley-Blackwell.

Herring, S. C. (2022). 'Grammar and Electronic Communication'. In *The Encyclopedia of Applied Linguistics* (pp. 1–9). Wiley-Blackwell. https://doi.org/10.1002/9781405198431.wbeal0466.pub2

Herring, S. C., Stein, D. and Virtanen, T. (2013). 'Introduction to the pragmatics of computer-mediated communication'. In S. C. Herring, D. Stein and T. Virtanen (Eds), *Pragmatics of Computer-Mediated Communication* (pp. 3–32). De Gruyter Mouton.

Horrocks, G. (2010). *Greek: A History of the Language and Its Speakers* (2nd ed.). Hoboken, NJ: Wiley-Blackwell.

Hyndman, S. (2016). *Why Fonts Matter*. London: Virgin Books.

Karyolemou, M. (2001). 'From linguistic liberalism to legal regulation'. *Language Problems and Language Planning*, 25(1), 25–50. https://doi.org/10.1075/lplp.25.1.03kar

Kemp, N. (2010). 'Texting versus txtng: Reading and writing text messages, and links with other linguistic skills'. *Writing Systems Research*, 2(1), 53–71.

Kemp, N., Graham, J., Grieve, R. and Beyersmann, E. (2021). 'The influence of textese on adolescents' perceptions of text message writers'. *Telematics and Informatics*, 65(August), 101720. https://doi.org/10.1016/j.tele.2021.101720

Luna, P. (2018). *Typography: A Very Short Introduction*. Oxford: Oxford University Press.

Lyddy, F., Farina, F., Hanney, J., Farrell, L. and Kelly O'Neill, N. (2014). 'An analysis of language in university students' text messages'. *Journal of Computer-Mediated Communication*, 19(3), 546–561. https://doi.org/10.1111/jcc4.12045

Nuessel, F. (2015). 'Deviant Orthography'. In P. P. Trifonas (Ed), *International Handbook of Semiotics* (pp. 291–301). Springer. https://doi.org/10.1007/978-94-017-9404-6

Ong, K. K. W. (2017). 'Textese and Singlish in multiparty chats'. *World Englishes*, 36(4), 611–630. https://doi.org/10.1111/weng.12245

Papadima, A., Ayiomamitou, I. and Kyriacou, S. (2013). 'Typographic practices and spelling convention for the written representation of a non-standard dialect: The case of the Greek–Cypriot dialect'. In M. Lachout (Ed), *Aktuelle Tendenzen der Sprachwissenschaft* (pp. 87–100). Verlag Dr. Kovač.

Papadima, A., Ayiomamitou, I., Kyriacou, S. and Parmaxis, G. (2014). 'Orthography development for the Greek Cypriot dialect: Language attitudes and orthographic choice'. In C. Dyck, T. Granadillo, K. Rice and J. E. Rosés Labrada (Eds), *Dialogue on Dialect Standardization* (pp. 63–80). Cambridge Scholars Publishing.

Papadima, A. and Kourdis, E. (2016). 'Global meets local: Typographic practices and the semiotic role of subtitling in the creation of parodies in Cypriot dialect on Internet texts'. *Social Semiotics*, 26(1), 59–75. https://doi.org/10.1080/10350330.2015.1051343

Papadima, A. and Photiadis, T. (2019). 'Communication in social media: Football clubs, language, and ideology'. *Journal of Modern Greek Studies*, 37(1), 127–147. https://doi.org/10.1353/mgs.2019.0004

Papapavlou, A. (2010). 'Language planning in action: Searching for a viable bidialectal program'. *Language Problems and Language Planning*, 34(2), 120–140.

Pavlou, P. (2009). 'The use of dialect in the primary classroom with particular emphasis on the influence of school subjects'. In A. Papapavlou and P. Pavlou (Eds), *Sociolinguistic and Pedagogical Dimensions of Dialects in Education* (p. 265). Cambridge Scholars Publishing.

Pavlou, P. and Papapavlou, A. (2004). 'Issues of dialect use in education from the Greek Cypriot perspective'. *International Journal of Applied Linguistics*, 14(2), 243–258. https://doi.org/10.1111/j.1473-4192.2004.00061.x

Shortis, T. F. J. (2007a). 'Gr8 txtpectations: The Creativity of Text Spelling'. *English Drama Media* (June), 21–26.

Shortis, T. F. J. (2007b). 'Revoicing txt: Spelling, vernacular orthography and "unregimented writing"'. In S. Posteguillo, M. J. Esteve and M. L. Gea-Valor (Eds), *The Texture of Internet: Netlinguistics in Progress* (pp. 2–23). Cambridge Scholars Publishing.

Shortis, T. F. J. (2016). *Orthographic Practices in SMS Text Messaging as a Case Signifying Diachronic Change in Linguistic and Semiotic Resources*. Doctoral thesis. UCL (University College London).

Sophocleous, A. (2006). 'Identity formation and dialect use among young speakers of the Greek–Cypriot community in Cyprus'. *British Studies in Applied Linguistics*, 21, 61–78.

The Routledge Handbook of Endangered and Minority Languages

Spilioti, T. (2012). 'Greek-Alphabet English: Vernacular transliterations of English in social media'. In B. O'Rourke, N. Bermingham and S. Brennan (Eds), *Opening New Lines of Communication in Applied Linguistics. Proceedings of the 46th Annual Meeting of the British Association for Applied Linguistics* (pp. 435–446). London: Scitsiugnil Press.

Spilioti, T. (2019). 'From transliteration to trans-scripting: Creativity and multilingual writing on the internet'. *Discourse, Context and Media*, 29, 1–10. https://doi.org/10.1016/j.dcm.2019.03.001

Spyrou, S. (2000). 'Education, ideology, and the national self: The social practice of identity construction in the classroom'. *The Cyprus Review*, 12(1), 61–81.

Stavrinides, P. and Georgiou, S. (2011). 'National identity and in-group/out-group attitudes with Greek–Cypriot children'. *European Journal of Developmental Psychology*, 8(1), 87–97. https://doi.org/10.1080/174 05629.2010.533989

Terkourafi, M. (2007). 'Perceptions of difference in the Greek sphere: The case of Cyprus'. *Journal of Greek Linguistics*, 8(1), 60–96.

Themistocleous, C. (2009). 'Written Cypriot Greek in online chat: Usage and attitudes'. In *Proceedings of the 8th International Conference on Greek Linguistics* (Vol. 30, pp. 473–488). University of Ioannina.

Themistocleous, C. (2010). 'Writing in a non-standard Greek variety: Romanized Cypriot Greek in online chat'. *Writing Systems Research*, 2(2), 155–168.

Themistocleous, C. (2015). 'Digital code-switching between Cypriot and standard Greek: Performance and identity play online'. *International Journal of Bilingualism*, 19(3), 282–297. https://doi.org/10.1177/1367006913512727

Thurlow, C. and Brown, A. (2003). 'Generation txt? The sociolinguistics of young people's text messaging'. *Discourse Analysis Online*. Retrieved from http://extra.shu.ac.uk/daol/articles/v1/n1/a3/thurlow 2002003.html

Tsiplakou, S. (2006). 'Cyprus: Language situation'. In K. Brown (Ed), *Encyclopedia of Language & Linguistics* (pp. 337–339). Elsevier Science. https://doi.org/10.1016/b0-08-044854-2/01790-9

Tsiplakou, S., Papapavlou, A., Pavlou, P. and Katsoyannou, M. (2006). 'Levelling, koineization and their implications for bidialectism'. In *Language Variation – European Perspectives. Selected Papers from the 3rd International Conference on Language Variation in Europe (ICLaVE 3), University of Amsterdam, 23–25 June 2005* (pp. 265–276). Amsterdam: John Benjamins Publishing Company.

Turner, K. H., Abrams, S. S., Katíc, E. and Donovan, M. J. (2014). 'Demystifying digitalk: The what and why of the language teens use in digital writing'. *Journal of Literacy Research*, 46(2), 157–193. https://doi.org/10.1177/1086296X14534061

Unger, G. (2007). *While You're Reading*. New York: Mark Batty Publisher.

Vandergriff, I. (2013). 'Emotive communication online: A contextual analysis of computer-mediated communication (CMC) cues'. *Journal of Pragmatics*, 51, 1–12. https://doi.org/10.1016/j.pragma.2013.02.008

Greek references

Armostis, S. (2022). 'Cypriot Greek and its writing' 'Η κυπριακή ελληνική τζαι η γραφή της'. In A. Achilleos, S. Armostis and E. Socratous (Eds), *Decolonisation: Linguistic Creations by Machines and Humans ΑΠΟαποικιοΠΟΙΗΣΗ* (pp. 13–33). Limassol: Ypogeia Skini.

Armostis, S., Katsoyannou, M., Christodoulou, K. and Themistocleous, C. (2012). 'Tendencies of Greek–Cypriots in writing Cypriot-Greek' 'Τάσεις των Κυπρίων ως προς τη γραπτή απόδοση των μεταφατνιακών συμφώνων της κυπριακής'. In Z. Gavriilidou, A. Efthymiou, E. Thomadaki and P. Kambakis-Vougiouklis (Eds), *Selected Papers of the 10th International Conference of Greek Linguistics* (pp. 663–678). Komotini/Greece: Democritus University of Thrace.

Armostis, S., Katsoyannou, M., Christodoulou, K. and Themistocleous, C. Αρμοστής, Σ., Κατσογιάννου, M. and Χριστοδούλου, K. (2016). 'Orthographic trends in a non-standard variety: The rendering of synizesis in Cypriot Greek' 'Ορθογραφικές τάσεις σε μια μη τυποποιημένη ποικιλία: η απόδοση της συνίζησης στην Κυπριακή Ελληνική'. In A. Ralli, N. Koutsoukos and S. Bompolas (Eds), *Proceedings of the 6th Modern Greek Dialects and Linguistic Theory Meeting*. https://doi.org/10.26220/mgdlt.v6i1.2670

Georgiadou, D. Γεωργιάδου, Δ. (2022, December 11). 'Our language quirks: What do you think?' 'Οι γλωσσικές μας φαιδρότητες'. *Alithia Αλήθεια*, p. 24. Retrieved from https://alithia.com.cy/wp-content/uploads/2022/12/Altihia.pdf

Karyolemou, M. Καρυολαίμου, M. (2000). 'Cypriot reality and sociolinguistic description' 'Κυπριακή πραγματικότητα και κοινωνιογλωσσική περιγραφή'. *Studies on the Greek Language Μελέτες Για Την*

332

Ελληνική Γλώσσα. Proceedings of the 20th Annual Meeting of the Department of Linguistics of the Faculty of Philosophy of the Aristotle University of Thessaloniki Πρακτικά 20ης Ετήσιας Συνάντησης Του Τομέα Γλωσσολογίας Της Φιλοσοφικής Σχολής ΑΠΘ, 23–25 May 1999 23–25 Μαΐου 1999, 203–214.

Karyolemou, M. Καρυολαίμου, M. (2010). 'Language policy and language planning in Cyprus' 'Γλωσσική πολιτική και γλωσσικός σχεδιασμός στην Κύπρο'. In A. Voskos, D. Goutsos and A. Mozer A. Βοσκός, Δ. Γούτσος, & A. Μόζερ (Eds), *The Greek Language in Cyprus from Antiquity to Present Day Η ελληνική γλώσσα στην Κύπρο από την αρχαιότητα ως σήμερα* (pp. 242–261). Athens: National and Kapodistrian University of Athens Αθήνα: Εθνικό και Καποδιστριακό Πανεπιστήμιο Αθηνών.

Katsoyannou, M., Papapavlou, A., Pavlou, P. and Tsiplakou, S. Κατσόγιαννου, M., Παπαπαύλου, A., Παύλου, Π., Τσιπλάκου, Σ. (2006). 'Bidialectal communities and the linguistic continuum: The case of Cypriot' 'Διδιαλεκτικές κοινότητες και γλωσσικό συνεχές: η περίπτωση της κυπριακής'. In M. Janse, B. Joseph and A. Ralli (Eds), *Proceedings of the 2nd International Conference on Modern Greek Dialects and Linguistic Theory* (pp. 156–171). Patras: University of Patras.

Kontosopoulos, N. Κοντοσόπουλος, N. (2008). *Dialects and Idioms of Modern Greek Διάλεκτοι και Ιδιώματα της Νέας Ελληνικής*. Athens: Gregori Αθήνα: Γρηγόρη.

Kostoula-Makraki, N. Κωστούλα-Μακράκη, N. (2001). *Language and Society Γλώσσα και Κοινωνία*. Athens: Metechmio Αθήνα: Μεταίχμιο.

Moschonas, S. Μοσχονάς, Σ. (2005). *Ideology and Language Ιδεολογία και Γλώσσα*. Athens: Patakis Αθήνα: Πατάκης.

Papadima, A. and Kyriacou S. Παπαδήμα, A. and Κυριάκου, Σ. (2014). 'The Cypriot-Greek dialect in school language textbooks of Cypriot education: orthographic conventions and typographic practices' 'Η ελληνική κυπριακή διάλεκτος στα σχολικά γλωσσικά εγχειρίδια της κυπριακής εκπαίδευσης: ορθογραφικές συμβάσεις και τυπογραφικές πρακτικές'. In *Studies on the Greek Language 34. Proceedings of the 34th Annual Meeting of the Department of Linguistics of the Department of Philology of the Aristotle University of Thessaloniki Μελέτες Για Την Ελληνική Γλώσσα 34. Πρακτικά Της 34ης Ετήσιας Συνάντησης Του Τομέα Γλωσσολογίας Του Τμήματος Φιλολογίας Του Α.Π.Θ.*, 323–335. Thessaloniki: Institute of Modern Greek Studies Θεσσαλονίκη: Ινστιτούτο Νεοελληνικών Σπουδών.

Papapavlou, A. Παπαπαύλου, A. (2011). *The Linguistic Landscape of Cyprus Το γλωσσικό τοπίο στην Κύπρο*. Athens: Kastanioti Αθήνα: Καστανιώτη.

21

"I ALREADY KNOW WHERE THAT PLACE IS ..."

The educational linguistic landscape of a language at risk

Kayhan İnan and Gülin Dağdeviren-Kırmızı

Introduction

There is a large volume of studies which has focused on linguistic landscape research in the different but related topics of multilingualism, language planning, language endangerment, and ethnolinguistic vitality. More recent attention has been paid to linguistic landscapes as a pedagogical resource (e.g. Rowland 2013; Hancock 2012; Sayer 2010). Landry and Bourhis (1997) emphasized the role of linguistic landscape experience in bilingual development. The linguistic landscape is a good source of real-life experience (Sayer 2010) for learners because it helps them to develop their critical literacy and pragmatic competence (Hewitt-Bradshaw 2014: 172). Linguistic landscape as a pedagogical tool also contributes to the awareness of linguistic diversity.

This study was therefore designed to investigate how the linguistic landscapes in a Gagauz educational setting align with the language policy of the Gagauz ATU as there has been no detailed quantitative or qualitative analysis of linguistic landscape and language pedagogy in the Gagauz context. To this end, as a first step, to explore the languages represented in the linguistic landscape of Gagauz educational settings, a group of photographs taken on a university campus. Then, how Gagauz speakers perceived the language choice in the Gagauz educational setting was investigated using those photographs.

Linguistic landscape

Shohamy and Gorter (2008: 1) defined linguistic landscape as "the attention to language in the environment, words and images displayed and exposed in public spaces". All forms of public signage such as "the language of public road signs, advertising billboards, street names, place names, commercial shop signs, and public signs on government buildings" are of interest in linguistic landscape research (Landry & Bourhis 1997: 25). In other words, anything written which includes a text in a public sphere can be the topic of investigation. It is seen that linguistic landscape can even include litter containers (Kallen 2010), restaurant menus (Kasanga 2012), and manhole covers (Tufi & Blackwood 2010). Apart from non-mobile ones, texts on transportation and any materials which can be transmitted can also show the representation of languages. Therefore, Sebba (2010) extended the scope of the sign in linguistic landscape research by

DOI: 10.4324/9781003439493-25

including "discourses in transit" and referred to signs on vehicles and related stickers, pamphlets, and banknotes.

Adopting a social psychological perspective, Landry and Bourhis (1997: 25) made a distinction based on the functions of language signs which have an informational and a symbolic function. Firstly, the informational function was described as one marking language boundaries informing both in-group and out-group members. Leclerc (1989) made a further classification and offered a distinction between private and government signs that have informational functions. As can be clearly understood, private signs are commercial signs which can be seen on streets and public transport, whereas government signs refer to public ones used in governmental contexts where the exertion of control is more visible compared with private signs. Second, the symbolic function of the linguistic landscape is related to how members of a language group feel in terms of in-group and out-group dynamics. Landry and Bourhis (1997) also emphasized the close relationship between the symbolic functions of linguistic landscape, ethnic identity, and ethnolinguistic vitality.

Linguistic landscape studies have also been instrumental in the understanding of language policy and planning. Hult (2018) categorized the relationship between linguistic landscape and language policy and planning into two parts: indirect and direct ways. The indirect way simply refers to the reflection of language ideologies in public spaces. On the other hand, direct ways can be exemplified as the regulations about specifically what and how a language should be used in those contexts. The results of language policy can be easily observed in top-down signs, which are official, and governmental signs, which are designed according to related regulations. However, Gorter and Cenoz (2007) suggested that language policy can also be visible in bottom-up signs, which are non-official ones, as in the case of the Catalan language. In the Catalonian context, the Catalan language is guaranteed with specific regulations designed for the use of this language together with Spain's mainstream language in both public and private domains.

Changes in language ideologies and policies can also be observed in the linguistic landscape. Ben-Rafael, Shohamy, and Barni (2010) criticized the perspective of Landry and Bourhis (1997) for their account of linguistic landscape as a 'given' one instead of an ever-changing and dynamic one. Backhaus (2005: 104) similarly suggested that "the coexistence of older and newer types of signs allows for the detection and reconstruction of ongoing changes in language use patterns" which demonstrates the dynamic nature of the linguistic landscape. In the same vein, Pavlenko (2009) emphasized the need to examine the linguistic landscape from a diachronic perspective. She pointed out that especially in politically changing environments and during nation-building processes, the linguistic landscape exhibits a dynamic nature (p. 253).

The current study was designed to investigate the linguistic landscape in one of these contexts, namely in the post-Soviet context and in autonomy where political and historical dynamism is relatively salient. Although extensive research has already been carried out on the linguistic landscape in this context, far too little attention has been paid to the visibility of the Gagauz language in an autonomous context. One of these studies (Dağdeviren-Kırmızı 2021) investigated the linguistic landscape of the Autonomous Territorial Unit (ATU) of Gagauzia in terms of bilingualism/multilingualism, the order of display of languages, the amount of information delivered, and the size of the texts in signage. The results showed the dominance of the Russian language in both public and private signs. Henzelmann (2022) further explored monolingual, bilingual, and trilingual signs in official administrative contexts in the ATU of Gagauzia from a semiotic perspective and found that linguistic combinations served different functions and audiences. Additionally, Romanian and Gagauz were found to be dominant in public signage in the study. However, the generalizability of the published research on this issue is problematic as it is limited, and still very little is currently known about the Gagauz context.

Linguistic landscape as a pedagogical resource

As an indispensable part of the linguistic landscape, educational institutions play an important role in multilingual contexts. Brown (2005: 79) used the term "schoolscape" to refer to "the physical and social setting in which teaching and learning take place". It is seen that schoolscapes are considered vital in the representation of the language ideologies in society. Adopting the framework of ethnolinguistic vitality, Landry and Bourhis (1997) placed particular emphasis on the relationship between linguistic experience and bilingual development. It is also said that public signage in a specific language influences the cognitive processes of the population (Sachdev & Bourhis 1993). Cenoz and Gorter (2008) further discussed the role of the linguistic landscape in the learning context. They asserted that it can be considered as an example of incidental learning, as well as a source of texts with various functions which help to increase learners' pragmatic competence and provide context for multilingual literacy skills.

Another relevant finding about linguistic landscape in educational contexts is its role in language awareness. Dagenais et al. (2008) found that linguistic landscape activities help learners increase their language awareness with a critical perspective. Similarly, Gorter et al. (2021) reported that although the signs used in everyday life are not designed to teach a language or aid its learning, exposure to them can help to increase awareness. Moreover, sensitivity to connotational aspects of language such as negative or positive attitudes can also be significantly developed with the help of linguistic landscape activities (Sayer 2010).

In everyday life, the representation of languages with fewer speakers has a positive impact on the encouragement to use the language and involvement of these individuals in language practices. Pennycook and Otsuji (2014: 168) suggested that translanguaging practices can "shape the linguistic landscapes" in a specific context, which can also be observed in educational contexts. Menken and Sánchez (2019) found that developing a linguistic landscape was one of the strategies for promoting translanguaging practices in the classroom. The representation of linguistic examples from home languages was also found to cause ideological changes in monolingual classes.

There is a growing body of literature (e.g. Andrade et al. 2023; Lourenço et al. 2023; Gorter 2018; Rowland 2013; Hancock 2012; Sayer 2010) and interest in investigating the importance of linguistic landscape in educational contexts. Its roles in developing pragmatic competence and literacy skills, raising linguistic awareness, providing an environment for translanguaging practices, and contributing to language policies and planning have been the object of research so far. In the context of the ATU of Gagauzia, however, far too little attention has been paid to the role of linguistic landscape in educational institutions. In one of the few previous studies addressing this, Henzelmann (2022: 106) reported a striking result that emerged from the data. Although Romanian appeared to be the first language represented on signposts at state schools, the Gagauz and Romanian languages were used at the entrances to the Comrat State University. Henzelmann (2022) also emphasized that despite these languages being used to welcome visitors, Russian was nevertheless the most functional language in the university context. In the same vein, Holsapple (2018) found that the participants found it more appropriate to use Russian in a higher education institution as they thought of it as more "official" and formal. As can be seen, previous studies have only partly shown the representation of these languages in an educational context.

The Gagauz language

The Gagauz language, which is a member of the southwestern branch of Turkic languages (Johanson 1998: 82), is spoken in specific parts of Eastern Europe. Bessarabia is the region that lies between the Prut and Dniester rivers, and the variety of Gagauz spoken here is categorized by

UNESCO as a definitely endangered language (Moseley 2010: 24), which refers to an interruption in the intergenerational transmission of the Gagauz language in this context. Recently, UNESCO has upgraded the language status of the Gagauz language spoken in the Republic of Moldova and categorized it as "potentially vulnerable". Similarly, Eberhard et al. (2023) labeled Gagauz a safe language in *Ethnologue*. This classification refers to a situation in which there is no sustainability of a language in formal domains, but it survives as a norm at home and in the community.

Following the declaration of the ATU of Gagauzia in 1994, three languages were declared official: Gagauz, Russian, and Romanian. The use and representation of these languages in different domains of everyday life have been protected by the Law on Languages of the Gagauzia ATU. Even so, a discrepancy between the policy and implementation has been observed as a salient feature in everyday life. To date, the problem has received little attention in the related literature (Henzelmann 2022; Dağdeviren-Kırmızı 2021; Holsapple 2018).

Considering this research gap, the current study addressed the following research questions:

1. How do the linguistic landscapes in Gagauz educational settings align with the language policy of the Gagauz ATU?
2. How do Gagauz speakers (academic, administrative staff, and students) perceive the use of Gagauz, Russian, and Romanian in an educational setting?

The current study

Methodology

For the current study, an ethnographic approach was adopted. Brewer (2000) defined this as a form of research that is conducted to "understand the social meanings and activities of the people in a given field and setting" (p. 11). For the methods used for ethnographic research, Willis and Trondman (2000) used the term "a family of methods" (p. 5), which includes formal/informal interviews, collecting documents and artifacts (Hammersley & Atkinson 2007), and observation (Malinowski 1922). With respect to linguistic studies, ethnography has been of interest because context is considered to be at the heart of the understanding of language (Gumperz 1982). Hornberger (2015) stated that in the late 1980s, "ethnographic on-the-ground methods" began to be used in the studies of language policy and planning as a result of paradigm shifts in related research (p. 10). Specifically, regarding linguistic landscape research, an ethnographic approach has frequently been adopted as it provides an emic perspective (Lou 2017).

In the current study, document analysis and interviews were used as the main data collection approaches. In the document analysis, policies related to language use and representation in macro-level examples such as the Law on Languages of Gagauzia ATU, and micro-level examples such as the Regulation of Comrat State University were interpreted. Photographs of the linguistic landscape to be used as prompts in the interviews were taken on the campus.

Adapted from Li (2022), the interviews were built on the questions concerning the language(s) used in lectures, the language of the signposts on campus, perceptions and comprehension of these signs, and the relationship between the signs and the language policy of the institution.

Data collection

Data were collected through the analysis of the relevant legislative documents and interviews with the members of the academic and administrative staff as well as students. Concerning the document analysis, documents related to the legal framework of the languages spoken in the ATU of Gagauzia were reviewed and their content was evaluated. The interpretative document analysis included both electronic and non-electronic documents. To this end, the analysis has focused on the Law of Moldova on Languages, the Law on Languages of the Gagauzia ATU, and the Regulations of Comrat State University.

In the interview preparatory phase, 206 photographs were taken using a Canon Eos 4000d and an internal 12MP camera of iPhone 7. The criteria employed in the selection of these 16 photographs were their representativeness of the available signposts, their locations within buildings, and their functions in campus life. The invalid photos were removed using the three criteria (exclusion of repetitive ones, unclear ones, and ones without texts) established by Lai (2013: 256). Within the scope of this research, 16 photos were selected from a total of 206 photos to be used in interviews. The selected photos consist of both permanent and temporary signs, some of which include visuals in addition to text. The photos were evaluated and chosen by two field experts. The information about the photographs is given in Table 21.1. The pictures were taken at Comrat State University, which was founded in 1991 in Comrat, the capital of the ATU of Gagauzia. The campus is composed of two connected buildings on Galatsana Street, Comrat. One of them houses administrative units and research centers, whereas the faculties of agro-technology, national culture, economy, and law are located in the other. The photographs were taken in both buildings.

Semi-structured interviews with five participants were held on campus. Each lasted for about 30 minutes, and they were recorded (with the interviewees' consent) using a SONY ICD PX333 digital voice recorder. The interview questions were designed to explore the perceptions of the students and members of the academic and administrative staff concerning the linguistic landscape and related language policies in the context of a higher education institution, Comrat State University. As mentioned before, during the interviews, the 16 photographs taken on the campus were presented to the participants as prompts, and they were asked to comment on them.

The participants

This study employed purposive sampling to investigate the perceptions of the linguistic landscape at Comrat State University. To explore a range of experiences and perceptions, interviews were held with five participants. Three students (Vera, Natalia, and Olga) and one academic/administrative staff member (Irina) were chosen to enable an understanding of the emic perspective, and a fifth participant, Mehmet, a Turkish visiting scholar, was selected to present the etic perspective as an outsider. Detailed demographic information about the student participants is given in Table 21.2.

As can be seen in Table 21.2, the student participants' ages ranged between 21 and 25, they were all female, and they were studying in different departments (Law, Turkish Language, and Literature) at Comrat State University. Additionally, they reported that they could all speak Russian, Gagauz, Romanian, Turkish, and English. The second group of participants comprised two members of the academic/administrative staff working at Comrat State University. Table 21.3 shows details about these participants.

The two members of the academic/administrative staff, as shown in Table 21.3, were working in the Accounting and Finance and the Turkish Language and Literature departments. Mehmet had been working at Comrat State University for several years and had previously worked as a lecturer at a university in Türkiye. On the question of languages, Irina reported that she could speak Turkish, Gagauz, Russian, Romanian, and English, whereas only Turkish and English were reported

"I already know where that place is . . ."

Table 21.1 Photographs used as prompts[1]

	Location	Languages	Order	Font Size
Photo 1	Conference hall entrance	Trilingual	Gagauz, Romanian, Russian	Gagauz (large font size), Romanian and Russian (small font size)
Photo 2	Entrance to the university	Quadrilingual	Visual: Gagauz, Romanian, Russian, English	Gagauz (small font size), Romanian, Russian, English (large font size)
Photo 3	Old block first floor	Trilingual	Romanian, Gagauz, Russian	Equal font size
Photo 4	New block third floor	Monolingual	Russian	Large font size
Photo 5	New block second floor	Monolingual	English	Large font size
Photo 6	Old block third block	Bilingual	Visual: English, Gagauz	Equal font size
Photo 7	New block ground floor	Monolingual	Visual: Russian	Equal font size
Photo 8	Old block first floor	Trilingual	Sign 1: Visual: Gagauz, Romanian, Russian	Equal font size
			Sign 2: Romanian, Gagauz, Russian	
Photo 9	Old block second floor	Monolingual	Russian	Equal font size
Photo 10	Old block third floor	Trilingual	Gagauz, Romanian, Russian	Gagauz and Romanian (large font size), Russian (small font size)
Photo 11	Old block third floor	Trilingual	Sign 1: English, Romanian, Russian	Equal font size
			Sign 2: Romanian, Gagauz, Russian	
Photo 12	New block ground floor	Monolingual	Romanian: Visual	Equal font size
Photo 13	New block fourth floor	Trilingual	Gagauz (title only), Romanian, Russian	Equal font size
Photo 14	Old block first floor	Sign1: Bilingual Sign: Monolingual	Sign 1: Visual: Romanian, Gagauz	Equal font size
			Sign 2: Russian	
Photo 15	Old block first floor	Monolingual	Gagauz	Large font size
Photo 16	New block first floor	Bilingual	Russian, Gagauz	Russian (large font size), Gagauz (small font size)

The Routledge Handbook of Endangered and Minority Languages

Table 21.2 Participants (students)

Participant name	Age	Gender	Department
Vera	21	Female	Law
Natalia	25	Female	Turkish Language and Literature
Olga	25	Female	Turkish Language and Literature

Table 21.3 Participants (academic/administrative staff)

Participant Name	Age	Gender	Department
Irina	45	Female	Accounting and Finance
Mehmet	40	Male	Turkish Language and Literature

by Mehmet. All five participants in this study were given pseudonyms to ensure their privacy and to maintain confidentiality. Their participation in this research study was completely voluntary.

Data analysis

Qualitative data analysis methods were used in the study. The first method involved taking photographs during a walk around the campus and then categorizing them based on the first language displayed, the amount of information offered, and the font size of the text and they were grouped according to the locations of the photo shootings.

Second, in the document analysis, laws, and regulations on the use of languages were identified and interpreted. As these documents were the primary sources of the university's language policy, they also provided valuable data for triangulation. Finally, the interview transcriptions were analyzed using thematic analysis to identify any recurring patterns related to the participants' perceptions of the linguistic landscape.

Results

Document analysis

In the document analysis part of the study, the Law of Gagauzia ATU on the Functioning of Languages on the Territory of Gagauzia (Gagauz Yeri) (LGA) (Halk Toplușu 1995), the Law of the Republic of Moldova on language (On Language Functioning on the Territory of Moldovan SSR) (LRM) (Ministerul Justiției 2021), and the Regulations of Comrat State University were analyzed. It is seen that the Gagauz language was granted equal status with Russian and Romanian.

The Law of ATU Gagauzia on the Functioning of Languages in the territory guarantees the use of these three languages. For the official names of the territories of Gagauzia ATU, one name, either in Gagauz or Romanian, can be used. According to the law, names of settlements of Gagauzia are allowed to have only one name, be it in Romanian or Gagauz or any other language (Chapter VI, Article 13). Under LRM, the Gagauz language must necessarily be present on the signs of Gagauz villages and towns without translation, while the LGA does not place this requirement (Chapter VI, Article 24). At this point, it can be said that the local laws do not sufficiently encourage the use of the Gagauz language on signboards. Sirkeli and Lisenco (2012) report that the signboards of Gagauz settlements in most of the cases have only Romanian names. Similarly, the Russian language in square and street names has not been changed since the USSR.

Moreover, the names of official institutions (Chapter VI, Article 14) and signposts of streets, squares, and other public spaces (Chapter VI, Article 15) can be executed in Romanian, Gagauz, and Russian. The texts are placed on the left (above) in Gagauz, in the center (below) in Moldovan, and on the right (below) in Russian. Although the regulation of Comrat State University states that education can be provided in Gagauz, Romanian, Russian, Bulgarian, and other languages, there is no regulation regarding the language of signs within the university.

Interviews

The questions put to the interviewees were primarily about the languages and their order of appearance on the signposts on the campus, multilingual practices, and their functionality in the academic/administrative context and language policy of Comrat State University. The majority of the participants who responded to the questions related to the linguistic landscape on the campus stated that they had used the signs to navigate in the buildings of the university. It was found that students, especially the freshmen, made use of signs in different languages. Olga's account was particularly informative in this respect.

If you go to the foreign languages department, you will use English signs. If you go to the Turkology department, it's Turkish. Therefore, Comrat State University is a place where many languages are used depending on the faculties. We communicate in different languages.

Additionally, Olga emphasized the informative function of the signs on campus. She said:

If I need to find a building or office, I pay attention. If there is no sign, I try to find out by asking where the place I am looking for is. It is easier to get lost in large buildings if there are no signs.

The interview showed the importance of the linguistic landscape, especially for the students, who have more mobility through time and space. Natalia said:

It is not a problem for me that there is only Gagauz. But for people of different nationalities, it is very difficult to understand. It should be in different languages.

The excerpts support the transformation of the Comrat State University to a more multilingual context. Despite being limited in number, foreign students, with their language and cultural backgrounds, positively contribute to the diversity. As a result of internationalization, the need for a more multilingual environment was echoed by the students.

On the other hand, awareness of these signs was not reported by one of the participants who had spent 20 years as an academic and administrative officer at the same university. Irina stated that she could navigate on the campus without using signs.

I usually don't look [at signposts]. Because we have been working here for twenty years, we don't look. We know everywhere. . . . [The signs] are written here for visitors . . . because it does not matter what is written here or in what language; I already know what that place is.

The Routledge Handbook of Endangered and Minority Languages

Irina's excerpt shows that for speakers who are familiar with the physical context, the signage does not have an informative function. In other words, for some speakers, the basic function of the signage, which is to guide and warn the reader, does not have descriptive, explanatory, and instructive functions.

Romanian as a state language

Romanian is one of the official languages of the ATU of Gagauzia, as stated in the Legal Status of Gagauzia within the Republic of Moldova. Additionally, it is the official language of the Republic of Moldova. It therefore has equal status with the Gagauz and Russian languages. The interviews in the current study showed that the participants' opinions differed in terms of the representation and the use of the Romanian language. Although it was one of the languages listed by the speakers in an ideal signage on the campus, some of the participants questioned its functionality. Some of them agreed that the representation of Romanian can be expected as it is the official language of the central state, Moldova. From this perspective, it can be seen that the language of the bureaucracy and the official correspondence with the Moldovan government is carried out in the Romanian language. Therefore, the discrepancy between the domains of use might cause problems, as Mehmet, a visiting scholar, points out:

> There is already a problem here. [They] prepare the official document, the document [they] will send to the Ministry of Education, in Romanian. But the language of education is Russian. This situation creates confusion. For example, when we prepare the curriculum etc., we prepare it in Turkish because it is the Turkish Language and Literature department. But while filling out the paperwork and entering students' grades, we write the course name in Romanian. When we write [students'] grades, for example, eight to nine, we write in Romanian. This creates confusion rather than multilingualism. This is a bureaucratic burden.

Mehmet identified the multilingualism in the official correspondence as a 'bureaucratic burden' and emphasized the inconsistency in the use of these languages. Responding to Photograph 3 (showing the emergency telephone number), a similar comment was made by Irina, who said that there was no standardization in the use and representation of these languages:

> Everyone knows this number (112). The texts are too small. It does not matter whether they exist or not. But there is no specific standard. Here [they] wrote it in Romanian first. There [they] wrote it first in Gagauz. There is no standardisation [in the order], which one comes first, and which one comes after.

The same lack of standardization and inconsistency could also be observed in everyday life practices. For example, Olga said, "If it is necessary to prepare and read documents, [I use] Romanian. I use Romanian for official university-related matters. But I very rarely speak Romanian as a spoken language". The sharp distinction between the domains of use for the Romanian language is quite salient in these examples. The limited use of Romanian was reported to lead to consequences such as the difference between the levels of proficiency in these languages. Supporting this, Irina stated that

> In twelve years, it is necessary for a child [student] to be able to talk a lot, both in Gagauz and in Romanian. But it doesn't work. Normally, our entire population, the Gagauz people,

"I already know where that place is . . ."

also need to speak Romanian. It is the state language. That's a big problem for the people of Gagauzia. They cannot find jobs in Chisinau because they don't know the language.

Generally speaking, contrary to the expectations related to the representation of the Romanian language, it can be seen that the Romanian language does not have functionality in daily communication in the context of the ATU of Gagauzia. It is obvious that it is the language of the top-down discourse such as the signage in public organizations, institutions, and announcements.

Russian as a post-Soviet language

Russian, as one of the official languages, has a vital role in the ATU of Gagauzia, as in most of the former Soviet countries. When it comes to functionality, however, some of the participants stated that Russian should be first in order and written in bigger font size as most people speak the Russian language:

> People speak Russian here. It would be better if Russian came first. Then Gagauz and Romanian, or Romanian than Gagauz. No difference to me, because you look at the upper text, the larger text, so that's why the larger text should be in Russian. Most of them speak Russian. You're looking at the large text, not the small text.

This view was supported by Mehmet, who said that the campus is mostly a multilingual place but emphasized the role of Russian. He emphasized that speakers of different ethnicities and languages can understand Russian. Mehmet also said:

> Well, there is some Romanian as well. You can handle all your work in Russian. Even if someone is a Romanian teacher or a teacher from Chisinau, he/she speaks Russian to everyone here. That's why Gagauz doesn't have much chance.

As mentioned before from this viewpoint, Russian seems to be the lingua franca of the region as a result of the Soviet past. In this context, the disadvantaged position of the Gagauz language when compared to Russian and Romanian reported by other participants as well. A similar opinion was expressed by another participant. Upon seeing the monolingual Photograph 7, Irina stated that as all students can speak Russian, so there is no need to use other languages. She said

> Students study in the Russian language. If a sign were written in another language, no one would understand it. No, who should they talk to? There is no use writing in another language. This information is provided for students who speak the Russian language. . . . Whether they [other signs] are in different languages or pictures, this information must still be in Russian because our students know Russian. . . . The language of instruction is Russian. So, there is no need [to use other languages].

As an administrative officer and a member of the academic staff who had worked in the same institution for several years, Irina also mentioned the use of Russian in announcements. However, when it comes to administrative communication, the inclusion of the Romanian language can be seen. Therefore, the participants' perceptions of the use of the Romanian is considered normal as it is the language of the central government. Irina commented on Photograph 10 which showed the course schedule written in Romanian and Russian, saying

> Well, these plans come from the Ministry, from Chisinau, from the Ministry of Education. Lessons are written in Romanian [in these plans]. That's why the course schedule should be according to this plan. But they write it in Russian so that students can understand whatever course they are taking.

As can be seen, to increase the intelligibility of particular documents, the Russian language was added. This also shows the status of Russian as opposed to Romanian as a state language.

On the other hand, Olga had a more moderate approach. When commenting on Photograph 1, which showed a trilingual sign, she stated that Russian can be considered a complementary language. According to Olga, Romanian should be available on this sign as it is the language of the state. However, when it comes to Russian, she emphasized the need for functionality, saying

> If visitors are coming from outside Moldova, which happens very often, it is written in Russian for them too. It is also good that it is written in Gagauz because we live in Gagauzia. The order of the languages is good. . . . Romanian is the state language and Russian is included here as a complementary language.

It is evident that the Russian language has still power and dominance in the ATU of Gagauzia which was formerly under the rule of the Soviet regime. The Soviet-era role of Russian as a lingua franca of the different ethnic communities is still observed.

Gagauz as a language at risk

In the current linguistic landscape, the status of the Gagauz language seems to be ill defined. Although most of the participants agreed on the representation of the signage, in some cases they also reported the limited use of and need for the Gagauz language. A possible explanation for this might be the official status of the language in the ATU of Gagauzia. Vera said, "Because we live in Gagauzia, this is the educational institution of our autonomous region. We live in Moldova, but we have our autonomy". Natalia similarly commented "Gagauz, Romanian and Russian. Since we live in Gagauzia, it is good that the Gagauz language comes first. Then, Romanian and Russian", commenting on Photograph 6, which showed a trilingual sign. These excerpts show that the participants were in favor of using Gagauz in the first place as they associated the order of representation of the languages with the political status of the ATU of Gagauzia.

In terms of the functionality of Gagauz in everyday life, however, the participants expressed their concerns. Olga said

> Since very few students study Gagauz [referring to the Gagauz department], Gagauz is not used much in such announcements. Having them in Romanian and Russian is good for those who know one of these languages. The lack of Gagauz may be because it is not widely used.

When commenting on Photograph 10, which showed a bilingual course schedule in the Romanian and Russian languages. Mehmet commented on the use of the Gagauz language as a medium of instruction and expressed his concerns about the inadequacy of the courses offered in the Gagauz language. He said

> For example, there are no elective courses in Gagauz in the departments. Not in any department. Therefore, it is not possible to offer law courses in Gagauz. Gagauz language courses are only available in the Gagauz Language and History department.

The courses given in the Gagauz language to which Mehmet referred are the Gagauz Language and Culture courses, which are only offered to students in the department of Gagauz Philology and History. Mehmet reported that these courses are not language courses but courses on Gagauz culture.

However, Irina was particularly critical of the courses in the Gagauz language. According to her, the Gagauz language should be taught at kindergarten when children are 5 to 6 years old instead of teaching at the higher education level. She said

> I do not see the benefit of understanding and using the Gagauz language at university. We cannot develop this language at university. They will never want to learn. They will say it is very difficult. They don't know what to do at university. Let's teach our mother tongue in kindergarten. If a five- or six-year-old child hears and speaks [it], s/he will speak it later and will speak this language for the rest of her/his life. Gagauz should be taught at a young age. Then, this problem will not exist in schools either. There are two courses at school. Gagauz Language and Grammar, and Gagauz Folk Customs. But let me tell you that Gagauz folk customs are included in the [university] curriculum, but students study the course in Russian because they don't understand [Gagauz]. They speak Russian. It's too late for [use at] the university and it's of no use. There is a training program, there is a standard program. How many lessons and how many hours should someone study? Why should I lose the Gagauz literature? I am now 20 years old. I have graduated from high school. They need [to be taught] more accounting at university, not the Gagauz language.

The functionality of the Gagauz language recurred throughout the interviews. Commenting on multilingual signs, Irina also emphasized that Gagauz would be non-functional as nobody speaks it and does not expect to see it in signage. She said

> There is no difference in the use of Gagauz here; it is the same whether the Gagauz language is written or not written here. Nobody speaks [it], so Gagauz will remain only in writing.

Irina suggested that higher education should enable occupational development and equip students with the skills needed in the relevant fields. She, therefore, regarded Gagauz as a non-functional language. The only reason for the need for Gagauz on signs echoed by some participants was its intelligibility for the Turkish students. For example, Vera commented on the multilingual Photograph 10 that

> It was probably written in Gagauz so that students from Türkiye could understand it because students from Türkiye do not know much Romanian and Russian in their first years. That's why Gagauz is used in the title for clarity.

As Gagauz and Anatolian Turkish are two linguistically close dialects of Turkic languages, the mutual intelligibility between the speakers is relatively high. It was therefore reported that the use of the Gagauz language on signs has a facilitative function for international Turkish students at Comrat State University.

Generally speaking, although the participants were in favor of the representation of the Gagauz language, they expressed their concerns related to its use in everyday life and education. It was clear that the non-functionality of the Gagauz language lowered the participants' perceptions about its use in signage.

English as a lingua franca

Another language which functioned as a lingua franca on the campus, according to the participants, was English. The majority of them agreed that English can be functional and informative for international students and academic staff. Commenting on Photograph 2 (showing no smoking), Olga stated

> I think this is better because it's also written in English here. English is an international language. It is more advantageous to write in English.

In the same vein, Irina suggested that some English expressions had become an integral part of urban signage. Commenting on Photograph 4 (showing the exit sign), she said

First, they have used international words a lot. If it were up to me, English would be enough. A person knows the words even if he doesn't know English. Most people know and understand 'Exit' and 'Welcome'. It might be better to use only English in such cases.

The participants reported that direction signs and signs of locality in English help people find their way around the building. Especially the basic vocabulary was found to be comprehensible by the participants for the speakers of different languages. Talking about the same photograph (Photograph 4), Mehmet commented:

> 'Exit' is comprehensible to everyone. But there is also a third language, Gagauz. But there are also people here who do not speak Gagauz. English could be better for everyone to understand, because 'Exit' is now an international word.

It was found that apart from the indigenous languages spoken on the campus, English had an important role as a language of globalization. Vera, who reported that she had taken extra courses to improve her English, stated that English should be included in the signs, commenting on Photograph 5. As can be seen from the responses reported previously, despite the low number of international students and lecturers at Comrat State University, the participants expected to see the presence of English in public spaces. It seems that after Russian, English was perceived to be the lingua franca in this particular educational context.

Language policy

To investigate the relationship between the linguistic landscape on the campus of Comrat State University and the related language policies, the participants were asked some particular questions during the interviews. The findings showed that the members of the academic and administrative staff, Mehmet and Irina, were more aware of the changes in the University's language policy over time. They reported that they had observed changes in the representation of the languages on the campus. For example, Mehmet, who had been working at Comrat State University for five years, stated that Romanian and Gagauz languages had become more visible over time:

> When I first came, all the signs were in Russian. Then the president [of the university] made a decision and had [something] added to those Russian signs. He added it in Gagauz. We have also been seeing signs in Gagauz for the last four years. . . . Romanian was also added at about the same time.

This excerpt shows that despite the multilingual policy of the Comrat State University, monolingual signage, mostly in Russian, was more widespread. It was found that the Romanian and Gagauz languages had been included later. Although this does not show a change in policy, it is evidence of the difference between in the implementation and the policy of the institution.

In the same vein, Irina, who had been working as an administrator at the University for longer than Mehmet, reported that the Gagauz language was only recently included on the signs. She also criticized the changes in the names of the faculties. She stated

> There used to be just Russian and Romanian. Five years ago, they added Gagauz to the Faculty of Economics. But I don't know whether I am right whether it is the Faculty of Economics or the Faculty of Jurisdiction. In other words, it is Juridical, not Law. They took these terms from another language. In our hospital, it says 'Meditsina center'.

Irina expressed her concerns about the Gagauzification of the words. According to her, although the words juridic and meditsina were used by the Gagauz speakers, they were borrowed words from Russian. Irina pointed out that Gagauz counterparts hukuk (justice) and saalık (health) were not used in these examples.

On the other hand, the student participants could not comment on the changes in the linguistic landscape of Comrat State University as their number of years on the campus was relatively shorter than that of the academic and administrative staff members. When they were asked about how they felt about the language policies of Comrat State University, they said that they supported and liked multilingualism on the campus. For example, Olga stated

> I think there are quite a lot of languages at Comrat State University. There are Romanian, English, German, Russian, Turkish and Gagauz. I think the language policy at Comrat University is quite good. The university attaches sufficient importance to multilingualism.

With this more international perspective, Olga emphasized the role of multilingualism for international students. In this excerpt, it has been shown that Olga was referring to the languages spoken on the campus rather than their representation on the signage. Multilingualism was appreciated without taking the standardization in top-down signage into consideration. Generally speaking, it could be said that the student participants did not have expectations related to the Gagauz language as a language learning resource or its symbolic function.

Discussion

The study examined the linguistic landscapes of Gagauz, Russian, and Romanian at a university in the Autonomous Territorial Unit of Gagauzia. It also revealed a lack of detailed qualitative analysis of the Gagauz context and language pedagogy. Specifically, how the linguistic landscapes align with the language policy of the Gagauz ATU and how Gagauz speakers perceive the representation of these languages was explored. The findings revealed a misalignment between policy and practice in the use of the three official languages, with Russian being the functionally dominant language. This highlights the need for further research on linguistic landscapes in educational settings.

The representation of the languages used in the educational domain plays a vital role in the construction of Gagauz's identity in this context. Although the region's autonomy, which survives in the economic and political turmoil of the region, has the power to foster the use of the Gagauz language, it was found that today Gagauz is a symbolic part of the Gagauz identity. Landry and Bourhis (1997: 28) commented that "[e]xclusion of the in-group language from public signs . . . conveys the notion that the in-group language is of little use for conducting public affairs, thus reinforcing a diglossic situation to the advantage of the dominant language". In the case of Gagauz, the expectations and perceptions of the linguistic landscape were found to be in favor of the Russian language and partly of the Romanian language.

One of the significant findings emerging from this study is the indispensable role of the Russian language. It was found that the participants perceived Russian as a local lingua franca which is spoken by most of the people in the context of the ATU of Gagauzia. The reason Russian is the most functional language is based on historical, political, and economic factors. Sağlam and Adıgüzel (2021) stated that the reason for the difficulties in reproducing Gagauz's identity is the institutionalization of the Soviet language and cultural heritage. The case of ATU of Gagauzia is similar to the situation in some post-Soviet countries. Kulbayeva (2018) exemplifies the change in nation-building language policies in Kazakhstan. She suggests that these policies evolved from nativism and derussification to the recognition of Russian as a local lingua franca. This seems also explanatory for the Gagauz case.

On the other hand, Gagauz nation-building efforts to promote the status of the Gagauz language have some reflections on the linguistic landscape. Holsapple (2022: 944) gives the example of the failure of attempts to rename Lenin Street. The controversies to replace Lenin Street with Stepan Topal, a Gagauz politician and activist, through referendum failed. According to Holsapple (2022: 944) economic constrictions, especially the costly referendum is one of the factors hindering the construction of Gagauz national identity indirectly.

The linguistic landscape data analysis in the current study shows that Comrat State University does not have a consistent language policy. The variation in the language choice in different locations on the campus can be easily seen. It was found that the participants mostly agreed on the visibility of the three official languages. Brown (2013: 238) suggested that this is evidence of the Soviet-era commitment to multilingualism. A relatively positive attitude towards multilingualism can therefore be observed. However, apart from attitudes and related expectations, the widely held perception was in favor of the necessity for the Russian language. The prestigious status of Russian also shapes employment opportunities in the ATU of Gagauzia. The functionality and status of the Russian language play important roles here, and it contributes to the maintenance of Russian's status as a lingua franca. In the broader context, as Pavlenko (2008) suggested, Russian is the local lingua franca as it is still "a major political, military, and economic superpower of the geopolitical region, its main energy supplier, and an important cultural, informational and academic center" (p. 301). In a kind of vicious circle, it can be seen that the more Russian is used, the more it is required.

Another theme identified in the current study is the role of internationalization at Comrat State University. In this context, English was perceived to have a facilitating role for international

"I already know where that place is ..."

students, although the signage in English was quite limited. The most striking result to emerge from the data was the role of the Russian language as a tool of internationalization. Contrary to the university's policy, the choice of the Russian language as a medium of instruction in practice shows that covert ideologies are structured around the Russian language. Sirkeli and Lisenco's (2012) analysis of Gagauz legislation and practice provided a strong critique of the status of Russian. (p. 15) According to the researchers (2012) the official status of the Russian and its widespread use in daily life resulted from socio-historical processes. In the Gagauz context, education had been one of the strategies of Russification.

When it comes to the consideration of the linguistic landscape as a pedagogical resource, it can be said that Comrat State University is a good example of the language ideologies of the Soviet regime. In addition to representing three official languages, it also shows the functionality of the Russian. In other words, as Duncan and Duncan (1988: 126) suggested, schoolscapes are the places where "transformation[s] of social and political ideologies" can be observed. Encouraging multilingualism at the same time as increasing the legitimate and functional power of the Russian language, Soviet language policy was marked by inconsistencies. Taking the discrepancy between the Soviet policy and practice into consideration (Grenoble 2003), a similar condition was observed in the ATU of Gagauzia. Kosienkowski (2021) pointed out that the Gaugazia ATU's pro-Russian stance is based on language use in bureaucracy, media, vocational training, and similar fields. Kosienkowski (2021) also reported the dominant use of the Russian language in bureaucracy except for meetings held with Turkish bureaucratic representatives.

Conclusion

Taking the gap in the related literature, the current study investigated the level of alignment of the linguistic landscape within the Gagauz educational setting in Gagauz ATU. Additionally, Gagauz speakers' perceptions of the representation of these languages on campus were explored. Document analysis and semi-structured interviews were used as data collection methods.

The findings show an inequality in the representation of the languages in the Gagauz educational context. It was found that detailed and formal announcements and signage were in Russian and Romanian, whereas relatively simple and short ones were written in the Gagauz language. When it comes to the speakers' perceptions, it was seen that although the participants agreed on the representation of the three official languages and English, they expected to see Russian as the most functional language in the region.

Acknowledgment

We would like to express our deepest gratitude to the participants.

Note

1 Signs analyzed in the research can be accessed via the QR code:

References

Andrade, A. I., Martins, F., Pinto, S., & Simões, A. R. (2023) 'Educational possibilities of linguistic landscapes exploration in a context of pre-service teacher education', in S. Melo-Pfeifer (ed.) *Linguistic landscapes in language and teacher education*. Hamburg: Springer, pp. 207–222. https://doi.org/10.1007/978-3-031-22867-4_11

Backhaus, P. (2005) 'Signs of multilingualism in Tokyo – a diachronic look at the linguistic landscape', *International Journal of the Sociology of Language*, 175–176, 103–121. https://doi.org/10.1515/ijsl.2005.2005.175-176.103

Ben-Rafael, E., Shohamy, E., & Barni, M. (2010) 'Introduction: An approach to an ordered disorder', in E. Shohamy, E. Ben-Rafael, & M. Barni (eds.) *Linguistic landscape in the city*. Bristol: Multilingual Matters, pp. xi–xxviii. https://doi.org/10.21832/9781847692993-002

Brewer, J. D. (2000) *Ethnography*. Buckingham: Open University Press.

Brown, K. D. (2005) 'Estonian schoolscapes and the marginalization of regional identity in education', *European Education*, 37(3), 78–89. https://doi.org/10.1080/10564934.2005.11042390

Brown, K. D. (2013) 'Language policy and education: Space and place in multilingual post-Soviet states', *Annual Review of Applied Linguistics*, 33, 238–257. https://doi.org/10.1017/S0267190513000093

Cenoz, J., & Gorter, D. (2008) 'The linguistic landscape as an additional source of input in second language acquisition', *International Review of Applied Linguistics in Language Teaching*, 46(3), 267–287. https://doi.org/10.1515/IRAL.2008.012

Comrat State University (2008) *Regulations of Comrat State University*. Available at: https://kdu.md/ru/o-kgu/ustav-kgu (Accessed: 10 May 2024).

Dağdeviren-Kırmızı, G. (2021) 'Gagauzia between the past and tomorrow: An analysis of the linguistic landscape', *Türkbilig*, 42, 241–252. https://dergipark.org.tr/tr/pub/turkbilig/issue/67357/1050663

Dagenais, D., Moore, D., Sabatier, C., Lamarre, P., & Armand, F. (2008) 'Linguistic landscape and language awareness', in E. Shoshamy & D. Gorter (eds.) *Linguistic landscape*. New York: Routledge, pp. 293–309. https://doi.org/10.4324/9780203930960

Duncan, J. & Duncan, N. (1988) '(Re)reading the landscape', *Society and Space*, 6, 117–126.

Eberhard, D. M., Simons, G. F., & Fennig, C. D. (2023) *Ethnologue: Languages of the world* (26th Ed.). Available at: www.ethnologue.com/guides/most-spoken-languages (Accessed: 10 May 2024).

Gorter, D. (2018) 'Linguistic landscapes and trends in the study of schoolscapes', *Linguistics and Education*, 44, 80–85. https://doi.org/10.1016/j.linged.2017.10.001

Gorter, D., & Cenoz, J. (2007) 'Knowledge about language and linguistic landscape', in N. H. Hornberger (ed.) *Encyclopaedia of language and education*. Boston: Springer, pp. 1–13. Available at: http://link.springer.com/referenceworkentry/10.1007/978-0-387-30424-3_160

Gorter, D., Cenoz, J., & van der Worp, K. (2021) 'The Linguistic landscape as a resource for language learning and raising language awareness', *Journal of Spanish Language Teaching*, 8(2), 161–181. https://doi.org/10.1080/23247797.2021.2014029

Grenoble, L. (2003) *Language policy in the Soviet Union*. Dordrecht: Springer. https://doi.org/10.1007/0-306-48083-2

Gumperz, J. J. (1982) *Discourse strategies*. Cambridge: Cambridge University Press. https://doi.org/10.1017/CBO9780511611834

Halk Topluşu (1995) *Law on languages of Gagauzia ATU (On language functioning on the territory of Gagauzia/Gagauz Yeri)*. Available at: https://halktoplushu.md/archives/46 (Accessed: 10 May 2024).

Hammersley, M., & Atkinson, P. (2007) *Ethnography, principles in practice*. London: Routledge. https://doi.org/10.4324/9781315146027

Hancock, A. (2012) 'Capturing the linguistic landscape of Edinburgh: A pedagogical tool to investigate student teachers' understandings of cultural and linguistic diversity', in C. Hélot, M. Barni, R. Janssens, & C. Bagna (eds.) *Linguistic landscapes, multilingualism and social change*. Frankfurt am Main: Peter Lang, pp. 249–266. Available at: www.peterlang.com/index.cfm?event=cmp.ccc.seitenstruktur.detailseiten&seitentyp=produkt&pk=59689&cid=448

Henzelmann, M. (2022) 'The Gagauz language and its semiotic landscape in the Republic of Moldova', *Studii de Ştiinţa şi Cultură*, 18(3), 97–108. www.revista-studii-uvvg.ro/files/SSC%202022/SSC%20nr%203%20-%20septembrie%202022.pdf

Hewitt-Bradshaw, I. (2014) 'Linguistic landscape as a language learning and literacy resource in Caribbean Creole contexts', *Caribbean Curriculum*, 22, 157–173. Available at: https://journals.sta.uwi.edu/ojs/index.php/cc/article/view/536

Holsapple, C. (2018) *The politics of belonging in Gagauzia: Negotiating language usage, ethnic labels, and citizenship*. Unpublished Master's Thesis. University of Tartu. Available at: https://dspace.ut.ee/server/api/core/bitstreams/fbdabbf1-ef8d-4dbf-a262-d2234bf3fd17/content

Holsapple, C. (2022) 'Bordering and strategic belonging in Gagauzia', *Journal of Borderlands Studies*, 37(5), 935–953. https://doi.org/10.1080/08865655.2020.1828142

"I already know where that place is . . ."

Hornberger, N. H. (2015) 'Selecting appropriate research methods in LPP research: Methodological rich points', in M. F. Hult & D. C. Johnson (eds.) *Research methods in language policy and planning: A practical guide.* Pondicherry: Wiley-Blackwell, pp. 9–20. https://doi.org/10.1002/9781118340349.ch2

Hult, F. M. (2018) 'Language policy and planning and linguistic landscapes', in J. W. Tollefson & M. Pérez-Milans (eds.) *Oxford handbook of language policy and planning.* New York: Oxford University Press, pp. 333–351. https://doi.org/10.1093/oxfordhb/9780190458898.013.35

Johanson, L. (1998) 'The history of Turkic', in L. Johanson & E. A. Csató (eds.) *The Turkic languages.* London: Routledge, pp. 81–125. https://doi.org/10.4324/9780203066102

Kallen, J. L. (2010) 'Changing landscapes: Language, space, and policy in the Dublin linguistic landscape', in A. Jaworski & C. Thurlow (eds.) *Semiotic landscapes: Language, image, space.* London: Continuum, pp. 41–58. Available at: https://shorturl.at/fiCG7

Kasanga, L. A. (2012) 'Mapping the linguistic landscape of a commercial neighborhood in Central Phnom Penh', *Journal of Multilingual and Multicultural Development*, 33(6), 553–567. https://doi.org/10.1080/01434632.2012.683529

Kosienkowski, M. (2021) 'The Russian world as a legitimation strategy outside Russia: The case of Gagauzia', *Eurasian Geography and Economics*, 62(3), 319–346. https://doi.org/10.1080/15387216.2020.1793682

Kulbayeva, A. (2018) 'Polycentricity of linguistic landscape and nation-building in post-Soviet Kazakhstan', *Central Asian Affairs*, 5(4), 289–312. https://doi.org/10.1163/22142290-00504001

Lai, M. L. (2013) 'The linguistic landscape of Hong Kong after the change of sovereignty', *International Journal of Multilingualism*, 10(3), 251–272.

Landry, R., & Bourhis, R. Y. (1997) 'Linguistic landscape and ethnolinguistic vitality: An empirical study', *Journal of Language and Social Psychology*, 16(1), 23–49. https://doi.org/10.1177/0261927X970161002

Leclerc, J. (1989) *La Guerre des langues dans l'affichage.* Montreal: VLB Éditeur. https://doi.org/10.7202/040655ar

Li, X. (2022) *Exploring linguistic landscape in a multilingual Finnish university.* Unpublished Master's Thesis. University of Helsinki.

Lou, J. J. (2017) 'Linguistic landscape and ethnographic fieldwork', in C. Mallinson, B. Childs, & G. Van Herk (eds.) *Data collection in sociolinguistics: Methods and applications.* New York: Routledge, pp. 94–98. Available at: www.routledge.com/Data-Collection-in-Sociolinguistics-Methods-and-Applications-Second-Edition/Mallinson-Childs-Van-Herk/p/book/9781138691377

Lourenço, M., Duarte, J., Silva, F., & Batista, B. (2023) 'Is there a place for global citizenship in the exploration of linguistic landscapes? An analysis of educational practices in five European countries', in S. Melo-Pfeifer (ed.) *Linguistic landscapes in language and teacher education: Multilingual teaching and learning inside and beyond the classroom.* Cham: Springer, pp. 93–121. https://doi.org/10.1007/978-3-031-22867-4_6

Malinowski, B. (1922) *Argonauts of the Western Pacific.* London: Routledge.

Menken, K., & Sánchez, M. T. (2019) 'Translanguaging in English-only schools: From pedagogy to stance in the disruption of monolingual policies and practices', *TESOL Quarterly*, 53(3), 741–767. www.jstor.org/stable/45214951

Ministerul Justiției (2021) *Law of the Republic of Moldova on language (On language functioning on the territory of Moldovan SSR)* Available at: www.legis.md/cautare/getResults?doc_id=125359&lang=ru (Accessed: 10 May 2024).

Moseley, C. (2010) *Atlas of the world's languages in danger.* Paris: UNESCO Publishing. Available at: https://unesdoc.unesco.org/ark:/48223/pf0000187026

Pavlenko, A. (2008) 'Multilingualism in post-Soviet countries: Language revival, language removal, and sociolinguistic theory', in A. Pavlenko (ed.) *Multilingualism in post-Soviet countries.* Bristol: Multilingual Matters, pp. 1–40. https://doi.org/10.21832/9781847690883-001

Pavlenko, A. (2009) 'Language conflict in post-Soviet linguistic landscapes', *Journal of Slavic Linguistics*, 17(1–2), 247–274. Available at: www.jstor.org/stable/24600143

Pennycook, A., & Otsuji, E. (2014) 'Metrolingual multitasking and spatial repertoires: Pizza mo two minutes coming', *Journal of Sociolinguistics*, 18(2), 161–184. https://doi.org/10.1111/josl.12079

Rowland, L. (2013) 'The pedagogical benefits of a linguistic landscape project in Japan', International *Journal of Bilingual Education and Bilingualism*, 16(4), 494–505. https://doi.org/10.1080/13670050.2012.708319

Sachdev, I., & Bourhis, R. Y. (1993). 'Ethnolinguistic vitality: Some motivational and cognitive considerations', in M. A. Hogg & D. Abrams (eds.) *Group motivation: Social psychological perspectives.* Wheatsheaf: Harvester, pp. 33–51. Available at: https://psycnet.apa.org/record/1993-98846-000

Sağlam, N. A., & Adıgüzel, Y. (2021) 'Gagauz identity in the post-Soviet period', *Journal of Economy Culture and Society*, 63, 279–296. https://doi.org/10.26650/JECS2020-0112

Sayer, P. (2010) 'Using the linguistic landscape as a pedagogical resource', *English Language Teaching Journal*, 64(2), 143–154. https://doi.org/10.1093/elt/ccp051

Sebba, M. (2010) 'Discourses in transit', in A. Jaworski & C. Thurlow (eds.) *Semiotic landscapes: Language, image, space.* London: Continuum, pp. 59–76.

Shohamy, E., & Gorter, D. (2008) *Linguistic landscape: Expanding the scenery.* New York: Routledge. https://doi.org/10.4324/9780203930960

Sirkeli, M., & Lisenco, S. (2012) *Implementation of linguistic rights of the Gagauz of Moldova. Youth Center Pilgrim Demo from Gagauzia.* Available at: https://piligrim-demo.org.md (Accessed: 10 May 2024).

Tufi, S., & Blackwood, R. (2010) 'Trademarks in the linguistic landscape: Methodological and theoretical challenges in qualifying brand names in the public place', *International Journal of Multilingualism*, 7(3), 197–210. https://doi.org/10.1080/14790710903568417

Willis, P., & Trondman, M. (2000) 'Manifesto for ethnography', *Ethnography*, 1(1), 5–16. Available at: www.jstor.org/stable/24047726

SECTION IV

Learning endangered and minority languages

22
ARTIFICIAL INTELLIGENCE–ASSISTED LANGUAGE LEARNING FOR *ALL* IN THE NEW GLOBAL CONTEXT
Threats and opportunities

Cristina A. Huertas-Abril and Francisco Javier Palacios-Hidalgo

Introduction

Recent developments in artificial intelligence (AI) have resulted in significantly increased interest and concerns regarding its application in education. This situation has triggered authors like Qu et al. (2022), Yang et al. (2022), and Yıldız (2023) to state that 'Integrating artificial intelligence and education will lead to a new education development model and promote better education' (Qu et al. 2022: 581).

Despite its relevance today, AI is nothing new. Instead, AI is a term coined back in 1956 by a group of scientists and engineers at the Dartmouth Summer Research Project following the work of Alan Turing on the potential intelligent reasoning and thinking of intelligent machines (Cristianini 2016). Since then, the definition of AI has grown. According to Fu et al. (2020: 4), AI 'refers to the reasoning, interacting and learning functions associated with human beings [. . . which] facilitates intelligent and adaptive behaviours through algorithm training to let machine learn from the environment.'

Despite AI having become a widely used tool in education, as pointed out by Crompton and Burke (2023), it poses significant challenges, including the risks of increasing technological dependence and reducing cognitive effort among students (Barr et al. 2015). Likewise, other studies indicate that AI not only requires that users have adequate digital literacy (Yang and Kyun 2022) but also certain accessibility features (Goldenthal et al. 2021).

The field of language learning, especially since the beginning of the 2020s, has witnessed an explosion of publications on AI, paying special attention to specific tools, including chatbots (Belda-Medina and Calvo-Ferrer 2022) or robot-assisted language learning (Chen et al. 2022), but also focusing on instructional methods (Mayer 2022) and personalised teaching and learning (Jia et al. 2022). It is particularly interesting when referring to language teaching and learning the assets of AI for the democratisation of learning, the promotion of equality, and the improvement of accessibility. Authors like Katsarou et al. (2023) and Lee and Lim (2023) suggest that AI tools are easy to use, accessible, and practical for users. Moreover, Huang et al. (2023) and Jeon (2022) pose that it can help foreshadow students' profiles, identify those at risk, and reduce dropout rates.

DOI: 10.4324/9781003439493-27

The Routledge Handbook of Endangered and Minority Languages

These ideas seem to be in line with the United Nations' fourth Sustainable Development Goal (UNESCO 2016), which should be considered a guiding principle for building an inclusive and equitable future where the educational benefits of AI are shared by diverse global populations. This goal is committed to ensuring inclusive and quality education for all learners; recognising education as a cornerstone for individual and social development; and advocating for equal opportunities regardless of gender, socio-economic background, or geographical location. In relation to this goal and its concern with breaking down barriers that hinder learning, AI stands as a powerful tool to revolutionise education by personalising learning experiences and tailoring them to individual needs (Karaca and Kılcan 2023).

Nevertheless, little research has been conducted about the implications of using artificial intelligence–assisted language learning (AIALL) to foster the access to and democratisation of language education in the new global context. For this purpose, this chapter uses qualitative analysis, and more specifically a strengths, weaknesses, opportunities and threats (SWOT) matrix, in order to gain insights into the potential of AIALL considering its strengths, weaknesses, opportunities and threats.

In this light, the overarching question for this study is: what are the implications of using AIALL to foster the access to and the democratisation of language education in the new global context? In order to answer this general question, two specific research questions (RQs) are posed to provide the information necessary to elaborate the SWOT analysis, as these details are important to know the internal and external factors that impact the use of AIALL:

- **RQ1:** What are the strengths and weaknesses of AIALL, especially regarding the access to and the democratisation of language education in the new global context?
- **RQ2:** What are the opportunities and threats of AIALL, especially regarding the access to and the democratisation of language education in the new global context?

Methods

A PRISMA (preferred reporting items for systematic reviews and meta-analysis for protocols; Moher et al. 2015) systematic review methodology was used to answer the two RQs guiding this study, and their principles have been utilised to provide an *a priori* roadmap to conduct a rigorous systematic review (PRISMA Statement 2021) and later elaborate upon the SWOT matrix (Samejima et al. 2006). According to Page et al. (2021), PRISMA principles are used to search, identify, and select articles to be included in the research and then in how to read, extract, and manage the secondary data gathered from the studies selected. Hemingway and Brereton (2009) argue that systematic literature reviews support unbiased syntheses of data in an impartial way. A qualitative inductive coding methodology was also used to analyse data and generate new theories on the use of AIALL (Gough et al. 2017), especially regarding the access to and democratisation of language education in the new global context.

The process begins with the search for the articles to be included in this study. The study parameters are defined, including the search years, quality, and types of publications to be included. Then, databases and journals are selected, and a Boolean search is created and used for the search. Once a set of publications is located, they are examined against inclusion and exclusion criteria to determine which papers will be included in the final study. The relevant data to match the RQs and elaborate the SWOT matrix is then extracted from the final set of studies and coded.

Regarding the SWOT analysis, it must be borne in mind that strengths and weaknesses are the internal (and therefore controllable) factors that support and hinder systems, organisations, or plans to achieve their mission, whereas opportunities and threats are the external (and therefore uncontrollable) factors that enable or not systems, organisations, or plans to accomplish their mission (Dyson 2004). Following Huertas-Abril and Shashken (2021), five stages of SWOT analysis were utilised in this study: (a) data gathering; (b) content analysis (after conducting PRISMA systematic review methodology); (c) classifying data into strengths, weaknesses, opportunities or threats; (d) specifying the weight of each factor; and (e) reporting the findings.

This methods section is organised to describe each of these processes with full details to ensure transparency.

Search strategy

Only peer-reviewed journal articles indexed in Scopus were selected for examination in this study, thus ensuring a high level of confidence in the quality of the papers selected (Gough et al. 2017). The search parameters narrowed the search focus to include studies published between 2013 and 2023 in order to ensure the research was up to date, which is especially important with the rapid change in technology, AI and AIALL. The data retrieval protocol employed an electronic search using the Scopus database (www.scopus.com/), the world's largest abstract and citation database of peer-reviewed research literature. Aligned with the research questions, the Boolean search was as follows (Figure 22.1).

Screening

Electronic search in Scopus resulted in 130 articles for possible inclusion, although 6 were removed from initial screening as they did not meet the inclusion criteria (academic documents different from peer-reviewed journal articles, texts not related to AI for education but rather to other subject areas, or retracted articles), leading to 124 articles to screen. Further screening was conducted manually, as each of the articles was reviewed in full by the two researchers to examine a match against the inclusion and exclusion criteria found in Table 22.1.

Following Belur et al. (2018), interrater reliability was calculated by percentage agreement. Both researchers had initially reached a 90% agreement for the coding process, while further discussion of misaligned articles resulted in 100% agreement. This screening process against inclusion and exclusion criteria resulted in the exclusion of 64 articles, leaving 60 articles for inclusion in this research (see Figure 22.2).

Coding

The selected 60 articles were coded to answer each of the RQs using an inductive coding method. A grounded coding methodology (Glaser and Strauss 1967) was selected for this study to allow

---

TITLE-ABS-KEY ("artificial intelligence" "language learning") AND PUBYEAR > 2013 AND PUBYEAR < 2024 AND (LIMIT-TO (SUBJAREA , "COMP") OR LIMIT-TO (SUBJAREA , "SOCI") OR LIMIT-TO (SUBJAREA , "ARTS") OR LIMIT-TO (SUBJAREA , "PSYC") OR LIMIT-TO (SUBJAREA , "MULT")) AND (LIMIT-TO (DOCTYPE , "ar")) AND (LIMIT-TO (LANGUAGE , "English")) AND (LIMIT-TO (PUBSTAGE , "final")))

Figure 22.1   Data query in Scopus database

Table 22.1 Inclusion and exclusion criteria

Inclusion	Exclusion
Peer-reviewed journal articles	Academic documents different from peer-reviewed journal articles (i.e., conference proceedings, book chapters)
Original research	Using AI for education but not related to language learning and teaching
Using AI for language learning and teaching	Retracted articles
Subject area limited to social sciences, computer science, arts and humanities, psychology, and multidisciplinary	Other subject areas (e.g., engineering, mathematics, materials science, chemical engineering)
Journal articles published between 2013 and 2024	
Journal articles written in English	

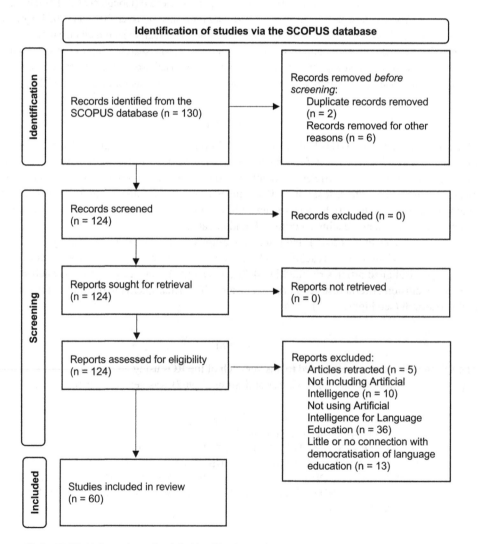

Figure 22.2 PRISMA flow chart of article identification and screening (adapted from Page et al. 2021)

findings of the internal and external factors that impact AIALL, with a special focus on the access to and the democratisation of language education in the new global context, emerge from the data. This process is essential as it allows a direct understanding about how AI is being used in the context of language education rather than how researchers may think it is being used and fitting the data to pre-existing perceptions or ideas.

The grounded coding processes was conducted *in vivo*, as *in vivo* codes are those that use language directly from the article to capture the authors' language directly from the original sources, thus ensuring consistency with their findings (Saldana 2015). For this, the researchers identified relevant text related to AI in language education from the articles, and through an iterative process initial codes led to axial codes. The two researchers coded and reached an interrater percentage agreement of 90%, and after discussing misaligned articles, a 100% agreement was achieved.

SWOT analysis

When 100% agreement was achieved in the coding process, the SWOT analysis was conducted. SWOT analyses provide researchers with the possibility of a detailed study of the directions of the increasing effectiveness of AIALL in two positions at the same time (internal vs external factor and positive vs negative impact), using a four-course matrix form of data presentation (Mushkarova et al. 2021). More specifically, this SWOT analysis will aim at exploring how AIALL can be used to advocate democracy, critical thinking, and freedom of speech, as well as to fight against authoritarianism, hegemony, and discrimination. Each course analyses two-folded combinations of the interaction of internal states and external factors to determine the principal directions of strengthening the positive development trends and overcoming the weaknesses of AIALL in terms of increasing the level of its effectiveness for supporting all types of students, and using its potential to improve a pluralistic, democratic, and critical language education in the new global context.

The total of weight scores for the codes was calculated and then classified into the appropriate SWOT categories: strengths, weaknesses, opportunities, and threats. The Rule Model (Thamrin and Pamungkas 2017) was followed to classify the factors based on the participants' responses.

The researchers first categorised the codes into two categories: positive and negative factors. Then the positive codes related to internal factors were considered 'strengths,' while external factors were considered 'opportunities.' Similarly, negative responses related to internal factors were labelled 'weaknesses,' and those related to external factors 'threats.' Once again, to check the interrater reliability of this phase, the researchers checked the data analysis. The cross-checking procedure showed high consistency, confirming then the reliability of the analysis.

Findings

The findings section is organised by the RQs guiding this study. Nevertheless, to have a better initial understanding of the connections among the topics present in the articles coded, VOSViewer was used to create a graphical network (Figure 22.3).

Moreover, regarding the distribution in time of the papers, Figure 22.4 shows the increasing interest in AIALL.

Bearing in mind these connections, Table 22.2 presents information about the articles that were selected, including the authors, research purpose, participants, context, and research outcomes.

The SWOT matrix (Table 22.3) presents the linkage between the strengths and weaknesses (internal factors) and threats and opportunities (external factors) of the use of AIALL to foster pluralistic, democratic, and critical language education in the new global context.

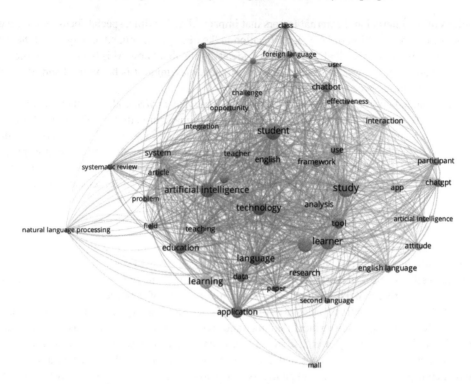

Figure 22.3 Network of most recurrent topics using VOSViewer

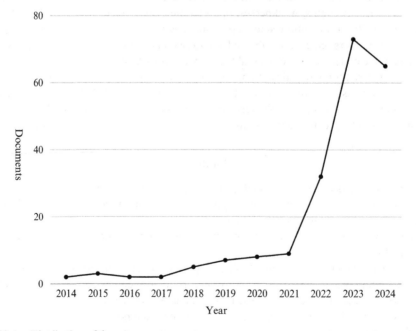

Figure 22.4 Distribution of the papers per year

Table 22.2 Summary of papers analysed and coded

ID	Authors	Research purpose	Context/participants	Democratisation of language education
003	Karaca and Kılcan (2023)	To analyse the bibliometric aspects of journal publications on AI technology in educational research.	Literature review	Feedback and personalisation. Enhanced teaching and learning quality. Ubiquitous, adaptive, learning. High financial investment needed.
005	Divekar et al. (2022)	To evaluate the effectiveness of cognitive immersive language learning environment (based on AI) for foreign language learning.	China/university students of Chinese as a Foreign Language $n = 10$	Improved learners' language skills, motivation, confidence, and engagement. New learning strategies.
008	Yıldız (2023)	To develop an instrument to measure the attitudes toward AI in language learning processes.	Turkey/university students $n = 174$	Effective feedback. Personalisation. Improved teaching and learning quality. Decrease of anxiety and stress.
010	El Shazly (2021)	To explore the role of AI-driven applications on anxious English learners.	Egypt/university students of English $n = 48$	Improved language skills. Increased multimodal language exposure. More opportunities to practice the target language.
012	Katsarou et al. (2023)	To study the potential of voice-based intelligent virtual agents for English language learning.	Literature review	Adaptive learning environments. Support personalised and collaborative learning. Exposure to diverse and authentic uses and contexts.
016	Chen et al. (2022)	To create an application system using robots as a tool for training English language tour guides.	Taiwan/master students $n = 2$	Personalised individual experiences. Decrease workloads. Help analyse large and complex data sets and monitor the learning process to offer just-in-time support.
019	Fu et al. (2020)	To explore why learners use AI-enabled automatic scoring applications.	China/foreign language learners $n = 260$	Automatic tutoring system to facilitate learning and as a supplement of face-to-face teaching. Immediate feedback.
021	Kent (2020)	To explore voice-user interface of digital assistants in the language classroom.	NA	Students with low self-confidence in their foreign language abilities prefer to interact with a chatbot over a human. Enhanced learner autonomy and intrinsic motivation for learning. Accessibility is essential.
022	AbdAlgane and Othman (2023)	To draw attention to the impact that AI has and its function in the teaching of English.	Saudi Arabia/university English teachers $n = 20$	Immediate feedback. Increased exposure to multimodal language. Opportunities for learners to practice the target language.

Table 22.2 (*Continued*)

ID	Authors	Research purpose	Context/participants	Democratisation of language education
028	Huang et al. (2023)	To investigate the trends, research issues, and applications of AI in language learning.	Literature review	Automated writing evaluation and error detection. Intelligent tutoring systems for reading, writing, pronunciation, speech training, and assessment. Computer-mediated communication. Personalised language learning. Natural language and vocabulary learning.
030	Li (2022)	To update the current spoken English learning methods using natural language processing technology and propose a natural language processing–based oral English teaching model.	NA	Renewal of teaching methods and models. Mobilisation of students' enthusiasm and initiative in learning spoken English. Accurate and timely pronunciation evaluation and feedback guidance.
035	Karakaya and Bozkurt (2022)	To examine research trends and patterns in mobile-assisted language learning research.	Literature review	Personalisation of learning through AI-supported mobile learning.
036	N and Kumar (2022)	To review the potential of AI-powered Google Assistant for teaching and learning languages.	Literature review	Effective and user-friendly tool for communication concerning people having intellectual and multiple disabilities.
037	Liao (2023)	To propose AI-based English vocabulary test research.	NA	Personalisation. Consideration of cultural influences based on cognitive web services.
039	Li and Peng (2022)	To evaluate a flipped class teaching model based on an AI language learning platform.	China/university students $n = 61$	Tracing, monitoring, and recording of users' behaviour. Accurate assessment of students. Promotion of external motivation. Real-time evaluation of students' listening and speaking. Ubiquitous, adaptive, flexible learning.
040	Zou et al. (2023)	To study the impact of social network-based interaction on students' English speaking practice with the assistance of AI speaking apps.	China/university students $n = 70$	Improved speaking skills. Enhanced teaching quality. Personalised feedback.
043	Wang (2022)	To explore students' expectations and perceived effectiveness of computer-assisted review tools.	China/university students $n = 188$	Meets personalised and diverse educational needs. Effective feedback. Flexible learning.

ID	Authors	Research purpose	Context/participants	Democratisation of language education
044	Jia et al. (2022)	To present the developmental process and methods used to develop and validate an AI-enabled English language learning system.	China/undergraduate and postgraduate students $n = 20$	Automated writing evaluation and corrective feedback. Enhanced writing performance, motivation, confidence, and engagement. Authentic and ubiquitous language learning.
045	Lin et al. (2022)	To investigate the intention to use AI-enabled English e-learning products.	China/users of online learning products $n = 584$	Personalised language education.
046	Chung and Bong (2022)	To study the intelligibility of Korean accented English through the implementation of AI applications in English education.	US/30 native English speakers and 2 AI apps	Corrective and personalised feedback. Low accessibility of programs, which are offered for a limited time and place only.
048	Dizon et al. (2022)	To explore language students' experiences, behaviour, and perceptions towards Alexa for language learning.	Japan/language students $n = 6$	Increased multimodal language exposure. Personalised learning.
050	Zhang (2022)	To study students' attitudes towards cross-cultural communication through AI.	NA/high school students $n = 263$	Enhanced intercultural skills.
051	Yang and Kyun (2022)	To analyse the trends and development of empirical research on AI-supported language learning.	Literature review	More personalised, flexible, inclusive, and engaging learning. Instant feedback. Reduced time, cost and learners' frustration and anxiety. Prediction of learners' future performance. Digital skills required.
052	Jeon (2022)	To investigate students' usage patterns of a self-directed interactive app.	South Korea/primary school students $n = 179$	Increased multimodal language exposure. Identification of students at risk. Reduction of dropout rates.
054	Goldenthal et al. (2021)	To examine the gap between availability and accessibility in AI-mediated communication tools.	US/diverse profiles $n = 519$	Not equally accessible to all users. Unbalanced, limited and standard language uses. Accessibility problems especially for older generations and people with disabilities. Non-native English speakers, or English speakers of minoritised dialects or with limited competence in English, face hurdles when using AI.

(Continued)

Table 22.2 (Continued)

ID	Authors	Research purpose	Context/participants	Democratisation of language education
055	Belda-Medina and Calvo-Ferrer (2022)	To examine the knowledge, level of satisfaction, and perceptions about integrating conversational AI in language learning among future educators.	Spain and Poland/university students majoring in education $n = 176$	Useful as language-learning partners. Available anytime and anywhere, particularly in contexts and settings where formal education and access to native speakers are not an option. Provision of various daily conversation contexts. Immersive environment. Reduced anxiety and increased self-confidence. Multimodal practice. Rich variety of contextual vocabulary. Effective feedback. Timeliness, ease of use and personalisation.
056	Nikonova et al. (2023)	To review existing online study courses, educational platforms, and AI technologies for teaching foreign language in higher technical institutions.	NA	More time for teachers' professional development. Personalisation. Optimisation of teaching and learning. Decreased repetitive/routine teaching workload. Virtual tutoring services. Provisions for teacher–teacher–learner communication and feedback.
061	Zhai and Wibowo (2023)	To examine the use of AI dialogue systems to enhance English university students' interactional competence.	Literature review	Improved interaction in safe, low-pressure environments.
062	Young and Shishido (2023)	To investigate the potential of ChatGPT to generate reference dialogues for an EFL chatbot system.	Literature review	Students can gain conversation experience in a safe, low-pressure environment. Simulation of real-life conversations. Possibility to practice anywhere and at any time outside the classroom. Increased language exposure. Opportunities to practice for students who may not have access to native speakers.
064	Kessler (2018)	To study how technology-mediated social interactions dominate our daily lives and how we can leverage such interactions to the benefit of learners.	NA	Immediate and effective feedback. Personalised learning. Improved language skills, motivation, confidence, and engagement, as well as new learning strategies. Enhanced teaching and learning quality.
065	Tafazoli et al. (2019)	To review and discuss issues surrounding the development and use of intelligent tutoring systems for language learning and teaching.	Literature review	Personalised learning, improvement of students' language skills, and possibility to create intelligent learning environments.

(Continued)

ID	Authors	Research purpose	Context/participants	Democratisation of language education
066	Zhang et al. (2023)	To investigate the incorporation of chatbots in the field of educational administration to improve language learning achievements among university students.	China/university students from Jiangsu *n* = 292	Exposure to diverse and authentic uses and contexts.
067	Yang et al. (2022)	To reflect on the role of machine learning in language acquisition and to explore its challenges.	NA	Improved quality of teaching and learning. Decrease of anxiety and stress among students.
070	Kannan and Munday (2018)	To examine the implications of AI for creating new trends in language education.	NA	Personalised learning. Exposure to diverse and authentic uses and contexts. Collaborative learning and social interaction. High financial investment required.
073	Klimova et al. (2023)	To explore different approaches to the efficient implementation of neural machine translation into language learning.	Literature review	Tools especially suitable for advanced learners. Good digital skills needed. Does not cater to specific needs.
075	Peña-Acuña and Crismán-Pérez (2022)	To examine learners' perceptions of the linguistic and learning potential of an AI-based English language learning app.	Spain/university students majoring in education *n* = 128	Improved oral skills. Enhanced memorisation of vocabulary. Opportunities for self-evaluation.
076	Wang et al. (2023)	To investigate how students interact with AI for learning English.	China/primary school students *n* = 16	Ubiquitous, flexible learning. Not equally accessible to all users. Unbalanced, limited, and standard language uses. Does not cater to learners' specific needs.
080	Godwin-Jones (2021)	To examine developments in big data collection related to language learning.	NA	Provision of specific feedback to learners. More guidance on learning strategies and behaviours. Opportunity to identify hidden groups of learners who may profit from differentiated instructional approaches/alternative learning materials.
083	Pack and Maloney (2023)	To highlight potential affordances of AI generative tools for creating language learning and teaching materials and assessment.	NA	ChatGPT can expose learners to diverse and authentic uses and contexts and facilitate resource design.

(Continued)

Table 22.2 (*Continued*)

ID	Authors	Research purpose	Context/participants	Democratisation of language education
085	Youn (2023)	To discuss recent research that reports the use of AI in teaching and assessing speaking.	NA	Exposure to diverse and authentic uses and contexts. Collaborative learning and social interaction. Ubiquitous learning. User-friendly communicative tools for people with disabilities.
087	Lin and Mubarok (2021)	To develop a mind map–guided AI chatbot approach in an English flipped speaking classroom to engage students in learning in a contextualised way.	Taiwan/university students $n = 50$	Immediate and effective feedback. Personalisation. Improved language skills. Provision of access to native speakers.
095	Zhai and Wibowo (2022)	To review existing studies on AI second language chatbots regarding the development of empathetic strategies for enhancing learners' learning outcomes.	NA	Improved motivation, confidence, and engagement. New learning strategies. Enhanced intercultural skills.
097	Ericsson and Johansson (2023)	To explore how conversational AI in language education is experienced for the learning and development of speaking skills.	Sweden/high school students $n = 22$	Personalisation Adaptive learning. Increased multimodal language exposure.
101	Hockly (2023)	To describe how AI is used in English language teaching and explore its opportunities and challenges.	Literature review	AI tools are free for learners to access and to use in their own time. Learners should be informed about data collection. Managers and administrators should be familiar with the basics of data protection law and ensure that these laws are respected by the AI used in their institutions.
104	Shaikh et al. (2023)	To evaluate the potential of ChatGPT for English language learning in formal settings.	Norway/university students $n = 10$	ChatGPT should not replace the human instructions in the language learning, but it can be used by language learners with human instructions to fully develop language learning skills.
108	Almelhes (2023)	To analyse the role of AI in improving pronunciation.	Literature review	Language learning and teaching using AI-driven chatbots could be effective in environments with low budgets and when sufficiently knowledgeable human tutors are lacking and there are language datasets with few resources.

(*Continued*)

ID	Authors	Research purpose	Context/participants	Democratisation of language education
109	Barrot (2023)	To explore the benefits and challenges of using ChatGPT for writing.	Literature review	ChatGPT cannot replace humans because it lacks the emotional depth and life experiences that contribute to an individual's voice, identity, and distinctiveness in writing.
110	Jeon et al. (2023)	To identify different chatbot features and how they can be categorised from a design perspective.	Literature review	Increased interactivity. Reduced anxiety. Authentic communication. Student-centred approach. Ubiquitous learning.
111	Crompton and Burke (2023)	To investigate the benefits and challenges of AI within university settings.	Literature review	Most of the research was conducted in high income countries revealing a paucity of research in developing countries.
112	D. Lee et al. (2023)	To design and validate an AI-based system to assist autonomous learning.	Korea/secondary school students $n = 3$	Need for human assistants. Technological problems.
114	Putra et al. (2023)	To build an automatic system that provides with discourse-level feedback, focusing on argumentative essays.	Tokyo Institute of Technology (Japan) and University of Cambridge (UK)	Assuming a single correct answer for a given input is common; however, there might be multiple correct argumentative structures and multiple acceptable arrangements.
115	Li and Mohamad (2023)	To develop and implement the latent Dirichlet integrated deep learning framework for the oral proficiency assessment of student speech recognition and classification.	Universiti Kebangsaan Malaysia	Personalised feedback for each student, focusing on areas of improvement such as vocabulary, grammar, fluency, and pronunciation.
116	N and Kumar (2023b)	To investigate the perceptions and problems concerning Google Assistant–assisted language learning.	India/university students majoring in engineering $n = 250$	AI could provide learners with meaningful content to learn the English language at feasible places at any time and any place. Students can access reliable English language learning tasks.
117	Lee and Lim (2023)	To develop and test a teachable agent that allows learners to interact with an AI conversational partner.	Korea	Interactive chatbots are capable of learning to interact with users according to different complexity levels. Chatbots are motivating and sustainable for teaching purposes.

(Continued)

Table 22.2 (Continued)

ID	Authors	Research purpose	Context/participants	Democratisation of language education
118	N and Kumar (2023a)	To investigate the perceptions and problems concerning AI-assisted English language learning, identifying the challenges faced by English learners.	India/university students majoring in engineering $n = 130$	The availability of AI apps based on language learning is very low. Students are not aware of AI apps. Technical issues and limited internet connectivity may hinder the use of AI-assisted language learning.
119	Liu et al. (2023)	To examine the effectiveness of a learning approach that integrates automatic writing evaluation and peer assessment based on the knowledge-building theory.	China/university students majoring in English $n = 64$	Opportunity for repeated practices, which effectively reduced learners' anxiety due to the fear of making mistakes during the writing process and improved writing skills.
120	Khampusaen et al. (2023)	To assess the uptake of English pronunciation skills using AI-powered lessons.	Thailand/tourism businesspeople $n = 15$	Learners' beliefs and emotions impact their language acquisition. Each locality has its own local wisdom, which varies from one society to the next.
121	Muñoz-Basols et al. (2023)	To study the potentialities of applied translation to promote critical thinking skills.	Literature review	Applying a critical ecological approach to applied translation can help learners navigate challenges by identifying power imbalances and societal inequities.
123	An et al. (2023)	To measure different variables related to teachers when using AI.	China/middle school teachers $n = 470$	Improved teaching efficiency and quality. If the government or schools want to promote AI and English teaching in middle school, they need to help teachers understand the usefulness of AI for their teaching.
124	J. H. Lee et al. (2023)	To study whether AI-based content generator activities benefit participants' foreign language enjoyment and interest in reading English books.	Korea/young learners $n = 121$	Increased information literacy and extensive reading enterprise. Unlimited and original texts available. Reduced teachers' workload.

Table 22.3 SWOT matrix

	Positive	*Negative*
Internal	**Strengths** • provides timely immediate and effective feedback (003, 008, 016, 019, 022, 028, 030, 035, 039, 040, 043, 044, 045, 046, 051, 055, 056, 064, 065, 075, 080, 087, 110, 115, 116, 119, 123) • facilitates personalised learning (003, 008, 012, 016, 028, 035, 043, 044, 045, 048, 051, 055, 056, 064, 065, 067, 070, 075, 080, 087, 097, 104, 108, 109, 110, 115, 119, 120, 124) • improves language skills (005, 008, 010, 012, 021, 030, 037, 040, 044, 046, 055, 062, 064, 065, 067, 070, 073, 075, 087, 104, 108, 110, 124) • improves students' motivation, confidence, and engagement, as well as new learning strategies (005, 008, 012, 021, 036, 039, 044, 048, 051, 055, 062, 064, 075, 095, 110, 119, 124) • improves the quality of teaching and learning (003, 008, 012, 016, 028, 036, 040, 056, 064, 067, 108, 119, 123) • decreases anxiety and stress (008, 021, 036, 044, 051, 055, 062, 067, 076, 110, 119) • exposes learners to diverse and authentic uses and contexts (005, 012, 036, 064, 066, 070, 080, 083, 085, 124) • decreases teachers' workload (016, 051, 104, 108, 118, 119, 123) • are easy to use, accessible, and practical (012, 055, 116, 117, 120, 123) • enhances learners' autonomy (005, 021, 037, 048, 062, 110) • fosters collaborative learning and social interaction (012, 070, 085, 118) • enhances students' intercultural skills (005, 037, 050, 095) • develops critical thinking skills (044, 075)	**Weaknesses** • is not equally accessible to all users on the basis of device access, internet access, and the cost of devices and internet connection (054, 070, 075, 076, 080, 101, 111, 112, 116, 118) • is restricted to unbalanced, limited, and standard language uses (012, 046, 054, 055, 070, 080, 104, 111) • requires teacher training (064, 070, 075, 076, 109, 121, 123) • is not adopted equally (054, 070, 075, 076, 080, 101, 111) • cannot imitate human–human interaction (012, 064, 066, 076, 121) • does not cater to learners' specific needs (046, 062, 073, 076, 112) • fails communication and interaction (012, 054, 055, 067) • requires high maintenance fees (046, 114, 116) • has accessibility problems (e.g., older generations, people with disabilities) (021, 054, 075, 101) • non-native English speakers, or English speakers of minoritised dialects or with limited competence in English, face hurdles when using certain AIALL tools (054, 066, 080, 111) • requires that users have good digital literacy (051, 054, 073, 112) • usually presents inaccuracies, misunderstandings, and errors (012, 054, 114) • does not provide corrective feedback (012, 080) • presents biased information and reinforces stereotypes (054, 104) • offers access to a limited range of content for learners to practice (046, 076)

(Continued)

Table 22.3 (Continued)

	Positive	Negative
External	Opportunities	Threats
	• can support ubiquitous, adaptive, flexible learning (003, 008, 009, 012, 019, 021, 028, 035, 037, 039, 043, 044, 051, 055, 056, 062, 075, 076, 080, 085, 097, 104, 115, 116)	• is affected by technical problems (012, 067, 111, 112, 116)
	• can increase students' multimodal language exposure (005, 010, 012, 022, 048, 052, 055, 062, 087, 097, 117)	• has ethical issues and threats academic integrity (008, 080, 104, 109)
	• can provide students with more opportunities to practice the target language (005, 008, 010, 022, 028, 055, 062, 087, 121)	• has privacy issues (021, 054, 101, 118)
	• can create intelligent learning environments (028, 030, 046, 051, 056, 065, 087, 111)	• provokes ineffective communication or machine–learner miscommunication (021, 055, 066, 109)
	• can improve interaction in safe, low-pressure environments (028, 030, 044, 055, 056, 061, 062, 075)	• requires high financial investment (003, 070, 101, 116)
	• can assist teachers' work (008, 019, 030, 040, 055, 056, 121)	• users have negative perceptions towards AIALL tools (008, 012, 051, 124)
	• can help predict learners' profiles, identify students at risk, and reduce dropout rates (028, 051, 052, 056, 080)	• causes frustration when user commands and questions, or their responses, are continuously misheard or misunderstood (021, 067, 104)
	• can be user-friendly communicative tools for people with disabilities (036, 085, 110, 116)	• has enormous data costs (101, 108, 118)
	• can provide learners with settings where (formal) education and access to native speakers are not an option (055, 080, 087, 117)	• teachers are expected to lead the change to integrate AIALL tools (064, 120, 123)
	• can assist teachers, administrators, and policymakers in making decisions (028, 045)	• can take control away from humans and threatens humanity (003, 008)
	• inclusive practices in language data collection and analyses are needed to redirection uses and research in AIALL tools (080, 111)	• can cause teachers to be supplanted (045)
		• can have limited accessibility (046, 080)
		• students may drop out of school with the advancement of AI technology (003)

Conclusion

In response to the call by Chu et al. (2022), this study provides unique results with an up-to-date examination of the use of AIALL from 2013 to 2023, trying to analyse how it can foster the democratisation of language education in the new global context. To facilitate the understanding of the main findings, the RQs of the study are revisited in the following lines.

Regarding RQ1 (*What are the strengths and weaknesses of AIALL, especially regarding the access to and the democratisation of language education in the new global context?*), the study has allowed unveiling considerable strengths of AIALL associated with the access to and the democratisation of language education in the new global context, as research shows how AI tools are both accessible and practical for users (Katsarou et al. 2023; Khampusaen et al. 2023; Lee and Lim 2023) and can promote social equality and facilitate personalised learning (Chen et al. 2022; Li and Mohamad 2023; Wang 2022). However, weaknesses related to the use of AIALL in this sense have also been revealed, such as the fact that AI tools are not equally accessible to all users due to device access, internet access, and the cost of such devices and internet connection (Hockly 2023; D. Lee et al. 2023; Peña-Acuña and Crismán-Pérez 2022). Moreover, different studies suggest that AI is restricted to unbalanced, limited, and standard language uses (Chung and Bong 2022; Katsarou et al. 2023) and the disadvantages in terms of users' limited linguistic competence in the target language (Godwin-Jones 2021). Likewise, AIALL seems not to cater to learners' specific needs (Young and Shishido 2023), has accessibility problems especially with respect to age and disabilities (Goldenthal et al. 2021; Hockly 2023; Kent 2020), requires that users have adequate digital skills (Klimova et al. 2023; Yang and Kyun 2022), and may present biased information that might eventually contribute to reinforcing stereotypes (Shaikh et al. 2023).

As for RQ2 (*What are the opportunities and threats of AIALL, especially regarding the access to and the democratisation of language education in the new global context?*), the findings of this study have shown several opportunities for AIALL to facilitate the democratisation of learning, promote equality, and improve accessibility. The analysed studies indicate that AI and AIALL can support ubiquitous, adaptive, flexible learning (Liao 2023; Shaikh et al. 2023) and provide learners with opportunities to practice the target language (Yıldız 2023) and with settings where (formal) education and access to native speakers are not possible (Godwin-Jones 2021). Furthermore, research also shows that these tools can help predict students' profiles, identify those at risk, and lower dropout rates (Huang et al. 2023; Jeon 2022; Yang and Kyun 2022), and be user-friendly communicative resources for people with disabilities (Jeon et al. 2023; Youn 2023). On the other hand, certain dangers have also been identified, such as the ethical issues and associated threats to academic integrity (Godwin-Jones 2021; Shaikh et al. 2023), the high financial investment required (Kannan and Munday 2018), its limited accessibility (Chung and Bong 2022), and the possibility of students dropping out of school as AI advances (Karaca and Kılcan 2023).

These findings should be considered in the light of certain limitations. First, only articles published in English have been considered for the present study, which may have led to potentially overlooking texts written in other languages and other types of research that might contain relevant information about AIALL. Second, and despite the attempts of the researchers not to let their personal views interfere with the revision, the information synthesis processes may have been biased. Third, only Scopus was used as a database for the review, with other research repositories neglected. Therefore, prospective review studies on the field of AIALL continue examining the potential of these tools to enhance language teaching and learning by relying on a broader variety of contexts, languages, and types of texts, as well as securing an ethical procedure when analysing the data. Moreover, specific studies need to be developed on how language teachers should be properly trained to meet the necessities of using AI in language education, not forgetting about the possible ways to meet the special needs of learners.

In any case, AIALL seems to have potential to democratise language education globally by offering personalised learning experiences, breaking barriers, providing real-time interactions, and fostering inclusion and cultural understanding. Nevertheless, with its rapid evolution, teachers, administrators, policies, and decision makers cannot be unaware of AI's potential risks, but rather they must make sure that education gets the most out of it to help bridge linguistic, social, cognitive, and geographical divides.

Availability of data and materials

The datasets used in this current study are available from the corresponding author on reasonable request.

References

AbdAlgane, M. and Othman, K. A. J. (2023). 'Utilizing artificial intelligence technologies in Saudi EFL tertiary level classrooms.' *Journal of Intercultural Communication*, *23*(1): 92–99. https://doi.org/10.36923/jicc.v23i1.124

Almelhes, S. A. (2023). 'A review of artificial intelligence adoption in second-language learning.' *Theory and Practice in Language Studies*, *13*(5): 1259–1269. https://doi.org/10.17507/tpls.1305.21

An, X., Chai, C. S., Li, Y., Zhou, Y., Shen, X., Zheng, C. and Chen, M. (2023). 'Modeling English teachers' behavioral intention to use artificial intelligence in middle schools.' *Education and Information Technologies*, *28*(5): 5187–5208. https://doi.org/10.1007/s10639-022-11286-z

Barr, N., Pennycook, G., Stolz, J. A. and Fugelsang, J. A. (2015). 'The brain in your pocket: Evidence that Smartphones are used to supplant thinking.' *Computers in Human Behavior*, *48*: 473–480.

Barrot, J. S. (2023). 'Using ChatGPT for second language writing: Pitfalls and potentials.' *Assessing Writing*, *57*: 100745. https://doi.org/10.1016/j.asw.2023.100745

Belda-Medina, J. and Calvo-Ferrer, J. R. (2022). 'Using chatbots as AI conversational partners in language learning.' *Applied Sciences*, *12*(17): 8427.

Belur, J., Tompson, L., Thornton, A. and Simon, M. (2018).' Interrater reliability in systematic review methodology: Exploring variation in coder decision-making.' *Sociological Methods & Research*, *13*(3). https://doi.org/10.1177/0049124118799372

Chen, Y.-L., Hsu, C.-C., Lin, C.-Y. and Hsu, H.-H. (2022). 'Robot-assisted language learning: Integrating artificial intelligence and virtual reality into English tour guide practice.' *Education Sciences*, *12*(7): 437. https://doi.org/10.3390/educsci12070437

Chu, H., Tu, Y. and Yang, K. (2022). 'Roles and research trends of artificial intelligence in higher education: A systematic review of the top 50 most-cited articles.' *Australasian Journal of Educational Technology*, *38*(3): 22–42. https://bit.ly/3NaZiOG

Chung, B. and Bong, H. K. M. (2022). 'A study on the intelligibility of Korean-accented English: Possibilities of implementing AI applications in English education.' *The Journal of AsiaTEFL*, *19*(1): 197–215. https://doi.org/10.18823/asiatefl.2022.19.1.12.197

Cristianini, N. (2016). 'Intelligence reinvented.' *New Scientist*, *232*(3097): 37–41. https://doi.org/10.1016/S0262-4079(16)31992-3

Crompton, H. and Burke, D. (2023). 'Artificial intelligence in higher education: The state of the field.' *International Journal of Educational Technology in Higher Education*, *20*(1): 22. https://doi.org/10.1186/s41239-023-00392-8

Divekar, R. R., Drozdal, J., Chabot, S., Zhou, Y., Su, H., Chen, Y., Zhu, H., Hendler, J. A. and Braasch, J. (2022). 'Foreign language acquisition via artificial intelligence and extended reality: Design and evaluation.' *Computer Assisted Language Learning*, *35*(9): 2332–2360. https://doi.org/10.1080/09588221.2021.1879162

Dizon, G., Tang, D. and Yamamoto, Y. (2022). 'A case study of using Alexa for out-of-class, self-directed Japanese language learning.' *Computers and Education: Artificial Intelligence*, *3*: 100088. https://doi.org/10.1016/j.caeai.2022.100088

Dyson, R. G. (2004). 'Strategic development and SWOT analysis at the University of Warwick.' *European Journal of Operational Research, 152*: 631–640.

El Shazly, R. (2021). 'Effects of artificial intelligence on English speaking anxiety and speaking performance: A case study.' *Expert Systems, 38*(3): e12667. https://doi.org/10.1111/exsy.12667

Ericsson, E. and Johansson, S. (2023). 'English speaking practice with conversational AI: Lower secondary students' educational experiences over time.' *Computers and Education: Artificial Intelligence, 5*: 100164. https://doi.org/10.1016/j.caeai.2023.100164

Fu, S., Gu, H. and Yang, B. (2020). 'The affordances of AI-enabled automatic scoring applications on learners' continuous learning intention: An empirical study in China.' *British Journal of Educational Technology, 51*(5): 1674–1692. https://doi.org/10.1111/bjet.12995

Glaser, B. and Strauss, A. (1967). *The discovery of grounded theory*. New Brunswick: Aldine Publishing Company.

Godwin-Jones, R. (2021). 'Big data and language learning: Opportunities and challenges.' *Language Learning & Technology, 25*(1): 4–19.

Goldenthal, E., Park, J., Liu, S. X., Mieczkowski, H. and Hancock, J. T. (2021). 'Not all AI are equal: Exploring the accessibility of AI-mediated communication technology.' *Computers in Human Behavior, 125*: 106975. https://doi.org/10.1016/j.chb.2021.106975

Gough, D., Oliver, S. and Thomas, J. (2017). *An introduction to systematic reviews* (2nd ed.). London: Sage.

Hemingway, P. and Brereton, N. (2009). 'What is a systematic review?' In Hayward Medical Group (Ed.), *What is . . .? Series*. https://bit.ly/49ZJloy

Hockly, N. (2023). 'Artificial intelligence in English language teaching: The good, the bad and the ugly.' *RELC Journal, 54*(2): 445–451. https://doi.org/10.1177/00336882231168504

Huang, X., Zou, D., Cheng, G., Chen, X. and Xie, H. (2023). 'Trends, research issues and applications of artificial intelligence in language education.' *Educational Technology & Society, 26*(1): 112–131. https://doi.org/10.30191/ETS.202301_26(1).0009

Huertas-Abril, C. A. and Shashken, A. (2021). 'Exploring the potential of CLIL in Kazakhstan: A qualitative study.' *Revista Complutense de Educación, 32*(2): 261–271. https://doi.org/10.5209/rced.68345

Jeon, J. (2022). 'Exploring a self-directed interactive app for informal EFL learning: A self-determination theory perspective.' *Education and Information Technologies, 27*(4): 5767–5787. https://doi.org/10.1007/s10639-021-10839-y

Jeon, J., Lee, S. and Choe, H. (2023). 'Beyond ChatGPT: A conceptual framework and systematic review of speech-recognition chatbots for language learning.' *Computers & Education, 206*: 104898. https://doi.org/10.1016/j.compedu.2023.104898

Jia, F., Sun, D., Ma, Q. and Looi, C.-K. (2022). 'Developing an AI-based learning system for l2 learners' authentic and ubiquitous learning in English language.' *Sustainability, 14*(23), 15527. https://doi.org/10.3390/su142315527

Kannan, J. and Munday, P. (2018). 'New trends in second language learning and teaching through the lens of ICT, networked learning, and artificial intelligence.' *Círculo de Lingüística Aplicada a la Comunicación, 76*: 13–30. https://doi.org/10.5209/CLAC.62495

Karaca, A. and Kılcan, B. (2023). 'The adventure of artificial intelligence technology in education: Comprehensive scientific mapping analysis.' *Participatory Educational Research, 10*(4): 144–165. https://doi.org/10.17275/per.23.64.10.4

Karakaya, K. and Bozkurt, A. (2022). 'Mobile-assisted language learning (MALL) research trends and patterns through bibliometric analysis: Empowering language learners through ubiquitous educational technologies.' *System, 110*: 102925. https://doi.org/10.1016/j.system.2022.102925

Katsarou, E., Wild, F., Sougari, A.-M. and Chatzipanagiotou, P. (2023). 'A systematic review of voice-based intelligent virtual agents in EFL education.' *International Journal of Emerging Technologies in Learning (iJET), 18*(10): 65–85. https://doi.org/10.3991/ijet.v18i10.37723

Kent, D. (2020). 'A room with a VUI – voice user interfaces in the TESOL classroom.' *Teaching English with Technology, 20*(3): 96–124.

Kessler, G. (2018). 'Technology and the future of language teaching.' *Foreign Language Annals, 51*(1): 205–218. https://doi.org/10.1111/flan.12318

Khampusaen, D., Chanprasopchai, T. and Lao-un, J. (2023). 'Empowering Thai community-based tourism operators: Enhancing English pronunciation abilities with AI-based lessons.' *Journal of Mekong Societies, 19*(1): 132–159.

Klimova, B., Pikhart, M., Benites, A. D., Lehr, C. and Sanchez-Stockhammer, C. (2023). 'Neural machine translation in foreign language teaching and learning: A systematic review.' *Education and Information Technologies, 28*(1): 663–682. https://doi.org/10.1007/s10639-022-11194-2

Lee, D., Kim, H. and Sung, S.-H. (2023). 'Development research on an AI English learning support system to facilitate learner-generated-context-based learning.' *Educational Technology Research and Development, 71*(2): 629–666. https://doi.org/10.1007/s11423-022-10172-2

Lee, J. H., Shin, D. and Noh, W. (2023). 'Artificial intelligence-based content generator technology for young English-as-a-foreign-language learners' reading enjoyment.' *RELC Journal, 54*(2): 508–516. https://doi.org/10.1177/00336882231165060

Lee, K.-A. and Lim, S.-B. (2023). 'Designing a leveled conversational teachable agent for English language learners.' *Applied Sciences, 13*(11): 6541. https://doi.org/10.3390/app13116541

Li, B. and Peng, M. (2022). 'Integration of an AI-based platform and flipped classroom instructional model.' *Scientific Programming, 2022*: 1–8. https://doi.org/10.1155/2022/2536382

Li, W. and Mohamad, M. (2023). 'An efficient probabilistic deep learning model for the oral proficiency assessment of student speech recognition and classification.' *International Journal on Recent and Innovation Trends in Computing and Communication, 11*(6): 411–424. https://doi.org/10.17762/ijritcc.v11i6.7734

Li, Y. (2022). 'Teaching mode of oral English in the age of artificial intelligence.' *Frontiers in Psychology, 13*: 953482. https://doi.org/10.3389/fpsyg.2022.953482

Liao, L. (2023). 'Artificial intelligence-based English vocabulary test research on cognitive web services platforms: User retrieval behavior of English mobile learning.' *International Journal of E-Collaboration, 19*(2): 1–19. https://doi.org/10.4018/IJeC.316656

Lin, C.-J. and Mubarok, H. (2021). 'Learning analytics for investigating the mind map-guided AI chatbot approach in an EFL flipped speaking classroom.' *Educational Technology & Society, 24*(4): 16–35.

Lin, H.-C., Ho, C.-F. and Yang, H. (2022). 'Understanding adoption of artificial intelligence-enabled language e-learning system: An empirical study of UTAUT model.' *International Journal of Mobile Learning and Organisation, 16*(1): 74–94. https://doi.org/10.1504/IJMLO.2022.119966

Liu, C.-C., Liu, S.-J., Hwang, G.-J., Tu, Y.-F., Wang, Y. and Wang, N. (2023). 'Engaging EFL students' critical thinking tendency and in-depth reflection in technology-based writing contexts: A peer assessment-incorporated automatic evaluation approach.' *Education and Information Technologies, 28*(10): 13027–13052. https://doi.org/10.1007/s10639-023-11697-6

Mayer, R. E. (2022). 'Instructional media and instructional methods in digital language learning: are we asking the right questions?.' *Bilingualism: Language and Cognition, 25*(3): 396–397.

Moher, D., Shamseer, L., Clarke, M., Ghersi, D., Liberati, A., Petticrew, M., Shekelle, P. and Stewart, L. (2015). 'Preferred reporting items for systematic review and meta-analysis protocols (PRISMA-P) 2015 statement.' *Systematic Reviews, 4*(1): 1–9. https://doi.org/10.1186/2046-4053-4-1

Muñoz-Basols, J., Neville, C., Lafford, B. A. and Godev, C. (2023). 'Potentialities of applied translation for language learning in the era of artificial intelligence.' *Hispania, 106*(2): 171–194. https://doi.org/10.1353/hpn.2023.a899427

Mushkarova, O., Mikheeva, M., Nefedova, I., Chepic, F. and Vasiliev, S. (2021). 'SWOT matrix analysis of the enhancing the effectiveness of education in the context of digitalization.' *IOP Conference Series: Earth and Environmental Science, 806*(1): 012023.

N, M. and Kumar NS, P. (2022). 'Amelioration of Google Assistant – a review of artificial intelligence stimulated second language learning and teaching.' *World Journal of English Language, 13*(1): 86–91. https://doi.org/10.5430/wjel.v13n1p86

N, M. and Kumar NS, P. (2023a). 'Investigating ESL learners' perception and problem towards artificial intelligence (AI) – assisted English language learning and teaching.' *World Journal of English Language, 13*(5): 290–298. https://doi.org/10.5430/wjel.v13n5p290

N, M. and Kumar NS, P. (2023b). 'Google Assistant assisted language learning (GAALL): ESL learners' perception and problem towards AI-powered Google Assistant-assisted English language learning.' *Studies in Media and Communication, 11*(4): 122–130. https://doi.org/10.11114/smc.v11i4.5977

Nikonova, E., Yakhyaeva, K., Pivkina, N. and Schetinina A. (2023). 'Using artificial intelligence tools in teaching a foreign language in higher technical institutions.' *European Journal of Contemporary Education, 12*(2): 578–589. https://doi.org/10.13187/ejced.2023.2.578

Pack, A. and Maloney, J. (2023). 'Potential affordances of generative AI in language education: Demonstrations and an evaluative framework.' *Teaching English with Technology, 2023*(2): 4–24. https://doi.org/10.56297/BUKA4060/VRRO1747

Page, M. J., McKenzie, J. E., Bossuyt, P. M., Boutron, I., Hoffmann, T., Mulrow, C., Shamseer, L., Tetzlaff, J. M., Akl, E.A., Brennan, S. E., Chou, R., Glanville, J., Grimshaw, J. M., Hróbjartsson, A., Lalu, M. M., Li, T., Loder, E. W., Mayo-Wilson, E., McDonald, S., . . . Moher, D. (2021). 'The PRISMA 2020 statement: An updated guideline for reporting systematic reviews.' *British Medical Journal, 372*(71): 1–9. https://doi.org/10.1136/bmj.n71

Peña-Acuña, B. and Crismán-Pérez, R. (2022). 'Research on Papua, a digital tool with artificial intelligence in favor of learning and linguistic attitudes towards the learning of the English language in students of Spanish language as L1.' *Frontiers in Psychology, 13*: 1019278. https://doi.org/10.3389/fpsyg.2022.1019278

PRISMA Statement. (2021). *PRISMA endorsers.* PRISMA Statement Website. https://bit.ly/41l676x

Putra, J. W. G., Teufel, S. and Tokunaga, T. (2023). 'Improving logical flow in English-as-a-foreign-language learner essays by reordering sentences.' *Artificial Intelligence, 320*: 103935. https://doi.org/10.1016/j.artint.2023.103935

Qu, J., Zhao, Y. and Xie, Y. (2022). 'Artificial intelligence leads the reform of education models.' *Systems Research and Behavioral Science, 39*(3): 581–588.

Saldana, J. (2015). *The coding manual for qualitative researchers* (3rd ed.). London: Sage.

Samejima, M., Shimizu, Y., Akiyoshi, M. and Komoda, N. (2006). 'SWOT analysis support tool for verification of business strategy.' *IEEE International Conference on Computational Cybernetics*: 1–4. https://doi.org/10.1109/ICCCYB.2006.305700

Shaikh, S., Yayilgan, S. Y., Klimova, B. and Pikhart, M. (2023). 'Assessing the usability of ChatGPT for formal English language learning.' *European Journal of Investigation in Health, Psychology and Education, 13*(9): 1937–1960. https://doi.org/10.3390/ejihpe13090140

Tafazoli, D., Gómez-Parra, M. E. and Huertas-Abril, C. A. (2019). 'Intelligent language tutoring system: Integrating Intelligent computer-assisted language learning into language education.' *International Journal of Information and Communication Technology Education, 15*(3): 60–74. https://doi.org/10.4018/IJICTE.2019070105

Thamrin, H. and Pamungkas, E. W. (2017). 'A rule-based SWOT analysis application: A case study for Indonesian higher education institution.' *Procedia Computer Science, 116*: 144–150.

UNESCO. (2016). *Education 2023: Incheon declaration and framework for action for the implementation of Sustainable Development Goal 4: Ensure inclusive and equitable quality education and promote lifelong learning opportunities for all.* Paris: UNESCO. https://bit.ly/2BfAvnY

Wang, X., Liu, Q., Pang, H., Tan, S. C., Lei, J., Wallace, M. P. and Li, L. (2023). 'What matters in AI-supported learning: A study of human-AI interactions in language learning using cluster analysis and epistemic network analysis.' *Computers & Education, 194*: 104703. https://doi.org/10.1016/j.compedu.2022.104703

Wang, Z. (2022). 'Computer-assisted EFL writing and evaluations based on artificial intelligence: A case from a college reading and writing course.' *Library Hi Tech, 40*(1): 80–97. https://doi.org/10.1108/LHT-05-2020-0113

Yang, H., Kim, H., Lee, J. H. and Shin, D. (2022). 'Implementation of an AI chatbot as an English conversation partner in EFL speaking classes.' *ReCALL, 34*(3): 327–343. https://doi.org/10.1017/S0958344022000039

Yang, H. and Kyun, S. (2022). 'The current research trend of artificial intelligence in language learning: A systematic empirical literature review from an activity theory perspective.' *Australasian Journal of Educational Technology*: 180–210. https://doi.org/10.14742/ajet.7492

Yıldız, T. (2023). 'Measurement of attitude in language learning with AI (MALL:AI).' *Participatory Educational Research, 10*(4): 111–126. https://doi.org/10.17275/per.23.62.10.4

Youn, S. J. (2023). 'Test design and validity evidence of interactive speaking assessment in the era of emerging technologies.' *Language Testing, 40*(1): 54–60. https://doi.org/10.1177/02655322221126606

Young, J. C. and Shishido, M. (2023). 'Investigating OpenAI's ChatGPT potentials in generating chatbot's dialogue for English as a foreign language learning.' *International Journal of Advanced Computer Science and Applications, 14*(6): 65–72. https://doi.org/10.14569/IJACSA.2023.0140607

Zhai, C. and Wibowo, S. (2022). 'A systematic review on cross-culture, humor and empathy dimensions in conversational chatbots: The case of second language acquisition.' *Heliyon, 8*(12): e12056. https://doi.org/10.1016/j.heliyon.2022.e12056

Zhai, C. and Wibowo, S. (2023). 'A systematic review on artificial intelligence dialogue systems for enhancing English as foreign language students' interactional competence in the university.' *Computers and Education, 4*: 100134. https://doi.org/10.1016/j.caeai.2023.100134

Zhang, Z. (2022). 'The cultivation of cross-cultural communicative competence in English teaching under the background of artificial intelligence and big data.' *Hindawi. Wireless Communications and Mobile Computing, 2022*: 9566066. https://doi.org/10.1155/2022/9566066

Zou, B., Guan, X., Shao, Y. and Chen, P. (2023). 'Supporting speaking practice by social network-based interaction in artificial intelligence (AI)-assisted language.' *Sustainability, 15*(4): 2872. https://doi.org/10.3390/su15042872

23

RAISING INTERCULTURAL AWARENESS IN EUROPEAN UNIVERSITY ALLIANCES

Opportunities, challenges and limitations

Cédric Brudermann

Introduction

Today's world is increasingly characterised by linguistico-cultural superdiversity (Vertovec 2007). In this context, cooperating, living, working, participating and thriving in society means being able to 'engage in open, appropriate and effective interactions across languages and cultures' (OECD 2020: 17). As these skills are not innate (Barbot and Gremmo 2012), education is regarded as responsible (Tawil 2013) for empowering students to deal with sociocultural diversity, increase their intercultural skills and develop appropriate reactions to various social situations.[1]

In higher education in particular, European University Alliances (EUAs) currently stand out as good potential candidates to facilitate socialisation in different languages and reconcile cultural diversity, as these institutions, for instance, offer built-in mobility opportunities and foster the creation of online/onsite plurilingual-cultural communities of practice gathering culturally and linguistically diverse peers from various countries. Nevertheless, while promoting understanding between and rapprochement of cultures and giving languages and cultures a central role to play in the learning opportunities offered, EUAs' affordances can at the same time create difficulties for students: when having to embrace cultural diversity beyond tokenism/stereotypes, to accept the existence of cultural dimensions/differences across cultures (Hofstede 1980) or to solve conflicts caused by cultural differences (d'Abreu et al. 2019: 3). Under such circumstances, merely communicating with people from different cultural backgrounds will consequently not 'automatically lead to intercultural learning' (Kitade 2012: 65), and this situation highlights the need to identify pedagogical solutions likely to help students overcome cultural differences in communication in the learning opportunities offered. In order to bridge this gap, this chapter argues that using the second language teaching and learning (SLTL) field to support the implementation of pedagogical initiatives relating to global citizenship education (GCE) may prove beneficial in EUAs to both ensure the sustainability of the continent-wide model of education they embody and formulate strategic responses to today's sociocultural needs. In order to sustain this argument, this chapter first defines what EUAs are and clarifies why some of their features might make them good candidates for broadening one's linguistic and cultural horizons. It then explains why the implementation of language-/culture-based GCE initiatives could prove relevant in this institutional framework to raise

DOI: 10.4324/9781003439493-28

students' intercultural awareness.[2] It further proposes a hypothetical reflection on what the implementation of such initiatives would imply in EUAs regarding instructional design, pedagogical engineering and course content. It concludes with a critical discussion on the opportunities, challenges and limitations which are likely to derive from the deployment of language-/culture-based GCE initiatives in EUAs.

Rationale

Today's interconnected and interdependent world has made communication and connections between individuals, peoples, nations and cultures closer and faster than ever before. At the same time, the current geopolitical context is paradoxically characterised by numerous tensions and other armed conflicts between countries and communities. In order to 'avert the dangers that might result from the marginalisation of those lacking the skills necessary to communicate' (Council of Europe 2001: 4), finding ways to make it possible for people with differences in language, ethnicity, race, nationality, religion, social background and age to break down cultural barriers, build bridges and commit to cultural awareness is therefore now crucial, and this is why 'education must fully assume its central role' (Tawil 2013: 1) in helping to achieve this societal objective.

Regarding this topic, in Europe, many 'strategies for diversifying and intensifying language learning in order to promote plurilingualism' (Council of Europe 1998: 33) have been implemented since 1954.[3] Besides, to facilitate intercultural ties and cooperation among peers with different languages or cultures, internationalisation has also now become a priority (Beacco et al. 2022) in the European higher education area. Regarding this subject however, strategies for internationalising tertiary education in Europe have long included institutions organised in international cooperation networks (bi- or trinational universities or cross-border universities) or establishing partnerships with post-secondary education providers abroad in order to pursue shared objectives on a certain number of actions.[4] These strategies have nevertheless now taken a new turn, and since 2019 many European higher education institutions' internationalisation strategies have been evolving towards new 'models of systemic, structural and sustainable transnational cooperation [designed to, *our addition*] reinforce the quality, performance, attractiveness and international competitiveness of higher education across Europe'[5]: European University Alliances.

European University Alliances: definition and characteristics

EUAs are integrated transnational consortia of higher education institutions located across Europe (member states of the European Union and countries participating in the Erasmus+ programme). EUAs have been created to 'play a flagship role in the creation of a European Education Area as a whole' (European Commission 2019: 125) by following a blueprint organised around four principles:

- Sharing 'an integrated, long-term joint strategy for education (. . .) that goes beyond any potential existing bilateral and multilateral cooperation' (*Ibid.*)
- Establishing 'a European higher education inter-university "campus"' (*Ibid.*: 126)
- Building 'European knowledge-creating teams' (*Ibid.*)
- Acting 'as models of good practice to further increase the quality, international competitiveness and attractiveness of the European higher education landscape' (*Ibid.*)

378

EUAs further aim at connecting like-minded institutions,[6] are implemented through Erasmus+ funding and have to 'be composed of a minimum of three higher education institutions . . . from at least three EU Member States or other Erasmus+ Programme countries' (*Ibid.*: 128).[7] Eventually, in EUAs, 'embedded mobility at all levels . . . is a standard feature and at least 50% of the students within the alliance should benefit from such mobility, be it physical, virtual or blended' (*Ibid.*: 126).

So far, 51 EUAs gathering 467 institutions based in 38 countries and including nine partners on average have been created. For example, the European University for Smart Urban Coastal Sustainability (EU-CONEXUS) comprises nine pan-European higher education partners specialising in coastal management and engineering[8] and aims at becoming an academic and research network 'covering the smart urban sustainable coastal development from a holistic perspective'.[9] For the smooth running of the continent-wide networks of local host institutions they bring together, EUAs are also committed to implementing joint transnational initiatives which can, for instance, include sharing academic catalogues, developing comprehensive mobility frameworks, creating sustainable governance structures or establishing common management structures (Brudermann 2023). Eventually, in this institutional model, providing stakeholders[10] based in different countries with dedicated social, recreational and learning opportunities requires to articulate various temporalities (a/synchronous, dis/continuous, etc.), spatialities (physical, bimodal, hybrid, virtual, etc.), scales (local, national, continental) and teaching-learning practices (formal, informal, individual, collective, etc.) and organising them (as far as possible) into coherent wholes. In EUAs, this effort is bound to translate into the implementation of continent-wide educational initiatives creating opportunities for (i) contact with members of other cultures/languages, (ii) international/intercultural learning or (iii) encouraging global mindsets in their students.[11] Under such circumstances, whether it be for the sustainability of the institutional framework EUAs embody[12] or to respond to today's barriers to cross-cultural communication,[13] ensuring students make maximum use of the learning opportunities offered ultimately means providing them with pedagogical initiatives/ teaching support designed to help them strengthen their capacities to adapt to diverse linguistic and cultural contexts. The difficulty which then arises in EUAs lies in the identification of pedagogical solutions likely to achieve this objective.

Addressing the challenges posed by cross-cultural communication in EUAs: a tentative approach

Openness to cultural diversity and the ability to speak multiple languages are a requirement in EUAs, as in this institutional model, languages and cultures are (i) situated at the crossroads of research, education and innovation; (ii) central to the creation and transmission of knowledge; and (iii) fundamental to ensure mutual understanding/facilitate socialisation. However, even if languages and cultures can be seen as ideal vehicles to achieve rapprochement between peers with different languages/cultures in EUAs, they may at the same time engender communication problems among users (cf. introduction). This can be explained by the fact that while being able to interact and cooperate with linguistically and culturally diverse others means both knowing how to operationalise one or several linguistic codes autonomously *and* having developed 'a mode of expression which members of a given linguistic community share' (Kramsch 2008: 35), cultural proficiency[14] for its part is not an innate skill. Ensuring that students develop as 'intercultural speakers or mediators who are able to engage with complexity and multiple identities and to avoid the stereotyping which accompanies perceiving someone through a single identity' (Byram et al. 2002: 9) therefore requires that specific training actions be offered in the educational sphere

(Barbot and Dervin 2011). In order to help students overcome cultural barriers and prepare them for the societal demands of the 21st century related to intercultural awareness, cultural diversity/ sensitivity and cross-cultural communication, dedicated learning opportunities thus need to be designed and implemented in EUAs. In this chapter, we argue that one way of addressing this challenge is to harness the SLTL field and use it to support the deployment of pedagogical initiatives relating to global citizenship education (GCE).

Promoting language-/culture-based global citizenship education initiatives in European University Alliances: a tentative reflection

Global citizenship

Global citizenship (GC) is a multifaceted term (Goren and Yemini 2017). It is a 'contested concept in scholarly discourse, and there are multiple interpretations of what it means to be a global citizen' (UNESCO 2014: 14). Despite this limitation, this chapter regards GC as:

> A sense of belonging to the global community and a common sense of humanity, with its presumed members experiencing solidarity and collective identity among themselves and collective responsibility at the global level. Global citizenship can be seen as an ethos or a metaphor rather than a formal membership. Being a framework for collective action, global citizenship can, and is expected to, generate actions and engagement among, and for, its members through civic actions to promote a better world and future
>
> (UNESCO 2017: 2)

In addition to this, the scientific literature of the field suggests that there are three dimensions which are generally associated with GC: '(1) social responsibility (concern for others, for society at large, and for the environment), (2) global awareness (understanding and appreciation of one's self in the world and of world issues), and (3) civic engagement (active engagement with local, regional, national and global community issues)' (Perry et al. 2013: 185).

Such dimensions are in turn very much in line with EUAs' internal needs and those of today's society[15] and can thus serve as pedagogical objectives to pursue within the framework of GCE-related initiatives.[16] Nevertheless, achieving these educational goals in EUAs (at least implicitly) requires users to be culturally proficient and linguistically competent in different languages so as to be able to play a constructive role, face and adapt to linguistic/cultural diversity and prevent (as much as possible) the occurrence of open conflicts in the learning opportunities offered. As being able to communicate in a foreign language (L2) is no more innate than is intercultural pragmatics (Kecskés 2014), pursuing GCE-related objectives in AUEs means (at least partially) leveraging the second language teaching and learning field to achieve them.

Fostering GCE-related objectives by leveraging the language teaching and learning field in EUAs

Using the SLTL field may prove useful in EUAs to support educational initiatives related to GCE if we consider that:

1. Language learning is in itself an experience of contact with diversity and that when engaging with languages, 'students not only learn about the target culture and language, but they can also

Raising intercultural awareness in EUAs

be moved to introspection, questioning themselves and their own perspectives and cultures' (Kim 2020: 523)

2. Language is itself a reflection of people's values, meanings and behaviours (Byram and Guilherme 2000)
3. 'Language teaching is potentially a most important site of learning for democratic citizenship' (Starkey 2002: 20)
4. 'There is also a long tradition of a humanistic stance in language learning aspiring to the ideal of democratic dialogues across languages and cultures. The objective goes beyond a mere proficiency in language to the construction of common values about peace and mutual understanding regardless of language, culture, gender, race, religion, age or income' (Derivry-Plard and Potolia 2023: 189)
5. Language teaching and learning is strongly connected with applied linguistics i.e., a research field providing tools to (for instance) (i) analyse and understand how different languages express different cultures, (ii) develop effective communication strategies with partners whose languages/cultures may differ from one's own and (iii) enhance one's ability to understand cultural differences

However, despite the strong interconnections which can be identified between SLTL and GCE, relying on their articulation to foster GCE in EUAs is far from self-evident since such an initiative has never been conducted before. This effort thus requires innovation by restructuring the SLTL field, but the short perspective justifies that a hypothetical reflection on the types of SLTL-based learning opportunities to pioneer in EUAs to pursue GCE-related objectives be conducted in the first place.

Restructuring the second language teaching and learning field to foster GCE in EUAs: practical implications

As a starting point for a reflection on the way the SLTL field could be restructured in transnational alliances to promote GCE, it can be assumed that, whether it be for their internal needs or those of society, part of EUAs' third mission statement is to shape 'responsible citizens who are both open to the world and able to take a step back when interpreting it' (Kern et al. 2023: 6) and, to do so, to equip students with the skills they need to 'decentre and take up the other's perspective on their own culture, anticipating, and when possible, resolving dysfunctions in communication and behaviour' (Byram 1997: 42). In EUAs, while such objectives are likely to lie at the interface between GCE and SLTL, they correspondingly imply on the SLTL side that:

- Language teaching should not only aim at fostering second language development among students but also at promoting the acquisition of skills susceptible to allow them to engage in plurilingual communication practices in line with the advent of the multilingual turn (May 2014) and in which genuine cultural misunderstandings can arise (UNESCO 2005: 58)
- Learning opportunities allowing students to 'successfully negotiate complex intercultural, transactional, and ideational dimensions of collective human interactivity' (Dubreil and Thorne 2017: 2) should be offered to them so as to 'take into account this social, community-oriented perspective on learning and to more fully comprehend, and contribute to, a diversity of culturally organized systems of activity' (*Ibid.*)
- Language teachers should play new roles in the learning initiatives offered,[17] like acting as 'facilitators who create the conditions for a learning environment which promotes student

interaction, critical reflection and inquiry by drawing on their plurilingual repertoires' (Walker 2021: 129)

- Languages and cultures should both be considered levers to foster students' communication skills in the chosen target languages and vehicles through which to transmit dedicated knowledge

These considerations further stress the need to address concerns related to the language and non-language specific knowledge, skills and attitudes to promote among students in the GCE-related learning opportunities offered and therefore to deal with (i) instructional design, (ii) pedagogical engineering and (iii) course content.

Instructional design

Regarding instructional design, in order to equip EUAs' multi-location students with a wide range of languages, proficiencies, experiences and expectations likely to help them create and sustain social connections with linguistically and culturally diverse others, implementing language-/culture-based GCE initiatives first necessitates that on-site/online opportunities enabling them to get together, collaborate and share their views on GCE-related topics be offered to them. Indeed, allowing students to form international communities of practice (Lave and Wenger 1991) can lead them to interact, collaborate, negotiate meaning and build networks with diverse others and, in doing so, to:

- Develop 'more extended capabilities in meaning-making and interpretation' (Kern et al. 2023: 4)
- 'Decentre their own perspectives and learn to view them from the outside as well as from one's own values' (*Ibid.*: 17)
- Engage critically 'with the place of language and culture in the interaction' (*Ibid.*: 10)

On a pedagogical level, providing students with opportunities to take part in dialogue, collaborative and relationship-building activities means having them to join forces to complete shared assignments based on real-life problems, needs, challenges or concerns. Seeking to operationalise such principles within language-/culture-based initiatives in turn raises concerns related to pedagogical engineering.

Pedagogical engineering

In EUAs, besides the fact that incorporating active learning initiatives[18] into university courses can enhance student learning experiences (Freeman et al. 2014), this teaching strategy dovetails naturally with the pedagogical approach to language learning and teaching which has now been standard for more than two decades in Europe,[19] that is, task-based language teaching (TBLT). With TBLT indeed, tasks[20] are the core unit of planning and instruction. TBLT is besides action-oriented and within this approach participants are viewed as '"social agents" i.e., members of society who have tasks (not exclusively language-related) to accomplish in a given set of circumstances, in a specific environment and within a particular field of action' (Council of Europe 2001: 9). Therefore, as is the case with project-based learning (PBL), with TBLT, students are expected to engage in interactive experiences with peers in order to tackle together various real-life situations.[21] Eventually, on both occasions, PBL and TBLT involve end products: 'we speak of "tasks" in so far as the actions are performed by one or more individuals strategically using their own specific competences to achieve a given result' (*Ibid.*).

In conclusion, in EUAs' language-/culture-based GCE initiatives, whether it be to deliver a topic-specific presentation, to prepare a slideshow or to submit a report (a business plan, a project outline or a book review, for instance), asking multi-location students to complete shared deliverables in international groups of peers amounts to having them simultaneously (and to varying degrees) (i) use various L2 to collaborate, solve problems, make decisions, or explain their ideas; (ii) navigate the difficulties posed by cross-cultural communication; (iii) draw on their store of personal knowledge in the topics dealt with; and (iv) exercise various soft skills (like critical thinking, teamwork, digital literacy or problem solving) to further complete the assignments given. Based on this reflection, it can be deduced that from a pedagogical engineering perspective, SLTL and GCE form an interface which can be relied upon in language-/culture-based GCE initiatives to foster intercultural awareness among students. One aspect which seems to require further developments within this framework, however, has to do with the course content to include in the learning opportunities offered to reach this pedagogical objective.

Course content

Given the three dimensions which are generally associated with GCE (cf. 'Global Citizenship' section previously) and the hybrid nature of the SLTL/GCE pedagogical initiatives, reflecting upon the learning materials to include in the educational opportunities offered to raise intercultural awareness among students means considering using one or several languages/cultures to address topics related to (for instance) philosophy, anthropology, sociology, civic education or history. Indeed, as these subjects can be geared in different ways towards critical thinking; serve to tackle sensitive and controversial issues about diversity, cultural otherness and inclusion; or allow to acknowledge cultural differences, they may prove useful to increase tolerance and respect for ethnic and cultural diversities among students (Utomo and Wasino 2020). For instance, according to the Committee of Ministers of the Council of Europe (2001), history can help students:

- Enhance their critical faculties, ability to think for themselves, objectivity and resistance to being manipulated
- Become acquainted with the events and moments that have left their mark on the history of Europe
- Eliminate prejudice and stereotypes (through the highlighting in history syllabuses of positive mutual influences between different countries, religions and schools of thought over the period of Europe's historical development)
- Critically study misuses of history, whether these stem from denials of historical facts, falsification, omission, ignorance or re-appropriation to ideological ends
- Study controversial issues through the taking into account of the different facts, opinions and viewpoints, as well as through a search for the truth[22]

In addition, foreign languages and cultures and the previously mentioned subjects also happen to share similar educational goals regarding multilingualism and multiculturalism since they are humanities disciplines and, as such, tend to place human relations and dialogue, linguistic/cultural backgrounds, cultural otherness and issues related to education for democratic citizenship at the core of concerns. However, if foreign languages/cultures and GCE can be leveraged in unique ways in EUAs to equip students with the knowledge, skills and values, they may need to become informed citizens and active participants in the educational sphere and society at large articulating them amounts to implementing a content and language integrated learning (CLIL) approach in the classroom.[23] On this matter, Beacco (2010), for instance, provides an in-depth look at the linguistic dimensions underlying knowledge building in history courses as well as insights into the way this very subject can be taught through an L2. This effort is nonetheless set to raise additional questions in EUAs regarding the balance to strike between the linguistic and subject-content objectives pursued because (i) CLIL can be implemented in at least two different ways,[24] and (ii) EUAs' learning ecosystems are anticipated to bring together users of various languages/cultures and may thus require delivering instruction in more than one L2 at a time to take this reality into account.

Interim report

By exploring the intersection between the SLTL field, GCE, soft skills training, the affordances of EUAs and the contributions of active learning/TBLT approaches to education, this reflection ultimately suggests that working towards intercultural awareness development in EUAs means promoting in parallel competences, knowledge and attitudes organised around three pillars (soft skills, dedicated subject-based knowledge and languages/cultures) and to envision them as levers to help students open up to the world, engage with others (in various languages) and get to know themselves better. This articulation is in turn very much in line with Narcy-Combes (2005), who postulates that languages, cultures and subject-based contents (knowledge) are likely to form a *transductive relationship*,[25] that is, an indivisible whole in which the pillars at play feed off each other to take shape together. Based on this model, it can be deduced that fostering intercultural awareness among students in EUAs means leveraging a specific transductive relationship made of up of the three previously mentioned components (Figure 23.1).

Indeed, in Figure 23.1, the 'Languages-cultures' component has to do with the fact that languages and cultures are essential in EUAs for the smooth running of the learning opportunities offered since they are the channels through which students of different origins, languages, nationalities, religions, values and cultures are required to collaborate, negotiate meaning, reach compromises and 'take positions between languages and cultures' (Kern et al. 2023: 10) to achieve mutual comprehension. In initiatives harnessing the potential of the language teaching and learning field to foster GCE, taking into account the 'Languages-cultures' component (Figure 23.1) could therefore invite EUA instructors to not only use the CLIL approach to deal with course content ('Subject-based contents' component in Figure 23.1) and foster soft skill development ('Soft skills' component in Figure 23.1) but also to rely on several L2s during class time ('Languages-cultures' component in Figure 23.1) to deliver instruction, encourage peer to peer interactions and further promote intercultural awareness/L2 development among students. Such pedagogical practices of

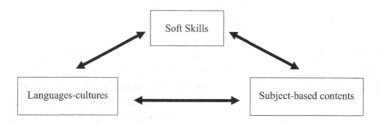

Figure 23.1 Delineating the contours of a transductive relationship related to GCE within EUAs

a new kind are anticipated to raise additional issues regarding the CLIL approach and thus to open new avenues for research/opportunities for innovation within EUAs.

In parallel to that, the learning opportunities offered in EUAs might as well be coupled with action-oriented experiences (volunteering or work placements for instance) taking place in the academia[26] or the workplace:[27] to allow students to apply and expand their knowledge in GC ('Subject-based contents' component in Figure 23.1) in real-life situations, gain hands-on cross-cultural field training, practice their language skills ('Languages-cultures' component in Figure 23.1), enhance their metacognitive awareness, engage in identity-building activities related to GC in the broad sense or increase their willingness/aptitude to engage in dialogue with others ('Soft Skills' component in Figure 23.1). In this respect, in EUAs, the associated partners from the civil society could prove instrumental in providing students with opportunities to undertake work placements in professional settings and, beyond, in helping them develop/enhance skills, knowledge and attitude related to the three pillars of the transductive relationship (Figure 23.1).

Eventually, communicating with people of diverse linguistic and cultural repertoires and in different L2 ('Languages-cultures' component in Figure 23.1) is not an innate capability and requires to rely on specific knowledge[28] ('Subject-based contents' component in Figure 23.1) and interpersonal skills ('Soft skills' component in Figure 23.1)[29] to further engage in meaning-making interactions. In this regard, if implementing learning experiences organised around the three pillars of the transductive relationship (Figure 23.1) could help promote intercultural awareness among students, such initiatives are at the same time anticipated to raise further questions as to whether EUAs should be involved (or not) in the evaluation or certification of soft skills or about the criteria against which to assess soft skills in EUAs.[30]

Discussion

Based on this reflection, it can be anticipated that if the principles of the transductive relationship (Figure 23.1) were applied to foster intercultural awareness among students in EUAs, such an endeavour would bring with it many implications regarding pedagogy. First, it would probably call for a 'rethinking of the ethical dimension of teaching and learning to prepare learners to become participants in the new experiences they are offered' (Kern et al. 2023: 18) and, in this respect, for a process of curriculum reform focusing on social inclusion, equality, participation and empowerment.

Then, implementing language-/culture-based GCE initiatives in EUAs would presumably generate new needs regarding initial and in-service teacher training programmes because active learning approaches to education and community-based learning (Miller and Archuletta 2013) place a greater degree of responsibility on the learner compared to more passive approaches (lectures for example). As such, as teacher mediation would be key to encourage peer to peer interactions or help students 'develop knowledge of self and other and the meanings they create and understand in interaction' (Kern et al. 2023: 10) in language-/culture-based GCE initiatives, this specificity would in turn require GCE instructors to draw on a specific expertise necessarily acquired ahead of time and within the framework of dedicated training programmes.

Besides, contrary to the objectives set forth in language modules for non-specialist language students,[31] in language-/culture-based GCE initiatives, language teachers would be set to rely on their specialised background knowledge in literature, history, linguistics or art to support instruction and enrich the educational experiences underway. Such practices would therefore necessitate re-examining the role played by language teachers in tertiary education and would raise the need for society to recognise them as content specialists in their own right.

Eventually, through the use of the transductive relationship related to GCE in EUAs, a question would certainly arise as to the criteria against which to evaluate one's ability to maintain social contacts with others or confront cultural differences. Regarding this issue, the CEFR (cf. note n°19) for instance promotes an integrated model encouraging to teach languages and cultures in an integrative way but does not deal with several areas, like (i) the definition of the knowledge, skills and attitudes needed to interact with diverse others, (ii) the standards to consider to determine if a given interaction can be deemed *intercultural* (or not) or (iii) the best pedagogical approaches to take to contribute to transformed thinking and intercultural insight among students. A grey area is thus expected to exist on these topics in EUAs' language-/culture-based GCE initiatives but the use of the transductive relationship (Figure 23.1) might serve as a working basis to address them.

Conclusion

This chapter has illustrated that while EUAs' affordances do represent an opportunity for bringing together stakeholders from various backgrounds and facilitating communication and understanding of diversity among them, focusing on 'relational dimension of language use' (Lewis et al. 2023: 152), discovering/comparing different mindsets and learning from/about one another are not innate abilities and require that specific educational initiatives be provided. In this vein, this chapter argues that deploying language-/culture-based GCE opportunities supported by the theoretical principles of a dedicated transductive relationship (Figure 23.1) could prove useful in promoting intercultural awareness in EUAs. As a hypothetical reflection on the subject, however, this chapter currently fails to provide concrete evidence about the benefits and complexities involved in implementing such learning experiences. It is a limitation which is due to the fact that EUAs are ecosystems of a new kind which do not offer enough hindsight yet to measure the learning outcomes of the projects they offer. Despite this, by offering new insights on the topic, this chapter constitutes a first step towards filling this knowledge gap.

In particular, it shows that by placing diversity at the heart of all considerations, the implementation of language-/culture-based GCE initiatives is anticipated to create a certain number of difficulties in EUAs regarding the languages of instruction to choose for communication with/ between users, the language management issues[32] they would bring in their wake or the decisions they would imply to take in terms of language policy.[33] On this last point, for instance, as students from at least three host institutions are expected to take part in EUAs' learning programmes, giving consideration to this variable in language-/culture-based GCE initiatives would mean that using peer-to-peer learning methods like tandem learning would bear little relevance to facilitate collaboration among students given the variety of languages/cultures involved. To circumvent this difficulty, communication between stakeholders would therefore most likely have to be reconsidered within a more plurilingual-cultural framework, as can be the case with tridems/quadridems (Audras and Chanier 2007); the use of teaching methods based on intercomprehension between (un)related languages (Melo-Pfeifer 2016); or the implementation of trans- and plurilingual pedagogies: translingualism (Jones et al. 2020), flexible bilingualism (Creese and Blackledge 2011), codemeshing (Canagarajah 2011), polylingual languaging (Jørgensen 2008) or translanguaging (García and Kleyn 2016), for instance.

Besides, despite the theoretical potential of EUAs' affordances to raise intercultural awareness and foster a culture of multilingualism among students, the smooth running of pedagogical approaches aiming at facilitating dialogue between languages and cultures in transnational ecosystems could be hampered by a certain number of obstacles for which solutions would need to be identified. This could for instance include funding constraints, resistance to pedagogical change or logistical difficulties in coordinating multi-location programmes.

Eventually, putting language-/culture-based GCE initiatives into service within EUAs would probably raise the question of the future of the language learning and teaching field in higher education. Indeed, if we consider that language professionals would seemingly have a coherent profile to be in charge of the language-/culture-based GCE initiatives offered in EUAs, what would become of the educational efforts (language classes, conversation workshops, etc.) or services (language departments, language centres, etc.) specifically fostering L2 development implemented at the local level of host institutions? Should language classes disappear or, on the contrary, exist alongside complementary language-/culture-based GCE learning opportunities? Would it be more appropriate to envision GCE and SLTL from a holistic vision of education? To encourage L2 development through incidental learning (online mobility, for instance) or exposure to comprehensible input (Winke 2015)? As these questions suggest, implementing language-/culture-based GCE initiatives in EUAs would necessarily require that informed decisions be made at the governance level on a certain number of issues relating to not only languages and cultures but also to domains which transcend this field. In this regard, deploying language-/culture-based GCE initiatives in EUAs might constitute a driving force for innovation and serve as a catalyst for new developments on issues for which the necessary distance is still currently lacking. This opportunity could besides be all the more welcome in the current context as in order to respond to the challenges of today's fast-changing world new educational solutions are needed. In this vein, if the advent of EUAs may be part of the long-term solution, leveraging the SLTL field to promote GCE in EUAs could mean more than providing students with opportunities for upskilling: it could hold potential for uniting various stakeholders around major projects for facilitating the exchange of ideas/resources and for building positive relationships in interdependent ecosystems (EUAs/planet Earth/the Internet, etc.) where people of diverse cultures and languages need to be able to navigate the complexities of cross-cultural communication to work towards the greater good.

Notes

1 Within the framework of their Third Mission Statements in particular.

2 To be understood in this chapter as an aptitude to display attitudes of curiosity and openness; to demonstrate the knowledge of how language and culture are related in the target culture, to possess skills of interpreting and relating; and to be able to use, in real-time conversations, an appropriate combination of knowledge, skills and attitudes to interact with speakers from a different country or culture (Chun 2015: 6).

3 Such initiatives for instance include the organisation of the First Intergovernmental Conference on European Co-operation in Language Teaching (1957), the creation of the European Centre for Modern Languages (1994), the launch of the project *Languages of Schooling* (2006) or the publication of the CEFR-Companion Volume (2018).

4 The promotion of international student mobility, the provision of joint degrees or the development of international collaborative research, for example.

5 Quotation extracted from the website of the EUA initiative: https://erasmus-plus.ec.europa.eu/news/opening-of-2024-erasmus-european-universities-call

6 The Eurotech alliance, for instance, brings together European universities specialising in science and technology; EU4ART is a strategic partnership of higher education institutions devoted to fine arts and so on.

7 Even if they can also 'involve associated partners who contribute to the implementation of specific tasks/activities or support the dissemination and sustainability of the alliance' (*Ibid.*: 135). Since 2022, Bologna Process member states like the United Kingdom and Ukraine have also been permitted to take part in EUAs as associated partners.

8 Frederick University (Cyprus), the Agricultural University of Athens (Greece), the Catholic University of Valencia (Spain), the South East Technological University (Ireland), the University of Zadar (Croatia), the University of Rostock (Germany), the Technical University of Civil Engineering (Romania), Klaipeda University (Lithuania) and La Rochelle Université (France).

9 Please visit the official website of this alliance for more details about the objectives set forth by this alliance: www.eu-conexus.eu/en/home/who-we-are/

10 Students, teaching, administrative and technical staff, researchers, librarians and associated partners from civil society (associations, NGOs, the business industry, etc.) in particular.

11 As can be the case with the deployment of internationalisation at home (Beelen and Jones 2015) activities, the provision of distance learning opportunities, the implementation of domestic immersion (Freed et al. 2004) programmes or the development of (physical, blended and virtual) mobility schemes, for instance.

12 By facilitating seamless mobility for all or collaboration in education and research, for instance.

13 Which, for instance, requires one to be able to navigate the complexities of cultural differences, to master various languages and to cooperate with people from different backgrounds/countries.

14 Nuri-Robbins et al. (2011: 23–24) define cultural proficiency as 'the policies and practices in an organization or the values and behavior of an individual, that enable the person or institution to engage effectively with people and groups who are different from them'.

15 Since on both occasions different stakeholders (students, staff and citizens in particular) are called upon to maintain regular contact with peers from different cultures/linguistic backgrounds and expected to engage in shared activities to further thrive.

16 Whether it be according to an approach envisioning them from a holistic vision of education or through the implementation of dedicated study programmes.

17 Compared to their roles in language classrooms where the main focus is more in line with second language development.

18 Like discussions, problem solving exercises, case studies or role plays, for instance.

19 Through the use of the CEFR (Common European Framework of Reference for Languages) in particular (Council of Europe 2001), an international standard for describing one's language ability.

20 According to Ellis (2003: 9–10), a task is a workplan which (i) involves a primary focus on meaning and real-world processes of language use, (ii) can involve any of the four language skills, (iii) engages cognitive processes and (iv) has a clearly defined communicative outcome.

21 On this topic however, contrary to PBL, with TBLT, students need to relate to others using a target language chosen ahead of time.

22 This list of bullet points is taken and adapted from the Recommendation on history teaching in 21st-century Europe to member states (Committee of Ministers of the Council of Europe 2001).

23 That is, a dual focus educational methodology where curricular content is taught through a foreign language.

24 One which is referred to as 'strong', when the approach chosen is content driven and the subject content given primary focus, and another one, which is known as 'weak' (language-driven) and which is more language-driven (even though, in this case, content is given more weight than is typical in the foreign language classroom).

25 On the one hand, because 'no content is ever co-constructed without language' (Liddicoat and Scarino 2013). On the other hand, because language is necessarily used in a 'particular biological, biographical and historical-cultural context' (Martinez 2014: 9, *our translation*).

26 Participation in (online/onsite) international communities of practice, domestic immersion, physical, blended and virtual mobility, student life and campus life.

27 Such as associations or NGOs (including in countries differing from one's own, cf. 'Languages-cultures' component in Figure 23.1) dedicated to helping youth/adult migrants, refugees or displaced persons meet their settlement challenges and needs (social protection, local inclusion, linguistic integration, etc.), for instance.

28 To avoid approaching 'the interaction with linguistically and culturally diverse others from a perspective in which the cultures and cultural identities are treated as fixed, typically nation-based, sets of attributes and characteristics' (Kern et al. 2023: 7) in particular.

29 Knowing how to explore different cultural perspectives, to handle conflict, to critically reflect on languages and cultures or to take up position between languages and cultures, for instance.

30 Since soft skills consist of a broad spectrum of non-domain specific (Bellier 2000) knowledge, aptitudes and attitudes which are sometimes listed in dedicated framework documents (Trilling and Fadel 2009;

OECD 2018; Council of the European Union 2018, etc.) and the examined literature shows that no clear and unique definition of what they mean and include exactly is provided and adopted internationally (Joynes et al. 2019: 8).

31 Whose objectives are generally more in line with second language acquisition, the promotion of specialized academic/professional vocabulary or the development of communication skills among students.

32 Code-switching, literal translation, nativization (Andersen 1983), divergence/convergence in speech accommodation or differences in language skill levels among participants, for instance.

33 Considering, for instance, that while English is today's most common *lingua franca* in the academic sphere, it qualifies as a minority language in EUAs since it is the (co-)official language of 23 institutions out of the 467 which take part in this initiative.

References

Andersen, R. W. (Ed.) (1983). *Pidginization and creolization as language acquisition*. New York: Newbury House Publishers, Inc.

Audras, I. and Chanier, T. (2007). 'Acquisition de compétences interculturelles'. *Lidil*. 36: 23–42.

Barbot, M.-J. and Dervin, F. (Eds.) (2011). *Rencontres interculturelles et formation*. Paris: Education Permanente.

Barbot, M.-J. and Gremmo, M.-J. (2012). 'Autonomie et langues étrangères: Réaffirmer l'héritage pour répondre aux nouveaux rendez-vous'. *Synergies France*. 9: 15–27.

Beacco, J.-Cl. (2010). 'Items for a description of linguistic competence in the language of schooling necessary for learning/teaching (end of obligatory education): An approach with reference points'. In J.-Cl. Beacco, D. Coste, H. Linneweber-Lammerskitten, I. Pieper, P.-H. van de Ven and H. J. Vollmer (Eds.), *The place of the languages of schooling in the curricula* (pp. 31–47). Strasbourg: Council of Europe.

Beacco, J.-Cl., Bertrand, O., Herreras, J. C. and Tremblay, Ch. (Eds.) (2022). *Pour une gouvernance linguistique des universités et des établissements d'enseignement supérieur*. Palaiseau: Éditions de l'École Polytechnique.

Beelen, J. and Jones, E. (2015). 'Redefining internationalization at home'. In A. Curaj, L. Matei, R. Pricopie, J. Salmi and P. Scott (Eds.), *The European higher education area: Between critical reflections and future policies* (pp. 67–80). New York: Springer.

Bellier, S. (2000). '"Compétence comportementale": Appellation non contrôlée'. In S. Bellier (Ed.), *Compétences en action* (pp. 125–133). Paris: Éditions d'Organisation.

Brudermann, C. (2023). 'Caractériser le sens de l'expression "internationalisation du supérieur" dans le modèle institutionnel des alliances d'universités européennes: analyses quantitatives et qualitatives'. *Revue internationale de pédagogie de l'enseignement supérieur*. 39(3).

Byram, M. (1997). *Teaching and assessing intercultural communicative competence*. Bristol: Multilingual Matters.

Byram, M., Gribkova, B. and Starkey, H. (2002). *Developing the intercultural dimension in language teaching a practical introduction for teachers*. Strasbourg: Council of Europe https://rm.coe.int/16802fc1c3

Byram, M. and Guilherme, M. (2000). 'Human rights, cultures and language teaching'. In A. Osler (Ed.), *Citizenship and democracy in schools: Diversity, identity, equality* (pp. 63–78). Stoke-on-Trent: Trentham Books.

Canagarajah, S. (2011). 'Codemeshing in academic writing: Identifying teachable strategies of translanguaging'. *The Modern Language Journal*. 95(3): 401–417.

Chun, D. M. (2015). 'Language and culture learning in higher education via telecollaboration'. *Pedagogies: An International Journal*. 10(1): 5–21.

Committee of Ministers of the Council of Europe (2001). *Recommendation of the Committee of Ministers to member states on history teaching in twenty-first-century Europe*. https://rm.coe.int/16804ec22c

Council of Europe (1998). *Recommendation no. R(98) 6 of the Committee of Ministers to member states concerning modern languages*. https://rm.coe.int/16804fc569

Council of Europe (2001). *Common European framework of reference for languages: Learning, teaching, assessment*. Cambridge: Cambridge University Press. https://rm.coe.int/1680459f97

Council of the European Union (2018). *Council recommendation of 22 May 2018 on key competences for lifelong learning*. https://eur-lex.europa.eu/legal-content/EN/TXT/PDF/?uri=CELEX:32018H0604(01)

Creese, A. and Blackledge, A. (2011). 'Separate and flexible bilingualism in complementary schools: Multiple language practices in interrelationship'. *Journal of Pragmatics*. 43(5): 1196–1208.

d'Abreu, A., Castro-Olivo, S. and Ura, S. K. (2019). 'Understanding the role of acculturative stress on refugee youth mental health: A systematic review and ecological approach to assessment and intervention'. *School Psychology International*. 40(2): 107–127.

Derivry-Plard, M. and Potolia, A. (2023). 'Looking back, moving forward'. In A. Potolia and M. Derivry-Plard (Eds.), *Virtual exchange for intercultural language learning and teaching: Fostering communication for the digital age* (pp. 183–202). London: Routledge.

Dubreil, S. and Thorne, S. (2017). 'Introduction: Social pedagogies and entwining language with the world'. In S. Dubreil and S. Thorne (Eds.), *Engaging the world: Social pedagogies and language learning* (pp. 1–11). Boston: Cengage Learning Inc.

Ellis, R. (2003). *Task-based language learning and teaching*. Oxford: Oxford University Press.

European Commission (2019). *Erasmus + Programme guide, Version 1 (2020): 05–11–2019*. https://erasmus-plus.ec.europa.eu/sites/default/files/2021-09/erasmus-plus-programme-guide-2020_en.pdf

Freed, B., Dewey, D. and Segalowitz, N. (2004). 'Context of learning and second language fluency in French: Comparing regular classroom, study abroad, and intensive domestic immersion programs'. *Studies in Second Language Acquisition*. 26(2): 275–301.

Freeman, S., Eddy, S. L., McDonough, M., Smith, M. K., Okoroafor, N., Jordt, H. and Wenderoth, M. P. (2014). 'Active learning increases student performance in science, engineering, and mathematics'. *Proceedings of the National Academy of Sciences*. 111(23): 8410–8415.

García, O. and Kleyn, T. (Eds.) (2016). *Translanguaging with multilingual students: Learning from classroom moments*. London: Routledge.

Goren, H. and Yemini, M. (2017). 'Global citizenship education redefined – a systematic review of empirical studies on global citizenship education'. *International Journal of Educational Research*. 82: 170–183.

Hofstede, G. (1980). *Culture's consequences: International differences in work-related values*. Beverly Hills, CA: Sage.

Jones, K., Preece, J. and Rees, A. (2020). *International perspectives on multilingual literatures: From translingualism to language mixing*. Newcastle upon Tyne: Cambridge Scholars Publishing.

Jørgensen, J. N. (2008). 'Polylingual languaging around and among children and adolescents'. *International Journal of Multilingualism*. 5(3): 161–176.

Joynes, C., Rossignoli, S. and Fenyiwa Amonoo-Kuofi, E. (2019). *21st century skills: Evidence of issues in definition, demand and delivery for development contexts (K4D helpdesk report)*. Brighton, UK: Institute of Development Studies.

Kecskés, I. (2014). *Intercultural pragmatics*. Oxford: Oxford University Press.

Kern, R., Liddicoat, A. J. and Zarate, G. (2023). 'Research perspectives on virtual intercultural exchange'. In A. Potolia and M. Derivry-Plard (Eds.), *Virtual exchange for intercultural language learning and teaching: Fostering communication for the digital age* (pp. 1–20). London: Routledge.

Kim, D. (2020). 'Learning language, learning culture: Teaching language to the whole student'. *ECNU Review of Education*. 3(3): 519–541.

Kitade, K. (2012). 'An exchange structure analysis of the development of online intercultural activity'. *Computer Assisted Language Learning*. 25(1): 65–86.

Kramsch, C. (2008). 'Voix et Contrevoix: l'expression de soi à travers la langue de l'autre'. In G. Zarate, D. Lévy and C. Kramsch (Eds.), *Précis du Plurilinguisme et du Pluriculturalisme* (pp. 35–38). Paris: Édition des Archives Contemporaines.

Lave, J. and Wenger, E. (1991). *Situated learning: Legitimate peripheral participation*. Cambridge: Cambridge University Press.

Lewis, T., Rienties, B. and Rets, I. (2023). 'Communication, metacommunication and intercultural effectiveness in virtual exchanges: The evaluate project'. In A. Potolia and M. Derivry-Plard (Eds.), *Virtual exchange for intercultural language learning and teaching: Fostering communication for the digital age* (pp. 133–155). London: Routledge.

Liddicoat, A. J. and Scarino, A. (2013). *Intercultural language teaching and learning*. Hoboken: Wiley Blackwell.

Martinez, P. (2014). *La didactique des langues étrangères*. Paris: Presses Universitaires de France.

May, S. (Ed.) (2014). *The multilingual turn: Implications for SLA, TESOL and bilingual education*. London: Routledge.

Melo-Pfeifer, S. (2016). 'Translanguaging in multilingual chat interaction: Opportunities for intercomprehension between Romance languages'. In C. Wang and L. Winstead (Eds.), *Handbook of research on foreign language education in the digital age* (pp. 189–208). Hershey: IGI Global.

Miller, C. R. and Archuletta, A. (2013). 'Macro community-based practice: Educating through community-based action projects'. *Journal of Community Engagement and Scholarship*. 6(2): 59–69.

Narcy-Combes, J.-P. (2005). *Didactique des langues et TIC: Vers une recherche-action responsable*. Paris: Ophrys.

Nuri-Robbins, K. J., Lindsey, D. B., Lindsey, R. B. and Terrell, R. D. (2011). *Culturally proficient instruction: A guide for people who teach*. Thousand Oaks: Corwin Press.

OECD (2018). *The future of education and skills: Education 2030*. Paris: OECD Publishing.

OECD (2020). *PISA 2018 results (Volume VI): Are students ready to thrive in an interconnected world?* Paris: OECD Publishing.

Perry, L., Stoner, K. R., Stoner, L., Wadsworth, D. P., Page, R. and Tarrant, M. A. (2013). 'The importance of global citizenship to higher education: The role of short-term study abroad'. *British Journal of Education, Society & Behavioural Science*. 3(2): 184–194.

Starkey, H. (2002). *Democratic citizenship, languages, diversity and human rights*. Strasbourg: Council of Europe.

Tawil, S. (2013). 'Education for "global citizenship": A framework for discussion'. *UNESCO Education Research and Foresight – Working Papers*. 7: 1–8. https://unesdoc.unesco.org/ark:/48223/pf0000223784

Trilling, B. and Fadel, Ch. (2009). *21st century skills: Learning for life in our times*. Hoboken: John Wiley & Sons.

UNESCO (2014). *Global citizenship education: Preparing learners for the challenges of the 21st century*. Paris: UNESCO. https://unesdoc.unesco.org/ark:/48223/pf0000227729

UNESCO (2005). *Indicators for evaluating municipal policies aimed at fighting racism and discrimination*. Paris: UNESCO. https://unesdoc.unesco.org/ark:/48223/pf0000149624_eng

UNESCO (2017). *The ABCs of global citizenship education*. Paris: UNESCO. https://unesdoc.unesco.org/ark:/48223/pf0000248232

Utomo, C. B. and Wasino, W. (2020). 'An integrated teaching tolerance in learning history of Indonesian national movement at higher education'. *Journal of Social Studies Education Research*. 11(3): 65–108.

Vertovec, S. (2007). 'Super-diversity and its implications'. *Ethnic and Racial Studies*. 30(6): 1024–1054.

Walker, U. (2021). 'From target language to translingual capabilities: Harnessing plurilingual repertoires for language learning and teaching'. *The Langscape Journal*. 3: 117–134.

Winke, P. M. (2015). 'The effects of input enhancement on grammar learning and comprehension: A modified replication of Lee (2007) with eye-movement data'. *Studies in Second Language Acquisition*. 35: 323–352.

24

RHIZOMATIC APPROACHES

A response to hierarchies, linearity, and isolation in language learning

Beatriz Carbajal-Carrera and Rita Prestigiacomo

Introduction

Conventional approaches to *language curriculum design* have increased the gap between dominant language varieties and non-dominant varieties. Dominant varieties have consistently been selected as the standard to acquire knowledge following a top-down approach that prioritises prestige and teacher authority, while non-dominant varieties and bottom-up approaches rarely find representation in language textbooks (Ducar 2019). The logic behind such a gap must account for the colonial legacies, globalisation processes, national projects, and standardisation processes as a multifaceted motor for increasing linguistic inequality and homogenisation. Regardless of its reasons, what draws the interest of our study is that this situation reveals the failure of conventional language curriculum design to recognise learner agency and linguistic and epistemic diversity appropriately. For that reason, counter-hegemonic educational design approaches offer valuable opportunities to reimagine the position of both learners and non-dominant varieties – including endangered and minority languages – in the curriculum. The current chapter addresses this matter through an integrative review of rhizomatic approaches applied to language learning.

The curriculum design of language courses has traditionally followed a *top-down* model. From this perspective, and in terms of *structure*, decisions about content, methodologies, and assessment are made by teachers, in their role of experts and possessors of knowledge, and then passed down to learners. In addition, there is a tendency toward a structured and deficit-based views of the curriculum geared toward predefined learning outcomes (Blaschke et al. 2021), with the primary aim to fill learners' knowledge gaps (Khine 2023). In terms of *content*, the top-down model often focuses on languages that hold dominant status in society, along with their established linguistic norms and standards. This has increased the gap between dominant and non-dominant language varieties, with dominant languages overwhelmingly outnumbering non-dominant languages in textbooks (Ducar 2019). By favouring hierarchies in the structure and content, conventional language curriculum design disregards a reality of language variation that learners inhabit. Such limitations foster homogeneity and inequality, disregarding agency, innovation, creativity, and independent thinking, which are ultimately defined solely by institutions (Blaschke et al. 2021).

In this context, *counter-hegemonic approaches* to language learning are increasingly implemented in contemporary learning settings. These approaches are anchored in the fundaments laid

DOI: 10.4324/9781003439493-29

by *critical pedagogies*, the ways of teaching and learning that empower learners by stimulating their agency and critical awareness of social hierarchies (Freire 1970). As such, counter-hegemonic approaches reject hierarchies among languages, their epistemologies, and learner identities, and, to do so, they encompass both new and longstanding concepts. Among the latter, the notion of rhizome counts over 40 years since its formulation and yet has re-emerged in rhizomatic learning to address current limitations in curriculum design. The emergence of counter-hegemonic approaches to language learning points to the limitations of conventional approaches, as extensively reported by applied linguistics research (Canagarajah 2005; Norton and Toohey 2004; Pennycook 1990). This chapter aims to advance research in the same direction with a focus on rhizomatic approaches to language learning.

The pedagogical applications of the rhizome directly challenge hierarchies, offering valuable opportunities to reimagine the position of learners and non-dominant varieties in the curriculum. Rhizomatic learning is based on the *rhizome* metaphor proposed by post-structuralist thinkers Deleuze and Guattari (1980) in their seminal work *A Thousand Plateaus* and developed by educational technology expert Cormier (2008) in the contemporary context of participatory culture. The term rhizome has botanical origins: it refers to an underground plant structure that grows horizontally, with no central root or hierarchy. In this sense, rhizomatic learning emphasises the interconnectedness and non-linearity of knowledge: there is no beginning, no end, or central point of origin (Khine 2023). Thus, rhizomatic approaches aim to empower learners, fostering their choices and voices as well as nurturing their agency, flexibility, and accountability to deal with the unknown (Selkrig et al. 2023). The central tenet of rhizomatic learning of "community as curriculum" transfers more agency to the learners (Cormier 2008), questioning traditional power structures. Digital technologies and participatory culture have provided experimental opportunities for the rhizome such as open learning courses, which allow for knowledge co-construction by community members.

Even though the rhizome metaphor has a long trajectory and has been applied to a range of disciplines and particularly developed as a disruptive pedagogical approach by educational technology, its application to language learning is still very limited. Thus, while rhizomatic learning has gained popularity in educational technology (Sherman 2021) and attracted interest in diverse fields such as geophilosophy (Gough 2007) and healthcare (Holmes and Gastaldo 2004), its feature in language learning has mostly addressed dominant languages (Lian 2004; Mestre and Lian 1985; Kairienė and Mažeikienė 2021). In addition, due to its counter-hegemonic nature, a lack of traditional measurement is observed in rhizomatic learning settings (e.g., pre- and post-scores). As Koseoglu and Bozkurt (2023) argued rhizomatic learning resists the metric-culture driven in education. The recent body of rhizome studies in education contain key takeaways for rhizomatic learning dispersed across different disciplines and applications, making it compelling to bring some cohesive understanding of its underlying principles, as well as the affordances and challenges this approach has demonstrated. The present chapter addresses this matter by conducting an integrative review of rhizomatic approaches applied to language learning, a method that "synthesizes and evaluates current knowledge of a topic to provide new insights therein" (Cronin and George 2023: 168).

As we review and apply key contributions from rhizomatic approaches to language learning, we pose the following research question: *How does rhizomatic learning respond to key limitations in language learning?* We hypothesise that while the rhizome inherently counters hierarchies in education, these are so entrenched in the curriculum that a paradigm shift is not without obstacles. Examples used in the chapter to illustrate limitations, principles, opportunities and challenges draw on Spanish-speaking contexts due to its representation of a diverse and hierarchised linguistic ecosystem. As a colonial language spoken across multiple countries, Spanish-speaking geographies not only encompass Spanish diatopic variations but also minority and endangered languages spoken in colonised territories. Therefore, transferring knowledge about Spanish-speaking contexts raises questions about the degree of representation and authenticity of community languages in the curriculum. Given that the notions of 'community' and 'curriculum' are central to rhizomatic learning, this counter-hegemonic approach attracts our interest.

Rhizomatic learning is presented here as an approach that organically addresses some of the prevailing challenges in language aligning with the ongoing evolution of communication and information technologies. Importantly, the chapter does not present rhizomatic principles as the new holy grail for language learning. Instead, by contextualising its emergence, the chapter seeks to explain why aspects of this approach, including the central role of learner and the perception of learning as a social, contextual, interconnected, non-linear, evolving, and unbounded process (Blaschke et al. 2021; Lian 2011, 2004; Ossiannilsson 2023), have/are increasingly been adopted by educational proposals, even those not necessarily defining themselves as rhizomatic.

The chapter first sets the grounds for understanding where rhizomatic principles fit by considering existing limitations in the conceptualisation of language learning. It then outlines rhizomatic principles and discusses their applications to language learning. It concludes with a section on opportunities and challenges, as well as some reflections on future directions.

Limitations in the conceptualisation of language learning

The current panorama of language teaching and learning evidences limitations in conceptualising language learning as hierarchical, linear, and isolable. This section provides an overview of the reasons behind each of these conceptualisations, the various dimensions they encompass, their impact on conventional pedagogical practices, and influence on language learning.

Hierarchies

Even though language teaching methodologies have moved from teacher to student-centred approaches, language learning is still influenced by hierarchies that limit the extent of a truly unbounded experience where the learning environment is open and independent, as conceived by rhizomatic principles. Hierarchical learning refers to the assumption that acquiring knowledge, including linguistic and cultural knowledge, implies sourcing it from a higher *authority*, either personal or material such as a teacher, a curriculum, or a textbook. As a primary model for learners, personal and material authorities have shaped attitudes to language, conforming a sociolinguistic hierarchy where dominant varieties are prioritised over non-dominant varieties (Ducar 2019).

In conventional learning settings, the locus of knowledge and authority has traditionally been identified in the role of the teacher (Flannery 1994). Based on early research on the sociology of teaching (Waller 1965), some educational studies support the demonstration of teacher authority to foster productive relationships with students (Elliott 2009). There is consensus over the fact that authority as a concept is not an issue, but the quality of authority needs to be carefully considered (Giroux 1986). In this sense, authority is defined as a social construction that plays a central role in classroom communication and that is under constant reshaping by teachers and students (Pace and Hemmings 2007). This body of studies argues for a need to change our understanding and transferring of authority through a call for students "to assume more authority, assign authority to their peers, and to value their own thoughts and ideas" (Hübscher-Younger and Narayanan 2003: 4). Given their interactive and collaborative core, language curricula will particularly benefit from a redistribution of authority to enrich divergence and convergence processes, in alignment with rhizomatic principles, as will be explained in subsequent sections. Specifically, transferring authority needs to be paired with the cultivation of critical language awareness, which encourages learners to critically examine power dynamics and sociolinguistic hierarchies in language use.

Hierarchies present in social structures affect how students see their own identity (ontology), the knowledge (epistemology) they access and the interplay between these two. Language courses usually introduce the notion that language matters and that it is closely connected to identity (Norton 2010). However, this intention to raise awareness may be overridden by the reproduction of sociolinguistic hierarchies in teaching materials. Research has observed that current language materials and publications continue to perpetuate stereotypes and biases through example sentences already identified in the '90s (Cépeda et al. 2021; Kotek et al. 2021). The studies found that men were overrepresented as subjects, agents, and gender-based stereotypes regarding occupations, violence, and romance themes. Besides their impact on identity, hierarchies are responsible for regulating what is considered legitimate knowledge and what ways of knowing are institutionally accepted. Thus, hierarchies affect what language variations are prestigious and which ones are stigmatised. For example, Castilian Spanish is generally adopted as the default variation by Spanish textbooks, leading to a lack of awareness and appreciation for the linguistic diversity in Spanish-speaking contexts (Ducar 2019; Moreno Cabrera 2011).

Rhizomatic learning counters these issues regarding authority, identity, and knowledge through its unbounded approach. If hierarchical learning can be conceptualised in the botanical metaphor of a root with a central source of knowledge, unbounded learning is decentralised with knowledge having multiple entry points. In terms of authority, unbounded is understood as a redistribution of the knowledge-generator role among students and sources. This way, it allows learners to create their own paths of inquiry as *learning subjectives*, acknowledging the ever-evolving nature of knowledge similarly to renowned educational systems, such as the Finnish one (Sahlberg 2021). In connection to identity, unbounded refers to decentralising the entry point of knowledge and enriching it with the diverse insights that each learner can bring. The lack of dependence on a textbook or a teacher translates into a more inclusive approach that challenges traditional power dynamics. At the same time, the unbounded quality recognises the legitimacy of all linguistic variations, stirring away from standardisation and moving towards linguistic diversity. This perspective acknowledges the equal value of all linguistic variations within a language and places emphasis on plurilingualism, communication efficiency and language use over monolingualism, correctness and language norms (Moreno Cabrera 2021). Finally, an unbounded structure allows for more fluid interactions across language proficiency levels, leading to transversal opportunities for debating knowledge and peer-to-peer mentoring.

Linearity

The linear and sequential organisation of learning processes has been consolidated as the prevalent model in education, a standard for planning courses and designing learning materials. Western perspectives conceptualise time and history in a linear manner as opposed to indigenous perspectives that conceptualise it in a cyclical manner (Carjuzaa and Ruff 2010; Sleeter 2010). Given that Western approaches were disseminated globally through colonisation and globalisation processes, it is not surprising that this understanding of time has also been consistently adopted in educational design. In the words of Marshall (1996: 2): "For three centuries the dominant scientific world view has been the image of a static, repetitive, predictable, linear, and clockwork universe. . . . We have been obsessed with linear systems and their effect has controlled almost every dimension of our

Table 24.1 The myth of the average learner[1]

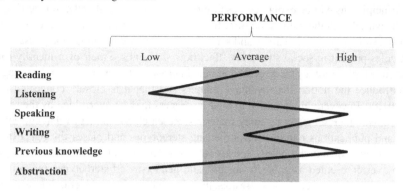

culture". From this logic, if time is linear, learning processes that involve time should develop parallelly. However, cognitive contributions to education posit that linearity is a limiting assumption that does not accurately represent the complexity and dynamism of learning processes (Bransford et al. 1999).

A key limitation to linearity lies in the assumption that learners progress in a homogenous manner. This illusion is institutionally created through a coordinated focus on learning goals as milestones rather than individual student performance across different skills. As a result, it is assumed that all students have uniformly achieved the overall learning goals at the end of a course. Linearity also affects the generalised perception of student profiles. Drawing on statistical averages introduced during the Industrial Revolution, educational approaches adopted this measurement to assess students' performance and potential and to design learning environments. The average learner myth perceives the performance of each student across skills in a linear manner in agreement with the descriptors of their correspondent language proficiency level. The notion of average is represented as a straight line in the central column of Table 24.1. Nevertheless, nowadays we know that systematic variability affects students, who display a jagged profile in their performance, rather than a straight line (Carbajal-Carrera 2024; Rose 2015). Each student shows a set of strengths and weaknesses that draw a ridged profile, per the irregular black shape in Table 24.1. Based on these findings, language curricula should abandon the idea of the average learner and explore non-linear paths, allowing learners to navigate their own linguistic journey.

Despite the linear organisation of course curricula towards learning outcomes, language learning is non-linear. Linguistic items are not learnt in a linear process that implies mastering one item and moving on to another one (Larsen-Freeman 1997). Rather, both progress and backsliding are common in language learning (Mallows 2002). For instance, when learning a given tense in the target language, the tense may be initially learnt as a lexical unit and used correctly in a controlled environment; this correctness "is followed by a period of chaos as exposure to the language increases and generalizations and random usage creep in" and that happens differently for each learner (Mallows 2002: 4). In fact, Larsen-Freeman (1997) and Mallows (2002) argue that even the term "target language" provides a distorted perception of language learning as linear "because there is no endpoint to which the acquisition can be directed. The target is always moving" (Larsen-Freeman 1997: 151); that is, the ideal of language proficiency dynamically evolves from the beginner to the intermediate learner. This misleading perception is dependent on prevalent metaphors in language learning that "are essentially hierarchical and . . . linear," and, for that reason, they limit our conceptualisation of teaching and learning (Bowers 1990: 128). Therefore, introducing non-linear approaches to learning, such as those proposed by rhizomatic approaches, is expected to enrich our conceptualisation of language learning.

These issues regarding homogenisation and rhetoric in language learning may benefit from non-linear pedagogical approaches. Linear conceptualisations are rooted in Eurocentric ideals such as the Aristotelian linear rhetoric, which lead to an inaccurate and oversimplified vision of language learning. This reduced vision may be overcome by non-linear approaches. First, non-linear conceptualisations provide a more diversified response to the sequential order of elements generalised by Western thought by offering alternatives to universalist linear conceptualisations. For instance, Mesoamerican cultures conceived time in a cyclical manner that contrasts with the linear sequence of history by Spanish colonisers (Aveni 2012). Second, non-linearity challenges homogenised representations of the student profile and the learning process that dismount the myth of the average learner and reveal the coexistence of progress and backsliding by allowing for multiple entry points to learning.

Isolation

Language learning methodology has historically shown some tendency to isolation as demonstrated in approaches that focus on one communicative skill, linguistic or cultural component (Richards and Rodgers 2007). For instance, early approaches to language learning focused on written skills (grammar and translation method), oral skills (audio-oral method), grammar (structuralist method), vocabulary (lexical method), or functions (communicative method). Isolating each of these components neglects the meaningful interrelations among them, their context and interlocutors, as well as their relationships and boundaries for successful communication. Acknowledging that language is an emergent and multifaceted phenomenon that arises from the interaction of multiple agents, texts, and contexts implies recognising the dynamism and interdependence of these components in the learning processes.

An important manifestation of isolation can be identified in the artificial boundaries among cultivated languages, which contradicts a reality of fluid boundaries among natural languages (Moreno Cabrera 2011). By acknowledging the fluidity of boundaries across languages and variations, opportunities emerge for integrating non-dominant varieties in the curriculum in combination with dominant languages. For instance, translanguaging practices allow for a more inclusive approach to language learning that embraces the interweaved coexistence of different languages in the collective repertoire of a community (Cenoz and Gorter 2022).

Another relevant realisation of isolation happens in the artificial boundary between in- and outside-class learning. Linguistic studies have argued that language learning is a dynamic process that transcends classroom boundaries (Benson and Reinders 2011). The artificiality of such separation is intensified by the currency of digital environments that blur boundaries across environments in learning and beyond (Choi and Nunan 2018). In the words of Bastian et al. (1985) "School isolation works to deny students a link between what they learn in the classroom and the environment they function in outside the school. . . . Isolation denies schools the energy, resources, and, ultimately, the sympathies of community members" (47). This issue works directly against the core values of rhizomatic learning, where the community is the curriculum (Cormier 2008).

The limitations emerging from isolation may find an answer in conceptualisations of language learning as interconnected and emergent. Specifically, rhizomatic learning proposes the concept of assemblages, which can be useful to combine interconnected and emergent qualities. Assemblages here refer to the dynamic and heterogenous relationships among learners, materials, tools, practices, and contexts that build meaning in emergent and evolving ways. In response to conceptualisations of language as isolable, assemblages can produce meaning and knowledge relations in more situated, authentic and comprehensive ways. For instance, language learners may form an assemblage by interacting with a wide range of input and output sources as well as among peers that they can choose according to their preferences and circumstances. In fact, this is the direction that digital behaviours in social media, artificial intelligence, forums and wikis are demonstrating. This includes the expectation for a more "on demand" or "prosumer" experience in language learning, where knowledge connections are not predetermined by teacher authority but are emergent and constantly evolving from the multiple elements involved in the assemblages.

This section has identified mis-conceptualisations in language learning as hierarchical, linear and isolable. In doing so, it explains why rhizomatic learning may have sparked the interest of educators. Next, rhizomatic learning and its principles are outlined as a prior step to understanding how they have contributed and can further contribute to language learning.

Mapping rhizomatic learning principles

Despite the growing popularity of rhizomatic learning, there is limited application to applied linguistics. In addition, educational research has reported difficulties in understanding its conceptual principles (Mackness et al. 2016). This makes it compelling to bring a cohesive understanding of its six principles – connection and heterogeneity, multiplicity, asignifying rupture, cartography, and decalcomania – originally proposed by Deleuze and Guattari (1980) in philosophy and further developed in education by many others (e.g., Cormier 2008; Cronjé 2023; Khine 2023). Their mapping is a necessary step preceding any implementation stages in any discipline or macrocontext. In what follows, we outline each principle and illustrate how it may translate to the macro-context of language learning.

Connection and heterogeneity

Connection and heterogeneity suggest that multiple elements or ideas can connect and interact freely leading to the creation of a network of unordered and complex array of links and nodes (Khine 2023). The mechanisms and processes through which individuals acquire new knowledge and skills encourage learners to compare, contrast and challenge knowledge. When individuals' internal systems of understanding meet new information or experiences, this can lead to cognitive dissonance or a need for convergence. It is this collision that prompts critical thinking, reflection, cognitive growth, the re-evaluation of existing beliefs as well as the development of more complex mental models. The principle of connection and heterogeneity questions the isolation and social boundaries outlined in the previous section (Cronjé 2023). It defies the invisible and intangible lines between elements influencing the learning environment, such as learner/learner, learner/teacher, or learner/materials. As proposed by critical pedagogies, rhizomatic learning transforms teachers into student-teachers and students into teacher-students (Freire 1970). Therefore, across disciplines, this principle translates into networked learning systems and transfer of authority that privileges learning subjectives over learning objectives.

In language learning, connection and heterogeneity entails dissolving language boundaries (L1/L2/LX) and promoting forms of social, teaching, and cognitive presence in the benefit of language practice. *Language boundaries* can be dissolved by introducing strategies for connecting knowledge across languages, forming networked repertoires, including opportunities for pedagogical translanguaging. For instance, practices adopted by Cenoz and Gorter (2022) such as alternating different languages in the input and output can be implemented. At the same time, connection and heterogeneity are crucial to the cultivation of *presence* in networked language learning (Carbajal-Carrera 2021). Social presence refers to learner to learner relations, teaching presence to teacher-student relations and cognitive presence to learner-material relations (Garrison et al. 2000). In rhizomatic learning, educational technology is used to maximise the connection of learners to other learners, teachers, and materials, shaping heterogeneous interactions. Thus, face-to-face interactions may be supplemented by Padlet, Mentimeter, Slido, discussion forums, and other interactional platforms that allow different forms of participation.

Multiplicity

Multiplicity recognises that there are numerous ways to approach a subject, explore concepts, and construct understanding. This concept challenges traditional linear, single-entry, and prede-termined learning paths to follow. With an extended number of possible entries that may lead to unexpectedly large exit points, individuals can enter the system from various angles, exploring and making contributions based on their interests and perspectives. As remarked by Cronjé (2023), "There are multiple ways of knowing. There are multiple knowledges. There are multiple perspectives. There are multiple pedagogies" (12). Multiplicity can be favoured by a co-constructed and emergent curriculum and the implementation of a discussion forum to elicit emergent themes proposed by learners (Koseoglu and Bozkurt 2023).

Applied to language learning, multiplicity refers to both language methodologies and content selection. In practical terms, a dedicated module on *language methodology* titled "Ways of learning a language" can serve as a collective questioning exercise for prevailing language methodologies. Some pre-existing knowledge of the historical contributions of key language learning methods will be necessary. To that end, a co-constructed Wiki can help outline some baseline knowledge on methods, followed by a discussion forum. Part of this would entail identifying methodological contributions and individual preferences for different methods, evidencing the lack of sufficiency of one single method. In terms of *content selection*, multiplicity challenges the idea that curricula should focus on dominant languages. By questioning this default selection, multiplicity challenges universalist approaches that present dominant languages and their epistemologies as valuable while neglecting non-dominant epistemologies. In the practice, multiplicity of content selection can be prompted in a dedicated module titled "Ways of knowing in Spanish-speaking contexts". A discussion forum and thought-provoking questions can serve as networked learning tools for eliciting the multiple historical and current epistemologies within Spanish-speaking geographies.

Asignifying rupture

Asignifying rupture refers to the fluid and ever-evolving definition of the learning activities implicit in the rhizome metaphor. In the words of Deleuze and Guattari (1980), "[a] rhizome may be broken, shattered at a given spot, but it will start up again on one of its old lines, or on new lines" (p. 9); if one path is blocked, the rhizome can transform into another. In this sense, the image of asignifying rupture epitomises the transformational role of learning, in line with critical pedagogy approaches (Freire 1970).

In language learning, asygnifying rupture connects to treatment of errors, language strategies and emergent assemblages. Regarding the *treatment of errors*, asygnifying rupture means embrac-ing them as learning opportunities. Treating errors as part of the learning journey can help over-coming common obstacles in the process, such as language anxiety. As such, asignifying rupture connects to the broader concept of self-regulation or language *strategies*, where the blockage of a learning path stimulates, rather than dissuading, the exploration of opportunities. Options for moderation and support should address the treatment of errors and language strategies to ensure that learners are equipped with the right tools. This can be implemented in the form of post-it notes with language strategies for each activity. Finally, asygnifying rupture is present in the concept of *assemblages* in language learning proposed by Kairienė and Mažeikienė (2021), which involves dynamic combinations of language skills (e.g., reading-listening, reading-writing, reading-speaking, speaking-listening, and listening-writing). While some of these assemblages are common in traditional pedagogies, the same notion can be implemented in cross-disciplinary projects, where learners may collaborate on real-world challenges, integrating language skills with problem-solving skills.

Cartography

As a rhizome is a network of links and nodes, cartography suggests that their relationship can be represented in a map. The art of graphically creating a mind map means engaging learners in the process of representing the multiple, non-linear, and dynamic nature of their language journey with their learning goals and preferred paths (multiplicity), reflecting on the language resources encountered across a variety of contexts (connection). Akin to linguistic cartography (Phillips Galloway et al. 2022), it can raise awareness of the learners' diverse repertoires, encompassing languages from different contexts and for different social purposes. Cartography substantially differs from traditional mind maps, where students trace a topic at the centre and, departing from here, various arms with headings and subheadings (Cronjé 2023). While traditional mind maps represent knowledge in a linear and isolated manner, cartography captures the dynamics and collective nature of the multiple and interconnected interactions and asignifying ruptures.

When implemented to language learning, cartography allows recording memorable language exchanges, cultural events attended, or personal reflections on language breakthroughs. The map becomes a dynamic reflection of learners' linguistic exploration and journey. Therefore, cartography can help dissolving learning ecology boundaries, understood as the barriers between inside/outside the classroom. *Learning ecology boundaries* may be overcome by introducing resources that elicit reflections on the spatial contexts, such as methods and tools from linguistic landscape research; these can promote shared reflections among learners on the languages spoken in their communities. For example, the situated language portraits (Carbajal-Carrera, forthcoming), by which learners actively and creatively record their surrounding linguistic landscape as an extended part of their linguistic self-representation, can serve as cartographic materials.

Decalcomania

Decalcomania is an artistic technique by which prints and engravings can be transferred to a surface, repeating endless patterns. This method offers learners a unique lens through which to recognise patterns that can help learners internalise language structures more effectively. Akin to artists, language learners can creatively combine linguistic elements (i.e., vocabulary and grammar structures) to express their thoughts and ideas. In addition, the principle of decalcomania can help explore and reshape traditional paradigms in language education, which has typically prioritised verbal communication, neglecting other modes such as visual and gestural. However, effective communication and meaning transfer occur through various modes of representation, including verbal, visual, and gestural. Hence, decalcomania epitomises the multiple semiotic options for representation and expression in a language. Incorporating multimodality into language learning acknowledges the value of multiple modes of representation and expression, in which learners make meaning, helping them develop the ability to predict the outcomes of their learning processes as they identify patterns.

In language learning, decalcomania has much potential when combined with visual creative methods such as language portraits. *Language portraits* are a visual creative method that allow for visual representations and interpretations of the linguistic repertoire of an individual within an outline of their body silhouette (Busch 2006). In the practice, language portraits may be decalcomania versions of a learner's hand, their foot or their whole body. The languages associated with each body part may be represented with a colour. Thus, decalcomania practices manifest aspects of the linguistic repertoire in a personal manner.

The illustration of these principles to language learning demonstrates that some of them are manifested in current trends in applied linguistics not derived from the rhizome metaphor itself, such as linguistic landscapes or language portraits. This insight aligns with educational research that conceives rhizomatic learning in a broad sense as a teaching philosophy and not as a strict model (Koseoglu and Bozkurt 2023). As discussed in the last section of the chapter, this view facilitates its implementation.

Rhizomatic principles applied to language learning

To understand how rhizomatic principles can be translated into language learning, some early (Mestre and Lian 1985) and more contemporary studies (Lian and Pineda 2014; Kairienė and Mažeikienė 2021) have been selected for laying the groundwork. Here, the rhizome is critically analysed as a relevant paradigm to counter pervasive sociolinguistic hierarchies in language learning, not defended as an ultimate solution.

In the study by Mestre and Lian (1985), a microsimulation environment was created for French students, who immersed themselves in a simulated village with distinct geographical, economic, and cultural features. This environment was designed with predefined roles, potential conflicts, and problems for learners to solve. Within this dynamic ecosystem, learners actively engaged with the French language across various *modalities*, encompassing speaking, listening, writing, and reading. The complexity of the simulated village mirrored the diversity of the French language, emphasising its connection to cultural, social, and historical contexts while also linguistically and psychologically engaging the learners from multiple perspectives. Per decalcomania, by combining multiple semiotic modalities, learners could creatively express their thoughts and ideas. In addition, the tasks they encountered within the simulated environment challenged their linguistic skills and logical and representational systems. This collision prompted them to approach subjects, explore concepts, and construct understanding from a *multiplicity* standpoint.

In the same microsimulation environment by Mestre and Lian (1985), per the asignifying rupture principle, the learners could move away from the idea of communication as an orchestrated and isolated interaction but rather as a motivating, natural and rich event that encompassed gestures, body language, linguistic elements, rhythm and intonation, and proxemic relationships with the rules for interaction. Engaging with language in an immersive, experiential and context-rich manner, considering the sensory, embodied and affective dimensions of communication, learners were encouraged to experiment with language in context and take risks by engaging in creative writing, role-playing, and storytelling. Also, they could critically analyze language usage, including the influence of power dynamics, socio-political contexts, and biases. This example of transformative language learning experience can help cultivate critical language and cultural awareness as well as the willingness to embrace language learning complexity versus simplification and simple memorisation.

The study by Lian and Pineda (2014) exemplifies a compelling application of the connection and heterogeneity principle. Thai speakers aiming to comprehend the nuances of "Yes/No" questions in English greetings engaged in a self-directed learning journey facilitated by a *connected and heterogeneous* learning environment. In this instance, the learners initiated their exploration both in physical and virtual spaces. They harnessed the power of networked learning systems, accessing a multimedia database that provided authentic instances of "Yes/No" questions in various contexts, including explanations and commentaries. This rich and heterogeneous database exposed learners to different perspectives and linguistic nuances, laying the foundation for a more comprehensive understanding of elements of the targeted language.

Their exploration, far from being linear, unfolded in a rhizomatic manner. Initially focused on understanding "Yes/No" questions within greetings, this was dynamically expanded by the learners. They further investigated the broader theme of greetings by analysing online movies and stopping at checkpoints to check their comprehension. This branching and re-branching of their heterogeneous exploration allowed for a more holistic grasp of language within its cultural and contextual dimensions. A pivotal aspect of their journey was the engagement with a multimedia database, where they observed authentic instances and actively discussed and experimented them with different scenarios. In their pursuit of understanding "Yes/No" questions, the learners reached out to their networks, including their teacher, a language expert, and native speakers, who provided answers and insights. This collective engagement addressed their unanswered questions and highlighted the diversity inherent in language use. Over time, their interactions and collected information were published in their networked platform, benefitting all system users. This collaborative and interactive dimension underscores the idea that learning is a collective endeavour involving heterogeneous perspectives, interactions, and contexts, which ultimately enriches learners' language proficiency and cultural understanding.

Kairienė and Mažeikienė's study (2021) aimed to reveal and map out secondary school students' English learning assemblages. The multiple learning assemblages of various English language skills were represented in a rhizomatic map, exemplifying the principles of connection and heterogeneity. Findings showed that students learned new English words and tenses by watching movies, music videos, or educational material with subtitles. Every English language activity was intricately linked. For instance, reading and writing skills formed assemblages, with a specific point on the map indicating learners' correspondence in English with peers from other countries. Learners practised reading and listening skills by engaging with global news sources like BBC and CNN and demonstrated a strong affinity for English music, regularly listening to diverse genres and artists. This example illustrates how learning ecology boundaries between inside/outside the classroom can be dissolved through connection, heterogeneity, and cartography principles.

Overall, the previous studies provided valuable groundwork for translating and applying the rhizomatic principles to language learning. They contribute to the ongoing discourse on effective pedagogical approaches, where learners and their needs are positioned at the centre of their language learning journey. With the agency and the autonomy to define and construct what learning is and the possible forms and paths it may take (Blaschke et al. 2021; Lian 2004), learners turn themselves into curators of knowledge – a moving target, not a final product, that is continuously constructed and negotiated without boundaries. However, the focus on two dominant languages (French and English) highlights the need to explore the impact of rhizomatic learning in non-dominant languages, creating opportunities to reflect the multilingual repertoires of language users and their translanguaging practices.

Rhizomatic approaches

Opportunities and challenges

The concept of rhizome has inspired educational innovation across disciplines, including languages. Its disruption of the hierarchical, linear, and isolable views of language and learning in conventional educational design has created opportunities and challenges to the learner's experience. On the one hand, learners who participated in rhizomatic learning environments pointed to the merits of this approach for its transformative, experimental, and positive nature (Caldwell et al. 2023; Mackness and Bell 2015). As traditional power structures dissolve, learners praised a sense of liberation from prescribed content, classroom spaces, and teachers without their free access to learning and its deterritorialisation being compromised (see Sherman). This created spontaneity and movement that enabled them to experience autonomy and self-organisation in a participatory, inclusive, and spiralling experience where learning can be adapted and built upon new viewpoints (Caldwell et al. 2023). They felt empowered to take charge of their educational journey, develop critical thinking skills, and participate in meaningful discussions (Bell et al. 2016; Mackness and Bell 2015). All of this was facilitated by the richness of communication systems and information and the power and the unprecedented mobility of social networks that permit "learning as just in time, just enough, just for me" (Lian and Pineda 2014: 6).

On the other hand, rhizomatic learning poses challenges to learners. They found rhizomatic learning environments "demotivating, demoralizing, disenfranchising and even disturbing" (Mackness and Bell 2015: 34). First, learners questioned the lack of content, learning outcomes, and limited conceptual depth and theoretical discussion, which the absence of a facilitator may have exacerbated (Mackness and Bell 2015). Second, learners accustomed to traditional educational frameworks struggled with the ambiguity and vastness of the learning landscape, requiring scaffolding, guidance, and direction (Knox 2014). This ambiguity and vastness can lead to learners experiencing social isolation, disconnection, overload, anxiety, and a loss of identity and individuality. In addition, some group cultures may become disempowered as they struggle to position themselves and make their voices heard (Bell et al. 2016; Knox 2014; Mackness and Bell 2015). Third, learners' distractions, lack of persistence, time management, or cognitive overload can result in a chaotic experience. Finally, lacking familiarity with digital tools and reliable and consistent availability of high-speed internet can hinder learners' engagement, participation, and equitable access to learning opportunities (Wallace et al. 2021), creating a set of challenges related to social, cognitive and teaching presence (Carbajal-Carrera 2021).

To address the previous challenges, proposals considering implementing rhizomatic principles in language learning should entail some preliminary steps regarding prompting, moderation and transition support, infrastructure, and philosophy. Facilitating thought-provoking prompts for learners is essential for enabling knowledge co-construction. Nevertheless, promoting the idea of learning as a collaborative endeavour should also acknowledge ethical and intellectual property considerations about who owns the content, how it can be used, and the rights of contributors' attribution and sharing. Additionally, requirements should be offered, including guidance, structure and practices that balance learners, tools, and resources (Ibnus 2022), as well as support and learner autonomy. For instance, early discussions of implementing rhizomatic learning environments should clearly communicate course expectations and a general understanding on how to cultivate a positive and collaborative learning environment (Bell et al. 2016). A facilitator moderation of social media and platform regulation can minimise harmful discourse and help establish trust and regulate social dynamics. Moreover, it is important to ensure that classroom authority and agency are transferred to learners who may find this unconventional. Further, for rhizomatic learning environment to work, any necessary participatory infrastructure for a networked learning system, including social media and blogs, should be set up. In addition to this, stable and extensive technological infrastructure and a suitable selection of resources are needed (Mestre and Lian 1985). Finally, educational research has reported the advantages of adopting rhizomatic learning in a broad sense as a counter-hegemonic teaching philosophy rather than as a strict paradigm (Koseoglu and Bozkurt 2023) widening the options for its implementation; indeed, the rhizome metaphor was proposed from the discipline of philosophy by its original proponents Deleuze and Guattari (1980). Failing to ignore these challenges can lead to an idealised illusion about the accessibility of rhizomes.

The relatively young convergence between technological advances and unbounded approaches to learning and communication leaves much potential for rhizome-inspired proposals to be implemented in language learning. Future studies in rhizomatic learning could qualitatively and/ or quantitatively analyse the impact of each of the principles outlined here in learners' experience. Research could also investigate the impact of counter-hegemonic approaches to educational design led by the community, including rhizomatic learning, on the revitalisation of endangered and minority languages.

Note

1 Table adapted from Rose (2015).

References

Aveni, A. (2012). 'Circling the square: How the conquest altered the shape of time in Mesoamerica'. *Transactions of the American Philosophical Society*, 102(5): i–116.

Bastian, A., Fruchter, N., Gittell, M., Greer, C., & Haskins, K. (1985). 'Choosing equality: The case for democratic schooling'. *Social Policy*, 15(4): 34–51.

Bell, F., Mackness, J., & Funes, M. (2016). 'Participant association and emergent curriculum in a MOOC: Can the community be the curriculum?'. *Research in Learning Technology*, 24.

Benson, P., & Reinders, H. (2011). *Language Learning and Teaching Beyond the Classroom: An Introduction to the Field*. Palgrave Macmillan. https://doi.org/10.1057/9780230306790_2

Blaschke, L. M., Bozkurt, A., & Cormier, D. (2021). *Learner Agency and the Learner-Centred Theories for Online Networked Learning and Learning Ecologies*. Unleashing the Power of Learner Agency. EdTech Books.

Bowers, R. (1990). 'Mountains are not cones: What can we learn from chaos'. *Linguistics, Language Teaching, and Language Acquisition: The Interdependence of Theory, Practice, and Research*, 123–136.

Bransford, J. D., Brown, A. L., & Cocking, R. R. (1999). *How People Learn: Brain, Mind, Experience and School* (Expanded ed.). National Academic Press. https://doi.org/10.17226/6160

Busch, B. (2006). 'Language biographies for multilingual learning: Linguistic and educational considerations'. In B. Busch, J. Aziza, & A. Tjoutuku (Eds.), *Language Biographies for Multilingual Learning* (Vol. 24, pp. 5–17). PRAESA.

Caldwell, H., Cuthell, J., Hall, S., Osman, H., Preston, C., Younie, S., . . . Shelton, C. (2023). 'Everyone is an expert: Rhizomatic learning in professional learning contexts'. *Rhizome Metaphor*, 25–52. https://doi.org/10.1007/978-981-19-9056-4_3

Canagarajah, S. (2005). 'Critical pedagogy in L2 learning and teaching'. In *Handbook of Research in Second Language Teaching and Learning* (pp. 931–949). Routledge.

Carbajal-Carrera, B. (2021). 'Mapping connections among activism interactional practices and presence in videoconferencing language learning'. *System*, 99: 102527. https://doi.org/10.1016/j.system.2021.102527

Carbajal-Carrera, B. (2024). 'Delimitación, visualización y metalenguaje: Hacia un diseño curricular de las emociones guiado por principios del DUA'. *Revista Española de Lingüística Aplicada/Spanish Journal of Applied Linguistics*. https://doi.org/10.1075/resla.23012.car

Carjuzaa, J., & Ruff, W. G. (2010). 'When western epistemology and an indigenous worldview meet: Culturally responsive assessment in practice'. *The Journal of Scholarship of Teaching and Learning*, 10(1): 68–79.

Cenoz, J., & Gorter, D. (2022). 'Pedagogical translanguaging and its application to language classes'. *RELC Journal*, 53(2): 342–354. https://doi.org/10.1177/00336882221082751

Cépeda, P., Kotek, H., Pabst, K., & Syrett, K. (2021). 'Gender bias in linguistics textbooks: Has anything changed since Macaulay & Brice 1997?' *Language (Baltimore)*, 97(4): 678. https://doi.org/10.1353/lan.0.0256

Choi, J., & Nunan, D. (2018). 'Language learning and activation in and beyond the classroom'. *Australian Journal of Applied Linguistics (Online)*, 1(2): 49–63. https://doi.org/10.29140/ajal.v1n2.34

Cormier, D. (2008). 'Rhizomatic education: Community as curriculum'. *Innovate: Journal of Online Education*, 4(5).

Cronin, M. A., & George, E. (2023). 'The why and how of the integrative review'. *Organizational Research Methods*, 26(1): 168–192.

Cronjé, J. (2023). 'What should we be teaching if Google gives the answer before we have even finished typing the question?' *New Directions in Rhizomatic Learning: From Poststructural Thinking to Nomadic Pedagogy*, 2.

Deleuze, G., & Guattari, F. (1980). *Mille Plateaux*. Les Éditions de Minuit.

Ducar, C. (2019). 'The sound of silence: Spanish heritage textbooks' treatment of language variation'. *In Iberoamericana Vervuert*, 21: 347–368. https://doi.org/10.31819/9783865279033-018

Elliott, J. G. (2009). 'The nature of teacher authority and teacher expertise'. *Support for Learning*, 24(4): 197–203.

Flannery, J. L. (1994). 'Teacher as co-conspirator: Knowledge and authority in collaborative learning'. *New Directions for Teaching and Learning*, 59: 15–23. https://doi.org/10.1002/tl.37219945904

Freire, P. (1970). *Pedagogy of the Oppressed*. Herder and Herder.

Garrison, D. R., Anderson, T., & Archer, W. (2000). 'Critical inquiry in a text-based environment: Computer conferencing in higher education'. *The Internet and Higher Education*, 2(2–3): 87–105.

Giroux, H. A. (1986). 'Authority, intellectuals, and the politics of practical learning'. *Teachers College Record*, 88(1): 22–40.

Gough, N. (2007). 'Geophilosophy, rhizomes and mosquitoes: Becoming nomadic in global science education research'. In B. Atweh, M. Borba, A. C. Barton, N. Gough, C. Keitel, C. Vistro-Yu, & R. Vithal (Eds.), *Internationalisation and Globalisation in Mathematics and Science Education* (pp. 57–77). Springer.

Holmes, D., & Gastaldo, D. (2004). 'Rhizomatic thought in nursing: An alternative path for the development of the discipline'. *Nursing Philosophy*, 5(3): 258–267.

Hübscher-Younger, T., & Narayanan, N. H. (2003). 'Authority and convergence in collaborative learning'. *Computers & Education*, 41(4): 313–334.

Ibnus, N. (2022). 'Rhizomatic approach to the 21st century EFL learning: A literature review'. *ELT Echo: The Journal of English Language Teaching in Foreign Language Context (Online)*, 7(1): 111–118. https://doi.org/10.24235/eltecho.v7i1.10810

Kairienė, A., & Mažeikienė, N. (2021). 'The assemblages of rhizomatic learning of English of secondary school students'. *Proceedings of EDULEARN21 Conference*, 1576–1585. IATED. http://doi.org/10.21125/edulearn.2021

Khine, M. S. (2023). *New Directions in Rhizomatic Learning: From Poststructural Thinking to Nomadic Pedagogy*. Taylor & Francis.

Knox, J. (2014). 'Digital culture clash: "Massive" education in the E-learning and digital cultures MOOC'. *Distance Education*, 35(2): 164–177.

Koseoglu, S., & Bozkurt, A. (2023). 'Rhizomatic pedagogy in higher education: A comparative analysis'. In *New Directions in Rhizomatic Learning* (pp. 142–157). Routledge.

Kotek, H., Dockum, R., Babinski, S., & Geissler, C. (2021). 'Gender bias and stereotypes in linguistic example sentences'. *Language (Baltimore)*, 97(4). https://doi.org/10.1353/lan.0.0255

Larsen-Freeman, D. (1997). 'Chaos/complexity science and second language acquisition'. *Applied Linguistics*, 18(2): 141–165.

Lian, A. (2004). 'Technology-enhanced language learning environments: A rhizomatic approach'. *Computer-Assisted Language Learning: Concepts, Contexts and Practices*, 1–20.

Lian, A., & Pineda, M. V. (2014). 'Rhizomatic learning: "As. . . When. . . and If. . ." A strategy for the ASEAN community in the 21st century'. *Beyond Words*, 2(1): 1–28. https://doi.org/10.33508/bw.v2i1.508

Lian, A.-P. (2011). 'Reflections on language-learning in the 21st century: The rhizome at work'. *Rangsit Journal of Arts and Sciences*, 1(1): 5–17.

Mackness, J., & Bell, F. (2015). 'Rhizo14: A rhizomatic learning cMOOC in sunlight and in shade'. *Open Praxis*, 7(1): 25–38.

Mackness, J., Bell, F., & Funes, M. (2016). 'The rhizome: A problematic metaphor for teaching and learning in a MOOC'. *Australasian Journal of Educational Technology*, 32(1): 78–91. https://doi.org/10.14742/ajet.2486

Mallows, D. (2002). 'Non-linearity and the observed lesson'. *ELT Journal*, 56(1): 3–10.

Marshall, S. (1996). 'Chaos, complexity, and flocking behavior: Metaphors for learning'. *Wingspread Journal*, 18(3): 13–15.

Mestre, M.-C. & Lian, A.-P. (1985). 'Goal-directed communicative interaction and macrosimulation'. *Revue de Phonétique Appliquée*, 185–210.

Moreno Cabrera, J. C. (2011). *Unifica, limpia y fija: La RAE y los mitos del nacionalismo lingüístico español.* https://dialnet.unirioja.es/servlet/articulo?codigo=8683636

Moreno Cabrera, J. C. (2021). 'Políticas lingüísticas en el Estado español: Del bilingüismo hegemónico al plurilingüismo armónico'. *Erebea. Revista de Humanidades y Ciencias Sociales*, 11: 21–43.

Norton, B. (2010). 'Language and identity'. *Sociolinguistics and Language Education*, 23(3): 349–369.

Norton, B., & Toohey, K. (2004). *Critical Pedagogies and Language Learning.* Cambridge University Press.

Ossiannilsson, E. (2023). 'Rhizome learning: A catalyst for a new social contract'. In *New Directions in Rhizomatic Learning* (pp. 65–79). Routledge.

Pace, J. L., & Hemmings, A. (2007). 'Understanding authority in classrooms: A review of theory, ideology, and research'. *Review of Educational Research*, 77(1): 4–27. https://doi.org/10.3102/003465430298489

Pennycook, A. (1990). 'Critical pedagogy and second language education'. *System*, 18(3): 303–314.

Phillips Galloway, E., Meston, H. M., & Dobbs, C. L. (2022). 'Linguistic cartography: Exploring the power and potential of mapping language resources within classroom communities'. *Journal of Language, Identity, and Education*: 1–16. https://doi.org/10.1080/15348458.2022.2147935

Richards, J. C., & Rodgers, T. S. (2007). *Approaches and Methods in Language Teaching* (2nd, 13th printing ed.). Cambridge University Press. https://doi.org/10.1017/CBO9780511667305

Rose, T. (2015). *The End of Average: How We Succeed in a World That Values Sameness* (1st ed.). HarperOne.

Sahlberg, P. (2021). *Finnish Lessons 3.0: What Can the World Learn from Educational Change in Finland?* Teachers College Press.

Selkrig, M., Dulfer, N., Harrison, M., Smith, C., Cochrane, T., & McKernan, A. (2023). *Keeping It Human: Learning Design in the Digital Age.* The University of Melbourne.

Sherman, B. (2021). 'A rhizomatic CALL: Technological becoming in the language classroom'. *Canadian Modern Language Review*, 77(4): 374–391. https://doi.org/10.3138/CMLR-2020-0069

Sleeter, C. E. (2010). 'Decolonizing curriculum'. *Curriculum Inquiry*, 40(2): 193–204.

Wallace, S., Schuler, M., Kaulback, M., Hunt, K., & Baker, M. (2021). 'Nursing student experiences of remote learning during the covid-19 pandemic'. *Nursing Forum*, 56(3): 612–618. https://doi.org/10.1111/nuf.12568

Waller, W. (1965). *The Sociology of Teaching.* John Wiley.

25

THE NON-FICTION PICTUREBOOK AS A TOOL FOR (RE)CONSTRUCTING CHILDREN'S AND TEACHERS' REPRESENTATIONS OF ENDANGERED LANGUAGES

Design and results of a multimodal educational project for the Aragonese language

Iris-Orosia Campos-Bandrés and Rosa Tabernero-Sala

An approach to the social and educational situation of the Aragonese language

Aragonese is a Romance language that has coexisted with Castilian and Catalan within Aragon – a region in northern Spain – and is considered a unique minority language (Extra and Gorter 2008). After a golden age in which Aragonese was used in the social, public, and private spheres of the Kingdom of Aragon, it began to be replaced by Castilian in the mid-15th century, as a result of a series of political developments mostly over the line of succession to the Crown of Aragon (Benítez and Latas 2023).

Nowadays, there are 56,235 self-reported Aragonese speakers in Aragon, representing 4.2% of the population. Of these, 44,439 state that they understand Aragonese, 29,985 that they can read it, 25,556 that they know how to speak it, and only 17,009 that they can write it (Reyes et al. 2017). According to the *Atlas of the World's Languages in Danger* (Moseley 2010), Aragonese is at a level two degree of endangerment, meaning that intergenerational transmission of the language as a native tongue has practically ceased, as evidenced by recent findings showing that the number of native speakers has fallen from nearly 13,000 in 2001 to approximately 8500 in 2011 (Gimeno 2019).

However, since the 1970s, with the advent of a number of bottom-up social movements (Ager 2001) focused on the recovery of the language, small-scale networks of new speakers have begun to emerge, resulting in a new group of Aragonese speakers. Authors such as Gimeno (2019) and Campos et al. (2023) have stressed the potential importance of these new speakers for the recovery and survival of the language. However, research on this group of speakers tends to reveal a

DOI: 10.4324/9781003439493-30

The Routledge Handbook of Endangered and Minority Languages

non-standardized appropriation of the language, one that corresponds more to a ritualized use that is linked to a situation of post-vernacularity (Shandler 2006).

From a legal point of view, *Law 3/2013 of May 9 on the use, protection, and promotion of the languages and linguistic varieties found in Aragon* provides a certain degree of protection for Aragonese. This partial protection recognizes the right of citizens in areas where the language is still spoken to learn it voluntarily or to use it to communicate with local public administrations. Moreover, the current law also establishes the possibility of developing actions in favor of Aragonese in areas such as the public media, but it does so under discursive formulas such as "it will be promoted" or "it will be favored." In practice, this leaves the decision to develop pro-language policies to the autonomous government of each legislature (López 2015). Aragonese therefore does not have the official status enjoyed by the regional languages of other Spanish territories, such as Catalan and Occitan in Catalonia, Catalan in the Balearic Islands and Valencia, Basque in Navarre and the Basque Country, and Galician in Galicia. On this issue, López (2021) notes the paradoxical, discriminatory reality of Aragonese as, contrary to trends in international, national, and regional legislation – in which equality is a fundamental principle – the absence of official recognition of Aragonese in its historical place of use and influence leads to discrimination of its speakers compared to those who speak the official language of the state or one of the languages recognized as official in other autonomous communities of Spain.

The weak institutionalization of Aragonese has posed challenges in all areas related to its social integration, including the media (Campos 2018c) and literature (Sánchez 2019). Glottopolitical actions, which are primarily carried out from a bottom-up perspective by the speakers themselves (Ager 2001), lead to initiatives that, while contributing to the maintenance of the language, tend to materialize in diglossic dynamics (Alén 2023). One of the main obstacles to the social normalization of Aragonese lies in the normative sphere, as the establishment of a standard variety with a supradialectal character has been a source of contention in the last decade (Nagore 2023). This situation undermines the mutual recognition of Aragonese speakers as members of the same linguistic community. Native speakers of the language therefore tend to identify exclusively as speakers of the local variant rather than a part of the Aragonese-speaking community (Postlep 2012).

In the educational context, the widespread adoption of a Castilian-only education at the beginning of the 20th century in the region where Aragonese was preserved resulted in language oppression within schools (Campos 2015), which was intensified by the Franco dictatorship. This oppression added to the institutional neglect of the language, which, at the time, was only preserved in rural areas of the province of Huesca among members of the lower socio-economic classes. In the case of Aragonese, the tepid and late arrival of institutional recognition of Aragon as a trilingual region (López 2021), with the consequent *assimilationist* practices in linguistic policy (Skutnabb-Kangas 2013), resulted in a late and deficient introduction of its two regional languages – Aragonese and Catalan – in formal education. Against a backdrop marked by glottophagy (Calvet 1974) and the implementation of a subtractive linguistic education (Campos 2015), in-school teaching of Aragonese began in 1997/1998 as a pilot program, taught outside of the core curriculum, after normal school hours, and only in four locales in the province of Huesca (northern Aragon).

Twenty-five years later, the reality of the Aragonese language in the educational system shows some improvement, mainly reflected in the creation of a curricular framework for its teaching and the increase in the number of schools where it can be learned. However, in most of these schools, the instructional practices are still far from the *enrichment* educational models (Siguán and Vila 2014) that would be consistent with the educational principles fostering a plurilingual citizenry,

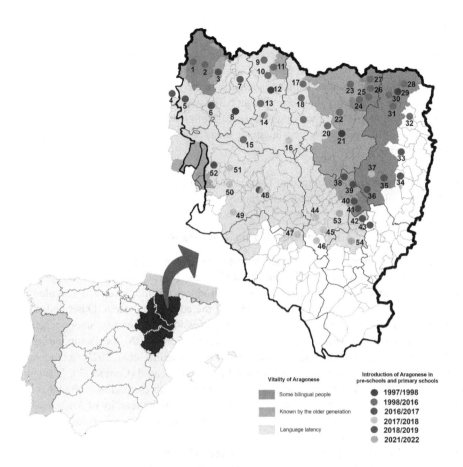

Figure 25.1 Evolution of the introduction of Aragonese in schools, superimposed on the language's vitality map as described by Postlep (2012) in the province of Huesca (Aragon)

and even from the *maintenance* educational proposals (Siguán and Vila 2014) that could ensure the future survival of the language.

As found by Benítez (2015) and Campos (2019), the primary obstacles to the educational normalization of Aragonese have been the delayed creation – 2016 – of a curriculum for primary and compulsory and post-compulsory secondary education and the decisive role played by the faculty of each center in determining whether to introduce the language as part of their educational project as well as the teaching model to be used.

As a result, the inclusion of the Aragonese language in the primary and secondary schools where it is taught varies widely, presenting a complex scenario with a wide range of cases that can be defined according to two main variables: the vitality of the language in the local context and the teaching model chosen by the educational institution. Thus, we can currently find:

- A wide variation in terms of language vitality, ranging from educational institutions in places where Aragonese is no longer the native language of the population to others where it is and where there is a certain degree of social bilingualism. Between these two extremes, we find contexts where the language is latent to a greater or lesser degree, from places where Aragonese is known by the older population to others where it remains only in the form of vocabulary or expressions among a population that has Castilian as its mother tongue.

- Great differences in terms of language planning in the educational context, as there are certain schools where Aragonese is a subject taught twice weekly – sometimes outside of the ordinary school day and to groups of varying degrees of proficiency – and others where the language is the medium of instruction for non-linguistic areas of content, such as social science or education in values.

In total, 1235 pupils in the province of Huesca (Aragon region, Spain) learned Aragonese in the 2022/2023 school year in pre-school and primary education.

Challenges facing the teaching of Aragonese

Since the introduction of Aragonese in the education system, its status and teaching outcomes have been explored almost exclusively by the ECOLIJ research group at the University of Zaragoza through longitudinal studies. Empirical research produced by the group has revealed the main roadblocks to the normalization of the language in the education system. Other endangered languages share some of these challenges such as low professional self-esteem among teachers owing to contextual factors that affect their status as teachers (Campos 2018a; Dompmartin-Normand 2002; Hammine 2020; Hickey and Stenson 2016; Pérez-Izaguirre et al. 2021); a tendency among adolescents to abandon study of the language after primary school (Campos 2021; Bangma et al. 2011); or the propensity for students to develop a diglossic representation of the language – as a thing of the past, belonging to rural locales or folklore – given the scarcity of Aragonese-speaking points of reference in their day-to-day lives and within the institutional and cultural spheres (Campos 2019; González and Armesto 2004).

From a pedagogical standpoint, Campos (2018a) identifies as the main problem the scarce reflection of teachers of Aragonese on the appropriateness, potential, and limitations of their teaching methods, a question that seems to be mediated by problems of the language in terms of educational, social, and normative normalization. Thus, issues such as variations in the teaching model implemented in each school or the lack of a standard variety of Aragonese sanctioned by an official language authority emerge as factors that lead teachers to make pedagogical decisions that, as occurs in other minority European languages (Hickey and Stenson 2016; Dompmartin-Normand 2002), do not align with the current curricular framework. With regard to literacy, this approach includes decisions such as greater attention to oral communication compared to writing and recurrent or exclusive use of texts drawn from popular literature and the oral tradition, as well as topics related to ethnological aspects, restricting the use of the language to a particular set of communicative contexts. This state of affairs poses the challenge of balancing reading and writing development with other linguistic skills and to do so using approaches based on a range of textual genres.

As stressed by Cheetham (2022), access to reading in the minority language promotes its acquisition; moreover, for children who have a minority language as their L1, achieving full literacy in that language is essential to attaining a balanced communicative competence in the two languages present in their lives. In line with the link between literature and identity proposed by scholars (Bruner 1988; Petit 1999), Díaz (2005) highlights the importance of an adequate and high-quality literary corpus for children and youth speakers of minoritized languages that helps them to build self-esteem, develop awareness of their cultural identity, and have quality ethical-aesthetic

The non-fiction picturebook as a tool

experiences that motivate them to read for pleasure in the regional language, not just as a means of reaffirming ethnic and social belonging.

In any case, the only available data regarding the frequency with which primary school-aged children in the province of Huesca read in Aragonese shows a precarious situation. As shown in a quantitative study conducted by Campos (2018b), only 3% of the participants mentioned titles written in Aragonese when asked to name the three most recent books they had read in their free time.

Practice with reading in the minority language is one of the challenges that Aragonese share even with other more widely institutionalized languages (Hickey and Stenson 2016). Furthermore, in the case of Aragonese, there is a scarce number of works of children's and young adult literature, among which modest editions predominate, far from the aesthetic level of works in majority languages (Campos 2018b). All these factors taken together are not beneficial to the development of motivation to read in this language on the part of the students who are learning it.

The awareness of both the problems of the Aragonese language in education and the opportunities offered by non-fiction picturebooks in literacy processes – thanks to the knowledge generated in the R&D project "Non-fictional readings for the integration of critical citizens in the new cultural ecosystem" (LENFICEC) – led the ECOLIJ research group to design teaching materials to promote reading in Aragonese through the multimodal project *O nuestro charrar*. Its objective was to stimulate the interest of teachers and students in the teaching and learning of reading in Aragonese in primary education. To determine how to accomplish this goal, once the materials were created, research was conducted with teachers who had incorporated such materials into their teaching programs. The objective of this research was to explore the ways in which the implementation of the materials could offer opportunities for changing teachers' thinking about the teaching-learning processes of reading in Aragonese, as well as students' representations of the language.

Non-fiction picturebooks in language education and their potential within endangered language teaching

As stated, literacy, including digital literacy, plays a fundamental role in acquiring an endangered language and is key to the survival of the language in the information society. Under this premise, a number of authors (Brouwer and Daly 2022; Foe et al. 2022; Gobbe-Mevellec and Paolacci 2021) have explored the role of picturebooks in the teaching of languages in danger, given their potential use as tools for multimodal literacy and their possibilities for this sphere of language education thanks to their construction. As evidenced by the current publishing landscape (Mascia 2023), non-fiction picturebooks are the sector with the greatest vitality among books aimed at children, works that respond to a combination of artistic and literary discourse that has characterized the way of addressing childhood from its origins (Tabernero and Colón 2023). Thus, non-fiction books for children combine art and knowledge, establishing an innovative discourse on traditional purposes that addresses a reader in training who is curious by nature (Tabernero 2022). The aim is not just to convey information but to evoke emotional attachments to the content, which, in the case of minoritized language teaching, becomes a fundamental aspect.

In their review of the genre, the research group led by Tabernero (2022) details the keys to reading contemporary non-fiction picturebooks, identifying the main paths taken by this publishing sector. Thus, through a blurring of the boundaries separating fiction and non-fiction, as in Bauman's (2017) liquid frontiers, or through the open reflection that breaks with the encyclopedic nature of earlier picturebooks, or a subjective, emotional evocation of the so-called "real world"

(Grilli 2020), or the physical dimension of reading, emphasizing materiality as the basis for construction (Salisbury 2020), non-fiction picturebooks (Tabernero 2022), break with the linear nature of discourse in a way that calls to curious readers (Von-Merveldt 2017). In line with the hybridization of language, content, and readers fostered by the multimodal nature of discourse (Pappas 2006; Von Merveldt 2017; Smith and Robertson 2019; Graff and Shimek 2020; Grilli 2020, among others), current non-fiction picturebooks blend art and knowledge in shaping a critical, creative reader that may be explained by the curiosity that evokes a sense of wonder.

The project *O nuestro charrar*

The project *O nuestro charrar*[1] comprises a set of analog and digital materials that aim to foster the interest of teachers and students toward the teaching and learning of reading in Aragonese during primary education.

The focal point of the project is a non-fiction picturebook that compiles a collection of 50 idiomatic expressions. Each expression is accompanied by a short text showing its meaning in an informative fashion, either by addressing its origin or by putting it in practice by presenting interesting information about Aragonese history and culture, combining narrative, descriptive, and expository texts. The aims of this proposal resemble those of phraseodidactics, an often overlooked field in teaching-learning processes, even within majority languages (Núñez-Román 2015). In addition, the metaphors and associations in the idiomatic expressions reflect cultural patterns that shape a particular way of interpreting the world (Dobrovol'skij and Piirainen 2005).

As for this aspect of the language, in cases of linguistic domination, it is common to come across a paradoxical situation in which, despite the transmission of the minority language across generations, it is *semantically colonized* by the dominant language. To explain this concept, Mühlhäusler (2012) points out that the characteristics of less-used languages that are associated with local conceptualizations are swallowed up by the change in the worldview of younger generations, which comes from their contact with the dominant language and its cultural framework. In this sense, Mühlhäusler (2012: 5) notes that "metaphor is a prime example of an endangered area of most traditional old-established languages"; similarly, Idström and Piirainen (2012) point out that "when a language becomes potentially endangered . . . metaphors and figurative nuances are the first to vanish, even if the language continues to exist" (Idström and Piirainen 2012: 18). In these same lines, in processes of literacy-building in endangered languages, Idström (2010) emphasizes the importance of offering educational materials based on idiomatic expressions to raise awareness among the speech community of the value and relevance of these components to conserve the language and also the culture.

O nuestro charrar meets the criteria to be considered a "bilingual" picturebook as described by Gobbé-Mévellec (2021). In their analysis of picturebooks containing different languages, Gobbé-Mévellec (2021) establish a classification system based on the degree of porosity or interaction between the book's different languages, marking the distinction between bi-/multilingual and plurilingual works. The latter are taken to be those in which languages do not merely coexist as in a redundant relationship, but rather are intertwined to propose an interaction based on interlinguistic reflection for meaning construction.

O nuestro charrar is primarily a "bilingual" work, as it presents a set, vertically symmetrical structure in which expressions in the Aragonese language and the short informational text meant to give meaning to the expression are mirrored by the corresponding expression in Castilian and a translation of the short text. Within this relation of redundancy, however, the visual discourse creates a sense of porosity, in terms of Gobbé-Mévellec (2021), both in the book

The non-fiction picturebook as a tool

Figure 25.2 Example of the contents of the book. Texts by Iris-Orosia Campos-Bandrés and illustrations by Delia Tello (Campos and Tello 2021)

itself and in the accompanying epitexts. These scholars define porosity, in the context of illustrated books written in several languages, as the result of the use of discursive strategies that promote interaction and interdependence between the different languages present in the book. As the aforementioned authors point out, these mechanisms compel readers to deploy linguistic intercomprehension strategies for the construction of meaning. In the case of *O nuestro charrar*, the porosity-through-illustration is a result of the way in which illustrations act as a bridge between languages, as references are made to the expression in Aragonese and not in Castilian – also playing with the literal and figurative meaning simultaneously at times, as can be seen in Figure 25.2 – thus compelling a model reader learning the minority language to pay attention to both the literal and figurative meanings of the expression in Aragonese and, to fully understand it, the corresponding translation in Castilian.

The project extends beyond the physical book by means of different epitexts, in a proposal that characterizes 21st-century readers as an "interactive audience" that demands full access to the universe of books through different formats or platforms in which content, characters, or plots are combined and complement each other, thereby providing a unique reading experience in the form of a "transmedia narrative" (Scolari 2013). Thus, the work is accompanied by a traveling exhibition that, in addition to Aragonese, includes Catalan, the second most commonly spoken regional language throughout the history of Aragon. In the exhibition, a selection of expressions is presented along a thematic journey, including expressions referring to animals, parts of the body, plants, places, objects, time, and money. Using a series of QR codes, students can listen to recordings of the texts that appear on the panels. While navigating the ten panels that make up the exhibition, students are prompted to resolve a number of "challenges" that lead them to reflect on the three languages of Aragon – Aragonese, Spanish, and Catalan – entering their responses on a short downloadable worksheet.[2] Once again, these activities reveal the interlinguistic porosity of the project.

The book and its accompanying materials also contain a digital epitext in the form of a book trailer available in Aragonese and Spanish,[3] which favors an initial approach to the book through promotion patterns typical of children's and youth literature that are closer to 21st-century readers (Tabernero and Calvo 2016).

It is also noteworthy that the regional variety used in the creation of these materials falls within the central dialectal complex of Aragonese (Nagore 2013). This fact may facilitate opportunities for interdialectal reflection among students who speak or learn other regional varieties of the language.

Research results linked to the didactic implementation of *O nuestro charrar*

After the creation of the materials in *O nuestro charrar*, we conducted a phenomenological research study (Hernández-Sampieri and Mendoza 2018) involving ten primary-school teachers of Aragonese who used the materials in their classroom during the 2022–23 and 2023–24 academic years. The aim of this research was to explore how the integration of the created didactic materials into their teaching programs could create opportunities to modify the participants' perspectives regarding the teaching and learning of reading in Aragonese, as well as the students' representations of the language.

From a theoretical point of view, we approach the study of teacher cognition following the perspective proposed by Cambra (2000), based on Woods (1996), which involves conceiving the construct of a system of teacher beliefs, assumptions, and knowledge (BAK) as a complex, dynamic network comprising theoretical concepts derived from scientific knowledge, assumptions tied to cognitive or emotional aspects, and meanings shared with social groups (Pérez-Peitx and Sánchez-Quintana 2019). These systems guide teacher decision-making and are made up of the following: teacher personality, their experience as learners, training, consolidated/shared principles or practices in their educational institution, their professional experience, and influences derived from the education system and society (Palou 2008). As for modifying these systems, Birello and Sánchez-Quintana (2014) underscore the relevance of the concept of tension, alluding to the moment in which a teacher encounters a case that destabilizes their BAK, and stress the importance of these moments as opportunities to readjust teacher cognition.

Taking into consideration both the previous theoretical framework and the scarcity of resources and methodologies for teaching reading in Aragonese, the implementation of the research project *O nuestro charrar* was carried out with the intention of generating tensions and promoting an evolution in the BAK systems of Aragonese teachers, as well as offering opportunities to overcome the diglossic representation of the language by the students (Campos 2019).

The participating teachers were selected using non-probabilistic purposive sampling (McMillan and Schumacher 2005), and the main selection criterion was their commitment to using the materials in their classrooms. In order to implement the project *O nuestro charrar* in their classrooms, teachers received several copies of the book and were given access to both the complementary digital resources as well as the traveling exhibition. No specific instructions were given for the use of the materials, in line with the exploratory and emergent approach of the research. In this sense, a certain complexity arose due to the necessary absence of guidelines and the uncertainty of the teachers involved. On the other hand, access to the participants was not without difficulties due to the effort required to participate in the study and the participants' resistance to unfamiliar materials.

Following the work and didactic experimentation with the didactic materials, which was completed between December and January of 2024, all participants took part in one in-depth interview (Kvale 2011). The interviews followed a semi-structured design that focused on three key issues: methodological keys for the teaching of reading throughout teachers' careers, how the *O nuestro charrar* materials had been integrated into their classroom programs, and outcomes observed. The interviews were transcribed verbatim and analyzed using a qualitative process based on extracting emergent categories (McMillan and Schumacher 2005).

The non-fiction picturebook as a tool

As for the results of the research, we confirm the emergence of some of the challenges detected in previous studies on the teaching of reading in Aragonese (Campos 2018a). Among these, the secondary role generally attributed to written communication compared to oral communication is of note. Teachers participating in the study related this fact to problems connected with the normalization of Aragonese in the education system as well as other social and normative impediments, such as the existence of different orthographical variants for the written representation of the language:

P2: [Regarding his teaching style in general, throughout his entire career as an Aragonese teacher] To be honest, I don't spend my time on reading. I try to work more on speaking and, then, I give them short texts, not very long because their communicative competence isn't very good overall . . . And, of course, because you're working with different levels, it's hard to do readings. . . . It's hard for me to work on reading because there are no available materials, that's the biggest problem. So, I end up working with short texts, such as riddles, to start motivating them, but most of all I offer them oral narrations. . . . I eventually end up doing the readings myself, orally, because it's easier for me . . . because another problem I encounter is dialectal varieties, or variations in spelling. . . . There are so many barriers, you often end up thinking: "Jeez, I just don't know whether I want them to read! I'd rather read it to them myself," because verbally you don't have those problems.

The most prominent tendency is to work on reading through literary texts, mostly from the oral tradition. As evidenced in the previous fragment, the teacher often reads these aloud to the class. With the exception of the few schools where part of the curriculum is taught in Aragonese, using a textual typology beyond the boundaries of literature is uncommon. Consistent with this finding, the teachers report that before taking part in the study based on *O nuestro charrar*, they had no in-depth knowledge of non-fiction works in the language and had never considered using them in class.

P6: The texts I tend to work with are more narrative: traditional stories, legends . . . that type of text. Although, at times, I've worked with other text types. I recall two years ago, we were working on the topic of plants in the area and, from there, I learned that the first female botanist in Spain was Aragonese, and I translated her biography and we worked with it.

Participating in the research set up tensions that cause certain destabilization in the teachers' beliefs system on the teaching and learning of reading in Aragonese, which may in turn lead to some resistance. As seen in Table 25.1, this comes out of a reflection process that promotes: (1) necessary review of the materials offered for use in teaching programs and (2) student responses to the experience.

As for the first question, in their approach to the work, the teachers discover the inclusion of certain simple expressions – understandable to speakers of Castilian, as the translation could be easily deduced by the students – along with others that were more complex – either without a correspondence with Castilian or one that was difficult to deduct – and the combination of different types of texts linked to each expression. This discovery leads to an in-depth reading of the book to select those expressions and texts that best fit the level and interests of students. Thus, despite initial resistance, the complexity of the material, due to its linguistic and discursive heterogeneity, favors an analytical approach that results in rich reflection on methodology and on the teachers' stances toward phraseology not just as teachers of Aragonese but also as speakers of the

Table 25.1 Synthesis of emergent categories arising from the data analysis

Topic	Macrocategory	Category	Key aspects
Challenges in existing tendencies regarding the teaching of reading in Aragonese	Priority of oral over written communication	Lacking motivation to read in Aragonese among students	
		Problems in the normalization of Aragonese within the education system	Elective nature of the school subject Mixed-level groups Lack of resources
		Problems in the standardization of Aragonese	Scarcity of resources adapted to dialectal varieties Variability in the orthographic norm used in the materials available
	Scant variety in text types used for reading	Considering literature the most motivating genre	
		Predominance of literature from the oral tradition	
		Lack of awareness of non-fiction books as a teaching resource	
		Exception in institutions where Aragonese is the medium of instruction for other subjects	
Tensions with the BAK system as a result of participation in the study	Importance of investigating the book as a source of initial reflection	Reflection on the value of idiomatic expressions to communicative competence in Aragonese	Integration of the material in the teaching program with a focus on student assimilation of the expressions, emphasizing investigation in the local setting
		Reflection on the value of idioms from the link language-culture-worldview	
		Reflection on one's own mastery of this aspect of lexical competence in Aragonese	
		Reflection on prior inclusion of this aspect within their teaching	
	Importance of student responses	Aesthetic proposal as a motivating factor to read in Aragonese and to reassess student assumptions toward the language	Importance of the book as an object (epitexts included) Importance of illustrations (source of hypothesis generation and reflection) Interest in resorting to the text to test hypotheses generated based on images Interest in taking the book home to be read during free time
		Student ways of reading	Dialectal variety as a factor motivating metalinguistic reflection Bilingual texts as promoters of reflection between language systems Bilingual texts as a tool for mixed-level groups Awareness on areas of student deficiency regarding competence in Aragonese

The non-fiction picturebook as a tool

language. As an example, some teachers reflected on their own knowledge of this aspect of lexical competence:

P3: I hadn't had much exposure to studying expressions, and I think it's very interesting to have these included in a picturebook like this one. Even if it weren't written in Aragonese, only in Castilian, I would find this to be interesting material, because I believe these expressions are being lost with the passing of time. Even in Castilian, which is not a language in danger. And in Aragonese, much more, of course. Some of the expressions in the book I didn't know myself (*laughs*).

The discourses bring to light a reflection on the value of this aspect of lexical competence from the perspective of developing communicative competence, which leads to the intention of focusing the students' experience with *O nuestro charrar* on the acquisition of the expressions they had worked with in class:

P2: I was interested in them eventually using these expressions, even if they mostly speak in Castilian. As a result, all the expressions that we worked with were related to what I was going to work on at the time in my syllabus. For example, as I have been working on describing, I brought the book to class to work on the expression "*estar más fiero que un totón*" [literally, "to be uglier than a ghost"]. Also, I integrated it around October 31, the excuse being that it was around the Nuei d'Almetas [similar to Halloween] because they already knew what a *totón* [ghost] was . . . And then, later on, I did ask them to recall it when we were coming up with descriptions. . . . And at other times I also "played" with other expressions that were easy to interiorize and use in day-to-day life. Expressions related to the weather, for example.

In line with this issue of awareness, we also observe a tendency to use the project materials outside of the school walls, with research projects outside of the contents of the book and auxiliary materials, thus involving the local community:

P4: After presenting the book in the first session, I told them they could investigate a little more. They could talk to their families, their parents, their grandparents . . . , so they could tell them other expressions in Aragonese used here. . . . Then, for the next session, I assigned them a research project involving their families and neighbors who know the language. And in that next session I really saw some very pretty things and, above all, things that showed that you can get more out of it, that there are things in there that are covered up, but if you look and ask, these can come to light. There are things that you can look for, investigate, and record for the time when those older people are no longer around, people who can contribute so much, so that these things are not lost. So that is how I set out to work . . . I believe the foundation is *O nuestro charrar*, but from there you can go to the context and work on some really nice things.

This way, teachers integrate the material over an extended period of time, as an essential element of their didactic program. The materials are used in didactic sequences and not just in a single moment of the course, looking for versatility in the material and thus incorporate phraseology as another part of the teaching program:

P1: It all comes out because, as there are 50 expressions that are so different from each other and linked to such a wide range of texts, you can work with a lot of topics and weave them together. . . . These are materials that transport you to other places, right? It may not seem so at first. . . . But yes, we travel with the book. It's a constant journey, because it isn't just the expression, but rather the content that you get with the text that comes along with it. Some of them tell you stories, others interesting facts. . . . But all of them make [the children] reflect. I'll keep working with this material throughout the school year, and also next year.

With regard to students' responses to the proposal as a tension-causing factor in the teachers' BAK system, we find two major themes that encompass the emerging categories in the discourses we analyzed. First, the teachers emphasize the value of the aesthetic and material proposal as a factor that motivates students to read in Aragonese, and how this proposal can result in a modification of students' representations of the language:

P2: This material is visual and attractive. There is hardly anything else like it in Aragonese. So often you find yourself giving them photocopies to read, which makes them lose their motivation. It's not the same, it doesn't draw them in. . . . And I believe it is important to note that there are attractive materials in the language, which is not a second-tier language. . . . For them, materiality is essential, it's essential.

As part of the aesthetic proposal, the role of illustration is emphasized as a point of attraction and a trigger for hypotheses and reflections on the text's content. Students spontaneously engage in reading, out of a desire to confirm their assumptions about the represented expression and its meaning. Additionally, the teachers note the students' interest in incorporating the expressions they have worked on, even in cases where competence in Aragonese is still very limited:

P6: Based on the illustration, they thought up many, many possibilities as to what the expression could be and its meaning. And then they would write it all down, mind you. . . . They are making their own notebook, their own set of vocabulary. And they even take it upon themselves to write things down, you don't have to tell them to do it. . . . They are hooked . . . it's pleasurable for them. I mean, they're waiting for the next day to come when they can work on the project. . . . For it to be next week so they can see what's next. You see, it's helped me motivate them. Because they had zero motivation before.

P7: The children were happy, because the book is very different and they were delighted to get to read something else. Keep in mind that they had always been told the typical stories and legends from around these parts. . . . And they had never realized that the expressions existed. They were really struck by it, because later they used the expression non-stop, saying it when they were out and about. It stuck with them.

Within the already mentioned students' spontaneous initiative to read the texts, one of the most important issues regarding teacher cognition is the opportunity to dispel a sometimes strongly held belief, that is, the dialectal variety of the books may condition children's potential interest in reading them. Thus, some teachers, who had not previously used texts written in other regional varieties of Aragonese because of this belief, note that this situation can become, rather than an obstacle, a stimulus for metalinguistic reflection:

P1: As for spelling, this really struck them. For instance, in the expression "*fer burro falso*", here it isn't "*fer*" but rather "*fe*", that is, it's written without a final -R. So they said: "here some

The non-fiction picturebook as a tool

things are missing while others are extras". . . . And, of course, they had no real exposure to another dialectal variety of Aragonese. For them it was all new.

On this issue, some teachers underscore how the experience has led them to reflect on the need to develop a supradialectal representation of the language among the students:

I: *And had you ever thought of bringing them a text – either oral or written – in another dialectal variety?*

P1: No, not yet. With P10 [another participant in the project, both working in a school with a different diatopic variety], we have talked about possibly making a video so that the students can say: "Wow, listen how they talk!" and analyze the videos a bit. For example, for a project we're working on now on the weather, in which the children are going to play the role of meteorologists, my idea was to send P10's students a video and have them send us another doing the art project they are working on, explaining something about painters or whatever they wanted.

Overcoming the reluctance to use materials in dialectal varieties other than the reference variety specific to the area in which they teach is supported not only by students' responses to the reading. The reactions observed in the families are also relevant in this sense: as a result of the motivation shown by the students, the book sometimes goes beyond the school and reaches the pupils' homes, where it does not provoke reticence in the families for being written in a variety of Aragonese different from the one used in the household:

P5: You see, I left the book in the classroom bookshelf so they could take it home with them if they wanted, and I thought, "I may get a message or something from parents criticizing me for it . . . " because there is a belief that teaching anything other than the local variety is frowned upon. But it wasn't like that, so good. It's as if it were a book in Castilian. They've read the book at home and then brought it back a few weeks later. Just like any other book.

Observing students' reading responses reinforces teacher awareness of the value of phraseology for developing communicative competence in Aragonese. The teachers note certain deficits in students' knowledge of expressions in Aragonese that are still used among the Castilian-speaking population in the province of Huesca. This stresses the need to pay greater attention to this aspect of lexical competence in teaching programs, and not only because of its value in developing communicative competence in Aragonese, but also because of its cultural importance:

P6: Well, I've realized that the children, when I've given them an expression in Castilian and ask them to imagine how to say it in Aragonese, they attempt to translate the expression literally from Castilian into Aragonese. This means they never think that an expression could exist in Aragonese on its own, an expression in Aragonese to say the same thing. So I believe that it has brought, in the first place, quality to their competence in the language they're learning . . . but also an awareness that language is not just syntax or grammar, but rather reflects a set of ideas, a culture; that language is a reflection of a culture. That is what it has given them. And they were surprised.

In sum, our analysis reveals that, thanks to the tensions in the teachers' BAK system sparked by participating in this research, there is an explicit awareness of their beliefs, representations, and knowledge concerning the process of teaching and learning of reading in Aragonese, which may ultimately bring about change or reassessment in teacher cognition:

P1: My biggest fear [right before introducing the book] was that they'd reject it on the basis of the dialectal variety it's written in, and I said, "Gosh, I don't know if they'll accept it or not." That was my biggest fear, though in the end it was unfounded. So sometimes, I don't know, we get ideas in our heads about what's going to happen, but these never actually happen.

P2: I realize that on a . . . , as a teacher, I still have to find a place for reading. Because I want to always start classes off with a text. But as the curriculum in primary school gives you so many things that you have to cover, I sometimes don't know how to fit it in, I don't know where to put a good reading that will draw them in. So, of course, that's a personal reflection of mine, I wonder, "How can I do it?" And I think I lack training in this regard.

Given the limitations associated with the exploratory nature of the present study, longitudinal research would be needed to determine the extent to which the triggering of tensions in the teachers' BAK system results in a change in their pedagogical approach.

Conclusion

The present study is innovative in the field of endangered languages literacy. Although there has been international interest in the publication of multilingual picturebooks featuring regional languages in recent decades (Hadaway and Young 2017), there are still few empirical studies that focus on the analysis of reading responses or teachers' thinking about these books. Research such as Daly (2019), Iwan (2023), Lewis and Nixon (2023), or Skaremyr et al. (2024) has focused on the discourse analysis of multilingual picturebooks, but few studies (Chateaureynaud and Oroz-Aguerre 2019; Hartmann and Hélot 2021) present empirical research with this type of books in regional or local minority language contexts. However, these few existing studies focus mainly on the case of fiction literature.

The project and the research presented in this chapter reveal how cooperation between researchers and teachers of an endangered language may create opportunities for the evolution of the teaching practice in the school context. *O nuestro charrar*, teaching material based on knowledge of non-fiction picturebooks generated as part of the research, development, and innovation project LENFICEC (PID2021–126392OB-I00), made it possible to discern the potential of this type of book in literacy initiatives worldwide.

With a firm belief that literacy, including digital literacy, plays a fundamental role in acquiring endangered languages and is a key to the survival of these languages within the information and communication society, we designed material that encouraged teachers to explore and experiment with new ways of introducing students to reading in Aragonese without sacrificing the idiosyncrasies and cultural context of this regional language.

The results, which support the theories of Bonnafé (2008) and Littau (2006), indicate that during childhood, reading is a physical act, which highlights the importance of the book as an object within the process of motivating children to read. This aspect takes on particular relevance in languages in danger to the extent that these often have a limited corpus of titles for children, and the books that do exist tend to be of lesser aesthetic and material quality.

Experimenting with a novel and coherent material, in line with the characterization of the 21st-century child reader led to the emergence of reader responses that prompted a change of the cognitive process of teachers of Aragonese and an evolution in the representation of the language

The non-fiction picturebook as a tool

among some students, who showed greater interest in incorporating the language in day-to-day communication.

Acknowledgments

This research forms part of the activity of the ECOLIJ (*Educación Comunicativa y Literaria en la Sociedad de la Información, Literatura Infantil y Juvenil en la construcción de identidades*) through the R&D project "Non-fictional readings for the integration of critical citizens in the new cultural ecosystem" (PID2021-126392OB-100), funded by the Ministry of Science and Innovation of the Spanish government; through Project S61_20R, funded by the Regional Government of Aragon; and through Project "Non-fictional reading in the teaching-learning process of the Aragonese language: a case study," funded by the Cátedra Johan Ferrández d'Heredia (University of Zaragoza and government of Aragon).

Notes

1 *O nuestro charrar* is the title of the project in Aragonese. It means "our way of speaking."
2 The roll ups designed for the traveling exhibition and the rest of the complementary materials can be viewed at: https://lenguasdearagon.org/o-nuestro-charrar/
3 The book trailer can be viewed at: https://www.youtube.com/watch?v=AoFQk8ItCPA

References

English references

Ager, D. (2001). *Motivation in language planning and language policy*. Clevedon: Multilingual Matters.

Bangma, I., Van der Meer, C. and Riemersma, A. (Eds) (2011). *Trilingual primary education in Europe: Some developments with regard to the provisions of trilingual primary education in minority language communities of the European Union*. Leeuwarden: Mercator European Research Centre on Multilingualism and Language Learning.

Brouwer, J. and Daly, N. (2022). 'Te Puna Pukapuka Pikitia: Picturebooks as a medium for supporting development of te reo rangatira with kindergarten whānau'. *Early Childhood Folio*. 26(1): 10–15.

Cheetham, D. (2022). 'The translation of children's literature into minority languages'. *Children's Literature in Education*. 54: 517–533.

Daly, N. (2019). 'The linguistic landscape of multilingual picturebooks'. *Linguistic Landscape*. 5(3): 281–301.

Dobrovol'skij, D. and Piirainen, E. (2005). *Figurative language: Cross-cultural and cross-linguistic perspectives*. Oxford: Elsevier.

Extra, G. and Gorter, D. (2008). 'The constellation of languages of Europe: an inclusive approach'. In G. Extra and D. Gorter (Eds.), *Multilingual Europe: Facts and policies* (pp. 3–60). Mouton de Gruyter.

Foe, C., Kelly-Ware, J. and Daly, N. (2022). 'Supporting language, culture, and identity using Pacific picturebooks'. *Early Chidhood Folio*. 26(1): 3–9.

Graff, J. M. and Shimek, C. (2020). 'Revisiting reader response: Contemporary nonfiction children's literature as remixes'. *Language Arts*. 97(4): 223–234.

Grilli, G. (2020). 'Beauty and the world: Some questions to five illustrators (often also authors) of non-fiction picturebooks for children on their work, poetics, inspiration(s)'. In G. Grilli (Ed.), *Non-fiction picturebooks: Sharing knowledge as an aesthetic experience* (pp. 267–293). Edizioni ETS.

Hadaway, N. L. and Young, T. A. (2017). 'Multilingual picturebooks'. In B. Kümmerling-Meibauer (Ed.), *The Routledge companion to picturebooks* (pp. 260–269). Routledge.

Hammine, M. (2020). 'Framing indigenous language acquisition from within: An experience in learning and teaching the Yaeyaman language'. *The Language Learning Journal*. 48(3): 300–315.

Hartmann, E. Ch. and Hélot, Ch. (2021). 'The three robbers in three languages: Exploring a multilingual picturebook with bilingual student teachers'. *Journal of Literary Education*. 4: 174–195.

Hickey, T. and Stenson, N. (2016). 'One step forward and two steps back in teaching an endangered language? Revisiting L2 reading in Irish'. *Language, Culture and Curriculum*. 29(3): 302–318.

Idström, A. (2010). 'Challenges of documenting the idioms of an endangered language: The case of Saami'. In J. Korhonen, W. Mieder, E. Piirainen and R. Piñel (Eds.), *Phraseologie. Global – areal – regional* (pp. 221–228). Narr Verlag.

Idström, A. and Piirainen, E. (2012). 'Endangered metaphors: Introduction'. In A. Idström and E. Piirainen (Eds.), *Endangered metaphors* (pp. 25–19). John Benjamins.

Iwan, L. (2023). 'Language preservation: The rise of Māori-language picture books in Aotearoa'. *International Journal of Languages, Literature and Linguistics*. 9(2): 152–156.

Lewis, K. and Nixon, S. B. (2023). 'Honoring indigenous languages through literature'. *Language Arts*. 100(3): 192–205.

Littau, K. (2006). *Theories of reading: Books, bodies, and bibliomania*. Cambridge: Polity Press.

Moseley, Ch. (Ed.) (2010). *Atlas of the world's languages in danger*. Paris: UNESCO Publishing.

Mühlhäusler, P. (2012). 'Prologue'. In A. Idström and E. Piirainen (Eds.), *Endangered Metaphors* (pp. 1–14). John Benjamins.

Pappas, C. C. (2006). 'The information book genre: Its role in integrated science literacy research and practice'. *Reading Research Quarterly*. 41(2): 226–250.

Pérez-Izaguirre, E., Châteaureynaud, M. A. and Amiama, J. F. (2021). 'Teachers' view on the elements that enhance and hamper Basque and Occitan teaching in southern France: An exploratory approach'. *Diaspora, Indigenous, and Minority Education*. 15(3): 151–165.

Salisbury, M. (2020). 'True stories and big books: New creative opportunities in non-fiction picturebooks'. In G. Grilli (Ed.), *Non-fiction picturebooks: Sharing knowledge as an aesthetic experience* (pp. 91–108). Eizioni ETS.

Shandler, J. (2006). *Adventures in Yiddishland: Postvernacular language and culture*. University of California Press.

Skaremyr, E., Hermansson, C., Abraham, G. Y. and Lindström, M. (2024). '(Re)thinking children's picturebooks as the mirror of contemporary society'. *Journal of Early Childhood Education Research*. 13(1): 343–367.

Skutnabb-Kangas, T. (2013). 'Today's Indigenous education is a crime against humanity: Mother-tongue-based multilingual education as an alternative?'. *TESOL in Context*. 23(1–2): 82–125.

Smith, J. M. and Robertson, M. K. (2019). 'Navigating award-winning nonfiction children's literature'. *The Reading Teacher*. 73(2): 195–204.

Tabernero, R. and Calvo, V. (2016). 'Book-trailers as tools to promote reading in the framework of the Web 2.0'. *New Review of Children's Literature and Librarianship*. 22(1): 53–69.

Von-Merveldt, N. (2017). 'Informational picturebooks'. In B. Kümmerling-Meibauer (Ed.), *The Routledge companion to picturebooks* (pp. 231–245). Routledge.

Woods, D. (1996). *Teacher cognition in language teaching: Beliefs, decision-making and classroom practice*. Cambridge: Cambridge University Press.

Spanish references

Bauman, Z. (2017). *La modernidad líquida*. Madrid: Fondo de Cultura Económica de España.

Benítez, M. P. and Latas, Ó. (2023). 'El aragonés: Historia de una lengua minoritaria y minorizada'. *Lengas: Revue de Sociolinguistique*. 94. https://doi.org/10.4000/lengas.7360

Birello, M. and Sánchez-Quintana, N. (2014). 'Tensiones en el sistema de creencias, representaciones y saberes de los docentes. ¿Oportunidades ante el cambio?'. In J. M. Sancho, J. M. Correa, X. Giró and L. Fraga (Eds.), *Aprender a ser docente en un mundo en cambio: Simposio Internacional* (pp. 82–88). Universidad de Barcelona.

Bonnafé, M. (2008). *Los libros, eso es bueno para los bebés*. Barcelona: Océano.

Bruner, J. (1988). *Realidad mental y Mundos posibles: Los actos de la imaginación que dan sentido a la experiencia*. Barcelona: Gedisa.

Campos, I. O. (2015). 'Más de un siglo de lingüicidio en las aulas: Aproximación al caso del aragonés'. *Studium*. 21: 199–230.

Campos, I. O. (2018a). *Lengua minorizada y enseñanza: Actitudes, metodologías y resultados de aprendizaje en el caso del aragonés*. Zaragoza: Prensas de la Universidad de Zaragoza.

Campos, I. O. (2018b). 'Literatura infantil y lenguas minorizadas: Imagen y paratextos en el caso del aragonés'. In R. Tabernero (Ed.), *Arte y oficio de leer obras infantiles. Investigaciones obre lectores, mediación y discurso literario* (pp. 87–96). Octaedro.

Campos, I. O. (2018c). 'Lengua minorizada y medios de comunicación: Prejuicio, activismo y fragmentación lingüística. El caso del aragonés'. *Studium: Revista de humanidades*. 24: 173–196. https://doi.org/10.26754/ojs_studium/stud.2018242606

Campos, I. O. (2019). '20 años de aragonés en la Educación Infantil y Primaria, ¿hacia su normalización en la escuela?'. In F. Nagore and J. Giralt (Eds.), *La normalización social de las lenguas minoritarias: Experiencias y procedimientos para la salvaguarda de un patrimonio inmaterial* (pp. 241–272). Prensas de la Universidad de Zaragoza.

Campos, I. O. (2021). *Las actitudes lingüísticas en los centros de Educación Secundaria del Alto Aragón: Evidencias para la actualización del estado de la cuestión*. Zaragoza: Prensas de la Universidad de Zaragoza.

Campos, I. O., Tabernero, R. and Colón, M. J. (2023). *El aprendizaje del aragonés en la vida adulta: Un estudio cualitativo sobre las representaciones del alumnado*. Zaragoza: Prensas de la Universidad de Zaragoza.

Díaz, L. (2005). 'Literatura infantil desde la frontera: Identidad cultural, didactismo y el placer de leer'. *Hipertexto*. 2: 66–71.

Gimeno, Ch. (2019). 'Neohablantes de aragonés: Retrato de un colectivo estratégico en la revitalización'. In F. Ramallo, E. Amorrortu and M. Puigdevall (Eds.), *Neohablantes de lenguas minorizadas en el Estado español* (pp. 89–109). Iberoamericana Vervuert.

Hernández-Sampieri, R. and Mendoza, C. (2018). *Metodología de la investigación: Las rutas cuantitativa, cualitativa y mixta*. Madrid: McGraw Hill.

Kvale, S. (2011). *Las entrevistas en investigación cualitativa*. Madrid: Morata.

López, J. I. (2021). 'Minoritarias dentro de la minorización: La doble discriminación de las lenguas no oficiales. El caso del aragonés'. *Revista de Llengua i Dret*. 76: 57–78.

McMillan, J. H. and Schumacher, S. (2005). *Investigación educativa: Una introducción conceptual*. Madrid: Pearson.

Núñez-Román, F. (2015). 'Enseñar fraseología: Consideraciones sobre la fraseodidáctica del español'. *Didáctica: Lengua y Literatura*. 27: 153–166.

Pérez-Peitx, M. and Sánchez-Quintana, N. (2019). 'Creencias de los docentes sobre la competencia plurilingüe'. *Lenguaje y textos*. 49: 7–17.

Petit, M. (1999). *Nuevos acercamientos a los jóvenes y la lectura*. Ciudad de México: Fondo de Cultura Económica.

Postlep, S. (2012). '"Este per no ye d'a mía tierra": Percepción científica y percepción inexperta del contínuum dialectal altoaragonés'. *Alazet*. 24: 77–116.

Sánchez, J. Á. (2019). 'La literatura en la normalización externa del aragonés. Ensayo de aproximación'. In F. Nagore and J. Giralt (Eds.), *La normalización social de las lenguas minoritarias: Experiencias y procedimientos para la salvaguarda de un patrimonio inmaterial* (pp. 273–282). Prensas de la Universidad de Zaragoza.

Scolari, C. (2013). *Narrativas transmedia: Cuando todos los medios cuentan*. Barcelona: Deusto.

Tabernero, R. (Ed.) (2022). *Leer por curiosidad: Los libros de no ficción en la formación de lectores*. Barcelona: Graó.

Tabernero, R. and Colón, M. J. (2023). 'Leer para pensar. El libro ilustrado de no ficción en el desarrollo del pensamiento crítico'. *Revista de Educación a Distancia (RED)*. 23(75). https://doi.org/10.6018/red.545111

Aragonese references

Benítez, M. P. (2015). '(De)construindo o marco lechislatibo ta l'amostranza ofizial de l'aragonés'. *Luenga & Fablas*. 19: 39–44.

Campos, I. O. and Tello, D. (2021). *O nuestro charrar: 50 esprisions en aragonés ta chicoz e grans*. Sabiñánigo: Comarca del Alto Gállego.

López, J. I. (2015). 'A Lai 3/2013, de 9 de mayo, u a infraproteuzión churidica de as luengas minoritarias d'Aragón'. *Revista de Llengua i Dret*. 63: 186–199. http://dx.doi.org/10.2436/20.8030.02.99

Nagore, F. (2013). *Lingüística diatopica de l'Alto Aragón*. Huesca: Consello d'a Fabla Aragonesa.

Nagore, F. (2023). 'Enta ra norma común de l'aragonés escrito: Una endrezera plena de barzals'. *Lengas: Revue de Sociolinguistique*. 94. https://doi.org/10.4000/lengas.7461

Reyes, Á., Gimeno, Ch., Montañés, M., Sorolla, N., Espluga, P. and Martínez, J. P. (2017). *L'aragonés y lo catalán en l'actualidat: Analisi d'o Censo de Población y Viviendas de 2011*. Zaragoza: Asociación Aragonesa de Sociología y Seminario Aragonés de Sociolingüística.

Asturian references

González, X. A. and Armesto, X. (2004). *Les llengües en Asturies: Usu y valoración de la so importancia educativa. Estudiu empíricu fechu col alumnáu de Maxisteriu de la Universidá d'Uviéu*. Oviedo: Academia de la Llingua Asturiana.

Catalan references

Cambra, M. (2000). 'Introducció. El pensament del profesor: Formació per a la pràctica reflexiva'. In A. Camps, I. Ríos and M. Cambra (Eds.), *Recerca i formació en didáctica de la llengua* (pp. 161–172). Graó.

Palou, J. (2008). *L'ensenyament i l'aprenentatge del català com a primera llengua a l'escola: Creences i actuacions dels mestres amb relació a les activitats de llengua oral a l'etapa de primària*. Barcelona: Institut d'Estudis Catalans.

Siguán, M. and Vila, I. (2014). *Multilingüisme i educación*. Barcelona: Universitat Oberta de Catalunya.

French references

Alén, C. (2023). 'Défense de la langue et développement des territoires: L'aragonais et ses promotrices/promoteurs'. *Lengas. Revue de sociolinguisticque*. 94. https://doi.org/10.4000/lengas.7550

Calvet, J. L. (1974). *Linguistique et colonialisme: Petit traité de glottophagie*. Paris: Payot.

Chateaureynaud, M. A. and Oroz-Aguerre, M. (2019). 'Aventure littéraire plurilingue en contexte scolaire frontalier: Développement des compétences de lecteurs chez les élèves allophones à travers la lecture d'une œuvre longue et de ses différentes traductions, Shola et les lions, de Bernardo Atxaga'. *Strenæ*. 14. https://doi.org/10.4000/strenae.3114

Dompmartin-Normand, Ch. (2002) 'Collégiens issus de Calandreta: Quelles représentations de l'occitan?'. *Langue et société*. 101: 35–54.

Gobbe-Mevellec, E. and Paolacci, V. (2021) 'Des albums plurilingues à l'école pour les lecteurs . . . plurilingues?'. *Publije: E-Revue de critique littéraire*. http://revues.univ-lemans.fr/index.php/publije/article/view/161

Italian reference

Mascia, T. (2023). 'L'evoluzione creativa della letteratura nonfiction per l'infanzia e l'adolescenza. Una prospettiva internazionale'. *Education & Sciences Society*. 1: 401–419. https://doi.org/10.3280/ess1-2023oa15697

26

MODULARITY AS A PRACTICAL APPROACH TO TEACHING AND LEARNING ABOUT THE LGBTQIA+ COMMUNITY IN JAPAN AND BEYOND

Nobuko Koyama

Introduction

Language educators and learners face two distinct realities. One is how the force of prescriptivism crashes with the world in a state of flux, and the other is how the COVID-19 pandemic has propelled the advancement of pedagogical technologies. Foreign-language textbooks often uphold antiquated or rigid norms and forms from the past. However, we live in a fast-paced and ever-changing world. Unsurprisingly, the Japanese language and culture are in a state of flux induced by the rapid development of new technology and changes in the political, social, and cultural climate. For instance, the Japanese language is well known for its gender-specific speech styles. However, 'the actual speech of Japanese men and women often diverges' from the gender norms presented in Japanese language textbooks (Siegal and Okamoto 2003: 53). This phenomenon has accelerated its pace as we have witnessed a global increase in the awareness of LGBTQIA+ communities. LGBTQIA+ stands for *lesbian*, *gay*, *bisexual*, *transgender*, *queer* (or *questioning*), *intersexual*, or *asexual*. The plus sign is an indicator of a different sexual orientation and allies. Japanese language educators have begun encountering female Japanese language learners in the US who intentionally choose to use the male pronoun *boku* (the male first-person pronoun) to express themselves in classrooms. In Japanese anime and comics, '*boku*-girl' characters create their own genres. Among teenagers in Japan, '*boku* girls' and '*ore* girls' ('*ore*'/a vulgar style of the male first person) challenge gender stereotypes (Honda 2011; Miyazaki 2004; Nishida 2011). They, especially, do so by pushing 'the gender-based linguistic boundaries' (Sato 2018: 1266). For instance, according to Honda (2011), 5% of female junior high school students in Yokohama used variants of male first-person pronouns. Similarly, Okamoto (1995) pointed out the trend in the early 90s that younger women were 'abandoning' stereotypical female speech patterns (p. 298). These gender-bending linguistic choices and behaviors are no longer idiosyncratic exceptions but are a part of our reality. This indicates that the fluidity of how language is used no longer fits language prescriptivism. Thus, adopting critical and descriptive approaches to teaching Japanese language and culture is imperative, now more than ever (Kubota 2003; Siegal and Okamoto 2003; Tai 2003). In terms of practice, language educators therefore need to be aware of

DOI: 10.4324/9781003439493-31

The Routledge Handbook of Endangered and Minority Languages

'the diversity that exists within the culture' (Kubota 2003: 70). More importantly, such approaches inevitably present opportunities for them to assume an active role as diversity and expressivity advocates in language learning instead of being gatekeepers of prescriptivism.

Another reality with which we must contend is the impact the COVID-19 pandemic has had on our lives. All of us have experienced 'Zoom fatigue' across the board (Bailenson 2021). In education, the pandemic has forced every educator to learn how to teach remotely using a multitude of applications (apps) and courseware. Although we have witnessed a 'great retirement' of experienced teachers (Montes et al. 2022), our collective experience surviving the pandemic may have a redeeming quality. Many have risen by acquiring a wide range of technological advancements. Currently, a variety of language-learning apps and pedagogical platforms are available, such as Anki (digital flashcards), Duolingo (free language-learning apps), WaniKani (kanji learning tools), inter alia. WaniKani is particularly popular among learners of Japanese keen to build their kanji proficiency on their own. Now we can deliver instructions completely remotely, on-demand, hybridized, in-person, and in flipped classrooms or modules.

Focusing on the latter specifically, the term modules or modularity has long been used in pedagogy (Burns 1972; Mariani 1981). For instance, the use of modules in courseware is a convenient way to monitor curricula. During the pandemic, modular distance learning (Insorio and Olivarez 2021) was implemented globally using instructional modules. Naturally, modularity is more than just that and will be discussed in more detail in subsequent sections.

More importantly, the two realities mentioned previously leave us equally with two issues that must be addressed: (1) How should we approach the fluidity and dynamics of language use when teaching and learning Japanese? and (2) How can such teaching be delivered in the classroom? To answer these questions, I explore modularity in this chapter as a sustainable method for incorporating critical approaches in teaching Japanese. Additionally, I propose ideas for potential modules that specifically address diversity. Critical approaches are used synonymously with critical pedagogy throughout this chapter. The latter allows both teachers and learners to critically examine their realities and struggles (Fairclough 1989, 1995; Siegal and Okamoto 2003).

In the following section, I first examine the state of Japanese language textbooks and the rationale behind the impracticality of adopting new textbooks in colleges and universities to address these two issues. Secondly, I propose a more sustainable method for both publishers and authors of long-standing popular textbooks. This involves creating well-designed and easy-to-access modules instead of new textbooks or curricula. The use of modules is not only a sustainable pedagogical method but also a small-yet-easy way to start with critical pedagogy and address the importance of learning about the LGBTQIA+ community in Japan. Eventually, well-curated modular materials will enable language educators to introduce a critical dialogue about LGBTQIA+ communities into their classrooms, laying the foundation for further discussions about discrimination, inequality, inequity, and injustice in as well as beyond our own lives.

New textbooks and our reality

The trend in new foreign language textbooks is to be more interactive with multimedia platforms, such as web-based platforms and apps, particularly at college and university levels. Smartphone applications have now replaced audio CDs, while visual aids are now available on YouTube. Both teachers and students have easy access to these supplementary course materials and aids online. Long-standing popular textbooks have periodically renewed their appearance and editions following similar trends. Consequently, finding reputable textbooks without a web presence has become almost impossible these days. Similarly, Japanese language textbooks follow the same trend by not only updating vocabulary to include contemporary expressions but also reflecting significant changes in our society and the world. As an illustrative example, new and long-standing popular textbooks were compared.

In recent years, the following two new additions have been widely promoted and advertised at professional conferences and workshops in the US: (1) *Compass Japanese Intermediate* (Azama et al. 2022) and (2) *Tobira I* and *II* (Oka et al. 2021, 2022). Both textbooks were published by the same company. However, similarities in content, structure, and specific aims simply reflect the current trend in Japanese pedagogy, which is more multimedia-based and more descriptive and critical than prescriptive. Pedagogically, (1) specifically targets middle and high schools as it is suitable for Advanced Placement (AP) and International Baccalaureate Diploma Programme (IBDP) in the US (Azama et al. 2022), whereas (2) was created as part of the *Tobira* series (Oka et al. 2009) that has been widely used at colleges and universities for intermediate and lower advanced levels.

Both (1) and (2) have dedicated websites for course materials (e.g., audio files, videos, vocabulary lists, flipped class instructional videos, tasks and activities, presentation slide samples, etc.). More importantly, the authors of these textbooks seem to be aware of the importance of critical perspectives in teaching the Japanese language and culture. Azama et al. (2022) stated that one's Japanese language learning 'journey must begin with an understanding of our fellow global citizens' (p. 2). Oka et al. (2021) explained that they 'have avoided run-of-the-mill cultural introductions in favor of discussions about Japanese traditions and customs' to 'lead to deeper discoveries about Japan and its culture' (p. 3). Their intent was further reflected in carefully selected topics and unit headings. This included diversity and intercultural experiences. None of these have traditionally been covered in the long-standing popular textbooks.

In (1), ともに生きる社会 (Diverse society) has subsections, 変わりゆく日本 (Evolving Japan) and アイデンティティ (Identity). In (2), the first lesson begins with自分を再発見する (Rediscovering myself) and covers 異文化を体験する (Experiencing different cultures) and 世界とつながる (Connecting with the world). Additionally, (1) has a section titled 探ってみよう (Investigate the world) in every unit with subsections such as いろいろな視点を学ぼう (Recognize diverse perspectives) and 文化の窓 (Take a look into Japanese culture). Clearly, these headings include social and pedagogical buzzwords such as diversity, identity, and other cultures. To emphasize diversity, (2) introduced characters from diverse backgrounds rather than portraying traditional gender roles, such as homemaker mothers and breadwinner fathers. Moreover, both textbooks steer away from teaching gender-specific expressions as characteristics of the Japanese language. In short, both textbooks aim to describe Japan in a state of flux and encourage learners to examine the status quo of Japanese language and culture from 'diverse perspectives' (Azama et al. 2022).

Conversely, long-standing popular textbooks have been widely used for close to three decades (e.g., *Japanese for Busy People*, *Nakama*, *Yookoso*, etc.) and present a striking contrast to the new textbooks. Siegal and Okamoto (2003) examined and analyzed seven popular Japanese textbooks in the US and found that these textbooks exhibit a tendency 'to portray stereotypical images of Japanese men and women' by assigning the characters' roles to 'conform to traditional gender norms' (p. 51). Furthermore, these popular textbooks underrecognize 'the diversity and change in gender roles and relations in contemporary Japan' (Siegal and Okamoto 2003: 51). Interestingly, Okamoto (1995) reported that 'reversed sex roles or images have appeared' in elementary school textbooks in Japan since 1992 (p. 310). Evidently, changes made to Japanese language textbooks lag behind what is unfolding in Japan. In other words, popular textbooks tend to preserve and reinforce cultural stereotypes and traditional views that deviate further from diversity, equality, and equity among men and women.

The Routledge Handbook of Endangered and Minority Languages

Teaching gendered speech is not necessarily harmful if language educators are mindful of its framing and introduction. While the actual speech of Japanese speakers is less likely to conform to gendered speech patterns, we encountered the manipulation of gendered speech in the media. With the popularity of Japanese pop culture (e.g., anime, manga), many Japanese language learners 'initially dabbled in Japanese out of curiosity and interest' in Japanese anime, manga, films, and TV programs (Koyama 2022: 652). In these media outlets, gendered speech patterns are purposefully manipulated and sometimes overexaggerated as role/character language, which is 'based on social and cultural stereotypes' (Kinsui and Yamakido 2015: 29). Role/character language has wide varieties and subgroups, from elderly male/female language to the samurai language (pp. 31–32). By utilizing role/character language, actors and characters in fiction can embody intended character traits. Some Japanese language educators teach gendered speech with caveats by carefully underscoring the usefulness of learning gendered speech. The rationale was that this could facilitate learners' better understanding of popular Japanese entertainment and fiction (Hatanaka and Kato, personal communication, July 2, 2023). When framed with caveats, teaching gendered speech helps learners better comprehend and enjoy their favorite media.

Compared to popular textbooks, the new textbooks aim to facilitate learners' critical thinking by focusing on diversity and worldviews. Simply put, the newer the textbooks, the more balanced the views they tend to bring forth. Switching to newer textbooks may be conducive to better teaching practices, consistent with critical pedagogy. In reality, however, changing textbooks every two or more years is not a viable option for many educational institutions. Changing textbooks typically entails clearing a multitude of hurdles, including costs, teacher labor (careful evaluation and examination of new textbooks and creation of a new curriculum), and issues with curriculum continuity from old to new textbooks. For example, our university (a public university in northern California) has roughly 500–700 students enrolled in Japanese language courses per quarter. Any change in the curriculum would affect a large student body and teachers. Several years ago, textbook changes were initiated. This took a few years to plan and gradually shifted to new textbooks across the board. Course materials also required constant evaluation and revision, which took a few additional years. Throughout these phases, all the language educators worked continuously to create new course materials and devise new assessments. They were constantly overworked and overburdened themselves. Justifiably, no educational institute would immediately switch to the new textbooks because they are better. In many cases, switching to a new textbook is neither sustainable nor viable.

LGBTQIA+ community in Japan

Despite its popular beliefs, Japan is neither a homogenous nor a monolingual nation. In addition to the indigenous Ainu and Ryuukyuu people, who have their own languages, Japan has also been home to Koreans and Chinese, who have been in Japan for generations. The same applies to foreign residents, who have grown rapidly in Japan. According to Immigration Services Agency (2022), the total number of foreign residents as of June 2022 was 2,961,969, which made up for 2.3% of the total population in Japan (Statistics Bureau of Japan 2022). Furthermore, while the population of Japanese citizens has been declining rapidly, that of foreign residents has been growing steadily (Statistics Bureau of Japan 2022). In reality, Japan is far from homogenous and has multiple layers of diversity. Considering this reality, Tai (2003) cautioned that Japanese culture is 'invented as an essence of the nation, as an integrated, homogeneous whole shared by the members of the nation' (p. 1). This 'invented' notion of Japanese culture also extends to the Japanese language.

Modularity as a practical approach

Within this 'invented' monolingual uniformity, the gender dichotomy is reinforced and manifested in gendered speech patterns. These are in turn associated with gender stereotypes and roles. Gender stereotypes are defined as either positive or negative self-concepts about one's desirable feminine or masculine side, based on societal expectations (Dohi 2014: 3). In addition, characteristics of both genders are 'extremely generalized', while individual differences are 'underestimated' (Dohi 2014: 5). Extensive gender dichotomies further reinforce the heteronormative beliefs and perceptions of the people living in Japan. Namely, the (mis-)beliefs run along the lines of 'there are only men and women in Japan', and 'you rarely run into people of the LGBTQIA+ community because sexual minority people are uncommon in Japan' (Endo 2016; Nakusoo SOGI Hara Jikkoo Iinkai 2019). This points to the unspoken tendency in Japan that, when individuals do not fit overgeneralized gender dichotomies, they are likely to be dismissed and considered exceptions or anomalies. Currently, Japan has not legalized same-sex marriage, although 255 local governments in Japan have a same-sex partnership system in place. Compared to other developed nations, Japan lags far behind in the legalization of same-sex marriage and the establishment of support systems for sexual minorities. What is worse, sexual minorities have long been referred to by pejorative terms such as おかま *okama* (literally 'male buttocks', which equates to gay people) and オネエ/オネエ系 *onee/onee-kee* (literally 'big sister', which equates to cross-dressers, transgender, and gay people altogether) in Japan. On TV, so-called オネエタレント *onee tarento* (cross-dressing entertainers) are popular for speaking and behaving comically in the shows. Inadvertently, this has led some to interpret it as the default image of gay people (Endo 2016).

In 2018, the Dentsu Diversity Lab conducted a nationwide LGBT survey of 60,000 individuals aged 20–59 in Japan. According to their data, 8.9% identified themselves as a sexual minority, which is equivalent to one in every 11 individuals. A similar survey was conducted in 2015. Thus, the 2018 survey has further revealed the following important findings: (1) A total of 68% understood that LGBT was one of the terms referring to sexual minority groups (37.6% in 2015); (2) about 76% expressed their willingness to learn more about LGBT; (3) the majority of LGBT people never came out to anyone because they were afraid of prejudice, bullying, and harassment; and (4) they witnessed a lack of support for the LGBT community in the workplace. These findings further explain the situations that sexual minority youths face at school. When 8.9% of adults are sexual minorities (Dentsu Diversity Lab 2018), we should expect to find 2 to 3 students to be sexual minorities in a classroom of 30 in Japan (Nakusoo SOGI Hara Jikkoo Iinkai 2019).

Nakatsuka (2013) surveyed 1,167 patients diagnosed with gender dysphoria at the Gender Clinic of Okayama University between 1999 and 2010. The data revealed that 70% of female-to-males and 33.6% of male-to-females began experiencing gender dysphoria before they entered school age. However, the majority of school-age children with gender dysphoria are afraid to seek support for fear that no one would accept or understand them (Katsuda and Shoji 2021). They are also subjected to bullying, harassment, and prejudice by their classmates, friends, teachers, and family members because of their ignorance or lack of understanding of sexual minority youths (Hidaka 2016). Furthermore, Hidaka's (2016) online survey of sexual minorities ($N = 15,141$ sexual minorities from teens to age 50 or over) revealed that 60% experienced bullying at school. Of these, 63.8% of bullying was verbal abuse with derogatory terms for the sexual minorities, and 18.3% were physical abuse. It is no surprise that sexual minorities are also known to be at a high risk of suicide (Endo 2016). All these data and studies reveal an alarming outcome, especially in light of the crises sexual minorities in Japan face at school, in the workplace, and at home.

Modules for learning about diversity and sexual minority in Japan

The status quo of Japanese language textbooks and the crisis sexual minorities encounter in Japan call for an eminent need for critical pedagogy to address the importance of learning about the LGBTQIA+ community in Japan. To address predicaments shared among language educators, Siegal and Okamoto (2003) made several suggestions that were also practical and remedial 'pedagogical responses to the social and linguistic diversity' (pp. 59–60). Two of these are worth mentioning: the use of authentic texts of different genres and allowing students to choose their own identities as Japanese-language speakers. Similarly, Tai (2003) suggested the use of 'excerpts from ethnographies' (pp. 21–22) for discussion topics by exploring newspapers and resources found on the internet. Their suggestions could supplement the not-so-new textbooks that language educators are stuck with. However, these suggestions may not be easily implemented, particularly when language educators are constantly overburdened.

The lack of understanding of sexual minorities in Japan results partly from a deeply rooted gender dichotomy, which is strongly tied to a heteronormative ideology. Men speak and act masculinely, and women speak and behave femininely. Teaching gendered speech in Japanese may inadvertently reinforce this ideology. In fact, some Japanese language textbooks continue to advocate it as an indelible part of Japanese culture (Siegal and Okamoto 2003), even though our reality is no longer a male-versus-female binary but more dynamic, diverse, and fluid. Therefore, Japanese language educators should refrain from upholding outdated heteronormative ideologies in their classrooms. Given the rapid changes unfolding in our world, the following section explores the use of modules as a sustainable way to move toward descriptive and critical approaches to teaching the Japanese language to ensure that both teachers and learners remain updated and well informed. Adopting descriptive and critical approaches simultaneously can empower language educators to advocate for diverse learners and sexual minority students in educational practice.

Modularity in language pedagogy

The meaning of a module, or modularity, depends heavily on the context. In this chapter, I define a module as a self-contained instructional unit or package that is structurally and functionally congruous with the proposed modifications to be made to long-standing popular textbooks. Conveniently, modules can be flexibly incorporated into teaching and learning and combined or used independently. These modules can serve as teaching aids and resources. They can be skill-, topic-, or form-based (i.e., focusing on a particular sentence or grammar structure, vocabulary set, etc.). Furthermore, the modules can be modified to meet different needs based on different language proficiency levels or groups. Authentic materials can be packaged into modules and used as supplements in primary textbooks (Butcher et al. 2020; Mariani 1981; Martin et al. 2013).

The ADDIE process is commonly adopted for designing modules (Martin et al. 2013; Molenda 2003). This includes *analysis, design, development, implementation,* and *evaluation*. This is a cyclical process for creating and improving the modules. Martin et al. provided a succinct explanation of this process by creating 'an interactive multimedia instructional module' and using ADDIE as a guideline (2013: 5–6). The analysis phase of the process requires a designer to develop 'a clear understanding of the gap that exists between the desired outcomes and the existing knowledge and skills of the learners' (Martin et al. 2013: 5). The design phase translates the information and knowledge gained from the analysis phase into an instructional program by focusing on the critical needs that the intended instruction must address and deliver (Martin et al. 2013). These two phases are consistent with the careful analyses and suggestions made by advocates of critical approaches

Modularity as a practical approach

in their careful examination of the status quo of Japanese language teaching (Kubota 2003; Siegal and Okamoto 2003; Tai 2003). The development phase involves producing a prototype that leads to the implementation phase, followed by the evaluation phase. The evaluation phase ensures a thorough assessment of the implemented prototype by measuring learning outcomes and asking for feedback from both users/learners and implementers/instructors (Martin et al. 2013: 5–6).

Why does a module matter to us now? Mariani (1981) discussed the place of modules in language teaching by highlighting how language educators 'cannot afford to spend vast amounts of time and energy to devise' new materials or aids (p. 42). The use of modules offers 'an extra choice of language activities, materials, and techniques' (p. 43). Note that these statements from the 1980s continue to be valid. These modules have the potential to bring diverse and authentic materials into classrooms. They can be more helpful and usable when created as supplementary materials for popular textbooks which contain multiple platforms, including websites and applications. Using their means and resources, the publishers of popular textbooks can create and store well-designed modules. Compared with new textbooks, modules are more sustainable and educator friendly.

How to start critical pedagogy with modules

Using authentic texts of different genres and the facilitation of discussions on sociocultural and politically critical topics are two simple methods of implementing critical pedagogy in Japanese (Koyama 2016, 2022; Siegal and Okamoto 2003; Tai 2003). These pedagogical approaches are relatively easy to adopt at advanced levels because teachers do not necessarily need to rely on specific textbooks as the learner's proficiency level is advanced enough to allow for the processing of various authentic texts. I have been teaching advanced Japanese courses in small seminar settings with 10–15 students at a university using a wide variety of genres, including a collection of readings from the LGBTQIA+ community in Japan. The depth of coverage spans terminology, statistical information, issues and problems, outings, and coming out. Based on my observations of student performance over the years, learning about the LGBTQIA+ community in Japan is clearly beneficial for students. Out of the many benefits, I have found the following two to be the most intellectually significant for students and to have useful implications for language educators in practice:

1. Students become equipped with the language necessary to critically discuss diversity and sexual minorities, which consequently leads them to gain critical language awareness (Fairclough 1989, 1995). Japanese language learners in the US are familiar with the various terms used to discuss sexual minorities; however, they may not know the equivalent terms and concepts in Japanese. Unfortunately, the Japanese media is fraught with misinformation, misrepresentation, and derogatory terms that refer to sexual minorities (Endo 2016; Nakusoo SOGI Hara Jikkoo Iinkai 2019). Owing to this distractive noise, sifting through the sea of information to consciously learn about sexual minorities and their struggles is not easy. In my advanced courses, well-curated readings on the LGBTQIA+ community in Japan helped students acquire appropriate linguistic tools and understand imminent issues and problems faced by sexual minorities. With the advancement of their understanding, students gradually gained what Fairclough (1989) defined as critical language awareness (pp. 239–240). This is a pillar of critical pedagogy and is crucial for a deeper exploration of sexual minorities in Japan.
2. Students' epistemological and intellectual expansion was promoted and encouraged through in-depth discussions of the LGBTQIA+ community in Japan. People still tiptoe when they address issues surrounding sexual minorities because of the fear of inadvertently offending

others.[1] Therefore, a careful examination of the LGBTQIA+ community in class opens the window for students to further their intellectual endeavors, as it helps overcome their inhibition and fear of addressing sensitive issues.

In the past, class discussions on sexual minorities in Japan and the US had evolved into lively debates and critical analyses of the identity crises and social injustices faced by minority students at home and in society. For example, Japanese heritage speakers explained their ideological clashes with their Japanese parents as being caught between their Japanese heritage and American culture. Another example is the Asian American experience in the US. One Asian American student shared her encounter with a white male stranger at a bus stop. This stranger overheard her conversation with her mother in Chinese and approached them to ask where they came from. Despite answering that she was from California, this white man repeatedly pressed her with the same question. This encounter left her bitter and with conflicting feelings, as she was an American citizen and a native speaker of English. Unfortunately, this type of offensive and discriminatory behavior is heard and observed everywhere, but people rarely talk about it.

The aforementioned Asian American student ended up examining racial discrimination against Asian immigrants in the US in her term paper. Similarly, many students considered and explored current social issues in their term papers. In doing so, they had unraveled the dominant social structures that nurture systemic discrimination, social injustice, and socioeconomic dysfunction. Moreover, by delving into the issues surrounding the LGBTQIA+ community in Japan, students were given a safe space and encouraged to discuss other social issues that mattered to them the most from diverse perspectives. Ultimately, classroom practice evolved into a genuine transformative process for the students.

Learning with care at the beginner level

Teaching and learning about the LGBTQIA+ community in Japan can be relatively easily incorporated into the most advanced levels of Japanese language learning. Doing so can provide excellent opportunities for language educators to explore social issues. With this knowledge, they can choose to advocate for sexual minorities. For Japanese language learners, learning to discuss this sensitive topic will expand their horizons and facilitate their critical thinking and language awareness. However, this will require language educators to spend a significant amount of time, energy, and investment in creating meaningful course materials, delivering such teaching, and constantly updating their information, when they may not have sufficient time to do so (Mariani 1981).

Care and attention are needed at the beginner level, where language educators are bound by the use of specific textbooks and obliged to build learners' linguistic foundations. Generally, the beginner level of any foreign language course is packed with basic essential materials, from new sets of orthographies to grammatical structures and esoteric verb conjugation paradigms. Therefore, beginner-level lessons tend to run on tight schedules, leaving no room for teachers to add additional activities or materials. Furthermore, popular Japanese language textbooks tend to be fraught with traditional heteronormative views, such as setting a stay-at-home mother as the default female role and assigning supervision roles exclusively to male characters. Therefore, the critical use of these resources requires care, attention, and time.

In the following section, I first examine a popular introductory Japanese language textbook, *Genki I Third Edition* (Banno et al. 2020), that is used in colleges and universities. I then suggest modules that can demonstrate the ways in which the authors and publishers of popular textbooks can incorporate well designed methods that can facilitate more critical approaches to teaching Japanese.

Genki I Third Edition (Banno et al. 2020) has 12 lessons (i.e., chapters), and a typical quarter-system curriculum covers 5 lessons per quarter (i.e., ten weeks). Each lesson takes approximately two weeks to cover, during which language educators are obliged to introduce (1) new vocabulary; (2) kanji characters; (3) new grammatical points; (4) dialogue practices; (5) composition writing; and (6) multiple assessments such as vocabulary, grammar, and kanji quizzes. Although it varies between institutions, universities usually designate foreign language curricula to ensure that the students learn about world cultures, intercultural communication, and oral skills, with specific criteria and metrics to follow. This further demonstrates the lack of room for divergence from the textbooks, as the higher the standards and quality of a language program, the more time constraints that language educators face.

This chapter has thus far examined the status of popular textbooks and their issues regarding the LGBTQIA+ community in Japan. This was sufficient for the ADDIE analysis phase to create the modules. The third edition of *Genki* has updated its materials by overhauling vocabulary and grammar, enriching the online course materials, and adding audio applications for smartphones. However, the primary characters in *Genki* – Takeshi, Mary, and Mary's host family (father, stay-home mother, and teenage daughter) – have not changed since 1999 in order to maintain the textbook's continuity and structure. As found in other popular textbooks (Siegal and Okamoto 2003), *Genki* also portrays stereotypical men and women, including their gendered roles. However, unlike other textbooks, *Genki* does not emphasize gendered speech patterns, and the model conversations are gender neutral (Siegal and Okamoto 2003: 62). This particular aspect of *Genki* exemplifies a move in the right direction.

Modules for *Genki I*

The target learners of *Genki I* (Banno et al. 2020) were beginners, limiting the incorporation of authentic materials. The content of a module may be limited for this reason; however, introducing notions of diversity and the reality of the LGBTQIA+ community in Japan at the initial stage of Japanese language learning continues to be worthwhile. Structurally, *Genki* has created multiple smartphone apps. Additionally, *Genki*'s official website provides a variety of resources for both teachers and learners: *self-study room, teacher's page*, and *examination copy*. A collection of short videos (most are less than a minute long, with the longest ones less than three minutes long) is available as 'pedagogical aids to accompany "Culture Notes" columns' in the textbook (Japan Times Publishing 2023). All the resources primarily focus on developing and improving linguistic skills, except for the 'Culture Notes' videos. In the textbook, each chapter has the main section (a vocabulary list, model dialogues, target grammar, and exercises), subsections, and optional items (*Useful Expressions* and *Culture Notes*, which always begin with 日本のXX *Nihon-no* XX (Japanese XX)). These structures of *Genki I* present multiple potential points for module insertion or replacement on websites and textbooks.

Genki I maintains gender-neutral dialogues, unlike other problematic textbooks; however, four pedagogical issues persist that require instructional interventions for critical approaches. I propose the following four non-intrusive modules for *Genki I* as a starter by optimizing their websites and apps. Note that non-intrusive here is functionally equivalent to 'sustainable' in a way that no major changes to the textbook or drastic revised editions are needed. Drastic changes in the main sections would require similar drastic changes in the course curriculum, placing a heavy burden on language educators. Thus, easy-to-access and easy-to-use modules must cause minimal disruptions.

The Routledge Handbook of Endangered and Minority Languages

Designers must keep in mind that small steps and changes are good starting points to facilitate a better understanding of diversity and other social issues over the long term. From the perspective of institutions and language educators, sustainability means that neither additional purchases nor curriculum changes are involved. Both the authors and publisher of *Genki I* can start with small changes, that is, the addition of supplementary materials on diversity as modules. In doing so, they assume advocacy roles for diversity, which subsequently provide opportunities for language educators to become advocates themselves.

Module 1: Model dialogues and gender roles

Genki I has one-off characters without names, such as perfect strangers, shop clerks, doctors, and nurses. In *Lesson 12* (Banno et al. 2020: 272–273), model dialogues demonstrated interactions between a patient (Mary, one of the primary characters) and a male doctor, with an illustration of them and a female nurse added. This male/doctor-female/nurse fits the perceived gender stereotypes within traditional views, which are reflected in the long-standing popular textbooks of men with higher status roles and women with more subordinate and supportive roles (Siegal and Okamoto 2003: 51). Unsurprisingly, Western professionals learning Japanese often find it problematic to learn the language 'loaded with traditional gender roles and gender inequality' (Itakura 2009: 29). The visual impact of seeing this specific gender dichotomy in the profession immediately captures learners' attention. Changing this particular illustration for future editions may be possible for the publisher; however, there is a less demanding solution that can be implemented immediately. Therefore, I suggest that the publisher replace the online dialogue video for *Lesson 12* with that of a female doctor. This visual representation of a female doctor provides a more balanced view of the careers and professions available to both men and women in Japan.

Module 2: Addition to Culture Notes *and accompanying short videos*

Online short videos on *Culture Notes* could be further enriched by publishers with their own resources, which language educators may lack in terms of resources. *Culture Notes* are titled 日本のXX *Nihon-no* XX (Japanese XX) and focus mainly on the unique aspects of Japanese culture and society, such as exchanging business cards, Japanese food and architecture, and religion. I suggest that online videos include 日本のプライドパレード (Pride Parade in Japan) to inform learners of the LGBTQIA+ movements in Japan. Such videos provide opportunities for teachers and learners to examine the status quo of sexual minority groups in Japan. In addition, a short video can accompany the narration of a brief history of 東京レインボープライド (Tokyo Rainbow Pride), which hosted the first 'pride parade' in Japan in 1994. Since then, the movement has grown and evolved into support for the community, educating the public, and disseminating accurate information about the community. Making their presence visible in learning materials not only advocates diversity in Japan but also supports learners of the LGBTQIA+ community in class.

Module 3: Pronouns

Logging into a Zoom meeting, we often notice a participant's choice of pronouns in the US. Similarly, it is becoming common practice to have our pronoun choice as part of our email signature. As our world continues to learn how to embrace diversity, more pronouns are being created and added to the list of pronouns, including *ze-zir-zir* (LGBTQ Nation 2022). This suggests the importance of having more options and choosing pronouns that are the most comfortable and identity-accurate for speakers. In general, Japanese speakers are not keen on using gender-based pronouns in addressing others. The most preferred way to address others is the use of a name (either a first or last name, heavily depending on the situational dynamics) together with a vast array of titles ranging from generic 〜さん /*san* (Mr./Ms./Mrs.) to intimate 〜ちゃん /*chan* (dear). Note that 彼 *kare* (he) and 彼女 *kanojo* (she) are commonly used not as pronouns but as nouns referring to 'boyfriend' and 'girlfriend,' respectively. Thus, the most contentious pronoun set is the first-person pronoun, based on gender. Choosing one's own pronoun is one of the many ways to manifest one's identity linguistically and publicly. In the Japanese language, this is demonstrated by the use of *boku* or *ore* (male first person) by female speakers (Nishida 2011).

Lesson 1 in *Genki I* has a small section explaining how uncommon it is to use the second-person pronoun あなた *anata* (Banno et al. 2020: 45). This section provides an opportunity for learners to begin exploring their pronoun choices and identities as Japanese language learners. To complement this section, I suggest the following options as modules to be made available online: a list of pronouns (and how they are used or not used by Japanese speakers) or a short article/essay on Japanese pronouns (for beginners, having an English article with a Japanese translation would be informative and helpful). Having this type of pragmatic knowledge increases student awareness of pronoun use in Japanese.

Module 4: Gendered speech

Genki I does not focus on gendered speech, unlike other popular textbooks. Teaching gendered speech patterns as norms may start painting an unrealistic picture of the Japanese language and culture. However, with caveats and caution, learners continue to benefit from becoming aware of the place of gendered speech in Japanese as part of their role/character language (Kinsui and Yamakido 2015). In reality, gendered speech may not be used by Japanese native speakers, but it can be manipulated in popular media outlets, such as anime and manga. Japanese pop culture makes for the first encounter with many people in the Japanese cultural experience (Koyama 2022). Thus, learning about gendered speech patterns facilitates better comprehension of media content, which furthers language learning and promotes long-term media literacy. A useful and informative module may be a short video or selective video clip on the role/character language used in the media, including popular anime and TV programs. This can help learners understand the highly stylized context of gendered speech patterns. Moreover, we can theoretically reconfigure a place for gendered speech as part of the role/character language. This further allows us to reframe and reposition it critically within the Japanese language and culture, without denying its place and presence.

Conclusion

In this chapter, I propose sustainable ways in which to incorporate more inclusive pedagogical interventions that coexist with popular Japanese language textbooks by suggesting that the publishers and authors of popular textbooks should create new modules instead of producing new textbooks. Popular textbooks continue to be used in higher education institutions, as demonstrated by Siegal and Okamoto's (2003) textbook analyses, which assert that such popularity 'attests to their excellence in many respects' (p. 51). As technology develops rapidly and the world changes, new textbooks reflect continuous attempts to meet these demands and challenges. However, switching from one textbook to another is not a simple task for educational institutions and language educators, as the larger the language program, the more onerous the switch. This is a pedagogical and educational reality.

Foreign-language textbooks tend to uphold prescriptive views of language and inadvertently reinforce cultural stereotypes in certain cases. Cultural stereotypes in Japan often dwell on the gender dichotomy and heteronormative ideology in which men are dominant and women are subordinate. This skewed image further distorts Japan's reality, which is neither homogeneous nor confined to established traditions. Similar to other cultures, Japan is characterized by diversity, although this particular aspect is gravely underrecognized (Kubota 2003). Therefore, recognizing sexual minorities in textbooks is a critical step toward acknowledging and advocating for diversity.

Popular Japanese language textbooks enrich their content using multiple platforms such as smartphone apps, audiovisual materials, and other teaching and learning materials stored on dedicated websites. By using these resources, publishers can create and add simple modules in various forms. These modules can be simple, complex, short, extensive, and easy or difficult to use. Modules are a convenient method for meaningfully incorporating authentic materials and assisting language educators. However, the modules must be relevant, reflect reality, and be created and provided by textbook authors and publishers. Accordingly, the authors and publishers of popular textbooks can actively contribute to environmental sustainability by not publishing new textbooks or print editions. They can also choose to become pedagogically sustainable by supporting language educators with easy-to-use online modules. Language educators are constantly overburdened by the daily grading and coverage of the required curriculum and have little time to create modules (Mariani 1981).

The modules proposed herein are less demanding and can be added to the *Genki I* (Banno et al. 2020) website. Illustrative examples include changing a one-off character in a model dialogue video, featuring a 'pride parade' in Japan, adding a list or brief explanations of Japanese pronoun paradigms, and featuring the use of role/character language in the media. Teaching gendered speech patterns as a norm has been criticized because it reinforces prescriptivism and an outdated linguistic reality (Kubota 2003; Siegal and Okamoto 2003; Tai 2003). However, teaching gendered speech has its own merits when it is reframed as a part of role/character language (Kinsui and Yamakido 2015).

Gendered speech patterns are often manipulated in the media to depict particular character traits as an easy way to portray sociocultural stereotypes. Although I do not subscribe to the enhancement of sociocultural stereotypes, I strongly believe that explaining the rationale and manipulation of gendered speech in the media will help learners to better understand their favorite entertainment forms. Gaining such an understanding and awareness may facilitate learners' long-term media literacy. Meanwhile, the Japanese media often features sexual minority entertainers as fun or comical characters (Endo 2016), which offends sexual minorities and allies and inadvertently contributes to the misrepresentation of the LGBTQIA+ community. More accurate information about and descriptions of the realities of Japanese society should be incorporated into Japanese language textbooks to ensure that learners gain critical language awareness and become well informed. Language educators can either choose to remain gatekeepers of traditional views or become diversity advocates. By incorporating modules on the LGBTQIA+ community in Japan, they can assume active roles as diversity advocates and help learners to critically examine their heteronormative ideologies. This can initiate learners' long-term transformative process.

The creation of inclusive and diverse modules will provide long-term educational benefits. Eventually, language educators' small steps (i.e., by incorporating new modules in their teaching) will lay the epistemological groundwork for learners to gain more critical views as they learn about Japanese language and culture. Teaching and learning about sexual minorities also provides the opportunity to acquire the language to debate and discuss sensitive social issues. This can enrich students' worldviews and allow them to examine the world more critically. Most importantly, it is an opportunity for both teachers and learners to become diversity advocates.

To conclude this chapter, I would like to share some memorable anecdotes. Since I began incorporating readings and dialogues about the LGBTQIA+ community into Japanese language courses, I have encountered a few graduates who have identified with the LGBTQIA+ community and said that 'I wish I could have learned about this [LGBTQIA+ and related issues] when I was a student'. Teaching and learning about the LGBTQIA+ community in class allows students to express their voices and creates a safe space. Thus, language educators can critically contribute to learners' subsequent growth by planting the seed at the beginner level.

Acknowledgment

This study was financially supported by Small Grant in Aid of Research funded by the University of California at Davis.

Note

1 When I presented a model curriculum with an annotated bibliography to introduce critical dialogues about the LGBTQIA+ community and other social issues at a regional conference (Koyama 2023), I found that there were no language educators or schools (including high schools) that incorporated sensitive and critical social issues into Japanese language curricula. Common reactions and feedback were either 'I wish I could try it in class someday' or 'I do not know how to start'. I also suddenly found myself considered an expert on the LGBTQIA+ community and was asked for advice on how to interact with students or family members of the LGBTQIA+ community. Clearly, most language educators remain unsure of or afraid to talk about the LGBTQIA+ community in their classrooms.

References

English references

Azama, Y., Kikuchi, A., Nishimura, M., and Lupisan, M. (2022) *Compass Japanese Intermediate: Interactive Workbook*. Tokyo: Kurosio.

Bailenson, J. (2021) 'Nonverbal overload: A theoretical argument for the causes of Zoom fatigue', *Technology, Mind, and Behavior* 2(1). APA Open. DOI:10.1037/tmb0000030

Banno, E., Ikeda, Y., Ohno, Y., Shinagawa, C., and Takashiki, K. (2020) *Genki I: An Integrated Course in Elementary Japanese, Third Edition*. Tokyo: Japan Times.

Burns, R.W. (1972) 'An instructional module design', *Educational Technology* 12(9): 27–29.

Butcher, C., Davies, C., and Highton, M. (2020) *Designing Learning: From Module Outline to Effective Teaching*. London: Routledge.

Dohi, I. (2014) *Gender Personality in Japanese Society: The Determinants of Femininity/Masculinity, Menal Health, Female-Male Relationships, and Cultural Factors*. Osaka, Japan: Union Press.

Fairclough, N. (1989) *Language and Power*. London: Longman.

Fairclough, N. (1995) *Critical Discourse Analysis: The Critical Study of Language*. London: Longman.

Immigration Services Agency (2022). *Regarding the Number of Foreign Residents as of the End of June 2022*. www.moj.go.jp/isa/publications/press/13_00028.html?hl=en

Insorio, A.O., and Olivarez, J.A. (2021) 'Utilizing Facebook and Messenger groups as platforms for delivering mathematics interventions in modular distance learning', *International Journal of Professional Development, Learners and Learning* 3(1). DOI: 10.30935/ijpdll/11290

Japan Times Publishing (2023) *Genki-Online*. https://genki3.japantimes.co.jp/

Itakura, H. (2009) 'Attitudes towards the use of masculine and feminine Japanese among foreign professionals: What can learners learn from professionals?', *Language, Culture and Curriculum* 22(1): 29–41. DOI: 10.1080/07908310802287681

Kinsui, S., and Yamakido, H. (2015) 'Role language and character language', *Acta Linguistica Asiatic* 5(2): 29–42. DOI: 10.4312/ala.5.2.29-42

Koyama, N. (2016) 'Introduction to a dubbing activity for a college first-year Japanese language course', *Applied Language Learning* 26(2): 69–86.

Koyama, N. (2022) 'Academic Japanese: Challenges and myths for learners of Japanese as a foreign language in the US', in C. Shei and S. Li (Eds.), *The Routledge Handbook of Asian Linguistics* (pp. 650–666). London: Routledge.

Koyama, N. (2023, November 4) *Let's Talk About LGBTQIA+ Communities and Social Issues in Japanese Language Classrooms* [Online conference presentation]. FLANC/NCJTA Hybrid Conference, Hayward, CA.

Kubota, R. (2003) 'Critical teaching of Japanese culture', *Japanese Language and Literature* 37(1): 67–87.

LGBTQ Nation (2022) *An (Incomplete) List of Gender Pronouns*. www.lgbtqnation.com/2022/08/incomplete-list-gender-pronouns/ Accessed July 3, 2023.

Mariani, L. (1981) 'The place of modular systems among foreign language teaching materials', *System* 9(1): 41–49.

Martin, F., Hoskins, O.J., Brooks, R., and Bennett, T. (2013) 'Development of an interactive multimedia instructional module', *The Journal of Applied Instructional Design* 3(3): 5–17.

Miyazaki, A. (2004) 'Japanese junior high school girls' and boys' first-person pronoun use and their social world', in S. Okamoto and J. Shibamoto-Smith (Eds.), *Japanese Language, Gender and Ideology: Cultural Models and Real People* (pp. 256–274). Oxford: Oxford University Press.

Molenda, M. (2003) 'In search of the elusive ADDIE model', *Performance Improvement* 42(5): 34–37.

Montes, J., Smith, C., and Dajon, J. (2022) '"The great retirement boom": The pandemic-era surge in retirements and implications for future labor force participation', *Finance and Economics Discussion Series*. DOI: 10.17016/FEDS.2022.081

Oka, M., Kondo, J., Tsutsui, M., Mori, Y., Okuno, T., Sakakibara, Y., Sogabe, A., and Yasuda, M. (2021) *Tobira I: Beginning Japanese*. Tokyo: Kurosio.

Oka, M., Kondo, J., Tsutsui, M., Mori, Y., Okuno, T., Sakakibara, Y., Sogabe, A., and Yasuda, M. (2022) *Tobira II: Beginning Japanese*. Tokyo: Kurosio.

Oka, M., Tsutsui, M., Kondo, J., Emori, S., Hanai, Y., and Ishikawa, S. (2009) *Tobira: Gateway to Advanced Japanese Learning Through Content and Multimedia*. Tokyo: Kurosio.

Okamoto, S. (1995) '"Tasteless" Japanese: Less "feminine" speech among young Japanese women', in K. Hall and M. Bucholtz (Eds.), *Gender Articulated: Language and the Socially Constructed Self* (pp. 297–325). New York and London: Routledge.

Sato, E. (2018) 'Constructing women's language and shifting gender identity through intralingual translanguaging', *Theory and Practice in Language Studies* 8(10): 1261–1269. DOI: 10.17507/tpls.0810.02

Siegal, M., and Okamoto, S. (2003) 'Toward reconceptualizing the teaching and learning of gendered speech styles in Japanese as a foreign language', *Japanese Language and Literature* 37(1): 49–66.

Statistics Bureau of Japan. (2022) *Current Population Estimates as of October 1, 2022*. www.stat.go.jp/english/data/jinsui/2022np/index.html#a15k01-a

Tai, E. (2003) 'Rethinking culture, national culture, and Japanese culture', *Japanese Language and Literature* 37(1): 1–26.

Japanese references

Dentsu Diversity Lab 電通ダイバーシティ・ラボ (2015) *LGBT調査2015 (Survey for LGBT 2015)*. www.dentsu.co.jp/news/release/2015/0423-004032.html Accessed June 22, 2023.

Dentsu Diversity Lab 電通ダイバーシティ・ラボ (2018) *LGBT調査2018 (Survey for LGBT 2018)*. https://www.dentsu.co.jp/news/release/2019/0110-009728.html Accessed June 22, 2023.

Endo, Mameta 遠藤まめた (2016) 先生と親のためのLGBTガイド　もしもあなたがカミングアウトされたなら *(Guidebook for Teachers and Parents to LGBT: What if Someone Does Coming-Out to You)*. 合同出版Tokyo: Goodoo Shuppan.

Hidaka, Yasuharu 日高庸晴 (2016) *LGBT*当事者の意識調査：いじめ問題と職場環境等の課題 *(Survey on Sexual Minorities: Problems and Challenges with Bulling and Work Environments)*. Health-issue.jp. https://www.health-issu.jp/reach_online2016_report.pdf. Accessed January 9, 2024.

Honda, Yuki 本田由紀 (2011) 学校の「空気」若者の気分 *(Atmosphere of Schools, Youngsters' Sentiments)*. 岩波書店 Tokyo: Iwanami Shoten.

Katsuda, Minori and Shoji, Ichiko 勝田みのり・庄司一子 (2021) '性的指向・性自認に違和感をもつ児童生徒に対する教員の意識と関わり経験' (Teachers' awareness and experience with students who feel uncomfortable with sexual orientation and gender identity)', *Journal of Educational Research for Human Coexistence* 2021(8): 3–30.

Nakatsuka, Mikiya 中塚幹也 (2013) 学校の中の「性別違和感」を持つ子ども：性同一性障害の生徒に向き合う *(Children with Gender Dysphoria at School: Supporting Students with Gender Dysphoria)*. 岡山大学 Okayama University.

Nakusoo SOGI Hara Jikkoo Iinkai 「なくそう! SOGIハラ」実行委員会 (Ed.) (2019) はじめよう! *SOGI*ハラのない学校・職場づくり—性の多様性に関するいじめ・ハラスメンをなくすために *(Let's Start Creating Schools and Workplaces Free of SOGI Harassment – To Eradicate Bullying and Harassment Against Sexual Diversity)*. 大月書店Tokyo: Ootsuki Shoten.

Nishida, Takamasa 西田隆政 (2011) '「ボク少女」の言語表現：常用性のある「属性表現」と役割語との接点' (Linguistic expression of 'Boku Shoojo': The relation between 'attributive expression' and role language)', 甲南女子大学研究紀要 文学：文化編 *(Konan Women's University Researches of Literature and Culture Volume)* 2011(48): 13–22.

Tokyo Rainbow Pride 東京レインボープライド (2023) 沿革 *(History)*. https://tokyorainbowpride.org/ Accessed July 2, 2023.

INDEX

abandonment 61, 318
aboriginal 22, 192, 194, 197, 200, 201, 203, 279
abuse 33, 192, 194, 429
accent 87, 138, 286, 289, 290, 300, 325, 326
accessibility 4, 43, 177, 311, 355, 361, 363, 369–371, 373, 404
accountability 26, 232, 239, 240, 393
activism 40, 41, 128, 140, 149, 152, 154, 209, 304, 404
adjectives 111
affordances 165, 166, 365, 373, 375, 377, 384, 386, 393
agglutinative 195, 196, 204
agreement 82, 107, 253, 263, 270, 308, 313, 357, 359, 396
American 29, 43, 47, 116, 118, 137, 147, 179, 180, 192, 210, 278, 283, 286, 288, 290–293, 295, 299, 300, 302, 304, 305, 308–310, 312, 314, 315, 404, 432
ancestral 49, 192, 200, 202, 205, 309
anonymity 99, 132, 191, 279, 323, 324, 329
anthropology 106, 109, 126, 132, 139, 153, 191, 210, 225, 272, 285, 287, 291, 299, 300, 383
Arabic language 2, 79, 80, 82–92, 304
Arctic 36, 43, 46, 60, 198, 201
Asia-Pacific 14, 28, 29
assimilation 1, 44, 81, 91, 141, 148, 188, 189, 192, 202, 219, 226, 256, 309, 315, 416
audience 31, 41, 51, 113, 161, 163, 164, 189, 190, 207, 319, 323, 328, 329, 413
Australasian 372, 375, 406
Aymara 3, 140, 143, 145, 147–151

Basque 62, 64–77, 95–97, 124, 130, 136, 138, 262, 265, 268, 272, 408, 422
bilingualism 30, 34, 36, 45, 54, 55, 59, 60, 73, 95, 103, 106, 137, 138, 152, 168, 169, 185, 220,

221, 253, 256, 264, 265, 267–269, 271–273, 277, 280, 281, 283, 284, 286, 287, 292, 294, 295, 299, 300, 310, 316, 332, 335, 351, 374, 386, 389, 410
biodiversity 18, 75
blending 298, 306, 309, 310
bordering 67, 93, 198, 244, 350
boundaries 25, 78, 81, 87, 91, 113, 118, 262, 263, 281, 295–297, 304, 307, 335, 397, 398, 400, 402, 411, 415, 425
British 13–15, 30, 54, 91, 163, 170, 172, 179, 196, 197, 210, 231, 232, 238–241, 268, 302, 309, 317, 320, 331, 332, 373, 375, 391

Canadian 192, 208, 301, 406
Cantonese 213, 216–220, 225, 290
capitalization 208, 210, 327
cartography 109, 315, 398, 400, 402, 406
Castilian 73, 268, 304, 305, 395, 407, 410, 412, 413, 415, 417, 419
Catalan 72, 73, 268, 270, 335, 407, 408, 413, 424
categorization 82, 98, 201, 310, 311, 323
censorship 225, 329
census 15, 28, 34, 49, 60, 128, 129, 139, 158, 171, 175, 179, 185, 241, 265, 270, 303, 310, 311, 314–316
ceremony 29, 287
Christian 3, 31, 109–112, 117, 149, 155, 301, 302, 309
citizenship 5, 14, 78, 80, 81, 87, 91, 125, 137, 152, 249, 350, 351, 377, 380, 381, 383, 389–391
civilization 78, 180, 222, 306, 309
classification 10, 30, 34, 43, 92, 94, 125, 171, 196, 226, 324, 335, 337, 367, 374, 412
climate 18, 26, 31, 89, 231, 238, 296, 425

Index

code-switching 132, 134, 137, 255, 279, 281, 321, 329, 332, 389

coexistence 62–64, 72, 221, 243, 263, 330, 335, 397, 439

cognitive 19, 54, 55, 63, 84, 85, 91, 92, 168, 181, 188, 206, 282, 336, 351, 355, 361, 362, 372, 374, 388, 396, 398, 399, 403, 414, 420

collaboration 29, 36, 304, 312–314, 386, 388

collective 2, 72, 76, 79, 80, 83, 150, 191, 202, 207, 208, 244, 257, 261, 379–381, 397, 399, 400, 402, 426

colloquial 79, 86, 245, 250, 256

colonization 2, 31, 143, 180, 191, 320

combination 88, 110, 178, 295, 306, 327, 387, 397, 411, 415

communicative 62, 110, 116–118, 161, 245, 253, 262, 276, 317, 321, 328, 329, 366, 370, 371, 376, 388, 389, 397, 406, 410, 415–417, 419

community-based 51, 58, 123, 151, 153, 263, 269, 373, 385, 391

competence 3, 57, 62, 64, 69, 74, 158, 161, 162, 179, 182, 229, 236, 241, 243–246, 251–253, 255, 263, 266, 269, 329, 334, 336, 363, 364, 369, 371, 376, 389, 410, 415–419

complexity 83, 85–87, 258, 275, 305, 320, 327, 367, 379, 396, 401, 402, 405, 406, 414, 415

comprehension 79, 163, 165, 166, 254, 327, 337, 384, 391, 402, 435

computer-assisted 161, 362, 375, 405

conceptualization 203, 206, 207, 275, 301, 311

conservation 29, 170

consolidation 206, 227

consonant 195, 196, 319, 325, 326

constitution 13, 16, 28, 36, 54, 73, 78, 96, 106, 115, 171, 172, 174, 177, 180, 182, 183, 185, 186, 215, 216, 218, 247, 251, 256, 263, 266, 268

construction 91, 105, 111, 126, 160, 206, 208, 261, 285, 293, 303, 307, 317, 323, 332, 348, 381, 394, 411–413

contextualized 184, 280, 296

convergence 47, 169, 389, 395, 398, 404, 405

conversation 18, 45, 132, 133, 165, 166, 179, 231, 232, 321, 364, 375, 387, 432

corpus 33, 37, 41, 44, 85, 112, 164, 174, 177, 221, 237, 309, 324, 410, 420

Creole 13, 310, 350

cross-border 64, 67, 78, 243–245, 247, 249, 256–258, 378

culturally 20, 27, 31, 39, 47, 89, 141, 191, 192, 194, 223, 254, 295, 301, 329, 377, 379–382, 388, 391, 404

danger 21, 23, 61, 86, 94, 106, 111, 140, 263, 351, 407, 411, 417, 420, 422

database 51, 194, 199, 357, 371, 402

debate 24, 36, 44, 214, 227, 240, 270, 273, 285, 300, 319, 436

decolonizing 44, 202, 209, 210, 406

deconstructing 207, 286

deficiencies 254, 321

democratic 73, 171, 359, 381, 383, 391, 404

demographic 49, 82, 129, 318, 323, 338

dependent 50, 52, 67, 76, 195, 328, 396

descriptive 109, 113, 116, 170, 342, 412, 425, 427, 430

dialect 4, 36, 38, 43, 45, 95, 96, 107, 132–134, 159, 163, 169, 196, 200, 210, 214, 217–221, 224–227, 245, 249, 250, 278, 280, 283, 288–292, 295, 298, 317–320, 322, 324–326, 328–331, 333

dialogue 2, 5, 25, 108, 112, 115, 271, 331, 364, 375, 376, 382, 383, 385, 386, 426, 433, 434, 436

diaspora 2, 14, 18, 77, 91, 92, 140, 143, 145–147, 150–152, 154, 156, 158, 165, 167, 305, 422

dictatorship 67, 72, 73, 408

dictionary 160, 200, 215, 225, 291

didactic 115, 244, 273, 414, 417

diglossia 58, 79, 83, 91, 92, 275, 285, 310, 330, 331

discourse 2, 76, 91, 127, 132, 139, 152, 158, 202, 219, 226, 231, 239, 267, 269, 273, 282, 286, 287, 306, 317, 319, 320, 323, 328–330, 332, 343, 350, 380, 402, 403, 411, 412, 420, 437

discrimination 191, 194, 283, 286, 289, 290, 300–302, 319, 359, 391, 408, 426, 432

dissemination 164, 191, 205, 319, 387

distance 63, 74, 162, 165, 168, 184, 269, 387, 388, 405, 426, 437

documentation 1, 10–12, 16, 27–30, 37, 40, 41, 44, 146, 156, 160, 170, 214, 222, 223, 314, 323

domestic 31, 304, 307, 388, 390

dualism 79, 91

eastern 35, 36, 78, 106, 172, 173, 252, 262, 263, 271, 336

ecological 10, 140, 226, 296, 307, 368, 390

economic development 128, 187, 219, 222–224

economy 11, 137, 173, 186, 256, 286, 321, 328, 338, 352

ecosystem 175, 176, 181, 183, 185, 394, 401, 411, 421

educational context 3, 5, 64, 67, 69, 259, 260, 336, 346, 349, 408, 410

emancipation 33, 41, 260

emergence 28, 66, 72, 74, 79, 164, 166, 175, 318, 321, 393, 394, 415, 420

emotional 137, 192, 207, 262, 313, 367, 411, 414

empower 89, 162, 280, 393, 430

English language 9, 13–15, 17–22, 25, 27–29, 92, 154, 158, 160, 210, 233, 242, 249, 255, 291, 293, 299–301, 312, 320, 322, 329, 352, 363, 365–367, 373–375, 402, 405

Index

entertainment 17, 158, 177, 187, 323, 428, 436
environmental 2, 154, 200, 296, 374, 436
episodes 49, 161, 166
epistemological 11, 278, 283, 431, 436
ethical 205–207, 370, 371, 385, 403
ethnic groups 16, 78, 99, 140, 145, 214, 217, 251, 264, 290
ethnographic 4, 124, 145, 153, 214, 323, 337
Eurocentric 109, 397

face-to-face 165, 321, 328, 361, 399
facilitating 2, 59, 86, 105, 177, 182, 235, 312, 327, 328, 348, 386–388, 403
familiarity 124, 318, 327, 403
federalism 96, 265
feminine 326, 429, 437, 438
fiction 41, 114, 170, 411, 420, 428
figurative 412, 413, 421
forbidden 67, 162, 192, 288
freedom 13, 31, 47, 154, 172, 215, 218, 219, 318, 329, 359
French 12, 13, 15, 20, 21, 24–26, 53, 55, 61, 64–66, 69–73, 93–107, 110, 114, 117, 125, 178, 204, 209, 229, 230, 233, 238, 262, 263, 266, 267, 274, 295, 390, 401, 402, 424

Gaelic 48, 52, 53, 56, 57, 60, 61, 137, 138, 169
gender 5, 31, 44, 99, 102, 196, 319, 322, 340, 356, 381, 405, 425, 427, 429, 430, 433–439
genocide 80, 152–154, 157, 188, 189, 192, 202, 209, 241
genre 41, 309, 323, 411, 416, 422
geographical 9, 11, 16, 40, 49, 65, 112, 113, 115, 130, 131, 151, 159, 165, 168, 191, 195–198, 200, 204–206, 243, 244, 265, 304, 356, 372, 401
German 14, 34, 36, 42, 47, 66, 70, 71, 93–104, 106, 110, 114, 148, 149, 162, 178, 184, 204, 229, 230, 233, 234, 238, 241, 242, 245, 246, 248–250, 262, 263, 266–268, 277, 286, 347
globalization 1, 73, 79, 143, 171, 180, 192, 200, 209, 267, 297, 309, 310, 320, 346
governmental 31, 97, 158, 205, 207, 305, 311–313, 335
grammar 1, 28, 30, 33, 85, 111, 116, 117, 132, 134, 166, 174, 215, 220, 222, 244–246, 248, 250, 251, 290, 314, 318, 319, 331, 345, 367, 391, 397, 400, 419, 430, 433
grassroots 24, 38, 172, 180–182, 184, 259

habitus 240, 258, 263, 272, 275
handwriting 98, 321
Hawaiian 188, 197, 208, 288, 300, 310
hegemony 180, 206, 227, 231, 269, 290, 301, 359
heritage 1–4, 17, 29, 30, 33, 38, 39, 41, 53, 80, 96, 104, 105, 109, 112, 113, 117–119, 124, 127, 136, 138, 144, 153, 156, 159, 165, 167, 168,

183, 188, 190–192, 194, 199, 202, 203, 209, 210, 221, 223, 224, 226, 232, 236, 251, 259, 261, 266–271, 273, 276, 285–287, 294, 300, 301, 305, 306, 311, 312, 322, 348, 405, 432
heterogeneous 54, 90, 251, 254, 327, 399, 402
hierarchy 157, 175, 178, 259, 260, 267, 393, 394
Hispanic 286, 303, 305, 306, 309–311, 315, 316
historical 2, 3, 11, 32–34, 38, 43, 47, 60, 67, 72, 73, 88, 96, 98, 105, 140, 158, 191, 192, 202–204, 208, 223, 240, 244, 245, 251, 255, 260, 261, 263, 265, 266, 273, 274, 279, 309, 335, 348, 383, 399, 401, 408
holistic 33, 39, 42, 76, 379, 387, 388, 402
homeland 140, 142, 143, 145, 146, 154, 307, 308, 314
homogeneous 78, 249, 428, 436
humanity 11, 112, 115, 185, 304, 370, 380, 422
hybrid 4, 36, 111, 183, 187, 279, 321, 379, 383, 438

Iceland 31, 38, 42, 114
ideological 3, 4, 44, 46, 48, 52, 106, 127, 135–137, 153, 218, 219, 226, 228, 232, 237, 238, 270, 274, 277, 279, 282, 284, 286, 287, 317, 319, 320, 329, 330, 336, 383, 432
idiomatic 110, 412, 416
illegal 181, 202, 306, 308
immigrants 44, 72, 91, 99, 125, 129, 136, 152, 153, 243, 252, 262, 295, 305, 306, 308, 310, 314, 432
imperialism 15, 29, 32, 45, 92
inclusive 1–5, 39, 63, 66, 76, 90, 203, 204, 233, 243, 272, 276, 286, 299, 330, 356, 363, 370, 375, 395, 397, 403, 421, 435, 436
independence 13–15, 31, 265
Indian 18, 22, 47, 82–85, 88, 92, 171–175, 177–180, 182–187, 192, 193, 208, 209, 308–310, 312, 315
indigenous language 3, 12, 15–17, 21–23, 25–27, 39, 40, 59, 104, 145, 147–149, 153, 155, 160, 167–169, 188, 189, 191, 194, 199–201, 204, 206, 207, 209, 278, 286, 287, 300, 312, 421
inequality 126, 205, 349, 392, 426, 434
innovative 1, 4, 5, 33, 152, 182, 201, 221, 270, 273, 285, 321, 411, 420
integration 2, 5, 63, 80, 81, 124, 125, 127, 129, 131, 135–138, 146, 202, 216, 374, 388, 408, 411, 414, 416, 421
intellectual 22, 55, 68, 111, 117, 142, 203, 260–263, 269, 270, 362, 403, 431, 432
interactions 20, 77, 81, 89, 126, 135, 237, 239, 254, 291, 307, 317, 321, 323, 328, 364, 372, 375, 377, 384, 385, 395, 399, 400, 402, 434
intercultural 5, 65, 148, 153, 225, 241, 251, 256, 271, 363, 366, 369, 372, 377–381, 383–386, 389, 390, 427, 433
interview 83, 89, 98, 102, 104, 105, 134, 164, 188, 338, 340, 341, 414

Index

intonation 321, 401
Ireland 48, 51, 52, 57, 58, 61, 97, 125, 129, 238, 265, 388
isolation 10, 63, 180, 294, 392, 397, 398, 403

Japanese language 5, 372, 425–428, 430–433, 435–438

Korean 184, 196, 274, 285, 363

laboratory 183, 243
lexical 44, 196, 206, 310, 318, 328, 396, 397, 416, 417, 419
liberation 46, 403
library 109, 118, 148, 193, 241, 315, 316, 375
linguistic anthropology 106, 126, 225, 291, 299, 300
literacy 5, 13, 19, 21, 24, 30, 31, 43, 79, 80, 85, 86, 89–92, 144, 147, 149, 158, 160, 163, 165, 178, 203, 204, 209, 213, 214, 216, 272, 278, 288, 290, 293, 297, 299, 301, 310, 312, 318, 332, 334, 336, 350, 355, 368, 369, 383, 410, 411, 420, 422, 435, 436
literature 41, 47, 55, 65, 69, 78, 80–82, 84, 108, 109, 111, 113, 114, 116–118, 126, 127, 132, 142, 143, 145–147, 157, 167, 189, 190, 207, 210, 217, 222, 228, 233, 277, 283, 284, 302, 304, 311, 318, 319, 321, 336–338, 340, 342, 345, 349, 356, 357, 361–368, 375, 380, 385, 389, 405, 408, 410, 411, 413, 415, 416, 420–422, 438, 439
loanwords 41, 45

Mandarin 3, 26, 97, 141, 213–215, 217, 220, 224–226, 236, 237, 241, 242, 274, 282
manipulation 309, 322, 328, 428, 436
masculine 326, 429, 437
meaning 17, 29, 81, 84, 208, 224, 236, 294, 314, 323, 382, 384, 388, 398, 400, 401, 407, 412, 413, 418, 430
medieval 49, 109–111, 119, 318
methodology 69, 79, 83, 85, 97, 98, 144, 194, 206, 323, 337, 356, 357, 372, 388, 397, 399, 415
migration 18, 44, 74, 78, 81, 88, 89, 91, 92, 124, 127, 129, 138, 139, 143, 147, 152, 154, 158, 162, 243, 246, 255, 256, 258, 264, 269, 270, 303, 305, 311, 312
modernization 79, 106, 223
morphology 108, 195, 196, 319, 328
multiculturalism 89, 227, 251, 294, 383
multilingualism 1, 3, 28, 30, 42, 44, 45, 60–64, 72, 74–76, 85, 89, 97, 105, 106, 138, 157, 162, 171, 172, 178, 180, 184, 215, 217, 220, 221, 226, 232, 237–239, 243, 251, 257–265, 267, 269, 270, 272, 273, 281, 289, 292–294, 297, 299, 301, 302, 312, 334, 335, 342, 347–352, 383, 386, 390, 421
multimedia 11, 161, 209, 402, 426, 430, 438

narrative 84, 114, 161, 200, 228, 236, 300, 412, 413, 415
nationalism 31, 46, 61, 87, 91, 209, 261, 263, 270, 272
nationality 81, 214, 218, 251, 306, 311, 378
native speakers 49, 56, 82, 117, 118, 132, 133, 136, 138, 244, 248, 249, 264, 270, 319, 364, 370, 371, 402, 407, 408, 435
neighborhood 295, 306, 351
neologisms 41, 164
normalization 67, 408–410, 415, 416
noun 29, 195, 196, 325

oppression 143, 189, 288, 289, 299, 408
orthography 16, 30, 33, 38, 40, 41, 93, 159, 168, 322, 324, 327–329, 331
otherness 65, 75, 310, 312, 383
outgroup 87, 88, 158

Pacific 2, 9–15, 17–26, 28–30, 170, 197, 201, 226, 310, 351, 421
pedagogy 3–5, 45, 56, 79, 117, 118, 147, 151, 161, 165, 167, 236, 285, 286, 294, 295, 298–302, 334, 348, 351, 385, 399, 404–406, 426–428, 430, 431
philosophical 90, 109, 111, 116, 207, 404
phonetic 138, 213, 227, 319, 322, 324, 327, 328, 330
phonological 65, 319, 328, 330
phrase 161, 166, 167, 208, 293
phraseology 415, 417, 419
pictographic 329
Pidgin 157
plurilingual 63, 73–75, 77, 269, 294–298, 301, 302, 313, 382, 386, 391, 408, 412
politeness 133
political 11, 13, 15, 44, 49, 67, 73, 86, 90, 91, 93, 94, 98, 99, 109, 115, 126, 137, 143, 151–154, 158–161, 172, 180, 205, 231, 235, 237, 238, 241, 251, 261, 265, 274, 275, 283, 286, 298, 304, 305, 309, 313, 317–320, 324, 329, 330, 335, 344, 348, 349, 407, 425
postcolonial 43, 188, 202
pragmatic 27, 327–329, 334, 336, 435
psycholinguistic 84, 281

qualitative 12, 64, 69, 97, 98, 124, 153, 164, 194, 199, 201, 334, 340, 347, 356, 373, 375, 414
quantitative 90, 97, 98, 324, 334, 411
questionnaire 82–84, 94, 252, 253

reading 103, 117, 147, 150, 163–165, 181, 252, 295, 311, 328, 329, 331, 332, 350, 362, 368, 374, 375, 396, 401, 402, 410–416, 418–422
religion 31, 60, 79, 87, 152, 158, 172, 184, 320, 378, 381, 434

443

Index

revitalization 1–3, 31–33, 36–49, 52, 53, 55, 57–60, 82, 89, 121, 137–140, 151, 153, 156, 157, 160–164, 167–170, 187–191, 194, 195, 197, 199–201, 204, 205, 209, 210, 214, 222, 223, 278–280, 282–284, 286, 287, 294, 300, 302

script 16, 41, 141, 172–174, 179, 195, 213, 215, 218, 220, 226, 319, 322, 324–327
semantic 190, 329
semiotic 41, 97, 281, 283, 318, 319, 321, 325–327, 331, 335, 350–352, 400, 401
sensitivity 75, 84, 85, 297, 336, 380
sentence 112, 134, 293, 327, 430
sociolinguistic 2, 4, 44, 60, 63–65, 67, 69, 74–77, 87, 99, 106, 107, 124, 130, 137, 157, 244, 272, 276, 280, 283–285, 295, 305, 313, 322, 331, 332, 351, 394, 395, 401
Spanish 4, 55, 64–73, 100, 114, 117, 123, 136, 145, 147, 148, 178, 184, 200, 204, 208, 229, 230, 233, 238, 262, 268, 274, 276, 277, 285–287, 300, 304, 305, 309–311, 313, 316, 350, 375, 394, 395, 397, 404, 405, 408, 413, 421, 422
speaking 16–18, 27, 31, 33, 68, 85, 89, 94, 103, 104, 110, 111, 118, 119, 127, 131–135, 142, 143, 148, 158–160, 164–166, 171, 178, 179, 182, 192, 202, 208, 219, 220, 222, 231, 245–248, 250–255, 263, 264, 275, 276, 278, 285, 290, 292, 300, 309–311, 343, 346, 347, 362, 366, 373–376, 396, 401, 415, 421, 429
standardization 33, 40, 41, 55, 56, 78, 79, 96, 158, 162, 226, 272, 274–276, 278–280, 283, 286, 287, 320, 331, 342, 347, 416
statistics 13, 16, 28, 60, 94, 239, 270, 428, 438
stereotypes 46, 159, 304, 369, 371, 377, 383, 395, 405, 425, 427–429, 434, 436
storytelling 43, 75, 194, 295, 309, 401

taboo 317
temporal 109, 112, 243
terminology 36, 40, 41, 78, 114, 203, 249, 301, 311, 431
territorial 4, 145, 262, 263, 335, 347
textbook 84, 110, 153, 191, 196, 200, 201, 277, 394, 395, 428, 432, 433, 435, 436
Tibetan 217, 219, 224–227, 282, 287

translanguaging 4, 74–76, 279–281, 284–287, 289, 294, 298–301, 336, 351, 386, 390, 397, 398, 402, 405
tribal 182, 189, 202, 306–308

universal 16, 114, 115, 169, 182, 214, 216, 309, 329
utopia 31, 32, 109, 114
Uyghur language 2, 3, 140–143, 145–147, 150–152

variation 36, 37, 40–42, 46, 138, 275–278, 283, 285, 292, 297, 299, 319, 332, 348, 372, 392, 395, 405, 409
varieties 13, 34, 36–38, 41, 42, 56, 93, 94, 213, 216, 223, 224, 261, 267, 268, 274–277, 279, 280, 283–285, 287, 289, 290, 292, 298, 309, 317, 320, 329, 330, 392–394, 397, 408, 414–416, 418, 419, 428
verb 166, 195, 432
vocabulary 85, 102, 109, 111, 117, 126, 132, 134, 161, 165, 166, 208, 215, 237, 254, 291, 300, 319, 321, 346, 362, 364, 365, 367, 374, 389, 397, 400, 410, 418, 427, 430, 433
vocative 326
voice 33, 153, 168, 204, 279, 338, 367, 373
voiced 127, 319, 324
vowel 325, 326, 328

western 11, 14, 15, 19, 22, 29, 41, 60, 81, 109, 110, 112, 113, 116, 125, 138, 147, 151, 190, 195, 196, 199, 202, 203, 206, 207, 213, 255, 263, 301, 351, 395, 397, 404, 434
worldview 180, 190, 206, 278, 404, 412
writing 43, 90, 108–110, 114, 118, 119, 147, 150, 162–164, 166, 179, 181, 195, 203, 210, 220, 222, 245, 252, 253, 275, 284, 292, 296, 300, 309, 311, 313, 317–322, 324, 327–332, 343, 345, 362, 363, 367, 368, 372, 374, 375, 389, 396, 401, 402, 410, 433

xenophobia 289, 302, 304
Xinjiang 140, 142, 147, 152–154, 217, 225, 226

YouTube 41, 43, 150, 156, 162, 175–177, 180, 182, 315, 421, 426
Yugoslavia 252, 263, 264, 273

9781032574288